The Genealogy of Demons

The Genealogy of Demons
Anti-Semitism, Fascism, and the Myths of Ezra Pound

Robert Casillo

Northwestern University Press
Evanston, Illinois

© 1988 by Robert Casillo

No part of this book may be reproduced in any form or
by any means without the prior written permission of
the publisher.

Published by Northwestern University Press
Evanston Illinois 60201
Printed in the United States of America

ISBN #0–8101–0710–4

Contents

To the memory of
Gennaro Casillo
1903–1977

Preface

A year ago in Venice, in the cemetery of San Michele, I stood at the grave of Ezra Pound. This was an act of homage to the writer who had contributed much to my aesthetic and cultural education. On this occasion I was conscious of Pound as the great revolutionary modernist and literary instigator, the catalyst of renaissances and restorer of neglected beauty. I was also aware of him as Ruskin's most distinguished heir in this century as an interpreter of Italian civilization to the Anglo-American world. Like Hugh Kenner's in *The Pound Era,* my itinerary through the Venetian labyrinth had been plotted along the course of "luminous details" which Pound had defined in *The Cantos* and other works. And yet this moment of reverence was disturbed by questions and qualifications. In spite of my admiration for Pound as a cultural figure, I had not forgotten his association with some of the most brutal and dehumanizing ideologies of this century and the inseparable relation between these ideologies and his major poem. Nor could I forget that Pound, for all his love of Italy and desire for its "resurrection," as he called it, had served a regime which brought the country to degradation. This book originated in doubts and questions such as these. Their exploration obliged me to suspend my admiration for Pound's literary and cultural achievements and to consider his ideology as objectively as possible.

When I began my project it was my impression that Pound criticism on the whole had failed to attain this level of objectivity. I am now convinced that, with a few recent exceptions, it still has not done so. Although we have many fine studies of Pound's poetry, aesthetics, criticism, economics, and other matters, nothing comparable exists on the subject of Pound's anti-Semitism and fascism. Critics who have ventured into this terrain have largely contented themselves with historical anecdotes, source hunting, special pleading, simple obfuscation, or evasion. Thus they have avoided the necessary task, which is to elucidate systematically the connection between Pound's work and the historical ideologies he embraces. All too often the demonic features of Pound's psychology have been ignored as an influence upon his political beliefs while Pound's own writings have been adduced as a reliable explanation of his political and other intentions. Rarely have critics attempted to stand outside Pound's text in order to situate it in the light of contemporary understanding, at once historical, sociological, and psychological, of anti-Semitism and fascism. As a result of these methodological and theoretical limitations, we have yet to understand the relation between the turbulent mind of this writer and the violent social and political currents in which he lived—in short, the apocalyptic, fearful, emarginated, atavistic, reactionary, and revolutionary setting which gave rise to fascism and from which *The Cantos* themselves emerged.

Among its other purposes, the chief aims of this book are threefold. First, I have sought to direct Pound criticism from its more usual focus on formalist analysis, merely factual biography, and research into literary references and influences, considered by themselves, to broader and more urgent questions of politics, society, and morality. I found it necessary to systematize the reading of the apparently unsystematic Pound and to uncover the deep structure of the Poundian worldview. Second, I have tried to demonstrate the limitations of explaining Pound chiefly according to the terms that Pound himself provides. Third, and most important, I have tried to show that Pound's anti-Semitism and fascism, far from being adventitious, aberrant, or marginal features of his mind and work, are inseparable from his linguistic strategies and personal psychology. It is impossible to understand Pound's cultural enterprise without realizing that this project is joined indivisibly to fascism and anti-Semitism.

In researching and writing this book I was supported by two Max Orovitz Summer Fellowships from the University of Miami. I am also grateful to the University of Miami Library and especially its Inter-Library Loan Department for the promptness and courtesy with which they responded to my requests for books and articles. The University of Miami was equally generous in making available its word processing service: I much appreciate the unfailing skill and courtesy of Patricia Stango and Ana Miyares. I would also like to thank Professor Donald Gallup, Curator of the Pound Collection of the Beinecke Rare Book and Manuscript Library, Yale University, for granting me permission to examine its Pound materials. The remainder of my research was carried out at Butler Library, Columbia University, Eisenhower Library, Johns Hopkins University, Sterling Memorial Library, Yale University, and the Library of Congress. Portions of this book have already appeared as scholarly articles, and I thank the editors of the following journals for allowing me to reprint them: *The Carrell, Criticism, Modern Language Studies, Modern Language Quarterly, Papers on Language and Literature, Texas Studies in Literature and Language,* and *San Jose Studies.*

This book reflects my indebtedness to many fine teachers and scholars. Among my undergraduate teachers I owe the deepest thanks to Stephen

Donadio, Joseph Anthony Mazzeo, and the late Lionel Trilling. I have always admired Trilling's concern with the relationship between literature and morality, that is, with the kind of questions I have raised in this book. In graduate school the late Donald Howard gave me assistance and encouragement while the late Earl Wasserman taught me the absolute importance of systematically defining the points upon which a poet has constructed his web. In my initial studies of Pound I was guided by Hugh Kenner, with his unsurpassed knowledge of the poet's life and works. My greatest debt, however, is owed to Avrom Fleishman. After having encouraged this book from its inception, he read its successive chapters with great speed and exactitude. It is a pleasure to be able to thank him now not only for supporting and recommending my work but for subjecting it to his rigorous standards.

This book benefitted as well from the attention of two other superb editors. My colleague John Paul Russo read the first version of the mansucript as well as its revisions, and I am most grateful to him for having pruned its prolixities and strengthened many of the positions I have taken. I also want to express my thanks to Gerald Graff, of Northwestern University Press, first for his interest in my manuscript and later for his tough editing of the book. I have valued both his improvements of its argument and style and his decision to allow me to expand the manuscript by well over a hundred pages.

Others who have contributed to this book include Clark Emery, with whom I had a stimulating conversation in 1979, and Noel Stock, who has allowed me to quote from his letters to Pound at St. Elizabeths. Darlene Tennerstedt and Alma MacDougall of Northwestern University Press were very helpful in preparing the manuscript for publication.

List of Abbreviations

ABC: *ABC of Reading*
ALS: *A Lume Spento*
C: *The Cantos* (references in the text give number of Canto and page, e.g., 99/ 697)
CEP: *Collected Early Poems of Ezra Pound*
CON: *Confucius*
EPVA: *Ezra Pound and the Visual Arts*
GB: *Gaudier-Brzeska*
GK: *Guide to Kulchur*
I: *Impact: Essays on Ignorance and the Decline of American Civilization*
J/M: *Jefferson and/or Mussolini*
L: *The Letters of Ezra Pound*
LE: *Literary Essays of Ezra Pound.*
NOH: *The Classic Noh Theater of Japan*
PD: *Pavannes and Divagations*
PER: *Personae: The Collected Poems of Ezra Pound*
P/J: *Pound/Joyce: The Letters of Ezra Loomis Pound to James Joyce, with Pound's Essays on Joyce*
P/L: *Pound/Lewis: The Letters of Ezra Pound and Wyndham Lewis*
RB: *"Ezra Pound Speaking": Radio Speeches of World War II*
SP: *Selected Prose of Ezra Pound, 1909–1965*
SR: *The Spirit of Romance*
WT: *Women of Trachis*

The Genealogy of Demons

Fear, father of cruelty,
        are we to write a genealogy of the demons?
                                Canto 114, page 793

Chapter One

Introduction

Ezra Pound was fascinated by two vast, disparate, and incommensurable orders of being: the luminous realm of divine wisdom, beauty, and order, and the dark, confused, and invisible realm of microbes. As Olga Rudge told a visitor to Venice in the 1960s, "EP was reading the PARADISO aloud to her and a book on microorganisms"; she added, "beyond me" (Stern, 2: 215). It would be easy to view this anecdote as another example of Pound's expansive sensibility, which can leap from high to low, great to small, and find in each the same indwelling presence and life. Rather, it is reminiscent of another and deeply disturbing contrast in Pound's thought and works, a contrast thus far beyond the comprehension of his critics: Pound the imitator of Dante and Cavalcanti, his mind filled with images of light, beauty, and benevolence, passing judgment on the world from his "Thrones" of justice; and Pound the violent anti-Semite and fascist, whose hatred and fear of Jews finally reduces them in his mind to the demonic status of germs and bacilli, invisible "carriers" of plague and disease, a swamp, an enormous "power of putrefaction" (SP, 317) and profanation preying invisibly on the body of the West. How is one to explain the disparity between the poet who envisions ideal polities in the later *Cantos* and who, with probable reference to the Jews, also speaks of "clearing fungus" (97/ 676) and "maintain[ing] antisepsis" (94/ 635). It would seem that there is an absolute and incommensurable difference between these two aspects of Pound, and yet they appear simultaneously and inseparably in the same man and the same works.

Although anti-Semitism is a frequent and explicit theme in Pound's writing, criticism has failed to weigh Pound the poet, and Pound the anti-Semite and fascist, in a single balance. Nor has it even attempted to investigate in a thorough, systematic, and truly serious fashion the relationship of anti-Semitism and fascism to Pound's poetic techniques and language, his cultural vision, and his politics. Our first step is to survey the historical development of Pound's hatred and to show the failure of previous attempts to explain its nature and origins. Then we will show why this explosive subject has been so long suppressed.

II.

Pound passed through four stages of anti-Semitism, followed by a late and famous recantation. According to Pound in a 1967 interview with Allen Ginsberg, his "worst mistake" had been the "suburban prejudice" of anti-Semitism (Reck, 2: 27ff). This painful self-evaluation, which has been made much of by some Pound critics, no doubt alludes to Pound's social origins in the upper-middle-class suburbs of Philadelphia (Wyncote, Pennsylvania), where anti-Semitism was probably common in the last decades of the nineteenth century. At the same time, Pound implies that in essence his anti-Semitism is more or less like the "polite" and literary version which appears in James's *American Scene* and Adams's *Mont St. Michel and Chartres*. It must, therefore, be emphasized that, however painful and sincere his recantation, the adjective "suburban" euphemistically describes Pound's anti-Semitism as a whole. The enormity of Pound's hostility to the Jews can hardly be characterized as a mere "mistake." The truth is that Pound's anti-Semitism, when it finally attains its fully developed and virulent form in the late 1930s and 1940s, figures within an elaborate cultural and political ideology and serves a politically manipulative purpose, and is thus quite different from polite prejudice or mere distaste. Indeed, it is in no sense a simple prejudice but rather a massive hatred. The distinction between suburban and ideological anti-Semitism is well stated by Leo Lowenthal and Norbert Guterman in their study of the American right-wing agitator, a figure whom Pound in his later career often resembles:

> It is as though the agitator were aware of the fundamental difference between the kind of "bona fide" suburban anti-Semitism, which is not usually associated with a conscious political purpose, and totalitarian anti-Semitism, in which the Jew is primarily an object of political manipulation. An anti-Semite of the traditional type may recognize that at least some Jews are good citizens, although he would not care to meet them socially. What the agitator aims at is to impress upon his audience the need to persecute all Jews. . . . (Lowenthal, Guterman: 69)

In Pound's case the term "suburban prejudice" defines only the first of a series of loosely definable stages through which his anti-Semitism gradually took the shape of a political and cultural ideology.

The second stage began with his return to America in 1910–1911, when Pound first became aware of the extensive Jewish immigration to American shores. Besides *Patria Mia*'s reference to the Jews' "detestable" and unalterable "qualities,"[1] Pound's poetry and prose of the early and late teens and early 1920s contain hostile and contemptuous remarks about Jewish artists, businessmen, publishers, women, social reformers, and more ominously, pawn brokers. *Hugh Selwyn Mauberley* presents a not totally unsympathetic caricature of Max Beerbohm, who in fact was not Jewish but whom Pound treats as a graceless, dandified, and deracinated Jew, "Brennbaum, the Impeccable." In "Imaginary Letters," Pound's thinly disguised alter ego Walter Villerant speaks contemptuously of the social reformer and feminist "Levine," who figures as a pimp or "procure[r]" (PD, 62). In the same work, Pound introduces as Villerant's his own rather free translation of Baudelaire's "Le Vampire," in which he expresses both anti-Semitic and anti-feminist attitudes; again, the Jews are associated with prostitution and promiscuity, and also with death, decay, and the moral corruption of luxury. In another early poem, "Near Perigord," the Provençal aristocrat Bertran de Born (another alter ego of Pound's) proposes an anti-Semitic stratagem which Pound himself appears to have endorsed in a conversation at St. Elizabeths Hospital (Van O'Connor, Stone, eds., *A Casebook*: 107). Bertran tells the Provençal barons that they should pawn their castles to Jewish pawnbrokers and then steal them back: "Let the Jews pay" (PER, 152). It is obvious that at this point Pound's prejudice was not polite or suburban but considerably more ugly. Even so, anti-Semitism was not yet important in his thought.

The third stage of Pound's anti-Semitism extended roughly from the late 1920s to the late 1930s and was marked by ambivalence and equivocation culminating in violent and open hostility. During the 1920s, with his increasing interest in politics, economics, and metahistorical speculation, Pound's latent hatred of the Old Testament and of "Judaic" Protestantism emerged strongly, as well as his idea that Jewish culture and religion were altogether foreign to the Occidental spirit. Pound also discovered in usury the root cause of economic distress and cultural stagnation. Thus, by the middle 1930s, Pound had come to associate certain actual and supposed Jews, such as the Rothschilds and Sir Basil Zaharoff, with international finance, war profiteering (munitions sales), and the domination of the press. But Pound did not yet condemn the Jews as a group or view all usurers as Jewish. Writing in April 1930 to Lincoln Kirstein, Pound attacked the press, the war profiteers, and the educational system; he did not mention Jews.[2] In his numerous articles in the *New English Weekly* between February, 1934 and April, 1936, Pound attacked mainly non-Jewish usurers. He insisted that his villains were "not in one chapel only," that "usurers have no race." Attacking not only the Rothschilds but usurious Quakers, Calvinists, and Genevans, Pound wondered "how long the whole Jewish people is to be sacrificial goat for the usurer."[3] He also said, in 1937, that "Race prejudice is a red herring. The tool of a man defeated intellectually, and of the cheap politician." Pound went on to observe that "it is nonsense for the anglo-saxon to revile the jew for beating him at his own game" (GK, 242, 243). Though Pound had a profound admiration for Mussolini and Italian Fascism by the early and middle 1930s, during the same period he had no use for either Hitler or Oswald Mosley, head of the anti-Semitic British Union of

Fascists. In *Jefferson and/or Mussolini* (written in 1933) Germany is "epileptic," with many of its "militars wanting pogroms" (J/M, 34). As for Hitler, in the *New English Weekly* of May, 1934, Pound labelled him an "almost pathetic hysteric," and cautioned his readers not to confuse Italian Fascism with the "Hun's travesty." Pound also found it "difficult . . . to believe that a number" of Mosley's prominent supporters "are supporting him for any save the foulest of reasons." Over a year later Pound disavowed the "travesties of [Italian] Fascism presented in alien newspapers" and the "antics" of Mosley.[4]

Nonetheless, writing to John Drummond in 1934, Pound said that it is "all right" if "Jew baiting opens the MIND," since it would disclose not only Jewish financiers but "nazarenes" and "connecticut yankees"; he added equivocally that "once the community wakes up to the POWER of credit and takes hold of it, the jew (or financier) conspiracy flops."[5] Far less equivocal was Pound's statement, in a 1937 article in the *British Union Quarterly* (the official publication of the British Union of Fascists), that the "schnorrer [Jewish] press" spreads "vagueness in communication."[6] This statement is an ominous development from the literary anti-Semitism which Pound manifests as early as *The Spirit of Romance*, in which he inveighs against the barbaric, profuse, and subjective "Carthagenian [sic] element" (SR, 18) in European writing; it is furthermore continuous with Pound's belief, especially intense after 1939, that the most pernicious literary and intellectual habits of Westerners derive from Jewish allegory, metaphor, hermeticism, and interpretation.[7] Even more ominously, throughout the 1930s Pound increasingly emphasized the necessity of dissociating true Christianity from Judaism; inveighing repeatedly against the "squalid" (SP, 64) and "gangster" (SP, 68) ethics of the Old Testament and Talmud and the pervasive cultural influence of the "Hebrew disease" (LE, 154), he found Christianity "verminous with Semitic infections."[8] These views were inspired in part by the anti-Semitic paganism of Thaddeus Zielinski, whom Pound probably discovered in 1927 or 1928. During the 1930s Pound became increasingly disposed to judge history, politics and culture in racial terms. As Pound said in the *New English Weekly* in 1936, in an article entitled "Race": "But to suppose that a difference of policy is due to a mere ideology or to mere reason, when it has its roots in blood, bone, and endocrines, is to take a very superficial view of society, humanity and human co-ordinations."[9]

Meanwhile, *The Cantos*, the major epic which Pound had begun in 1917, became more and more obviously anti-Semitic. In addition to such political and economic slurs as his reference to Wellington as a "jew's pimp" (50/ 248) and his serious consideration in Canto 48 of the idea that the Jews were responsible for the American Civil War, *The Cantos* contain Pound's survey of Jewish Mitteleuropa (Vienna) in Canto 35. Disgusted by what he considers the utter formlessness of Jewish familial, emotional, and intellectual life, Pound speaks contemptuously of "the almost intravaginal warmth of / hebrew affections" (35/ 172–173), the Jews' "general indefinite wobble," their "sensitivity / without direction," their "communal life of the pancreas" (35/ 173). He also satirizes in this canto what he considers typically Jewish cowardice, cheap theatricality and sentimentality, cultural prostitution and mercantilism, in short, the virtual opposite of his system of values. Later, in Canto 52, written in the late 1930s, Pound denounces the Rothschilds, speaks of the "few big jews' vendetta on goyim" (52/ 257), and implicitly endorses a quotation, falsely attributed to Benjamin Franklin, recommending the total quarantine of Jews from America. The American universities, said Pound in 1939, "have never faced the Jew as a problem," while "the short cut for England," as he told R. McNair Wilson in a letter of the same year, is "VIA Mosley."[10]

The fourth stage of Pound's anti-Semitism began in the 1940s. Strongly colored by biological racism, and bearing an unmistakable resemblance to the Nazi version, it now figured within a political ideology. Broadcasting during wartime in favor of the Axis cause over Rome radio, Pound referred to the Jews as "the rot eating in since Cromwell" (RB, 190), as an "alien race" which had "wormed into the system" (RB, 199) and "infected the world" (RB, 340). The vengeful and power-hungry Jews stood "against the rest of humanity" (RB, 310), fomenting "chaos" (RB, 320) and "racial enmity" (RB, 329), seeking the "ruin" of "all goyim [Gentiles]" (RB, 284). Now Pound saw the Jews not so much as human beings or individuals but as "rats" (SP, 317), "bed bugs" (RB, 253), "vermin" (RB, 74–75, 86), "worms" (RB, 59), "syphilis" (RB, 86), "plague" (RB, 74), "disease incarnate";[11] "until a man purges himself of this [Jewish] poison," said Pound, "he will never achieve understanding" (SP, 320). Thus Pound called for a "purge" (RB, 62), a program of "RACIAL survival" (RB, 203), a "RACIAL solution" (RB, 153) of "world prophylaxis" (RB, 115). The "choice" was now "between Europe and Jewry" (RB, 310). As for the Nazis, they "wiped out bad manners in Germany" (RB, 32).

Nor is there any reason to believe, as do some critics, that Pound's attitudes changed after his supposedly restorative and purgative encounter with Nature during his imprisonment in Pisa.[12] After the war, Pound spoke of Hitler as a "martyr" and celebrated him in the later *Cantos*;[13] these also contain references to the "*dung flow*" of the "*kikery*" (91/ 614) among many other instances of racial and cultural anti-Semitism, and encrypt an historical tradition of Aryan kings which includes Hitler and Mussolini. During his confinement for insanity at St. Elizabeths Hospital, Pound told Charles Olson that a lunatic is "an animal somewhat surrounded by Jews" (Olson: 75, 55). For Pound America had become "Baruchistan" or the "Jewnited States," with "NOTHING but bloody kikery visible as an element in the soc[ial] scene" (P/L, 291, 299, 284, 286). Pound's anti-Semitism persisted in his poetry, prose, and letters into the 1960s, when he finally recanted.[14]

III.

According to one unnamed observer, Pound became anti-Semitic through contagion; anti-Semitism was "in the air" in the teens and 1920s, and he caught a strain of it.[15] Another explanation is that Pound's anti-Semitism derives from his American nativism and especially his Populism, for like Pound the Populists denounced the tyranny of Eastern banks and had strong agrarian and middle-class values.[16] Other critics argue that Pound's anti-Semitism springs entirely or mainly from his hatred of usury, which he then mistakenly identified with the Jews.[17] And others argue that it stems from his anti-monotheism and paganism, and is a "logical corollary" of these beliefs.[18]

The idea that Pound "caught" anti-Semitism fails to explain why his anti-Semitism is far more virulent than that of other writers in his milieu, including Wyndham Lewis. Like most attempts to exonerate Pound's anti-Semitism, this diagnosis suggests, mistakenly, that its sources are external to Pound and his work. As for the image of Pound's anti-Semitism as a form of Populism, it is true that Pound had Populist affinities and values and even appealed to the Populist tradition in the broadcasts against the Jews; it has also been argued that Populism is perhaps the first major instance of political anti-Semitism in the United States.[19] Even so, Populism was largely anti-European and anti-intellectual, and thus opposed to many of the values to which Pound appeals in his anti-Semitism. Nor can it be equated with fascism. But even more dubious is the very common idea that Pound's anti-Semitism is primarily of economic origin, a deduction from his opposition to usury. It has been shown repeatedly that anti-Semitism is only partially connected with materialism or any other kind of economics, often having its deepest roots in religion, cultural tradition, racist theory, and the psychology of individuals and groups.[20]

Much more plausible is the idea that Pound's anti-Semitism stems from his hatred of monotheism and that his paganism is thus a "logical corollary" of his religious and moral beliefs. But the problems in this case are twofold. For one thing, this interpretation would largely ignore personal and social interests as well as unconscious psychological factors. For another, no one has shown in detail in what sense anti-Semitism is the logical corollary of Pound's other beliefs.

Although C. David Heymann has said that Pound's anti-Semitism is finally inexplicable, the correct view is that critics have not tried very hard to explain it—as opposed to explaining it away. Bernard Bergonzi argues that there is a "striking lack of actual or responsible criticism" of Pound, the sort that is "prepared . . . to ask awkward questions."[21] Such criticism would presumably study the roots of anti-Semitism (and fascism) and, making use of the large body of post-war research, explore its thematic, formal, and structural role in Pound's works. But if it seems scandalous that no such criticism has yet been attempted, its reason is clear. In an effort to rehabilitate Pound and protect his reputation, the Pound cult and the "Pound industry" have produced an ingenious body of critical writing in which Pound's anti-Semitism has been arbitrarily discounted, ignored, in short, repressed. This apologetic tradition began in the late 1940s under New Critical auspices and it achieved its fullest expression in the controversy over the Bollingen award.

In February, 1949, the Fellows of the Library of Congress awarded Pound the first Bollingen Prize for poetry for the Pisan *Cantos*. Since the judges were all distinguished poets and writers, normally the award would not have been questioned. But in this case a national institution had honored a writer for a work that contained strongly fascist and anti-Semitic passages. Only six years earlier, Pound had been charged with treason for his radio broadcasts, and may well have avoided conviction and execution through his successful insanity plea, which led to his confinement in St. Elizabeths Hospital in Washington.[22]

The focus of the controversy was this passage from the jury's statement:

> . . . To permit other considerations than that of poetic achievement to sway the decision would destroy the significance of the award and would in principle deny the validity of that objective perception of value on which civilized society must rest.[23]

In general, Pound's support came from critics who asserted the principle of aesthetic autonomy, the independence of poetic judgment from all "extrinsic" facts and values. In their view, Pound's poetry should be judged according to "intrinsic" standards of poetic style, form, technique, language. In no way was the value of his poetry diminished or affected by his personal beliefs or their expression in his work; such matters were irrelevant to poetic judgment. The award of the Bollingen Prize to Pound was thus a major victory for ascendant New Critical formalism.

Many critics, mainly liberals, had moral and political reservations about the award, questioning whether a poem which contained anti-Semitic and fascist avowals, and whose author had broadcast for the fascist cause, deserved the Bollingen Prize. Clement Greenberg and George Orwell were disturbed by what they viewed as the jury's indifference to content and moral value as criteria of literary judgment (*A Casebook*: 58–61). William Barrett, though he accepted the jury's decision with reservations, found it "so obsessed with formal and technical questions that it . . . [had] time only for a hasty glimpse at content" (*A Casebook*: 53). Similarly, the poet and political conservative Peter Viereck questioned a "method of analysis" that tends to "treat a poem by itself, like a self-created airtight-sealed object,

outside cause and effect," thus discarding its supposedly *"irrelevant* historical, psychological, and 'moralizing' incrustations" (*A Casebook*: 100).

In this group of critics one finds the frequent assumption that the New
Critics were absolute formalists, indifferent to content and meaning and
interested only in verbal technique. Robert Gorham Davis rebuked the
Bollingen jury for allowing form and content to fall into an "abstract polar-
ity," and he reminded the jurors that Pound viewed these as inseparable;
Peter Viereck said that "the issue is whether, as some 'new critics' believe,
form and technique can be considered apart from content and meaning."[24]
Other critics, however, mainly protested the presumably detachable content
of Pound's work, his objectionable subject matter or ideas considered separately from poetic technique or form. As Barrett said, the Bollingen controversy raised the question: "How far is it possible, in a lyric poem, for
technical embellishments to transform vicious and ugly matter into beautiful
poetry?" (*A Casebook*: 53). For Barrett, style or formal technique are a mere
external or "inorganic" embellishment of some more important internal
content.

One understands why Allen Tate resisted the attack on the award, for
the New Critics themselves opposed the dissociation of form (or style) and
content (*A Casebook*: 63–64). If anything it was such liberal critics as
Barrett who invoked the form-content distinction, treating content as "inside" and style or form as the "outside" of the text, and attacking Pound
primarily for his content or ideas. The New Critics never concerned themselves only with form and technique, nor did they banish content from
poetry or deny poetry the status of a kind of knowledge; in fact, at some
points they argued that poetry presents experiential, psychological, imaginative, and moral truth, thus covertly or overtly endorsing extrinsic criteria.
Generally speaking, what the New Critics objected to were propositional
and assertive statements in poetry. They saw a good poem as organic and
nonassertive; it should not mean but be. It should marry form and content,
technique and meaning, so that ideas lose their discursive, propositional,
and assertive status within the autonomous verbal context defined by the
poem. Content thus becomes dramatized and embodied, providing an occasion for immediate experience and unified feeling; beyond mere paraphrase,
meaning was supposed to be organically inseparable from the language that
embodies it. A poem is thus to be judged as bad or weak if its ideas (or
content) are so badly assimilated that they appear as mere propositional or
dogmatic opinions, untransformed by sensibility and reducible to paraphrase. No longer an autonomous object, the poem thus becomes merely
"about" something, inviting judgment according to unpoetic or extrinsic
standards, such as the rightness or wrongness or logicality of its ideas.[25]
When Allen Tate said that *The Cantos* were "not about anything,"[26] he
most likely meant that they were not propositional or dogmatic, that they
"dramatized" experience and made no isolatable truth claims or assertions;

and moreover, that those parts of *The Cantos* that did make such claims might therefore be judged inferior *not* for what they said, but for the fact that the ideas stood out as such.

Given such assumptions, there could be little meaningful debate between the New Critics and most of Pound's opponents, for whom "extrinsic" standards were sufficient to devaluate his work. Irving Howe condemned Pound's poetry because of Pound the man: Pound, he said, was "beyond the bounds of our intellectual life." Karl Shapiro, a dissenting member of the Library of Congress jury, argued that "the poet's political and moral philosophy ultimately vitiates his poetry and lowers its standards as literary work." Taking a more historical perspective, Robert Gorham Davis spoke of a "whole set" of bankrupt and reactionary "values" for which *The Cantos* were "a test case," and implied that such values led to the poem's bankruptcy.[27]

Nonetheless, Davis was one of the few critics to suggest a possible alternative to the dichotomy between form and content which the New Critics held in suspicion and which had led many liberal critics into facile moralizing. *The Cantos*, he said, fail not only in moral or historical but in formal terms; their incoherence is "real incoherence"; it is not "achieved form" (*A Casebook*: 57). In short, Davis believed that the poem's incoherent value system or content must produce formal incoherence. Davis's position resembled that of Viereck in his criticism of the New Critics. It is doubtful, said Viereck, "that artistic form can be considered apart from its content or moral meaning." In "discarding the *relevant* historical, psychological, and ethical aspects [of a text], they [the New Critics] are often misreading the text itself" (*A Casebook*: 100–101). Both Davis and Viereck thus challenged the idea of the autonomous poem, and both were undaunted by the heresy of paraphrase; insisting that a poem must mean, Viereck referred to a propositional and finally discriminable content. On the other hand, both critics denied that "extrinsic" matter is really extrinsic; rather it is *in* and part of the poem, and has structural consequences. Form and content are, therefore, discriminable but interconnected: demonstrable coherence at the level of ideas is demanded if the poem is to have final coherence at the level of language and form.[28]

Neither Davis nor Viereck nor anyone else pursued this kind of analysis. Having condemned Pound for his beliefs, placing him "beyond the bounds of our intellectual life," the liberal critics largely ignored him and thus ironically paved the way for his more recent cultural rehabilitation as a poet of ideas. In the meantime, it still remained possible to minimize the importance of the ideas in Pound's poem. One could still argue that anti-Semitism, once assimilated into the organic structure of *The Cantos*, becomes something essentially different from what it is in the world of political discourse. Or one could argue that anti-Semitism, as an "idea" or "theme" or "opinion," is only part of the poem's paraphrasable content or logical "scaffolding,"[29] which vanishes once ideas are successfully dramatized within the work. Anti-Semitism is thus a mere abstraction, an isolated element which one can freely ignore. The most striking example of this argument was Archibald MacLeish's "Poetry and Opinion," which was written during the Bollingen controversy and sought to insulate Pound's poetry against the contaminating presence of anti-Semitism and fascism. Admitting that *The Cantos* contain contemptible attitudes, Mac-Leish nonetheless said that the poem, if it is to be attacked or condemned, must be attacked intrinsically, as a poem, and not for its ideas. MacLeish distinguished between the poet's opinions, such as anti-Semitism and fascism, which he saw as false, abstract, and external, and his dramatized artistic "intuitions," which are based on concrete experience and thus have a claim to truth as well as to our admiration.[30]

New Critical formalism, however, hardly characterizes present views of Pound or the main trend of Pound criticism. In fact, the last three decades have witnessed the accumulation of a large body of criticism which examines Pound's historical and cultural theories and which admires his cultural values. Critics such as Christine Brooke-Rose stress the inseparability of Pound's ideas and values from the language and form of his works (Brooke-Rose: 66–73). This new Pound differs strikingly from the purely formalist or liberal versions of the late 1940s. More than just a technical master, this culturally rehabilitated Pound is the misunderstood and benevolent prophet of various transhistorical and mythical values essential to the survival of modern culture. Only incidentally a fascist and anti-Semite, he is primarily an enemy of "the capitalist-imperialist state."[31]

It was inevitable that criticism should have come to emphasize Pound's content. Karl Shapiro observed in 1949 that Pound's poetry is often didactic, and that Pound must therefore protest any judgment of his works which neglects his ideas and opinions, his subject matter, and his moral values. Pound himself described *The Cantos* as a "political weapon," implying that they demand to be judged on the validity of their truth claims.[32] Critical practice has also demonstrated repeatedly that Pound's poetry cannot be adequately understood exclusively by New Critical methods. Far from constituting their own autonomous or intrinsic context, *The Cantos* require the reader to go outside the text for elucidation and understanding. Constantly expanding their reference, they presuppose knowledge of Pound's other poems, his cultural, political, and economic writings, numerous historical sources, places, and cultural artifacts. They also intersect with discursive statements contained in Pound's broadcasts. And finally, it is impossible to understand *The Cantos* without knowledge of the poet's life and personality: as Eliot said, *The Cantos* are "wholly himself."[33]

IV.

Yet the acceptance of extrinsic ideas and standards in Pound criticism has not led to any serious examination of his anti-Semitism. Although Cookson argues that there is no "fundamental split" (SP, 7) in Pound's works, critics continue to treat anti-Semitism as an incidental, "peripheral," isolatable, and finally detachable subject matter clinging to the margins of Pound's text. Even G. S. Fraser, by no means a Pound idolator, argues that anti-Semitism is not "central" to Pound.[34]

Of all attempts to explain away Pound's anti-Semitism, none is more absurd than Henry Swabey's idea that Pound was persecuted for a putative fascism and anti-Semitism in order to distract attention from his earth-shaking radical economics.[35] Nor is there any substance in Wendy Flory's updated dissociation of Pound's "true" or essential emotions from his supposedly adventitious ideas and opinions. According to Flory, the true, good, and essential Pound is emotional and intuitional, and instinctively inclines toward benevolence and humanitarianism as long as he keeps in touch with his "real feelings." When Pound writes great poetry, he is expressing his deepest, most authentic emotions. By contrast, the bad Pound is fearful of introspection and loses touch with his emotions, thus getting lost in theory and propaganda, opinions, abstract formulas, and dogmas, and making "choices on a theoretical rather than emotional basis." Flory's radical separation of Pound's "poetic" self and his propagandizing self enables her to dismiss as false or insincere anything which, either in his poetry or prose, smacks of intolerance, authoritarianism, and anti-Semitism.[36]

Apart from the contradictory fact that Flory has no difficulty in discussing many Poundian ideas as expressed in verse, her distinctions are vague, arbitrary, and psychologically dubious. *The Cantos*, besides being lyrical and emotional, are didactic, and their didactic purpose carries over into lyrical passages. Nor are the radio broadcasts an example of extraneous and emotionless ideology. Constantly illuminating the ideas of *The Cantos*, they are also among the most psychologically revealing of Pound's writings, a "repellent analytical session," as Bacigalupo calls them (Bacigalupo: 102). As for Flory's strenuously argued thesis that Pound's violence and political excesses result from his imitation of Wyndham Lewis, this is a forced attempt to make Lewis into a scapegoat for Pound. Lewis became disenchanted with Hitler by the late 1930s, whereas Pound went on to make broadcasts in the 1940s. In their commitment to fascism as in their violence, Pound's broadcasts surpass anything in Lewis. If Pound was imitating anyone when he made these broadcasts, his models were Benito Mussolini and Adolf Hitler.

Another persistent idea is that Pound's anti-Semitism is only economic. It takes little trouble to show that his prejudice is essentialist, racial, and biological, these being fundamental aspects of modern anti-Semitism. Other critics argue that Pound's anti-Semitism is a mere "label" or "bias," belied by the fact that some of his friends, such as Louis Zukofsky, were Jewish. Such reasoning is a staple of anti-Semitic apologetics, and one has only to recall Wagner, who enjoyed having Jews as disciples and in his entourage, to realize that Pound's friendship with individual Jews proves nothing.[37] Other critics, following Pound, view anti-Semitism (and fascism) as an "error" or "mistake," an "embarrassment," "aberration," or temporary "infatuation" within his works.[38] The notion that Pound's anti-Semitism is a mistake underlies some critics' attempts to determine the truth or falsity of Pound's statements on the Jews, and then to measure their significance by the frequency of such statements in his work. Pound's prejudice would thus consist of "spurious matter," and, to quote George Dekker, would as a purely "peripheral" element "account . . . for a great deal less in . . . [*The Cantos*] than is often supposed."[39] Not only does Dekker erroneously suggest that Pound infrequently lapses into anti-Semitism in *The Cantos,* but it is doubtful that a simple numerical tally of Pound's anti-Semitic references can disclose its full significance.[40]

For other critics, Pound's anti-Semitism is not so much a historical ideology as a historical symbol or myth. As Ray West suggests, in using the word "Kike," Pound employs a time-tested and "conventional symbol" which does not register any actual hatred of Jews. Rather, in Pound the Jew is a symbol of a certain form of ugliness; for "so much of literature deals with the ugly," and "Beauty is difficult" (*A Casebook*: 69). This idea, which has reappeared in a variety of forms, suggests that for Pound the Jews have no real connection with the evils which he has them represent; their ideological victimization is neither risked nor intended. The fact, however, is that Pound distrusts symbolism and employs it only when he believes the symbol is intimately related with its referent. Pound also refers to specific Jews as evil and treats them as objects of ideological violence. It therefore makes no difference that Pound's anti-Semitism relies on spurious material, or that it is a kind of phantasmatic delusion. None of this would make his hatred any less actual, or the Jews any less figures of evil in his work.[41]

The notion that Pound's anti-Semitism is a myth has served other attempts to deny its reality and importance. Writing on Pound in the *Sewanee Review* in 1950, James Blish argued that since all myths are cognitively meaningless, it makes no difference what myth an artist uses, so long as it helps his creation. All poetic myths are delusional systems, so there is no point in criticizing Pound for his anti-Semitic delusion. Blish also argued that liberal critics found Pound's anti-Semitism offensive only because this particular myth posed "a clear and present danger." As memories of fascism faded, and critics attained a broader historical perspective, Pound's anti-Semitic myths would seem no more reprehensible than Shakespeare's or Marlowe's (Blish: 185–226).

Few if any Pound critics now believe that Pound's myths are meaningless. As for Blish's argument that Pound's anti-Semitism is a "myth" comparable to Shakespeare's or Marlowe's, this is an early attempt to minimize and misrepresent Pound's hatred by placing him in distinguished literary company. Yet there is a difference between Pound's anti-Semitism and the earlier, largely Christian versions. Peter Viereck observes that the anti-Semitism of Shakespeare was not in "blunt defiance of the limited information available to . . . [his] age [indeed it reflected the ruling ideas of his period]." Viereck rightly adds that "pre-Belsen and post-Belsen anti-Semitism, though both unjustified, are qualitatively different: the former (Shakespeare or Voltaire) cannot be logically compared to the latter (Pound or Céline)" (*A Casebook*: 98–99).

In his disregard for historical differences, Blish anticipates those critics for whom Pound, as an already timeless classic, must be judged not primarily within his immediate historical context but rather as the repository of mythical in the sense of "timeless" values.[42] Pound's connection with fascism and anti-Semitism is thus necessarily deemphasized, since neither is a transhistorical or mythical value. To put it another way, Pound had the bad luck or "bad timing" or committed the "great error" of choosing the "wrong side" in World War II, just as Milton chose the "wrong side" in the English Revolution[43]—again, as if Pound's political stance and ideology has nothing to do with his poem. But, of course, such arguments are preposterous, since it would be impossible to understand *The Cantos* or *Paradise Lost* apart from their historical and political affiliations. For all their mythologizing, *The Cantos* also contain a specific historical ideology and are written in response to specific historical needs. Any attempt to project their meaning to a mythical plane beyond history must neglect their more immediate and relevant significance.

Along with anti-Semitism, Pound's most troublesome ideology is fascism, which was originally the main subject of this book. Thus far we have no accepted definition of Pound—to use William Chace's phrase—as a "political identity." The matter is complicated by Pound's radically nominalistic denial of fascism. In a 1958 letter to Thomas Horton, Pound complained that E. E. Cummings refused to collaborate in one of his political schemes "cause Mosley wuz 'fascist' / nice package word."[44] Or, to quote a 1951 letter from Pound to Wyndham Lewis, Pound's broadcasts were his "OWN stuff, NOT axis" (P/L, 264), for in fact Brooks Adams, one of Pound's favorite historians in the broadcasts, had preceded fascism by decades. These remarks reflect Pound's irritation that some consider him a fascist, when in his view both his and other so-called fascists' politics are so unusual and individualistic as to resist any abstract categorization. There is no need to adopt Pound's characteristic distrust of abstraction and generalization. Though the concept of "generic fascism" has been called in question in recent years, many scholars believe that the preservation of the concept is preferable to a chaos of "radical nominalism."[45] Fascism forms a loose but distinct political typology, and Pound's ideology falls within it. Following the now accepted practice of historians, this work refers to the generic concept of fascism with a lower-case "f," reserving the upper-case "F" for the Italian variety of fascism. This distinction is necessary because, as we shall see, Pound's political ideology sometimes conforms chiefly to the Italian Fascist model, while at others it follows other patterns within European fascism, especially National Socialism.

The reasons for my shift of emphasis from fascism to anti-Semitism are also worth considering. It is evident, as Ernst Nolte shows, that anti-Semitism or racism is insufficient to constitute fascism. Nonetheless, Nolte points out that anti-Semitism is ideologically indispensable to Nazism as well as to Maurras' *Action Française* (which Nolte views as a fascist movement); it is also indispensable to numerous other fascist ideologies.[46] Far more than Pound's economics, whose importance is much exaggerated by his apologists, anti-Semitism is the crucial factor in the development of his fascism. Simply put, anti-Semitism goes further to explain Pound's fascism than vice versa.

And yet, serious questions persist concerning the place and effect of anti-Semitism not only in Pound's work but in literature generally. If we assume, for instance, that anti-Semitism is only a "present danger," would it not be inconsistent for us "to praise Dostoyevsky merely because Czarism is a distant memory and castigate Pound because the enormity of fascism is of recent date?" (*A Casebook*: 17). Is it not also true that any work will contain attitudes that some persons will find objectionable and even insupportable? Perhaps we can read Pound as we read Dostoyevsky, Homer, and numerous other authors, without troubling too much over what may be erroneous, retrograde, and even inhuman but finally incidental attitudes? Is it not possible to make allowances for Pound, separating the good from the bad or ugly elements in his work? One can seriously ask what is required for anti-Semitism to have verbal, formal, and thematic significance in Pound's text. At the same time, what are the conditions under which the presence of anti-Semitism might seem to vitiate that text, or at least seriously qualify our judgment of it?

V.

Anti-Semitism is not a mere idea or theme that Pound picks up somewhere and then "uses" or "applies" in his work. Apart from its historical, cultural, and sociological influences, the inner logic, content, and motivation of Pound's anti-Semitism emerges from within his works and the mind of their creator. Far from being adventitious or extraneous to Pound's texts, anti-Semitism is a characteristic manifestation of Pound's thought and language, a virtually inescapable response to the most pressing intellectual and poetic difficulties. In short, there are certain irresistible ideological and poetic reasons why Pound assigned negative meanings to the Jewish "parasite,"[47] who is as necessary to Pound's text as he is to his thinking and personal psychology.

This book rejects entirely the most common and influential view of Pound's anti-Semitism. Although Pound criticism now accepts the importance of "extrinsic" elements such as ideas, in dealing with anti-Semitism it still adheres implicitly to a protective distinction which, if it is not structured on the earlier antithesis of "intrinsic" and "extrinsic," still preserves the idea of a hierarchical textual difference between "core" or "central" and peripheral meanings: the primary and subsidiary, the essential and extraneous, the authentic and the factitious. Thus, there is an enclosed and organic central core of familiar Poundian truths, a harmonious and univocal constellation of themes, values, and definitions; there is also the extraneous, marginal, and implicitly "parasitic" theme of anti-Semitism, a theme that has no place within the organic core and is thus both discontinuous with and different from it. One needs little subtlety to see that in quarantining anti-Semitism Pound criticism is curiously repeating (imperfectly to be sure) Pound's cultural strategy against the Jews. For just as Pound seeks to define an absolute difference between the organic core culture of the West and the presumably disruptive Jewish strangers who yet dwell familiarly within it, and uses the violent charge of parasitism to establish this difference, so Pound critics have used a similar and no less arbitrary violence in quarantining Pound's text from another disruptive, extraneous, and yet familiar presence. Where Pound treats the extraneous Jews as the dangerous embodiment of otherness and confusion, critics treat anti-Semitism as a textually foreign substance, the dangerous "other" of Pound's text.

It is erroneous for a number of reasons to think that anti-Semitism stands like an unbidden guest within Pound's supposedly harmonious semantic household. Not only does it dwell manifestly within the text, but it figures within its verbal and especially its metaphorical economy. As we shall see later, Pound's writing is pervaded by an elaborate system of metaphors. Virtually every metaphor through which Pound represents the Jews and expresses his anti-Semitism—the swamp, bacilli, plague, castration, parthenogenesis, erosion, the parasite—first appears elsewhere, and without any reference to the Jews, in Pound's attacks on the Gentile community. This suggests that Pound's anti-Semitism belongs within his metaphorical system and is linked to the rest of his writing by a chain of metaphorical displacements and substitutions. Anti-Semitism is thus part of the economy of Pound's language—not as a single theme so much as a cluster or tangle of varied images and metaphors which are deployed throughout Pound's writing. For this reason, it cannot be understood in isolation from Pound's text. Nor, for that matter, can Pound's text be understood in isolation from his anti-Semitism.

Nonetheless, Pound insists on defining the Jews as parasites. As to what, at the deepest level, Pound's charge of parasitism might serve, and why anti-Semitism has been excluded from the core of Poundian themes, these questions can be answered fully only over the course of this book. However, two points can be made here. J. Hillis Miller points out that the "parasite" is often characterized by a threatening confusion and uncertainty, particularly in the eyes of those belonging to the closed community in which the parasite appears.[48] The parasite calls in question the community's (or text's) operative meanings and distinctions, the laws and limits it sets for itself and its self-identity. Neither exactly within nor exactly without the community, neither totally other nor acceptably familiar, but moving freely across (and thus transgressing and obscuring) all margins, the parasite has the uncanny capacity to make the familiar strange and the strange familiar, to destabilize the conventional meanings on which a social or textual order depends. Since the parasite is not the sheer opposite of the community, is not sheer other, its mystery and confusion cannot be viewed as entirely foreign. Rather, he is the community's uncanny double, whose very presence reminds men of the mystery and confusion that exists within a community (or text) and which it normally conceals. This brings me to my second point, namely that the charge of parasitism is an essential feature of the process of projection and scapegoating described by René Girard. According to Girard, not only is the "parasitic" scapegoat held responsible for the violent breakdown of cultural distinctions and differentiations, in short confusion, he is himself the monstrous embodiment of such confusion, a symbol of all that the community considers other: a monster. And yet, in his very confusion the scapegoat is also the secret, uncanny, and projected image, the very double of the community that expels him (Girard, 3: *passim*). Only an arbitrary act of exclusionary violence can establish the distinction between the parasitic scapegoat or "other" and the core community itself.

My contention in the second half of this book is that the Jews, whom Pound treats as intolerably other, are essential to his text in precisely the manner defined above. They are the unrecognized double of the confusion and uncertainty which lurks at the putative center or core of Pound's writing, that is, his definitions, ideas, and cultural values. Without the Jews, without the arbitrary assignment of difference and confused otherness to this group, without the arbitrary repression of the parasite through violence, Pound would never be able to carry out, if only provisionally and questionably, his major project of calling things by their right names. His anti-Semitism, then, does not exist in itself, as a detachable theme, nor should one look for its explanation outside the text or in explicitly anti-Semitic statements. The possibility of anti-Semitism is always present in Pound whenever his text either consciously or unconsciously transgresses its own categories, laws, and assumptions, at moments of confusion, contradiction, and undecidability. In short, anti-Semitism is inseparable from those instances in which Pound cannot command meaning, where univocal significance is undercut by the overdetermination or polysemousness of metaphor, where his essential and seemingly fixed and univocal concepts, such as Nature, usury, and luxury, prove to be inherently confused and finally undecidable. Besides being an obviously historical issue, and apart from its social and cultural sources, Pound's anti-Semitism is no less a problem of signification, language.

Nor can Pound's anti-Semitism be treated apart from his personality, which as Eliot recognized, pervades *The Cantos.* In *Anti-Semite and Jew* Jean-Paul Sartre rejects the idea that anti-Semitism is a molecule that can enter into combination with other molecules without undergoing and causing any alteration. Instead, it is inseparably and necessarily connected with the anti-Semite's personal being and total view of the world: "If the Jew did not exist the anti-Semite would invent him."

> Anti-Semitism is a free and total choice of oneself, a comprehensive attitude that one adopts not only toward Jews but toward men in general, toward history and society; it is at one and the same time a passion and a conception of the world. (Sartre: 13, 17)

Less convincing is Sartre's existentialist assumption that anti-Semitism is a purely conscious choice of one's being (and hence an act of bad faith or false consciousness pure and simple). Ernst Simmel has argued that "psychoanalysts must infer that . . . [anti-Semitic] accusations have a symbolical significance, i.e., they stand for something else."[49] Simmel treats anti-Semitism neither in isolation from the personality nor solely in terms of its manifest content. Nor is it exclusively a conscious choice, as in Sartre. Anti-Semitism reflects the tension between conscious and unconscious impulses, is an overdetermined symptom of psychic contradiction and ambivalence. The Jews figure within a process of repression and projection, are associated with that which the subject cannot acknowledge within himself.

Increasingly in Pound the Jews are the object on which he projects not only his anxieties and fears but also his own ambivalent attitudes towards numerous other things. The contradictory and confused representation of the Jews in Pound's writing testifies not to any confusion in the Jewish "object" but rather to his persistently undefined attitude towards Nature, History, the feminine, instinct, sexuality, the unconscious, production and many other concepts whose precise definition is demanded within Pound's project of cultural reconstruction. Pound's accusations of Jewish violence have little relevance to the Jews themselves but are beyond question a reflection of the confusion and violence that dwells within Pound. Anti-Semitism, then, at once conceals and reveals Pound's personality, a personality which dominates his works. Far from being any reason for dismissing it, the massive incoherence of this hatred is precisely what makes it so important. As the most unstable and irrational element in the entire Poundian corpus, anti-Semitism helps to reveal incoherences concealed elsewhere in his writings. All this explains why, for long stretches of this study, the direct examination of anti-Semitism will be suspended as a central subject and our attention will be shifted to "something else." But logically and inevitably the narrative will always return to its main theme.

It is perhaps unnecessary for me to emphasize that I am not treating anti-Semitism from within an organicist conception of Pound. A common assumption of organicism is that any single element of a work or corpus, no matter how small, marginal, or seemingly insignificant, should reflect and fit into the whole; the larger work, meanwhile, is a continuous, coherent, and unified entity, a seamless web in which every element is logically related to every other. Thus Cookson, quoting Pound in a different context, says that Pound's entire work is "one, indivisible" (SP, 7), like a tree. The truth is that this indivisible whole is constantly disrupted and intersected by fault lines, intellectual rifts, metaphorical hiatuses, discontinuities and ambiguities. Anti-Semitism is a major symptom of inorganic fracture, of that discontinuous, grotesque, irrational, and demonic element which Yeats was perhaps the first to note in *The Cantos*.[50]

To prove the preceding contentions would be to show the poetic, ideological, and psychological importance of anti-Semitism in Pound's writings. But this does not answer our earlier question, namely, in what way might its presence vitiate Pound's work, or at least seriously qualify our judgment of it. Obviously, the mere presence of anti-Semitism in Pound should probably not in itself be considered a serious flaw, since it is also present in Dostoyevsky and Eliot, neither of whose reputations much suffer for it. On the other hand, it might seem that anti-Semitism, insofar as it is dependent on a dubious charge of parasitism, and insofar as it is not only incoherent but symptomatic of a greater textual incoherence, would formally and ideologically vitiate Pound's work. Nonetheless, the charge of parasitism and the scapegoating strategy are often found in various (and usually non-lethal) forms in both literature and culture, while many great works of art are arguably in some way or other incoherent, transgressing their own assumptions and laws. If anything, this question involves not a formal issue or even the relation of formalism to morality but rather the problem of evil in literature. For it must be emphasized that Pound's anti-Semitism is quite different from Dostoyevsky's and Eliot's.[51] Not only is it a massive and prevalent theme, but at a number of points in Pound's poetry and prose it becomes so virulent that Pound hints covertly at the extermination of the Jews. This is a fact later to be demonstrated and always to be kept in mind, for it would be difficult if not impossible to find a truly great work or writer in Western tradition embracing such acknowledged evil.[52]

VI.

In its method and scope this study should reflect its subject. Pound's anti-Semitism or any version of this prejudice is not a single phenomenon with a single cause, such as economics. Like fascism, it is an overdetermined and multidimensional phenomenon demanding multiple and linked strategies of explanation (Loewenstein: 65). Thus, instead of confining itself to Pound's psychology and language, this study will define Pound's anti-Semitism within his cultural and political ideology and within the entire religious and secular tradition of anti-Semitism in the West. Nor can it discount the historical, social, and economic pressures—the catastrophes of class and status—under which Pound's anti-Semitism acquired its virulent ideological form. The "genealogy" mentioned in the title is not meant to imply that Pound's anti-Semitism can be traced to a single origin: though the term derives from a passage in Pound, its meaning is closer to Nietzsche's notion of genealogy as an endless decipherment of "sign chains," a tangle of significations without issue in a single meaning, cause, motivation, univocal truth.[53] The book thus begins synchronically, with a survey of Pound's fully-developed anti-Semitic ideology, and only later, to avoid synchronic distortions, moves backward in order to pick up the various strands which formed that ideology. Since anti-Semitism figures in many of Pound's works, and since his works constantly intersect with and inter-illuminate each other, the focus is not only on *The Cantos* but on Pound's entire corpus. If his radio broadcasts seem to have been overemphasized, my justification is that these works have never been seriously examined, and that they are frequently continuous with *The Cantos* and other Poundian texts in their language and themes.[54]

Though it conforms in one sense to familiar critical practice, this book applies to Pound a variety of critical instruments and methods that Pound criticism has largely resisted or ignored. It is indebted to the modern social sciences, to the extensive historical, psychological, and sociological research on anti-Semitism and fascism in the post-war period, and to the theories of the Frankfurt School, which brings twentieth-century Marxism within its scope. It is also indebted to Derrida, chiefly for his critique of logocentrism and metaphor; to Lacan, who casts light on Pound's pervasive phallocentrism; and especially to René Girard, whose theories of scapegoating and sacrifice provide an entirely new perspective for Pound studies. Freud is a pervasive influence. It should be emphasized that there is a good reason for the use of such "alien" methodologies.[55] Many Pound critics have been deeply influenced by Pound himself and, without necessarily being anti-Semitic, share or reflect his ideology and values. Often they have chosen methodologies which agree with Pound's assumptions and explain him in the terms (often taken from his prose) which he provides. The influence of Pound's belief in mythological values on Poundian myth criticism is but one example of this development. To be sure, a critic should first attempt to understand an author on his own terms. However, at the present time much of Pound criticism appears not only as an apology for Pound but as a mirroring of the Pound canon. Instead of offering a truly critical analysis, it all too often repeats or reflects his work in a sophisticated paraphrase or commentary, and in this way carries out the protection of his text. This activity is far removed from the ultimate task of criticism, which should never only restate an author's position or re-present his work. A critic should also attempt to stand outside the Poundian text by adopting methods whose assumptions are sharply opposed to Pound's, should analyze his works with different mediating terms than those which critics generally employ. Only in this way is a genuinely critical understanding possible.[56]

The title of this book raises the question of myth, which is in need of some clarification. In one sense the word simply alludes to Pound's belief that mythological understanding is essential not only to his work but to the salvation of Western culture. Actually, rather than emerging out of any truly primitive or prehistorical consciousness or transmitting archetypal content or value, as some critics believe, most of Pound's myths serve historical and ideological purposes and are consciously manipulated by Pound; their specific historical, personal and practical significance should therefore be examined. It is no less important to remember that in Greek rationalism (for instance Plato and the Sophists) and Old Testament prophecy—two traditions Pound generally disliked[57]—myth means a false structure of thought, a fiction serving to mislead the multitude and preserve power; it thus calls forth the enterprise of demythification.[58] And so, in the broadest sense, myth here refers not only to anti-Semitism but to a whole set of Poundian fictions and deceptions, whether ideological or personal or both.[59]

Finally, let me again emphasize that Pound's anti-Semitism and fascism can be fully understood only if they are considered in relation to the whole of his work and his widest cultural aims. Just as Pound's anti-Semitism requires us to look beyond his explicit anti-Semitic statements, so an understanding of his fascism requires more than an enumeration of Pound's overtly pro-fascist avowals. Many Poundian values which critics do not consider fascistic—among them his anti-monotheism, his agrarian paganism, his solar worship, his phallocentrism, his anti-feminism, his attacks on abstraction, his anti-usury, his longing for mythical rather than historical time, his demand for a ritualized and hierarchical society—are characteristic of many versions of fascist ideology. All too often Pound critics treat his values in a fragmentary way, and thus make much of his thinking seem not only innocent but attractively "vital" and affirmative of humane values. Indeed, by a careful selection of Pound's statements one might present him, as have many critics, as a misunderstood apostle of benevolence, justice, and humanitarianism. One might do the same for Adolf Hitler, a writer whom Pound resembles as much as he resembles any other. Only when one systematically examines Hitler's most "positive" statements within the whole panoply of his thought do they appear incoherent and dangerous. Similarly, the full fascist implication of Pound's ideas and values can never be grasped if they are treated in isolation. Only when taken together, and examined in their interrelation, do they reveal the form of a single (but by no means coherent or organic) fascist whole.

Within this totality, as within the Poundian psychology and the Poundian text, anti-Semitism has a necessary and indispensable place. Nor is this all. Far more than any other of his themes, anti-Semitism exemplifies the inner contradictions of Pound's writing and discloses the incoherence of his psychology and values. It is thus easy to see why critics have neglected this subject for so long.

Part I

The Intellectual and Psychological Foundations

Chapter Two

The Jews as Negative Principle

A resolute anti-dualist and deeply influenced by Neo-Platonism, Pound rejects the separation of spirit and matter and views all Nature as a continuum pervaded by the "life-force" (SR, 95). In a late version of a long tradition, he identifies light with the divine essence and intelligence and thinks of physical nature as informed by light, the perpetual efflux of the divine. But light is not uniformly distributed throughout Nature. As in Neo-Platonism, Nature is an order, a cosmos, with hierarchical differences and gradations between things, which contain or reflect the divine essence in varying degrees. The sun, or "Pater Helios" (113/ 786), is the first of physical beings and the most obvious symbol of the divine intellect or Nous. As the source of light, it enables men to see the marvelous order, diversity, and "splendour" (GK, 282) of Nature, in which "all things" themselves "are lights" (74/ 429).

Because the divine light is "alive" and constantly interacting at all levels of cosmos, Pound's universe is open-ended and metamorphic, "germinal" (SR, 92) and "abundant" (92/ 620). No wonder then that Pound was deeply attracted to pagan polytheism. Like Pound, the polytheist has a mind "close on the vital universe" (SR, 93), sees no absolute separation between the divine and the natural, the god-like and the human. The divine is immanent in creative Nature, and it manifests itself concretely and diversely, in natural phenomena and even in man. Such phenomena are for Pound quite literally "gods" (SR, 93), the "permanent" (SR, 92) basis of the pagan mythology and pluralistic pantheon. Besides recognizing and cherishing the differences within Nature, polytheism cherishes the differences between men: "the truth is the individual" (LE, 355). It therefore "never asserted a single and obligatory path for everyone. . . . It never caused an attempt to force people into a path alien to their sensibilities" (SP, 56).

Pound connects light with thought and the sun with language. The sun is "god's mouth" (77/ 466); it is the means by which the word or *logos* is transmitted, while the *logos* itself is identified with intelligence and light.

The sun is thus a logocentric sign, a symbol of the divine origin or parent (Pater Helios) of speech, reason, and order. Insofar as man has reason and speech, which are part of his endowment of light, he can understand and imitate the order over which the sun presides as a good son imitates his parent. And so light is connected with one of Pound's favorite themes, the need to recognize the natural, preexistent, and hierarchical differences among things, to call things by their right names, to attain intellectual and verbal clarity.[1] In establishing "correct denominations" (Cheng Ming), man creates a discursive structure or "pattern" which is a mimetic reflection of Nature's "pre-ordained" hierarchy: discourse is itself a hierarchical and organic system of meanings, of "root[s]," "center[s]" (85/ 549), "branches," and "twigs."[2]

In Pound's mythology the paternal *logos* and the light of the sun are associated interchangeably with the phallus and its seed, the plough and the farmer's sowing.[3] Fecundating Mother Nature and causing things to grow, the sun is masculine, paternal, while Nature, or matter (HYLE), is maternal and feminine. In Canto 106, envisioning a "center," node, or vortex of the universe, Pound speaks of a "great acorn of light bulging outward" (106/ 755). In Canto 116 he asks: "Can you enter the great acorn of light?" (116/ 795). Pound plays on the Latin *glans* (as in *glans penis*), which also means acorn (Sieburth, 2: 153). In *Guide to Kulchur* he quotes favorably an un-named Stoic philosopher who discusses creation in terms of a " 'creative Fire' " from God and " 'spermatic *logoi*,' " which are a " 'gradual and organic distribution of an unique and spermatic word (*logos*)' " (GK, 128).

Pound adheres to the Aristotelian distinction between the formative and active masculine principle and the passive, material, and receptive feminine: his thought is both logocentric and phallocentric.[4] To quote Wang, "man's phallic heart is from heaven / a clear spring of rightness" (99/ 697). So too, "the heart shd/ be straight, / the phallos perceive its aim" (99/ 702). Every-thing that Pound values in Nature, society, and culture—distinctions, clar-ity, *telos*, order, hierarchy, abundance—testifies to the priority of the origi-nating masculine principle and specifically the phallus in its various forms. Like light, plough, seed, and word, and perhaps interchangeably with them, the divine and human phallus differentiate and hierarchize physical Nature, rendering it nameable and distinct; the mark of the phallus repeats and traces to the ultimate origin or father and is a sign of the informing light.[5] Man's "job" is to "build light" (94/ 642) and "make cosmos" (116/ 795).

Man's essential energies are thus expressed most fully in thinking and sexuality. As early as *The Spirit of Romance* Pound speaks of those whose thoughts are "germinal" (SR, 92).[6] Pound also thinks of the head of the genius as a kind of lesser sun, as a luminous sphere radiating order and clarity: "light," he suggests in his Postscript to Gourmont's *Natural Philoso-phy of Love*, "is a projection from the luminous fluid, from the energy that is in the brain" (PD, 210). In the same essay Pound speaks of the "integration of the male in the male organ" (PD, 204) and speculates that the human brain, either through sublimation or a surplus of genital substance, may derive from the coagulation of sperm transmitted to the skull via the spinal cord.[7] For Pound, who boasts of driving ideas "into the great passive vulva of London" (PD, 204), and whose head was represented as a marble phallus by Gaudier-Brzeska (Norman: 136), the creative artist's brain "exteriorizes" (PD, 204) forms as does a spermatazoa.

Though the artist sublimates sexuality, cultural health also depends on coitus, which is "the mysterium" (SP, 70). Since it makes men vitally aware of those natural energies called "the gods," Pound gives sexual intercourse a religious significance. In "Terra Italica" he quotes an anonymous Italian text which, though it reads clumsily in translation, perhaps distills his religious beliefs:

> Paganism, which at the base of its cosmogonic philosophy set the sexual phenomena whereby Life perpetuates itself mysteriously throughout the universe, not only did not disdain the erotic factor in its religious institutions but celebrated and exalted it, precisely because it encountered in it the marvellous vital principle infused by invisible Divinity into manifest nature. (SP, 55)

Paganism grasps what Western civilization has forgotten, that "civilizations or cultures decay from the top" (SP, 55). The meaning of this remark is implicit in Pound's anonymous Italian author, who says that "it was natural that the woman should have in the various rites the feminine role that holy nature had given her" (SP, 55). The decay of cultures "from the top" refers to the decline of political power and authority, which Pound associates with masculine energy; his Mussolini is often "bo" or "boss," affectionate variations on the Latin *bos*, meaning bull.[8] The phrase also refers obliquely to the male's "naturally" dominant position in the sexual act and culture's supposed dependence on his dominance and priority.

According to Frazer, whom Pound apparently followed, primitive copulation rituals originate in an agrarian setting and reflect primitive man's belief that "copulation . . . [is] good for the crops" (LE, 85). More precisely, copulation is a mimetic act: as in Cantos 39 and 47, it imitates and promotes Nature's fecundity. In "Religio" Pound mentions "other rites" (SP, 70), presumably of Adonis (the yearly slain), Demeter, and Kore, which imitate Nature's seasonal cycles of death and renewal and thus integrate man within its "timeless" order. These rites are the "festivals of fecundity of the grain and the sun festivals, without revival of which religion cannot return to the hearts of the people" (SP, 70). As Pound told Douglas Fox: ". . . The only vigorous feasts of the Church are grafted onto European roots, the sun, the grain, the harvest and Aphrodite."[9]

By the late 1930s Pound's values belong mainly to the premodern world. Their proper setting is the family "homestead," either Western or Chinese, which Pound calls the true "basis" (RB, 152) and repository of civilization.[10] Besides being the source of primary economic production, Pound's agricultural homestead stands for man's continuity with Nature, his appreciation of its beauty and bounty, and his rootedness within its "process" (74/ 425). As a traditional institution, the homestead escapes the discontinuities of historical life and seems almost to derive from Nature itself. Its very structure reveals the same fidelity to distinctions and differences which Pound discovers in the natural world. Just as Nature reveals traces of the *logos,* so the family order traces to an origin or father. This patriarchal system emphasizes hierarchy (subordination to the father), distinctions (between families and family members), individual identity (through familial and proper names), and individual ownership; one might say that Pound, projecting bourgeois individualism to a transhistorical plane, views property rights as natural and time-honored.[11] Finally, the family homestead repeats in its division of labor the order of cosmos and thus maintains the "natural" and hierarchical distinction between masculine and feminine roles:[12] "One big chap not plow / one female not weave / Can mean shortage" (99/ 709).

Like the pagan, the agrarian (or peasant, as Pound often calls him) sees Nature as a benevolent and all-encompassing "process" (74/ 425) infused with vital energies called "gods." Hence his mythology, through which he represents Nature to himself, his seasonal rituals, which harmonize Nature and man, and his votive images, by which he worships the gods in specific form. Because he adapts his activities to seasonal rhythms and thus conforms to the "intelligence" (CON, 193) in Nature, agrarian man reaps Nature's benefits: social order, sexual vitality, offspring, abundance. This is why Pound views the agrarian consciousness of Europe and China as the basis upon which any future paganism, or indeed any healthy society, must build.

By contrast, modern man neglects natural beauty and knows nothing of the "process" or the intelligence within Nature; he thinks of mythology as merely a collection of pretty stories. Divorced from natural instincts, his sex is mechanical, the very antithesis of the erotic "mysterium" of pagan religion. His art is thoroughly desacralized, lacking the beauty and reverence of ancient votive images. But nowhere is his denaturalization more evident than in his economic system, which gives him "stale rags" for bread and sets "corpses" at his "banquet" (45/ 229, 230). Instead of adapting to Nature's rhythms, instead of recognizing Nature as the true source of abundance, modern economics obeys its own laws and cycles and confuses true wealth with the usurious multiplication of money. The result: not only poverty, but the modern economic paradox of overproduction and scarcity, enormous waste and enormous deprivation.

The return to the homestead and paganism requires a massive transformation of Western consciousness, a return to Nature and to myths. This is the meaning of Pound's statement: ". . . the gods exist. . . . Without gods, no culture. Without gods, something is lacking" (GK, 125, 126). Only through mythology, man's "totalitarian" (SP, 87) expression of a holistic universe, can the modern world defeat usury, which supplants Nature, condemns man to economic misery, and plunges Europe into fraternal strife. As Pound says in "A Visiting Card": "Who destroyed the mystery of fecundity, bringing in the cult of sterility?" (SP, 317).

An examination of the immediate and broader context of these questions will reveal an obvious conclusion: the Jews are to blame. By the early 1940s Pound conceives the Jews not only as an alien presence. Enemies and deniers of light, haters of life and instinct, parasitic destroyers of agriculture and the homestead, they are for Pound a disease, a poison, a plague attacking the putatively organic body of the West.

II.

In a letter to Marianne Moore, Pound speaks of "Semite . . . hatred of light." To judge from his translation of Voltaire's "Genèse," which was published in 1920, Pound is speaking literally.[13] In "Genèse" Voltaire says that in ancient times "men saw [light] spread through the air before sunrise and after sunset." Thus the Jewish author of the Hebrew creation myth believes that "light did not come from the sun," and "lumps in light with the other objects of creation." Bowing "to the vague and stupid prejudice of his nation, he has the sun and moon made four days after the light."[14] So the Jews are guilty of a primal sin against the light; they deny light's purity (Pound's "Light tensile immaculata," 74/ 429) as well as the sun's ontological priority and superiority. Such beliefs run counter to Pound's solar worship as well as to his Neo-Platonic idea of the cosmos as a hierarchy, each thing infused in varying degrees by a divine and original light.[15]

For Pound the worst of Jewish errors is monotheism. Pound correctly saw the Jews as the primary inventors of the monotheistic idea and the ultimate source of Christian (and Islamic) monotheism and anti-paganism. Nor is this all. By the late 1930s Pound blames the Jews and Jewish influences for a massive and increasing impoverishment of Western life; thanks to them, the Occident moves steadily toward "intolerance, monopoly, and uniformity,"[16] toward what Nietzsche saw as the Judeo-Christian diseases of *ressentiment*, guilt, authoritarianism, and repression.

In a letter of 1927 Pound speaks of the "god damnability of all monotheistic Jew, Mohammed, Xtn. buncomb" (L, 215). Unlike the pagan, the monotheist reduces divine plurality to unity and removes God from Nature; his God is transcendental and spiritual, invisible and infinite. Because of monotheism, men no longer seek divinity in the individual being but in the more abstract concept of a timeless and permanent Being. Now Nature, deprived of its immanent gods, is no longer an endless flux of metamorphic creation, containing within itself the forces of growth and generation; it is no longer *natura naturans* (Nature naturing). Instead, like the usurer, and unlike the Greek philosophers, the Jewish monotheist believes in creation *ex nihilo:* the one God, by fiat, brings material reality into being. This means that the principle of creation is outside of Nature, and that Nature is already complete and static: *Natura Naturata* (Nature natured). For Pound, monotheism necessarily results in a decline in man's awareness of the life and energy within Nature and a devaluation of natural existence. It also creates an insuperable abyss between spirit and matter, God and man.

With monotheism comes a change in men's attitude towards myth. According to Pound, the decline of mythological awareness occurred with the appropriation of myths for a "moral purpose" and an abstract and rationalizing end. Because "some unpleasing Semite or Parsee or Syrian" used myths for "social propaganda," thus degrading the myth "into an allegory or a fable," the "gods no longer walked in men's gardens" (LE, 431). Pound said of myths that they never "level out all differences" (GK, 128); faithful to the concrete perceptions of those who made them, they embody Pound's belief that "the truth is the individual" (LE, 355). The mythmaker thus makes only a limited claim for his truth; he does not theorize about "what he doesn't know" (GK, 128), nor does he expect everyone to believe his particular myth. But as exploited by the Jews, myths are allegorized, transformed into moral abstractions in order to reach as many minds as possible.[17]

And so, unlike the pluralistic "polytheistic anschauung," monotheism dogmatically ignores the spiritual and temperamental differences between men and the multiplicity of possible truths. Dogma, says Pound, is "bluff based upon ignorance" (SP, 49): it "builds on vacuum, and is ultimately killed or modified by, or accommodated to knowledge" (LE, 153). Such dogmatizing reflects monotheism's abstract and universalizing tendency; just as monotheism abstracts one God from Nature's diversity, so it asserts the "one" and "universal truth" (SR, 95) for all men. Thus Pound connects dogmatic monotheism with "bigotry, mess" (LE, 238), and intolerance, with the emergence of "curious fanaticisms" (RB, 238, LE, 154, SP, 57, 90) of all kinds within Western civilization. For Pound the monotheist is "the bestial," "the fanatical" (GK, 223); he is "the man on fire with God and is anxious to stick his snotty nose into other men's business or reprove his neighbor for having a set of tropisms different from that of the fanatic's" (GK, 223). The Talmud is a "species of gangster's handbook" (SP, 68), while the Old Testament is the "record of a barbarian tribe, full of evil" (L, 183). These are the chief sources of the Christian impulse to sacrifice others and create "hells for one's enemies" (LE, 150), of numerous forms of "excess" (SP, 86).[18]

Like Nietzsche a hater of priests, Pound has no doubt that monotheism in whatever form attacks religious freedom in order to create religious tyranny and to control and exploit the masses.[19] "The greatest tyrannies," says Pound, "have arisen from the dogma that the *theos* is one, or that there is a unity above the various strata of theos which imposes its will upon the sub-strata, and thence upon human individuals" (SP, 51). The Jewish religion originated when Moses, "having to keep a troublesome rabble in order, . . . [invented and scared] them with a disagreeable bogie, which he . . . [called] a god" (SR, 95). For Pound the Jews are from the very beginning of their history not so much individuals as members of a "servile" (SP, 91) tribe or herd.

Another pernicious instrument of monotheistic tyranny is ethical abso-lutism or "code-worship" (GK, 164). For Pound there are only two possi-ble sorts of ethical systems: a "graduated system in which all actions . . . [are] relative good or evil, according to almost millimetric measurement, but in the absolute," and a system in which "everything was good or bad without any graduation, but as taboo" (SP, 151). The first system belongs to ancient and medieval Europe, to Dante and Aquinas, while the second belongs to the Jews, who in Pound's view developed a law rather than an ethical system, and whose Old Testament ethics are "merely squalid" (SP, 64). Pound believes that the Jews, being ignorant of gradations in Nature, are also ignorant of moral gradations. Unlike the flexible Greeks, they follow rigid laws and formal procedures and a categorical set of moral standards (the Ten Commandments) which now have a wide if not univer-sal application. Pound also argues that the real purpose of the Jewish law is fraudulent and monopolistic, namely "to provide FINES, payable to a gang or tribe of allegedly religious superiors" (RB, 118). The Semitic, then, is "excess," lacking "proportion" (SP, 90), and opposing "ANY scale of values" (SP, 86).

Nor is this the only evil of code worship. According to Pound, the "attempt to square nature with the code, leads perforce to perverted think-ing" (GK, 164). As monotheism severs man from Nature, so its categorical morality alienates man from his natural impulses. This is why Pound consid-ers Judaism the religion *par excellence* of punishment and repression, of the "forbidden," of "taboo" (SP, 150). Repeatedly he emphasizes the "brute disorder" (SP, 150) of Jewish taboos and the Jews' responsibility for the "sadistic and masochistic tendencies" (SP, 58) of Christianity. All of these supposedly Jewish qualities trace to "the utterly damnable and sadistic and altogether loathesome concept of JHV [Jehovah], daddy slap / em / with / slab," who gave the Jews a "sort of roving commission . . . to bash all and sundry."[20] Jehovah is a "narsty old maniac" (L, 339) and, as the god of John Calvin, who "revived" the "brutal and savage mythology of the Hebrews" (SP, 265), a "maniac sadist" (SP, 70), symbolizing paternal repression and the bad father.[21] Pound would "prefer other qualities in one's immediate parenthood" (SP, 70).

At points one is tempted to think that hatred of sexuality is for Pound the essence of Jewish code worship. Having destroyed the glad pagan animal-ism, Jewish "sadism" penetrates Christianity and infects it. As an example of "perverted thinking" produced by Hebraic code worship Pound offers Protestantism and especially Puritanism, which "lacks a scale of values" (GK, 196), "semiticly . . . efface[s] grades and graduations," and limits "mental corruption" to the "single groove of sex" (GK, 185). Elsewhere Pound speaks of the "Hebrew disease," which leads variously to guilt, "asceticisms," the "belief that the body is evil" —in short, to every feature of Christianity which is "anti-life" and "anti-flesh" (LE, 150–154). Pound also finds the "Hebrew disease" in the darkest and ugliest features of medieval architecture, bad physique, laziness, Christian strictures against feminine hygiene, and the love or acceptance of filth (LE, 150, 154); "being clean is a pagan virtue," notes Pound's hero Poggio Bracciolini, and "no part of the light from Judea" (PD, 99). For Pound, as for Nietzsche, these are symptoms of dwindling life, of "maiming" and "curtailment" (LE, 152), of castration.[22]

Pound's attack on Jewish ethics goes further. In Canto 113 he writes: "As to sin, they invented it—eh? / to implement domination / eh? largely" (113/ 789). He probably refers to the Jews, who gave the world (but themselves rejected) the idea of original sin, and whom Pound blames for man's pernicious fear of moral transgression and punishment.[23] The very idea of sin has no place within Pound's essentially naturalistic conception of man. Pound believes that all men have, in greater or lesser degrees, a natural intelligence and a natural "will toward the light" (LE, 59), a Dantescan and Confucian "Directio Voluntatis" (SP, 84). Human "evil" is not sinful but rather the result of intellectual error or ignorance or else "the [mis]direction of the will" (LE, 62). Its remedy is not punishment but education. This rejection of sin is an attempt, similar to Nietzsche's, to lessen human guilt, even to eliminate the powerful superego, which is perhaps the Jews' most important contribution to Western moral life.[24]

According to Pound, Europe has only sporadically resisted code worship and monotheism. After the decline of Rome and the rise of Christianity emerged in Provence from the underground traditions of paganism the love cults of the troubadours and the solar religion of Montségur. These short-lived movements, which Pound traces to the fertility cults and Eleusinian mysteries, were "the strongest counter force to . . . asceticism" (SP, 58). Not much later arose in Tuscany, thanks in part to troubadour influence, the "radiant world" (LE, 154) of Dante and the early Italian Renaissance. Here, as in Provence, but to an even greater degree, man regained his full physical, sexual, and sensory life, his accurate perception of natural phenomena, his love of beauty and art, his ability to make clear intellectual discriminations. Here was a world of "moving energies," where every thought met every other with a "clean edge" (LE, 154). But soon the partially pagan Renaissance fell into mere material opulence and was aborted by the Reformation, and with Protestantism, says Pound, came the revival of Hebrew texts and habits of thought. From this point Pound marks the decline of life in Europe into the present century, which he finds riddled with Jewish influences, a "morass" of intellectual confusion.[25]

Pound, who despises theorizing and identifies artistic and scientific truth with the precise definition of things, considers the great modern disease to be "abstraction," which has "spread like tuberculosis" (LE, 59). For this, too, the Jews are largely responsible. In the essay on Cavalcanti the Jews are hostile to moral gradations and the "clean edge" of intellect. Elsewhere Pound suggests that the Jewish mind, which invented an invisible and immaterial God, is speculative, abstract, and theoretical, therefore encouraging man's fascination with metaphysics, his fuzzy thinking, and his flight from palpable reality. In modern mathematics and science men ignore the visible forms of things and create purely mental and invisible constructs, such as waves and atoms.[26] In psychology attention passes from observable actions to theories of the instincts and the unconscious, the invisible and unrepresentable inner life. Deploring these "immoral" modern "geometries" (GK, 78) of subjectivity, Pound associates them with Bergson and Freud (RB, 115), two Jewish explorers of the unknown. In Western philosophy Pound finds a deplorable tendency towards theory, which leads to the "jungle" (SP, 78) of idealism and the "desiccation of culture" (GK, 40–41), an intellectual tyranny like that of monotheism: the theorist "is constantly urging someone else to behave as he, the theorist, would like to behave" (LE, 46). Although Pound does not always associate these developments with the Jews, in "A Visiting Card" they have an outstanding place among those who destroy both intellect and faith through "abstract" (SP, 306) and "theoretical argument" (SP, 317). Hyam Maccoby correctly argues that, for Pound, the Jews "play endlessly with ideas spun from their own entrails," with "soft bodiless conceptions which are squeezed and molded, not hacked out by strength and courage from the hard stuff of reality." As "the chief exponents of discursive rational thinking" (Maccoby: 67, 69), they are the primary enemies of Pound's image and ideogram, those votive and aesthetic objects whose concrete immediacy "move[s] the soul to contemplation and preserve[s] the tradition of the undivided light" (SP, 307).[27]

For Pound the most pernicious form of Jewish abstraction is usury. Besides finding a connection between sensory and intellectual discrimination and reverence for Nature's beauty and vitality, Pound believes that "any high development of the perceptive faculties" is "dangerous to avarice" (GK, 281). The reason is that perceptive men recognize the difference between abundance and sterility, productive and unproductive work, labor and exploitation, true wealth and false. The money-changer and usurer thrive only where men are confused about these differences. "Usury and mercantilism" are therefore "syphilis rotting all things moving concurrently with all deficiencies in discrimination."[28]

With their gift for abstraction, the Jews are supposedly in an ideal position to create and benefit from this confusion. Money in their hands becomes a mere "symbol" which, bearing no correspondence or relation to the production or existence of actual goods, multiplies itself endlessly and assumes demoniacally "an infinite number of shapes or of meanings" (Maccoby: 65). Thus, while Pound is by no means hostile to all forms of money, he obsessively attacks that form of it—namely usury—which he thinks the Jews created and which figures in economics as the virtual equivalent of the abstract and monopolistic Jewish God, who creates reality *ex nihilo*.[29] At the same time, Pound is certain that Jewish usurers exploit honest labor and impede the forces of production. He believes implicitly that the Jews, for whom labor is "the curse of Adam," reject the principle of work (Berezin: 267, 269, 273–274). The usurers, says Pound, are "against the natural increase of agriculture or of any productive work" (LE, 211). Elsewhere he reveals that, while some usurers may be non-Jews, the system of usury or "Jewsury" is essentially Jewish: "It is, of course, useless to indulge in antisemitism, leaving intact the Hebraic monetary system which is a most tremendous instrument of usury" (SP, 351).[30]

Pound's attacks on Jewish usury are complicated by his knowledge that the Jews originated the usury prohibition. Not only does he refer frequently to *neschek* ("the bite"), which is Hebrew for usury, but in *Guide to Kulchur* he recognizes the difference in ancient Jewish law between *neschek* and *marbith*, the latter meaning fair or permissible increase; as Pound says, "the age of abundance" may have ended "when the *marbit* swelled out into *neschek*" (GK, 42). This suggests that Pound knew Deuteronomy 23:19–20. As Benjamin Nelson observes, this text "forbade the Hebrew to take *neshek* . . . from his brother, but permitted him to exact it from the *nokri*," that is, the stranger, or non-Jew. It also prevented him from taking *neschek* from the *ger*, or "protected sojourner," and the *toshab*, the "resident stranger"; in some instances, in fact, the *gerim* are to be treated exactly as Jewish brethren.[31]

Obviously, the Deuteronomic text can serve anti-Semitism, since it might be taken as an example of Jewish tribalism and exclusivity.[32] Pound, however, seems to have examined it with some care. In *The New English Weekly*, he asks whether "the Jew has the power to dominate," and adds that "the law of Moses forbids usury in many cases. It stamps it as a hostile act. If permissible, permissible only against mortal enemies of the tribe."[33] Pound may be making the distinction between the *nokri* (Pound's "mortal enemies") and the *ger* and *toshab*, the sojourning and resident stranger with whom usury is prohibited. Elsewhere Pound argues that the Jews, while living among strangers, have ignored their own laws:

> The two-standards system of Geneva cannot be blamed on the Semites, but the Semitic avoidance of their own law on usury while wishing to be accepted as neighbours is on a par with Geneva, . . . the usurer's stronghold. (SP, 64)

This is confusing. Although Pound attacks the Jews for following a double standard, Deuteronomy permits the Jews to take usury from foreigners. Still, Pound may be interpreting Jewish law under modern national conditions. Since the Jews are living among strangers who are also neighbors, they are obliged not to take usury. In any case, usury remains the Jews' distinctive "problem": "At this point, and to prevent the dragging of red herrings, I wish to distinguish between prejudice against the Jew as such and the suggestion that the Jew should face his own problem. . . . DOES he in his individual case wish to observe the law of Moses?" (SP, 299–300).

Pound shares with Houston Stewart Chamberlain the idea that "the Jews do not take seriously the moral content of their texts" (Berezin: 270). Nowhere is this assumption more evident than in Pound's attacks on the Old Testament, in which he has to explain why that book, which he loathes, contains prophetic teachings whose moral greatness even Pound recognized. Pound argues that the exception proves the rule: "The prophets ceased not to object to the conduct of . . . [their] coreligionaries" (RB, 117).[34] This does not mean, though, that Pound now recognizes any value in the Jewish code. Rather, anti-Semites invariably condemn the Jews for contradictory errors. They fail to observe the law or code of Moses, to which Pound appeals in attacking them; and yet they follow their code all too closely, whether in the Old Testament or the Talmud, the "code of vengeance" (RB, 118).[35]

Although usury seems only an economic evil, Pound reaches the conclusion that economics is the key to history, and that cultural vitality depends on the proper use of money. He accordingly finds evidence of usury throughout Western society and culture.[36] This is why, when we speak of usury, it will also refer metaphorically to usury's effects. Nowhere is usury more disturbing to Pound than in art, his *summum bonum:*

> You can probably date any Western work of art by reference to the ethical estimate of usury prevalent at the time of that work's composition; the greater the component of tolerance for usury the more blobby and messy the work of art. The kind of thought which distinguishes good from evil, down into the details of commerce, rises into the quality of line in paintings and into the clear definition of the word written (SP, 76).

Pound, following Thaddeus Zielinski, perhaps his favorite anti-Semitic writer, would no doubt trace these symptoms not just to usury but to the Jewish prohibition of images, another example of Jewish abstraction and anti-naturalism (Zielinski, 1: 15).

What remains unclarified is Pound's attitude toward Christianity—a problem which can only be outlined here. Believing that the true Christianity is Catholicism and that it descends from pagan roots, Pound attacks Protestantism as largely Judaism in disguise. For Pound, Jesus is a kind of individualist and perhaps even a pagan, a great reformer who had sought to "provide an antidote for Judaism" (SP, 57), but who, being a Jew and thus afflicted with Jewish "provincialism" (SP, 193), "invented no safeguard against fanaticism" (SP, 57). Elsewhere Pound may be indebted to Nietzsche's idea that the apostle Paul had betrayed Christianity and given it an indelible Jewish imprint. Jesus is "not wholly to blame for the religion that's been foisted on him" (L, 183); "we know that . . . [Paul] neither wrote good Greek nor represented the teaching of the original Christian" (L, 54).[37] Thanks to Judaism, says Pound, Christianity has "become the slogan of every oppression, of every iniquity" (SP, 193), is imbued with fanaticism and hatred for the body.

III.

Pound's anti-Semitism is not entirely the product of irrational hatred and prejudice but claims its weak justification in a form of pagan naturalism and vitalism; whatever its ultimate political implications, and despite its obvious wrongness, at some points it is ostensibly motivated by Pound's interest in increasing man's happiness and thus by a kind of dubious humanitarianism. Moreover, Pound's anti-Semitism is often unoriginal, having analogues in the Enlightenment, Romanticism, and Nietzsche. Broadly speaking, it figures within what Peter Gay calls the rise of modern paganism.[38]

Even after this survey, it is necessary to emphasize that Pound was truly anti-Semitic. Critics have argued that Pound's anti-Semitism is really economic rather than cultural, racial, and biological, and that it develops mainly from his identification of the Jew with the usurer. Others have claimed that Pound never attacked all Jews, only Jewish usurers, and that when he did, he did not attack them as Jews. And others believe that Pound's application of the terms "Jew" and "Kike" to various Gentiles reveals the vagueness, the empty generality of his hatred.

This book shows repeatedly that Pound attacks the Jews for mainly noneconomic reasons. As Pound told Wyndham Lewis, "I object as much to semitism in matters of mind as in matters of commerce" (P/L, 218). The sentence is in fact phrased in the form of a question, but the question leaves little room for doubt. In this reference to "semitism," as in his later references to Jews as a race of alien blood, Pound believes that he has found something that characterizes both Jews and Jewish culture and that supposedly sets them apart eternally and unmistakably from other groups. According to Leon Poliakov, the chief difference between medieval or Christian anti-Semitism and the modern version lies in the modern belief in the existence of permanent Jewish traits. Medieval anti-Semitism is really anti-Judaism; the Jews are accused of deicide (the murder of Christ) but can remove their sin and guilt through conversion. Modern or secular anti-Semitism (that is, anti-Semitism proper) denies that conversion will help the Jews; it condemns them as an unchanging, collective, ethnic, and even biological or racial essence.[39] In no sense limited to or defined by economics, this is the form of anti-Semitism which Pound embraces in his later career.

Later it will be shown that Pound's hatred includes not only Jewish usurers but "small" Jews. As for his tendency to speak of Gentiles as Jews, that is, "to use the word Kike regardless of race" (RB, 387), this odd habit has perplexed commentators.[40] In the radio broadcasts Pound speaks of "Jews, sub-Jews" (RB, 42), "crypto" (RB, 52) Jews, "hyper-kikes" (RB, 105), "demi-kikes" (RB, 341), and doubts whether his enemies are "born Jews," or "have taken to Jewry by predilection" (RB, 21). Elsewhere he wants a "list of the citizens of YIDDonia whether semite, chazar [Khazar] or full-buttocked Briton."[41] But Pound's imputation of Jewish traits to non-Jews cannot possibly mean, as some critics believe, that Pound does not hate Jews.[42] These statements reveal his belief that "semitism," the Jewish essence or ideology, is as communicable as a disease, and that certain Gentiles, having been infected by Jews, are its "agents" (RB, 238) and "carriers" (SP, 317, RB, 238). Indeed, they are "honorary Jews" (RB, 387). Pound thus resembles Hermann Goering, who consciously or unwittingly echoed the famous remark of Karl Leuger, the anti-Semitic mayor of Vienna around the turn of the century: "I decide who is a Jew."[43] No one could seriously argue that these men, any more than Pound, are not anti-Semitic.

Still, one cannot remain satisfied with a purely ideological analysis, nor can one explain Pound's anti-Semitism simply by placing it in cultural tradition and robbing it of its distinctive character. By the 1940s Pound's anti-Semitism is a systematic delusion and reveals the same irrationality and fanaticism which Pound condemned in the Jews. It is therefore necessary to connect Pound's ideology with its psychological and emotional sources, and to examine the metaphorical system which governs and articulates it.[44] Thus examined, Pound's anti-Semitism has its closest affinity not with Voltaire and Nietzsche but with Rosenberg and Hitler.

Chapter Three

The Jews, Castration, and Usury

Perhaps the most frequent and persistent of Pound's anti-Semitic accusations is that the Jews are ungenerative and anti-generative. To a large extent these charges have their foundation in Pound's phallocentric ideology, which celebrates the male generative power at once literally and metaphorically, and within which the Jews for a variety of reasons become the negative principle. Yet Pound's phallocentrism is by no means a purely intellectual construct. It develops out of and at the same time serves to allay some of his deepest personal fears, above all a fear of castration. Personally and historically Pound embodies this threat in the figure of the Jew.

Probably in June, 1915, Pound wrote a letter to James Joyce, who at this point had never seen Pound: "I have," says Pound,

> several copies of a photo of a portrait of me, painted by an amiable Jew who substituted a good deal of his own face for the gentile parts of my own. . . . Dante, you remember at the beginning of the epistle to Can Grande (at least I think it is there) mentions a similar predicament about presenting one's self at a distance. It is my face no I can not be represented in your mind by that semitic image (P/J, 35).

Pound then mentions other portraits of himself, in one of which, according to Pound's landlady, he resembles Jesus of Nazareth, a Jew. But the last portrait which Pound mentions is no doubt closest to his self-conception. The work presumably of Gaudier-Brzeska, it depicts Pound's face "immortalized by vorticist sculpture. . . . This bust is monumental, but it will be no use to the police, it is hieratic, phallic. . . ." Pound is probably referring to a photograph of Gaudier's bust of Pound in the shape of a "marble phallus" (P/J, 35).

The Jew's portrait had a lingering effect on Pound. Several months later, in another letter to Joyce, Pound needlessly mentioned again the "photo of a portrait painted by a Jew in Paris four years ago," and went on to castigate the "resoluteness with which some people believe all beauty is made in their own image" (P/J, 58). Yet this portrait may have been a good likeness: not only does Pound in the first letter allow that "it may have been my face as it may have been years ago," but he also speaks of the "gentile parts" of his own face, thus suggesting that some of his features are not Gentile, and even refers to the photo as "my face" (P/J, 35). Apart from his landlady's notion that Pound looked like Jesus, Pound at a number of points in his career was taken to be a Jew. Arnold Leese, the rabid British anti-Semite, thought Pound Jewish after seeing his profile by Gaudier on a letterhead, and Wyndham Lewis recalled the absolute certainty with which his friends at the Vienna Cafe labelled Pound a "pukka kosher."[1] Pound also felt the need to explain his "worrisome" Hebraic name to Douglas Fox.[2] To judge from Pound's letter to Joyce, the basis of this anxiety lies in his identification of the Jews with falsification and fragmentation as well as in their supposed opposition to the "phallic." Even at this early point in his career, Pound conceives of the Jews as the virtual antithesis of his personal identity as a phallic hero.

Although its ultimate sources are probably psychological, Pound's opposition between the Jews and the phallus runs throughout his work and finally comes to figure within a broad transhistorical antithesis between Western and Near Eastern culture, between the forces of generation and the forces of aridity. In "Date Line" (1934) Pound remarks that Frazer had shown that the "opposing systems of European morality" derive from two "opposed temperaments": "those who thought copulation was good for the crops, and the opposed faction who thought it was bad for the crops (the scarcity economists of pre-history)." "The Christian," argues Pound, must "at least decide whether he is for Adonis or Atys, or whether he is Mediterranean." Pound adds that he sees no point in "dyeing Europe with a mythology elucubrated to explain the thoroughly undesirable climate of Arabia Petraea. . . ." Indeed, he finds "the peculiar frenzies of the Atys cult" to be "unadapted to the pleasanter parts of the Mediterranean basin" (LE, 85).

In referring to the pleasanter parts of the Mediterranean, Pound undoubtedly means Europe. But the choice which he demands is phrased somewhat ambiguously: are Adonis and Attis together opposed to the more pleasant Mediterranean, or is this ideal embodied in Adonis? In Frazer's *Golden Bough* Adonis and Atys (or Attis) are cognate yet different figures.[3] In ancient myth, and in the ritual which Pound celebrates in Canto 47, Adonis is a nature god who sleeps with the Great Mother (Aphrodite, in this case), is killed by a boar, and is resurrected, with the crops, in the spring. The Attis myth is much less attractive. Attis, the son of the Great Mother (in this case Agdistis or Cybele), sleeps with the goddess and then castrates himself in an act of frenzy and horror. It is to this act, no doubt, and its ritual commemoration by the castrated priests of Attis, that Pound refers in speaking of "peculiar frenzies."

In *The Golden Bough* Frazer shows that the cult of Adonis thrived not only in Europe but in Asia Minor, and that even the early backsliding Hebrews performed mimetic acts of copulation to honor Adonis, Tammuz, and other gods (Frazer: 17–18). Nonetheless, Pound believes that the Attis cult, which originated in Asia Minor and was resisted strenuously by Greece and Rome,[4] is a characteristically Semitic product of the arid Near Eastern climate. The opposition between Adonis and the castrated Attis is thus between two kinds of matriarchal religion, and two sorts of influence, one vital and the other sterile, on European culture. As for the metaphor of dyeing, this figure of contamination carries with it the idea of Tyrian or Carthaginian purple dye (Punic red, Pound would call it), and suggests that the passage is anti-Semitic in the broadest sense.[5]

This passage is also anti-Jewish in its implications. Presently it will be obvious that Pound views the Jews as basically indistinguishable from other Near Eastern groups. Similarly, when Pound speaks of the scarcity economists of prehistory, one recalls Pound's association of Jewish monotheism with repressors and in particular nineteenth-century scarcity economics. Around the same time as "Date Line" Pound suggested more directly a connection between Judaism and the Attis cult: "The god of the old testament was beast. . . . Later corruption in Europe, due not to Adonis (dangerous) but to Atys worship which is more corrupt than anything save possibly Hindoo mess."[6]

One would expect the erudite Pound to have distinguished the Attis cult from Jewish religion. The Bible reveals the Jews as the patriarchal people *par excellence,* and the earliest Hebrews were horrified and repelled by the orgiastic violence of Canaanitic rituals, among them the Attis cult.[7] Curiously, Pound's outrage at such cults suggests a patriarchal rigor which may have developed in the Hebraic atmosphere of the Protestant Sunday school. But historical arguments are useless in dealing with a systematic delusion; repeatedly Pound identifies the Jews with the "demonic" matriarchies of the Near East.

So far as I know, only Donald Davie and Alan Durant have noted the castration theme in Pound's anti-Semitic writings.[8] For Pound, not only are the Jews castrated, they are either overtly or implicitly mutilators and castrators. In short, castration is for Pound the common denominator between the Jews and the Attis cult, and supplies the link between them.[9]

One consequence of the "Hebrew disease" in the Cavalcanti essay is "curtailment" and "maiming" of the sexual instincts. Later Pound says that, because of usury and Cromwell's readmission of the Jews into England, American school books are "wholly castrated" (RB, 330). A similar idea appears in *Guide to Kulchur,* where Pound observes that the Old Testament is a barbaric document from the "first lies of Genesis" to the "excised account" (GK, 330) of the decapitation of Holofernes by Judith. Why does Pound mention this omitted or "excised" work? Pound, we remember, equates head and phallus. This means that the decapitated Holofernes is also a castrated Holofernes, Gentile victim of Judith, a demonic "chewess" (RB, 297). In suggesting that the Bible is itself incomplete or mutilated, Pound finds evidence of castration at the very core of Judaism. Nor should we forget Pound's reference to the "unFreudian chewess eating like a boll weavil [sic] into the creative will of her victim" (RB, 297); the phrase "chewess" evokes the idea of the vagina dentata.[10] In *The Cantos*, quoting Herr Marcher, the man who reared his daughter Mary, Pound summarizes his conception of the Jews in a punning phrase which defines their equal propensity for economic exploitation: "Der Jud will Geld" (89/ 600).

A variation on the metaphor of castration appears in Pound's references to Jewish syphilis, sexual immorality, and prostitution, all of which have analogues in the writings of Adolf Hitler, in whose *Mein Kampf* Pound found history "most keenly analyzed" (RB, 133, 140).[11] In the broadcasts Pound speaks of "financial syphilis" (RB, 80), "economic syphilis," and "political syphilis" (RB, 29). These statements refer to the Jews, the "syphilis bugs" (RB, 74). Pound also mentions a "syphilitic organization" composed of "born Jews" and those "who have taken to Jewry by predilection" (RB, 21). Indeed, he asserts that Jewry, not merely the financiers who lead it, is "more deadly than syphilis" (RB, 86). Thus having isolated the disease whose symptoms appear in the Usury *Cantos*, Pound calls for "world prophylaxis" (RB, 115) against the Jews. Earlier, in Canto 45, the first usury canto, usury defiles the color azure with a "canker" and, like syphilis, "slayeth the child in the womb" (45/ 230); so too, it brings no doubt syphilitic "whores" (45/ 230) to the sacred rites of Eleusis. This reference to prostitution intersects with Pound's observation that the Eleusinian mysteries probably declined from "bacteriological causes" (SP, 59). In the broadcasts, and with ostentatious casualness, Pound connects the Jews with prostitution and the monopolization of "pornography" (RB, 217). Thanks to the Jews, "the spirit of England, immortal spirit of England's May Day," with all its associations of purity and fertility, will find itself "chained in a brothel" (RB, 58).

In *Moses and Monotheism* Freud traces one source of anti-Semitism to the fearful and "uncanny" associations produced by the Jewish practice of circumcision. According to Freud, circumcision "reminds" non-Jews "of the dreaded castration idea and of things in the primeval past which they would fain forget."[12] Freud has also shown that, wherever an abnormally great amount of worth is attached to a particular human quality or characteristic, one should look for its opposite. This rule applies to Pound's fascination with and great estimation of phallic potency, which discloses a deep anxiety over sexual debility and castration, both of which Pound associates with the Jews. Jehovah is for Pound the punishing, avenging, and forbidding deity, who forces man to repress his sexual instincts. He is the castrating father god.

Pound counters this threat with a projective mechanism which characterizes his anti-Semitism. Not Pound but the Jews are castrated. By the middle of his career Pound frequently refers to the Jews as "jews." This shift from the capital (signifying head, signifying phallus) to the lower case is his way of cutting the Jews down to size—a linguistic gesture all the more striking since Pound, in his fascist polemics and self-promotion, favors a "capital" style, often printing whole words and sentences in capitals.[13] Or consider this passage from Charles Olson's memoir of Pound during his stay at St. Elizabeths. "There was a Jew," said Pound,

> "in London, Obermeyer, a doctor of comparative . . . of the endocrines, and I used to ask him what is the effect of circumcision. That's the question that gets them sore," and he begins to be impish as hell, "that sends them right up the pole. Try it, don't take my word, try it." And then, with a pitiful seriousness, turning directly toward me he says: "It must do something, after all these years and years, where the most sensitive nerves in the body are, rubbing them off, over and over again." (Olson: 55)

Not only is Pound's fascination with circumcision apparent in that he asked Obermeyer about it again and again, but the mysteriousness of the practice is reemphasized by Pound's apparently needless mention of Obermeyer's expertise in glandular disorders. He is linked, as are the Jews repeatedly in Pound's work, with that which is most mysterious and familiar, foreign and intimate—the interior of the body. As for the Jews, implicitly they are incapable of understanding another mystery, namely coitus (the "mysterium"). They have suffered serious damage to their genital nerves, a mutilation which, for some unexplained reason, they suffer "over and over again." In the broadcasts usury attacks the "nerve centers" (SP, 317) of nations.

This passage reveals the uncanny—the familiar in the unfamiliar, the return of the repressed. Pound was first about to refer to Obermeyer as a specialist in comparative anatomy, a slip of the tongue which suggests that his real interest is the difference between the Jews' anatomy and his own. His question moreover repeats the effects of circumcision; it was, says Pound, the question that "gets them sore"—a phrase reminiscent of Pound's references to Jewish syphilis. It turns out, then, that Pound must confirm, or re-mark, the original mark of mutilation. And yet, ironically, his question sends the Jews "right up the pole"—a phallic image which suggests that the Jews, in spite of mutilation, are priapic, as Pound conceives himself. Even more curiously, the language of Pound's speculations concerning Jewish circumcision has little to do with circumcision: "after all these years, where the most sensitive parts of the body are, rubbing them off, over and over again." Circumcision occurs only once. Pound's language more appropriately describes masturbation or coitus, both of which involve repeated rubbing. The real danger of mutilation seems much closer to home, within the sexual act.[14]

II.

When Pound speaks of the phallus he usually refers t
object. But Pound also conceives of the phallus as does Jacques ᴸᵃᵪ
abstract signifier or principle beyond any specific object which may bᴜ
thought to represent it. It is a symbol or idea, carrying with it the ideas of
presence, the denial of lack, the filling of space, power, language, differentiation, and the paternal, as opposed to absence, emptiness, lack, and speech-
lessness, which are identified with the mother and the feminine.[15]

Lacan argues that the paternal interdict on incest, which concludes the
Oedipal crisis and initiates the castration complex, decisively distinguishes
father from son and so confers the child's identity. The interdict is a differentiating act of speech by which the "name" and authority of the father is
recognized, obeyed, and granted priority, and the child himself comes to
pursue a paternal role in imitation of the father. Thus the recognition of
logos, name, and difference coincides with the appearance of the phallus as
the differentiating sign of the father and as something to be sought and
imitated: the powers of the word and language are connected with the idea
of the phallic origin or phallus as a symbol of total plenitude, freedom from
lack. Lacan would thus afford a possible explanation for Pound's conception of the originating sun as "god's mouth" and "Pater Helios." For Pound,
whether as *logos,* thought, or seed, light orders and differentiates reality.
Pound furthermore conceives of the essence of man's being as light and
hence as continuous with the creative, paternal phallus: "Man's phallic
heart is from heaven / a clear spring of rightness." Man must therefore
"illumine the words of procedure" (99/ 698), for only then can he imitate
the paternal authority which is the sun.

Nonetheless, Lacan emphasizes that the mythical phallus is unattainable, for no such object, no full presence, really exists. The phallus can only
be known through its differentiating marks and traces, through real and
imaginary objects, none of which can successfully overcome the subject's
initial and persistent sense of lack (the castration complex). In short, the
castration complex engenders a whole series of symbolic and metaphorical
substitutions for what the subject perceives to be missing. Pound's entire
project of reestablishing cultural plenitude is implicit in the title of his early
series of essays, "I Gather the Limbs of Osiris," which alludes to Isis' search
for the scattered limbs and lost phallus of the dead Osiris. Nothing better
reveals the importance of the phallus in Pound's quest for cultural unity.
Similarly, Pound obsessively multiplies signifiers of the phallus throughout
his work: the head, the sun, the pen, the chisel, the monument, the artifact,
all pointing to the mythical phallus but capable of representing it only as an
endlessly repeatable and constantly endangered trace, a presence which is
also an absence. Meanwhile, a theme of castration, absence, and effacement
appears persistently in Pound's writings on the Jews.

Given Pound's association of sperm and light, and given his belief in the "Semite hatred of light," one sees why he could then portray the Jews as the essence of the ungenerative, as transmitters of allegories "against procreation" (RB, 253). Like the Nazis, he believes that the Jews, having originated in an arid and undesirable climate, and hence divorced from agriculture, are sexually and culturally sterile.[16] Such accusations, of course, jar with Pound's associations of the Jews with great numbers and "excess"; but this is not the place to consider his confusion. When in the radio broadcasts he accuses his British listeners of having succumbed to Jewish influences, theirs is a failure of "breedin' " (RB, 203) in a double sense of maintaining race and population. In his fear of sterility and emphasis on breeding Pound conforms to a familiar fascist pattern.[17]

Sterility is only one symptom of the Jews' attack on the Western homestead. Whether as a herd, crowd, host, rabble, or bacilli, the Jews reveal all the defects of a tribe which "had not evolved into agricultural order" (SP, 90). They are an indistinct, deracinated, and destructive mass, an "atavistic" (RB, 302) force "[alone] proclaiming the ethos of a nomadic era" (SP, 66). These desert wanderers infect the communities they infiltrate with their rootless and indistinct spirit, their complete disregard for Nature and property.

The homestead is the triumph of phallic man, who reveres mythology, imitates the sun, and who understands the value of generation, property, and inheritance. Thus in Canto 87:

> Baccin said: I planted that
>   tree, and *that* tree (ulivi)
> Monsieur F. saw his mentor
>   composed almost wholly of light. . . .
> Butchers of lesser cattle, their villain the grain god.
> Fell between horns, but up . . .
>   and the murmur: "salta sin barra,"
> There is no such play for a goat.
> Tho' Mr. Paige has described Ligurian butchery,
> And the hunting tribes require some preparation.
> Mont Ségur, sacred to Helios . . . .
>
>   (87/ 573–574)

Baccin is an Italian farmer "familiar with every tree he has planted and watched as it grew" (Bacigalupo: 248). Patriarchal man, husbandman to Mother Nature, Baccin has won mystical and yet concrete possession of the earth. As for the mystic Monsieur F. (Flaubert), he has visions of that generative light whose source is the sun—the very light which the agriculturalist imitates, and which enables him to call things, such as trees, by their right names. Pound also links Baccin to the Spanish bullfight, characterized by "clean" killing, and Montségur, for Pound the highest example of European solar religion. "Butchers of lesser cattle" looks back to Pound's *Meridiano di Roma* article of November 1, 1942, in which Pound again argues that true religion derives from agriculture. The Hebrew religion, by contrast, "with its deity who was a shark and a monopolist, was the religion of the 'butchers of lesser cattle.' " Instead of hunting wild beasts, these tribes "fattened cows and sheep and then killed them at leisure, with no danger to themselves" (Stock, 3: 513). The Jews thus fail to make those discriminations which come easily to the hard-working agriculturalist, and they are cowardly, unlike the Spanish matador. One sees a connection between the butchers of lesser cattle and the Jewish usurer or monopolist, who prefers the abstract symbol of wealth to work and the bounty of the soil, and who, through mortgages and foreclosures, eats away slowly at the "rights of ownership" (SP, 298) and drives the peasant and aristocrat from his traditional lands.

This is precisely the social and cultural usurpation to which Pound refers in Canto 103, in which David Blumenthal, having bought Talleyrand's former castle in Provence, wittily names himself "Dalleyrand Berrigorrr!" Pound adds that this event took place "800 years after En Bertrans," that is Bertran de Born, one of Pound's aristocratic troubadour heroes, who knew how to circumvent usurers' machinations with tricks of his own. In a famous sestina Bertran tells the other Provençal barons to follow him in pawning their castles in order to acquire funds before the outbreak of war: "[Baros, metetz] en gatje [gatge]!" ("Pawn your castles, Lords") (103/ 749). If victorious, Bertran will retain his castles without paying back the usurers; if not, he will be unable to pay his debts anyway. In "Near Perigord" Pound gives this passage an anti-Semitic slant lacking in the original and anticipating his identification of the pawnbroker with the Jew: "Pawn your castles, Lords, / Let the Jews pay!" (PER, 152).

Somewhat less obvious is Pound's identification, from the late 1930s on, of the Jews with Communist Russia. In *Guide to Kulchur,* Communism is "barbarous and Hebrew" (GK, 270), "a return to the Anschauung of the nomad" (RB, 302).[18] Later, in the broadcasts, Pound like Hitler and his ideologist Alfred Rosenberg sees no difference between Jewish finance capital and its supposed enemy; he reaches the preposterous conclusion that Jewish usurers and Communism are in alliance, that Communism and Marxism are no more than the instrument of "Judah" (RB, 155).[19] But even these absurdities reveal a kind of logic once we realize that for Pound both Jewish usury and Communism challenge the patriarchal system of ownership and property which traces to the phallic origin, the paternal sun. According to Pound, the usurer and the Communist aim for the destruction of the homestead and "the abolition of ALL private ownership" (RB, 50); they destroy the "grain symbol" and the symbols of "the sun and fecundity" (RB, 155). But as for whether Pound's attacks on Communist materialism consort with the "Jewish" tendency towards abstraction, or, for that matter, whether Jewish materialism consorts with Jewish abstraction, Pound never asks these questions.

Pound's anti-Semitism figures within an inheritance plot whose implications are phallocentric and patriarchal: who shall inherit the concrete body of Western culture? To quote Sartre:

> The anti-Semite has a fundamental incomprehension of the various forms of modern property: money, securities, etc. They are abstractions, entities of reason related to the abstract intelligence of the Semite. A security belongs to no one because it can belong to everyone; moreover, it is a sign of wealth, not a concrete possession. The anti-Semite can conceive only of a type of primitive ownership of land based on a veritable magical rapport, in which the thing possessed and its possessor are united in a bond of mystical participation; he is the poet of real property. . . . To put it another way, the principle underlying anti-Semitism is that the concrete possession of a particular object gives as if by magic the meaning of that object. (Sartre: 23–24)

While Sartre goes too far in claiming that a single principle underlies anti-Semitism, the attitude he describes corresponds exactly to Pound's treatment of the farmer Baccin.

One might argue that Pound has a reasonably clear idea of money as an abstract sign of wealth, and that he is aware of money's purely functional character as a means of exchange. Nonetheless, Pound's monetary proposals and attacks on usurious abstraction demonstrate his preference for concrete wealth. The primary purpose of such proposals, for instance Gesell's stamp scrip, is to eliminate abstract expressions of wealth and to transform money into a counter signifying a certain number of things. Pound never ceases to insist that real wealth is not money but concrete possessions, such as works of art, machinery, and land.[20]

In any case, it is wrong to think that usury is only an economic disease, for in many instances its economic significance is at best secondary. Though Pound associates usury with indefinition, he never defines it precisely, and it finally is a negative principle, overdetermined in its meanings and multifarious and contradictory in its effects. Still, there is a common denominator in all its manifestations: usury is always a failure of man's distinctions; again and again it attacks the "forméd trace" (36/ 178). This process has less to do with economics than with castration.

Pound relates language, the identifying name, to the phallus: as man's sexual energies trace back to Pater Helios, so the sun is an utterer or "mouth" creating clarity and definition. Language is thus linked to the phallic origin, while the written trace is itself a phallic mark. It therefore follows that, if the Jews are the enemies of light, they are also the enemies of the paternal *logos* or word; their purpose, as "falsification incarnate" (RB, 184), is to distort, misrepresent, and conceal language, to "castrate" (RB, 330) school-books, literature, origins, and traditions, to promote "the Atys element in all Anglo-Educ[ation]" (L, 264). As we shall see later in detail, Pound blames the Jews for introducing obscurity, verbiage, equivocation, and allegory into language. Like many fascists, proto-Fascists, and conservatives, he is equally convinced that "the American press and radio are mostly in Chewisch hands" (RB, 290), and that the "Jewspapers" and the "schnorrer press" spread "vagueness in communication."[21] "Exist[ing]" only to "lie," whether in print or in the airwaves, Jewish "news agencies" (RB, 228) most fully exercise their enormous powers of "falsification" (RB, 284) in concealing the usurious corruptions of liberalism while misrepresenting the benevolent intentions of Mussolini and Hitler: "There is nothing surprising," says Pound, "in a Goy [Gentile] nation falling under the domination of the Jewish print" (RB, 217). As a further instance of the Jewish inheritance plot, Pound claims that the Jews are the destroyers of Western historical tradition. He speaks of the Talmud "wanting to annihilate all history" (RB, 198). Indeed, "wherever one looks—printing, publishing, schooling—the black hand of the banker blots out the sun" (L, 263).

With the destruction of language proceeds the destruction of other traces, monuments which preserve "the tradition of the undivided light" (SP, 307). As Pound says in "A Visiting Card," "tradition *inheres* . . . in the images of the gods," while "history is recorded in monuments, and *that* is why they get destroyed" (SP, 322). In the same essay Pound speaks of the "power of putrefaction" which aims at the obfuscation of history by "destroying the symbols" (SP, 317). Pound is thinking primarily of Jews. As he says in the broadcasts, "Insofar as there are monuments to OTHER races he [the Jew] is against them . . . . They are . . . useless to him until they are reduced to fragments that can be sold in antique shops" (RB, 219). In Canto 96 the Colossus of Rhodes, representing the sun-god Apollo, is destroyed and sold in fragments "to a jew" (96/ 657). The Jews play a central role in the cultural dissolution which Pound encapsulates in Canto 87:

> Chief's names on a monument,
> Seepage,
> the élan, the block,
> dissolution.

> (87/ 575–576)

Though the names are fated to dissolve, Pound introduces the *chih* (wisdom) sign, masculine and erect, asserting man's resistance, his "phallic heart" (99/ 697).

As written records and monuments are signs of the phallus, so are artifacts and graven images, on which the artist, imitating Nature, traces his marks. Donald Davie argues that Pound treats poetry as a form of sculpture and conceives of the activity of stone-carving as sexual (Davie, 1: 155–156). For Pound, the sculptor's or engraver's way with a stone is like a man's way with a woman; the artifact reveals man's imprint, the phallic trace, on the feminine substance.

In the Usury *Cantos* Usura causes "the girl's needle [to go] . . . blunt in her hand" (51/ 250); it keeps "the weaver . . . from his loom," and the "stone cutter . . . from his stone" (51/ 250). Meanwhile, the force of "Judah" is "destructive EVEN of the mason's trowel" (RB, 155). Usury thus produces a form of castration leading to impotence. It attacks the very instruments and impulses of art and forestalls the very moment of art's inception. So far as the finished art product is concerned, usury either causes its lines to "grow thick" (45/ 229), or else to fade, blur, and finally disappear. Here Pound plays on at least one of the meanings of usury. As Jacques Derrida observes, usury in one sense means wear and tear, abrasion and rubbing, the deterioration suffered by the side or face of the coin. Usury can thus mean, as it does at some points in Pound, the loss of metallic value in weight sustained by the coin in use. But usury can also refer to the simultaneous corrosion of the engraved mark on the coin's face. Pound considers the corrosion of this human image or face as significant as the loss of the coin's weight.[22]

In European and other societies the face implies identity, and identity is always attributed to that which confers it, the phallus or father, which "moulds the face of the child."[23] Hence Pound's fascination with heads, which he associates with fecundity, intelligence, light, and the phallus. But Pound is also interested in the images and "characters" (86/ 565) on coins, images which usually represent the heads and faces of rulers and leaders, and which have a monumental significance: he was no doubt aware that the Latin word *moneta,* meaning money, is related to the word monument. All this is enough to establish the phallic significance of coin. Not only is the coin the product of the engraver's tools, but the ruler's image is implicitly phallic, while the ruler himself is the father of his nation and the temporal surrogate for the heavenly father (God, the origin).[24] One also understands Pound's obsession with the preservation of a lost numismatic art: its purpose is to preserve the trace, which testifies to general cultural health, stability, and authority (SP, 327; GK, 36). Pound would return to the Renaissance, when the great Pisanello engraved coins and medallions for the "deification of emperors" (74/ 425), and when a Sigismundo Malatesta, an "entire" (GK, 194) or complete man, was worthy of being represented upon them.

Pound's phallocentrism, as well as his castration anxiety, had a profound influence on his politics, as we shall see throughout this book. Not only does Pound admire the Italian Fascist corporate state for its analogies with the organic unity of the human body, he wants the totalitarian and phallic dictator (Mussolini, the "bull," "Big Stick," SP, 261, and "male of the species," LE, 83) at its political "apex" (88/ 581) or "summit" (88/ 580).[25] Such values are entirely consistent with Pound's phallocentrism, that is, his worship of the phallic sun (and *logos*) as the originating and necessary center of an all-embracing cosmic system of preordained hierarchical relationships. In short, Pound considers non-fascist political systems to be implicitly disorderly, incomplete, and castrated. One can now comprehend the horror which the "enormous tragedy" of Mussolini's assassination inspires in Pound. The hanging of the murdered Mussolini "by the heels" signifies the total inversion of hierarchy and authority as represented in the properly "erect" figure of the leader, who is himself the symbol of the organic and corporate unity of the nation. At the same time, in death Il Duce has ceased to be a bull and become a "bullock," a castrated bull, upon whose carcass feeds an undifferentiated and profaning horde of human "maggots" (74/ 425).

Chapter Four

Medievalism, Corporatism, and Totalitarian Culture

Pound's interest in the Middle Ages persists in his life and works and has its most important statement in the section on "Medievalism" from the 1934 essay on Guido Cavalcanti. Unlike many of his Romantic predecessors, Pound refuses to ignore medieval diseases of mind and body. The first include superstition, intolerance, extremism, "hell obsession" (LE, 153), and religious fanaticism; the second, "idiotic asceticism" (LE, 150), "anti-flesh" (LE, 154), masochism, "bad physique" (LE, 150), the suppression of hygiene, the worship of filth, and the "belief that the body is evil" (LE, 150). For Pound, these medieval diseases bespeak a general confusion and lack of proportion which finds expression in the darker and more confused forms of medieval art. Yet Pound is most interested in the pure, "clean" (LE, 153), and ideal form of the Middle Ages, a permanent model for later artists. Inspired by a love of light, intelligence, and moderation, this ideal has its symbol in the healthy and active human body and above all in the Italian Gothic and Romanesque cathedral, whose "clear lines and proportions" (LE, 154) bespeak religious, social, and cultural order. Defined as the "Mediterranean sanity" (LE, 154), such medieval beauty and restraint is the antithesis of medieval asceticism and intolerance, the "Hindoo disease" and the "Hebrew disease" (LE, 154).

Pound's medievalism also feeds his social and political thought. After about 1930, Pound follows Ruskin and the medievalizing Guild Socialists in advocating craft ideals and the guild organization of society;[1] His attacks on usury, his quest for the "just price," his emphasis on economic morality, all reflect medieval Catholic models.[2] His notions of political authority owe something to Dante's *De Monarchia,* which envisions European unification under a benevolent Catholic king. But by the late 1930s and early 1940s Pound's medievalism has more sinister implications. Praising Ruskin's and Morris's guild and craft ideals in his radio broadcasts, Pound finds their salvation and fulfillment in the corporate state of Mussolini. The Romanesque and Gothic cathedrals of the Cavalcanti essay have "place and right . . . in corporate order" (RB, 197); Italian Fascism is the means by which medieval harmony will be restored.[3]

According to Jeremy Cohen, in the later Middle Ages there developed the theory of the Christian Church and state as a "corporate" and "organic unity," whose hierarchical organization is comparable to that of a human body and the mystical body of Christ. The organization extends from the Pope, or ruler, as head, to the various levels of the ecclesiastical and secular hierarchy, to each component of society, all of which are required to subordinate their interests and activities to the good of the whole. Cohen adds that this "totalitarian" ideal finds its perfect cultural expression in the cathedral, symbolizing harmony, order, and universality (Cohen: 248–252). Though Italian Fascism looked much more to Rome than to the Middle Ages, Pound was not altogether mistaken in linking it with medieval political and cultural values. Whether in politics, culture, or society, Pound envisions Italian Fascism as aspiring toward a totalitarian completeness and unity, toward organic harmony, hierarchy, and proportion. The state, says Pound, is "totalitarian" (SP, 158)[4] and its power, centered in Mussolini as "head" or "apex" (88/ 581), is "absolute" (SP, 306). Its purpose, meanwhile, is to direct and unify virtually every aspect of social and cultural life, to mould it, upon the analogy of the human body or well-functioning organism, into a corporate or organic unity: "The State is corporate / as with pulse in its body" (99/ 707). This means that the state must transform the various branches of labor and industry into self-managing but at the same time state-directed and even state-controlled syndicates and corporations, which Pound views as Italian Fascism's improvement on the somewhat anarchic because monopolistic medieval guilds; the state must define for each group of producers its rightful "place" and its rightful reward within a hierarchical social structure. As in the Middle Ages, society is hierarchized on the basis of occupation and estate rather than on the basis of the competitive and "inorganic" concept of class. The integration of social groups replaces the divisiveness of class interest, and each group is made to perform its economic function for the good of society as a whole.[5]

As Pound's Fascism derives at least partly from his medievalism, so his anti-Semitism confirms the argument that some of the main sources of modern anti-Semitism lie in medieval religious beliefs. "If the Jew is today despised and feared," writes Joshua Trachtenberg, "it is because we are the heirs of the Middle Ages," and thus share something of the "medieval psychology." Norman Cohn likewise argues that modern anti-Semitism is a "secularized version of the popular medieval view of Jews as a league of sorcerers employed by Satan for the spiritual and physical ruination of Christendom," and that the drive to exterminate the Jews springs from "demonological superstitions inherited from the Middle Ages."[6]

To be sure, these scholars go too far in claiming that medieval and other religious influences are decisive in the formation of modern anti-Semitism.

Modern anti-Semitism in Pound's case as in all others depends heavily on the unique psychology of individuals and on their historical, economic, social, and cultural circumstances.[7] Nor is Pound's anti-Semitism perfectly comparable to the Christian and medieval form. Like most modern versions, it focuses not on the problem of the Jew as non-Christian and supposed killer of Christ, as in medieval times, but on supposedly ineradicable ethnic and racial differences between Jews and Gentiles.[8] Nonetheless, Pound's and Hitler's accusations against the Jews often resemble those that appeared in the crisis-ridden society of the late Middle Ages, a society of millenarian longings and apocalyptic fears. The resemblance can be explained partly by the fact that Pound, like Hitler and the Nazis, made use of an underground tradition descending from medieval times.[9] However, its ultimate explanation lies probably in Pound's and Hitler's profound attraction to medieval models of corporatism, hierarchy, and totalitarianism.

Jeremy Cohen observes that up to the thirteenth century the Church followed St. Augustine's teaching that the Jews have a right to exist in Christian society. One consequence of the thirteenth century drive towards corporate and totalitarian unity in politics and culture was a massive outbreak of violent, even exterminatory anti-Semitism. "In a society which was committed to an ideal of organic unity, . . . no room existed for infidels"; the Jews faced conversion or purgation (Cohen: 14–16, 254, 296). Pound's anti-Semitism takes inspiration from the medieval ideal of a corporate and organic society, an ideally healthy "body" from which the Jews are necessarily excluded. Indeed, his 1940s proposals to "purge" (RB, 62) Europe of its Jewish "bacillus," to eliminate the "Jewish poison" (SP, 320), are anticipated in the essay on Cavalcanti, where medieval evils trace to the "Hebrew disease."

II.

In 1935 Pound observed that "The Crusading Spirit was and is full of semitic intolerance," while present day Christianity "is riddled with semitism." This statement not only endorses medieval anti-Semitism but expresses Pound's desire for its revival in modern times. Earlier, in "Ecclesia," Pound said that "when the Church was real it was anti-semite. Whatever privileges and immunities were granted the jews, the Church regarded herself as the opponent of semitism." The church, he added, conceived of itself as "the OPPONENT of ancient error (and devilment), built the cathedrals," and "evolved a dialectic and a few clean economic ideas."[10] The source of "devilment" is clearly "semitism," and so the Jews appear, as in the Middle Ages, as a satanic power. Five years later, writing to Ronald Duncan on the eve of war, Pound repeated that "Christianity is (or was when real) anti-Semitism" (L, 340).[11]

Among the many medieval anti-Semitic accusations, the most persistent were that the Jews had spread plague and disease and had contaminated

wells; that they had poisoned Christians, often through drugs and medicines; that they, as an unclean people, gave off a distinctive odor known as
the *foetor judaica* (the medieval devil was associated with bad smells); that
they had sought the blood and heads of Christians; that they had collabo-
rated with the Tartar and Mongol enemies of Europe; and that they had
violated the purity of the ritually consecrated blood of Christ and the Communion wafer itself (a charge linked to the idea of Jewish deicide).[12] But in
the broadest sense, probably the most important similarity between Pound's
and medieval anti-Semitism is that both involve an essentially corporate
concept of society and social responsibility (Trachtenberg: 113, 162).

Some critics argue that Pound never really attacked all Jews but only
corrupt and reprehensible financiers, who happened to be Jewish. In Canto
52 Pound distinguishes between "big jews" (the Rothschilds) and "poor
yitts," who must suffer for "a few big jews' vendetta on goyim" (52/ 257).
According to Kimpel and Eaves, by the middle 1930s Pound believes that
the "small" Jews bring pogroms upon themselves for failing to expose and
denounce their evil "big" brothers.[13] In the broadcasts as well Pound sometimes resists total condemnation of the Jews. Nonetheless, Pound in *Guide
to Kulchur* states that the Rothschilds seek to "avenge" (GK, 315) the
Jewish race as a whole— an idea implicit in many of the broadcasts. Moreover, the above passage from Canto 52 is followed by a quotation recommending the total quarantine of Jews in America. As for Pound's distinction
between big and little Jews, this is no less an example of anti-Semitism.
What is the purpose of bringing up the ethnic or racial identity of such
persons except to imply that such factors constitute an essential difference in
their behavior? Similarly, when Pound attacks "semitism" and vilifies the
Jewish race, or "Jewry," he no longer thinks of the Jews as individuals or as
representatives only of a particular religion, as in the Middle Ages. He
attacks that essence that is the true object of modern anti-Semitic hatred.
Ultimately Pound adopts his own version of the Nazi *Judenrein* concept, the
idea of a Europe freed or "purged" of Jewish influence either through
banishment or elimination of the Jews: as Pound says in the broadcasts, the
"choice" is "between Europe and Jewry" (RB, 310).[14]

Given Pound's organic and corporate vision of European society, it is
consistent that his anti-Semitic accusations repeatedly return to the language
of organic health and disease. Pound's propensity for such language is intensified by his phobic personality: like Hitler's his works are almost from the
beginning filled with images of contamination, infection, decay, of crawling
and slimy creatures leaving filthy trails on the face of the earth. By the
middle of his career Pound applies such imagery repeatedly to the Jews.

In the *Meridiano di Roma* in 1942 Pound defines the Jews as "malattia
incarnata," the very embodiment of disease (Norman: 373). Whether as
"rats" (SP, 317), "bed bugs" (RB, 253), "lice" (RB, 157), "vermin" (RB, 74,
75, 86, 253), "worms" (RB, 59), or bacilli, these parasites prey on the body

of Western culture and are identical with the Jewish "rats" and "vermin" of Hitler's obsession, those "Jewish colonies of parasites" in which Hitler sees the permanent enemies of mankind (Hitler: 31, 153). The Jews, writes Pound, are "the rot eating in since Cromwell" (RB, 190), who readmitted the Jews into England; the big Jew "has rotted EVERY nation he has wormed into" (RB, 59). Thus responsible for the slow, secret, and invisible decay of the West, the Jews constitute an enormous "power of putrefaction" (SP, 317). For Hitler, the Jews "produce the symptoms of decay of a slowly rotting world" (Hitler: 259). Where Pound would cut out usury, the "cancer of the world" (SP, 300, RB, 73), Hitler speaks of the Jews as "incurable tumors," of lancing abcesses and finding, "like a maggot in a rotting body, often dazzled by the sudden light, a kike!" (Hitler: 29, 57). Pound and Hitler also associate the Jews with unhealthy and unpleasant smells, as if they gave off the odor of disease and decay. Pound refers to the Jews as "big noses" (RB, 346), associates them with miasmatic bogs, "sewers" (RB, 345), and "odorous swindles" (RB, 345), and alludes to the intolerable "stink" (RB, 302) of their nomadic camps. Hitler tells in *Mein Kampf* of being made "sick to . . . [his] stomach from the smell of these caftan-wearers" (Hitler: 57). These accusations revive the medieval idea of the *foetor judaica*.

As in the Middle Ages, when the Jews were blamed for spreading plague, Pound in his later writing views the Jews as bacilli. Defined as the "pervasive, the ubiquitous Yidd" (RB, 188), and comparable to an infinitesi-mally small army of invaders, the Jews carry not only syphilis but typhus, tuberculosis, and a "more than bubonic plague" (RB, 74). Again Pound resembles Hitler, who refers to the Jews' "shameful numbers," describes them as bacilli, and compares the Jewish "pestilence" to the Black Death of medieval times; as Pound said, Hitler was "clear on the bacillus of Kikism."[15] Pound also suspects that many Middle and East European Jews are "Mongol" (35/ 174). This erroneous insinuation anticipates Pound's version of the medieval charge that the Jews incite and collaborate with the enemies of the West, particularly the orientalized horde of Russian Commu-nists, to invade and overturn European nations.[16] In this instance he only slightly varies his more familiar accusation that the Communist masses are allies or pawns of world Jewry.

During the Middle Ages the Jews were frequently charged with poison-ing Christians with drugs and medicines, of which the Jews, as traders and physicians, had special knowledge (Trachtenberg: 91–96, 97–98). In the radio broadcasts and *The Cantos* Pound denounces Jewish opium racketeers for befogging the mind of Europe; if any member of his audience must see a doctor, advises Pound, he should not "send for Rosenman" (RB, 346).[17] In fact, Pound speaks of poison or "*veleno*" (74/ 437) as a metaphor for the total contamination of Western culture by usury and hence the Jews. Eliot, says Pound, "has not come through uncontaminated by the Jewish poi-son. . . . Until a man purges himself of this poison he will never achieve understanding" (SP, 320). A similar obsession with poison appears in Hit-ler's writings, where the Jews are the "rats that politically poison our na-tion" (Hitler: 31, 233). In spite of obvious differences, Hitler's accusation of poisoning also resembles the familiar medieval blood accusation. Trachten-berg observes that medieval Christians believed that the Jews needed Chris-tian blood for their rituals and even sought to defile the symbolic blood (wine) used in the Communion service. Hitler's updated version of this accusation is his allegation that the Jews corrupt the Aryan race through a continuous stream of blood poisoning—in short, racial contamination.[18] In similar fashion Pound in the radio broadcasts says that the "Kikes" have "squirted . . . follies" (RB, 61)— implicitly poisons—into English and Ro-man veins and threatened Gentile blood with racial contamination. Pound also speaks, somewhat ambiguously, but also with direct reference to the "bloodthirsty" Jews, of "bleeders" (RB, 25, 60) and "sons of Blood" (RB, 24) drawing blood from Gentile victims and nations.

Pound's fears of racial and personal debilitation through blood-poisoning precede his virulent anti-Semitism and originally had little or nothing to do with the Jews. Well over a decade before his anti-Semitism had become obsessive and ideological, Pound revealed his fears of blood-poisoning in his correspondence with William Carlos Williams. Writing to Williams on November 10, 1917, Pound expresses two contradictory atti-tudes towards nationality. He quotes against Williams's nativist stance Gourmont's defense of literary cosmopolitanism, which also serves to de-fend Pound's decision to remain temporarily in Europe rather than return to America. But despite Pound's anti-provinciality, and despite his statement that Williams is as "Amurkun" (L, 123) as himself, he also asserts over Williams his superior authenticity as an American as well as his more pene-trating knowledge of the "heart" (L, 123) of the country. Whereas Wil-liams's family had recently immigrated to America, and the mixed-blood Williams has been confined to the Eastern seaboard, the Idaho-born Pound has not only seen the Western prairies and mountains but can trace his ancestors back three centuries to the Anglo-Saxon colonists.[19] He boasts to the "foreign" (L, 123) Williams that "I (der grosse Ich) have the virus, the bacillus of the land in my blood, for nearly three bleating centuries" (L, 124)—a statement which Williams quoted in the Prologue to *Kora in Hell.* But there is a certain ominousness in Pound's metaphor of the bacillus. Three years later, in another letter to Williams, this boast of racial priority and superiority has turned to anxiety. Now Pound describes Williams as having the "fresh blood of Europe in . . . [his] veins," a portion of which Pound knew to be Jewish, while Pound, like Eliot, belongs to a colonial stock which had grown enervated over the centuries. Pound laments that he had absorbed only the "thin milk" of New York and New England—a veiled complaint, perhaps, against his mother's lack of affection—and that this weak mixture had denied him such strength as enabled the racially "younger" (L, 158) Williams to see things objectively. It turns out that "there is blood poison in America"; Pound has "cursed blood," a "disease" which he has to "fight day and night" (L, 158). These passages repeat the anxiety of *Patria Mia,* in which Pound, returning to America in 1910–1911, and observing with fascination and loathing the immigrants' vigorous animality, fears that the nation's colonial legacy will be swamped in a rising tide or "pool" (SP, 108) of new races. Even more important, the second letter to Williams perhaps marks Pound's first assertion of race as something like an ideological concept: "I don't care . . . about nationality. Race is probably real. It is real" (L, 158). In the light of this evidence, one must view Pound's accusations of Jewish blood poisoning as the ultimate rationalization and projection of a fear not originally of the Jews but of his own racial inferiority and marginality, a fear for which the Jews came for a variety of reasons to be the most convenient object.

One accusation remains, namely Pound's version of the medieval charge that the Jews seek to violate the communion wafer symbolic of the body of Christ.[20] First, though, it should be emphasized that Pound's economics is inseparable from his basically unobjectionable belief that nutrition is of primary importance in all cultures. Pound's horror of the adulteration of food, his fondness for alimentary metaphors in reference to the consumption of cultural knowledge, these reveal the major importance of food and nutrition in his thought. For Pound, the "strength of men is in grain" (106/752), while Princes must "Feed the people" (99/695).

Pound reveres those times when bread was "sanctified . . . and . . . regarded as the bearer, in concentrated form, of the vital powers of the cosmos."[21] "The religious man," he says, "communes [with the deity] every time his teeth sink into a bread crust" (SP, 70). In Canto 104 Pound links the ideas of mastication, grain, and solar religion:

> Luigi in hill paths
>   chews wheat at sunrise,
>   that grain, his communion
>   (104/741)

William Desmonde notes that for primitive and modern man food symbolically represents the body of the father, toward whom, as Freud has shown, man harbors feelings of love and hatred (oral aggression). Desmonde also observes that "the fertility spirit . . . was often the sacrificial victim in the ritual meals which were at the center of the social organization" of early European cultures, and that the "holy repast was an occasion at which each communicant reidentified himself," through eating and incorporation, "with the divinity" (Desmonde: 72–73, 75). Some cultures achieve such identification through the symbolic substitution of totemic animal victims for the fertility spirit, who is thereby consumed symbolically in the totemic feast, but Pound apparently conceives of the grain as the body of the god:

"Only a WHEAT GOD," he says, "can save Europe."²² These rituals of incorporation can be taken as sublimated versions of an original act of social violence against a human scapegoat victim, whose death stands at the origin of social order and who can thus be viewed as society's father. This idea was known to Pound not only from Frazer but from Allen Upward.²³ As Pound says, in a phrase suggesting the Wheat God's simultaneous role as progenitor, victim, and nourishment: "The whole tribe is from one man's body" (99/ 708). In these terms, Pound's grain rite is a personal and pagan version of the Catholic Communion.

So for Pound "the only vigorous feasts of the Church" are pagan, are "grafted onto European roots, the sun, the grain, the harvest. . . ." Pound envisions society as a sacred and communal feast, through which each person, in the act of eating, participates in the deity and incorporates his share of the social substance. Thus in the agrarian China of Canto 98:

> Each year in the Elder Spring, that is the first month
> > of it,
> The herald shall invite your compliance.
> There are six rites for the festival
> > and that all should converge!
>
> > (98/ 693)

These lines pun implicitly on the idea of incorporation. The social order in Cantos 98 and 99 requires the incorporation of the Chinese people within an organic, hierarchical body, a "corporate" state like that of Italian Fascism: "High & low, top & under / INCORPORATE / & one body" (99/ 707). But the injunction to incorporate is also to participate in the communal feast, to share in the vitalizing body of the deity; for the "whole tribe is from one man's body" (99/ 708).²⁴

Anti-Semitism has been traced to the devouring instinct and attitudes towards food, particularly to the Gentile's sense of the strangeness of Jewish eating habits and the exclusiveness which such habits seem to imply.²⁵ This helps to explain why, in the communal feast which Pound envisions for the West, there is no room for the Jews. Pound identifies the Jews with the devouring instinct, unclean eating habits, the contamination and adulteration of food, and above all, oral aggression. Because of usury the peasant "does not eat his own grain" (51/ 250), and man's "bread [is] ever more of stale rags," is "dry as paper, / with no mountain wheat, no strong flour" (45/ 229). As Pound says in Canto 45, "corpses are set to banquet / at behest of usura" (45/ 230).

Pound found worthy of "attention" Voltaire's "Ezekiel," from *The Philosophical Dictionary*. In this essay Voltaire quotes derisively a presumably typical Biblical passage in which the Lord helps the prophet and the Jews to "knead" their food with "shit."²⁶ Generally, however, Pound focuses on the supposed violence of Jewish orality. As he notes, the Hebrew word *neschek* means "the bite," and refers to the tendency of usury to "gnaw into" (I, 96) wealth and abundance.[27] Thus, in Pound's prose, as in Hitler's, the Jews "gnaw" (RB, 340) into the body of Western culture and have "the power to starve the whole of mankind" (RB, 7). The Jews are "always eating away at the life inside the nation" (RB, 153), are the "rot eating in since Cromwell" (RB, 190). "The kikes," Pound tells England, "have sucked out your vitals" (RB, 61).[28] But the most remarkable of these accusations are Pound's references to the "chew[s]" (RB, 330; P/L, 218). Mimicking a Yiddish accent—an oral and aggressive imitation of the Jews— Pound fulminates against the "chewisch peers" (RB, 253) in Britain, warns of the "Chewisch problem" (RB, 255), and asserts that America's "press and radio are mostly in Chewisch hands" (RB, 290). Nothing could more fully represent Pound's image of the Jews as orally aggressive than their metaphorical reduction to the oral function.

The question remains: What could possibly motivate such accusations? What is the difference, if any, between the Jews, or "chews," and Luigi, the sacred hunchback who "chews wheat at sunrise," so achieving "his communion"?

As we have seen, food symbolically represents the body of the father, and Pound's grain rite involves incorporation of the deity. Pound's rite is thus comparable with the Catholic Communion. Whatever their differences, these rituals serve to emphasize identification and participation with the god, while concealing man's violent and devouring tendencies towards him. Even so, in both cases the god must be viewed as having been originally a sacrificial victim: the prototype of the Catholic ritual, as of Pound's perverse parody of it, is the totemic feast and sacrifice of the father deity or human scapegoat, from whose "body" derives the organic unity of "the whole tribe."[29] Pound's grain rite thus contains a repressed, unacknowledged, and even violent impulse of oral aggression. As Pound told Douglas Fox: "I keep chewing on that. Wheat God."[30] Nor is Pound, any more than Gentile society, altogether satisfied spiritually with such highly sublimated forms of sacrificial ritual as the grain rite. In The Cantos and Pound's Confucian translations the sacrifice and incorporation of totemic animals have a prominent place in maintaining order and promoting abundance. Such animal sacrifices reveal a more direct and violent form of aggression against the god (in the form of a totemic animal) than does the grain rite.

All this means that Pound's violent oral impulses toward the divinity must be denied, concealed, and projected onto the Jews. Pound's hatred thus resembles that of some Christians who blame the Jews for Christ's death and accuse them of host desecration. In both cases, these accusations are denials of hostility toward the father figure or savior, whose necessary sacrifice and death are commemorated symbolically, while the hostile impulses are projected onto a Jewish pariah society.[31]

Pound's attribution of demonic qualities to the Jews discloses an obvious self-deception which could never have been far from his consciousness.

For Pound knew that European history over the last two centuries is hardly comparable to a ritualistic communal feast. If anything he thought of the modern cultural crisis as a violent outburst of oral aggression from within. Quoting Jefferson on the fraternal strife of Europe during the nineteenth century, Pound says that the "cannibals of Europe are eating one another again" (32/ 159). This observation calls to mind Desmonde's suggestion that the competitive spirit of capitalism may coincide with an increase in oral aggression throughout Western culture (Desmonde: 92). Pound, however, locates such violence outside the European community and outside capitalism, in Jewish usury, which he treats as a foreign perversion of capitalism. Pound again resembles Hitler, who said: "The Aryan peoples, related in blood and culture, who have hitherto been tearing each other to pieces, must understand that it is the Jew who is the enemy of mankind." Hitler was thoroughly convinced that the Jew "would really devour the peoples of the earth."[32]

Pound's projective strategies reveal the essential nature of all Jewbaiting. For if the Jews fail to show the expected orally aggressive behavior, they must be provoked into acting like angry and violent animals, such as dogs.[33] Jewbaiting thus achieves its end only if the Jewbaiter first shows oral aggression, as in Pound's comparison of massacred Russian Jews to "fresh meat on the Russian steppes" (*A Casebook:* 15). According to Michael Reck, Pound raged repeatedly against Franklin Delano Roosevelt at St. Elizabeths. Such actions are explicable if we recall that in the broadcasts F.D.R. or "that brute Rosefield" (RB, 7) is indistinguishable from his supposed liberal Jewish "accomplices":[34]

> When raging against Roosevelt, whom he called "old Sowbelly," Pound assumed a Jewish accent (for some obscure reason) and actually bit his thumb. He could and did talk for twenty minutes straight on this subject. He told me that his hate for Roosevelt was sufficient to dam up the Potomac River.[35]

Pound manifests not only infantile and oral aggression against the patriarchal Jews but a curious mimesis of Jewish behavior (the Jewish accent). This confirms the truth of Jewbaiting, which requires the Jewbaiter to imitate unconsciously his idea of his enemies. Caught in a mimetic cycle of fascination and hatred, Pound most resembles his conception of the Jews when he attacks them. Here we have glimpsed the hidden pattern of his anti-Semitism.

Chapter Five

The Enlightenment and Orientalism

The preceding chapter has shown the links between Pound's anti-Semitism and that which prevailed in the Middle Ages. Even so, the essential spirit or core of Pound's hatred owes much less to medieval and Christian models than to that secular, ethnological, and finally racial anti-Semitism which emerged in the Enlightenment and whose chief inspiration is probably Voltaire. Although a number of critics, among them Hugh Kenner, have noted Pound's deep admiration for Voltaire and the French Enlightenment, they rarely mention that Pound admired not only Pound's style but his rabid anti-Semitism. Nor is it mentioned that Pound appeals to the Enlightenment in order to give a kind of dignity and legitimacy to his hatred of the Jews.[1]

Arthur Hertzberg observes that most of the *philosophes* "had their own 'enlightened' reasons for regarding Jews . . . [as outside] the pale of culture." Horkheimer and Adorno speak similarly of "the dialectical link between enlightenment and domination, and the dual relationship of progress to cruelty and liberation which the Jews sensed in the great philosophers of the Enlightenment."[2] Pound too was perhaps aware of the connection between liberation and persecution. In Canto 44 he surveys the social transformation of Northern Italy after the French Revolution:

> The citizen priest Fr Lenzini mounted the tribune
> to join the citizen Abrâm
> and in admiring calm sat there with them the citizen
> the Archbishop
>
> (44/ 225)

An ambassador of Napoleon, Abrâm is in all likelihood a Jew. In accordance with Napoleon's policy of integrating the Jews within their host communities (an idea which Pound largely ignores in his hero), the Jews are now citizens.[3] But liberty exacts its price: in the following passage the Jew is the victim of the violent anti-Napoleonic resistance which arose in the Northern Italian countryside in 1799:[4]

and on June 28th came men of Arezzo
past the Porta Romana and went into the ghetto
there to sack and burn hebrews
part were burned with the liberty tree in the piazza
and for the rest of that day and night
1799 anno domini

(44/ 225)

While it is not clear what Pound thinks of these events, it is possible that he disapproves of such violence as undermining the reforms of his hero, Napoleon. Yet in moving toward fascism Pound is increasingly critical of the Declaration of the Rights of Man, and so in Canto 44 he may regret Jewish emancipation as a consequence of the Enlightenment. By the broadcasts Pound treats the Jews as instrumental in the "chaos" (RB, 320) of the French Revolution.[5]

Most of the *philosophes* were not virulently anti-Semitic but attacked Judaism as part of their assault on religion, myth, and superstition. What characterizes Voltaire's anti-Semitism is its extraordinary intensity. As the "patron saint" of modern anti-Semitism, Voltaire generally ignores the Christian arguments against the Jews and gives anti-Semitism an entirely new justification.[6] In Voltaire's theory of Western culture neither the Jews nor Biblical history nor even Christianity is "central." Rather, the "normative" culture of the West had been disseminated by classical Greece and Rome, which are Europe's authentic foundations, and whose Golden Age of paganism the Enlightenment would restore. As for the Jews, they belong to a "different family," and their religion is rooted in their character. So too, Christianity is for Voltaire the Jewish religion, an alien superimposition on the pagan West. Voltaire further argues that since the Jewish character (like the Jewish religion) is innate, the Jews must remain "radically other, . . . hopeless[ly] alien," immune to enlightenment. These views, though not specifically racial, were later assimilated to Nazi racism.[7]

While Pound was deeply read in Voltaire, his anti-Semitism was most profoundly influenced by "Genèse," an article in *The Philosophical Dictionary* which he translated and to which he referred obliquely but approvingly in his correspondence with Marianne Moore. In what follows the translations from "Genèse" are mainly Pound's.

We have seen that Voltaire attacks the Jews for their supposed denial of the priority of the divine light and hence their hostility to the Enlightenment. In "Genèse" Voltaire is equally certain that the Jews are just another "Arab tribe" (PD, 172) or "horde."[8] This attack is part of Voltaire's attempt, similar to Pound's, to deny the uniqueness and value of the Old Testament—an aim perhaps ironic and self-contradictory, since Voltaire also wants to show the absolute uniqueness of the Jew as other. It is inconceivable, writes Voltaire, that "our laws, our fortunes, our morals, our well being," are "tied up with . . . poor shirtless Arabs," with "the ignorant chiefs of an unfortunate barbarous country, . . . always peopled by thieves." Why bother, he asks, to determine "whether there were kinglets in one canton of Arabia Petra before they appeared in the neighboring canton to the west of lake Sodom" (PD, 184–185). Later Pound protests against the dyeing of "Europe with a mythology elucubrated to explain the thoroughly undesirable climate of Arabia Petraea" (LE, 85).

Far from being unique, the Jews are for Voltaire the least notable of Semitic peoples, parasites on surrounding cultures, "plagiarists in everything."[9] These charges of Jewish cultural sterility, in the *Philosophical Dictionary* and elsewhere, anticipate Pound's and the Nazis' arguments that the uncreative Jews are experts in plagiarism, falsification, and slander (Hitler: 232). Voltaire also resembles Pound in presenting distorted evidence that the Jews viewed fertility as evil.[10] Here, however, a familiar contradiction appears, one which is implicit in Voltaire's references to Jewish licentiousness and in Pound's reference (actually an interpolation) to "the carnal Jews" (PD, 168). Such charges of infertility are hard to square with another fundamental anti-Semitic assumption, that the Jews are carnal and materialistic. For all his hatred of Jewish abstraction, Pound associates the Jews with material excess and sexual depravity and wantonness. Voltaire, on the other hand, ignores Jewish abstraction and views the Jews as crude pagan materialists. The Bible, he says, is really a polytheistic document, while the Jews are idolatrous; they "constantly believed god corporal, as did all the rest of the nations" (PD, 170). Even worse, the Jews love forbidden sexuality. According to Voltaire, whose fantasies may have inspired Pound, they worshipped and had sex with angels, whom they "represented . . . as bulls and as sparrow hawks, despite the prohibition to make graven images" (PD, 176). Voltaire also suggests that the Jews are incestuous, and that their sexual and childbearing practices resemble those of animals.[11] In this way he, like Pound, seeks metaphorically to reduce the Jews to beasts.

Voltaire is horrified by circumcision. In "Genèse" he tells the story of Sichem, son of King Hemor, who falls in love with Dinah, a Jewish girl. King Hemor permits Dinah's family to enter his city and even submits his people to a debilitating circumcision; then the Jewish strangers "massacre the king, the prince, his son, and all the inhabitants" (PD, 183). Like Pound, Voltaire is equally certain that Jehovah foments "brotherly enmity" and desires the bloody sacrifice of his own children.[12] Having damned mankind "for an apple," and "slaughtered his own son [Adam] quite uselessly," Jehovah supposedly incites Cain against Abel. After Abel's murder he takes Cain "under his own protection" (PD, 177), thus seeming to condone fratricide. Voltaire gives one the misleading impression that Jehovah's marking of Cain serves only incidentally to prevent escalation of fraternal enmity, and that it is primarily a sign of his "execrable" (PD, 177) tolerance of murder. Ironically, it is Voltaire who himself suggests that Abel should be avenged.

Voltaire's perverse and erroneous assumption that Judaism is a sadistic religion of "torture" probably helped to inspire Pound's later excursions against Jewish "sadism" and bloodthirstiness of all kinds.[13] As in the later Pound, Voltaire's blindness to his own persecutory impulses enables him to project upon the Jews the urge to sacrificial violence. It also enables him to fantasize a just and violent revenge against those two Jews who implausibly attacked King Hemor's kingdom: ". . . One would defend oneself against two scoundrels, one would assemble, surround them, finish them off as they deserved" (PD, 183).

Inspired by their common Hellenism and classicism, Voltaire and Pound will do virtually anything to discredit the Jews. Voltaire anticipates Pound in attributing practices to the Jews which they may have once performed but which they later condemned; as is often the case in anti-Semitism, Judaism appears as a static, transhistorical entity. This taxonomical approach results from Voltaire's idea, typical of his age, that historical research should determine "the identifying characteristics of each people," to "discover . . . [their] marked, abiding, and stable traits . . . rather than to trace their development . . ." (Katz, 2: 41, 42–43). Voltaire's thought could thus easily be adapted or transformed by racial theorists, as it was by the Nazis and Pound. And yet, since Voltaire accuses the Jews of being falsifiers, and since Pound describes them as "falsification incarnate" (RB, 184), such indifference to historical and textual truth is ironic. No less ironic is both writers' tendency to accuse the Jews for attitudes or behavior which resemble their own. Pound, in his translation of "Genèse," neglects to register his undoubted reservations concerning Voltaire's mocking notion that the Jews, as much as the "vulgar" (PD, 178) pagan peoples, believe in the sexual union of gods ("Eloïm") and the daughters of men. Aside from the inaccuracy of this charge, which holds true perhaps only for the earliest stages of Hebrew religion, it is hard to see why Pound should allow the Jews to be faulted for a belief which constitutes a central myth of *The Cantos*.

II.

When Voltaire calls the Jews just another "Arab tribe," he anticipates and contributes as did the Enlightenment in general to that European historical tradition which Edward Said defines as Orientalism.[14] This tradition, which becomes systematic and dominant in the nineteenth century, asserts an ontological, cultural, and sometimes racial inequality between Europe and the Near East. Not only does it view the Jews as radically different from Hellenes, it also treats them as members of an inferior culture. Orientalism is thus anti-Semitic in the broadest sense, a "secret sharer of Western anti-Semitism" (Said: 2, 27). Pound was in this tradition when, in *Guide to Kulchur*, and following Leo Frobenius, he spoke of the "racial tropism[s]" of the "code worship[ping]" and implicitly Semitic peoples. These "near-eastern races . . . [are] a group to themselves" (GK, 164). Pound likewise conformed to Orientalist tradition when, in the broadcasts, he spoke of the "Jew Asia" (RB, 45).*

Orientalism conceives of the Near East as hopelessly backward and ahistorical; unlike the Western world, which possesses a historical destiny, the Semitic is historically arrested and, from our "historical" point of view, is permanently dead. Given such assumptions of incompleteness and absence, and given its implicit identification with the timeless cycles of Nature, the Orient repeatedly appears in Western scholarship and literature as implicitly feminine and hence castrated. It is a place of "obscurity" and darkness, is without the creative and regenerative power of the masculine *logos,* which brings light, clarity, and distinction. It therefore lacks everything which the Orientalist defines as European and which Pound himself sometimes espoused: order, reason, objectivity, consecutive or logical thinking, stability, historical direction, perhaps above all personality, freedom, individuality; hence Orientalists treat Orientals as an undifferentiated mass or horde. Again, in lacking *logos,* the Orient cannot complete itself, make itself, historicize or represent itself; typified by the defeated feminine Asia in Aeschylus' *Persians,* it has no voice, and must be represented by the West. Like Pound's feminine matter (HYLE, the Greek ὝΛΗ of Canto 30), it is supine and passive, awaiting the formative power of the masculine principle.[15]

Inseparable from a male-dominated and patriarchal view of the world, Orientalism also reflects the West's ambivalence toward many things—chiefly women, sex, and nature itself—with which the Near East has often been identified: its representations of the Near East are often rich in contradictions, ambiguities, and uncertainties. Orientalism, however, enables the Occidental to ignore or banish this ambivalence and confusion. For, while the Orient "always resembles the West in some way," Orientalism is a system of "paranoia" whereby Europe, through projection, creates a supposedly decisive difference between the familiar and normal (Europe, the West) and the strange and abnormal (the Near East or East, "them") (Said: 70–72, 43).

In *Guide to Kulchur* Pound says that "the enemies of mankind are those who petrify thought, that is KILL it, . . . as countless . . . fools and fanatics have tried to in all times, since the Mohammedan decadence and before then" (GK, 277). He probably relies on Renan, who argues in *Averroès and Averroism* that Moorish civilization in Spain perished because of an inveterate religious fanaticism.[16] Elsewhere Pound admits that the Mohammedans

---

*Although Orientalist thought encompasses the Far East, the term Orientalism as used here and as applied to Pound's works refers exclusively to the mainly Semitic Near East. It has nothing to do with China, which Pound deeply admired. In P/L, p. 271, Pound wants Wyndham Lewis to clarify that his use of the word "oriental" refers to the Near Eastern "filth" rather than to China.

"had a few centuries," but thanks to their "stinking near eastern fanaticism" they lacked "the constructive sense to build anything" (L, 330), and in any case their inspiration was from "Greece or Persia" (L, 332) and hence non-Semitic. And so, because of the same "fanaticism" and "code worship" which Pound noted in Judaism, the Near Eastern races are "a group to themselves" and are paradoxically "arrested" at the "nomad level." Pound adds that "The attempt to square nature with the code, leads . . . to perverted thinking." Thus the Mohammedans "killed off their own civilization, or at least truncated and maimed it out of 90% of its vitality. All through an exaltation of conformity and orthodoxy" (GK, 164). Besides associating the Orient with incompleteness, Pound implies that the unbounded vitality of Nature is beyond the narrow definitions of the Semitic code. Meanwhile, the assumption of fanatical conformity enables Pound to view all Orientals as essentially the same.

Pound also identifies the Orient with the feminine, the timeless, and the unmeasured:

> The study of savages has in our time come to be regarded as almost the sole guide to anglo-saxon psychology. If we reflect on African and oriental vagueness as to time, if we reflect on what is often called "feminine" lack of punctuality among our more irritating acquaintances, it shd. not unduly astonish us that the idea of a MEASURE of value has taken shape slowly in human consciousness. (GK, 162–163)

Although Oriental and African traits are irritatingly present in the West, the Near Eastern mind implicitly lacks *logos,* order, history, accuracy (Said: 38, 105–106). This idea appears early in Pound. In a *New Age* article Pound defines the historical stasis and desiccation of the Orient, which, as he says in Canto 84, reaches "to Tangier" (84/ 447).

> This stasis you could have seen in Tangier before the arrival of the wireless telegraph; costume of the desert prescribed by the necessity to keep out dust, stasis of two thousand years; king's dinner music, dating supposedly from the year 700, etc.
> Doughty's "Arabia Deserta" is, perhaps, the one full study of such a stasis; . . . . It is the only book I know which in the least persuades me to endure the evils of occidental civilization.[17]

It seems curious that Pound condemns Near Eastern society for a stability and tradition which resembles that of Confucian China, which he admired. He also paradoxically opposes Semitic culture not only to history but to the unbounded freedom and vitality of Nature; the Semitic for Pound is always the unnatural. But this cannot be Pound's meaning in all cases. The Anglo-Saxons, he says, do "not howl for a return to the ethos of their more savage days. In fact you can see only the Jew proclaiming the ethos of a nomadic era (unless the *Koran* does)" (SP, 65–66). Here the Semitic is associated not with desiccation but with the wild, savage, and unbounded life of Nature, the *selva,* linked etymologically to the word savage. Pound also refers to North Africa, specifically the dusty Barbary Coast, as a "jungle," thus employing an image of natural luxuriance to describe an apparently sterile desert land.[18] For him the Near East bears a distinct resemblance to that fecund, feminine, and troubling Nature whose name is "HYLE" (Matter, uncut forest) (30/148):

> Jungle:
> Glaze green and red feathers, jungle,
> Basis of renewal, renewals;
> Rising over the soul, green virid, of the jungle,
> Lozenge of the pavement, clear shapes,
> Broken, disrupted, body eternal,
> Wilderness of renewals, confusion
> Basis of renewals, subsistence,
> Glazed green of the jungle;
> Zoe, Marozia, Zothar,
>   loud over the banners,
> Glazed grape, and the crimson,
> HO BIOS,
>   cosi Elena vedi. . . .
>   (20/ 91–92)

In the fecundity of its confusion the jungle is the basis of cultural energy, order, and renewals, of those measured shapes (lozenges) which rise above the jungle's soul and then sink back into chaos. In this canto the luxuriant jungle is associated with the Lotos-Eaters, who wear burnouses (Arab clothing), eat "natural" drugs (the lotus), sniff incense (an Oriental luxury), and sink into a vegetable stasis which may bring aesthetic clairvoyance. Of the four vamp figures above, Zoe and Helen are associated with the Asiatic world (Byzantium and Troy), while Zothar is undoubtedly Semitic. She appears in Canto 17 in contrast with the restrained and virginal beauty of ancient Greece (Nausicaa and Athena):

> Zothar and her elephants, the gold loin cloth,
> The sistrum, shaken, shaken,
>   The cohorts of her dancers. . . .
>   (17/ 78)

The elephants recall the jungle, their origin, and Carthage, which unleashed elephants against Rome and the West. The sistrum is Egyptian, and signifies frenzied Semitic religion. As for Zothar, she is a Semitic temple priestess or prostitute, and thus fit to appear in the promiscuous jungle. She exemplifies the "Carthagenian [sic] element" (SR, 18), the "African and Oriental inflow" upon the "Mediterranean clarity" (SR, 18n), the Near Eastern mind which "delight[s] in profusion" (SR, 18).

Zothar is also reminiscent of Flaubert, whose Carthaginian novel *Salammbô* greatly influenced the sexual ambience of *Hugh Selwyn Mauberley*.[19] Believing that all Semitic groups are the same, Flaubert presents Carthage against a background of "Canaanitic" usury, greed, exotic and erotic splendor, and barbaric luxury. The priestess Salammbô devotes herself to the goddess Tanit, "l'Omniféconde," symbol of the primal matriarchal principle.[20] As Said suggests, the Orient invariably smacks of prostitution and incest, the Fatal Woman.[21] In Tanit's chamber Matho and Spendius discover images celebrating her parthenogenetic power. As a "dazzling light made them drop their eyes," they saw

> an infinite number of beasts, lean, panting, brandishing their claws, and mixed one on top of the other in mysterious and frightening confusion. Serpents had feet, bulls wings, man-headed fish were eating fruit, flowers were blooming in crocodiles' jaws, and elephants with raised trunks passed proud as eagles through the blue sky. Their incomplete or multiple limbs were swollen by their terrible exertions. As they put out their tongues they looked as though they were trying to force out their souls; and every shape was to be found there, as if a seed-pod had burst in a sudden explosion and emptied itself over the walls of the room. . . . The turbulent soul of Tanit streamed forth expansively. (Flaubert, 2: 78, 79)

This is Flaubert's version of Pound's swamp or jungle. Vegetable and animal, chthonic and celestial, marine and terrene, spring from a primal egg and join in promiscuous, monstrous, but "natural" confusion. Nothing here is normal; everything is either multiple or incomplete. A castration motif figures in the blinding flash of light and the monsters who put out tongues but cannot speak—apt images of a feminine world without *logos*.

Like Pound, Flaubert presents the paradox of Oriental fecundity and sterility, enormous abundance and enormous barrenness (Said: 187). For if L'Omniféconde represents Nature's profusion, her generation is pointless, lacking *telos,* incomplete. Salammbô, her priestess, is neurasthenic and frigid, and when she touches the veil of Tanit, she dies. Thus the Semitic is both natural and unnatural, exists where the natural and the unnatural merge in "confusion." Or this paradox may have more to do with Flaubert's and Pound's ambivalence toward Nature itself.

III.

Pound's identification of Near East with the Fatal Woman is partly explained by his affiliation with a Decadent and late Romantic tradition, in which these themes are often conjoined.[22] Explicitly or implicitly a courtesan or harlot, the Oriental femme fatale of the Decadents often appears (as in Swinburne and Wilde) amid the luxuriant growth and promiscuous confusion, the bizarre metamorphoses of the swamp.[23] She also symbolizes human luxury (and sensuality) in all its dangers and attractions. Gautier's Cleopatra, Moreau's Salomé, Flaubert's and Mallarmé's Herodias, these lavishly ornamented and perfumed creatures inhabit dazzling palaces and temples: the ripe, opulent fruit of Semitic commerce. Perhaps the *locus classicus* of this theme in Anglo-Saxon culture is Pater's rhapsode on the *Mona Lisa.* An archetype of Fatal Beauty, Pater's "vampire" and threatening spider has trafficked for "strange webs with Eastern merchants." Thus she combines demonic sexuality with a suggestion of corrupt, perhaps usurious wealth.[24]

If Semitic luxury signifies excess transformed into sterility and enervation, it also inspires aesthetic clairvoyance and sensory refinement. Consider Pound's free translation of the octet of Baudelaire's sonnet "Le Vampire." Although presented as the work of the fictional Walter Villerant, the translation is Pound's:

> One night stretched out along a hebrew bitch—
> Like two corpses at the undertakers—
> This carcass, sold alike to jews and quakers,
> Reminded me of beauty noble and rich.
> Although she stank like bacon in the flitch,
> I thought of her as though the ancient makers
> Had shown her mistress of a thousand acres,
> Casqued and perfumed, so that my nerves 'gan twitch.
>
> (PD, 74)

Repelled and fascinated by the "carcass," the speaker finds in its teeming ripeness the thought of a perhaps desirable luxury and beauty.

A more significant example of Semitic ambiguity is Pound's free translation of Jules Laforgue's "Salomé," which appears in Laforgue's *Moralités légendaires,* and which Pound translated as "Our Tetrarchal Précieuse."[25] It should be emphasized, though, that while Laforgue ridicules literary Orientalism and leaves it at that, Pound gathers from Laforgue motifs which figure in his anti-Semitism. This is perhaps why "Our Tetrarchal Précieuse" appears in *Pavannes and Divagations* after Voltaire's "Genèse."

Endowed with "Canaanitic" attributes, Laforgue's Salomé is the beautiful daughter of the Tetrarch of the Esoteric Islands, a kingdom of metaphysical dilettantes who shun reality's "other world" (PD, 190). Her main haunt is this luxuriant hanging garden: "En trois pâtés aux pylônes trapus et nus, cours intérieures, galeries, caveaux, et le fameux parc suspendu avec ses jungles viridant aux brises atlantiques. . . ."[26] These murky "jungles viridant" appear elsewhere in Pound. It is here that he locates Zoe, Marozia, Zothar, and Helen of Troy: "Jungle: / Glaze green and red feathers, jungle, / Basis of renewal, renewals: / Rising over the soul, green virid, of the jungle." As in Canto 20 Pound associates the jungle with Zoe and HO BIOS, or Life, his hanging garden is also a zoo; "the zoo," says Pound, "was loose all over the place" (PD, 192). But this profuse and feminized environment is not exclusively fecund or vital or natural. Ornamented with monstrous excrescences, the Tetrarch's palace may evoke the barren excess of usury. Besides the zoo, in which animals run wild yet are under restraint, there is the aquarium, and below this the "hareem" from which emanates a "decomposed odor" and a "droning osmosis" (PD, 193) of eunuch slaves. "Esoteric" (PD, 194) creatures, the Tetrarch's children suggest that Oriental incest which figures in Flaubert (Flaubert, l: 108).

Her "hair dusty with exiguous pollens" (PD, 195), Salomé embodies this confusion of excess and barrenness. In Laforgue she feels a sexual attraction for the imprisoned Iokanaan but also desires to retain her virginity and emotional inviolability. By contrast, Pound ignores Salomé's tenderness towards Iokanaan and her struggle for purity (Ramsey: 226); to him she is barren, "anemic" (PD, 195), and abstract, an androgynous recluse who wants to preserve the "uniqueness . . . of her autochthonous entity" (PD, 195)—that is, to deny the masculine principle and give birth to herself. Like Laforgue, Pound defines Salomé's metaphysical thinking as "cosmoconception" and "parthenospotlessness" (PD, 197); he associates her with the sterility of virgin birth. For after all, Salomé's feminine universe is only one of the "nurse-maid cosmogonies" (*cosmogonies de Maman*) (PD, 196): "Isolated nebulous matrices, not the formed nebulae, were her passion; she . . . sought but the unformed, perforated, tentacular. Orion's gaseous fog was the Brother Benjamin of her galaxy. . . . She felt peer to these matrices, fecund as they in gyratory evolutions" (PD, 199). Salomé has this vision of the empty circularity of the feminine just before ordering Iokanaan's decapitation. But these fecund matrices are not a cosmos. Their disconnections and perforations evoke absence and incompleteness, even chaos. With "tentacular," the gaseous fog suggests the jungle's obscure emanations.

Salomé's inner life might be characterized as the "jungle" (SP, 78) of idealism. At one point Salomé reduces all distinctions to nullity and praises the emptied, pure, abstract, and infinite consciousness. Pound also runs together Laforgue's gibe at metaphysical idealism with another passage in which Salomé sings the passive and nearly vegetable life of the unconscious.[27] The abundant, self-duplicating ("Medusae of gentle water," PD, 196), and incestuous spawn of unconscious ideas denies that "other world" (PD, 190) of external reality, reduces it to the "excellent nothingness" of "Canaan" (PD, 196), everything interchangeable with everything else. A singer of "Fatal Jordans, abysmal Ganges" (the Cavalcanti essay links the "Hebrew" and "Hindoo" diseases) (PD, 196), Salomé represents the feminine or parthenogenetic principle in Nature, religion, and thought—the very idea, perhaps, of creation *ex nihilo*. No less important, she is distinctly Semitic, while her sympathetic listeners at the Tetrarch's feast are "racially, so very correct" (PD, 197).

As elsewhere, Pound identifies "Canaan" with the abstract, the incomplete, the metaphysical, the anti-empirical, the repressive, the unnatural, the vague. But for all its unnatural sterility, he also associates it with the unconscious (and hence the instincts), with the primitive jungle or zoo, profuse with life, and, in its cultural form, with the abundance of luxury and hence with sensuality. Consider again Zothar's elephants in Canto 17. These beasts may tally with "the panthers chained to the cars" (20/ 94) in Canto 20—an image of repression under Oriental despotism; they may also belong to the enclosed zoo in "Our Tetrarchal Précieuse." Yet they may also evoke Zothar's unrestrained and raw "jungle" sexuality, as of the Near Eastern Mother cults. To quote Pound, in a phrase which covers the abstractions of monotheism and the lubricity of Astarte, the Semitic is "excess" (SP, 86). Hence its nomadic hordes, its proliferating and parthenogenetic bacilli, the orgiastic "cohort" of Zothar's dancers.

IV.

Throughout Pound's writings, as throughout Enlightenment and Orientalist anti-Semitism, one encounters a sinister, contradictory, and finally paradoxical image of the Jews. Like the Near East, they combine but never reconcile the qualities of Nature and anti-Nature, passivity and aggressiveness, fertility and sterility, abstraction and materialism, the patriarchal and the matriarchal, the masculine (Jehovah) and the feminine (Cybele), the anti-natural and the anti-historical, the desert and the swamp. These ambiguities and contradictions have little to do with any putative Near Eastern "essence," but rather reflect the ambivalences and confusion of the Western observer, namely Pound. Meanwhile, Pound's attribution of such contradictory qualities to the Jews fits neatly and typically within the processes of scapegoating and sacrificial victimization. As René Girard has shown, the best candidates for scapegoating are those marginal individuals or groups which, in their apparent indefinition, are most easily associated with confusion, ambiguity, and monstrous plasticity. Pound's adoption of Enlightenment and Orientalist models of cultural prejudice thus marks a most ominous phase in the development of his anti-Semitism.

Chapter Six

Modern Anti-Semitism and Millenarianism: Zielinski, Frobenius, Rosenberg, and *the* Protocols

Profoundly influenced by Voltaire, the "patron saint" of modern anti-Semites, and by nineteenth-century literary Orientalism, during the 1920s and 1930s Pound comes to embrace other and more virulent versions of anti-Semitism as well as a number of extremely dubious cultural ideas. Through Thaddeus Zielinski, Pound receives the idea, which is also typical of fascism and proto-fascism, of the absolute difference between Christianity and Judaism. Pound is also indebted to Leo Frobenius, who emphasizes the racial basis of culture, and who distinguishes between agrarian-based culture and a soulless, calculating modern civilization. Both of these ideas serve to strengthen two of Pound's emerging beliefs, one, that the Jews are typical, unchanging, and alien products of the Near Eastern cultural zone, the other, that Jewish rationalism and commercialism, as the primary forms of modernity, have corrupted Western agriculture and the sacred homestead. No less important is the unquestionable similarity between these and other Poundian myths and those of Alfred Rosenberg, unofficial cultural theorist of the Nazi party; consciously or not, in the 1930s and 1940s Pound is often in the main line of Nazi cultural speculation. Finally, in his reliance on Zielinski and in his acceptance of the authenticity of the Jewish conspiracy supposedly secreted in the *Protocols of the Elders of Zion*, Pound in the broadcasts and after figures within a modern tradition of millenarian prophecy, a tradition in which Nazism has the most prominent place and which is in many ways a modern version of the anti-Semitic Christian eschatology of medieval times.

Writing in the magazine *Edge* in October, 1956, Pound said that "The American milieu is filled with poison that did not get there by accident." He added: "Since 1927 I have known that."[1] This is probably an oblique reference to Pound's discovery of the Polish classical scholar Thaddeus Zielinski's *La Sibylle,* an anti-Semitic work which he probably came upon in that year, and which was partially translated in *Edge* at Pound's instigation. Although Pound may have read Zielinski's *Religion of Ancient*

Greece, so far as I know he refers only to *La Sibylle: Trois essais sur la religion antique et le christianisme,* which contains the core of Zielinski's anti-Semitic ideas.[2] According to Pound, Zielinski "seems . . . imbued with sincere piety," but "sees Judaism in direct contrast, spiritual, theological contrast, with the Christian faith" (RB, 410).

When Zielinski speaks of Christianity he means essentially Catholicism, for which paganism provided not only the "psychological preparation" but supposedly the vast proportion of early converts; according to Pound in a most questionable statement, Jews remained "pertinaciously opposed" to the "new religion of Christianity." As for Protestantism, Pound follows Zielinski in viewing it as "REJEWdiazed [sic] religion" (RB, 411). The historical link and affinity between paganism and Christianity (or Catholicism), as well as their opposition to Judaism (and Protestantism), hinges on the fact that Christianity might be viewed as a modified polytheism. Having been psychologically prepared by paganism, converts easily understood the Trinity and the worship of the mother of God. Furthermore paganism and Christianity confer sanctity on certain human beings, the pagan in the cult of gods and demigods, the Christian in his cult of the saints. As Zielinski says, paganism and Christianity believe in "the dogma of the man-god; that is of a man, a son of god," who was "born of a mortal mother under purely human conditions," and who "earned ascension into heaven and apotheosis through his superhuman exploits." In paganism, notes Zielinski, the classic example of this dogma is Hercules, while in Christianity it is Christ; thus Mary is essentially the Christian equivalent of Alkmene as of numerous other mortal mothers of divine heroes. This theanthropic dogma appears too in the Christian idea of sainthood, for saints are a form of the man-god.[3]

Like Zielinski, Pound is fascinated by heroes who, like Hercules, "claimed" or else earned a "divine heritage" (PD, 210) through superhuman exploits. Not only does Pound allude frequently to the sexual union of mortal women with immortals, but he personally identifies with Hercules, son of Zeus and Alkmene, whom Zielinski describes as a messianic figure seeking to restore the age of gold (Zielinski, 1:22, 24). He also identifies with Apollonius of Tyana, a late pagan rival of Christ who belongs among the "doers of holiness" (94/ 638), that is, is a pagan saint (Philostratus, Vol. 1: xii, 503).

The Jews, on the other hand, represent for Zielinski a unique form of cultural sterility and formalistic "aridity" which results largely from their exclusive concern for the paternal principle and their denial of the erotic and spiritual bond uniting Father Sky and Mother Earth (Zielinski, 1: 17–31, 53–57, 94). "Unhellenic" in their supposed lack of feelings for the land, "which had never been . . . [their] mother," the dualistic and theocratic Jews create an insuperable abyss between divine and human, spirit and matter, masculine and feminine. Whereas Jesus Christ, like the Greek Messiah, claims a mortal mother and asserts literal rather than merely metaphorical kinship with God, the Jews strenuously deny his divinity, for they (like the Protestants) refuse to "honor the Mother of God in any form" (RB, 411).[4] Nor do the Jews (again like the Protestants) accept the existence of saints, since in their eyes "None is holy but God" (Zielinski, 1: 31–37). Zielinski further insists that the Jews' belief in an invisible, monotheistic deity and their rejection of religious images condemned them, as opposed to Greek and non-Protestant Europeans, to cultural sterility. These views are indistinguishable from those of Pound, who speaks of that Jewish "power of putrefaction" which destroys "all intrinsic beauty." They may also derive from Zielinski's association, again reminiscent of Pound, of the Jews with a vengeful, brutal, and ugly god, a god of fear rather than love, as among the Greeks.[5] Though Pound does not really believe in universal love, he too invokes it to attack the Jews: "Jehovah," he says, " . . . has no connection with Dante's God. That later concept of supreme Love and Intelligence is certainly not derived from the Old Testament" (SP, 91).[6]

Zielinski posits a transhistorical difference between the Occident and the Orient on the basis of their different views in ancient times of the maternal image. Strictly speaking, however, his discussion of Near Eastern matriarchal cults has no connection with the Jews, whom Zielinski identifies with religious patriarchy. It is a specific form of his general hatred of the Near East and his preference for the culture of "les peuples aryens."[7] But since Zielinski's remarks on Attis and Adonis influenced Pound, his argument is worth examining.

Zielinski observes that the priesthood at Galles in Phrygia consisted of castrated priests who, in commemoration of Attis, worshipped the Great Mother (Agdistis or Cybele) as a "shapeless idol." This cult, he adds, reveals "some disgusting" and "ecstatic" features which "taken together stamp it as unhellenic." Indeed, though we "should not generalize about myths," Zielinski is sure that the castration is not Greek: the Phrygian "institution of castrated priests . . . [was] banished from the Greek or Hellenized cult of the Great Mother. . . ." By contrast with the Phrygian myth, in the Greek myth Attis commits suicide. Also, in the Phrygian myth Agdistis' plan to restore Attis' life is foiled by Zeus, who denies her wishes. But in the Greek myth, which celebrates the devotion of the mother of the gods to her son, Attis' life is restored. Besides linking the myth of Attis' resurrection to the Eleusinian mysteries, which Pound admired, Zielinski argues that the resurrected Attis prefigures the myth of Christ.[8]

These two myths underlie Zielinski's (and Pound's) distinction between positive and negative matriarchal religions. Zielinski argues that Greek culture revered women, but not in the exclusively sexual or carnal sense. Rather, in contrast with the Semites, with their "repulsive" and "barbarian" custom of temple prostitution, the Greeks and Romans recognized woman as a spiritual being and celebrated her (as in Demeter) as the goddess of hearth and field. This is as much as to say that they valued the mother cults only when the dangerous and promiscuous mother goddess became a matron and mother, like Demeter, and was thus installed within an agricultural and patriarchal order. In *La Sibylle* this idealized maternal figure emerges from the resolution of the "primordial antagonism" between the cults of the maternal earth and those of the sky and sun—that is, violence. After the solar god Apollo murdered the symbolic maternal "dragon," Earth and Zeus, Mother principle and Father principle, were reconciled. Earth recognized the eternity (and authority) of Zeus, and Zeus recognized the venerable maternity, sanctity, and fruitfulness of Earth (agriculture). Apollo, however, had to expiate the murder of the maternal dragon by descending, mortal for a year, to Earth, and so became the prototype of the man-god; like Jesus, Apollo springs to renewed life from the body of the divine Mother (Earth) and ascends to the immortal realms of light. Zielinski adds that the Hercules myth, which is important to Pound, is related to this conflict.[9]

In spite of their passion and erudition, neither Zielinski nor Pound makes a convincing case for the exclusively or even mainly pagan character of Christianity. Zielinski recognizes but glosses over the fact that neither the cult of saints nor mariolatry figures in the Sermon on the Mount or Paul's epistles (Zielinski, 1:35). The truth is that both writers' attraction to Christianity lies mainly in its residues of pagan sexual mysticism, vitalism, ritual, polytheism, and on aesthetic possibilities in the cult of graven images. Neither Zielinski nor Pound shows any strong interest in the Imitation of Christ, universal love and self-renunciation, or the great ethical and social revolution which Christianity performed in the pagan world, in short, in those things which most people consider fundamental to Christianity. To put it another way, they have no interest in the Sermon on the Mount. Perhaps this is because much of Christ's ethical teaching has Jewish foundations. As Jesus said, he came not to destroy the Jewish law but to fulfill it.[10]

It is not on the face of it clear why Zielinski and especially Pound should promote these blatant distortions of historical and religious truth. What motivates Pound's assertion that Christianity is "infected" with alien Jewish influences? Despite his nostalgic and sentimental attachment to certain Christian beliefs, rituals, and forms of domination, the truth is that Pound remained on the whole an enemy of Christianity, and if anything his dislike of it intensified over his career. By the radio broadcasts he finds not only in Judaism but in most of Christianity the same objectionable "humiliation doctrine" (RB, 199). And yet Pound always avoids a thorough condemnation of Christianity, for he is unwilling to shatter his own historical delusions or to alienate large numbers of his readers and listeners, with whom he wants to identify. Instead, in a manner typical of many anti-Semites, above all his master Voltaire, Pound attacks Christianity indirectly, by attacking its parent religion, which is Judaism. Once again anti-Semitism proves indispensable to Pound. Among its other deceptive functions, it serves as a mask for his profound anti-Christianity.

II.

Pound's strong advocacy of Zielinski in the late 1930s reveals his increasing affinity with Nazi cultural and racial theory. Indeed, though Zielinski was not a fascist, Pound places him in the main line of fascist speculation and recommended him as essential reading for all fascists (Stock, 3: 520). Not for nothing is Hitler linked in Canto 90 to a Sibyl, an allusion to Zielinski's work. As Pound told Douglas Fox in 1938, Germany, in the next forty years, will be a "force toward a purgation."[11]

Besides Zielinski, Pound recommended Fox's teacher Leo Frobenius, head of the Research Institute for Kulturmorphologie in Frankfurt, as indispensable fascist reading.[12] Frobenius's cultural thought emphasizes the idea of the *Kulturkreis,* the culture zone or circle, which Frobenius borrowed from Bachofen.[13] According to this theory, each culture springs from an original seed and fulfills its destiny in a kind of organic exfoliation of cultural forms: all of the forms of a particular culture are thus imbued with a distinct character or essence. Frobenius also inspires Pound's distinction between that knowledge which is merely conscious "understanding," and that which "will stay by a man, weightless, held without effort" (GK, 53), which remains an instinctive "part" of one's "total disposition" (GK, 28). For both writers the true basis of culture is what Frobenius terms the Paideuma, which consists not of formal, conscious, or discursive concepts but rather of that form of instinct which is cultural, of those "gristly roots of ideas" which penetrate a culture at its deepest levels of instinct and tradition and are "in action" (GK, 58). Underlying this antithesis in both writers is the essentially Germanic distinction between *Kultur* (Culture) and *Civilization,* a distinction which often leads toward anti-Semitism.

Norbert Elias notes that the Culture-Civilization distinction originates in Kant and Goethe and opposes rural, agrarian, and small town societies to the life of the big and cosmopolitan city, typified by Paris. The first is defined as Culture, and is identified with a supposedly organic, creative, spiritual, and spontaneous life. The second is mere Civilization, associated with the weight of custom and formality, the organic and the mechanical, logic and abstract analysis (Elias: 3–50). During the nineteenth century this distinction is appropriated, twisted, and vulgarized by such proto-Nazi and *Volkisch* writers as Lagarde and Langbehn, who react phobically to the increasing rationalization and calculation of the expanding modern urban centers. Based on the organic and communal life of the peasant, Culture figures in their fantasies as an unconscious and instinctive rootedness in the soil and group, the intimate folk community or *Gemeinschaft* which Civilization had destroyed. For them, only Culture in this sense can provide an

antidote to the deadening process of modernization, world politics, centralization, urban money economy, machine technology, and specialization.
Many *Volkisch* writers identify this process with the image of the cosmopolitan and rationalistic Jew, supposedly the embodiment of a sterile and calculating modern civilization.[14]

In some ways Frobenius resembles his pupil Spengler, who uses the
organic metaphor to argue that Western Culture is moving into moribund
Civilization and finally death.[15] As Robert J. Welke says, "[For Frobenius]
each paideuma participates in . . . an organic cycle of birth, growth, zenith,
decay, and death . . . ." Reaching its "high point in mythology, especially
the solar and lunar cults," it descends into "senility with materialism, world
economics, specialization, and the 'machine age.' " This means that a culture comes closer to "dissolution" and "semantic depletion" the further it
moves from its "source [*Ursprung*]." But Frobenius denied that this process
would necessarily lead to cultural death. Though a culture might be brought
to the brink of death by analysts and specialists, at this point it would be
"stripped of its refined but meaningless hierarchy and reduced to the radix,
the source of cultural impulse" —the peasantry, standing in "awe and continuous appreciation" of nature's primal mysteries: the process of culture
"could start all over again" if the peasantry survived.[16]

Pound's idea of "Kulchur," an irreverent spelling with distinctly Germanic overtones, often corresponds to what Fritz Stern calls the "vacuous,"
"specious," and mystical distinction between Culture and Civilization.[17]
Increasingly dissatisfied with centralized urban megalopolises (New York,
London, Paris), Pound took refuge in the more intimate and spontaneous
"local centers" (I, 75, 82) of Rapallo and Venice and followed Frobenius in
locating the true source of cultural tradition in agrarian mythology. Where
the *Volkisch* writers and the Nazis idealize organic rootedness in the soil,
Pound speaks of the "gristly roots of ideas" that "go into action." This
phrase probably alludes to the agrarian basis of culture, which Pound seeks
to protect from the deracinated and international usurer, in short the Jews.

Although he rejected Nazism (and was rejected by the Nazis), Frobenius
believed that the origin and basis of each culture or *Kulturkreis* is racial, and
thus defined "a stable of racially-labelled cultures competing with one another in the Mediterranean basin" (Surette, 3: 129). Pound uses the term
Paideuma in a racial sense, as when he tells the supposedly pro-Semitic
English that they are at the end of their "paideuma," that is their "race
conviction," their "race consciousness" (RB, 168). This does not mean,
however, that Pound accepts the Nazi conception of Aryanism or Nordic
supremacy. Admittedly he sometimes nods toward Aryanism and even
Nordicism: he admires the Aryan race in a letter to Lewis,[18] seeks to defend
the "Aryan Peoples" (RB, 124), and declares that "the problem," namely
the "abolition of all ARYAN ownership," is "RACIAL" (RB, 71); he also
favors a Fascist "federation" (the dream of Vidkun Quisling) of "nordic"

(RB, 403) nations, and in *The Cantos* charts a mythical tradition of Aryan kingship extending from Sargon's Sumeria to Hitler's Germany. But generally speaking Pound uses "Aryan" more or less as does Céline (Céline, 2: 215), as a blanket term covering all "native" and non-Jewish groups within Europe. A "Mediterranean man," Pound conceives of the Occident as a single culture composed of related nations and races.

Nonetheless, there are numerous similarities between Pound and Alfred Rosenberg, unofficial cultural theorist of the Nazi party. According to Rosenberg,

> . . . Each race has its soul, each soul its race— its own unique inner and outer architectonic shape, its characteristic form of appearance and characteristic expression of life style, and unique relationships between the strengths of will and reason. Each race cultivates, as its fixed goal, only *one* high ideal. If this should be transformed or overthrown by another system of allegiance or by an overpowering intrusion of foreign blood and foreign ideas, the external consequence of this inner metamorphosis is chaos, designated as epochs of catastrophe. . . .[19]

Thus Europe "can produce a unity only through impartial delimitation; a unity which, firmly rooted and experienced, will one day be strong enough collectively to protect a thousand year old *Kultur*, a thousand-year-old humanity . . ." (Rosenberg: 196). This *Kultur* is that of the Third Reich, which, according to the Nazis, would last a thousand years.

For Rosenberg, the true culture of the West is Aryan and above all Nordic. Its great enemy, the Semitic world, comprises a single culture zone, a "collective Orientalism" of confusion, ambiguity, sterility, luxury, and usury. Near Eastern religions, including Judaism, constitute a single "religion of frenzy" (a phrase borrowed from Frobenius) which is "borne by Afro-Asian races and race-mixtures" into the West. "We can," says Rosenberg, "draw a straight line from daemonic King Saul to the earth-bound lust of Dionysus (who was nevertheless ennobled by the Greeks)" and then to the whirling dervishes of later Islam. Deeply fearful of cultural contamination, Rosenberg's mission is to "cleanse the European motherland," to defeat those "ever-expanding disease centers" and "overwhelming powers of Asia Minor," which had "infiltrated through a thousand channels, poisoned Hellas and, in place of the Greeks, deposited effete Levantines" (Rosenberg: 56, 51, 47, 80).

In Rosenberg the Jews embody rootless, *Kultur*-less cosmopolitanism and internationalism. He associates them with parasitism, poison, pestilence, disease, usury, incest, sterility, and aridity. But despite his conception of the Semitic world as "collective" and unified, his image of it is as paradoxical and contradictory as Pound's. Like Pound, Rosenberg identifies the Semitic world with a crude carnality and sensualism as well as with the most reprehensibly "abstract," monotheistic, and even parthenogenetic spirituality. Another paradox appears in his conception of Semitic culture as an "overwhelming" power and its association with softness, femininity, and the "wasteful extravagance" of Asiatic luxury.[20] And, for all the supposed sterility of the Near East, this image jars with passages in which Semitic culture is orgiastic and identified with the profusion of the swamp.

Like Pound's, Rosenberg's works are filled with images of swamps, swamp diseases, and swamp monsters, all symbolizing the Semitic world. Just as Pound describes usurious post-war London as a "bog" (14/ 63), and later accuses the Jews of making a "bog of things" (SP, 320), so Rosenberg describes the Weimar Republic, in which the Jews had considerable cultural and political influence, as a *Sumpf*.[21] Perhaps in the broadest sense, Rosenberg's swamp symbolizes that monstrous indistinction, that chaotic growth *ex nihilo* which he, like Pound, considers Semitic. Rosenberg hates partheno-genesis and the "abstract" or "Jewish" blurring of sexual distinctions; objects to the "non-Aryan" doctrine of Virgin Birth because it means the "demise of natural union"; and attacks St. Paul's idea that "there is neither male nor female" in the realms of the spirit (Rosenberg: 71). In other instances Rosenberg's swamp seems decidedly matriarchal, like the Near East. Following Dante, Rosenberg denounces "amphibious Geryon," the swamp monster symbolic of Fraud and Usury in both the *Inferno* and *The Cantos*. According to Rosenberg, Dante's Geryon preserves a dark recollection of the Asiatic Etruscans and a vast Semitic matriarchy resurgent in Italy after the fall of Rome: the "savage mother goddesses" of the Near East, the Furies (chthonic goddesses of blood vengeance and violence), witches, Medusas, castration, and priestly sacrifice—all that the Aryan West has supposedly transcended (Rosenberg: 64). It is evident why Rosenberg demands the defense of Europe against that "Hydra-headed race-chaos," those Semitic and Mosaic "systems which arose from the swamps of the Nile, the waters of Asia Minor and the wastes of Libya." Implicitly Rosenberg's hero, like Pound's, is the patriarchal and solar Hercules, who destroyed the swamp Hydra (symbolic of Usury in Addendum to Canto 100) and ushered in an age of abundance and order (Rosenberg: 70, 51, 48).

In contrast with the Near East, Rosenberg conceives of the West as a patriarchal culture. The true Western or Nordic gods originate in the patriarchal religions of Greece, in the essentially masculine Pallas Athena, Zeus "the heavenly father," and Apollo, the "golden haired . . . defender" of "order." Apollo, he says, "is the ascending light of dawn" and symbol of spiritual harmony and "piety" (Rosenberg: 48). Where Zielinski examines Apollo's defeat and murder of Python, the maternal and chthonic dragon, which led to the development of agriculture, the domestication of women, and the rise of Greek patriarchal religion, Rosenberg treats the same conflict and works it into a comparable cultural antithesis. Despite considerable evidence to the contrary, Rosenberg denies that the culture of ancient Greece had matriarchal beginnings. The dark, sensual, chthonic, and "inferior" element in Greek culture supposedly derived entirely from "racially alien" influences, namely the Semitic and Asiatic world. In their matriarchal "phase" the Greeks "assumed characteristics which were both physically and spiritually alien to their culture" (Reich: 85–88, 91–95). This conclusion follows from Rosenberg's belief that, "If the Greek gods were heroes of light and heaven," then "the gods of the non-Aryans of Asia Minor bore all the mundane values" (Rosenberg: 49). The victory of Greek patriarchy produces a purifyed Aryan Nature, transforms the demonic matriarchal image into an unthreatening helpmate of patriarchy, as in the asexual Athena.

Apart from his Nordic emphasis, Rosenberg's other myths resemble Pound's. As Pound's gods are associated with light and solar mythology, and as Pound finds divinity in the radiant head of the culture hero (Hercules or Apollo), Rosenberg's Nordic gods are "figures of light who bore . . . the cross and the swastika, and were crowned with haloes, symbols of the sun, of ascending life." Rich in "cosmic symbolism," the swastika or "circle with four spokes" represents "the heavenly cross," while its "six-part division indicates the . . . summer and winter solstices" (Rosenberg: 108–109n). In short, the swastika's rotating arms symbolize the natural cycle, the cyclical movement of the sun.[22] This symbolism calls to mind Pound's statement that "the only Christian festivals having any vitality are welded to sun festivals, the spring solstice, the Corpus and St. John's Eve, registering the turn of the sun."[23] In the Pisan *Cantos* Pound speaks of a cross different from the Christian, a cross which "turns with the sun" (74/ 443). As we shall see, this cross is probably the swastika.

The swastika has a deeper meaning. Wilhelm Reich has shown that it unconsciously symbolizes the sexual act; its interlocking shapes represent the union of Father Sun and Mother Earth, Man and Woman, masculine and feminine principles (Reich: 101–103). It thus expresses the agrarian and sexual mysticism which characterizes Pound's and Nazi ideology. The admiration for patriarchal authority, the cults of the sun and soil, the insistence on clear-cut sexual roles, these go hand in hand with the Nazis' mystic reverence for the sexual union of man and woman. Pound was aware at some level of these features of Nazism, and this is why, in a letter to Lewis in 1939, he twisted his first initial into the shape of the swastika.[24]

What remains to be examined is the relationship of such solar worship to Christianity. Peter Nathan noted in 1943 that there is "a large literature in Germany devoted to anti-Christianity," of which he gave this example: "The Cross must fall to make Germany live. The Christian religion must be destroyed" (Nathan: 116). Nonetheless, many Nazi ideologists relied on a long-standing Germanic distinction between "positive" and "negative" Christianity in order to prove that their message was consistent with that of Jesus. While Goethe was perhaps the first to make this distinction, its fullest statement is in Nietzsche. In *The AntiChrist* Nietzsche argued that true Christianity had been transformed (as Pound also believed) by the Jew, St.

Paul, into the otherworldly, sadistic, and masochistic religion of the suffering herd. Nietzsche thus dissociated the Judaized Pauline evangel of death and crucifixion from the message of Jesus' life: "Only Christian *practice*, a life such as he *lived* who died on the cross, is Christian."[25]

In Nazism, as in Pound, this kind of thinking masks a pagan hatred of Christianity and justifies programmatic anti-Semitism. Rosenberg believed that Jesus' great personality had been obscured by "the sterility of Near Eastern, Jewish, and African life," in short, the brutality of sacrifice, and that Christianity had been corrupted by that "Jewish preacher of race-chaos, St. Paul." Thanks to St. Paul, the world was not elevated "because of the *life* of the Saviour, but because of His death. . . ." "This," he adds, "is the sole motif of the Pauline Scriptures," against which Rosenberg praises a non-Jewish "*positive* Christianity," based on the example of Jesus' life. Hitler too demands "positive Christianity" in *Mein Kampf* and in the twenty-five points of the official Nazi programme.[26] In view of these religious perversions, the swastika takes on a new significance. It represents not only the solar cycle but the ascendant solar god, who instead of dying on the cross rises with the immortal sun, source of Nature's energy and vitality. This is the symbol of "life affirmation" under which millions of Jews were exterminated.

If the swastika is thus quite different from the Christian cross, what then of the cross Pound mentions, which "turns with the sun"? Pound's probable meaning is determinable through Allen Upward's *Divine Mystery*, which Pound reviewed most enthusiastically, and which, though Upward himself has no connection with Nazism, is sometimes reminiscent of Nazi cultural speculation (SP: 403–406).

Upward argues that the earliest religions depended on the brutal murder of religious victims and scapegoats in the belief that sacrifice promoted abundance and order. But at a key historical moment there emerged from the Aryan North "successive waves of Aryans" bearing the "good tidings" of solar religion; it was discovered that the sun, not the victim on the cross, caused the earth to germinate. So the living sun rather than the dying savior victim became the deity. Upward adds that the Aryan religion even made inroads into the Semitic world, enlightening some cultures which might have remained sunk in death-worship and ignorance of Nature's vitality (Upward, 2: 116, 137, 139–146). This idea underlies the following passage from the Pisan *Cantos*, which also explains the cross which turns with the sun:

> begotten of air, that shall sing in the bower
>   of Kore,   Περσεφόνεια
> and have speech with Tiresias, Thebae
>   Christo Re, Dio Sole

>   (83/ 533)

Christ assimilates to the unconquerable pagan sun-god (Dio Sole or Sol Invictus)[27] in his recurrent journey from Heaven to Hell and back to Nature and light. Pound's emphasis, then, is not on Christ's crucifixion (whose meaning and value he denies in Canto 80), but on Christ's pagan role as the unconquerable rising god of natural process and vitality. This Christ has the same significance, and the same frightening implications, as one finds in Nazi positive Christianity and in the symbolism of the swastika.

This discussion only touches on the numerous inaccuracies and distortions which riddle these Poundian and Nazi ideas. Nor does it disclose what will become increasingly evident in this book, namely the full presumption, hypocrisy, and irony of Pound's vitalistic and "instinctive" pagan religion. Pound's and the Nazis' disparagement of "negative," brutal, and sacrificial worship, as well as their repeated desire for a religion of "life affirmation," conceals a counter-impulse toward anti-Semitic victimization and even ritual murder as the originating moment of the new pagan culture.

III.

Norman Cohn has traced the fascist idea of a Jewish world conspiracy to a Christian apocalyptic tradition whose major sources are the Jewish eschatological writings, the Roman Sibylline books, and the Christian Johannine writings, including the book of Revelation. Christian fears of apocalypse increased at the end of the Middle Ages, when the millennium was supposedly at hand. According to prophecy, at the apocalyptic moment or "Last Days," Anti-Christ would emerge to lead to the massed forces of evil. Filthy, black, and horned, a monster or serpent with a powerful army of lesser demons, Anti-Christ embodies the bad father and bad son. His opponent is the radiant Warrior Christ or Savior, who assimilates to the Warrior King and the Emperor of the Last Days. This messiah bears all the attributes of the Divine Father and Son. Colossal, superhuman, and omnipotent, he pours forth the radiance of his supernatural power. After defeating Anti-Christ in a desperate battle, the Messianic King would journey to Jerusalem and there establish an empire of a thousand years, an age of bliss preceding the world's end.[28]

In the Middle Ages the figure of Anti-Christ was often projected onto outgroups, such as the Jews, who were thought to be his demons, while Anti-Christ was thought to be a Jewish Messiah and perhaps even a Jew himself. Anti-Christ "would be born at Babylon; he would grow up in Palestine and would love the Jews above all peoples; he would rebuild the Temple [of Jerusalem] for them and gather them together from their dispersion." Thus the Jews embodied that evil which had to be eliminated before the age of bliss (Cohn, 2: 86–87, 77–78, 75).

After the Middle Ages millenarianism lingered in the folk imagination, fed utopian prophecy, and reemerged in the Nazi idea of a millenarian kingdom or Holy Roman Empire (the Third Reich) and of the Jews as the satanic enemy of mankind. It is no accident that Moeller Van den Bruck, the proto-Nazi publicist, envisioned a Third Reich—an allusion to the millenarian kingdom of earlier prophecy.[29] Hitler later speaks of the "blood Jew and tyrant over peoples." Underlying this phrase is the image of the Jew as Anti-Christ. Indeed, Hitler saw himself as the Christian Messiah in his fight against the Jews: *"by defending myself against the Jew,"* he said, *"I am fighting for the work of the Lord."*[30]

The Nazis and other fascists also believed in the authenticity of the *Protocols of the Elders of Zion* and in a supposedly conspiratorial Jewish organization known as the Kahal. As is well known, the *Protocols* are a forgery disseminated by pro-Tsarist Russian emigrés after World War I and intended to blame the Jews for anarchy, liberalism, the French Revolution, and Russian Communism.[31] But for such Nazis as Hitler and Rosenberg, the *Protocols* offered proof of a secret Jewish government of sorcerers and priests. The goal of this conspiracy is a messianic age, in which the whole world will be united under Judaism and ruled by a King in the House of David (Cohn, 1: 179–180, 42, 64). Hitler thus used the *Protocols* (as Pound did) to show that the Jews' existence is a "continuous lie" (Hitler, 307). As for the Kahal, it frightened not only the Nazis but the American anti-Semite Henry Ford, whom Pound claimed as a kindred spirit.[32]

Pound was aware of millenarian prophecy at least as early as 1927 or 1928, when he first read Zielinski's *Sibylle*. Besides presenting a cyclical view of history, Zielinski's last essay, "The Sibyl and the End of Rome," examines the Sibylline prophecies of Roman paganism. Prophecy held that Rome would either collapse or renew itself after a thousand years. A great leader or king would arise and defend Rome in a great battle, either dying with her or leading her to resurrection and an age of gold. The leader is Christ, the man-god, who now rules the world from Rome, and who is now beset by enemies, such as the Jews. Zielinski also refers to medieval millenarianism and the return of Anti-Christ.[33]

Elements of millenarian prophecy appear in *The Cantos* in conjunction with Pound's celebration of fascism:

> Castalia like the moonlight
> and the waves rise and fall,
> Evita, beer-halls, semina motuum
> to parched grass, now is rain
> not arrogant from habit,
> but furious from perception, Sibylla, . . .
> (90/ 606)

The oracular Hitler, "furious from perception," is linked to beer halls, Zielinski's Delphic Sibyl, and Eva Braun, referred to with an affectionate diminutive and apparently the Führer's Muse (Castalia being the fountain of the Muses). But as history is a cyclical process ("Castalia like the moonlight / and the waves rise and fall"), and since Pound writes after the collapse of fascism, the tone is elegiac; for Pound Hitler is a "martyr," a "Joan of Arc," a "saint," a messiah who, like Zielinski's king, perished at the apocalyptic moment.[34] Canto 90 thus anticipates a passage in the next canto, where Pound is covertly an Italian Fascist martyr ("martire"); for he too suffered in this great collapse (Bacigalupo: 297).

At a more optimistic moment the Führer, through his deputy and Reichsminister Rudolf Hess, attacks usury in Canto 51, which precedes the next canto's barrage against the Jews:

> Grass; nowhere out of place. Thus speaking in Königsberg
> Zwischen die Volkern erzielt wird
> a modus vivendi
>
> (51/ 251)

The message of Nazism is delivered from Königsberg, the King's Mount, a prophetic or messianic place.[35] For Pound the message is of European unity, the Roman Imperium, a fascist era or millennium: "We have achieved a modus vivendi between the folk."[36] "The grass nowhere out of place" anticipates Canto 90, where Hitler is the "rain" that falls on "parched" grass, and the opening of Canto 92: "and from this Mount were blown / seed" (92/ 618). These are probably those seeds of motion ("semina motuum") referred to in Canto 90. One sees now why Pound praises Germany over England in the broadcasts: Germany was "nearer the centre" of the "Roman IMPERIUM" (RB, 156). The theme of empire also figures in the Pisan *Cantos,* where Pound "surrender[s] neither the empire nor the temples / plural" (74/ 434). The empire is that of the fascist millennium, which had been averted.

Quite predictably, Pound also uses the *Protocols of the Elders of Zion* to prove that the "Kike is out for all power" (RB, 120).[37] The frontispiece of Pound's edition reads: "Near is the Coming of Anti-Christ and the Kingdom of the Devil on Earth."[38] Pound's idea of *neschek* as the Jewish "serpent" resembles that serpent which, in the *Protocols,* symbolizes Jewish world dominance (*Protocols:* 18). With this paranoid fantasy Pound introduces his listeners to the Kahal, the Jews' "central committee of bleeders" (RB, 60).[39] Noel Stock says that Pound's fears of the Kahal were fed by Ms. Lesley Fry's *Waters Flowing Eastward,* based partly on supposed revelations about Jewish community life (the Kahal) by Jacob Brafman. In a March 24, 1940 article in the *Meridiano di Roma,* Pound charged that Jewish communities were under the control of "a central authority called the Kahal and . . . this organization . . . was behind the war, partly in order to control nickel production."[40] The same fear surfaces in Addendum to Canto 100, where "Finland is nickel" (Addendum to 100/ 799),[41] and in Pound's correspondence with Noel Stock in the 1950s. Stock wrote to Pound concerning the supposed role of Jewish bankers in fomenting and exploiting the Russian Revolution: "Who was and/or is using who not yet clear; tho Messianic idea, Chosen Few, etc obviously guiding factor, no matter whether the agitator is atheist swine like Marx or a pillar of the synagogue. KAHAL."[42] Underlying this anti-Semitic fantasy is the medieval conception of the Jews as the demons of Anti-Christ, and of Anti-Christ as the Jewish Messiah.

Chapter Seven

Bachofen and the Conquest of the Swamp

Writing in 1942, Pound speaks of the Jews as a "poison" which "already by the time of Scotus Erigena . . . had begun to make a bog of things" (SP, 320). Elsewhere he refers to the "Jew slime" (RB, 219), the "morass of high kikery" (RB, 189), the "sewers of Pal'stine" (RB, 345), the vague and "stinking pea-soup of near-eastern superstition, overlaid with crass ignorance of all origins,"[1] the "crawling slime of a secret [Jewish] rule" (RB, 73), and the "chaos" (RB, 320) brought about by the Jews. This last phrase is reminiscent of the swamp, which suggests chaos itself, the original confusion. Pound also refers to the Jews as an atavistic and primeval race of "subcrocodilian vitality" (RB, 187). The image of the swamp thus absorbs many of Pound's ideas about the Near East and the Jews: the feminine softness (*mollezza*) and "oriental flummery" of luxury,[2] the "squish" (L, 342) of Near Eastern thought, Jewish regressiveness, the decay of the "Hebrew disease," the tangle of the "jungle" in Canto 20, the timelessness of the Near East, the typically Semitic confusion, "excess," and anarchy of usury, the Jewish attempt to "submerge" (RB, 340) and efface cultural "ORIGINS" (RB, 9).

The swamp had a profound significance for the fascist mind and is often found inseparably from anti-Semitism in fascist writings. Along with Hitler's references to the Jewish Hydra, "jelly-like slime," and the contemporary "morass," and Rosenberg's attacks on Jewish swamps and the "*Sumpf*" of Weimar,[3] consider this typically fascistic and unintentionally parodistic passage from *Qu'est-ce que le Fascisme?* (1961) by the unregenerate French fascist Maurice Bardèche:

> [Democracies] allow all aspects of life to be open to all sorts of inundations, to all sorts of miasma, to all sorts of fetid winds, building as they do no dikes against decadence, expropriation, and especially mediocrity. They have us live on a steppe where anyone can invade us. There is one purely negative password: to defend liberty. . . . The monsters who make their nest on this steppe, the rats, the toads, the snakes, they transform it into a cesspool . . . . As

for mediocrity, it takes over like an insidious poison in peoples whom democracies cram with education without ever giving them a goal and an ideal: it is the leper of the souls of our time.[4]

The French fascist (or radical conservative) Charles Maurras similarly feared "the victory of the swamp and its catabolic, dissolving power"; he found it a "miracle" that "beauty" had survived in the midst of the swamp's "delirium" and "gloomy stagnation." Besides representing the original confusion, in Maurras the swamp symbolizes two related evils which tend toward the slow dissolution of Western hierarchy, distinction, tradition, community, order, beauty, and Nature. One is liberalism, the "dominating thought pattern of the modern age." The other is the Jews. In Maurras the first barbarian invasion is that of Martha, the Near Eastern prophetess and witch, whose coming forbode future "emanations" of the "Jewish miasma" into Europe. Having settled in the "primitive confusion" of the marshes, she called up devils by her magic arts and confused the mind of European man.[5]

Despite its uniquely vicious political emphases and goals, fascism cannot lay exclusive claim to the swamp as symbol of the Near Eastern world; nor does it originate the concept of an absolute cultural antithesis between classical and modern Europe and the Near East. These ideas can be found in Homer, Aeschylus, Herodotus, Virgil, and Catullus, among many ancient authors, and perhaps most impressively in modern times in the nineteenth-century Swiss classical scholar Johann Bachofen.[6] Though Pound gives no indication of having read him, Bachofen belongs here because no one has defined more thoroughly the significance of the swamp in the Western imagination as a combined symbol of matriarchal, Near Eastern, and hence "non-European" culture. This is not to deny that modern scholarship, though confirming Bachofen's discovery of a matriarchal stage of religion (rather than politics, as he believed) in Greece, has discredited many of his theories, including that of a universal stage of matriarchy.[7] Nonetheless, Bachofen defines a number of key oppositions which run through the mythical imagination of ancient and modern Europe and many of the myths Pound knew and admired. Because we are dealing not so much with historical truth as with the myths which inform Pound's perception of it, Bachofen remains most useful. Above all he helps to explain why, when threatened with the Semitic "swamp," Pound, Rosenberg, Maurras, and other fascists looked to classical Greece and especially Rome as the recoverable origin and bulwark of Western tradition.

II.

The inventor of the concept of the *Kulturkreis*, Bachofen believed that each culture has one original informing idea or "seed force," from which derive organically its fundamental thoughts and primary symbols. Western culture had moved through three stages: hetaerism, or unregulated naturalism; Demetrian matriarchy, or regulated naturalism, symbolized by the tilled field; and paternity, the triumph of the masculine and solar principle and in Bachofen's view the highest stage of culture. Originating in agriculture, Demetrian matriarchy coincides with the development of the concept of wife and matron and the recognition of phallic man and his participation in generation. However, in Demetrian culture the male principle is subordinate still to the natural principle of generative motherhood and obeys the feminine law of matter; men are not yet sons of their fathers but of their mothers. Demetrian matriarchy thus conceives of man's individual identity as indistinct and impermanent. Lacking the clearly differentiating paternal mark, men are like the myriad leaves of the trees.[8]

Bachofen defined another form of feminism symbolized by the unbidden and tangled growth of the swamp. This is demonic hetaerism, which precedes the Demetrian and into which it threatens to lapse. Hetaerism follows one law, that of self-generating sexually promiscuous matter, locked in perpetual and incestuous self-embrace. This unregulated naturalism rejects all patriarchal restrictions and authority, all taboos against parricide, incest, and adultery, all claims of monogamistic exclusivity. Like the swamp, it is entirely hostile to barriers and distinctions. The male or paternal principle goes unacknowledged and there is no such thing as legitimate birth; rather, all human life traces to the same fecund, parthenogenetic, and undifferentiated source.[9]

Greek patriarchy, Bachofen's third stage, asserts the primacy of the male ordering principle over both the promiscuous and material tyranny of Nature (the swamp) and the regulated naturalism of Demetrian matriarchy. Patriarchal culture is associated with light as a spiritual and seminal substance and with such solar heroes as Hercules, whose defeat of the Lernaean Hydra represents the triumph of masculine force over the matriarchal cultures of the swamps. Only with father right and marriage, the determinate mark of the phallus on the feminine substance, do men trace their origin and identity through the father. Now emerges the concept of personal, cultural, and national authenticity, which depends on being able to make distinctions, to define genealogies, to call things by their authentic names, to distinguish mine and yours (the idea of private property and patriarchal ownership), to hierarchize relations, to name oneself, one's tribe, and one's origin. Patriarchy grants man identity and prepares him for what Bachofen considered ethical and historical life.[10]

According to Bachofen, the chthonic maternal cults originated in the African and Near Eastern world. But in Greece and Rome these cults met resistance: they were transformed first into Demetrian religions and ultimately acquired that patriarchal and solar character which Bachofen considered distinctly Western. Far from developing into true historical life, as did the Romans, Africa and the Near East "held ... fast" to "the lowest tellurism," the "laws of matter" locked like swamp vegetation in cyclical self-embrace. Bachofen identifies Near Eastern groups with promiscuous sexuality, feminism, disorder, aimless and endless self-propagation, incestuous tribalism, and general indistinction, as of the swamp.[11]

Rome, says Bachofen, saved Europe from the "sensual maternity" of Asia. Though its roots were partly Oriental, Rome sternly repressed the "purely natural" Near Eastern view of man and the world and established the paternal principle and the "masculine imperium." Rejecting the Oriental concept of the debased Hercules, "enslaved by the woman's abuse of her sensual charms," it substituted the Roman matron and wife for the Near Eastern harlot. Thanks to Rome, the West emancipated itself forever from the "fetters of Oriental tradition." In this great struggle the Punic Wars and the destruction of Jerusalem figure decisively. For Bachofen, Rome's destruction of Carthage is the "greatest turning point in the destinies of mankind." It completes the "millennial struggle" of the West against the East by winning a clear "victory of the higher ethical principle of Western European mankind" over the "base sensuality" of Asia. Rome's destruction of Jerusalem is the other great turning point in history. Having liberated the West from "Mosaic Orientalism," Rome takes Jerusalem's place as the true spiritual center of the West. "Our Western life," says Bachofen, "truly begins with Rome."[12]

III.

Pound does not consistently pursue a patriarchal ideal. Besides worshipping the classical mother-goddesses, he greatly admires Catholicism, which has fairly successfully balanced and harmonized the two sexual principles in its images of the deity.[13] Indeed, Pound says that he is not entirely "patriarchal or matriarchal [in] disposition" (GK, 243). Nonetheless, something like Bachofen's hetaeristic stage of culture appears in *The Cantos*. Canto 2 alludes to Helen of Troy:

> Moves, yes she moves like a goddess
> And has the face of a god
>   and the voice of Schoeney's daughters,
> And doom goes with her in walking . . . .
>   (2/ 6)

Helen is ambiguous—with "the face of a god" she seems both feminine and masculine—and dangerous; her beauty and promiscuity throw the world into confusion. This is why Pound links her to the unrestrained daughters of Schoenus. Schoenus "the rush man" belongs to that stage of hetaeristic promiscuity in which women, like the tangled growth of marsh grass, ignore monogamistic laws and acknowledge no paternity.[14] Helen's voice is perhaps like the vague "high-murmuring" (40/ 199) sound of rushes which Hanno's sailors hear in Canto 40 as they explore the African "bayou." One should recall that Helen is related to the luxurious entanglements of Asiatic Troy, and that the name Asia may have originally meant fen or swamp.[15]

To this passage, which is preceded by a scene of unstable littoral metamorphoses, compare another from Canto 29, in which woman, as yet untouched by man, is a rootless littoral growth: "drift of weed in the bay" (29/144), "submarine" (29/145), and "octopus" (the Lernaean Hydra was an octopus). In Canto 16 Pound confronts the Palux Laerna:

> Palux Laerna,
> the lake of bodies, aqua morta,
> Of limbs fluid, and mingled, like fish heaped in a bin,
> And here an arm upward, clutching a fragment of marble,
> And the embryos, in flux,
>   new inflow, submerging,
> Here an arm upward, trout, submerged by the eels;
>   and from the bank, the stiff herbage
> the dry nobbled path, saw many known, and unknown,
> for an instant;
>   submerging,
> The face gone, generation.
>
>   (16/ 69)

Here nothing can be called by its right name, and origins are effaced. Generation is abundant and yet everything is abortive, indistinct, impermanent, fragmentary. As René Girard observes, the father "mold[s] the face of the child."[16] But here the "face" is gone, the ego or identity submerged. In short, the swamp represents generation without the paternal principle and the identifying phallic mark. At best there is a narrow path, "dry" and "stiff."

The next passage moves toward order:

>   an oasis, the stones, the calm field,
>   the grass quiet,
>   and passing the tree of the bough
>   The grey stone posts,
>   and the stair of grey stone . . . .
>   (16/ 69)

Demarcations (posts) and hierarchy (stairs) have emerged in the permanent form of stone; and this is an agricultural order, for the bough is the golden bough, while the stone posts signify property, agricultural civilization, and the primeval homestead. They are probably *hermae*, phallic objects in honor of Hermes, god of exchange, fertility, and boundaries. Not only is Hermes one of Pound's favorite deities, at least in his rustic and pastoral rather than urban form, but the *hermae* confirm Pound's identification of the phallus with agriculture and clear distinctions.[17] Shortly appear Sigismundo and Malatesta Novello, the "founders" and hence fathers of a temporary Paradiso, "gazing at the mounts of their cities" (16/ 69). Since Pound generally thinks of cities as feminine, "mounts of their cities" probably puns on Venus mount. In the next section Pound speaks of the "nymphs of that water," who spread "garlands" and weave "their water reeds with the boughs" (16/ 69–70). This is an image of the feminine (the water reeds symbolic, as in ancient tradition, of feminine pubic hair) ordered and harmonized by the masculine (the tree or phallus).[18] And so, to complete the sequence, "one man rose from his fountain / and went off into the plain" (16/ 70). Here, with the emergence of identity, the Palux Laerna is inverted.

The crucial Cantos 39 and 47 focus on Odysseus' conquest and transformation of Circe, an event which Horkheimer and Adorno interpret as a victory for patriarchy over the disorderly, unprogressive, and "unenlightened" instinctualism of putatively "feminine" Nature. Linked to the swamps "by Circeo" (41/ 202), a mountain which remembers her name, Circe is a dangerous witch and harlot belonging specifically to the world of hetaeristic and pre-patriarchal promiscuity. To quote Horkheimer and Adorno, she "is the daughter of Helios and the granddaughter of Oceanos. The elements of fire and water are undivided in her, and it is this non-differentiation as opposed to the primacy of a definite aspect of Nature (whether matriarchal or patriarchal) which constitutes the nature of promiscuity." Circe further signifies "the hopelessly closed cycle of Nature, to which—as an older theory has it—the name Circe alludes."[19] Pound, who mentions Circe's genealogy in Canto 39, thus identifies her with a feminine lack of order and measure. Once Circe transforms Odysseus' men into pigs, passive attendants of this unpurified version of the Great Mother, they forget their historical life and sink into a world without linear time or agriculture, in which the order and distinctions of the seasons are lost: "Spring overborne into summer / late spring in the leafy autumn" (39/ 193). "The stars," Pound later says of Circe, "are not in her counting, / To her they are but wandering holes . . ." (47/ 237). Like Salomé a figure of absence or lack, she neglects those natural signs by which man measures time and organizes his world.

Nevertheless, Circe ultimately frees Odysseus' men and joins with him in sexual union. Hence the rites of marriage, which establish the hierarchical dominance of man over woman, and which contrast with the promiscuous sexuality of the "fucked girls" (39/ 193) at the beginning of the canto. Hence too the rites of agriculture, which Pound associates with sex and patriarchy:

> With the crocus (spring
>   sharp in the grass,)
> fifty and forty together
>   ERI MEN AI TE KUDONIAI
> Betuene Aprile and Merche
>   with sap new in the bough
>   (39/ 195)

The quinces of Ibycus ("ERI MEN AI TE KUDONIAI") denote agriculture, through which men grow attentive to seasonal distinctions ("spring / sharp in the grass") and organize time by the sequence of months. Thanks to agriculture, the powerful and potentially chaotic germinal forces of the spring are tempered by the "measure" of ritual music and dance:

> With jasmine and olive leaf,
> To the beat of the measure
> From star up to the half-dark
> From half-dark to half-dark
> Unceasing the measure
> (39/ 195)

With the emergence of agricultural order and the marriage rites, Circe is associated with Aphrodite in her positive, that is purified form. Her statue stands in clear definition on the promontory at Terracina:[20]

> with the Goddess' eyes to seaward
> By Circeo, by Terracina, with the stone eyes
> white toward the sea
> (39/ 195)

And finally the paternal principle is asserted: a divine child is conceived or "made" during Odysseus' union with the goddess, a renewal which coincides with the spring:

> With one measure unceasing:
> "Fac deum!" "Est factus."
> Ver novum!
> ver novum!
> Thus made the spring . . . .
> (39/ 195)

But in Canto 47 emerges the awareness which characterizes Demetrian matriarchy—a sense of man's impermanence as of those marks (here notches) which man makes on the body of Mother Earth. During the sexual act (Odysseus with Circe) the speaker intuits the insubstantiality of his ego:

> Forked shadow falls dark on the terrace
> More black than the floating martin
>   that has no care for your presence,
> His wing-print is black on the roof tiles
> And the print is gone with his cry.
> So light is thy weight on Tellus
> Thy notch no deeper indented
> Thy weight less than the shadow
> Yet hast thou gnawed through the mountain,
>   Scylla's white teeth less sharp.
> Hast thou found a nest softer than cunnus . . . .
> (47/ 237–238)

Ignored by and yet resembling the martin, man (and his phallic trace) is a shadow-like presence on the earth, a "print" (or text) fated to fade. This passage anticipates Pound's encounter with Gea Terra (Earth Mother) in Canto 82, which conflates sexual union with Mother Earth and ultimate release from identity in the darkness of death and Nature. In both cases Pound is ready to sink into a maternal nest which is, paradoxically, "soft," "fluid" (82/ 526), and yet impenetrably hard, resistant to man.

Generally, however, Pound fears and resists swamp-like "softness." Much of his attraction to fascism's anti-feminism and its masculine cult of "hardness" (RB, 194) stems from his reaction to that "fluidity" and "under-tow" (Notes for Canto 111, 783) which characterizes not merely usury, *contra naturam,* but chthonic, unregulated, feminine Nature.[21] In fact the masculine principle finally asserts itself in Canto 47. "Begin thy ploughing" is Pound's invocation from Hesiod, and the canto concludes with sexual triumph and a celebration of the solar and seminal light: "The light has entered the cave. Io! Io!" Pound combines a Greek cry of jubilation with the Italian first person pronoun, which imports the masculine ego, the mark of the "prong" (47/ 238).

To what extent do Pound's politics and poetry reveal a matriarchal "disposition"? Erich Fromm notes that many socialists praised Bachofen for having demonstrated a link between the matriarchal ideal and such values as democracy, fraternity, communism, sexual liberation, and personal happiness. Indeed, Bachofen was in many ways impressed by the social freedom of matriarchy. But German conservatives fastened onto what is most distinctive in Bachofen, a belief in fixed, universal, and all-important differences between the sexes; the importance of religion; the worship of the "blood bond and earthly ties"; and a reverence for patriarchal authority, under which the maternal image is subsumed.[22] As Fromm says, in the conservative

> the desire to be loved by the mother is replaced by the desire to protect her and place her on a pedestal. No longer does the mother have the function of protecting; now she is to be protected and kept "pure." This reaction formation . . . is also extended to other mother symbols, such as country, nation, and the soil; and it plays an important role in the extremely patricentric ideologies of the present day.[23]

Since Pound sometimes gives a protective role to the goddesses, and since in some instances he seeks and receives their love, he does not fit this description perfectly. Nonetheless, Pound never wavers in his belief in the ontological differences between the sexes and in the religious status of the feminine. Meanwhile, his cultural enterprise is symbolized by his desire to "replace" (SP, 45) (and also protect) the marble goddess on her pedestal at Terracina. With Aphrodite belongs Artemis, whose profanation brings destruction, and the Princess Ra-Set, who enters the "protection" (91/ 611) of hard crystal in Canto 91. At the height of his fascism, Pound celebrates the Immaculata or Virgin Mary and the "Mother Church" (SP, 323), which he desires to protect against Jewish usury. If "Zeus lies in Ceres bosom" (81/ 517), Zeus remains superior to Ceres as light is superior to the earth it fecundates.

IV.

Writing in the *Meridiano di Roma* in January, 1940, Pound told his readers to accept only European or Chinese traditions:

> All that is obscure and distorted results from an almost pathological attempt to cause to conceal or to make correspond some Greek perception of the truth with some Near Eastern ambiguity.
>
> In the laws of Antoninus Pius, of the Emperor Constantine, of Justinian, we have the most elevated concepts of justice. . . . But between the Chinese "key economic space" and the Roman key space, we find an obscurantist space. It may be said that in the Near Eastern space the tribe and the people with little sense of the State were trying for millennia to block traffic between West and East, profiting from it, raising prices, etc.
>
> Greece was disturbed by foreign doctrines; fathers and Roman senators were alarmed from time to time by the effeminacy introduced into manners: "Persicos odi, puer," etc.[24]

Ambiguous and obscurantist, the Near East is a penumbra between the West and Far East; and "penumbra is the mother of bogies" (SP, 157). Meanwhile, Oriental luxury produces debilitating "*mollezze*" (softness) reminiscent of the swamp. Quoting Horace's well-known condemnation of Near Eastern excess, Pound appeals to those Roman "fathers" and senators who once resisted the onslaught from the usurious Near East.

Pound's Fascism stems in part from his belief that Rome's traditional mission is to protect the West from the Semitic world and even to extend dominance over it. An admirer of the anti-usurious legislation of Antoninus Pius and Justinian,[25] Pound speaks of Rome as the "CENTRE, . . . eterna" (RB, 155) of that Mediterranean civilization which fought against its "ENEMIES external and internal" (RB, 118). In Canto 78 he regrets the loss of imperial and legal "knowledge" once embodied not only in Justinian and Antoninus but in Titus, the conqueror and destroyer of Jerusalem, all of whom anticipate Mussolini in his struggle against the "monopolists" and "loan swine" (78/ 479). Or as Pound said, quoting a famous palindrome, "ROMA = AMOR" (SP, 327). One better understands the meaning of this love in the following passage from Canto 93, an elegy for Italian Fascism after its collapse:

> . . . the stone rose in Brescia,
> > Amphion!
> And yet for Venus and Roma
> > a wraith moved in air
> And Rapicavoli lost for a horse-jump.
> > Quarta Sponda
> > > transient as air
> Waste after Carthage.
>
> (93/ 630)

The stone lions of Brescia signify not only royal authority, as do the other great cats in the later *Cantos*, but the masculine potency of ascendant Fascism, which Pound likens to the emergence of Thebes from Amphion's inspired harmonies. But though Italian Fascism promised to renew Roma and Amor, together symbolised by the Temple of Venus and Roma in the delapidated Forum, this proved an illusion, a mere "wraith in air." Like the sexual athlete Mussolini, who often had himself photographed in the saddle and even horse-jumping, and whom Pound views as a condottiere on horse-back, the equestrian Rapicavoli evokes chivalric gallantry and poignant (though vaguely defined) defeat. As for "Quarta Sponda / transient as air," this is Semitic Libya, which Italy colonized in 1911–1912 and lost in World War II, and which the Italian Fascists conceived of as the nation's "Fourth Shore" in their fantastic dream of restoring the "Mare Nostrum" of the ancient Romans. As Pound implies, it was a misfortune for the Libyans that Mussolini's colonial venture failed, for their land, fated to typical Semitic sterility, had remained mere "waste" after Rome's destruction of Carthage. It is not clear whether this waste is that of the desert or the swamp, but it probably encompasses both.[26]

Pound again resembles Hitler and Rosenberg in his belief that the Roman Empire perished from Jewish usury (RB, 61). For Rosenberg, Rome is the central pillar of patriarchal authority, the "Apollonian parenthood principle," marriage, and race-preservation. Rosenberg praises Rome's destruction of Carthage, which spared Europe from the "breath of . . . [the] Carthaginian pestilence," but laments that Jerusalem "had already extended its strongest tentacles" to Rome itself: "The act of Titus," namely the destruction of Jerusalem in 70 A.D., "came too late." The praetor Cato, he adds, "stood like a lonely rock in this quagmire . . . [of] corruption, usury, and wasteful extravagance."[27]

The project of Mussolini's which most obsessed Pound was the draining of the Pontine and other marshes. Pound gave these events far more attention than they warranted because he found in them enormous symbolic significance.[28] In the radio broadcasts, for approximately two weeks preceding the passage quoted below, Pound evoked the Semitic evil in terms which imply the swamp: microbes, deadly gases, infection, the entrapments of softness and usury; then he praised Mussolini for draining "a powerful lot of swamp land" which had bred "malaria for over two thousand years. . . . But the FASCIST regime lit in and got quite a lot of [it] dried, and under healthy cultivation" (RB, 101).[29] The draining of the Pontine Marshes also figures at the opening of Canto 41, whose first lines ("MA QUESTO") are written in Roman letters:

> Having drained off the muck by Vada
> From the marshes, by Circeo, where no one else wd.
> > have drained it.
> Waited 2000 years, ate grain from the marshes;
> Water supply for ten million, another one million
> > *"vani"*
> that is rooms for people to live in.
> > XI of our era.

> > > (41/ 202)

As Odysseus transforms Circe into an agricultural goddess, so Mussolini drains the swamps by Circeo and makes them suitable for Italian farmers.[30]

According to Pound in *Jefferson and/or Mussolini*, the Duce can "pick out the element of immediate and major importance in any tangle" (J/M, 66). In Canto 41, confronting the "tangle" of the swamp, Mussolini creates the determinate out of chaos. Where usury destroys walls and barriers, he builds them; and in classical tradition the wall is essentially a phallic object.[31] Mussolini also figures in Pound as Cato in Rosenberg, as the enemy of that usurious corruption and wasteful extravagance which Pound associates with the Jews and which he symbolizes in the unredeemed swamps of Europe's ancient past. A supporter of the Italian family, Mussolini encourages breeding and the survival of the race against the "rotten" and deracinated "mezzo-yit" (41/ 202) of Canto 41.[32] Pound's reference to the eleventh year of the Italian Fascist Era (in the 1930s Pound often followed the Italian Fascist calendar) thus commemorates a cultural order which begins in 1922 with Mussolini's decisive "March on Rome" and continues with his draining of the Pontine Marshes: "the revolution continues" (J/M, 113). This revolution, however, is no less a return to true paternal and agrarian origins, the recovery of Roman (and anti-feminist) values from the chaos of the swamp.[33]

In *Jefferson and/or Mussolini* Pound explains the meaning of the Fascist axe by means of two Chinese ideograms:

(J/M, 113)

The first ideogram on the left (*hsin*) shows the axe, which clears away rubbish and establishes order, and a tree, signifying organic vegetable renewal; the other shows the sun, symbolizing natural and cultural renovation, which presumably the axe brings about. Implicitly the Italian Fascist revolution makes Nature and Culture new. At the same time the axe implies the *fasces,* from whose cut and bound rods an axe projects as the central and dominant element.[34] Taken together, the axe and rods signify the mark and the boundary, the recovery of Roman tradition, the emergence of definition and order from Nature's confused feminine tangle, and above all the unity of the family and nation; in the Chinese *Cantos* society collapses when men "wd/ not stand together / were not rods in a bundle" (53/ 271–272). Finally, the *fasces* is a logocentric sign. In *Jefferson and/or Mussolini* Pound notes that he had found the phrase "Dio ti benedica [God bless you]," addressed tó Mussolini, "on a shed where some swamps were" (J/M, 40). Representative of God the Father (Zeus, Pater Helios), Mussolini is also an avatar of the demi-god Hercules, who destroyed swamp monsters and bogeys and established patriarchal order.

Chapter Eight

Waddell and Aryan Tradition

Although some critics are willing to concede that Pound "flirted" with racism and fascism before World War II, they frequently assert that he abandoned these ideologies as a result of his imprisonment at Pisa by the U.S. Army in 1945 and his later thirteen year confinement at St. Elizabeths Hospital in Washington. According to David Gordon, Pisa renewed Pound's contact with the awesome and purifying forces of Nature and enabled him to see "the world from the point of view of the wasp and the ant." Thanks to this lesson of humility, Pound at last discovered "the dimensions of compassion" and tolerance and revealed a "wider range of sensibility to human values." Thus, though Pound had apparently been "affected" and misled by the mildly "suburban" and yet paradoxically "hysterical" anti-Semitism of other writers, such as Eliot and Yeats, "all that was completely altered by the things he learned so quickly in Pisa." This abandonment of anti-Semitism supposedly follows Pound's rejection and indictment of fascism during the early 1940s, when Mussolini, by joining with Hitler, betrayed the "mandate" of the people (Gordon, 1: 357–358). James J. Wilhelm more or less agrees with these views, arguing that Pound, who had learned his "lesson of humility at Pisa," and who had never been seriously committed to fascism anyway, turned inward after the war and abandoned fascism as a "lost political cause." Wilhelm also believes that Pound's anti-Semitism disappears from the later *Cantos*, which were written after the "chastening experience of Pisa and St. Elizabeths" (Wilhelm, 2: 5, 183).

These arguments are false. Apart from Pound's pro-Axis wartime broadcasts, *The Cantos* early and late refer favorably to Mussolini's and Hitler's policies. Pound's poetry and correspondence also provide abundant proof that his anti-Semitic cultural mythology persisted after the war, when he was confined to St. Elizabeths Hospital and still charged with treason. At this point, however, it was highly imprudent for Pound to express overtly many of his political and cultural views. As early as *The Spirit of Romance*, Pound had observed that the inspired visionary who holds unusual notions resorts to deception and mythical concealment to evade persecution (SR, 92). Besides prefiguring Pound's self-fulfilling conception of himself as a persecuted visionary, this observation suggests the necessary strategy of the later *Cantos*, in which the "SECRETUM" (L, 329) or "arcanum" (91/ 615) becomes increasingly important. If Pound in the 1940s and 1950s wanted to include fascistic and anti-Semitic themes, then, to borrow a term of Bacigalupo's, he had to "encrypt" (Bacigalupo: 64) them. As Reno Odlin argues from Pound's own statements, "detail after detail in the later *Cantos* is code language 'to get by the Kikes'. . . ."[1] Pound thus affords a non-Jewish example of that evasion of political censorship which Leo Strauss treats in *Persecution and the Art of Writing* and to which Freud alludes in *The Interpretation of Dreams*.[2]

At St. Elizabeths Pound discovered a work of historical and archeological fantasy and filled with dubious anti-Semitic and other cultural speculations: L.A. Waddell's *Egyptian Civilization: Its Sumerian Origin and Real Chronology and Sumerian Origin of the Egyptian Hieroglyphs* (1930) (Waddell, 2). Although Kimpel and Eaves rightly note that Pound was "inclined" to take Waddell's "radical reconstruction of history seriously," they create a strongly misleading impression in saying that Pound's references to Waddell "have nothing about the Jews" (Kimpel and Eaves, 2: 66). This statement typifies Kimpel and Eaves's approach, which is to confine Pound's anti-Semitism to explicitly anti-Semitic statements or references while ignoring those numerous instances in which it figures contextually, implicitly, unconsciously, or potentially in Pound's text. To be sure, Pound's borrowings from Waddell make no mention of the Jews, but in fact one can never comprehend Waddell's radical reconstruction of history without understanding his anti-Semitism.[3] Furthermore, as I have been arguing here, if one considers Pound's borrowings in the context of his correspondence in the 1950s, his political activities, his personal psychology, his ideological aims, and above all his need to conceal his true political opinions during his confinement at St. Elizabeths, then one has no difficulty in seeing Waddell as the arcane vehicle of Pound's anti-Semitic mythology.

Waddell sought to show that Egypt, far from owing its civilization to indigenous Semitic peoples, had been colonized and civilized around 2780 B.C. by Aryan Sumerians led by Sargon of Akkad. Sargon, he argues, was descended from Ikshvaku, the "immortal Aryan," who, as the "greatest" culture hero of all time, is the founder of agriculture and solar religion. Carrying on this tradition, and operating from the original culture center, Sargon and his successors disseminated Aryan culture and language to the Indus valley, where the Sumerians were known as Aryans, to Europe, China, and Indo-China, to the Indian Ocean and the Pacific. Waddell's book thus holds that Sumeria is the source of European civilization and the Aryan languages.[4] It also enables Pound to introduce into *The Cantos* a favorite myth of the Aryan and Nazi cultural theorists, that of the "Aryan migration."[5]

It should be emphasized that Waddell argues neither for German nor for any other form of fascism; he simply believes that the Aryan peoples—of which he takes the Nordics to be a subgroup—are superior to other groups. Waddell's racial interpretation of history is based on the idea that, while cultural aptitudes can be learned, Semites are inferior to Aryans and have contributed nothing of real value to world civilization.[6] To determine the race of Menes, Aryan king of Egypt, Waddell relies on Egyptian sculpture. Unlike the Egyptian aborigines whom the Aryan Sumerians had conquered, Menes has a straight, round-tipped nose, "long and square jaw," and tall stature, while his head is the "Aryan broad-browed and long-headed." In Menes' statue "the iris was inlaid . . . with lapiz lazuli stone . . . to represent the blue eyes of the Aryan race."[7]

Pound mentions Menes once in Canto 94 and later in Canto 97, in both cases relying on Waddell. The second passage reads:

> Came then autumn in April and
> > "By Knoch Many now King Minos lies"
> > > (97/ 680)

Waddell argues that Menes is also King Minos of Crete, who, in transmitting Aryan culture from Egypt to Europe, Crete, and Ireland, founded an Aryan world empire. Like Pound's Hercules and Hanno, Menes is a solar hero, a follower of the sun's "periplum," and a great explorer of distant Western lands. Evidence for his death in Ireland Waddell adduces from the name Knoch Many, in County Tyrone, where he locates Menes' tomb, which Pound mentions above (Waddell, 2: x, 31–69).

Perhaps Waddell's most curious idea is that Sargon and his successor Menes were Goths. After Sargon conquered the Indus valley, according to Waddell, he issued seals naming him "Gut" or Goth. This title Waddell takes as evidence that Sargon and his people were Aryan Goths; he thus asks us to believe that the Goths of late Roman times created the "Golden Age" of Sumeria and played a "leading part" in the civilization of Egypt and the world.[8] Pound's presentation of this fantasy appears in Canto 94, where Sargon is "Goth" (94/ 635), and in Canto 97, where Pound writes mysteriously: "gothic arch out of India" (97/ 679).

Waddell also inspires these lines:

> Panch, that is Phoenician, Tyanu

 lion head[9]

> (97/ 680)

Descendants of Menes and the Aryan dynasties of Egypt and India, the "able Panch" are the Phoenicians, sea-going merchant princes whom Waddell treats not as Semites but originally Sumerians and Aryans; hence probably Pound's inclusion in Canto 97 of the square-nosed Phoenician "lion head," which serves to distinguish this forthright Aryan people from their presumably hook-nosed and morally crooked Semitic neighbors, among them the "hook-nosed exotic" (RB, 85) Jews. The colonizing Phoenicians brought the Aryan alphabet to Europe, says Waddell, who also wrote a study of the alphabet's Phoenician origins, but their great achievements occurred before the Greco-Roman period, when they were "somewhat semitized" (Waddell, 2: 167–172). Waddell's fanciful attribution of the Greek alphabet to a non-Semitic source fits in neatly with one of Pound's major cultural projects of the early 1940s, namely the elimination from Western writing of all Semitic taints: "Not a jot or tittle of the Hebraic alphabet must pass into the text" (SP, 320).[10] Meanwhile, Tyanu links the Phoenicians to the supposedly Gothic peoples of Asia Minor and evokes Apollonius of Tyana, who comes from the region of Tyanu, and who appears prominently in the later *Cantos* as a pagan rival of Christianity (and hence Judaism). Opposed in his dealings with the Emperor Vespasian by the "schnorrer Euphrates" (94/ 640), a man not the river, Apollonius is associated with the Sumerian theme in Canto 94. Following Philostratus' account of Appollonius' voyage to the Straits of Gibraltar, Pound interpolates a detail of his own, that the pillars at Cadiz had "Sumerian capitals" (94/ 638) (Philostratus, Vol. 1: 463, 473–475). Besides picking up the idea of the solar voyage (Apollonius, like Hercules, Menes, and Hanno, follows the sun's western track), this discloses evidence of the diffusion of Sumerian culture as reported in Waddell (Philostratus, Vol. 1: 471, 473).

Pound's most important borrowing from Waddell is in Canto 94, where he introduces Waddell's reproduction of the seal of Sargon of Akkad. The same seal also appears in Canto 97 (with additional signs signifying vegetation), where Pound reproduces it twice:

(94/ 635)

Sargon's seal contains three signs: the lower sun sign and the middle temple sign, both enclosed in a cartouche or "shield," and the upper hawk sign. The sun sign is Sargon's "Solar title," indicating that he is not only a king and sun-worshipper but representative and son of the Sun-God. It thus testifies to a solar religion which the Sumerians (Aryans) originated and spread from Mesopotamia to Egypt and then to Europe. Waddell also connects solar religion, patriarchal authority, and agriculture; the Sumerian sun-worship-pers, he says, with their father gods, introduced agriculture into the ancient world. Where Pound celebrates a European "grain god" and agrarian and solar traditions, Waddell reproduces Aryan images of the solar deity, cham-pion of good over evil, and his son, the "Corn-god" and "patron of agricul-tural life," who figures in pre-historic monuments and coins.[11] These figures and images appear within the same cultural antithesis one finds in Pound, Upward, Zielinski, Bachofen, and Rosenberg, between the dark and de-monic chthonic gods of the Orient, and the European gods (in this case also Egyptian and Sumerian). Sun-worship, Waddell says, "is a wholly non-Semitic cult" which, once introduced by the Aryans into the Semitic world, replaced the brutalities of animal totemism and sacrificial butchery. Nor is Waddell any more gratified by the Semitic cults of the "wolf demon" (Set, the swamp monster, of great significance to the later Pound), the Serpent Mother, and the "aboriginal mother cow goddess" (Hathor)—all evoking the unrestrained, feminine, parthenogenetic earth, a reptilian realm untamed by agricultural man.[12]

Pound repeatedly relies on Waddell in order to weave into his "arcanum" elements of a far-diffused and Aryan religion, a religion of agrarianism and hence anti-Semitic. In Canto 97 Pound writes of "Aswins drawing the rain cloud" (97/ 679), which is followed by his reference to the diffusion of the Gothic arch out of India. The Aswins are Aryan spirits which appear in the *Rig-Veda*.[13] In a subsequent passage Pound writes murkily of "torchlight, at Multan, offer perfume," of the "Son of Herakles, Napat son of Waters," and then of "Panch, . . . Tyanu" (97/ 679–680). Multan is a place of worship mentioned in Waddell's *Indo-Sumerian Seals*, which quotes a Buddhist pil-grim on "a temple dedicated to the Sun, very magnificent and profusely decorated," which is also a "house of mercy." The son of Herakles, Napat, and Phoenician Panch are all versions of Assias, "one of the most famous ancient Aryan Vedic Fire-priests" (Waddell, 1: 108, 130). Finally, "Tyanu" again points us toward the no less oracular and prophetic figure of Apollonius of Tyana, whom Pound celebrates in this section of *The Cantos*, and whose name, evoking Apollo, the sun-god, also defines for him a place within Aryan tradition. In Canto 94 Pound spells the name of Apollonius' birthplace "Tyana," which according to Wilhelm emphasizes the Indo-European root "to shine," and which connects the sun-worshipping Apollonius to such Indo-European (Aryan) solar gods as Dyaus, Tiw, Zeus, Ju-piter, and Diony-sus (Wilhelm, 2: 89; Philostratus, Vol. 1: 217).

It might be argued that Pound's borrowings from Waddell imply only Aryanism rather than anti-Semitism, although the two are rarely if ever very far apart. The fact is, however, that the context of these borrowings is heavily anti-Semitic, and it is therefore most probable that Waddell serves an anti-Semitic purpose in Pound's poem. In Canto 94 Apollonius of Tyana takes pity on a lion in which, he claims, is lodged the soul of Amasis, King of Egypt.

Apollonius then sends the lion to a temple, where priests sacrifice to Amasis, and the lion becomes a venerated object (94/ 640; Philostratus, Vol. 1: 569–571). Pharoah and founder of the XVIIIth Dynasty (c. 1700 B.C.), Amasis delivered Egypt from the domination of the nomadic Hyksos, whom Pound describes in Canto 93 as "butchers of lesser cattle" (93/ 623). But since we have already seen in Chapter Three that Pound applies the same derogatory phrase to the nomadic Jews, it is entirely plausible that this detail is an example of that anti-Semitic code-language of which Reno Odlin speaks. Besides proving him an alter ego of Pound, who identifies cats with royalty and worships all members of the feline tribe, Apollonius' adoration of the lion confirms him as an Aryan, for the "Aryan" Phoenicians are associated in Canto 97 with the "lion head," and it links him as well to Fascism, which Pound symbolizes in the later *Cantos* in the "Brescian lions" (110/ 780; see also 93/ 630), whose record is threatened with effacement and historical "black out." So again, in Canto 97 Pound writes of the "octonary sun-worshipping Baltic," where the Prussians, imbued with divine wisdom, struck in 1806 bank notes that "ran 90 years" (97/ 673). These lines probably look back to Pound's 1938 letter to Douglas Fox, in which Pound speaks of Germany as a "force toward a purgation," praises rituals in Lithuania (the Baltic region), and says that "the only vigorous feasts of the Church" are of "the sun" and "the grain."[14] Like Waddell's other solar symbols, such as the Aryan swastika (Waddell, 2: 165), Sargon's seal represents what Pound calls "Sagetrieb," a sometimes concealed tradition both living and latent in myth (Sage) and instinct (Trieb). Pound considers this tradition as irrepressibly vital as the growth of corn and plants. Hence his use of the vegetation symbol in connection with Sargon's cartouche (see 97/679); like the tree sign in the *hsin* ideogram, it signifies growth and renewal.

Anti-Semitism appears at numerous other points in the later *Cantos*. In Canto 96 the Colossus of Rhodes, which had stood for "thirteen sixty years," and which represented the sun-god Apollo, is "sold" in fragments "to a jew" (96/ 657), another instance of the Jewish destruction of Sagetrieb. In Canto 100 a revolution in paper money in Amsterdam in 1572 leads to the establishment of the bank of Amsterdam in 1609, which leads in turn to the destruction of the Jewish "Wissel bank" and the forbidding of the Jews from dealing in exchange (Pearlman, 2: 175). Pound also conceals his racial theme in reference to the Venetian San Vio family, in which the physical marks or traces of past generations and Nature itself are preserved, and in which Sagetrieb is thus written into the genetic code.[15] Unlike the denatured Jews, the San Vios physically reflect their natural environment: their eyes recall those of the sea-goddess:

> with eyes pervanche,
> three generations, San Vio
> darker than pervanche?
>
> (97/ 676)

Canto 97 contains the elliptical and seemingly threatening phrase: "And as for who have a code and no principles . . ." (97/ 678). Although these lines may refer to Protestants, they probably also refer to the Jews, who follow the Mosaic code. Cut off from Nature, ignorant of divine origins (the sun), the Jews supposedly prefer a rigid and repressive legalism to the flexible and intuitive "natural" morality which the Aryan claims as his birthright.[16]

II.

One of the most prominent and important symbols in the later *Cantos* appears in the upper register of Sargon's cartouche or "shield." Pound isolates it four times in Canto 97:

The temple ⊔⊔ is holy,
because it is not for sale.
(97/ 676)

Waddell also thought this the hieroglyph of a temple (Waddell, 2: 21–22). Implicitly this temple belongs to a solar religion, one whose agriculturally-based rites are different from those of Semitic peoples, whose villain is the grain god. Menes' Crucifixion Monument, dedicated to the Sun-god, details his "simple fruit offering" comparable to that of Cain, who "incurred the wrath of the Semitic god for not offering the sanguinary Chaldean sacrifices, as did his 'brother' Abel" (Waddell, 2: 50–51). In Canto 97 Pound imagines a bloodless sacrifice within the inner temple or *Temenos*:

> Flowers, incense, in the temple enclosure,
> no blood in that *TEMENOS*
> When crocus is over and the rose is beginning
> (97/ 681)

These lines are preceded by Sargon's seal, and Sargon appears later as the founder of a long and non-Semitic tradition:

> From Sargon to Tyana
> no blood on the altar stone
> (97/ 680)

Earlier, in Canto 94, Pound had announced his newly-felt revulsion from animal sacrifice in celebrating Apollonius of Tyana:

> Apollonius made peace with the animals
> Was no blood on the Cyprian's altars
> (94/ 635)

For students of anti-Semitism, this is familiar mythological territory. Whereas Pound follows Apollonius in constructing a presumably bloodless cult,[17] he associates the Jews and Semites, as do Waddell and Upward, with blood sacrifice and the butchery of herd animals (Waddell, 2: 50–51, 90).

And yet, as in Voltaire, Rosenberg, and Hitler, Pound's dislike of blood sacrifice is ironically accompanied by an unabated impulse to persecute the Jews. It is also accompanied, as in the case of two notable anti-Semites, Hitler and Wagner, by a kind of vegetarianism.[18] In Canto 97 Pound gives another example of the bloodless and primitive European solar rite:

> Luigi, *gobbo*, makes his communion with wheat grain
> in the hill paths
> at sunrise

(97/ 679)

The *tan* sign, signifying dawn, means that this ceremony is open only to Aryan initiates, like the hunchbacked and hence sacred Luigi.

The third and dominant figure in Sargon's seal is the hawk, specifically a Sun-hawk, symbol of masculine power and political authority. As Pound says, "πανουργία" ("panourgia") is now "at the top" (97/ 678), and "When kings quit, the bankers begin again" (97/ 672). Earlier, Pound had introduced these lines on Sargon, his wife, and Menes:

> From the hawk-king
> Goth, Agdu
> Prabbu of Kopt, Queen Ash
> may Isis preserve thee
> Manis paid for the land
> 1 bur: 60 measures, lo staio, 1 mana of silver[19]

(94/ 635)

The later *Cantos* refer to a number of historical figures who stand implicitly in the tradition of the great Sumerian world empire. One is Alexander the Great, who "paid the debts of his soldiery" (85/ 549), and whom, as Sikandar, "tigers mourn" (87/ 576), presumably because he attempted what Sargon's immediate successors attained and Pound himself hoped for, a cultural rapprochement between East (China) and West:

> and there was that Führer of Macedon, dead aetat 38

(97/ 676)[20]

It is anachronistic for Pound to refer to a Macedonian king as a Führer, but Waddell's book is pervaded by a Germanic, Nordic, and Gothic theme which Pound picks up with fondness as he builds "Sagetrieb." He praises the "octonary sun-worshipping Baltic" and monetary reforms in Cologne and Amsterdam; speaks of Sargon as "Goth," and of the Gothic arch out of India; praises the Germanic Lombard kings; and commemorates "dawn," his sacred theme, by a German phrase, "Der Tag" (97/ 677). Toward the end of Canto 97, after Sargon's seal appears yet again, Pound writes:

> That he wrote the book of the Falcon.

(97/ 682)

The author of the *Book of the Falcon* is Frederick II (Von Hohenstaufen), the half-German King of Sicily in the Middle Ages, whose mastery of falconry and poetry indicates fitness for rule (both hawk and falcon are royal birds), and whom Dante admired as the just claimant to the throne of the Holy Roman Empire. Pound knew that Frederick's reign saw early signs of the ultimate divorce in Europe of Church and State. This line may thus look back to "A Visiting Card," where Pound implicitly blames the Jews for setting "the Church against the Empire" (SP, 317). Pound's Frederick would then be a lesser version of that Sargon who, as priest-King, possesses both political and religious authority. As Waddell notes, the title "Sag," a form of Sargon, means "seer" or "Diviner" (Waddell, 2: 30).

Sargon finds other avatars in several rulers who figure with him in Cantos 94 and 97. One is Antoninus Pius, whom Pound praises in *The Cantos* and elsewhere for having established a just and anti-usurious law of marine insurance (the Lex Rhodi). But this is not Antoninus' only claim to importance, since, as we have seen in the preceding chapter, Pound views him as a chief protector of European civilization from its "external" enemies, namely the Jews. The same is true of Constantine and Justinian, the first of whom is mentioned in Canto 94, the second in Canto 94 and again in Canto 97 following the ideogram of Sargon's seal. In the *Meridiano di Roma* Pound links Constantine and Justinian with Antoninus as examples of the "most elevated concepts of justice," concepts which stand opposed to those of the "Near Eastern space." Toward the conclusion of Canto 94, English tradition is shown to be a part of this "Sagetrieb" as Pound alludes to King Edward I, the so-called "English Justinian," under whose reign (1272–1307) England made advances in law and constitution. According to Carroll F. Terrell, Edward "rhymes" with Pound's themes of "thrones and justice," which are increasingly prominent in the later *Cantos*, and indeed Edward accomplished much as a ruler.[21] But if one wants to know his perhaps most dubious accomplishment, which Pound neglects to mention here, but which he undoubtedly has in mind, one must turn to the broadcasts. Addressing the English, Pound observes that Edward, like a medieval Hitler, "determined to solve the Jewish question as it existed in England and in the Statutum Judaismo [Statutum de Judeismo]," giving Jews permission to "engage in commerce and handcrafts" and even agriculture but forbidding them to lend at interest. Unwilling to take advantage of these opportunities, the Jews resorted to "highway robbery" and coin-clipping. "As a consequence," says Pound,

> in 1278 the whole of English Jewry was imprisoned and in 1290 finally expelled. Many settled in the ghetto of Paris. As to whether Edward the 1st was interested in the welfare of England, we must leave Mr. Ullstein to decide for you [the English], as you seem averse (to) making clear-cut decisions. (RB, 219)[22]

Canto 97 carries us to more questionable oracles and renewals. Midway in Canto 97, after again introducing the *hsin* sign (tree and axe), Pound writes: "So hath Sibilla a boken ysette" (so hath Sibyl set in a book) (97/ 675). This phrase, from Layamon's *Brut,* refers as well to Zielinski's *La Sibylle,* and calls us back to Cantos 90 and 91 (Bacigalupo: 268–269). The same phrase appears in Canto 91 immediately before a long tirade against democracy, Marx, Freud, and the "*kikery*" (91/ 614) of the American universities, which is followed by Pound's self-vindication as a Fascist "martyr." In Canto 90 the martyred Hitler is "furious from perception" (90/ 606) and appears in the company of Eva Braun (or more remotely "Evita," wife of Juan Perón) and Zielinski's Sibyl. The Sibyl had prophesied a pagan emperor whose millenarian kingdom will replace Christ's. In Canto 51, Hitler is the messianic king who from Königsberg (King's mountain, an oracular place) attacks usury, proclaims a "modus vivendi" for the "Volkern" (folk), and sees that the "grass," namely the usury-wracked multitudes of Europe, is "nowhere out of place." This is the same grass which, in Canto 90, having been "parched," at last receives Hitler's life-giving "rain" (90/ 606). In short, Hitler has established order in the manner suggested in Canto 97: "When kings quit, the bankers begin again" (Bacigalupo: 64, 268, 269). Although these passages are rarely noted by Pound critics, they demonstrate the intensity of his pro-Hitlerism, which persists from the late 1930s into his St. Elizabeths years. Hitler fits neatly with this canto's themes of Aryan and European tradition, sun-worship (a Nazi obsession), anti-Semitism, kingship, and world empire. He is in fact the modern avatar not only of Sargon, who appears in Canto 94 in the company of his consort Queen Ash, but of those ancient Aryan priests, the Aswins, who "draw down the rain cloud."

Canto 97 also conceals Italian Fascism and Mussolini within its panoramic vision of cultural authority. Like Pound's Mussolini, Waddell's Sargon is associated with the Bull, while Aryan kings are commemorated by the sacred axe symbol, a sign of the great Father God (Waddell, 2: 30, 166, 73–74). But where Waddell associates Sargon with the weapon of Zeus, the leading god of Mediterranean patriarchy, Pound mentions only Sargon, not his axe. Nonetheless, a symbolic axe appears in Canto 97:

New fronds,

novelle piante 新

what axe for clearing?

 ch'in¹   tan⁴   ch'in¹

(97/ 675)

The presence of *tan* (the dawn sign) in conjunction with *hsin* (the axe) signifies a secret doctrine or "arcanum" known only to the initiated and cast in mythical form to save the visionary from persecution. As we have seen, Pound associates *hsin* with the establishment of distinctions and the calling of things by their right names, a task which for Pound is inseparable from fascism. The axe also has a major symbolic significance in relation to Mussolini's clearing of the Pontine Marshes. If one remembers that Pound's commitment to fascism never wavered during his St. Elizabeths period, it seems likely that the axe is that of Italian Fascism. Like Sargon, Mussolini is an axe worshipper, having chosen the bound rods and axe (*fasces*) as symbol of his power and authority. Mussolini's worship installs him within Pound's royal ideology, the long tradition of Aryan kings.

Chapter Nine

Nature, Race, and History, I

Like many fascists, Pound appeals to a normative idea of all-encompassing Nature as the objective, absolute, and permanent basis of proper human conduct and the true human society. This ideal supposedly would enable fascism to transcend the mere accidents of history and ideology. Yet Pound's and the fascist conception of Nature is highly problematic. Not only does it fail to meet its claims of totality and transhistorical truth, but it is inconsistent with fascism's other historical values and aims. Far from defining objective truth, the fascist conception of Nature is an extremely attenuated ideological construct, founded on a narrow and impoverished view of human nature, and created under pressure of unique historical conditions and to serve specific historical needs. Moreover, this "totalitarian" appeal to a true and holistic Nature inevitably requires that Pound and the fascists invoke its paradoxical opposite, namely anti-Nature, which is indispensable to the preservation of the fascist idea of the natural, and which ironically seems at least as powerful as Nature itself. This anti-natural principle comes to be embodied most prominently in the Jews. Finally, fascism holds conflicting views of Nature and History. Despite their interest in a natural order beyond history, fascists were in truth ambivalent towards Nature, and in many cases celebrated not the natural but the historical. Nowhere is fascism's anti-naturalism more evident than in its glorification of technology at Nature's expense. At the same time, for all their pursuit of the transhistorical, the fascists often subscribed no less contradictorily to a relativistic and irrational historicism, holding the position that everything is historical and ideological rather than natural.

When Pound speaks of Nature he usually means external Nature, the world of physical process, in whose bounty, beauty, and efficiency he finds evidence of divine intelligence or "design" (95/ 645). Natural forms are for Pound the model and standard by which human creations are measured, while cultural and economic catastrophes result from man's foolish introspection, his lapses of attention and intelligence, his failure to recognize

Nature's order and to integrate himself within it: "Le Paradis n'est pas artificiel" (76/ 460). Man realizes his human nature and ethical life only when he harmonizes his actions with the abiding order without. Ideally, Man and Nature are "two halves of the tally" (82/ 526). Pound wants to unite Nature, whose symbol is the abundant growth of vegetation, with man, culture, whose symbol is the stone monument.[1] Once society adapts itself fully to natural process, its existence becomes organic and unified, like Nature's: "one, indivisible, a nature extending to every detail as the nature of being oak or maple extends to every part of the oak tree or maple" (SP, 82).

The familiar mythical reading of Pound, as of modern poetry in general, is typified by Daniel Pearlman's *The Barb of Time*. Summarizing Pound's views, Pearlman argues that man can attain harmony with Nature only by escaping linear or historical time into a ritually sanctified world, in which time is an unchanging cyclical process and culture is linked inseparably to the seasons. For Pound, history amounts to what Pearlman describes as a mere "series of unique and repeatable events," a "realm of suffering" characterized by violence, discontinuity, and above all usury, all of which separate man from Nature and destroy those myths and traditions which link man to natural process. By contrast, organic or mythical time is based on the "perpetually recurrent cycles of birth, death, and rebirth in organic nature." Abandoning history for Nature, man recovers an unceasing present in which he represents, follows, and renews the timeless seasonal pattern in the permanent forms of myth and ritual. Thus Pound's fundamental dramatic conflict pits cyclical time against history. Throughout *The Cantos* Pound contrasts the "organic," non-linear, repeatable yet endlessly renewing mythical time of ritual with the profane, quantifiable, mechanical and merely linear time of the modern world—a world of meaningless repetition and increasing debts, in which time is not renewed or lived but numerically accumulated and "consumed." Not only does all of history or linear time "violate" or negate Pound's ideal natural order, but Nature, "in the eyes of those who represent the forces of negation" —namely history—"is fraught with danger and must be suppressed." Pearlman further asserts that Pound is properly understood in mythical terms: Pound comes "to grips with the time world" and defeats it by treating human activity in relation to mythical constants and also by employing, curiously enough, the distinctly modern techniques of spatial form.[2]

My view of Pound's myths differs from Pearlman's. Myth, which Pound praises for its concreteness and reality over the merely abstract and theoretical, is really his form of abstraction, his way of distancing himself from modern actualities which he never really understood, just as his Nature is an ideological construct, thoroughly "contaminated" by history. Mythical criticism makes sense only if we believe Pound's myths. It can tell us little of why Pound espoused fascism and became a rabid anti-Semite. Though Pound preferred "not to write 'to the modern world' " (SP, 75), he wrote, inescapably, in that world, with ideological, cultural, and historical purposes. In suggesting that Pound confronts the "time world," Pearlman falsely objectifies and hypostatizes time and gives the mistaken impression that Pound can write from a privileged position not in time but outside it. Pound cannot avoid a contaminating relationship with the "time world" for the simple reason that, as Lillian Feder observes of *The Cantos*, he "reverses, extends, and controls time to suit his vision of the self, society, and history" (Feder: 110–111n).

Actually, the common view of Pound's project as a mythic transcendence of history does not even square with Pound's declared intentions. Pound repeatedly emphasizes the importance of unique historical needs and conditions. He adopts the Italian Fascist term "anti-storico" (SP, 148) to condemn those modern political movements which in his view ignore the historical actualities, habits, and traditions of nations. Mussolini, he says, conducts a "continual gentle diatribe against all that is 'anti-storico,' all that is against historic process" (J/M, v). Pound also praises Jefferson's insight "when faced with a particular problem *in* a particular geography, and when faced with the unending problem of CHANGE" (J/M, 11). Both Mussolini and Jefferson recognize that there is "a TIME in these things," that "we do not all of us inhabit the same time" (LE, 87).

Still, Pound's concept of the *anti-storico* enables him to move all too easily from the historical to the "natural" or trans-historical, for it opposes "ideologies hung in a vacuum or contrary to the natural order of events as conditioned by race, time, and geography" (SP, 148). Put simply, Pound believes that all nations possess a "root" that underlies all change and assures a "natural" permanence amid change. Mussolini, whose thoughts are like the "seeds" of the genius, has supposedly "never asked nations with a different historical fibre to adopt the cupolas and gables of fascism." In fact, were he in England, "he would drive his roots back into the Witanagemot . . ." (J/M, v). Yet these statements, which assume the possibility of some kind of historical prediction and even prophecy, as well as the unfolding of national history organically and perhaps teleologically, as from a germ or seed, beg the question of how a Mussolini or even a Jefferson really knows (or decides) what is "naturally occurring" in a nation or what is in keeping with its historical process and tradition.

Pound reveals contradiction or at least ideological equivocation in two other key points. Despite his appeal to history as an organic and roughly calculable development, he also praises political and historical opportunism, justifying them on the grounds that history is essentially contingent, unpredictable, and fluid: unlike Mussolini, "human theorizing has proceeded from an Euclidean stasis, from statecraft to music the theoreticians have dealt with a still world, and received derision, quite properly." By contrast, Mussolini's "opportunist politics has dealt with a flowing world and succeeded" (SP, 304–305). Untroubled by ideological inconsistency, and unwilling to define a specific form for his political programme, Il Duce never prejudges situations but instead trusts in his own intuitions while keeping all avenues open. These are precisely the virtues of Italian Fascism as defined by the Italian Fascist historian Gioacchino Volpe in a work Pound seems to have much admired (Volpe: 22, 27, 28, 56, 78, 81, 91; Heymann: 146). Thus for Pound Italian Fascism has both a discernible "AIM" and "great elasticity."[3] Meanwhile, Pound views Mussolini as a "voluntarist" (J/M, viii) and revolutionary genius for whom (as Mussolini himself believed) virtually anything is possible: not only has Mussolini the "opportunism of the artist, who has a definite aim, and creates out of the materials present" (J/M, 15, 16); he has "convictions," and "drives them through circumstance, or batters and forms circumstance with them" (J/M, 18). This suggests that Mussolini, instead of trusting to the conservative *senso storico*, follows the "DIRECTION OF . . . [his] WILL" (J/M, 16) and so forms History and Nature in revolutionary fashion and after his own personal conception: Nature or reality is mere passive matter for this active, voluntarist "*artifex*" (J/M, 34).[4]

Pound's celebration of Mussolini as a wilful political artist probably derives ultimately from his misreading of Jacob Burckhardt's *The Civilization of the Renaissance in Italy,* in which Burckhardt describes the Italian Renaissance state as a "work of art" created by amoral "virtuosi" and overreachers. Strictly speaking, Burckhardt's famous phrase refers to the objective and systematic treatment of politics which the Italian Renaissance ushered in and within which there is in fact little room for artistic originality or caprice.[5] Pound, however, took the phrase literally and thus had no hesitation in applying aesthetic and stylistic standards to politics even to the confusion of politics and art: "I can cure the whole trouble simply by criticism of style," observes Pound: "Oh, can I? Yes. I have been saying so for some time" (J/M, 17). As Pound says of Mussolini's speech of October 6, 1934 in Milan: "The more one examines the Milan speech the more one is reminded of Brancusi, the stone blocks from which no error emerges, from whatever angle one looks at them. . . . Lily-livered litterati might very well exercise their perception of style on this oration" (J/M, viii). Since Pound insists that form and content are inseparable, one might argue that in admiring Mussolini's style he never neglects the content of his statements. But in actuality Pound's interest in political style can and does lead to an emphasis on style for its own sake, irrelevant aesthetic criteria, mere surfaces. For instance, Pound derives a sense of Fascist political hierarchy or "*gerarchia*" (an Italian Fascist byword) from the "four tiles and the dozen or so bits of insuperable pottery, pale blue or pale brownish ground, in the ante-room of the Palazzo Venezia" (J/M, 85). The notion of Mussolini as an artist persists into the Pisan *Cantos,* in which Pound, enraptured by memories of Mussolini's hollow pronouncements during the Salò Republic, the puppet state of the Nazis, speaks of "the old hand as stylist still holding its cunning" (78/478). Mussolini, who also thought of himself as an artist, would probably have admired this passage.[6]

Few writers confirm more strikingly than Pound does Walter Benjamin's observation that fascism aestheticizes politics.[7] Thanks to his equation of politics and art, Pound is able not only to explain Mussolini's actions but to explain away their contradictions. Insofar as the Duce is a passionate and privileged personality, for whom politics is a form of artistic expression, his actions are comprehensible not by logical analysis but only through the synthetic and sensuous immediacy of aesthetic intuition: "I don't believe my estimate of Mussolini is valid," says Pound, "unless it starts from his passion for construction. Treat him as *artifex* and all the details fall into place. Treat him as anything save the artist and you will get muddled with contradictions" (J/M, 33–34). This indifference to detail permits Pound to identify Mussolini and Jefferson; one should not, says Pound, trouble oneself over the "un-Jeffersonian details of his [Mussolini's] surfaces" (J/M, 34). The same indifference, most curious in a writer who usually demands close attention to concrete facts, also enables Pound to assert the perceptual superiority of his earliest favorable intuitions of the Italian Fascist movement: "It may be, of course, that one's intuition takes in the whole, and sees straight, whereas one's verbal receiving station or one's logic deals with stray detail, and that one's intuition can't get hold of the particular, but only of the whole" (J/M, 50). Pound justifies his perception of Fascism on essentially the same subjective and unanalyzable grounds as he justifies Mussolini's actions.

In keeping with these Poundian assumptions, Mussolini similarly celebrated "voluntarism," the power of the intensely subjective will to shape matter and to dominate, even create reality: in short, Mussolini claimed not so much that Italian Fascism transcended ideology but that everything was ultimately ideological. To quote Dante L. Germino: "Permeating the [Italian] Fascist *Weltanschauung* is the idea that reality possesses no principle or structure independent of those created by the human will."[8] Such imperiousness helps to explain why Pound, like Mussolini, was largely indifferent to political means so long as they fulfilled desired ends; as Pound said of Mussolini, "who wills the ends wills the means" (J/M, 34). It turns out, then, that "the orders of an omniscient despot and of an intelligent democracy would be very much alike in so far as they affected the main body of the country's economics" (SP, 248). Just as Pound is willing to accept a dictatorship in order to achieve economic "benevolence," so he praises Mussolini for his lack of interest in political forms as such, what Pound dismisses as "governmental machinery" (J/M, 62). Given Pound's constant praise of objectivity and his emphasis on the priority of the external world, it is entirely inconsistent for him to endorse so subjective and capricious a political philosophy. According to Karl Mannheim, Mussolini's "irrationalism of the deed" negates the possibility of a coherent interpretation of historical events, for history is understood finally to be without structure. Mannheim rightly adds, though, that "Not everything is possible in every situation."[9]

George L. Mosse finds a tension in Italian Fascist thought between the desire to cling to the nation's "immutable" and eternal roots in Nature and a more "dynamic" emphasis on speed, efficiency, and revolutionary change. He believes that Fascism was unable to reconcile this tension, the modernizing impulse or "time" winning out in the end. Pound's attitude toward Nature likewise reveals a deep ambivalence born of his commitment to time, history, change, voluntarism, and even progress, to that order which man forces or rescues from Nature itself (Mosse, 8: 240–241, 245). His much-vaunted faith in Nature is no greater than his fear of the encroaching and "beclouding" (SP, 332) HYLE, those vegetative powers which, in their effacement of man's historical marks, curiously resemble usury, supposedly their opposite. Although Pound traces intrinsic cultural value to Nature and the "teleological" power of plants to "increase" (GK, 357), he also perceives spontaneous growth and abundance as dangerous, akin to those instinctual forces which require civilizing restraint and measure. To quote Canto 51, which celebrates Hitler and fascism, the grass should be "nowhere out of place" (51/ 251).

It is no wonder that Pound admired technology and the masculine and aggressive ethos of the technocratic Italian Fascist state.[10] In Canto 18 Dave [Hamish?] in Ethiopia brings technology to a barbarous and ahistorical Nature; his power saw conquers in an instant the intractable jungle. This same conquest is repeated on a grander scale in Canto 40, in which Mussolini and Hanno conquer the primitive African marsh and "bayou." In Canto 38 Pound contrasts regressive Vienna, where "gothic type is still used / because the old folks are used" (38/ 189) to it, with the Russian Communists, who "put up a watch factory outside Moscow / And the watches kept time" (38/ 188), that is, brought Russia into the twentieth century. These are purely historical and technological events carried out in the interests of a long-delayed historical progress and patriarchal domination. There is nothing natural or mythical about them, nothing that really resembles them in Nature and myth, not even Hercules' defeat of the Lernaean Hydra.

The historical meaning Pound drew from Mussolini's conquest of Nature is further evident in numerous instances in which Pound identifies the bog or swamp not only with the usurious but with the static or ahistorical: the "soggy" and "inchoate . . . mess" of Communism (after the heroic Lenin), the "bog" of the "Hun hinterland" (J/M, 34), the harbor drained by Palmerston in Canto 52, atavistic and miscegenous Vienna in Cantos 38 and 50.[11] Such a commitment as Pound's to the historical enterprise means that violence of some sort must inevitably be done to Nature, which is not the same as history. But in an ideology such as his, which appeals to timeless Nature as a normative idea, the violence that man does to Nature—and this includes the human instincts—must be disguised and concealed. One of Pound's ways of concealing such violence is to create a myth of cyclical time, whereby all historical changes that he happens to advocate are referred back to original and seasonal myths. Another way is to create a myth of naturalized technology, whereby technological man, instead of arbitrarily delimiting and imposing his will upon Nature and instinct (human nature), lovingly educes from both the forms and capacities latent within them. And another way is to rely on a broad and overdetermined concept such as usury (and the Jews) as a kind of metaphysical opposite of both natural and historical life.

II.

In one of the most pessimistic moments of the radio broadcasts Pound speaks of a multifarious evil that he is nearly powerless to combat:

> [This evil] destroys all scale and all sense of proportionate values. It calls to the basic laziness of the mind, the basic softness of human organism. It profanes. It soils, it is greasy and acid. It revolts all men who have any desire toward cleanliness. But it entangles the clean, it entangles them because of their inconsequentiality, their inability to see the connection between one thing and another. *Facilis descensus*. (RB, 238–239)

Besides usury, "tangle" suggests a swamp-like growth. The Latin phrase comes from the *Aeneid*, where it is easy to descend to the swamp of Hell but hard to find the way back up to the light. Here, though, the swamp has no clear connection with the Jews. Nor does it seem unnatural. It resembles the chaos mentioned in a later broadcast:

> . . . The Fascist ideal is well nigh unattainable; not from wrong direction, not from lack of aim toward organization, but from the natural chaos of man, the unfailing laziness of the average man, who WILL not be bothered to organize, who can not be persuaded to organize . . . . (RB, 287).

To defeat the swamp, Fascism must overcome not only the Jews but the natural human tendency towards softness, something Pound here doubts can be accomplished.

And yet, though Pound is capable of seeing chaos as typically human, he finds its most developed representation in Jewish Mitteleuropa (read Vienna), which appears in Canto 35. This canto opens with the implication of Jewish cowardice in Mr. Corles (Mr. Heartless, man without a core, based on the half-Jewish writer Alfred Perles), who, as a "commander of machine guns" (35/ 172) left his post but escaped court martial by having his family send him to a "mind sanitorium"; this suggests what Pound states elsewhere, that psychoanalysis is an evasion of moral responsibility. Shortly Pound announces:

> this is Mitteleuropa
> and Tsievitz
> has explained to me the warmth of affections,

the intramural, the almost intravaginal warmth of
hebrew affections, in the family, and nearly everything else. . . .
pointing out that Mr. Lewinesholme has suffered by deprivation
of same and exposure to American snobbery . . . "I am a product,"
said the young lady, "of Mitteleuropa,"
but she seemed to have been able to mobilize
and the fine thing was that the family did not
wire about papa's death for fear of disturbing the concert
which might seem to contradict the general indefinite wobble.
It must be rather like some internal organ,
some communal life of the pancreas . . . . sensitivity
without direction . . . this is . . .

(35/ 172–173)

"Intravaginal warmth" hints at Jewish incest, a concept inseparable in Pound's mind from Freud. "Communal life of the pancreas" represents the Jews as tribal and hence lacking individuality and the impulse to struggle actively with the external world.[12] It also reflects Pound's recurrent tendency to identify the Jews, such as Obermeyer, the endocrine specialist, with the vague and mysterious stirrings of glands, microorganisms, and rebellious cells. Protected by their tribe, and owing their sensitivity to an "internal organ," rather than the protrusive phallus, the Jews are sensitive "without direction," see no need actively to shape and understand external reality. If anything they are merely passive "product[s]" of their environment. Pound thus shows surprise at the emotional restraint and even martial forcefulness ("mobilized") of the young lady from Mitteleuropa, a rare exception to the "general indefinite wobble" of Jewish life. In short, the Jews are the primary form of the "natural softness of man." Their essential femininity stands at the farthest remove from Pound's "entire man" and "factive personality" .(GK, 194), the warrior Sigismundo Malatesta, who represents the "direction of the will." Nor can the Jews appreciate the phallic artist, who actively struggles with the stone.[13]

Pound's hostility to Jewish sensitiveness depends not on a complete rejection of emotion, but on the assumption that Jewish culture is entirely sentimental, a far cry from Anglo-Saxon self-control (Maccoby: 64):

Mr. Elias said to me:
        "How do you get inspiration?
"Now my friend Hall Caine told me he came on a case
"a very sad case of a girl in the East End of London
"and it gave him an i n s p i r a t i o n. The only
"way I get inspiration is occasionally from a girl, I
"mean sometimes sitting in a restaurant and
            looking at a pretty girl I
"get an i-de-a, I-mean-a biz-nis i-de-a?"
        dixit sic felix Elias?
The tale of the perfect schnorrer: a peautiful chewisch poy
wit a vo-ice dot woult
meldt dh heart offa schtone

and wit a likeing for to make ahrt-voiks
and ven dh oldt ladty wasn't dhere any more
and dey didn't know why, tdhere ee woss in the
oldt antique schop and nobodty knew how he got dhere
and venn hiss brudder diet widout any bapers
he vept all ofer dh garpet so much he
had to have his clothes aftervards pressed
and he orderet a magnifficent funeral
and tden zent dh pill to dh vife.

(35/ 174)

Elias's egoistic inspiration contrasts with Cavalcanti's true penetration of erotic mystery in the next canto; it results from a casual and sentimental encounter while eating a meal. Pound also implies that Elias exploits his emotions for profit: he writes best-sellers. A similar emotional opportunism is evident in the "schnorrer," who has a mere "likeing" for art, hangs around antique shops (thus acting as a parasite on Western culture), and organizes a sentimental funeral for which he is unwilling to pay. Pervading this passage is Pound's belief that the Jews lack good manners. Although Pound generally tries to endow his conception of civility with a Confucian ethical aura and legitimacy—the line "Confucius later taught the world good manners" appears in the Ur-*Cantos*—for all practical purposes his conception is that of the Gentile middle class.[14] In *Hugh Selwyn Mauberley,* Brennbaum cannot relax "into grace" (PER, 193), a failing which encompasses social clumsiness and impropriety (for which Pound himself was well known) and exclusion from the Christian community. Not only does this caricature conform with Pound's view of the Jewish tribal records' hostility to "polite civilization" (GK, 330), it looks forward to the radio broadcasts, in which Pound praises the Nazis for having "wiped out bad manners in Germany" (RB, 32). The schnorrer's voice, meanwhile, does the opposite of Pound's stonecarver, who preserves the stone's outlines; it can "meldt dh heart offa schtone," induce cheap and flabby emotions in an audience. Nothing could less resemble the ideal of fascism or of Confucius, who placed "constant emphasis . . . on the value of personality, on the outlines of personality, on the man's right to preserve the outlines of his personality . . ." (SP, 193). Nor is it difficult to see the attraction of Confucian hardness to a poet who, according to the novelist Phyllis Bottome, "wore his brain outside of him like a skin," and whose "terrific exposure" thus "made him always vulnerable and frequently hostile."[15]

Insofar as Vienna is the capital of the Austro-Hungarian Empire, which Pound later describes as the home of "embastardized cross-breeds" (50/ 247), Canto 35 cannot be dissociated ideologically from his later attacks on the American "melting pot" (RB, 157, 94/ 641). At the same time, Pound's denunciation of Jewish culture in Canto 35 anticipates his later overt proposals to purge America of Jews and to establish a quarantine against Jewish immigration. This is evident if one considers Canto 35 in relation to Canto

34, in which Pound, drawing upon the diary of John Quincy Adams, twice refers to the Jewish-American journalist, diplomat, and publisher Mordecai Noah (1785–1851). In the first instance Adams observes that "Mr. Noah has a project for colonizing Jews in this country / and wd. like a job in Vienna" (34/ 168). Adams's diary shows that Noah sought the post of Chargé d'Affaires in Vienna to further his plans for Jewish colonization; it also reveals Adams's dislike of Noah, who as consul at Tunis was recalled for "indiscretions." Later in this canto one learns that Noah had established the city of Ararat, which Adams passed through in 1843 on a trip to Buffalo, and whose founding Noah commemorated with a pyramid inscribed in English and Hebrew.[16] The pyramid and inscription are given on the last page of Canto 34. Although the references to Noah are presented without comment, their political significance becomes obvious in relation to Canto 35: Noah seeks to import onto American soil all the chaos of Jewish Mitteleuropa, the center of which is Vienna. In Canto 38 Pound mentions that "gothic type" is "still used in Vienna," further evidence of its cultural regression from Roman order, and then records a remark by an unidentified speaker who may have been a "stool-pigeon against the Anschluss" (38/ 189), that is, Hitler's forceful unification of Germany and Austria. Undoubtedly Pound favored the Anschluss as a necessary means of draining the Viennese "bog."

There is a certain irony in Pound's attempt to identify the Jews with a reprehensible confusion, interiority, and softness. In fact, America in Canto 29 is characterized by the "chaos" of the undried "feminine" and the vague "osmosis of persons" (29/ 144–145). Yet Pound most frequently associates the Jews above all others not only with the fluidity of the body's inner life but with the diseases that afflict it: bacilli, glandular disorders, etc. He also associates the Jews and one Jew in particular with a realm as mysterious as the inner body: the unconscious mind, in which are buried man's repressed feelings and instincts. In the broadcasts the swamp (and the Jews) is the source of dangerous bacilli which, like usury, are incommensurable and unnameable. Earlier, in the *New English Weekly*, Pound had identified the unconscious with the swamp and bacillary infections. The "whole subject" of psychiatry, wrote Pound, is a "quagmire," the "submarine" road to "insanity." Emphasizing the "subjective" and ignoring the "relative importance of the total external world," Freud is probably a neurotic while psychiatrists themselves are " 'going bugs' ": "The whole system of poking round with a forceps for minute bits of mental dust, that an invigorated organism would extrude itself, is, to put it mildly, open to question." Later in the article Pound says that "if a civilized man to-day cuts his finger, he swobs on a little iodine (when possible) and goes on about his affairs uninterrupted, he doesn't normally set up as amateur bacteriologist to see what he can grow in the fissure."[17]

As in his earlier reference to "mental dust," Pound conflates two different orders of understanding: physical processes and mental states. Pound had little grasp of Freud and his metaphor of infection makes little sense. Obviously, iodine on a cut prevents infection from without, but what is the equivalent of iodine for a serious psychic wound? The best that Pound can recommend is a version of stoicism and enforced forgetfulness; one should proceed with one's affairs. But bacilli "can grow in the fissure" and, as Pound implies, lead an unacknowledged life of their own. Thus the growth of unnameable and invisible bacilli is identified with the proliferation of unconscious mental states which Pound wants to forget or repress. It is evident why Pound denounced the "germy epoch of Freud" (L, 260).

In *Jefferson and/or Mussolini* Pound confronts again the issue of Freud and psychoanalysis:

> As one of the Bloomsbury weepers once remarked, "Freud's writings may not shed much light on human psychology but they tell one a good deal about the private life of the Viennese."
> They are flower of a deliquescent society going to pot. The average human head is less in need of having something removed from it, than of having something inserted.
> The freudized ex-neurasthenic, oh well, pass it for the neurasthenic, but the general results of Freud are Dostoievskian duds, worrying about their own unimportant innards with the deep attention of Jim drunk occupied with the crumb on his weskit.
> I see no advantage in this system over the ancient Roman legion. NO individual worth saving is likely to be wrecked by a reasonable obedience practiced to given ends and for limited periods. So much for commandments to the militia as superior to psychic sessions for the debilitated.
> That which makes a man forget his bellyache (physical or psychic) is probably as healthy as concentration of his attention on the analysis of the products or educts of a stomach pump. (J/M, 100–101)

Miscegenous and deliquescent Vienna, a "slough" of "embastardized crossbreeds" (50/ 247), imports not just Freud but the Jews.[18] Indeed, it cannot be emphasized enough that by this point Pound identifies the processes of the unconscious with the Jews; like the "sewers of Pal'stine," the "sewers" of Freudian and Jewish Vienna threaten the supposedly natural life of man.[19] Writing of Pound at St. Elizabeths, E. Fuller Torrey observes that the "fact that Freud was Jewish clearly contributed to Pound's dislike of him. . . . And on at least two occasions Dorothy Pound referred to psychiatrists as if they were all Jewish" (Torrey: 250). Pound also identifies the Jews with the unconscious, specifically a kind of instinctive automatism, in a letter of March 11, 1940 to T.S. Eliot: "Possibly all semitic activity is evil, I mean unconsciously and without their meaning it."[20] The Semitic infection is thus "carried" by creatures which, like rats or vermin, and equally disposable, are "wholly unconscious of their role" (SP, 317). Meantime, in *Jefferson and/or Mussolini* Pound again represents the inner mind in terms of the body, in this case that part of it which is most familiar, intimate, appetitive,

and primordial: the stomach.[21] He implies that the contents of the unconscious are like the poisonous educts of a stomach pump. Although this
metaphor seems odd, Pound often compares mental processes to the consumption and digestion of food, and he also compares Europe's usurious
diseases to gastric disorders. These metaphors suggest that the external
invasion upon the body of Europe is indistinguishable from an invasion
from within the European mind itself.

Even so, Pound denounces the impulse to examine one's "unimportant
innards" and suggests that one should forget one's mental bellyache. Yet the
antidote to introspection that Pound proposes is most disproportionate to
the insignificance of the innards and their disease. It is nothing less than his
version of the Roman legion, which insures forgetfulness and promotes
obedience and order. Here Pound is pitting both Mussolini and Italian
Fascism against Freud. In his deep hostility to psychoanalysis, as in his desire
for "a language to deny the unconscious," Pound again conforms to a
familiar fascist pattern.[22]

Unquestionably Pound's hatred of the Jews stems in part from their
connection with the modern and "Mitteleuropaisch" philosophies of introspection and subjectivity. As Pound wrote to Lewis:

> Proust and Freud are unmitigated shit/ they pass for intelligentsia because
> their shit is laid out in most elaborate arabesques . . .
> A good socking platitude in the jaw may be a perfectly good way of
> clearing off a lot of this sewage. (P/L, 218)

Outraged at the disclosure of what should remain hidden (excrement, with
unconscious associations of guilt), Pound responds violently and repres-
sively.[23] In the broadcasts the same hostility and fear is apparent when
Pound says that Freud and Bergson are "crawlin' through the crevices"
(RB, 115).

Pound's reptilian imagery is telling. He attacks the Jews not because
they are unnatural, as he believes, but because these supposedly "primitive
types" (RB, 85) represent the all-too natural: the "quagmire" of the instinctual and appetitive inner life, which is ever present to man and yet ever alien,
which can never be adequately represented or known. At the same time
Pound identifies the Jews with the "excess" of the feelings and the emotions,
with all that seems to him fluid, soft, and feminine.[24] Finally, he identifies
them with stages of man's historical development which seem prehistorical,
close to unbounded, undifferentiated, chaotic nature. Thus the Jews stand
for everything which fascist civilization must overcome in its pursuit of
definition and hard outline, of monolithic rigidity and solidity. One understands, then, why Pound accuses the Jews of being "atavistic" (RB, 302),
and why he associates them with crocodiles, "big noses" (RB, 346), "sewers," "odorous swindles" (RB, 345), "stink" (RB, 302), and, more specifically, the "stinks" of "Doctor Freud" (RB, 144). Not only is the sense of

smell the most intensely repressed of all the senses, it also possesses preeminently (as Proust and Eliot understood) the power of unlocking the doors of memory and the unconscious, what Pound referred to as "instink" (P/L, 203). To quote Otto Fenichel: "One's unconscious is also foreign. Foreignness is the quality which the Jews and one's own instincts have in common." He adds that "rejected instincts and rejected ancient times are revived" in the minds of Gentile observers "in these incomprehensible people who live as strangers in their midst." In the Jews "that which they had believed overcome appears to rise again and again like a hydra, and they try to cut off its heads."[25]

III.

The foregoing may seem to contradict Pound's stated interests and intentions, for he is attracted to the instincts and seeks to draw on their vital powers. Besides celebrating sexuality in his translation of Gourmont's *Natural Philosophy of Love,* Pound claims that the Vortex is driven by "RACE, RACE-MEMORY, instinct."[26] It is also well known that fascism extolled the primitive and instinctual as an answer to bourgeois repressiveness.[27] Nonetheless, Pound's appeal to Mussolini, fascism, and the Roman militia undoubtedly signals repression. We should therefore examine Pound's conception of instinct and show where that conception is problematic.

Pound argues not just for the complementarity of intelligence and instinct, but for the inadequacy of that "scholastic" distinction, and perhaps for the superiority of instinctual over purely conscious or intellectual activity.[28] Far from being in all cases prior to intelligence, instinct may also be its "result," the last stage "of countless acts of intellection, something after and not before reason" (GK, 195). Since Pound distrusts intelligence in the sense of merely conscious thought, he desires that it pass over, through education, into that instinct which is distinctly "cultural" (GK, 134, 195) and which manifests itself in "action" (J/M, 18). There are, says Pound, "ideas, facts, notions" that are "in one's stomach or liver [again the inner organs are metaphors for the unconscious], one doesn't have to remember them, though they now and again make themselves felt" (GK, 56–57).

What seems problematic is the weight placed on forgetfulness and un-self-consciousness in this conception of cultural instinct and activity. There is an analogy here between Pound and Carlyle, another renegade from Protestant culture who surpassed Pound in his awareness of the instincts and the dependence of high cultural achievement on sublimated instinctual energy. Central to much of Carlyle's work is his anti-self-consciousness theory: in order to evade the obstructing worm of consciousness and introspection, and to harness instinctual forces for socially productive ends, the self must forget itself: only in self forgetfulness can it fulfill itself in activity or work.[29] But Carlyle's anti-self-consciousness reveals the same ambiguity as appears in Pound. For it is entirely possible to confuse the un-self-conscious vitality of free instinctive activity with the self-forgetfulness that accompanies such repressive acts of automatism as the goosestep. Just as Carlyle moved from a theory of anti-self-consciousness to a celebration of Prussian militarism and authoritarianism, so Pound gave the Italian Fascist salute on a number of occasions and appealed to the "Roman legion" to enforce forgetfulness of the unconscious.[30] This is not to imply that Pound always thought this way; but such thinking is implicit in his fascism and anti-Semitism.[31]

Chapter 10

Nature, Race, and History, II

Although Pound's view of Nature and human nature already seems contradictory, there is no question that he saw himself on Nature's side. It therefore remains to be shown in greater detail what this concept means to Pound. First, however, let us briefly consider the twentieth-century French political theorist Charles Maurras, whose concept of "Nature" bears a striking resemblance to Pound's, and who helps in the definition of Pound's political identity. Such a comparison is not undermined by the fact that Pound criticizes Maurras and *Action Française* for ignoring finance and usury,[1] and that Pound was not a thoroughgoing and obsessive monarchist, as was Maurras; such differences are finally trivial. Nor is it especially significant that Maurras favored localistic rather than centralized government, whereas Pound, despite his admiration of local government and defense of state's rights, came to accept a high degree of political centralization and authority in his later career. Nor would this comparison necessarily hinge on Maurras's alleged fascism. Although Maurras was a rabid anti-Semite, one can make the argument that he was not a fascist but a radical conservative, an exponent of traditional values and hierarchy. Were Pound's politics finally of the Maurrasian type, then one might perhaps find a place for him as well within radical conservatism; he too would be an apostle not so much of fascist mass revolution as of traditional order, as in Confucian China. On the other hand, it is equally plausible that many of Maurras's values, especially his concepts of Nature, anti-Nature, and the Jewish "enemy," not only anticipate fascism but are compatible with it. Maurras, and Pound at the very least, marks that point where radical conservatism becomes "pre-" or "proto-fascism."[2]

Maurras conceives of Nature as a permanent, beautiful, and ordered unity (*cosmos*) which exists prior to man. Being within rather than outside of Nature, man is properly the faithful follower of her immutable decrees. The healthy state must recognize man's unchanging essence or nature and hence the unchanging natural laws of human society. Far from being abstract or theoretical, or based on human "caprice," this society must cohere with concrete reality, the truth of Nature. As Maurras says, "there are ideas which are consistent with reality and these are the true ideas." Man, then, "work[s] with Nature," and so creates a society attuned to the "natural rhythms of the manifold and the beautiful." Human society is the "offspring of nature's union" or marriage "with reason."[3]

In pursuing the "natural" basis of society, many fascist and proto-fascist thinkers arrived at the idea of preserving "naturally" occurring and "traditional" groups. Individual fascists, however, were not in agreement on the character of these entities. Hitler embraces biological racism while Pound emphasizes racial theorizing, a defense of various national identities, and a corporate view of Europe. But in Maurras the racial idea in the biological sense is less important. For him the nation, specifically non-Jewish France, is the permanent form of the naturally-occurring group (Nolte: 182–183, 140–143).

Since Nature, according to Maurras, is a beautiful and all-encompassing unity, human societies must be unified and inclusive too. Moreover, since Nature is hierarchical, characterized by "beautiful inequalities" among creatures and things, and since biology decrees natural inequalities among men, sharp hierarchical distinctions must be maintained within the group. The purpose of the state is twofold: to build unity among men; and to differentiate each individual and each group within society according to the organic functions which it provides for the whole. When a society is truly hierarchical, organic, and functional, it reflects the beauty of cosmos itself.[4]

Maurras has only contempt for democracy, pluralism, and the entire emancipatory movement which the French Revolution had set into motion. He repeatedly asserts that the "hysterical yearning for independence" and the doctrine of "indeterminate freedom" have imposed a false concept of "general" or "absolute" humanity on a differentiated society and so reduced it to an aggregate of warring atoms; these doctrines and impulses have isolated the individual, raised self-interest over the common interest, and ignored the permanent and natural inequalities between men. Freedom for Maurras is not a right but a duty to perform one's natural function within the social hierarchy; rather than authorizing men "to break ranks in disorder, it is the binding force against death, it is the defensive force against division." Maurras thus asserts the primacy of the natural and the social over the individual. His recurrent tendency is to think in terms of families and corporations rather than individuals. He envisions state and society as an enormous family reflecting patriarchal authority at each level of the social hierarchy.[5]

For Pound as well Nature is an immutable order or "cosmos": "I take it [cosmos] to mean a *sense of gradations*. Things neither perfect nor utterly wrong, but arranged in a cosmos, an order, stratified, having relations one with another" (SP, 150). Like Maurras, Pound locates the origin of this idea

in the Mediterranean: Athens and Sparta developed a "system of graduations, an hierarchy of values" (SP, 150). But by comparison with Dante,
Pound as modern necessarily has a more attenuated and yet open-ended
conception of cosmos. Where Dante had an "Aquinas-map" (L, 323),
Pound has only a general sense of the interconnection of one thing with
another.

Cosmos implies that the world or Nature is an organic whole with
concrete differences and "detail[s]" (92/ 620) and hierarchical relations
among its component parts: the sun is "under" and over "it all" (85/ 544).
No matter if the usurers and "barbaroi" (76/ 459) seek "lopsidedness" (99/
700) and division, the center holds, the "cosmos continues" (87/ 573) as a
total, all-inclusive "process" (74/ 425). Historical errors and cataclysms
result from man's failure to recognize the ontological priority of Nature and
his place within it: "First came the seen, then thus the palpable / Elysium,
though it were in the halls of hell" (81/ 521). They result too from his failure
to grasp the "enduring constants in human composition" (GK, 47), the
"permanent human process" (SP, 86).

The true human society cannot be based on "abstract," subjective, or
"theoretical" (SP, 168) constructs, but must reflect the actual nature of
reality and man. Pound gives beautiful poetic expression to this idea: "Learn
of the green world what can be thy place / in scaled invention or true
artistry" (81/ 521). The key words are "scaled" and "place," implying that
Nature (and human society) form an organic system of "manifest" (92/ 620)
gradations and differences; this is precisely what Pound, borrowing a central
term and concept of Italian Fascism, means when he speaks of the
"*gerarchia* (hierarchy) in nature" (J/M, 116). Just as Nature is differentiated, so there are "biological" (J/M, 114, viii) differences and inequalities
among individuals and groups, each of which must find a proper natural
and social "place." In order to reflect cosmos, which is synonymous with
order and Beauty ("TO KALON," RB, 193), human society must be arranged into organic hierarchies and functions. It must aspire toward that
totality and unity which the "process" constantly reveals.

Pound's support of fascism and his Confucianism develop directly from
his ideas of Nature and man. Not Italian Fascism, however, but Confucian
China most fully exemplifies Pound's ideal society. As Pound remarks in
1941, "Mussolini and Hitler follow through with magnificent intuition the
doctrines of Confucius," and he later attributes the shortcomings of both
leaders to their failure to conform to Confucian ideals.[6] This does not mean
that Confucian thought is fascistic, but that Pound tends to ignore the
differences between fascism and Confucianism. As early as Canto 62 Pound
sees in Hitler's motto "Schicksal" (Fate, Destiny, implying Nature's sanction
and retributive justice) (62/ 345, SP, 66) the nearest modern equivalent to
the teachings of *The Sacred Edict of K'ang Hsi*. In the Chinese *Cantos* he
links China's agrarian system to the "ammassi" (53/ 262) or grain pools of

Fascist Italy and makes an anachronistic reference to a Chinese "charter of labor" (54/ 287) in the seventh century A.D. One is thus to believe that the ancient Chinese anticipated the Italian Fascist Carta del Lavoro. When Pound traces Chinese social divisiveness to the failure of men to co-exist as "rods in a bundle" (53/ 272), he is referring to the *fasces*. In Canto 55 those Chinese bureaucrats who resist the economic reforms of the minister Ngan are "sent to the confino" (55/ 297); the analogy is with Mussolini's policy of punishing his political enemies with exile and confinement (*confino*), as in Canto 41. In the later *Cantos* Confucian China is no easier to distinguish from fascist order. Pound's injunction to "Incorporate" (99/ 707), applied to Chinese society, connects ancient China and the fascist corporate state: the Chinese "State is corporate, / as with pulse in its body" (99/ 707). Likewise, the "organization[s]" of Confucian society are "functional" (99/ 696), reflecting the idea that people should attend to their proper callings— that is, fit within a traditional hierarchy of roles. Although these may be examples of creative translation, Pound is aware that the terms "corporate" and "functional" derive not from a Confucian but Italian Fascist lexicon. Pound, after fascism became a liability, expresses his Fascist ideology under cover of Confucianism, just as he expresses his hatred of Jews under cover of a Confucian attack on Buddhists and Taoists. Nor should one forget that Pound constantly identifies the axe in the *hsin* ideogram with the axe of Italian Fascism.

Pearlman writes that "Confucian philosophy, founded on the essential nature of things, is universally applicable to the social condition of man regardless of time and place" (Pearlman, 1: 212). Thus, in Canto 99, Confucians "seek to include" (99/ 702), to observe that "plan" which "is in nature" (99/ 709), to link "Heaven, man, earth" (99/ 698) in an indissoluble unity: this is partly what Pound means when he says that Confucian society, like myth and like fascism, is "totalitarian" (SP, 87). Such a society is supposedly based on original principles or *arche* existing in Nature, an "awareness" of the "filiality that binds things together" (98/ 686). This really means that Confucian society is a rigid traditional hierarchy character-ized by patriarchal and feudal values and the ideals of the "homestead." As in Maurras, an "inclusive" filiality "binds" sons to fathers, wives to hus-bands, and all men to their rulers. If Pound has more praise for Confucius than for Mussolini, it is because he stabilized social life, subordinated the "anarchic" claims of the individual to those of society and the state. Nowhere in Cantos 98 and 99 does Pound, elsewhere a great defender of "personality" (SP, 193–195, 207–212), reveal suspicion that personality may have been repressed, undernourished, and even sacrificed by the Confu-cians. He contemplates a human order whose "colour" (98/ 689, 693) is the same as Nature's and which, in its traditional continuity, seems as unchang-ing as Nature itself.

Insofar as Pound would collapse as much as possible the difference between Nature and Culture, man's social behavior finds its true sanction in incontrovertible natural laws and regularities, supposedly objective "facts." This is a version of what Karl Popper terms "naive monism," which he traces to Plato and earlier, and which he views as the characteristic outlook of ancient and modern versions of the "closed society." Like Pound's China, such a society exists in a "closed circle of unchanging taboos, of laws and customs which are felt to be as inevitable as the rising of the sun, as the cycle of the seasons, or similar obvious regularities of nature." In this mystified environment Nature and society are linked in a magical rapport. By contrast, the open society is characterized by "critical dualism," the belief that normative human laws derive not from Nature but from human decisions and conventions, and hence are subject to criticism and change. For the critical dualist natural facts or occurrences are neutral, and therefore provide no basis for moral decisions. According to Popper, critical dualism was discovered by the Greek philosophers. Predictably, Pound complains of the "unvital" or "unnatural" dualism of the Greeks as opposed to the "holism" and "organicism" of Confucius, a classic intellectual exemplar of the closed society.[7]

II.

Given his conception of Nature, Pound, like Wyndham Lewis, sees himself as a conservative opponent of the historicist tendencies of the modern world. Pound also resembles many conservatives in rejecting modern doctrines of historical progress and especially the utopian ideologies of Marx and Rousseau, who supposedly ignore the concrete facts of Nature (and human nature), create historical abstractions, threaten to overturn tradition, and confine man in an ideological straightjacket.[8] The greatness of Mussolini, observes Pound, is that he pursues not an "ideal republic situated in a platonic paradise but an arrangement possible in Italy in the year VIII or IX of the Era Fascista" (J/M, 57). A problem arises, however, in Pound's endorsement or acceptance of the new "functional" hierarchy of Italian Fascism. As George L. Mosse points out, the true conservative thinks in terms of traditional, inherited hierarchies, hierarchies of status. But the fascist, being a revolutionary, conceives of hierarchies of function, which are theoretically "fluid" in their "circulation" and "open to all."[9] Another problem lies in the fact that Pound has not only an ideology but a strong utopian impulse.[10] The emergence of such utopianism, inseparable from Pound's embrace of revolutionary fascism, discloses perhaps the most glaring contradiction in his thought. Obviously, the conservative who envisions utopias and speaks glowingly of the "Fascist revolution" (J/M, 113, 127) has ceased to be a true conservative: herein is what Fritz Stern describes as the "characteristic predicament of conservative revolutionaries."[11] The deeper question is why the true society must be achieved by violent revolutionary action? If, as Pound says, "the nature of things is good" (SP, 87), why doesn't the natural and conservative society exist naturally? Why is it that "disease," the negative principle, "is more contagious than health" (SP, 227)?

Pound's position is characteristic of fascism. Beginning as a conservative counter-revolutionary, Hitler had wanted to anchor man and society within an immutable and "inviolable" natural order based on instincts and laws. Yet Hitler discovered that Nature itself was under attack by "one great process" of disease; unable to let Nature simply take its course, he was forced to take arms against its numerous enemies, chief of whom were the Jews. Hitler thus arrived at a formula identical to Pound's: "disease, . . . the negative [principle], . . . emerges more strongly than the positive, . . . good health."[12]

Still, there would seem to be little similarity between Pound and either Hitler or Maurras. Where Hitler and Maurras fear for the continued vitality of culture, Nature, and cosmos, the anti-dualistic Pound often appears as a kind of cosmic optimist and meliorist. Yet the note of cosmic pessimism and anxiety makes its appearance in Pound's most revelatory moments. "We find," says Pound in "A Visiting Card," "two forces in history: one that divides, shatters, and kills, and one that contemplates the unity of the mystery" (SP, 306). Earlier, Pound had denied that

> the history of China, or Chinese historic process, suffers a dichotomy or split into two opposite forces, as does that of Europe. Not, that is, unless you want to set Buddhism and Taoism together as a sort of Guelf party. And even then that wouldn't be a decent analogy. (SP, 67)

This anxiety is nothing compared to that expressed in the radio broadcasts. For Pound, as for Hitler, cultural and racial deterioration is indistinguishable from the natural struggle for existence:

> . . . You [the U.S.] don't even know whether your various races of European origin will or CAN survive on a continent that has seen the fade-out of Mayas and Aztecs. And you have an ORGANIZED minority of a different race amongst you. A race that never tires, a race possessed of subcrocodilian vitality. (RB, 187)

The subcrocodilian race is the Jews, who obliterate—but in an entirely natural if "invisible" way—the natural marks inscribed in the European genetic code. In another passage Pound notes the repeated attrition of the European fiber:

> . . . Simple-minded European tribesmen fell for it [the Jewish religion, masquerading as Christianity], were weakened during about 1600 years, continual attrition. Wonder we're here at all. Must be something tough in European and Mediterranean fibre. (RB, 188)

Such constant attrition implies the inherent weakness of the European nature; it even seems miraculous that Europe and Nature itself should have survived. But Pound, ever the "optimist," covers himself by taking such tenuous survival as a proof of strength.

Far from being naturally dominant, the forces of Nature and good know only a precarious circumscribed success; ironically, Pound must attribute this success to miracle:

> Machiavelli Senior remarked: "Men live in a few, and the rest are sheep." The idealists struggle against that. An occasional miracle happens. In China men have set up a series of dynasties. Acts of heroic creation, 160 to build or continue, and 160 years to decline. (RB, 287–288)

Pound's utopias, like those of Maurras, are not so much the products of Nature as of chance and luck; only at rare and unpredictable intervals do the culture heroes (Mussolini, Napoleon, Malatesta, Confucius) succeed in imposing their wills upon human nature, the natural softness of human sheep.[13] In these terms the historical vision of *The Cantos,* so often taken as optimistic, can better be read as an example of fascist despair over the gradual "fading" of "paideuma" (87/ 569), the "unnatural" and perhaps finally inexplicable attrition wreaked by history against the "true" human nature and the natural society. Nor is it accidental that Pound's most memorable poetic confrontations with history are elegiac, and that his elegiac voice is characterized by a falling rhythm which is unique to Pound and which evokes the melancholy of historical attrition and decline.

Undoubtedly Pound finds himself in the same contradictory position as do Hitler and other fascists. "The *way,*" he says, "is the process of nature, *one*" (SP, 87). Yet everywhere he looks Pound sees a massive disruption of natural process by bacilli, parasites, cancers. He thus encounters the difficulty that increasingly characterizes radical conservative thought since the French Revolution: "that of explaining the illegitimate power of the enemy in all its limitless facticity." To explain this power Pound must implicitly invoke a concept which splits his world apart. This concept, as in Hitler, is anti-Nature, and its chief representative is the Jews.[14]

III.

For Maurras one of the most dangerous forms of "anti-Nature" is abstraction, which he identifies with virtually all kinds of metaphysical, theoretical, and political thought; his unyielding classicism demands "precise definitions" ("Définitions certaines") and abhors all that is "blind or symbolic" (Maurras, 1: lxxiii; 2: 22–23). Like Maurras, Pound locates Leibniz at the transition between scientific concreteness and speculative abstraction: "After Leibniz' time the professional philosopher was . . . too damned lazy to work in a laboratory . . . [or] at an art. . . . I assert that there are immoral mathematics" (GK, 78).[15] Of these, Pound most deplores the "immoral geometries" of the Jews Freud and Bergson. The tendency to obliterate "moral gradations" is also "Semitic," and the mental and moral corruption of Europe begins with "the revival of semitic texts as a basis of metaphor, as mythology."[16] Elsewhere Pound charges that the Kabbalistic Jews have introduced allegorical interpretation into the West and thus distracted men "from the plain sense of the word, or the sentence" (RB, 284).[17]

The most dangerous form of abstraction affects man's spiritual life. Maurras "never had any doubts as to the most prominent indication of the anti-natural in man." It is the "[human] heart, which is capable of dedicating itself to a single absolute and thus of transcending and destroying the beautiful unity of the manifold, its true domain." Maurras therefore sought to "render harmless the infinite and absolute principle . . . in human relations," and especially those "secularized monotheisms" such as liberalism, which in Maurras's view had their origin in Jewish monotheism. With its pretentions to universality, monotheism leads man beyond Nature, disintegrates human relations within the naturally-occurring group, and destroys the love of beauty and order. Maurras furthermore rejects the "sovereignty" of "any human will and of the conscience," that socially-destructive "profession of faith" which reduces religious life to "the god within oneself."[18]

When Pound says that each nation should appear "in the name of its god" (79/ 487), he challenges the original text of Micah (4: 5) and affirms his belief that each nation must create its god or gods under its local and "natural" circumstances.[19] Pound thus abhors any transcendental or universalizing impulse whereby men "want to bust out of the kosmos" (105/ 750) or the "universe" (102/ 731), to establish a "parasitic relationship with the unknown" (SP, 216). This explains his attacks not only on Jews but Hindus, Buddhists, and Taoists. Where Confucians "seek to include" (99/ 702), Hindus "lust after vacuity" (95/ 646) and seek an "escape mechanism" in the "Ultimate Unity" (SP, 75), while Buddhists define "Man by negation" (99/ 702) of his natural qualities, and Taoists are "wholly subjective," seeking drugs and "pills" to quell the "moaning Dragon" (99/ 696) of inner life and "babbling" of "elixir[s]" (54/ 288) that promise man immortality. They all would "destroy" those "5 human relations" (98/ 687) which bind man to society and concrete, immediate Nature: "their mania is a lusting for farness / Blind to the olive leaf, / not seeking the oak's veins" (107/ 762–763). Pound altogether prefers Confucianism, which is as "natural" to the Chinese "as is water to fishes" (54/ 285) (Nolde: 74).

Like Maurras, Pound believes that interest in absolute spirit or personal immortality leads man away from Nature and tends toward the destruction of social responsibility and the social fabric: "the concentration or emphasis on eternity is not social" (GK, 38). The same is true of introspection and the conscience, to which Pound pays lip service in his Confucian essays and in defense of his radio broadcasts, but which he distrusts on a social level. On reading Mencius, one should not look for the idea of "something deeper" (SP, 96) in one's personal nature. Similarly, in praising Confucius Pound speaks contemptuously of those "nasty people fussing about their own mangy souls to exclusion of everything else."[20] Pound's focus is largely on the proper performance of social roles and rites, and, through these, the integration of individuals within society.

Thus the Confucians have a "sense of responsibility," thinking of the "whole social order" and creating a "balanced system" (GK, 29). By contrast, the Socratic injunction to "Know Thyself" is "glib," and the "Christian examination of conscience not much better." As Pound explains, "Saving one's soul may be of interest *in a system,* but in ignorance of that system, . . . your Xtian examination degenerates into mere cerebral onanism" (GK, 79). As a "modus vivendi," solely "for the individual" (SP, 57), Christianity cut man off in a "semitic" and "schizophrenic" (SP, 96) fashion from reality; there was no "sense of social order in the teachings of the irresponsible protagonist of the New Testament" (GK, 38).[21] Besides the Christian concept of immortality, Pound probably alludes to Jesus' distinction between things owed to God and things owed to Caesar, and to his claim that Christianity would, if necessary, force men to reject familial ties for higher spiritual truth.[22] One sees why Pound contrasts Jesus with Apollonius of Tyana, who consulted with kings and was concerned with the Roman Empire, and why he complains of the "disruptive" (SP, 65) influence of the Jesuits in imperial China.

According to Pound, Christianity is "anti-statal" (SP, 65). And yet, somewhat paradoxically, when he defines the ideal institutional organization of the West, it is either the Roman Empire ("The responsible ruler," GK, 38) or its heir, the Roman Catholic church, which is "equivalent to the ideal of the empire" (SP, 67). Later Pound asserts that "the Church of Rome was an imperial church at the outset," while "a Protestant sect is by definition cut off from universality" (RB, 411). Again Pound resembles Hitler, who rejected Catholicism but admired the Catholic "form of dominion."[23]

IV.

Pound has an exceedingly arbitrary and circumscribed view of what is natural for man. Man must confine himself to the visibly and concretely manifest and ignore two vast orders of fearful mystery and incommensurability: the microscopic (and mental) realm of bacilli and atoms, known only by "millimetric measure[s] and microscope[s]" (GK, 223), and the nameless and abstract infinite. In this realm of spiritual "inebriation" (GK, 223), an "unknown" (L, 333) realm transcending any existing social standard and incomparable with any earthly being, Pound locates the monotheistic Jewish god. Pound longs for "one of the primal images of mythic power" in the Heraclean epic cycle—the power to eliminate, exorcise, the "incommensurable."[24]

There are other reasons why Pound opposed monotheism. As Maurras recognized, monotheism, by asserting a transcendental absolute for all men, tends to destroy society's "beautiful" and natural "inequalities."[25] Even where social inequalities exist, monotheism democratizes the realm of the spirit and thus lessens differences between men. This is why Maurras finds in Jewish monotheism the ultimate enemy of hierarchy and the ultimate source of liberalism.[26]

Taking Pound's statements at face value, William Cookson believes that Pound's anti-monotheism proves his hatred of intolerance and "monopoly" and his love of freedom: monotheism is to spiritual life what usury is to economics. Cookson quotes Pound: "The glory of the polytheistic *anschauung* is that it never asserted a single and obligatory path for everyone" (SP, 9). The sophistry of Cookson's argument is obvious in light of Pound's intolerance of potentially universal religions such as Judaism, Buddhism, and Taoism, his criticism of Protestant sectarianism and praise of Roman Catholic imperialism, and the inadequacy of his comparison of monotheism and monopoly. A monopoly, such as usury, is highly exclusive. There is, however, nothing exclusive about monotheism, whose adherents do not usually consider themselves, as do the victims of usurers, to be exploited. Monotheism is largely anti-exploitative, implying that the same spiritual truth and salvation is available for all men. In the sentence after the passage quoted by Cookson, Pound praises polytheism for never having "caused the assertion that everyone was fit for initiation." What this attack on "monopoly" really means is that the majority of mankind are granted the freedom to recognize their unfitness to belong to a spiritual elect. Pound's attacks on monotheistic tyranny conceal the fact that his religious beliefs are spiritually elitist, hierarchical, and monopolistic, as are Maurras's and those of mandarin China. Pound believes that transcendence, if it is available to man at all, is available only to a few.

Jewish monotheism, by removing God from Nature, also destroys mythology and thrusts man into history and linear time. This helps to explain why Pound insists on connecting monotheism and usury, the second of which he views as history's identifying characteristic. This also helps to explain why Pound singles out the Jews as the representatives of anti-Nature. In a sense the Jews are the historical people par excellence. Not only is the Bible an historical rather than mythical work, but, as Ernest Renan recognized, the history of the Jews provides a model for modern and liberal attempts to transcend the limitations of human nature through the historical process (Nolte: 70).

What then of Pound's assertions that the Jews are entirely ahistorical and regressive, that they seek to "obscure all history" (RB, 158)? For all his attraction to myth, Pound is still interested in history as such, the products of linear time; William Vasse's phrase, "timeless history," aptly conveys the ambivalence that runs down the center of his work (Vasse: 325). No one should be fooled by Pound's claim that the Jews are the enemies of history. The truth is that Pound connects monotheism, the Jews, and usury with historical tendencies he hated and arbitrarily condemned as simultaneously anti-Natural and anti-historical: liberalism and progress. Once Pound discovers "one enemy" (GK, 31), the dissociated phenomena of usury and liberalism produce a nearly identical impression. As Pound asks absurdly in *Impact:* "Why are usurers always liberals?" (I, 105).[27] Nowhere is the identification between Jewish monotheism and liberalism more evident than in the radio broadcasts, where Pound, like Maurras and following the *Protocols of the Elders of Zion,* concludes that the Jews were instrumental in creating the "chaos" (RB, 320) of the French Revolution—in short, are linked to the historical source of those liberal ideologies which fascism opposes.[28] Elsewhere Pound inadvertently reveals the nature of the "Jewish" attack on "history." It is inseparable from historical progress, the "emancipatory process" which is liberalism (Nolte: 170): The Jews, in all truth a symbol of destructive modernity, "dazzle men with talk of tomorrow" (RB, 283).[29]

If anti-Semitism is not a sufficient explanation for Pound's fascism, it is its primary rhetorical vehicle. By the 1940s Pound, like Hitler, traces a vast number of history's negative forces to the same "plastic demon" of revolution, to the "single enemy."[30] Just as the usurer is the enemy of all peoples, the Jew is "the enemy of all mankind."[31] At the same time, anti-Semitism enables Pound to assert the factitiousness of all political doctrines other than fascism. Communism and Socialism have no true historical basis, but, as in Hitler, are manifestations of a single Jewish plot; America is "judeo-democratiche," its liberal and parliamentary system a pawn in the hands of Jewish usurers.[32]

This is not the only instance in which Pound attacks fundamental assumptions of liberalism. It is granted that Pound, in *Guide to Kulchur* (1937), praises the Declaration of the Rights of Man and especially the classic liberal doctrine that liberty is the "right to do what harms not others." Nonetheless, Pound judges this principle to have been "betrayed" in practice. Unjustifiably equating laissez-faire liberalism and modern liberalism, he observes that "in our time the true liberal has asked for almost no freedom save freedom to commit acts contrary to the general good." Hence "liberalism is a running sore" (GK, 254). This passage amounts to Pound's attempt to cast doubt on the efficacy of the liberal doctrine of rights, which, as he had earlier remarked contemptuously in *Jefferson and/or Mussolini,* had "started the enthusiasms of 1776 and 1782" (JM, 43). In "Freedom de Facto," which was written in 1940–1941, after Pound had cast his lot with fascism, he is much more critical of the Declaration of the Rights of Man and the concept that liberty is the right to do what harms not others. Though this concept is, he is willing to admit, "among the best formulations of principle that mankind has produced," it actually illustrates "the incapacity of abstract statement to retain meaning or utility," for it has "led to unending quibble and distortion and sophistry as to what actually does injure others" (SP, 303). Pound's ultimate solution to these difficulties is a radical rejection of the liberal principle of rights and an endorsement of the Italian Fascist doctrine of duties. In the true fascist manner, Pound asserts the primacy of social and political responsibility and the need for "statal" authority to enforce it: as in Maurras, Liberty is "not a right but a duty" (SP, 306, RB, 316); it imposes obligations on the individual to perform positive acts for the good of society.[33] Thus Pound opposes the liberal tradition of individualism, tolerance, and negative liberty.

All of the movements which fascism opposes, and which it views as "unnatural," originate in the French Revolution: democracy, liberalism, socialism, communism. In fact, Mussolini and Hitler stated that the purpose of fascism was to nullify the effects of the French Revolution and to substitute for representative democracy the authority of the state and hierarchy.[34] Thus no one should be fooled when Pound in the broadcasts pays lip service to parliamentary democracy; he could not afford to challenge American and British beliefs directly. Nor can one take seriously the idea that Pound was not recommending fascism for America and England. Mussolini made the same claims, but by the 1930s he saw fascism as a "universal phenomenon" and an "article for export": how else explain his support of Franco in Spain or his invasion of Ethiopia?[35] Apart from their approval of fascist intervention in Spain[36] and Ethiopia and of a fascist union of nations in northern Europe, Pound's works instruct America and England in the superiority of the Italian Fascist guild system, eugenics, racism, corporatism, and "statal" authority. Admittedly Pound in the 1930s doubted whether American democracy needed "corporate practice" (GK, 173), and even in the broadcasts he asserts that Italy and Germany "worked out a new system suited to EUROPE. It is NOT our American affair" (RB, 19). But this statement expresses not so much Pound's desire to limit fascism to Italy and Germany as his hope of persuading the United States not to intervene militarily against the Axis. The broadcasts also contain Pound's claim that the only "trace of sanity" in Roosevelt's program is "IMITATED from Mussolini and Hitler," although he adds that unfortunately Roosevelt has omitted the "essential parts" (RB, 45). Objecting to the lack of "syndical organization" in America's "internal government" (RB, 47), and recommending that his American listeners consult the Italian Fascist "Charter of Labor" (RB, 53), Pound demands to know whether America is "going to try to have as GOOD a brand of the corporate State as is now provided in Europe? If not, why not?" (RB, 46). Thus recommending fascism for export, Pound regrets the failure of the American industrialist and financier to see that "the solution" of his "problem . . . is a corporate solution, in the sense of that word now current in Europe" (RB, 22).

V.

The social vision of the later *Cantos* is based on the idea that any attempt to seek beyond the natural and corporate order of society, to cast off traditional authority and traditional human relations, to abandon the here and now and to pursue the infinite, to value the self over the collective— in short, any attempt radically to transform, enlarge, and finally generalize the concept of human nature—is dangerous and suspect. To borrow Nolte's terminology in his study of fascism, these "negative" impulses represent man's desire for theoretical and practical *transcendence*. Man seeks to escape submergence in the finite and repeatable pattern of nature and individual bondage to the local and racial group. In escaping the group he lays claim to the broader, more abstract, and more difficult concept of humanity—an idea which Pound held in contempt. At the same time man attempts to replace localistic social norms, religious and tribal rituals, and traditional social authority with individual and universal standards— internalized morality, the individual conscience, and the single god. Man reaches out not for a partial but for an "absolute whole." Nolte emphasizes, however, that the goal of theoretical transcendence can only be achieved through practical means. Without industrialization and technological progress, what Nolte defines as the core of practical transcendence, it is impossible to complete that process of universalization and emancipation which constitutes the essence of modernity.[37] In these terms, immanence and transcendence would seem to stand in an antithetical relation in Pound's as in fascist thought.

Yet this judgment of Pound's politics raises problems. Recent scholarship questions Nolte's view of all versions of fascism as anti-transcendental phenomena. If one thinks of transcendence as virtually synonymous with modernity, as do a number of Nolte's interpreters, then Italian Fascism seems to manifest at least some transcendental features (Payne: 188). Nor does Pound's thought appear anti-transcendental in every respect. Is he not one of the first and greatest of the modernists? The proper characterization of the tendency of Pound's political thought requires the sharpest discrimination between the two most prominent forms of fascism as well as a careful assessment of the true goals of the Italian version.

Alan Cassels and other historians argue that Nazism, in spite of its intensive continuation of the industrialization of Germany, was anti-transcendental in spirit and ultimate goals. Gravitating toward the "primitive," primordial, and mythical, the Nazis "wanted the products of industry without industrial society."[38] Through industrialization they would achieve not modernization but a return to *Volkisch* conditions, an "anti-modern utopia" in which society once more harmonized with Nature and the individual was absorbed within the racial group.[39] One might argue that even these ideas contain a transcendental component, since the individual Aryan is asked to sacrifice his individuality, "transcend" it, for the higher values of the collective. However, such social and cultural aims have little to do with what the West has generally come to conceive as transcendence, which includes individual autonomy or the freedom to resist and judge merely natural and local circumstances. An anti-transcendental purpose also underlies the thoroughgoing naturalism of Nazi racial theories. Once they had restored the Aryan race to its natural purity and unity, and installed all other races within a static biological hierarchy, the Nazis would have closed off the frightening "open-endeness" of history.[40] The profound pessimism of much Nazi thinking reflects a constant fear of racial deterioration through race-mixing, the defeat of "Nature" as a result of the historical "progress" proclaimed by liberals and socialists. In order to dispel such fears, many Nazis indulged in cyclical theories of history, which deny historical movement and always hold out the possibility of a return to *Volkisch* origins (De Felice: 103).

Italian Fascism does not conform to this pattern of anti-modernization and anti-transcendence. It pursued a policy of industrialization with the aim not of ultimate regression but of technological modernization; moreover, to some extent it achieved its goals. Italian Fascism reflects Mussolini's belief in "progress," his residual faith in human reason and even the Enlightenment idea of the "perfectability" of man.[41] Unlike the Nazis, Mussolini lacks a cyclical theory of history. Even Italian Fascist corporatism, which Pound endorsed and profoundly admired, and which one might suspect as an impractical and reactionary throwback to medieval notions,[42] develops out of a continuous and distinguished intellectual tradition and may perhaps be viewed as a worthy attempt to confront the problems of industrial society. One scholar describes Italian Fascist corporatism as an "eminently rational" and "credible" solution. In any case it does not propose a "retreat to a pre-industrial, rural paradise."[43] Although Mussolini suspected all utopianism, as Pound did not, he manifests the same sort of forward-looking spirit as one often finds in Pound. After all, it was Mussolini who drained the Pontine Marshes.

Nor is it true that Mussolini, even after his decisive move to the Right in the early 1920s, altogether rejected the legacy of the French Revolution.[44] By contrast with Nazi conservatism and reaction, Italian Fascism owes a considerable debt to left-wing influences, above all syndicalism, and seems dedicated in theory not merely to technological modernization but to a modernizing social and economic policy; A. James Gregor goes so far as to call it a Marxist heresy (Gregor, 3: 63, 91, 102, 244). One can understand why some historians, and some Italian Fascists as well, have seen the movement as an attempt to implement or fulfill at least some of the ideas of 1789.[45] But probably the deepest debt of Italian Fascism to the French Revolution lies not in liberal ideas, which the Fascists largely tamed, transformed, or rejected, but in its bold adoption of the "new politics," the "totalitarian democracy" which the French Revolution ushered in. The Italian Fascist Revolution resembles the earlier one in its use of mass cults and national festivals to mobilize the masses, although it does so to a far lesser degree than Nazism; its populist appeal to the state as the embodiment of the general will; and in its messianic political dictatorship.[46]

Italian Fascist racial doctrines show important and finally decisive differences from those of the Nazis. George L. Mosse points out that in Nazi doctrine the ideal Aryan man has already been created by Nature and therefore can only be preserved or else restored to his former biological purity. In contrast with Himmler, Hitler was not interested in breeding along "Social Darwinist" lines a new or better master race. The thrust of Nazi racial thinking was toward the recovery of the Aryan racial past rather than toward the uncertain future. But the Italian Fascists, with their belief in progress, were chiefly interested in the "creation" of a new man, a new Italian, for whom Mussolini was the model. By comparison with the static goal of Nazism, this aim must be viewed as in some way transcendental.[47] Nor did the Italian Fascists, in spite of their late passage of "racial" laws against the Jews, view the coming race of Italians mainly in racial or naturalistic terms. The new race was primarily a "spiritual" and nationalistic rather than a biological or naturalistic concept. To quote one Fascist theorist: "the highest spiritual values are a conquest of conscience, the consequence of effort and perpetual choice and, as such, not determined by natural fact."[48] Similar assumptions underlie Mussolini's much vaunted "voluntarism" (which Pound admired) and Giovanni Gentile's philosophy of "Actualism." Most Italian Fascists believed that man is "no longer subject to Nature," and that the new man of Fascism must "transcend" the old society.[49]

There is much in this description of Italian Fascism that applies to Pound. For all his Mussolinian distrust of "utopic stagnation" (SP, 195), Pound accepts some notion of progress toward a "Utopia" (SP, 336).[50] His aesthetic roots are in Vorticism, which, as Wyndham Lewis said, "accepted the machine world."[51] Admittedly such acceptance for aesthetic purposes is not the same as identification and endorsement, and Reed Way Dasenbrock has shown that the Vorticists, rather than uncritically or programmatically accepting technology, as is usually supposed, often viewed it pessimistically: the modern industrial world evokes disgust in Lewis, and Epstein's *Rock Drill*, especially in its second, drill-less version, depicts mechanized man as a "sinister" and "mutilated" figure (Dasenbrock: 42–48; Cork, Vol. I: 30, 32). But this qualification would not hold for Pound. His typically favorable attitude to technology, and his indifference to the frightening implications of Epstein's sculpture, are manifest in *Rock-Drill*, as Pound chose to call a long section of the later *Cantos;* this, remarked Pound to Wyndham Lewis, was his "attempt to drill something into the pliocene occiput of the b. bloody pupLick" (P/L, 294). The Vorticists' nearest Continental analogues and rivals are the Italian Futurists, whom Mussolini encouraged and finally at least tolerated in his regime, and whose modernizing and pro-technological aesthetics were not incompatible with Fascist ideology.[52] Like the Italian Fascists and the Futurists, Pound admires the aesthetic and social potential of machine technology; as he happily observes in *Jefferson and/or Mussolini,* "some of the sane [modern] principles are already accepted [in Italy], the idea of steel, aluminum, glass, contemporary material . . ." (J/M, 106).

In the same work Pound speaks favorably of "factories" as necessary for American "independence" and of machines as labor-saving devices (J/M, 39, 99).[53] Another indication of Pound's forward-looking attitude is his rejection of original sin. Besides separating Pound from most conservatives (Viereck, 1: 13–14), this belief testifies to a certain utopian optimism which conservatives do not share, even a faith in the perfectability of man. As in Italian Fascism, something of the Enlightenment influence is at work in Pound.

The residual "Jacobin" and "1789" element in Italian Fascism helps to explain what might remain the most outrageous paradox in Pound's political thought. How can Pound simultaneously espouse the American (and indirectly the French) Revolution and Italian Fascism? These two movements seem categorically opposed in their liberalism and anti-liberalism, but Pound did not view them in this way. For Pound their affinity lies in their commonly populist forms of participatory democracy in combination with such authoritarian leaders as John Adams and especially Napoleon, whom Pound came increasingly to admire.[54] In Canto 33 Pound quotes John Adams's praise of Napoleon as the transmitter through military dictatorship of the populist legacy of the French Revolution. Napoleon had led people's revolts against moribund monarchies and had imposed meritocratic and anti-feudal (and hence pro-centralizing or statist) values.[55] All of these achievements could seem agreeable to an Italian Fascist, as would Napoleon's claim as dictator to bypass parliament and to embody the general will or "mandate" of his nation. So too would Napoleon's claim to oppose the forces of usury, as well as his legal defense of private property in the Code Napoleon. In short, Napoleon is for Pound a precursor of Mussolini's "totalitarian democracy," in which the "state" is based on the "will" and "spirit of the people" (J/M, v, viii).[56] At the very least these men are united by their dictatorships, their anti-monarchism (which Mussolini never fully achieved), their anti-parliamentarianism, their commitment to a middle class (and essentially petit bourgeois) concept of elitism (careers open to talents), and their mobilization of the masses. Most of these political phenomena trace to the French Revolution.

Nonetheless, Pound's attempt to reconcile Jefferson and Mussolini is dubious indeed. According to Pound, Fascist corporatism assimilates to American values in a spirit of "continuing revolution." Not only had Mussolini "rewritten the Declaration of Independence," but Pound also believed that the Constitution must be kept "modern" by conforming to corporate practice. At his most extreme Pound asserts the "identity" (SP, 313) of the American and Italian Fascist Revolutions: in the days of Jefferson and Adams geographical representation by state supposedly coincided with different vocational interests and ways of life, so that the "thirteen colonies formed, more or less, a chamber of corporations," as in Italian Fascism; hence the supposed "betrayal" (SP, 314) of the democratic system in our time. Notwithstanding this defense of "democracy," Pound praises Jefferson for guiding a "governing class" and a "*de facto* one party . . . system" (J/M, 19, 125). In the broadcasts Pound goes so far as to say that Italy and Germany "make EFFECTIVE what had been INTENDED in the United States by Adams and Jefferson" (RB, 112). It is easy to see the resemblance between Pound, who wants to institute social reform by adding a "few gadgets" (RB, 205) in the "machinery" provided in the Constitution, and the supposedly conservative right-winger, who wants to "tinker" with the Constitution for radical purposes. Pound said far more than he intended when he remarked that "It is only in our time that anyone has, with any shadow of right, questioned the presuppositions on which the U.S. is founded" (SP, 152). His reforms really seek to undermine the longstanding, consensual, and essential liberalism of American politics. His proposal to reestablish voting rights on the basis of vocational organizations, rather than geographical or individual representation, would eliminate the concept of citizenship (one man, one vote) which derives from the French and American Revolutions. Nor can one take seriously Read's and many others' argument that Pound reveres the Bill of Rights. Everyone knows that the First Amendment guarantees free speech. Convinced by the late 1920s that usury had corrupted parliamentary debate and journalistic opinion, Pound reaches his odd "solution" to liberal corruption by endorsing Mussolini's suppression of all but state-controlled or -filtered opinion; this is the upshot of the evasive chapter nine of *Jefferson and/or Mussolini*, as it is the implication of the statement by which the Italian Fascist government introduced a number of Pound's radio broadcasts, namely that free speech is the prerogative only of those qualified to hold it. To quote *Jefferson and/or Mussolini:* "As the Duce has pithily remarked: 'Where the press is "free" it merely serves special interests' " (J/M, 41). The same idea emerges contemporaneously in *The Cantos:* "Pays to control the *Times,* for its effect on the market / 'where there is no censorship by the state / there is a great deal of manipulation . . .' / and news sense?" (41/ 205). As for Pound's appeals to free speech during and after his trial, these are self-serving in defense of his broadcasts.[57]

Pound's claims to an ideology of transcendence must be sharply qualified, even rejected. From the late 1930s on, in *The Cantos,* his letters, and critical prose, Pound stands closer to the Nazi than to the Italian Fascist position on the issue of race. For the later Pound, race is a biological fact of paramount importance. Not only is individual behavior linked inextricably to racial instincts, but Nature dictates that individual races be preserved (or improved). It is therefore dangerous for any individual to overstep or "transcend" the naturally-determined limits of his race. Such biological determinism and racial exclusiveness differs from the Italian Fascist concept of race, whereby individuals (even Jews) may rise above their merely biological origin by acts of will and attain a higher level of spiritual life and cultural universality (De Felice: 96). But though racism and anti-Semitism were far less significant in Italian Fascism than in Nazism, Mussolini's regime in its later phase moved toward an equivocally defined racism which excluded the Jews.

In 1938 Mussolini instituted anti-Semitic racial laws, and in the same year his ideologues issued a manifesto of race. It is often assumed that Mussolini was not personally or ideologically anti-Semitic and that he introduced these measures as a consequence of German pressure and also in order to solidify on ideological grounds the newly forged Rome-Berlin Axis. His anti-Semitism would thus figure as another example of his opportunism. But Meir Michaelis has recently shown that Mussolini had been obsessively anti-Semitic from the start of his career, and that he was the "moving spirit" behind the "racial campaign." Even during the years in which he derided Nazi racial theories and assumed the role of "protector" of the Italian Jews, Mussolini denounced Zionism and "international Jewry," blamed many of the world's troubles on Jewish finance, linked the Jews, as Pound did, to a Masonic conspiracy (Mussolini banned the Masons from Italy), and held that the Jews had led the Communist Revolution. Nor is there any evidence "whatsoever" that Mussolini's growing animosity toward Jewry was due to German influence. The "decisive turning point" in Mussolini's relation with the Germans and Jews was the invasion of Ethiopia and his pursuit of a strongly imperialistic policy. In the belief that Italian imperialism required the strengthening of his nation's identity and solidarity, Mussolini instituted laws against miscegenation with Ethiopians and soon after extended similar laws to Italian Jews. Besides flattering the Italian Fascists' totalitarian pretentions of "monolithic" national unity, these laws were intended to transform Italy into an imperialistic nation, a worthy partner in the Axis Alliance, which Mussolini has joined for largely imperialistic reasons. But A. James Gregor insists that Mussolini's social legislation in Ethiopia was motivated by a concern for Italy's "prestige" rather than the protection of the "biological patrimony" or "racial superiority" of the Italians. Although Italian Fascist academic experts did conceive of eugenic measures for the breeding of a new race, the Italian Fascists largely eschewed biological racism and instead assimilated racism into "totalitarian nationalism." Even in the Italian Fascist manifesto on race it is unclear whether the Jews are excluded from Italian society on racial or nationalistic grounds. Ultimately Mussolini's anti-Semitism lacks the massive murderousness and ideological centrality of Hitler's.[58]

As we shall see in the next chapter, Pound favors Nazi-style eugenic breeding. His position thus differs from the Italian Fascist concept of spiritual transcendence insofar as it is, like the Nazis', thoroughly naturalistic. Its pretensions to transcendence are undercut by its implicit denial of individual autonomy and the worth of the individual apart from his fixed natural endowment. If anything such a proposal implies the individual's submergence within the racial group. The radio broadcasts furthermore suggest that the ultimate purpose of Pound's eugenic schemes is a new race which, as in his conception of ancient China, shall remain protected, static, and hence pure or "thoroughbred" (RB, 155). The Chinese "breed" (99/ 707) to which Pound refers in the later Cantos is almost certainly a biological one. To achieve such goals would be to forestall transcendence once and for all, would "close off history," just as the Nazis had intended. Despite his continued assertions of hope, Pound's espousal of biological racism marks his sharp divergence from the comparative historical optimism of Italian Fascist ideology. His most frequently repressed and therefore profoundest historical feeling is one of pessimism and despair, the same as the Nazis felt, and this tone returns insistently in Pound's prose and poetry to the very end.

What then is one to make of Pound's recurrent theme of natural metamorphosis, his notion that the Divine Mind is "unceasing," "abundant," "*improvisatore*" (92/ 620)? At some points Pound's naturalism seems to have affinities with modern evolutionary theory, with its conception of mutation as rapid change and discontinuity. Pound can imagine sudden and violent metamorphoses of human nature taking place without genetic manipulation:

> I believe, and on no better ground than that of a sudden emotion, that the change of species is not a slow matter, managed by cross-breeding, of nature's leporides and bardots, I believe that the species changes as suddenly as a man makes a song or a poem, or as suddenly as he starts making them, more suddenly than he can cut a statue in stone, at most as slowly as a locust or longtailed Sirmione false mosquito emerges from its outgrown skin. It is not even proved that man is at the end of his physical changes. Say that the diversification of species has passed its most sensational phases. . . . (PD, 208)

Is Pound speaking of actual change within a species or of its diversification and development? The latter may be understood, as Gourmont says, as an augmentation of specializing traits.[59] Pound's fanciful comparison of man with the false mosquito confuses the issue, since the insect's emergence from its outgrown skin is not really a change of species. But whatever human changes Pound has in mind, he does not abandon his naturalistic model of man: these changes are all part of Spinoza's *Natura naturans,* "Nature actively creating herself and deploying her essential powers in her infinite attributes and in the various modes of these attributes."[60] Pound still thinks of man as properly installed not within a realm of transcendental possibility but of immanence. Physical Nature, virtually indistinguishable in Pound's mind from the divine, itself gives the impulse and provides the justification for changes in humanity. Though such thinking lacks the lethal implications which appear in the later Pound, it does not conform with the idea of transcendence as Nolte conceives of it.

Not only Pound's but the Italian Fascist conception of transcendence is suspect for other reasons. While the Italian Fascists do not stress submergence of the individual within a biological race, they emphasize (as does

Pound) the priority of the social and hence the necessity of the individual's subordination first to the group, then to the nation, and finally to what Pound calls the "power" of the "absolute" (SP, 307) Fascist state.[61] To quote Mussolini (or Giovanni Gentile) in "The Doctrine of Fascism," "individuals or groups are 'thinkable' in so far as they are within the state," which "transcends the brief limits of individual lives."[62] Thus the Italian Fascist state undermines the dialectical relation between the individual and the state by making the former altogether dependent on the latter. Transcendental aims are defined by and reachable only through the state. If there is, as Eugen Weber insists, a transcendental element in many forms of fascism, it is attainable only at the price of the loss of personal autonomy and resistance to the status quo as the state defines it (Weber, 2: 75–76). Instead of fostering the impulse towards Nolte's "absolute whole," that is, a transcendence of the peculiar conditions and local forms of life, the Italian Fascist state defines transcendence only in partial terms, within the narrow confines of a national political organization. One can also argue that Italian Fascism was willing to use modern technology while pursuing, as did the Nazis, fundamentally anti-modernist ends. Edward R. Tannenbaum believes that Italian Fascism was a failed revolution whose social conservatism disqualifies it from any serious claims as a modernizing movement. He refers to its preservation of many traditional values, its labor policies, and especially its anti-feminist social attitudes, all of which Pound admired and celebrated in his works.[63]

No less questionable are the supposedly transcendental or modernizing goals implicit in Pound's admiration for technology. It is true that Pound glorifies the machine and desires to promote Italian and American industry; industrial entrepreneurs such as Henry Ford are among his heroes. Yet the theme of industrial development receives far less emphasis in Pound's writing than a pastoral and agrarian theme inspired by a remote and sometimes even prehistoric past. The great social and economic institution celebrated in *The Cantos* and the radio broadcasts is not the factory but the patriarchal homestead, which Pound views as the basis of civilization, but which by his lifetime had taken a subordinate role to industry in America and the most technologically advanced European countries. Pound to the contrary, not the usurer but the industrialist was largely responsible for eclipsing and saving Western mankind from what Marx called the "idiocy" of rural life. Pound's fundamental suspicion of modernization and technology, and his fears of the unavoidable "decadence" they would bring, emerges even in *Jefferson and/or Mussolini*. At first Pound doubts strongly that the energetic Mussolini "expects to take 80 years" in modernizing Italy. Yet he adds more forcefully that "It is possible the Capo del Governo wants to go slow enough so as not to see in his old age, an Italy full of fat peasants gone rotten and a bourgeosie stinking over the peninsula as Flaubert saw them stinking through Paris" (J/M, ix). In his description of an Italian Fascist utopia in

"Gold and Work," Pound says little about industry, mentions a considerable range of commercial activities, and underscores the value of agriculture: "They attach the importance to skill in agricultural tasks that I attached in my youth to skill at tennis or football. In fact, they have ploughing contests to see who can drive the straightest furrow" (SP, 337). This utopia originates in images of a Latin or "Sabine" (SP, 337) past. The "organic" Italy for which Mussolini supposedly shows "affection" is in Pound's view "composed of the last ploughman and the last girl in the olive yards" (J/M, 34). Insofar as industrialization, as Nolte argues, constitutes the primary form of practical transcendence, then Pound's obsession with the "homestead" seems reactionary and raises serious doubts about his commitment to modernization. It may be that, like the Nazis, whom he had come increasingly to resemble, he embraces modern technology only as an instrument for restoring an idealized agrarian past.

One may conclude that Pound, like many other fascists, remains in constant equivocation between past and present, tradition and revolution, Nature and History. For good reason Cairns Craig suggests that Pound chose Italian Fascism because it promised to provide both modernization and preservation of the past, technical improvement and respect for agrarian traditions (Craig: 272–273). But despite his earlier interest in a revolutionary future, the later *Cantos* show that Pound's ultimate utopian model, again as in Nazism, lies in a pre-modern, mythical, ethnocentric, and "closed" agrarian setting: not the utopia of the Aryan Volk, but Confucian China.[64] This remote, unattainable, and yet "permanent" example provides the standard by which merely "historical" fascism was bound to fail.

Meantime Pound continues to attempt to avoid the tension between Nature and History through his notions of myth and metamorphosis. For although metamorphosis means that all is in flux in time, underlying all changes is an immutable form or root, a recurring pattern, as in Ovid and Agassiz.[65] As Pound says, "what has been shall be" (113/ 786). In Canto 97 Fortuna presides over the flux:

> All neath the Moon, under Fortuna,
> splendor' mondan',
> beata gode, hidden as eel in sedge,
> all neath the moon, under Fortuna
> (97/ 676)

Fortuna's wheel symbolizes the retributive balance of sub-lunar and cyclical Nature, which is unchanging in its changefulness. Perhaps ironically, Pound also associates Fortuna with the mysteries of the swamp ("hidden as eel in sedge"), elsewhere the antithesis of historical movement. Pound's reverence for this traditional figure confirms his opposition if not to historical change then to progress, the idea, common to Jewish monotheism and to a number of modern ideologies, that history has a goal. Indeed, C. S. Lewis notes that

Fortuna has always appealed to those who dislike historical teleology (Lewis: 176–177). Maurras was similarly attracted to "a Greek and even Oriental image which is in sharp contradiction to the entire European understanding of history: 'The great wheel that turns and turns has made no progress, although nothing halts it.' "[66]

Chapter Eleven

Nature, Race, and History, III

Although a form of naturalism pervades Pound's whole outlook by the late 1930s, he was moving in this direction perhaps as early as 1921, when he translated Gourmont's *Natural Philosophy of Love* (*Physique de l'amour*). Gourmont holds quite plausibly that Nature has no finality or *telos;* its only "goal" is the perpetuation of life. Nor can man transcend the natural. Man is not "the culmination of nature," writes Gourmont, "he is *in* Nature, he is one of the unities of life, that is all." Man is "an animal, submitted to the essential instincts which govern all humanity; there being everywhere the same matter animate with the same desire: to live, to perpetuate life" (Gourmont: 4, 6, 7).

Maurras similarly defines the "ontological basic" principle in "human relations" as the natural tendency of being to "persevere in being." This Spinozistic and anti-transcendental principle also means that "naturally occurring" or existing social groups, such as the French, are to be considered as permanent and necessary types (Nolte: 183, 363). Pound too accepted the Spinozistic law stated by Gourmont in *The Natural Philosophy of Love*. "The duty of [a] being," said Gourmont, "is to persevere in its being and even to augment the characteristics which specialize it."[1] Pound was probably remembering Gourmont when he said in the broadcasts: "First essential of life is to keep livin', to keep on living, not DIE" (RB, 112). Perhaps again recalling Gourmont, Pound also said: "Fight from instinct, ... Fight for survival, that's health. Man ought to fight for survival, and for RACIAL survival" (RB, 203). At this point, however, Pound had gone well beyond the merely irresponsible naturalism of Gourmont. His statements figure within a political ideology more closely resembling Nazism than Italian Fascism.

Gourmont holds that each being should "persevere in its being *and* [my italics] even . . . augment" its specializing characteristics. The second part of this statement was not lost on Pound. By the 1920s Pound saw modern man as having arrived at what Gourmont called a parthenogenetic "sign-post"

(Gourmont: 28), a point of cultural conformity closing off all possibilities of development within the species. Pound's discovery of this stasis coincided not only with his desire to "work out a view of life suitable to the new pagan era [the Pound Era, as Pound called it]," but with his increasing emphasis on "the biological aspect of life." Man's "impasse," noted Pound in 1922, is "biological," and "there is *no* easy way out."[2]

Richard Sieburth argues that Gourmont saved Pound from the dualistic Judeo-Christian view of man, in which man is the summit of Nature and lord over the animals (Sieburth, 2: 134). However that may be, many of Gourmont's ideas are curious and suspicious in their complacent assertion of the essentially predatory and combative character of all life, including man. Pound probably remembered the following passage in the late 1930s and 1940s:

> Life is made out of life. Nothing lives save at the expense of life. The male insect nearly always dies immediately after the mating; . . . why, if this is for the good of the species, should he not be eaten? Anyhow, he is eaten. It is his destiny. . . . It is really a matter of ritual, not of accident or of crime. (Gourmont: 168)

In Canto 47 man's earliest rituals are based on natural destiny: "Moth is called over mountain / the bull runs blind on the sword, *naturans*" (47/237).

Although Pound asserts vacuously that "the nature of things is good, . . . in the sense that the chemist and biologist so find it" (SP, 87), Nature, as he and Gourmont present it, is fundamentally amoral. To quote Gourmont:

> . . . Causes blindly engender causes; some maintain life, others force it to progress; others destroy it; we qualify them differently, according to the dictates of our sensibility, but they are nonqualifiable. . . . Life, like the pebble thrown by a child, will fall into the abyss, and with it all the good and evil, all facts, all ideas, and all things. (Gourmont: 157)

Yet Gourmont also uses Nature to justify certain forms of human behavior. He notes that enslavement of enemy species is a common and successful practice among the ants. By contrast, thanks to "sentimentalism" and Christianity, the white race lost its "opportunity" to enslave the black, which would have been "the complete and logical development of its civilization." Gourmont adds that there is nothing anti-natural in making neuter a part of the population, for the insects, far superior to man, have "managed it so well." Reminiscent of Pound's statement that "objections to slavery are in part ideal and sentimental" (SP, 234), this passage anticipates the eugenic schemes of the broadcasts.[3]

Nature's infinite variety can never provide the basis, as Pound believed, for ethical norms. This does not prevent Gourmont from suggesting that "animal cruelty" might be "edifying in this era of sentimentalism," might teach us that "the first duty of a living being is to live, and that all life is nothing but a sum sufficient of murders." Gourmont adds that "to eat grass, is not much better than suicide: ask the lambkins" (Gourmont: 257). In the late 1930s Pound remembered Gourmont: "The law of nature is that the animal must either adapt itself to environment or overcome that environment." Besides explaining Pound's disgust with "soft life and decadence" (SP, 246), this statement anticipates the broadcasts, in which Pound tells his listeners that they must not choose to die like sheep at the hands of Jewish slaughterers (RB, 206, 296, 339, 409). It also coincides with his support of fascism, which celebrated an exaggerated masculine toughness, and held that "to grow fat is the ideal of the lower species of animal."[4] Writing in the *Popolo d'Alessandria* of November 21, 1944, at the height of his commitment to fascism, Pound told his readers that it was "very well" for them "to believe in law," but that they should remember the "eternal law of nature," whereby the "strong shall dominate the weak."[5] Elsewhere, in a discussion of sacrifices, Pound says that "the sight of a killing can remind" a stupefied "mercantilist" public "that life exists by destruction of other life"; indeed, "the sight of one day's hecatomb might even cause thought in the midst of our democracy and usuriocracy" (SP, 68). Although some critics, following Frazer, view Pound's sacrificial rituals as an imitation of natural process, here ritual sacrifice apparently imitates Gourmont's "rite" of natural violence and death, the "Darwinian" struggle for existence.

Pound's point is that democracy and usury—an odd combination, to say the least—interfere with natural struggle by permitting the unworthy to live. Canto 30 opens with the "Compleynt against Pity," the song of Artemis, goddess of the moon and hunt:

> Compleynt, compleynt I hearde upon a day,
> Artemis singing, Artemis, Artemis
> Agaynst Pity lifted her wail:
> Pity causeth the forests to fail,
> Pity slayeth my nymphs.
> Pity spareth so many an evil thing.
> Pity befouleth April,
> Pity is the root and the spring.
> Now if no fayre creature followeth me
> It is on account of Pity,
> It is on account that Pity forbideth them slaye.
> All things are made foul in this season,
> This is the reason, none may seek purity
> Having for foulnesse pity
> And things growne awry:
> No more do my shaftes fly
> To slay. Nothing is now cleane slayne
> But rotteth away.
>
> (30/ 147)

Despite its apparent justification of such fascist values as natural struggle and systematic brutality toward the weak and unfit, most critics deny that this lyric is fascist or proto-fascistic. Nor do they believe that Pound refers literally to violence. Interpreted in the widest possible terms, the lyric condemns only Judeo-Christian dualism, which undermines man's reverence for natural process and causes him to pervert those beneficent and self-regulating operations which Artemis represents. Interpreted more narrowly but no less symbolically (and safely), the lyric rejects not all forms of pity and compassion but only "cheap sentiment," the "false tolerance" by the weak of others' weakness, incompetence, mediocrity, and imprecision, none of which Nature, cast in the form of unstinting Artemis, ever condones. In literature and criticism Pity leads to the acceptance of "fraudulence of communication, a stylistic counterpart of usury."[6] One might thus conclude that Artemis' violence represents nothing more lethal than a rigorous attitude toward life. Even if Pound meant to apply her hard lessons to human societies, they might figure within a conservative tradition inaugurated by Nietzsche and continued, with major alterations, by the Catholic Max Scheler. Attributing the impoverishment of modern life to herd- and slave-morality and the *ressentiment* of the mass man for all forms of excellence, these writers have nothing but disdain for liberal humanitarianism and sentimental altruism, which they identify with some but by no means complete justification with a fear of rigor, dishonest love, and a diminished sense of being.[7]

Actually, Pound does not merely condemn pity but argues for human and natural violence as its proper alternative: "No more do my shaftes fly / to slay. Nothing is now clean slayne. . . ." Moreover, while Artemis' "pruning" is directed at animals, her human victim Actaeon cannot be far from Pound's consciousness. Leon Surette correctly observes that Artemis for Pound represents "a beneficent cleansing through the death of the weak and malformed." She is the "weeder of life's garden," and Pound regrets that "she is no longer permitted to perform her bloody but necessary function" (Surette, 3: 203). In short, "Compleynt against Pity" is inseparable from the fascism which it in fact adumbrates. In Canto 106 the goddess and Italian Fascism appear in conjunction: "At Miwo the moon's axe is renewed" (106/ 755). The moon signifies Artemis, goddess of cyclical process and natural retribution, while the axe is interchangeable with the axe of Italian Fascism, which maintains purity and clarifies, by pruning, those natural distinctions which usury obscures.[8] Canto 30 also anticipates the radio broadcasts, in which Pound applies his own concept of Nature to human societies and relations.

Ernst Nolte has shown that an important foundation of fascist ideology was unwittingly established by Nietzsche when he traced the impoverishment of Western life partly to the Judeo-Christian sentiment of pity. Nietzsche argued that pity, in preserving those who are "ripe for destruction," and in glorifying the "psychologically retrograde" and "weak," had made "suffering contagious" and weakened man's natural vitality.[9] It is therefore especially noteworthy that Pound, writing in the *British Union Quarterly* in 1938, speaks of the Jews' "moments of pity." Admittedly in this instance Pound uncharacteristically finds pity to be a praiseworthy emotion, an indication of the Jews' slight superiority over the more ruthless "ariyo-kike."[10] But generally speaking Pound shares Nietzsche's profound regret that Nature is no longer allowed to select its best specimens from among its many failures. Pound's rejection of pity is also inextricably connected with another theme implicit in Canto 30, namely retributive Nature, a theme to which Pound returns in the later *Cantos,* and which is also prominent in Nazism.[11] According to Hitler, the idea that man should and can "overcome" or transcend Nature is "Jewish nonsense" and effrontery. Man should resist the impulse to replace "the natural struggle" with the "desire to 'save' even the weakest and most sickly at any price." This violation and "mockery of Nature and her will" can only summon forth the cruel forces of retribution or vengeance within Nature itself: human life will sicken and die. To illustrate this retributive process Hitler employs a feminine symbol which resembles Artemis in Canto 30. He rebukes those "humane" men who think they know "better" than Nature, the "cruel queen of wisdom."[12]

II.

Like Pound, Hitler repeatedly appeals to Nature and instinct and argues that human life is a natural and "eternal struggle" against "putrefaction." He means, of course, struggle between human beings. Through natural warfare man rises to "the highest accomplishments," achieves a "thoroughgoing selection" of the best individuals along biological lines. In Hitler as in Pound such ideas probably derive not from paganism but from the age of natural science and "scientific" racism, which stressed "the natural elements in historical life in order to glimpse reality."[13]

Ultimately, says Hitler, "only the urge for self-preservation can conquer"; or, to quote an American right-wing agitator of the 1930s and 40s: "We have been reduced to that one simple elementary problem of self-preservation." These statements mean essentially the same thing as Pound's notion that every organism must persist in and augment its own being. However, this conception of Nature (and society) as a battlefield ironically calls to mind the open conflict of the atomized bourgeois society which fascism supposedly opposes. The question is how to translate "natural" struggle between individuals into ideological and cultural warfare? By a dubious logic Hitler subsumes individuals under biological races and nations, which he finds analogous to animal species, and which stand as animals in Nature supposedly stand, in relations of physical superiority and inferiority. Nature, says Hitler, demands that races, like species, conserve their purity, delimit themselves, and overcome their biological inferiors. If a species or race perishes, whether by struggle or unnatural mixture, it lacks the requisite "instinct of self-preservation" and cohesion.[14]

Pound never endorses slavery. Although he considers "objections to slavery" to be "in part ideal and sentimental" (SP, 234), in *The Cantos* he admires Cunizza and John Randolph of Roanoke, who freed their slaves, as well as Mussolini, who suppressed the "slave trade" (78/ 479) in Ethiopia even while imposing a harsh domination of his own. In the broadcasts slavery is "evil" (RB, 164). However, like Hitler and the American right-wing agitator, Pound speaks of human beings as animals, particularly sheep and cows, and of the differences between men as analogous to those between animal species.[15] From here it is a short step to the equation between species as a fixed type and race (Nolte: 527–528). But though Pound early inclined toward racial thinking, only around the middle 1930s do his racial ideas acquire an ideological and even "super-ideological" cast. To quote Pound's 1936 article on "Race": "But to suppose that a difference of policy is due to a mere ideology or to mere reason, when it has roots in blood, bone, and endocrines, is to take a very superficial view of society, humanity and human co-ordinations." It is a "sign of health" for races to resist racially alien types of government, while "submission to any one of them by a race whereto it is alien is a sign of decay."[16] Later, in the radio broadcasts, the idea of the "RACIAL survival" (RB, 203) of Europe and America is obsessive.

Another instance of Pound's naturalism in politics appears in Canto 48, in which the retributive forces of Nature are not to be held down:

> Falling Mars in the air
> bough to bough, to the stone bench . . .
> Fell with stroke after stroke, jet avenger
> bent, rolled, severed and then swallowed limb after limb
> Hauled off the butt of that carcass, 20 feet up a tree trunk,
> Here three ants have killed a great worm. There
> Mars in the air, fell, flew.
>
> (48/ 243)

In *Jefferson and/or Mussolini* Pound praises the "remarkably full and perfect knowledge," in short "instinct," with which "a flying ant or wasp . . . cut up a spider at Excideuil [in Provence]." He adds that human "genius" consists in "an analogous completeness of knowledge, or intelligence carried into a third or fourth dimension," and "capable of dealing with a NEW circumstance . . ." (J/M, 18, 19). In Canto 48 the great worm, or spider, is probably symbolic of the monster Geryon or usury; it also resembles the usurious "worm" of Addendum to Canto 100 and Usura, the spider-like "beast with a hundred legs" (15/ 64) of Canto 15. Its enemies, the three warrior ants, are most likely Italy, Germany, and Japan, three allies rising up by intelligent instinct as it passes over into genius (read Mussolini and Hitler). To be more precise, what Pound saw "there," in Excideuil, is now seen "here," in Rapallo, as "Mars," meaning concerted war against international usury: three nations, according to Gourmont's formula of survival, persevering in their being (Bacigalupo: 91–92). If one judges from the context, this worm and war also imply anti-Semitism. Canto 51 closes Pound's Inferno in Königsberg, where Rudolf Hess speaks out for Hitler against usury and for the folk. In Canto 52, Pound fulminates against *neschek* and the Rothschilds and recommends that the Jews be excluded from American soil.

By the 1940s Pound had arrived at a solution to the "biological impasse" which threatened man with permanent undifferentiation and mediocrity. Having once speculated that the new era (he called it "the Pound Era") might be characterised by "a sort of eugenic paganism" (SP, 103), Pound finds his prophecies confirmed. Noting that the "human race . . . [is] worth as much attention as the British fanciers give to whiffets [very small dogs]," Pound says that the world's "next move" is "eugenic," the "production of thoroughbreds" (RB, 132). Unfortunately, England and America have neglected "breeding itself, whereof RACE is a component"; "instead of . . . breeding . . . thoroughbreds," they have "encouraged the most fatal admixtures," in short the Jews. By contrast, "the Nazi revolution was based on the BREED" (RB, 155). The first "point" of the "Hitler program" is to "Breed GOOD, and preserve the race," and then to "breed thorough, . . . and conserve the BEST of the race." This program is "opposed to" the "race suicide" encouraged by the "Talmudic Jews" (RB, 140).

Pound's racism derives less from Frobenius than from nineteenth- and twentieth-century naturalism.[17] Race, as Pound conceives of it, is first a biological and then a cultural idea. Nor did Pound's thinking change after the war. Like the broadcasts, the later *Cantos* celebrate "breed" (99/ 707) and warn against the "melting pot" (RB, 157, 94/ 641),[18] while Pound remarked to the American racist ideologue John Kasper in 1956 that there was "less sense in breeding humans (eugenics) than is used for cattle and sheep." In the same letter he labelled blood banks "infamy" and attacked "miscegenation, bastardization, and mongrelization of everything."[19] Consider too the editorial policy of the magazine *Edge*, whose guru was Pound: ". . . We are in a death-struggle against certain diseases of THOUGHT which have afflicted various races. . . . We believe in eugenics."[20]

One sees again why Pound conceives of the Jews as the essence of the unnatural. As symbols of rootless cosmopolitanism, monotheism, legalism, spiritual abstraction and egalitarianism, modernism, subjectivism, and a host of other things, the Jews lead men beyond Nature's laws. And yet, as if in revenge against them, Pound attempts metaphorically to reduce the Jews to the purely natural state to which they in theory are alien; he speaks of them not just as animals but as despised animals—vermin, bacilli, germs, beings which exist at the level of deindividualized, instinctive, *unconscious* automatism. This degraded metamorphosis prepares the Jews for the violent retaliation which Hitler, and Pound's Artemis in Canto 30, define as proper for those who fail to "understand the fundamental necessity of Nature's rule" (Hitler: 245). To put it another way, Pound is claiming, with enormous presumption and arbitrariness, the privilege of carrying out Artemis' purifying and retributive justice, of enforcing "the kharma," the Dantescan *"contrapasso"* (RB, 135, 148).

By conceiving human beings, not merely Jews, as breeding animals, Pound has revenge against history, which refuses to conform to Nature. He treats human society and human beings as entirely natural, thus fixing them permanently within a natural order. This object, however, renders ironic his accusations that the Jews treat Gentiles as "sheep" or "cattle" for slaughter. Apart from the fact that Pound seeks to "preserve" rather than slaughter them, he conceives of them in the same way.

Although eugenics is as much a human intrusion into Nature as the humanitarian "sentimentalism" which Pound deplores, Pound provides his apologists with a ready means to eliminate such problems. At the heart of Pound's Confucian thought, Pound critics tell us, is the idea that man is a part of Nature and can adapt his activities to Nature's ends; as in the case of eugenics, man can intelligently "aid" in the "process." But this idea, apart from its utter banality, is virtually empty of content and must always be arbitrary in its application, depending entirely on the conception of Nature that one cares to choose. So vague is it that Pound can speak of the feminine masses as cows, sheep, and "malleable mud" (L, 181), and of Mussolini as an artist, educing a pre-existent shape from within society exactly as a sculptor uncovers the shape concealed within the stone (J/M: viii, 33–34, 92). The greatest danger of this natural mythology is that it can serve to conceal and justify human violence as "natural" and "mythical," as part of the true order of things.

III.

Pound's "mythical" form of violence is directed at human beings who, like the Jews, appear to belong to that aspect of Nature which culture views as anti-natural and which it seeks to repress and overcome—the jungle or swamp. In Canto 39 Pound treats Odysseus' sexual union with Circe, whereby the witch, assimilated within a patriarchal economy, becomes Aphrodite. Pearlman's interpretation of this encounter is ambiguous. At one point Circe is "dominated . . . by . . . Odysseus," at another Odysseus is "Everyman, . . . entering a harmonious relationship with Circe . . . ," and at another, Odysseus "adjusts" himself to Circe's natural world. Again, Odysseus "transforms" Circe "into his willing concubine and [sexual] mentor," thus "achieving harmony." Circe, Pearlman concludes, "could very well symbolize Nature as order. . . . Hope is seen for man if he adjusts the rhythms of his life to those of organic time" (Pearlman, 1: 41, 44, 162, 45). But adjustment, transformation, harmonization, and domination are contradictory ideas. Perhaps this ambiguity results from Pound's omission of the passage in which Homer recounts Odysseus' handling of Circe. Protected by the drug *moly* given to him by Hermes, Odysseus is immune to Circe's potion; and when she orders him with her "long stick" into her sty, he draws his "sharpened sword" and holds it against her throat. Then the suppliant Circe tries to seduce and unman him, feigning that "mutual trust may come of play and love." But Odysseus, with his sword still drawn, demands that she swear a "great oath" that she will "work no more enchantments to . . . [his] harm."[21]

In Homer, only after Circe yields to Odysseus' threats does her "dangerous bed" become her "flawless bed" of love. She swears by the patriarchal Zeus, "binds" herself to Odysseus, and helps him to venture to the prehistoric world of the dead. Yet it would be wrong to speak here of harmony or adjustment between man and Nature, man and woman. The order which Odysseus demands is impossible without the cutting edge of the sword, the mark of the masculine ego. Without at least the threat of violence, Odysseus could never place Circe on her pedestal at Terracina.

Pound's elision of this passage in Canto 39 may mean that victimization has nothing to do with his envisioned harmony and order. But in Cantos 41 and 40 this elided violence reappears with special relation to Fascism.

Like Odysseus' conquest of Circe, Mussolini's draining of the Pontine Marshes in Canto 41 asserts masculine identity and marks a victory for patriarchy. Still, there is no overt violence in Canto 41. Violence emerges in Canto 40, which concludes with Pound's translation of *The Periplus of Hanno*. Written in Greek, and recording events from the sixth century B.C., the *Periplus* narrates the colonizing mission of the Carthaginian Hanno along the West Coast of Africa. This adventure suggests nothing of harmony or adaptation to Nature but rather aggression against the prehistoric jungle or "bayou": again the swamp.[22]

Few Pound critics have considered Canto 40, and then only in the most general terms. The most likely reason for such neglect is that this canto discloses what Cantos 39 and 41 tend to conceal, that Pound's attitudes toward Nature are repressive and fascistic. Pearlman, however, views Hanno's voyage as an escape or "exit" from the time-ridden, feminine, materialistic, and usury-ridden Victorian world: "AGALMA, haberdashery, clocks, . . ." (40/ 199). "Hanno's world," he says, "is mythic, heroic, Odyssean, a world of brutally direct confrontation of man with nature." Surette observes that Pound's voyagers seek an exit out of "the brutality, dishonesty, and violence of commercial exploitation."[23]

Considered mythically, Hanno is an avatar of Odysseus and Hercules the solar hero. Like Hercules' journey beyond the straits of Gibraltar to kill Geryon (in Canto 23), his voyage follows the sun's "great periplum" (76/ 452), which brings order and clarity to the earth. Like Mussolini, Hanno has a cultural mission in the African jungle: he will "lay out Phoenician [Carthaginian] cities. . . . / house[s]" (40/ 199). But in fact the Hanno section is from the very start "contaminated" by history. Though it transports us to a seemingly mythical time and place, not only is Hanno's voyage an historical fact, but Canto 40 was written in response to unique historical and ideological needs: the Italian Fascist invasion of Ethiopia, which it celebrates in advance.[24] Indeed, if one considers this canto historically rather than mythically, Mussolini should be substituted entirely for Hanno. After all, it was not Hanno but Mussolini who claimed to reject the decadence, repression, and materialism of nineteenth-century bourgeois society, what Pound called "soft life and decadence" (Finer: 46–49, 172–173). Still, one should not exaggerate the differences between Pound, Mussolini, and the bourgeoisie. Pound supports Italian Fascism for distinctly "bourgeois" reasons, and Mussolini is engaged in the same sort of activity which Surette believes Pound to be escaping—brutality, dishonesty, commercial exploitation.[25]

With its frequent references to beasts (crocodiles, sea-horses, elephants), this canto looks forward to Canto 47, where great rulers have "the power over wild beasts" (47/245). The Carthaginians and their friendly interpreters, the Lixtae, who speak a comprehensible language, are distinguished from human groups which keep no domestic animals and which are nearly indistinguishable from animals: the "aethiopians living with untamed beasts," the "misshapen men swifter than horses,"[26] the "folk" who "wear the hides of wild beasts / and threw rocks to stone us, / so prevented our landing" (40/199, 200). These belong to the primeval jungle:

> for 12 days coasted the shore
> Aethiops fled at our coming
> Our Lixtae cd. not understand them.
> 12th day rose the woody mountain
> with great soft smell from the trees
> all perfumes many-mingling
> Two days, the wide bayou or inlet.
> (40/200)

Hanno's sailors encounter the swamp or "bayou." This realm of "softness" resembles that referred to in the radio broadcasts, which "calls to the basic laziness of the mind, the basic softness of human organism . . . entangles . . . [men] because of their inconsequentiality, their inability to see the connection between one thing and another" (RB, 238–239). Pound evokes this confusion in olfactory terms. The jungle's "soft" exhalation is an indistinct combination of odors represented by sound values unusual in Pound: "great soft smell from the trees," "perfumes many mingling." Where Pound usually sculpts "blocks" of sound, here sounds are of indefinite shape and duration. The sharp "t" fades into the prolonged and sibilant "s," the "f" and "r" of "from" and "perfumes" lack hardness, while the repeated merging of "s" and "m" ("smells," "perfumes many mingling") evokes blurring or indefinition.

Pound was apparently repelled by olfactory confusion and by bad, unknown, or mysterious smells. Eliot's poetry dwells on mingling odors, but known, or mysterious smells. Eliot's poetry dwells on mingling odors, but Pound's on the whole lacks olfactory imagery; and when it appears, Pound defines smells with precision, as in the Japanese incense ceremony, or the Byzantine perfumers' regulations, or else responds to them phobically, as in his frequent references to "stench" (in Canto 15, "stench like the fats at Grasse" connects the fermentation of perfumes with Hell).[27] It is not clear why Pound has a phobia of smells, but one possible answer is that the sense of smell can destroy the barrier between subject and object, and enable one, in a sense, to absorb the essence or emanation of another person or thing. In Eliot as in Proust (whose work Pound pronounced "unmitigated shit"), mingled odors unlock the doors of unconscious memory. Although Canto 40 is not concerned specifically with the individual's archaic past, it depicts a voyage into the ahistorical past of mankind, and this archaic world appears as Pound elsewhere represents the individual unconscious—that is, as a swamp or jungle. This encounter is fraught with anxiety, for the breath of the jungle threatens to submerge man in prehistory:

> And by day we saw only forest,
> > by night their fires. . . .
> The diviners told us to clear.
> Went from that fire fragrance,
> Flames flowed into sea. . . .
> > (40/ 200)

The climax of the voyage occurs at South Horn, another swamp or "bayou," as Pound translates it for contemporary (and "timeless") effect. Here the cultural violence elided in Canto 39 appears openly:

> By flame for three days to South Horn, the bayou,
> The island of folk hairy and savage
> whom our Lixtae said were Gorillas.
> We cd. not take any man, but three of their women.
> Their men clomb up the crags,
> Rained stone, but we took three women
> Who bit, scratched, wd. not follow their takers,
> Killed, flayed, brought back their pelts into Carthage. . . .
> > (40/ 200–201)

Where Hanno's explorers build stone walls and cities, these primitives rain down stone and live in permanent dilapidation.[28] There is a suggestion in the phrase "their women" of primitive sexual communism and promiscuity, a violation of patriarchal order as in Circe. It is not clear, though, whether these primitives are animal or human. Although one normally refers to male and female gorillas, Pound also refers to them as men and women. But since they are undomesticated and ahistorical, from the "human" or Carthaginian point of view they appear as unnatural animals.[29] Hence the pelts brought back to Carthage, trophies flayed from the bodies of savage women who bit and scratched like beasts. Pound's true commitment in this passage is not to mythical, organic, or natural time but to history. Whether human or animal, these primitives obstruct the project of empire.

By the 1930s Pound tried to "justify and rationalize" the invasion of Ethiopia by arguing that Ethiopia was a "colonial settlement" rather than "invaded territory." One recalls Pound's distinction between the good and bad forms of empire building, the first of which is benevolent and constructive colonialism, in the Roman manner, and the second of which is corrupt, exploitative, and usurious imperialism.[30] Although Canto 40 does nothing to clarify this distinction, its conclusion evokes not violence but eternal knowledge, permanent mythical values, the masculine NOUS. The records and trophies of Hanno's voyage are sacred objects:

> To the high air, to the stratosphere, to the imperial
> calm, to the empyrean, to the baily of the four towers
> the NOUS, ineffable crystal:
> Karxèdoniōn Basileos
>   hung this with his map in their temple.
>   (40/ 201)

Mirroring the "imperial calm," the Prince knows the eternal "dimension of stillness," and has "the power over wild beasts" (47/ 245). As for the heavenly and redundantly phallic "baily of the four towers," it is an ideal city (like Pound's mental Dioce), an imperishable archetype which inspires Hanno's city building. This is an example of what Mircea Eliade calls the "royal ideology," which always implies "the ascent to Heaven," and in which Mussolini figures as Roman dictator, the modern substitute for the hereditary king.[31]

Canto 40 requires us to see Hanno's and Mussolini's combined acts of destruction and creation in relation not so much to history as to a timeless cosmogonic myth (the sun's periplum, the labors of Hercules), a "primordial event" without which their efforts would be meaningless, merely historical:

> . . . Recollection and re-enactment of the primordial event [Mircea Eliade writes] help "primitive" man to distinguish and hold to the *real*. . . .
> Myth assures man that what he is about to do *has already been done*, in other words, it helps him to overcome doubts as to the result of his undertaking. There is no reason to hesitate before setting out on a sea voyage, because the mythical Hero has already made it in a fabulous Time. All that is needed is to follow his example. Similarly, there is no reason to fear settling in an unknown, wild territory, because one knows what one has to do. One has merely to repeat the cosmogonic ritual, whereupon the unknown territory ("Chaos") is transformed into "Cosmos," becomes an *imago mundi* and hence a ritually legitimized "habitation." The existence of an exemplary model does not fetter creative innovation. The possibilities for applying the mythical model are endless. (Eliade, 7–8, 21–24).

The danger of such mythological thinking is that, like the Jungian archetypes, or those of Northrop Frye, the primordial myth can cover a multitude thing. Contrary to Pound's idea that myths never "level out the differences," in Pound's hands myth is a form of evasive abstraction justifying the most brutal historical actions. Mussolini has no reason to hesitate on his voyage, because "the mythical Hero has already made it" in mythical time. "All that is needed is to follow his example."[32]

Pound's translation of *The Periplus of Hanno* is part of his Fascist mythology. It reveals his latent hostility toward Nature and his desire to suppress it by violent and historical means. At the same time, Canto 40 celebrates violence directed toward human beings. This violence is justified by a form of myth. It is also justified by metaphorically turning human beings into beasts, and then by treating them as beasts. The same mind is at work here which would later refer not only to Jews but to Gentiles as "cattle," "sheep," "lambs," and "swine."[33]

IV.

As we have seen, the link is not incidental but profoundly intimate between Pound and the various anti-Semitic and fascistic ideologies of our time. Point by point Pound's ideas and values figure unmistakably within that wide current of proto-fascist and fascist thought which culminates at Auschwitz and Buchenwald. Nor are these links confined to Pound's prose or to his merely abstract, discursive language. They emerge in his poetry as well, not only in its ideas but in its symbols, images, and metaphors. One must conclude, then, even on the basis of the incomplete evidence thus far presented, that *The Cantos* are a fascist poem, that is, a poem whose real meaning cannot be grasped without reference to its fascism. However, it is inadequate to confine this study mainly to the definition of the content and historical background of Pound's ideology. One must also seek its social and economic roots as well as its ultimate social, economic, and political purposes. Beyond these, one must examine the role of anti-Semitism and fascism within the verbal economy and structure of *The Cantos,* showing above all else that the fascist ideology is indispensable to the poem's linguistic strategies and formal development. Finally, one must pursue the psychological origins of Pound's hatred, of which his ideology is, to no small extent, a cover and rationalization. These are the aims of the next three parts of this book.

Part Two

Among the "Goyim"

Chapter Twelve

America and London

The Jews did not always appear in a sinister form to Pound. As we have seen, Pound's anti-Semitism manifests itself through a complex metaphorical system. He associates the Jewish presence in the West with numerous negatives—filth, disease, castration, sterility, the feminine, etc.—which proliferate like the swamp itself. Yet this metaphorical system is not dependent on the Jews, and most of it is complete before Pound's anti-Semitism becomes ideological. Moreover, the majority of Pound's anti-Semitic metaphors first appear in reference not to the Jews but to Pound's numerous "enemies" in the Gentile world. This suggests that Pound's anti-Semitism is, if only in part, a deflection or displacement of hostile impulses from many groups to a single group.

Before the Other, there were others. Pound's anti-Semitism has much to do with his experiences in America and England, from which Pound came to believe himself in "exile," and which, by the 1940s, he believed to be in Jewish hands—in short, with situations which have little obvious connection with anti-Semitism. The next three chapters unfold the process by which Pound, imagining himself the persecuted "enemy" of a violent and divided society, came to identify with that society and to view it in organic terms. At this point the Jews become society's enemy and candidates for persecution.

The transformation of Pound's enemies and obstacles into the single form of the demonic Jew is a complex process involving psychological strategies of displacement, denial, projection, and condensation. In order for us to examine this process, the subject of anti-Semitism must remain submerged over long stretches of the following narrative. But here and there it will reappear, until it emerges fully, as if by necessity, in its ideological as well as poetic form.

II.

When Pound began his cultural mission in America and London in 1908 he encountered many obstacles: the bourgeoisie, the universities, the parliamentary system, the moneyed interests, the literary establishment, and worst of all, newspapers and magazines, obstructors of communication and critical thought. Until at least 1934 Pound was mainly critical of Gentile rather than Jewish editors and publishers.[1] Setting out to purge these negative forces, Pound conceived of himself as a "drainage" and "sanitation" expert like Flaubert, who had accomplished in thought what Mussolini had accomplished in action: a return to distinction, order, clarity.[2] Even as late as the 1930s Pound applied these sanitary metaphors to non-Jews and non-Jewish institutions. Christianity, he said, is a "sink" (SP, 77), the newspapers are "mental sewage" (SP, 76), democracy elects "sewage" (91/ 613), literary people are "vermin" (SP, 76) needing to be eliminated, music has been turned into a "swamp" by "oily" and "vulgarian virtuosi" (GK, 253), some of whom may have been Jews. As for America, "after Grant" it had "mainly slumped into bog and sewage" (GK, 264).

In what sense is America a bog? When Pound returned from England to America in 1910–11, he was taken aback by "the sort of floating bog of our national confusion" (SP, 115). In New York Pound had encountered the masses, a "great swarming" (SP, 106) of "new strange people" whose "gods are not the gods whom one was reared to reverence" (SP, 104), and in whose vast "pool of . . . races . . . the static element of the Anglo-Saxon migration" had been "submerged" (SP, 108). Only Henry James had sensed the phallic origins, "the uprights, . . . the piles that are driven deep, and through the . . . floating bog" (SP, 115).

One of the "new strange people," notes William Chace, was the Jews.[3] Even so, anti-Semitism is not prominent in *Patria Mia* (written in 1912–1913, published in 1950), nor does Pound, himself a sort of nomad, condemn the new nomadism of American life. Rather, the "sort of man who made America is nomadic" (SP, 108), and Pound condemns that portion of the Anglo-Saxon race which had remained static and was thus submerged. And so the idea of the crowd, like America's newly attained commercial wealth, remains ambiguous. Although the "surging" and "pagan" American crowd has "an animal vigour unlike that of any European crowd" (SP, 104), its energy remains unconscious, inorganic, undirected, undifferentiated, and so in a sense monstrous: formerly "two thirds of the animal [the U.S.]," New England and the South "are no more than the ears of some new monster that is almost unconscious of them" (SP, 121). In the absence of what Pound calls a "centre" (SP, 121) of authority, the crowd lacks order, hierarchy, identity, consciousness, and thought: the conscious mind and ego must shape this raw material as Mussolini organizes the swamp in Canto 41.[4]

In the early poem "N.Y.," written before *Patria Mia,* Pound addresses New York City not as a crowd or monster but as a young girl who awaits the affectionate poet's informing energies:

> My City, my beloved, my white! Ah, slender,
> Listen! Listen to me, and I will breathe into thee a soul.
> Delicately upon the reed, attend me!
> . . . .
> My City, my beloved,
> Thou art a maid with no breasts,
> Thou art slender as a silver reed,
> Listen to me, attend me!
> And I will breathe into thee a soul,
> And thou shalt live for ever.
>
> (CEP, 185)

Pound often thinks of cities as feminine, and of the feminine as unformed matter, the Greek HYLE, meaning uncut forest. In "N.Y." the girl is a silver reed, and thus belongs to the swamp. The mythical analogue is perhaps the story of Syrinx and her lover Pan who, to substitute for the object of his natural desire, played upon a notched reed, and so replaced Nature's uniform murmur with clearly differentiated sounds: music, poetry. Hanno's Carthaginian sailors do something similar in Canto 40, amid the "high murmuring rushes" of seaboard marshes.

For Pound America is basically feminine. "I don't know," he says, "how America is going to explain herself to England, considering that she has never permitted her writers to explain her to herself."[5] America thus remains like the vague and decentered feminine entity in "Ortus." As "beautiful as the sunlight and as fluid," but lacking a "name" and a "place," a "being" and a "separate soul," this creature cannot be brought to "birth" save through the poet's "labor." Only through him can she attain "a name and a center"; without him she cannot even "learn to say 'I' " (PER, 84).[6]

And yet, in the italicized middle section of "N.Y." Pound is aware of the incongruity between New York and its personification as a girl:

> *Now do I know that I am mad,*
> *For here are a million people surly with traffic;*
> *This is no maid.*
> *Neither could I play upon my reed if I had one.*
> (CEP, 185)

Far from being passive and feminine, New York jostles with economic competition: "traffic" anticipates Pound's later economic themes. The crowd is ambiguous. On the one hand it awaits the poet passively, like the swamp; on the other, it is mobile and perhaps even violent ("surly"). The crowd reveals the same ambiguities as later appear in the Jews.

III.

After leaving America in 1908, Pound took up residence in London, and, as he was to say in the broadcasts, "the charm of London is feminine."

He added: "London is romantic. That is, the three or whatever million surplus females in England open up possibilities to the traveler" (RB, 245). Reminiscent of the human proliferation of the American "bog," the phrase "surplus females" evokes London as a crowd of women. Yet far from being a full presence, such material abundance only "opens up" possibilities, a phrase which suggests the vagina and thus associates women with phallic absence and inactivity. With more obvious crudity Pound compares London with the female sexual organ in a letter of March 5, 1926 to William Carlos Williams. Again noting the "great proportion of females above the males" in England, Pound describes it as "THE land of the male with phallus erectus." As for London, it is "THE cunt of the world."[7] The last statement calls to mind Pound's notion of the brain as phallus and the necessity of the male intelligence to "charge" and form the "female chaos" (PD, 204). "Even oneself has felt it," said Pound, "driving any new idea into the great passive vulva of London, a sensation analogous to the male feeling in copulation" (PD, 204). Here is the probable inspiration for Gaudier's sculpted head of Pound in the shape of a marble phallus, commemorating his assault on the feminine city (Norman: 136).

Between 1908 and 1921 England was Pound's base in his attempt to set off a cultural revolution in mass society. This project was interrupted and finally aborted by World War I, in which T. E. Hulme and the promising young artist Gaudier-Brzeska had been killed, and which Pound believed to have virtually destroyed English civilization. Increasingly discouraged by English politics, society, and cultural life, and deeply depressed by the death of Gaudier, Pound in the immediate post-war period came to view England as dominated by usury. By the spring of 1921 Pound had permanently abandoned London for Paris, which he subsequently abandoned for Rapallo. These developments coincide with Pound's emergent Anglophobia. In *Guide to Kulchur* (1937), Pound describes London as a "bog or clog in the world's sub-sewage" (GK, 249). By 1940 England appears to Pound as an "outpost" (RB, 62) of usury and "judea" (P/L, 217), a nation in the hands of the enemy.[8]

Pound said that the "hell cantos are specifically LONDON, the state of English mind in 1919 and 1920" (L, 239). These cantos serve to "bottle" Pound's enemies within a hell of his own devising and to dramatize his abandonment of the city.[9] They are also Pound's fullest—and most ambiguous—representation of London as "female chaos."

Having pronounced in *Mauberley* that "age-old" (PER, 190) usury is the disease of modern civilization, Pound introduces into Hell an insidious and monstrous insect: Usura, "the beast with a hundred legs" (15/ 64). The Hell *Cantos*, though they never refer to the Jews,[10] contain the same kind of imagery as appears in Pound's anti-Semitic polemics: fragmentation, darkness, bogs, swamps, impotence, monstrosity, falsification, loss of origins, infection, plague, castration, organic disease, vermin, prostitution, filth, stench, sadism, and violence. But in London usury is only one of a number of sins, and Pound inculpates all of English society rather than any particular evil. Hence this Hell contains great numbers of unidentified people: "politicians," "crowds," "multitudes," "respecters," "conservatives," "invisible, many English," "back scratchers," "bores," etc. As if to suggest their anonymity and interchangeability, Pound introduces a kind of stage direction: "THE PERSONNEL CHANGES" (14/ 62). Curiously, this Hell lacks that Dantescan sense of moral gradations and clarity which Pound believed Semitic influences had destroyed in the West.

Like America, Hell is also a "bog" or swamp, whose inhabitants are "liquid animals": "multitudes in the ooze, / newts, water-slugs, water-maggots," "Dead maggots begetting live maggots" (14/ 61, 63). Observing journalists and their products, Pound hears Plotinus say that "this sort breeds by scission" (15/ 65). Pound thus equates human generation with insect and animal parthenogenesis—a metaphor which probably derives from Gourmont's *Natural Philosophy of Love.*

Especially common to the lower forms of aquatic animals and to "nearly all vegetables," parthenogenesis is reproduction by self-duplication (scission) or else solely by means of feminine sexual organs; the first is asexual generation (long treated as a form of parthenogenesis), while the second is parthenogenesis as Gourmont normally describes it. To put it another way, parthenogenesis is "generation without the aid of the male"; as such it is undifferentiated and hence "primitive." For Gourmont, as for Pound, the male is the bearer of difference.[11] However fecund, the feminine can only cast off undifferentiated duplicates of itself. Thus Gourmont's feminine or "primitive" Nature resembles Pound's "female chaos."

Swamps, parthenogenesis, and primitive generation are especially apt to evoke Pound's idea of the crowd, since they suggest chaos, undifferentiation, primitivism, monstrosity, passive femininity, and the mechanical repetition and contagious proliferation of received ideas: Pound refers to "scission," "flies carrying news" (14/ 63), and "howling, as of a hen-yard in a printing house" (14/ 61). Such imagery also suggests the masses' ephemeral existence, as of those "Bohemias" which Pound's Walter Villerant finds "worth avoiding. The poor ones are like pools full of frogs' eggs, and hordes of these globules perish annually" (PD, 64–65). Comparable to Gourmont's mouthless ephemera, which "hover in clouds . . . among the reeds," and which live, copulate, and die "without even having looked at the sun" (Gourmont: 15–16), the human crowds of Pound's Hell know nothing of Pater Helios, to whom Pound flees at the end of Canto 15. Meanwhile, these parthenogenetic images probably import the sterility of usury, whereby money falsely increases its value by monstrous duplication. Gourmont's hydra, which reproduces itself by "fragmentation," anticipates the self-duplicating Hydra of Usury in Addendum to Canto 100 (Gourmont: 21–24).

Gourmont argues that parthenogenesis tends toward a debilitating undifferentiation and sterility within the species. He points out, however, that parthenogenesis need not be "taken literally." Just as "there is no indefinite scissiparity without coupling," so there is no unlimited partheno-genesis without "fecundation," which inevitably restores a species to differ-entiation, energy, and health. Gourmont adds that "Parthenogenesis is a sign-post." Though the female "appears to be the whole show, without the male she is nothing" (Gourmont: 21–29).

The Hell *Cantos* thus reveal that man, suffering from the undifferen-tiating diseases of democracy (the crowd) and usury (often associated with democracy and liberalism in Pound), has reached the parthenogenetic sign-post. Pound suggests the dominance in London of a kind of demonic matriar-chy, what he elsewhere calls "gynocracy" (PER, 239); he speaks of "hens," "sows eating their litters," and "sadic mothers driving their daughters to bed with decrepitude" (14/ 62). Implicit too in the Hell *Cantos* is the motif of phallic absence, the disappearance of those differentiating marks which signify the originating masculine *logos*. Hell is an amphibious place of inde-terminate origins, of "mobile earth," "repetitions" (15/ 65) without differ-ence, "lost contours, erosions" (14/ 62), "ooze" (14/ 61); everywhere Pound finds evidence of lost cultural beginnings and distinctions. To overcome this chaos, civilization must return to the differentiating and fecundating mascu-line principle, which Pound himself represents (Gourmont: 114).

And yet, if London is essentially feminine and impotent (compare the "impetuous impotent dead" and the "sickly death's heads" of Canto 1, in which Odysseus is in Hades), why is it so actively threatening and difficult to control? Actually, Pound's Hell reveals femininity in its aggressive form: phallic "lady golfers" (15/ 64), "sadic mothers," and carnivorous sows. The "feminine" crowd is also characterized by violence: "the courageous vio-lent, ... the cowardly inciters to violence" (15/ 64). Toward the end of Canto 15 Pound sees unknown figures who, though they have "no confi-dence among them [et nulla fidentia inter eos]," appear threateningly:

> with daggers and bottle ends, waiting an
> unguarded moment . . . .
> (15/ 65)

To Pound's rescue comes Plotinus, bringing the decapitated head of the Medusa, which he controls. Thanks to the Medusa's petrifying gaze, Pound hammers the swamp of London into a narrow bridge which enables him to escape. As the myth has it, no man could look directly at the Medusa without turning to stone. Plotinus tells Pound to keep his eyes on "the mirror," the "unsinkable shield" presumably of Perseus, who received it from Athena and used it to decapitate the Medusa:

> Keep your eyes on the mirror.
> Prayed we to the Medusa,
> petrifying the soil by the shield,

Holding it downward
    he hardened the track
Inch before us, by inch,
    the matter resisting,
The heads rose from the shield,
    hissing, held downwards . . . .
The serpents' tongues
    grazing the swill top,
Hammering the souse into hardness,
    the narrow rast,
Half the width of a sword's edge.
    By this through the dern evil,
now sinking, now clinging,
    Holding the unsinkable shield.
            (15/ 66)

Pound staggers out of Hell into the light of Pater Helios, the masculine symbol of order, identity, and differentiation.

In a brief essay Freud sought to explain the horror which is often associated with the decapitated head of the Medusa. His explanation hinges on a connection as characteristic of Pound's thinking as of Freud's: the head and the penis are, symbolically speaking, interchangeable. Thus, says Freud, "to decapitate = to castrate. The terror of the feminine Medusa is . . . a terror of castration that is linked to the sight of something." Freud argues that the terror springs from the sight of the feminine genitals, the discovery by the child that the female is, in a sense, castrated, and that he might be castrated too.[12]

Pound's Hell implies parthenogenesis, which is a kind of incest, as well as phallic absence and aggressive matriarchy. Consider too the aspect under which the Anglo-Saxon American, consciously or unconsciously, must view England. It is his second home and the Mother or "mama" (RB, 378) Country. But in this case England figures as the bad mother, who refuses Pound's attentions, destroys her young, and yet supports an endless spawn of worthless parasites. To add further to Pound's terror, his assailants threaten him not only with knives but with the jagged mouth of a broken bottle—an image which suggests the vagina dentata rather than the "passive vulva" of London. Yet Pound has a means of protection and escape: the Medusa's head, which he uses as a weapon or shield, and which forges a bridge out of London. The use of the Medusa for attack or defense is based on homeopathy: Pound believes that what frightens him—the Medusa's head—will frighten others. By controlling the Medusa through the intervention of Plotinus, who represents conscious thought and hence the ego, Pound, like Mussolini in the draining of the Pontine Marshes, symbolically enacts the restitution of the missing phallus. Freud writes:

    The hair upon Medusa's head is frequently represented in works of art in the form of snakes, and these once again are derived from the castration complex. It is a remarkable fact that, however frightening they may be in themselves, they nevertheless actually serve as a mitigation of the horror, for they replace the penis, the absence of which is the cause of the horror. This is a confirmation of the technical rule according to which a multiplication of penis symbols signifies castration.

The sight of the Medusa's head makes the spectator stiff with terror, turns him to stone. Observe that we have here once again the same origin from the castration complex and the same transformation of affect! For becoming stiff means an erection. Thus in the original situation it offers consolation to the spectator: he is still in possession of a penis, and the stiffening reassures him of the fact.[13]

This would explain the snakes which "rose from the shield" and "hammered the souse into hardness." The bridge is a phallic object, hardening to resist the encroachments of the swamp. Pound also compares the bridge to the thin edge of a sword: one recalls Odysseus' sword, which he uses in Canto 1 to resist the impinging crowds of the dead, and in Canto 39 to bend the threatening Circe to his will. Like the unsinkable shield, Pound's sword implies demarcation, protection, and power; its edge can cut and mutilate, can do that which Pound fears will be done to himself.

IV.

The anxiety of the Hell *Cantos* has a sociological as well as psychological basis. Pound's assumptions of masculine political and sexual dominance were repeatedly challenged at the beginning of this century by parliamentary democracy, the woman's suffrage movement, and by a growing desire among women for sexual liberation.[14] Pound's distrust of the suffragette and the "new freewoman" resembles that of his Vorticist colleagues.[15] In "L'Homme Moyen Sensuel" Pound ridicules the ineffectual American "hero" Radway as the "finest flower" of the American "gynocracy" (PER, 239), and in his translation of *The Natural Philosophy of Love* he comments on the dominance of the female among North American animals: "O sinistre continent" (Gourmont: 57n). In each case American democracy implies either the rule or dominance of women. In "Imaginary Letters" Pound's thinly disguised alter ego Walter Villerant remarks that one "Levine," an all-purpose "procurer," had been called "the brains behind the female suffrage movement in England" (PD, 62). This passage combines anti-Semitism and anti-feminism, a link which we have already suggested, and which appears in fascism.[16] Pound also resents such Cheyne Walk Circes as Lady Valentine, whose "commands" (PER, 196) he, not Mauberley, awaits in a London drawing room.

It is less easy to explain Pound's representation of London in Cantos 14 and 15. Although Hells are traditionally violent, and although post-war London experienced considerable social unrest, the Hell *Cantos* almost certainly exceed the facts of the case. For all his claims of objectivity, of having "exaggerated nothing,"[17] Pound probably had no justification for his fears of contact with and contamination by London's inhabitants, nor had he any reason to fear unknown assailants. Nor would he seem altogether justified in referring to London as a swamp. Even if we accept the argument that Pound had to leave London because of the hostility of conservative editors, this would not account entirely for the violence of Pound's characterization.

In psychoanalysis the crowd is often interpreted as a symbol of the unconscious; Freud, who had a crowd phobia, drew an analogy between the seething masses and the "deeper strata of the human psyche." Furthermore Pound later speaks frequently of the human unconscious as a bog-like place of bacillary proliferation.[18] The presence of human and non-human crowds within the swamp of London in the Hell *Cantos* suggests that Pound's representation of the city is saturated with unconscious or latent content. Indeed it is evident that his faith in the protective power of the Medusa depends ultimately on homeopathy, the projection of unconscious fear onto the crowd. Pound believes that what frightens him will have a comparable effect on London. But if London's terror is a projection, the same thing might be said of its violence; it too is a projection, represented in the form of the crowd, of Pound's unconscious impulses of violence against the crowd. The Hell *Cantos* are a distanced representation of the Hell within.

It is necessary, then, to reject Hugh Kenner's view that the Hell *Cantos* successfully embody Pound's ideal of artistic and even scientific objectivity, that Pound's Hell, like a series of exhibits in a museum, "exists tamed, as an ideal order, behind glass."[19] In one sense Kenner is right to describe the Hell *Cantos* in terms of scientific objectivity, hygiene, fixity, and detachment. Insofar as Pound fears London as violent and contagious, and insofar as its chaotic flux resists his desires, he wants to "bottle," sterilize, and control the city. But Eliot was also right to say that Pound's Hell is for "the *other people*," and thus to imply that Pound fails to acknowledge both the violence within himself and the fear from which it emerges (Eliot: 47). Pound's evasion and self-recognition requires not scientific objectivity but the ability to distance and fix the hated and feared object by visual means, to present it not in its actual resemblance to himself but as entirely other and entirely loathesome. It requires, as Kenneth Burke says of Wyndham Lewis, that "eye-mindedness" which enables one to "project the enemy, to look at it by subterfuge" and "without risk," to attack it from afar and with the "artistic equivalent of a long fuse."[20]

To be sure, Herbert Schneidau is correct to remind us that there was no "visualization requirement" in the theory of the Image formulated by Pound and his circle. In response to those who thought only of the "STATIONARY image," Pound insisted that Imagism also includes the "moving image." Far from seeking to convey static perception, argues Schneidau, Imagism and Vorticism sought to convey dynamic, formal energy, the "shock and stroke of experience," which means that images "must be felt rather than merely seen"; hence Pound's concern for tactile as well as visual values.[21] Nonetheless, eyemindedness is perhaps Pound's primary quality as a poet, and an essential part not only of the Hell *Cantos* but of his poetic theory, whether of Imagism or Vorticism (Gage: 13–15). To quote Pound's discussion of Vorticism: "An image, in our sense, is real because we know it directly" (GB, 86). We know it with a "subtle and instantaneous perception . . . such as savages have of the necessities and dangers of the forest."[22] According to John Gage, this definition of the image indicates Pound's belief in poetry as a "visual" and "concrete" (though not necessarily mimetic) language (Gage: 15). Nor is it altogether correct to say that Pound prefers a dynamic to a static art. Apart from such "phallic" qualities as solidity, compactness, and hardness, Vorticism "took stasis as a general goal," as in Wyndham Lewis's statement that "The Vorticist is at his maximum point of energy when stillest."[23] Pound approaches this idea in the *New Age,* in 1918, observing that "art is perhaps a stasis. A painter or a sculptor tries to make something which can stay still without becoming a bore. He tries to make something which will stand being looked at *for a long time*" (EPVA, 78). This state-ment defines art as a means of visual control and dominance, of freezing or paralyzing external reality; it grants to it precisely that power which is possessed by the Medusa.

Cantos 14 and 15 tempt one to explain in psychological terms why Pound favors finely etched outlines and fixed and bounded images, an art of clear shapes and orderly, sometimes even geometrical or abstract patterns. Following Wilhelm Worringer, Pound's colleague T. E. Hulme viewed the abstract and geometrical as opposed to the vital and empathic image as an indispensable means of objectifying and arresting experience, and thus of escaping the otherwise uncontrollable external and internal flux. Although some critics have sought to deny the significance of Hulme's influence on Pound, Michael North has shown that Pound was sufficiently impressed by Hulme's theorizing to borrow his (and ultimately Worringer's) distinction between vital and geometric art.[24] As in Hulme, Pound's aesthetic values of concreteness, objectivity, and stasis may reflect a fear both of the chaotic outer world and of the unconscious in its fluidity and unrepresentability: certainly the Hell *Cantos* would support this view. One might also say that the paralyzing Medusa, suggestive of primitive terror of the unconscious as well as control over it, and with the capacity to freeze the image within the flux, is Pound's symbol of Imagism and perhaps of Vorticism.[25]

There are, however, a number of drawbacks to such direct and instanta-neous perception in representing social reality. The object, once fixed in time, gives no further feedback. The suppression of temporality lessens and even eliminates the possibility of further knowledge about the object and the reinvestment of such knowledge within it. Thus the direct and instantaneous perception which Pound admires may be merely an untested first impres-sion, saturated with projective elements, as in the Hell *Cantos*. Horkheimer and Adorno have pointed out a similar tendency to isolate the object, to refuse feedback and the testing of projections through temporal reflection, in the classic anti-Semite's perception of the Jews; such perceptual habits enable the anti-Semite to project hateful and guilty feelings onto the Jewish "other."[26]

   In the end Pound's Hell is neither "tamed" nor "ideal." Though Pound wants to "bottle" London, the "exhibits" will not stay "in their places," and his fuse is not long enough (Vasse: 113). As Pound looks beneath him in Canto 15, he finds "nothing that might not move, / mobile earth, a dung hatching obscenities" (15/ 65). The Medusa is capable of protecting and saving Pound, but not of controlling this chaos. Pound has no choice but to flee London and its "impetuous impotent dead."

Chapter Thirteen

Persecution and Power

This is Paul Rosenfeld's portrait of Pound as he appeared on the streets of Paris in the early 1920s:

> On the evening of my arrival in that city, sitting behind the privet-hedge of a small restaurant in the Latin Quarter, I became aware of something slightly disturbing on the sidewalk. This was a tall individual in the later thirties who, while obviously an Englishman or American, appeared to have stepped straight out of the opera *La Bohème*. A swarthy sombrero covered his head. The collar of his Wotan-blue shirt lay widely open on the lapels of his coat, which had a good English cut, setting off a ruddy, well-trimmed beard. He sported a cane. Resembling the 1830's artists in Puccini's opera, he also resembled a Norse pirate, but an ornamental Norseman, who had infrequently been to sea. His glance, as momentarily he lingered, took in the diners; not, however, it seemed to me, so much in order to gather their identities as to gather the impression he was making.[1]

Pound lingers before a passive crowd of already occupied and "respectable" people whom he seeks to astonish, provoke, and master. In the Hell *Cantos* Pound reveals an apparently different but in fact similar attitude toward the modern crowd. Filled with nameless conspirators, persecutors, and enemies, it chooses Pound as its innocent victim. This sense of persecution by great numbers increased over Pound's career. Describing Pound in the 1950s, Charles Norman speaks of "his mysterious, implacable persecutors, and it was not clear to the reporter whether they were men or demons." A visitor to St. Elizabeths also observed that whenever Pound read anything which concerned "the Conspiracy" or involved his delusions, "his voice would tremble and his hand would shake." By this time Pound believed that many, perhaps even most, of his persecutors were Jewish or allied with the Jews. A lunatic, he said, is "an animal somewhat surrounded by Jews."[2]

The projective strategies and metaphors of the Hell *Cantos* prefigure these anti-Semitic obsessions. What needs to be examined is the process by which one hostile crowd or group of crowds (the Gentiles or "goyim" as Pound calls them) is replaced by another, and how Pound's aggression against the Gentile world is displaced onto the Jews. First, though, it is necessary to consider Pound's conception of himself as a persecuted artist, and the pervasive themes of violence and power in his works.

In Canto 110 Allen Upward is one of those few artists who held out against his enemies: "Bunting and Upward neglected, / all the resisters blacked out" (110/ 781). Earlier Pound had implicitly identified with Upward:

> sd/ the old combatant: "victim,
> withstood them by Thames and by Niger with pistol by Niger
> with a printing press by the Thomas [Thames] bank"
>
> . . .
>
> and shot himself;
>
> (74/ 437)

Having withstood the savages of the Niger with a pistol, Upward as "combatant" only temporarily withstood the savages of the Thames with his printing press. In 1926 Upward committed suicide. In a statement remarkable for its lack of subtlety, Pound observed that the real cause of Upward's death may have been his "discouragement" on learning that George Bernard Shaw had received the Nobel Prize.[3]

Upward's *New Word,* which Pound reviewed enthusiastically in 1914 (SP, 407–412, 403–406), attempts to define the meaning of the word "idealist" as used by Alfred Nobel in his bequest of the Nobel Prize. For Upward the great literary artist is a quasi-religious figure capable of saving a benighted world. He is an avatar of what Upward, in his later work, *The Divine Mystery* (of even greater importance to Pound), called the Divine Man, a shaman, demigod, and genius of uncanny powers. But unfortunately society cannot tolerate its saviors, and pursues a "policy of crucifixion." Because of man's "fear and hatred of genius," it is, as A.D. Moody paraphrases Upward, "the fate of genius . . . to be crucified."[4] In man's "march upward out of the deep into the light. . . . the giants are cut down" on the "Procrustean bed" of Humanity. "Man's march upward" suggests an unconscious (and megalomaniac) pun, evoking the image of Upward himself leading mankind out of darkness. Besides resembling Pound's lament that all men are "cut down to worm-size" (87/ 572), the image of the Procrustean bed conveys Upward's notion that humanity is a uniform mass. The false "religion of Humanity," which derives from the French Revolution, signifies the revolt of the slaves against their natural superiors, whom the envious slaves attempt to infect with fear, guilt, and self-doubt (Upward, 1: 94–100, 302–303; SP, 409).

From the very start Pound assumes that the artist inevitably suffers persecution because he possesses a special truth. In "Masks," from *A Lume Spento,* Pound speaks of "tales of old disguisings," the "strange myths" invented by souls who "found themselves among / Unwonted" and "hostile . . . folk" (CEP, 34). The experience which they need to conceal or mask by myth is apparently the intuition or memory of immortal or god-like existence ("The star-span acres of his former lot"). Later, in *The Spirit of Romance,* Pound observes that "Greek myth arose when someone having passed through delightful psychic experience tried to communicate it to others and found it necessary to screen himself from persecution." This experience is probably that "certain sort of moment" when a man is privileged to feel "his immortality upon him" (SR, 92, 94).

According to Pound, the public is "sure to hate . . . the germ of original capacity" (L, 234), while genius "arouses any amount of inferiority complex" (J/M, 19), and inferiority is the real source of the public's patronizing belief that "genius" is "akin to madness" (ABC, 82). In his poem "The Rest," Pound addresses his fellow artists in America as "enslaved," "broken," "lost," "mistrusted," "spoken against," "shut in," "thwarted," "hated"; he, meanwhile, has "beaten out his exile" (PER, 92–93). Though it is unlikely that Pound and other artists suffered such massive persecution (much less enslavement), Pound's later experiences in London strengthened his idea of the artist as society's sacrificial victim. "There is no truce between art and the public," remarks Walter Villerant in "Imaginary Letters." "The public celebrates its eucharists with dead bodies. Its writers aspire to equal the oyster: to get themselves swallowed alive" (PD, 55). During the *Blast* period Pound observed that the public's habit had been "for long / to do away with good writers," and that he could "feel" the public's "hates wriggling about his feet."[5] He even found intense personal hatred among the guarantors of *Poetry* magazine (L, 237).

In spite of and even because of persecution, the artist always wins. For Upward persecution confirms the artist's special status: victimization proves election. This idea is consistent with Upward's argument in *The Divine Mystery* that primitive religions originate in scapegoating and victimization, and that the victim of religious persecution in primitive times is often indistinguishable from a divinity (Upward, 2: 56–59, 92–99). All this was not lost on Pound in his Postscript to Gourmont's *The Natural Philosophy of Love:*

> . . . In a primitive community, a man, a volontaire, might risk it. He might want prestige, authority, want them enough to grow horns and claim a divine heritage, or to grow a cat head; Greek philosophy would have smiled at him, would have deprecated his ostentation. With primitive man he would have risked a good deal, he would have been deified, or crucified, or possibly both. Today he would be caught for a circus. (PD, 210)

At the end of his last work, *Some Personalities* (English edition, 1921), after observing that he had been a "man of strife," Upward named himself a "foundation-victim," apparently of a new religious order of which some other artist would be the leader (Upward, 3: 302). This phrase, which forecasts Upward's suicide five years later, also serves to confirm his special status. Yet it is not clear that Upward, in committing suicide, was in fact the victim of others. The enmity which Upward saw in the public was not greater, indeed was less than his own hostility toward mass society. One might say that Upward, far from finding himself in an adversary position, instead chose the role of adversary to provoke that enmity which signifies the artist's special status. In the absence of actual persecutors, Upward had to enact personally society's supposed victimization of himself. There is a kind of schizophrenia in Upward's ultimate gesture.[6]

Pound, of course, did not commit suicide, for the suicide is "not serious from conviction," and the potential suicide should "first bump off some nuisance" (93/ 625). Nonetheless, Pound's assumption that the artist suffers persecution and his own adoption of a histrionic relationship to the public brings him close to Upward's position and binds him—as we shall see in the radio broadcasts—to increasingly schizophrenic and self-destructive behaviour. Instead of recognizing that society is largely indifferent to the artist, Pound assumes the presence of obstacles and enemies and creates them where none exists. His example confirms René Girard's argument that it is not society's hatred but its indifference which most frustrates the artistic revolutionary.[7]

Pound sometimes recognizes the public's indifference: "Hulme wasn't hated by the old bastards, because they didn't know he was there."[8] Pound also quotes Yeats's remark about artists: "Fortunately they don't know we are here, otherwise they wd. abolish us all" (L, 221). But even here Pound exaggerates the artist's unacceptability, just as he normally assumes that society is conscious of his challenge. His real situation in the face of society's indifference is conveyed in Charles Norman's description of Pound in the 1930s. Living in Rapallo, Pound repeatedly and vainly castigates America, a "very provoking" dunce that "neither knew nor cared," that "never listened" (Norman: 286). Pound is by no means indifferent to the masses he despised: the public must be made to pay attention, must be provoked to curiosity, hatred, even to violence. Upward's Divine Man (and victim) is also a "performing god" who requires an audience which he seeks to control by magical means (Upward, 2: 1). In similar fashion Pound's masks not only screen the artist from persecution but also gain, by histrionic means, the attention of the crowd.

In the radio broadcasts Pound seeks to attract and control a crowd which has supposedly gone over to the Jews. Much earlier he was frequently observed in theatrical poses and in "the operatic outfit of 'stage poet' "—a description tallying with Paul Rosenfeld's portrait of the Bohemian and exhibitionist Pound in Paris in the early 1920s (Norman: 68, 51). Such histrionics serve to support Pound's self-conception as a persecuted man and social outcast. This is obvious if we consider the impression which Pound sought to create and its analogues in social life.

Otto Fenichel observes that artists, stage actors, gypsies, and Jews have often created a similar impression within Western societies, and that each has suffered social persecution in widely varying degrees. Each is identified in some way with the exotic, the curious, the strange, the forbidden—the gypsies with black magic, the Jews with the mysterious mimesis of their rituals, the artist with the magical mimesis of art. All of these activities are felt by society to be powerful and even dangerous; their practitioners are *sacer*, at once sacred and taboo, holy and untouchable. These groups are also frequently identified with an archaic and nomadic rootlessness which sets them off from others and which differs sharply from everyday domestic life. But their most disturbing effect derives from their uncanny quality in Freud's sense, their simultaneous unfamiliarity and familiarity; for these "undomesticated" ones strike close to home. These groups often revive in the ordinary observer the memory of his own archaic, repressed, and now alien impulses: free mimetic activity (of all kinds), the refusal of normal social obligations, an apparently open and expressive emotional and sexual life. At the same time these groups revive the memory of historical periods in which social existence had a seemingly less repressive form. Undoubtedly the impulse to attack them has its partial basis in the desire to suppress reminders of the archaic instincts.[9]

That artists are persecuted and are objects of suspicion does not undercut the main point that society generally ignores the artist's challenge. One must also recognize that the modern artist has helped to create his own alienation, and that this posture is often welcomed or at least expected. This goes far to explain Pound's early identification if not with Jews then with gypsies, actors, prostitutes, and circus animals.

In "Fifine Answers," Pound's speaker and heroine is Browning's Fifine from *Fifine at the Fair*. An actress, loose woman, and member of a band of travelling players, Fifine experiences social degradation and economic hardship but also an exultant freedom and mastery inseparable from torment. She is a Christ figure whom society "exiles" and crucifies and whose crucifixion, endlessly repeated, provides a spiritual release unavailable to the cowardly bourgeois. More interesting and much less melodramatic is "The Gypsy," where Pound speaks without a mask. The poem commemorates his encounter with a gypsy in Southern France after the Feast of St. John:

> That was the top of the walk, when he said:
> "Have you seen any of the others, any of our lot,
> "With apes or bears?"
>   —A brown upstanding fellow
> Not like the half-castes,
>   up on the wet road near Clermont.
> The wind came, and the rain,
> And mist clotted about the trees in the valley,
> And I'd the long ways behind me,
>   gray Arles and Biaucaire,
> And he said, "Have you seen any of our lot?"

I'd seen a lot of his lot . . .
                    ever since Rhodez,
Coming down from the fair
          of St. John,
With caravans, but never an ape or a bear.
                              (PER, 119)

Like Fifine, these gypsies perform as exotic curiosities at the feasts, fairs, and carnivals of an alien religion. But Pound's relation to the gypsy is ambiguous. It seems as if the gypsy is one of his own, as if he took Pound for a gypsy too: the possessive "our" can include both the gypsy and Pound, and would thus imply that Pound, in more ways than one, is one of the "others." The similarity is brought out by Pound himself, who had "the long ways behind" him. As for Pound's comment, "I'd seen a lot of his lot," this is ambiguous, since "his lot" both dissociates Pound from the gypsies and implies a further identification: Pound has known the gypsy's lot, is himself a kind of gypsy.

Submerged in this poem is a theme of human degradation and victimization. One notes the link between gypsies, apes, and bears, the fact that the circus animals resemble (ape) human beings, and their performance at the feast of a Catholic saint, which would invariably involve sacrificial ritual. Indeed these exotic performances of gypsies and their animals are a sublimated form of religious sacrifice. Fenichel observes that fairs originated in divine worship, and "are still called 'Messe' in German," which means "mass." At fairs, moreover, "people are offered dreadful sights which are otherwise forbidden or inaccessible." Fenichel explains the significance of such sights, and why they appear at carnivals and "messes," both of which imply flesh and eating. They signify the foreign, persecuted, uncanny, beautiful, and "ugly" god, the god who is overcome and victimized and whose image revives in the foreigner and his histrionic retinue of exotic animals.[10] To quote Pound on his "horned god," in modern times he "would be caught for a circus." Incidentally, Fenichel connects such carnival performances with the typical anti-Semite's conception of the Jews, and Pound later refers to the Jews as "messes" (SP, 313).

There is another reason why Pound identifies with the nomadic outcasts of Western civilization. As early as "Anima Sola" in *A Lume Spento*, Pound apostrophizes "Loneliness" and speaks of himself as a "god man," a "weird untamed," who eats of "no man's meat" and drinks "the wine of sleet" (CEP, 20). A weird is an uncanny figure, at once familiar and unfamiliar, *heimliche* and *unheimliche*. As Pound says in a letter to Thomas Hardy on March, 1921, he comes "from an American suburb—where I was not born—where both parents are really foreigners, i.e., one from New York and one from Wisconsin." "The suburb," he adds, "has no roots, no center of life."[11] One recalls Pound's *New Age* article of January 8, 1920: "I was," says Pound, ". . . brought up in a district and city with which my forbears had had no connection, and I am therefore accustomed to being an alien, and it is just as homelike for me to be alien in one place as in another."[12] Pound, whether in America, England, or France, not only feels estranged from his environment, but thinks of himself as producing an alien and even uncanny impression upon others. His anti-Semitism is thus fed by a desire to deny or suppress his own social alienation and marginality. He projects onto the nomadic and uncanny Jews his simultaneously strange and familiar sense of his own foreignness.[13]

II.

Pound is by no means society's passive victim, nor are Bohemian histrionics the only means by which he alerts society to his presence. Pound believes that there is a "war" between the artist and the public, a war "without truce"; the artist should revolt against his "oppressors." Because the "dangers" faced by the artist are "subtle and sudden," he must live his life as would a "bushman" or "Tahitian savage," by "craft and violence." The artist worships "violent gods" (EPVA, 181). But in truth the artist's hostility, like his histrionics, really serves to provoke society and create opposition where none originally exists. It also places him in the cherished role of enemy, outcast, even criminal.[14] The public, says Pound, "would do well to resent these 'new' kinds of art" (EPVA, 182) created by himself and his colleagues.

Pound's need for opposition is manifest in his identification with the red-haired Bertran de Born, the "stirrer-up of strife."[15] It also goes far to explain the persistent "apostolic fury" (L, 267) and "blood lust" (SP, 229) of Pound's letters and prose—not physical but verbal violence of extraordinary intensity. Far from reflecting Pound's mistaken imitation of Lewis's "enemy" pose, as some critics think, this violence is a lasting character trait of a poet who, to quote Phyllis Bottome, "spoke in short staccato sentences like the bark of an angry dog."[16] As Pound said in 1934:

> . . . I personally would not feel myself guilty of manslaughter if by any miracle I ever had the pleasure of killing Canby or the editor of the Atlantic Monthly and their replicas, or of ordering a wholesale death and/or deportation of a great number of affable, suave, moderate men. . . . (LE, 58)

Pound told Eliot that "nine tenths of your Criterion writers . . . ought to be killed" (L, 281), and that the "the buggars back of the bank of Paris are . . . worth killin' " (L, 283). Two decades earlier, in 1916, Pound complained to Joyce of those "[literary] vermin [who] crawl over and be-slime our literature," and whom "nothing but the day of judgement can . . . exterminate" (P/J, 65).

One need not consider the impulse behind such statements as genuinely homicidal; Pound is probably speaking metaphorically. Even so, they seem ironic in view of Pound's charges that the Jews seek to eliminate vast portions of the Gentile population: the Talmudic Jews, he says, want to kill off "75% of the goy" (RB, 189). In such accusations Pound is probably projecting onto the Jews his own violence toward Gentile society, some of whose members he would have liked in some unspecified way to exterminate.

Although Pound on rare occasions recognizes his own tendency to "violence" (L, 182) and "anger" (LE, 391), he more often seeks to justify his "blood lust" against the contemporary system: it is, he says, "because of what I have seen done to, and attempted against, the arts in my time" (SP, 229). Many critics accept Pound's self-justification. For them Pound's situation recalls his description of Lewis's *Timon*: "The fury of intelligence baffled and shut in by circumjacent stupidity" (GB, 93). Pound's rage is thus not irrational but rather the "fury" that comes from "perception" (90/ 606), to borrow Pound's description of Hitler. Pound, observes Peter Makin, is not really hostile or violent but merely given to a "pugnacity" which makes him "unsuitable" in a second-rate world (Makin: 30). His increasingly aggressive tone expresses his legitimate frustration at a hostile society which, foolishly ignoring his advice and values, was staggering toward chaos. Pound's persecution complex results specifically from his rejection after the *Blast* period, when, thanks to his notoriety, he was deliberately ignored by important editors.

In truth this ostracism, though certainly damaging to Pound's career and finances, resulted not from any original and inveterate hatred of Pound but from his antagonistic behavior, of which *Blast* was the culmination. Noel Stock justly remarks that even in its "sad state" the "stolid" London literary world might have appreciated Pound's brilliance; Pound "failed to become an arbiter of opinion" in London because of "a lack of prudence and humility—which threw up a barrier between him and his objective."[17] Nor does Pound's hostility towards Anglo-Saxon society result from a long accumulation of grievances. As early as *Patria Mia*, under the delusion that he had been "hunted out" of America, Pound identifies with Farinata degli Uberti, Dante's aristocratic exile from Florence. Addressing his homeland on behalf of the "constantly railed at expatriates," Pound announces: "We have tomorrow against you" (SP, 133).

The Jewish desire for vengeance is a recurrent theme in Pound's anti-Semitic polemics of the 1930s and 1940s. Canto 52 vilifies the Rothschild dynasty, which carries out a "vendetta on goyim" (52/ 257). In *Guide to Kulchur* Pound says of Meyer Anselm Rothschild, the dynasty's founder, that he had "a race (his own race) to 'avenge.' " He thus "used the ONLY weapons available for a tiny minority, for a lone hand against organized goy power, pomp, militarism, rhetoric, buncombe" (GK, 315). In the radio broadcasts Pound has no doubt that the Jews, following the Talmud, seek retribution against the West. Such charges are probably a projection of Pound's vengefulness, particularly against England and America. Just as

Rothschild's position as the "lone hand" of a "tiny minority" resembles Pound's as the self-proclaimed head of a tiny and beleaguered minority of oppressed artists, so Pound's tendency to speak of Gentiles exactly as the Jews might, that is, as "goyim," reflects his alienation—far deeper than he ever realized—from Gentile society. It also shows his unconscious identification with the persecuted Jews as they confront and name the other.

Pound was working at cross purposes. While his desire for the artist's social integration leads him to celebrate medieval-style guilds, Pound also conceives of the artist romantically, either in opposition to society or above it. Here is a further explanation for Pound's violence, which reveals his desire for power and control over society. As early as 1914 Pound said that the artist

> has been at peace with his oppressors long enough. He has dabbled in democracy and he is now done with that folly. We turn back, we artists, to the powers of the air, to the djinns who were our allies aforetime, to the spirits of our ancestors. . . . The aristocracy of entail and of title has decayed, the aristocracy of commerce is decaying, the aristocracy of the arts is ready again for its service . . . and we who are the heirs of the witch-doctor and the voodoo, we artists who have been so long the despised are about to take over control. (EPVA, 182)

"I shall hang out myself," wrote Pound to Harriet Monroe, "until the U.S. is ready to start a ministry of Beaux Arts, and put me in charge" (L, 182). Usually such remarks are made kiddingly, but Pound was probably more than half serious: Richard Aldington, who knew him well, noted that Pound wanted and sought the literary dictatorship of England, precisely what T. S. Eliot attained.[18] Nor is Pound's megalomania confined to the arts, for the "party that follows" the artist "always wins" (SP, 215). This follows directly from Pound's statement in *Poetry* in 1914:

> It is true that the great artist has in the end, always, his audience, for the Lord of the universe sends into this world in each generation a few intelligent spirits, and these ultimately manage the rest.[19]

Since violence often accompanies and validates power and authority, it is no wonder that this artistic revolutionary and "criminal" twice identifies with the policeman.[20] The artist, says Pound, should hold "the whip hand" (L, 220). As for men, it "is the nature of homo canis to follow. They growl but they follow" (PD, 147). If Jewish monotheism was invented to keep a "troublesome rabble in order" (SR, 95), Pound desires similar control over the modern crowd.

III.

Pound's desire for power takes on an ironic cast in view of his charge that the "Kike out for all power" (RB, 120) over the entire Gentile world. A great age, or "era of brilliance" (GK, 266), says Pound, comes into existence when "men of a certain catholicity of intelligence come into power" (SP, 130), when the intelligentsia mingle freely with the ruling aristocracy. Ignoring the great variety of class origins among modern intellectuals, Pound envisions (as does Maurras) an intellectual and cultural elite bound by common interests, a separate meritocratic "class" (SP, 229) to which he belongs and which is indistinguishable from the traditional aristocracy, the *"beau monde toujours qui gouverne"* (SP, 313).[21] Inseparable from such elitism is the idea that power, the better to be exercised, should not be shared or diffused. This is Pound's belief, despite lip service to democracy, and it explains his hostility to the parliamentary system and his fascination with those cliques which govern by personal contact and "conversation" (J/ M, 15). As Makin says, Pound believes (as does Maurras) that the governing classes govern with a "superior knowledge of what is going on" (Makin: 73). These assumptions, implicit in Pound's statement that "universal peace will never be maintained unless it be by a conspiracy of intelligent men," motivated his visit to America in 1939, to "keep hell from breaking loose in the world," and his visit to Mussolini, to advise him as a Renaissance courtier would his Prince.[22] The same assumptions are stated openly in the later *Cantos*, in which Pound praises Italian Fascism for having "started with a limited (if not by dogma, but in practice) / suffrage of the qualified" (97/ 678), and in which he asserts the "necessity" of "liberty for a small privileged class" (101/ 724). The last passage condenses a remark of Napoleon's as reported by Madame de Rémusat. Napoleon said that "liberty is needed by a small and privileged class, who are gifted by nature with abilities greater than the rest of mankind. It can therefore be restricted with impunity."[23] This statement is impossible to square with the American democracy which Pound pretended to defend, but it does consort with fascism, and it agrees as well with another statement which Pound attributes favorably to Napoleon in Canto 44: "Artists [of] high rank," said Napoleon," are "in fact [the] sole social summits / which the tempest of politics cannot reach" (44/ 227). Such remarks no doubt encouraged Pound's mistaken notion that he, as an artist, was at once above and beyond all ideologies.

In spite of this fascination with cliquish and elitist politics, Pound was a brilliant publicist and often attacked the press and publishers for failure to make important ideas public. This concern culminates in the radio broadcasts, where Pound charges that the Jews possess secret information, obstruct the normal processes of communication, and use their privileged position to gain control over the Gentile world. Pound is here proclaiming the need for openness in communication and he is proclaiming it publicly.[24] Nonetheless, Pound himself advances a conspiratorial view of knowledge. By contrast with Frobenius's collective Paideuma, "Pound's Eleusis . . . is a hidden and even mysterious cultural heritage" which is possessed by a few fortunate souls (Surette, 3: 132).

Whether as the "secretum," the "arcanum," or the "mysterium," the mysteries "are *not* revealed, and no guide book to them has been or will be written" (L, 327). In *Guide to Kulchur* Pound speaks of a "secret history," consisting of the "constructive urges," a "*secretum*" which either "passes unnoticed" or which "no human effort can force . . . on public attention" (GK, 264):

> The minute you proclaim that the mysteries exist *at all* you've got to recognize that 95% of yr. contemporaries will not and can not understand *one* word of what you are driving at. And you can *not* explain. The SECRETUM stays shut to the vulgo. And as H. Christian said years ago re Catholics: "For god's sake leave 'em *in there* (i.e., church). If they weren't in there doing that, they wd. be out here pour nous embêter." (L, 328–329)

Since the mysteries are inaccessible and "fools can only profane them" (GK, 145), it is not clear why Pound proclaims their existence in the first place, or why the ignorant mob is a threat. The word "*embêter*" is the key. Besides suggesting annoyance, "*bête*," meaning beast, suggests Pound's familiar attitude toward the crowd. Pound fears becoming like the crowd by contact with the curious herd of human beasts. To keep the mysteries free of their contact is to maintain authority and control. Thus even the Catholic Church, in which Pound would contain the stupefied majority of European mankind, must also have its own "secretum." As Pound told the Reverend Henry Swabey, "Mass ought to be in Latin, unless you cd. do it in Greek or Chinese. In fact, *any* abracadabra that no bloody member of the public or half-educated ape of a clargiment cd. think he understood" (L, 339). Secrecy is a way of keeping distance, and both secrecy and distance, as Elias Canetti observes, are "at the very core of power," are indispensable to its attainment and preservation.[25]

Pound's accusations of Jewish conspiracy in the broadcasts are probably projections of his desire secretly to manipulate events. Generally, however, the purpose of Pound's elite is to create civilization and pass judgment on mankind. In the later *Cantos* Pound ascends to those "thrones" which will not "sqush [sic]" (88/ 581) and from which he judges human history; from here he announces the "domination of benevolence," which he drives into the rocklike mass of the human brain with the force of a pneumatic drill.[26] This project is anticipated as early as 1922, when Pound told Felix Schelling that "all values stem ultimately from" poets' "judicial sentences" (L, 181). Like most judges, Pound "reckons himself" a member of "the kingdom of the good, as though he had been born a native of it" (Canetti: 296–297).

Pound passes judgment over the living as the dead, human beings as herds. In a letter Pound called himself the "last living Rhadamanthus" (L, 274), an allusion to the king who judges the dead in Hell. Elsewhere Pound takes his aristocratic credo from Machiavelli: "gli uomini vivono in pochi" (LE, 83)— "men live in a few." These statements reflect Pound's assumption that the majority of men are not truly living and hence may be viewed as already dead. Pound told his father that a main theme of *The Cantos* is the descent of the "live man" to the "world" of the "Dead" (L, 210). This theme figures prominently in Canto 1, in Cantos 14 and 15, and in Canto 7, in which Pound, again in London, wanders among "thin husks . . . [he] had known as men," "Dry casques of departed locusts / speaking a shell of speech / . . . A dryness calling for death . . ." (7/ 26). These dead locusts anticipate the crowd of insects in the Hell *Cantos*. Meanwhile, Pound pursues Nicea, a bright invulnerable goddess of whom only he is aware. Thanks to her beauty, he rises momentarily to a god-like state: "being" (7/ 26), a property of the gods. Throughout his poem Pound identifies with Odysseus, "the live man among duds" (LE, 212).

In his letters and prose Pound similarly assumes that he, and a few members of his elite, are the sole truly living human beings. By 1918 Pound believes that "there is no longer any intellectual *life* in England save what centres in this eight by ten pentagonal room; now that Remy and Henry [James] are gone and Yeats faded. . . ."[27] Later he wonders whether Gourmont was the "last frog fit to consider a human being,"[28] and asks Harriet Monroe for a committee that "can at least *look* as if it wuz galvanized" (L, 238). These remarks tally with Pound's reminiscences of London and Paris. "London stank of decay in 1914," remarks Pound in *Jefferson and/or Mussolini*. "The live man in a modern city feels this sort of thing . . . as the savage perceives it in the forest" (J/M, 48–49). In "Terra Italica" Pound says that "mental corpses lay about in the streets [of London]," while the streets of Paris had also been filled with "carrion" (SP, 54).

Implicit in these passages is an extraordinary fantasy which also figures in the radio broadcasts, in which Pound believes that the Gentile crowds, infected by the "Jewish" plague, are deprived of their inmost being. As Pound surveys the crowds of anonymous "dead," he imagines himself a victor, maybe even an exterminator, but in any case one of the "surviving members of the human race" (L, 328). Indeed, Pound has a kind of survivor-complex. There is, he notes in 1922, "no organized or coordinated civilization left, only individual scattered survivors" (L, 172n). Writing to Basil Bunting in 1935, Pound observes that "it is very distressin [sic] to see the blokes die by the wayside."[29] In another letter Pound says that he, Eliot, and Santayana are the only persons who "got out" of America "alive" (L, 338), and in another he calls himself the "last survivin' monolith" (L, 343).[30] In 1956, quoting a remark of Hemingway's, Pound refers to himself as "the ONLY man who ever got out . . . [of England] alive" (P/L, 299). Besides their resemblance to statements by Mussolini, D'Annunzio, Céline, and Lewis, such fantasies reveal Pound's desire for power over the stricken other. "The moment of *survival*," observes Canetti, "is the moment of power. . . . All man's designs on immortality contain something of this desire for survival."[31]

Generally, though, Pound grants a certain kind of being to the mass of mankind. Rather than reducing them to non-entity, he places them in the class of animal herds and packs "bordering on the human" (PD, 147). To quote Pound's "student" in "An Anachronism at Chinon," "humanity is a herd, eaten by perpetual follies" (PD, 92), among them Judaism and Christianity. If Pound's alter ego Walter Villerant claims "affection" (PD, 60) for mankind, it is the contemptuous sympathy of a man forced to live amid "herds" of "live stock" (PD, 59), amid the "milkable human cows, the sheerable human sheep" (SP, 430). The student and Villerant implicitly follow Pound's Machiavellian credo: not merely that men live in a few, but that "the rest are sheep" (RB, 287). These typically Poundian statements are again ironic. Throughout the broadcasts Pound tells his listeners that the Jews view them as mere "human material, just browsin' round, innocent as lambkins at Easter . . ." (RB, 206). "To die not knowin' why," says Pound, "is to die like an animal. What the kike calls you: goyim or cattle" (RB, 409). The irony is that Pound, not the Jews, favors the last epithet, and continues to do so in the Pisan *Cantos*. There "the goyim are undoubtedly in great numbers of cattle," while the Jew "will receive information" (74/443).[32] One should be wary of Pound's remark that Jefferson and Mussolini "had sympathy with the beasts" (J/M, 63). It is uncertain whether he refers to animals or men, and in any case such sympathy is inseparable from contempt (Canetti: 210).

In other instances Pound reduces men to those lower forms of life which gather in pestilent crowds: vermin, maggots, worms, and lice. In the broadcasts the charge that the Jews are vermin is conspicuous, but this is preceded much earlier by Pound's comparison of the crowds of London with maggots and other insects. As Pound wrote to Harriet Monroe, "I take it somebody has got to provide insecticide or even squash the individual cockroach. In the general cause of health" (L, 236). For Pound, one must choose between dictating to vermin or being dictated to by them. "Do you expect," says Pound, "Col. Louse to dictate before or after the collapse?" (L, 243). The transformation of men into insects protects Pound from feeling "guilty" (LE, 58), for "the destruction of these tiny creatures is the only act of violence which remains unpunished even *within*" ourselves (Canetti: 205).

Let us consider one more instance of dehumanization. In Canto 27 Pound tells the story of the peasant "tovarisch," who stands for the Russian peasant during and after the Russian Revolution. For Pound this revolution must fail because, unlike fascism, it destroys natural hierarchy, confuses the "down" and the "up" (27/132):

> And that tovarisch cursed and blessed without aim,
>> These are the labours of tovarisch,
> Saying:
>> "Me Cadmus sowed in the earth
>> And with the thirtieth autumn
> I return to the earth that made me.

Let the five last build the wall;
I neither build nor reap . . . .
. . . Nothing I build
And I reap
Nothing; with the thirtieth autumn
I sleep, I sleep not, I rot
And I build no wall . . . .
"Baked and eaten, tovarisch!
"Baken and eaten, tovarisch, my boy,
"That is your story. And up again,
"Up and at 'em. Laid never stone upon stone."
                                    (27/ 131–132)

Unlike "tovarisch," the "five last" Greeks who followed Cadmus created a revolution "from the top." "Tovarisch," notes Mary de Rachewiltz, "is the Russian campagno. In Russia there is no civilization because there is no stone and they had a revolution without arriving at anything." "Tovarisch," however, is not so much human as vegetable. He is, adds de Rachewiltz, "like the corn, unconscious; like the corn, being sowed in the earth. . . ." Thus he resembles those human cornfields in Canetti's description, whose "pliancy" signifies "submissiveness," and which are "like an assemblage of loyal subjects, . . . [bowing] down simultaneously."[33] If "tovarisch" in his crude state bears no civilizing mark, he has two choices: either he "rots," falling back into the natural cycle, or is digested by the authoritarian culture which presides over his cultivation. For Pound the second is the proper choice: he must be baked, subjected to fire (the very mark of culture), and then "eaten."

Nothing better represents man's power over a thing or object than its total incorporation and digestion (Canetti: 210). Canto 27 thus lends a sinister character to Pound's Fascist agrarianism and his injunction to "IN-CORPORATE" (99/ 707). Not only does this word suggest oral aggression, but, in light of Canto 27, it may mean that the peasant rather than the mythical "Wheat God" is society's true victim. Likewise, the opening line of the Pisan *Cantos* —"the enormous tragedy of the dream in the peasant's bent shoulders" —suggests a sentimental agrarian fantasy founded not on any true sympathy with the peasant but on a reading of the Cambridge anthropologists. Though Pound claims to fight for the "peasantry" (RB, 181) against the monopolists—and incidentally "peasant" has an anachronistic and even reactionary ring in the twentieth century—such sympathy is combined with enormous contempt. This contempt emerges most strongly in the radio broadcasts, in which Pound observes no doubt wishfully that "the peasant never does more than grumble a bit, he never bothered about his landlord gettin' something," for "so long as he ate he was happy." Indeed, so stupefied and ineffectual is the peasant that, "LONG after he ceased to get a just portion of the returns from his own labor, he was certainly wholly innocuous" (RB, 195).

If one views the masses as herds, they can either be devoured or fed, though in either case they are to be politically controlled.[34] Pound, one is relieved to say, more frequently emphasizes feeding the people. "Food is the root, / Feed the people" (99/ 695), is one of his mottoes of paternalistic government, and in Canto 93 he admires the Catholic pastoral ideal: it is "easier to convert" the flock "after you feed 'em" (93/ 623). This line looks back to Canto 52, where Pound rebukes the Catholic bishops for allowing ornamental "fat" to cover their "croziers" (52/ 258), that is, for ignoring their pastoral responsibilities. Paternalism also figures in the *Unwobbling Pivot* (Chung Yung), where family authority is the model for an all-encompassing paternalistic state: "All who have families and kingdoms to govern have nine rules to follow," one of which is "to treat the people as children" (CON, 155–157). This idea resembles another in *Jefferson and/or Mussolini,* where the child Gigi, aged two, has this basic political intuition: "Gigi . . . used to stand up on his chair after lunch and say 'Popolo ignorante!' as a sort of benediction, one day he added the personal note 'And the worst of all is my *nurse*' " (J/M, 53). One understands why Pound abbreviates this anecdote in Canto 41, which celebrates Mussolini's draining of the Pontine Marshes. Despite his experience in the "female chaos" of London, Pound in 1933 still views the populace as passively feminine, like Gigi's foolish nurse; it is "ductile" (PER, 82), subject to the "factive" personality. Mussolini is an *"artifex"* (J/M, 34), while humanity is "malleable mud" (L, 181), another version of the feminine HYLE, having no choice but to take the shape of the artist's mould. Whether Pound considers the populace as sheep, children, mud, or women, his conception of its existence is entirely consistent with that of fascism.[35]

IV.

Writing in the *New Age* in 1919, not long before his departure from London, Pound said:

A man judges his own age according to his digestion; secondly, according to whether or no, as a small boy in school, he encountered more skunks than decent fellows.

Reflection engendered by scene at Tarascon, where two small boys had just forced a piece of horse-dung into the mouth of a third, who departed weeping, terrified, and threatening impotent vengeances.

There is in Bourrienne's Life of Napoleon no more significant picture than that of the young Buonaparte bullied by his schoolmates, and muttering, "I hate these French and I will do them all the harm that I can!" I don't imply that this sort of thing is indelible.

Thirdly, a man judges in accordance with the element of necessity in his own life—i.e., the extent to which he is constrained by poverty, or by the terror of poverty, to do certain things that he dislikes.

There are also the effects of experience, largely to be considered under heading A (digestion)—that is to say, a man's character makes his destiny.

There were in the past bugaboos, and Ovid, an extremely intelligent person, "went to pieces" in exile.[36]

This passage is probably self-referential. Not only does the impersonal subject of the first sentence include Pound, but the humiliating scene at Tarascon evokes in him such sympathy as springs from identification and knowledge.[37] Pound probably experienced a similar humiliation in his own childhood, one which filled him with a desire for vengeance, and which he connects with his own personal and economic distress. Ovid stands for the brilliant and persecuted artist destroyed by passive exile, while Napoleon later appears in *The Cantos* as the nineteenth century's most formidable opponent of usury.

In this passage, as in *The Cantos,* Pound deeply identifies with Napoleon. His relationship to English society, as he conceives of it, parallels Napoleon's to France. As the Corsican speaks French with a colonial (Italian) accent and suffers ridicule, so Pound speaks English with an American accent and suffers the animosity of the English. Napoleon's youthful hatred of France and his desire for revenge also parallel Pound's increasing Anglophobia. In 1918, Pound confessed a desire for "vengeance" against England.

During the 1930s Pound's resentment increased against those two nations from which he had supposedly been exiled and whose masses resisted his direction and control. Its culmination is in the radio broadcasts, in which Pound charges that England and America are in enemy hands. But Pound's true antagonism toward both nations is rarely overt in the broadcasts, and Pound insists that his interest is solely in their welfare. Instead, his hatred is always expressed indirectly, by means of anti-Semitism. Unable to acknowledge his own aggression against the Gentile world, and unwilling to acknowledge fascist imperialism, Pound attributes such aggression to the Jews. It is the Jews, not Pound, who desire vengeance, who are out for all power, who seek to eliminate the "goyim," who are obsessed with secrecy, who treat the Gentiles as passive animals and herds. These projections have two other purposes. By insisting that Anglo-Saxon society is in the hands of the Jews, Pound can express his alienation from the "goyim," as he himself calls them, without actually revealing it as alienation as such. He can also maintain his identification with the Anglo-Saxon community, an identification which, for all his hostility, Pound never gave up.

Chapter Fourteen

Society, Economics, and Politics

Apart from its sources in Western tradition and his personal psychology, Pound's anti-Semitism as well as his fascism has economic and social roots. We may begin to trace them by examining a complex of images and themes recurrent in Pound's writings, and out of which finally emerges his description of the Jews as "chews" (RB, 330), that is, as the supposedly demonic embodiment of the devouring instinct in Western culture. Encompassing the ideas of oral rage, oral aggression, and oral deprivation, this complex elucidates Pound's ever-increasing sense of social conflict in the West, his overwhelming and even violent ambitions, his immense hostility toward other human beings, and his resentful emargination from the indifferent society he had sought persistently to conquer.

The world of *Mauberley* is an enormous and threatening mouth. Not only does Pound resemble Capaneus, the hero who blasphemed the gods even in Hell, he is something to be tricked and eaten: "trout for factitious bait" (PER, 187). The age presents an unattractive, perhaps threatening show of teeth: though it has only "the press for wafer" (PER, 189)—which suggests a brawl for spiritual sustenance—it demands an "image / for its accelerated grimace" (PER, 188). Unlike Philistia, the true European culture lacks bite: it is "an old bitch gone in the teeth, . . . a botched civilization" (PER, 191). As Philistia triumphs, the youth of Europe perish in the First World War: "charm, smiling at the good mouth" (PER, 191). In the literary and social world of London, one can either "butter reviewers" like bread and "crack" (PER, 194) critics like nuts, or take refuge like the more passive "stylist" (Ford Madox Ford) in a maternal shelter which "offers succulent cooking" (PER, 195). One can "await the Lady Valentine's commands," or "hook" (PER, 196) her by means of poetry, or else pursue past beauty, as Pound does in "Envoi," dreaming of "some other mouth" (PER, 197), a mouth less threatening than that of the insatiable Messalina or the Cheyne Walk Circes. Mauberley does neither: he sits "amid ambrosial circumstances" and eats "insubstantial manna" (PER, 202), and pays the price in impotent rage:

> Mouths biting empty air,
> The still stone dogs. . . .
> (PER, 200)

Pound ironically compares Mauberley's inability to face down the "monster" of London to the unfitness of the "red-beaked steeds of / the Cytherean for a chain bit" (PER, 201). If anything, it is Pound, by contrast with Mauberley, who deserves the comparison, for he has neither taken the bait nor succumbed to the bit. His teeth, instruments of power and phallic aggression, remain intact.

London holds greater terror in the Hell *Cantos*. In Canto 16 Pound looks back to London and sees "hell mouth" (16/ 68). One recalls Canetti's observation that the "teeth are the armed guardians of the mouth and the mouth is indeed a strait place, the prototype of all prisons. . . . Hell still presents the same appearance today" (Canetti: 209). In escaping London, Pound frees himself from the very entrails of economic greed and power.

By the broadcasts the Jews embody oral aggression and are the cause of the social, economic, and military conflict within the Gentile world; thanks to the "chews," the "cannibals of Europe are eating each other again" (J/M, 79). These accusations are ironic. Pound, whose speech sometimes resembled the "bark of an angry dog," repeatedly attacks his numerous Gentile "enemies." By blaming the Jews for oral violence, he is able to ignore or deny its true origins not only within Gentile society but within himself. There is irony too in Pound's charges in the radio broadcasts and elsewhere that the Jews are guilty of parasitism upon his Mother or "mama" country. In Cantos 14 and 15 London pullulates with newts, water-slugs, water-maggots, lice, etc. It is thus cast in the image of the bad mother who ignores Pound but allows herself to be consumed by a horde of (in this instance) non-Jewish parasites.[1]

Although Pound exaggerates London's violence, the Hell *Cantos* reflect his persistent and probably accurate awareness of the English literary world as an increasingly hostile scramble. In 1915 Pound observed that in the literary world "The power is with the group who can provide a man food or inhibit his dinner." In 1934 he said of other writers that most were "maggots living in or on the mental activity of their time but contributing nothing to its life, parasitic in the strict sense." These "anonymities . . . slouch[ed] crumbling and cringing on the margin of the literature that provides them with beef and board." Meanwhile, "a god damn morgue like the Criterio [sic] exists . . . to feed a few clean authors."[2] Yet even Pound must sometimes have felt lost in the indistinct "crowd" or swarm of writers and intellectuals: Kensington, said Pound, "[was] SWARming with 'em" (Hutchins: 71). In a letter to Eliot Pound said that an editor "OUGHT to know which of his pullulating swarm of contributors CONTRIBUTES and which are mere parasites and insignificant riders."[3] Within this community, such as it is, one can choose either to eat or be eaten. Pound proposes that lesser writers should be "made to pay" to be printed in "good company," since "sharks catch suckers that way in far countries" (L, 281).

Pound sees himself more frequently as economic victim, first of editors and publishers, later of a usurious economic system. Writing in *The New English Weekly* in 1934, Pound says that "the 'pore' and a few of the most unruly writers have been up against hunger, or the imminent danger of hunger"; he also says that he had "always been a banned writer."[4] In the same year Pound remarks to Felix Schelling that "You know damn well the country [America] wouldn't feed me" (L, 256), and in 1939, with frustration and anger, he writes to Lewis and asks "why the blighters never print me."[5] Something like bitterness is evident in two letters of Pound's to Louis Zukofsky in the middle 1930s, in which Pound complains of being "short of cash for three years," and wonders "how I bloody live ennyhow."[6] In the broadcasts Pound defies his now Jewish obstructors, who threaten him and the West with "starvation" (RB, 7) through usury.

Pound's obsession with images of hunger and oral aggression had by this point culminated in a Manichean conception of contemporary and indeed the whole of economic history. How was it that Pound had come to believe that usury, personified chiefly by Jews, sought the monopoly of the world food supply and the starvation not merely of Pound but of mankind? By 1930 and perhaps even earlier, Pound was absorbed, sometimes even to the neglect of his poetry, in the problem of explaining and solving the economic crisis of the West: chronic underemployment, poverty, impeded production and investment, national and personal debt, underconsumption, and usury. This turn to economics was largely inspired by Major C. H. Douglas, the founder and leader of the Social Credit movement, whose *Economic Democracy* (1920) and other works had an overwhelming and permanent impact on Pound's thought.

Douglas was most disturbed by one fact. Although the productive capacity of the world's industrial plant had increased enormously in modern times, the world economy was still afflicted periodically by grave crises, such as gluts and depressions. These crises generally coincided with overproduction, that is, the failure of goods to clear the market at or above cost price, and the consumer's inability to purchase due to the shortage of money. Douglas had noticed, however, that overproduction and insufficient demand had largely ceased during World War I, when government regulated certain industries and the prices of certain goods, and when production was up and money plentiful.[7] He thus resisted Marx's interpretation of gluts and crises, that they result from the capitalist's extraction of surplus value from exploited labor and from the falling rate of profit (due to competition leading to overproduction).[8] For Douglas, crises have one primary cause, namely that the power to create credit, which he views as a communal and public value, is in private hands and an instrument of private gain. In order to buy plant and machinery, the industrialist needs bank or "loan credit," on which he is required to pay (often exorbitant) interest, and which his cost-accounting system includes as part of the total cost (and hence the price) of the goods he produces. These added costs due to interest charges constitute delusory or non-existent values; they result from a faulty accounting system and the misuse of credit by financiers. Moreover, this system of loan credit inevitably leads to a deficiency of purchasing power and hence underconsumption and crisis. For besides raising the price of goods, interest payments on bank charges necessarily withdraw money from circulation, money which the industrialist would otherwise distribute in the form of wages and salaries and which would clear the market of goods. Because of loan credit, bank charges, and interest payments, the total cost of production must exceed total purchasing power.[9]

Pound accepted Douglas's main arguments and came to trace economic crises to a conspiracy of usurious financiers. Operating both nationally and internationally, the usurers sabotaged purchasing power, impeded production by charging exorbitant interest, withheld funds from productive investment, and manipulated credit in order to profit from individual and national debts. In alliance with munitions manufacturers, they fomented European wars, which they helped to finance and from whose subsequent debts they reaped enormous profits in interest payments. Since they either controlled or were in alliance with the press, they also engaged in a conspiracy against culture, keeping the public ignorant of original and critical thought.[10]

According to Douglas, once money and banking are freed from unscrupulous financiers and placed under local (rather than national) control, the public or "community" will be able to regulate the quantity of money for purposes of investment, production, and consumption. Furthermore, it will be able to create "social credit," a dividend issued to all members of the community. Thus society will achieve true freedom, what Douglas, in the title of his first and most famous book, called "economic democracy." Pound was especially attracted to such proposals because he believed that they would give artists increased leisure and the means for creative work.[11] To be sure, Pound deviates in a crucial way from Douglas's position. Although Pound sometimes praises local control of purchasing power (for instance the Wörgl experiment celebrated in Canto 74), in general he favors the nationalization of banking, as under Mussolini. Nonetheless, Douglas had helped Pound to discover the supposed instigators of the bitter conflict not only in London literary culture but in the entire economy of the West: social conflict came not from within society but from an external financial conspiracy.[12] In the late 1930s Pound quoted Henry Ford's axiom: "Crises are not scourges from God; like wars, they are the work of a small number of people who get profit from them."[13]

This discovery had ominous implications. Finlay says in his study of Social Credit that Douglas originally thought in terms of a "very deeply laid and well considered plot of enslaving the world to the German-American-Jew financiers." But soon "the German-American element faded into the background, leaving the Jews as the real villains of the piece."[14] In 1941 in the *Meridiano di Roma* Pound paid tribute to Douglas as an astute anti-Semite: "C. H. Douglas . . . from 1919 he clearly saw the danger, saw that hebraic politics tended to the total ruin of Europe."[15]

II.

Post-war research has shown that the Jew has been the convenient scapegoat for persons and groups that have suffered poverty, defeated or frustrated social and economic expectations, a dwindling sense of social prestige and status, or the repeated effects of social and economic misfortunes. Such persons are most often found within the lower-middle and middle classes. Their hatred is partly nourished by the long-standing identification of the Jew with economic exploitation, as well as by resentment of successful Jews. The unsuccessful Jew also gives these persons and groups an object on which to project their own self-hatred, thus enabling themselves to punish themselves indirectly, by means of anti-Semitism.[16]

In Canto 3, in which Pound remembers his visit to Venice in 1908, economic insecurity is linked to anti-Semitism:

> I sat on the Dogana's steps
> For the gondolas cost too much, that year,
> And there were not "those girls," there was one race. . . .
>
> (3/ 11)

Besides a lack of funds, Pound feels "erotic deprivation" (the "one face") (Bacigalupo: 55–56). Shortly he encapsulates a section of the *Poem of the Cid,* in which the medieval Spanish hero, also deprived of funds (and mistakenly banished by his king), manages to "get pay" for his "menie" or band of soldiers and carry on his struggle against his persecutors. Two Jewish money-lenders, Raquel and Vidas, agree to provide the Cid with money in exchange for a box which, supposedly filled with treasure, is really filled with sand. Having tricked the usurers, the Cid, a Hermes figure and "factive personality" on the order of Malatesta and Mussolini, breaks his way to Valencia (Brown: *passim*).

Status anxiety is not an adequate sociological explanation of Pound's anti-Semitism in its virulent and ideological form, but it undoubtedly contributed to its development. Pound's origins were entirely "respectable" and upper middle class. On his mother's side he was related to the earliest settlers of Massachusetts and Henry Wadsworth Longfellow; his grandfather, Thaddeus Pound, was a lumber and railroad magnate in the Middle West and a lieutenant governor and congressman of Wisconsin. Yet his father Homer Pound was neither a high elected official nor a private entrepreneur but a relatively minor public servant in the United States Mint in Philadelphia; nor did he achieve great financial success. Although he provided a comfortable existence for his family, Wyncote, Pennsylvania, the suburb in which Pound grew up, was populated increasingly by new money, and Pound, as Noel Stock suggests, may have suffered a resentful sense of relative deprivation (Stock, 3: 26). A hint of status anxiety appears in *Patria Mia,* where Pound returns to America to find the Anglo-Saxon "uprights" (SP, 115) nearly submerged in the bog of vigorous new races, such as the Jews. Much later, in the broadcasts, Pound laments the racial corruption of the Anglo-Saxon stock, calls the melting pot a failed "experiment" (RB, 157), and envisions an "America that no longer exists" (RB, 312), a pastoral, professional, and middle class America untainted by Jewish influences.[17]

During the teens in London, and thanks to his choice of a poetic career, Pound found himself close to the economic margins of society. His difficulties increased when, as a result of post-war economic and social pressures, the Edwardian literary world collapsed (Davie, 2: 9). Although Pound sometimes shows contempt of mere material respectability, in the 1920s he sounds a new note. Where "poverty" in Europe "is decent and honorable," in America "it lays one open to continuous insult on all sides, from the putridity in the White House down to the expressman who handles one's trunk" (L, 204). In this passage Pound's anxiety over class and status is overt. Later he asks Williams whether Zukofsky wanted to come to Europe. "What sort of degradation," says Pound, "is he willing to undergo?" (L, 229).

Pound's official attitudes toward the middle class need qualification. Admittedly one of the mottoes of *Blast* is "Curse abysmal inexcusable middle-class (also Aristocracy and Proletariat),"[18] and Pound remains convinced that the artist "never has been part of the bourgeoisie" (RB, 294). Apparently he shares Mussolini's disdain for the "borghesi" (98/ 686), sunk in materialism and decadence. But the radio broadcasts reveal that Pound is not entirely a social renegade. In one broadcast he tells England that, thanks to the Jews, "your middle class will be engulfed" (RB, 319); in another, his sympathy goes out to middle class professionals, small landowners, and the lower middle class, all wracked by usury. "All of 'em," says Pound, have been "steadily LESS AND LESS represented; their interests, their power to LIVE, their power to USE the statal mechanism as a means to the good life, were eased OUT of their grip" (RB, 111). Elsewhere, in a discussion of the Italian Fascist corporate system, Pound observes that he, as an artist, should be represented not as an isolated individual but as a member of the "confederation of artists and professional men, painters, doctors, writers, dentists" (RB, 102). One appeal of Italian Fascism for Pound is that it will supposedly return him to his middle class origins.[19]

Neither class anxiety, nor economic deprivation, nor social dislocation, can in themselves or taken together explain why Pound was led finally to the ideological and apocalyptic belief that the Jews are the enemies of Western society. At most they could only produce isolated and imagined economic grievances against the Jews. Undoubtedly something else was required.

In *Disaster and the Millennium* Michael Barkun states that millenarian movements "almost always occur in times of upheaval, in the wake of cultural contact, economic dislocation, revolution, war, or natural castastrophe." They usually arise among impoverished, marginal, and socially threatened segments of society, groups constantly afflicted by culture shock and a sense of social "stress," crisis, and "relative deprivation." Gravitating around charismatic and messianic leaders, who promise imminent salvation, economic well-being, and utopian solutions to the social impasse, these groups view the world as a Manichean conflict, in which they represent good and all others evil. They also manifest the political (rather than the psychological or clinical) form of paranoia, which is chiefly marked by a preference for the conspiracy theory of history; hence their inclination to blame social ills on out-group scapegoats, such as Papists, witches, Jacobins, and Jews. Whatever form it takes—and Barkun mentions Social Credit and National Socialism as millenarian movements—the millenarian impulse emerges after a series of disasters in which the "reference points in life are lost."[20] Although such disasters cause "anxiety, fatigue, psychotic episodes, recurrent catastrophic dreaming and depression," they can be "therapeutic": "Disaster is a leveler."[21]

By the middle 1930s Pound was aware of what Barkun calls the "disaster syndrome," one of whose symptoms is depression (Barkun: 52–57). It is worth remarking that in our time the term depression has come to refer to economic as well as mental disorders, and that Pound believed that most mental problems stemmed from economic rather than psychological causes.[22] Both kinds of depression are implicit in a 1935 article of Pound's: "The next depression (not the financial one that Perkins [Frances Perkins, U.S. Secretary of Labor] is so anxious about, but the *next* depression) is upon us. It is mental, consisting in the low spirits induced by three years of F.D.R. and the men who 'now look to 1940.' "[23] Less than a year later Pound writes of the removal of familiar social "reference points" as a result of economic crisis. In a *New English Weekly* article pessimistically entitled "Last Words on Economic Democracy," he speaks of a social "warfare" so "subtle" and "penetrative" that "six or eight . . . English [social] categories" are endangered and several have "almost ceased to exist." Where Pound usually attacks the masses and fellow artists for their presumed hostility and stupidity, he now identifies not only with artists but with groups for which he normally had little real sympathy, "pinched white collar suburbanities," "small clerks," the trades, the artisans, the farmers, mere laborers. Now there is no reason to engage in aesthetic or class "snobbism" or to make invidious comparisons; everyone is the victim of a pervasive social warfare; "all" are "caught in the same set of snares," and there is "no reward for diligence. They cannot save themselves by production." Society is thus unified by a crisis which has destroyed distinctions between men and led to "prayers" for a leader,[24] the same sort of "leader" (RB, 56, 58) as Pound recommends for England in the broadcasts. From here is a short step to the idea that the Jews are to blame.

Pound's "last words" on economic democracy help to explain one of the most peculiar and paradoxical developments of his career. How is it that Pound, a distinguished (though impoverished) poet, free-lance intellectual, and professed elitist, should have found his way into an overtly mass movement such as fascism? For there is no question that fascism, despite its elitist philosophy, gained power through its mass appeal. An at least partial explanation is that Pound, both in mentality and in economic and social circumstances, had like numerous other members of the intellectual elite been driven into the ever-swelling ranks of the lower-middle class, that amorphous social body which, as numerous historians have shown, formed much of the support for fascism. Like the petit bourgeois victim of capitalism and industrialization, Pound suffers a profound sense of social emargination, anxiety, and resentment, longs for authoritarian order and stability, and finally allays his fear of social apocalypse by worshipping at the feet of the messianic leader. He affords a prominent example of what Hannah Arendt describes as the "disturbing alliance between the mob and the [intellectual] elite, and the curious coincidence of their aspirations," which results from the fact that these groups had been "the first to be eliminated from . . . the framework of class society." "They found each other so easily," notes Arendt, and "they were followed by unending masses."[25]

III.

Although anti-Semitism is insufficient to explain fascism, Ernst Nolte and George L. Mosse have shown that it is central to the "dynamic" of many of its versions (Mosse, 1: 7). Indeed Pound, as a fascist ideologue, has no more potent weapon at his disposal. It is indispensable to his effort to undermine liberalism, to divert and defuse socialism and communism, to define a "corporate solution" (RB, 22) for modern Europe, to unify society, and to "purify" capitalism. Pound's example lends support to Horkheimer and Adorno's observation that bourgeois anti-Semitism has a specific reason, which is "the concealment of domination in production."[26]

Despite Pound's repeated attacks on bourgeois society and the "capitalist system" throughout the 1930s[27] he does not attack capitalism as a whole. He rarely considers the exploitation of labor by the industrial capitalist, discounts class domination and warfare, and basically opposes the Marxist theory of surplus value. Pound also defends the rights of property and never challenges the material basis or class structure on which capitalism rests.

Like the French literary fascist Drieu la Rochelle, Pound wants to repair and "spiritualize" capitalism (Soucy, 2: 125).

Pound's "anti-capitalism" hinges on a crude and typically proto-fascist and fascist distinction between "*producers*" and "monopolies of *exploiters*."[28] Not only does Pound sympathize with the creative and innovative capitalist or entrepreneur (such as Henry Ford or his grandfather Thaddeus Pound), who uses private property to provide the public with the products it needs, but he extends the category of production to include such property owners as the artisan, artist, tradesman, small businessman, industrial worker, professional, farmer, in short, all who engage in what he considers useful, productive, and honest "work."[29] These men are linked by mutual dependence and a common interest in production and labor. Their common enemies, meanwhile, have no appreciation of honest labor, craft, or the rights of ownership. These are the exploiters or "NON-producers" (RB, 73), in whom money, or usury, stands revealed as the true form of unproductive, parasitic, and monopolistic wealth.

Pound would thus distinguish between capital and property. "Property means control over things," Charles Berezin writes of Pound's theory, "while capital means control over men."[30] Despite some equivocation on this point, Pound generally believes that exploitation has little to do with the extraction of surplus value in the form of profit from hired labor and through the private ownership of the means of production; the industrialist or property owner controls not men but things. The control of men results chiefly from financial manipulation, to which Pound gives the name of capitalism: "The doctrine of Capital . . . has shown itself as little else than the idea that unprincipled thieves and anti-social groups should be allowed to gnaw into the rights of ownership" (SP, 298).[31] Pound often seems convinced that, with the elimination of usury and the adoption of a national dividend and the corporate system, goods can be produced and distributed at fair prices and with fair profits accruing to the capitalist.

This distinction between production and financial exploitation is traditional in proto-fascist, Italian Fascist, and Nazi thought. Although the proto-fascists "did not accept the existing capitalist order," their "enmity . . . was directed toward finance capitalism only: the banks and the stock exchange," which symbolized "the power of unproductive wealth confronting the producers who unjustly lived in misery and want."[32] Later Hitler endorsed Gottfried Feder's distinction "between . . . pure capital as the end result of productive labor and a capital whose existence and essence rests exclusively in speculation."[33] In *Mein Kampf* Hitler says that "the fight against international finance and loan capital [is] . . . the most important point in the program of the German nation's struggle for its economic independence and freedom" (Hitler: 214). In "What is Money For?" Pound praises Wyndham Lewis for "magnificently" (SP, 299) isolating this passage, and he praises it again in an article on the Nazi movement.[34]

The identification of the Jews with loan capital is frequent too in proto-fascist and fascist thinking, as in Edouard Drumont, of whose *La France Juive* Pound was aware, and in the corporate theory of de La Tour du Pin, who blames class conflict on Jewish usury or "capitalism."[35] Many of these writers long for the corporate, pre-capitalistic, and anti-Semitic Middle Ages, free of financial manipulation. By the time of his radio broadcasts, Pound shares Hitler's view of international usury as essentially Jewish (Hitler: 148, 193): "The enemy is Das Leihkapital . . . . The big Jew is so bound up with this Leihkapital that no one is able to unscramble that omelet" (RB, 59). As in fascism, Pound's attack on "Jewish" loan capital serves a variety of ideological purposes. In isolating "parasitic" usury, he asserts that economic crises originate outside the institution of private property and capitalist production. By embodying loan capital in the Jew, Pound diverts hostility away from other forms of capitalist exploitation and dominance and directs the proletariat against its supposedly true enemies. Finally, by blaming the Jews for social unrest and class conflict, he defuses and subverts the arguments of Marxists and socialists.

Despite his curious and misguided flirtation with the left which terminated as late as 1937, and despite his admiration for Lenin as a heroic man of action, Pound rejects Marxism.[36] In Canto 16 the Russian Revolution is the product of demagogic crowd manipulation which ironically resembles the fascist variety. It is a sign of Pound's anxiety for the West that he repeats that "nobody," not even "the leaders," "knew it was coming" (16/ 75). For Pound, as for Douglas, monetary reform is the necessary response to the socialist danger (SP, 212; Finlay: 112–116). Instead of advocating a thoroughgoing socialism for the nations of the West, Pound wants to "socialize the medium of exchange," for this is supposedly the "one factor of economic life which is subject to socialization" (I, 247–248) without carrying the threat of bureaucratic collectivism which Pound and Douglas feared. Pound also argues that the Marxist analysis fails to focus on the real economic evil, namely usury. The Communists and Socialists only "pretended to . . . attack . . . capital" (RB, 301, 175), they had merely "attack[ed] . . . private property" (RB, 294), thus ignoring "the Jew capital" (RB, 301) and leaving "the pawn broker . . . in full control of the exploitation system, milking the producer" (RB, 294). In *The Cantos* Pound tells Stalin that an intelligent monetary policy will make it unnecessary to "take over the means of production" (74/ 426). Nor does Pound believe in the necessity or even perhaps the actuality of class conflict under capitalism.[37] The usurer, he says in the broadcasts, "starts the class war; class war does NOT come from the bottom" (RB, 195).[38] Once usury and the Jews are eliminated, and monetary reforms carried out, the class war will supposedly vanish.

By the time of the radio broadcasts Pound's worst fears had been confirmed. Having taken Communist Russia as an ally against Germany and Italy, America (and England) are "headin' for Communism" (RB, 361), toward "the abolition of ALL private ownership" (RB, 50). Now Pound's anti-Communism merges with anti-Semitism. Denouncing "Communist millionaires" (RB, 356), decrying the "Jewish factor in Russian politics" (RB, 403), Pound insinuates that the American Communist Party is "governed by Wall Street" (RB, 356), in short by Jewish interests. Anti-Semitism has become the chief element in Pound's attempt to "expose" Marxism and to discredit it entirely in the eyes of the Western proletariat.

IV.

Pound's anti-Semitism serves other major political purposes. Like Mussolini, Pound seeks to reform Italian capitalism, and capitalism in general, along the organic, functional, and corporate lines of Italian Fascism; his economic reforms are linked indissolubly to a social policy. According to Pound's organic and corporate ideal, a unified and harmonious society of producers must replace a divisive society of wasteful economic competition and class rivalry. Nonetheless, the continued presence of latent or actual antagonisms, as well as massive social inequalities, gives the lie to Italian Fascist corporatism; as in the corporate society of the Middle Ages, such outgroups as the Jews serve as a convenient, indeed indispensable means of deflecting and disguising unresolved social conflict. It is understandable that Mussolini turned officially to anti-Semitism in the late 1930s, when the numerous cracks and unfulfilled promises of his corporate system were becoming increasingly visible. During the same period Pound follows Hitler and the later Mussolini in relying on anti-Semitism to create not only national but pan-European unity. As Pound writes in the *Meridiano di Roma,* the Jewish usurocracy is the "enemy of all the people."[39]

Many critics believe erroneously that Pound's support of Italian Fascism resulted mainly from his mistaken notion that it intended to combat usury and to implement financial reforms similar to those of the Social Creditors.[40] Social Credit, observed the Social Creditor Walter Hampden, was both anti-Communist and anti-fascist, indeed anti-statist and anti-totalitarian (Douglas's *Economic Democracy* proposes alternatives to Prussian tyranny and militarism); it was intended to promote "economic freedom." Far from endorsing the nationalization of banking, Douglas sought to place credit under local control. By contrast, Pound combined Social Credit economic democracy with fascist political totalitarianism: "American Social Creditors," said Hampden, "did not like that."[41] They also disliked Pound's anti-Semitism, although Major Douglas was himself anti-Semitic. The truth is that Pound endorsed Italian Fascism not only for economic reasons but because it promised, under totalitarian dictatorship, a corporate state and society.[42]

Pound saw in fascism a modern version of the corporate, hierarchical, paternalistic, and pre-capitalistic Middle Ages. Through fascism Europe would return to something resembling those days when each estate recognized its proper place and function; church and state constituted a benevolent and all-encompassing authority; money had not yet replaced land as a measure of wealth; social morality and tradition enforced the just price; labor, not yet alienated by industrialization, was organized into regulated guilds; a mystic bond united aristocrats and peasants; and every social right or privilege was balanced by social obligations.[43] In his attraction to medieval corporatism Pound was preceded in the nineteenth and early twentieth century by radical conservatives and national socialists (to use Mosse's broad designation) such as Maurras, Drumont, and de La Tour du Pin.[44] Like Pound, these men were attracted to the Catholic idea of the just price and the Aristotelian idea of distributive justice which Pound believed he had found in Mussolini; for them, the only alternative to socialism and liberal atomization was national unification under a centralized or localistic corporatism.[45] They also found anti-Semitism to be ideologically indispensable in combatting liberalism and socialism, in integrating social classes, and in forging an "organic" national unity (Mosse, 6: 121).

By the late 1920s, after his exposure to English Guild Socialism, Pound was ready to commit himself to Italian Fascist corporatism. He now conceived of state-regulated guilds—or syndicates, as the Italian Fascists called them—as a necessary basis for economic production and social and political organization. Like the more conservative versions of Guild Socialism, which it in some ways resembles, Italian Fascism rejected class warfare and stressed the ideals of organicism, hierarchy, and functionalism, which it opposed to what it considered the conflictual and impractical political ideas of the modern world.[46]

Pound despised liberalism, socialism, and communism not only as "Jewish" but as inherently divisive, self-contradictory, mechanical, and inorganic. Like Mussolini, he believed that liberalism treated society as a warring chaos of individual atoms. Moreover, as the philosophy of a plutocratic laissez-faire capitalism, it supposedly promoted and was dominated by usury, which Pound perversely linked with liberal thinking. Thus, like the Italian syndicalists, Pound rejected the parliamentary system of representation.[47] As for labor, it aimed selfishly and irresponsibly toward the tyranny of one class over all others, while Communism and socialism fostered the herd instinct and entirely subordinated the individual to the collectivist state.[48] Only the Italian Fascists had found the way to an organic, functional, yet hierarchical society, a kind of middle way between capitalism and socialism.[49] Rather than discriminating among individuals according to class, the Italian Fascist state sought to eliminate this divisive idea and to define them hierarchically according to their economic vocation and function, their contribution to the general welfare.[50] Each major group of producers in each branch of national economy was to have its self-governing guild or syndicate. In the early days of Fascism workers and employers were often combined in the same guild, the so-called "mixed syndicate." But ultimately mixed syndicates were abolished, and businessmen and employers were grouped within the separate organizations which they had demanded (William S. Halperin: 54–55; Salvemini: 20).

The Italian Fascist state organized the separate employer's and worker's syndicates into collective political bodies known as corporations, which were intended to serve as the representative bodies and governing institutions within each branch of industry. Composed of representatives of capital and labor, and hence supposedly reconciling their interests under a common purpose, the corporations and their councils were theoretically granted the power to promote and coordinate their own production, to supervise in questions of labor relations, and to reconcile collective labor disputes. Representatives drawn from the syndicates composed the assembly of the National Council of Corporations, for which Mussolini, in 1933, claimed to envision genuine legislative powers (G. Lowell Field: 15–16, 29, 61–63, 138, 144, 180–182).

In Pound's opinion the Italian Fascist guild and corporatist system is the antidote to an atomistic, deceitful, and usury-wracked parliamentarianism. Since, according to Pound, "Most men want certain things IN their own lives, largely inside the sphere of their own trade or business" (RB, 18–19), Fascism endows the "people by occupation and vocation with corporate powers" (SP, 297–298), and thus installs them within an "organic" system of needs and functions. Mussolini, he says, "wants a council where every kind of man will be represented by some bloke of his own profession. . ." (J/M, v). In the United States as well, "any or every state could organize its congressional representation on a corporate basis," whereby each profession "could have one representative" (RB, 204). This idea, which Pound endorses for the United States as late as 1960, and which he shares with Mussolini, would overturn the concept of citizenship as it descends from the French Revolution.[51] Meanwhile, the American "big employer" should pursue a "corporate solution" (RB, 22) in the Italian Fascist sense. Trade unions, however, should be denied legal status because they lack "RESPONSIBILITY" (RB, 52) and are hence dysfunctional.

Although Guild Socialism, like Fascist syndicalism, had originally favored local and autonomous guilds, Guild Socialist theory gradually developed the idea of "joint management" in which all producers are partners of the state and the state is endowed with "coercive functions" in disputes between producers.[52] In Italian Fascism there similarly developed the conception of the state as the coordinator, supervisor, sometimes even the nullifier of social and economic conflict. The state was to integrate classes, reward the fulfilment of economic functions, place labor and capital on an "equal footing," and encourage economic "collaboration" between capital and labor within the corporation, all in the interests of the nation as a whole.[53] To quote Mussolini's Consegna of the Fascist year XI (1933): "Discipline the economic forces and equate them to the needs of the nation" (RB, 154).

In order to advertise its good intentions toward labor, the state issued its Carta del Lavoro (Labor Charter) (1927), which some syndicalists lauded, and which expressed concern for the rights of workers. This, however, was a statement of principle rather than a decree-law.[54] The truth is that the corporations were hardly free of state interference, since they were also intended to represent the interests of the state. Not only did they include state officials and experts within their representative councils, but the Ministry of Corporations possessed veto power over the representative process within the individual syndicates. As G. Lowell Field says, the corporation like the syndicate "is defined as an organ of the state." After 1933 the National Council of Corporations functioned only through a central committee of limited power.[55] Thus there is considerable justification for the claim that, despite Mussolini's constant advertisement of corporate principles, the "corporate state" was never more than a facade (Salvemini: 114–115, 134, 147–148; Schmidt: 67–68).

A fair assessment of Pound's corporatist beliefs requires one at least to consider the possibility that Pound, being highly susceptible to Mussolini's propaganda, partly mistook the reality of Italian Fascist labor organization. Perhaps one of his major errors was in assuming that Mussolini had fulfilled the apparent intentions of his speech of October 6, 1934 in Milan, a speech which Pound praises at the opening of *Jefferson and/or Mussolini,* and in which Mussolini promised to Italian workers the final achievement of corporatism, whereby they would enjoy increased economic benefits as well as genuine participation in politics (Salvemini: 141–142, 161). Pound may also have accepted the dubious claims of the propagandist Gioacchino Volpe that the National Council of Corporations had by 1930 not only a "consultative" but legislative function within the state; that Mussolini's legislation of February, 1934 had "increased" the power of the syndicates and "developed" the "revolutionary principles" of Italian Fascism; and that the Charter of Labor, which Volpe acknowledges to be less than a decree-law, had nonetheless preserved equality of classes, promoted the welfare of workers, and succeeded in subordinating capital and labor equally to the needs of the nation (Volpe: 7, 144–147). In any case, during the late 1930s and 1940s Pound assumes that a kind of corporatist "democracy" had been established under Italian Fascism.

Pound's attraction to syndicalist and corporatist ideas reflects his Guild Socialist heritage. It also marks him if not as a full scale socialist then as an affiliate in some sense of the so-called "Fascist left," which included such influential theorists and politicians as Sergio Panunzio and Pound's hero Edmondo Rossoni. Fathered by syndicalism, drawing on certain Marxist categories, and amounting perhaps to a "Marxist heresy," the Fascist left pursued the "proletarian" goal of the corporate autonomy of labor and the recognition of "producers" over parasites (for instance financiers) in the economic life of the nation. Their dream was the independence of labor from the industrial employer and his frequent ally the centralized state. Some even dreamed of a takeover by labor of the state administration.[56] The presence of an important and highly visible corporatist left wing in Italian Fascism gives the movement a socialistic coloring and impulse lacking in Nazism, which Hitler purged of corporatism almost from the very beginning.[57]

The Italian Fascist left never realized its hopes and in fact found itself increasingly at odds with the Fascist Party.[58] Mussolini began his career as a syndicalist and socialist, and he often opportunistically adopted a pro-labor and anti-bourgeois stance. As late as 1933, Pound quotes an Italian Fascist cabinet minister's description of Mussolini: " 'Once of the left, always left.' Uomo di sinistra, sempre sinistra" (J/M, 28). But by 1922, the year of the "March on Rome," Mussolini was moving toward the Right and beginning to manifest a more conservative attitude toward corporatism. Yielding to the pressure of such nationalists as Alfredo Rocco, who would not allow the corporation to "overshadow" the state, Mussolini made the syndicates and corporations increasingly subordinate to centralized power. Far from intending to overthrow capitalism or the rights of property, Mussolini was convinced that capitalism still had an historical role to carry out with the help of a reformed, non-parasitic bourgeoisie, and he therefore made special concessions to "productive" capital from the very beginning of his regime (Salvemini: 131, 406; Volpe: 123). Indeed, the history of the Fascist left might be seen as a long term of waiting for Mussolini to make good on his corporatist promises.[59] He attempted to do so as late as 1943, when, as Hitler's puppet and the head of the newly-formed Salò Republic, he perhaps opportunistically and no doubt desperately returned to the socialist and corporatist ideals of his early career.[60] Impressed by Mussolini's economic and social policies as announced in the Verona Manifesto, Pound celebrates his abortive government in the Pisan *Cantos:* "to dream the Republic" (78/478).[61]

It would be wrong, however, to overemphasize Pound's affinities with the Italian Fascist "left," or to claim that his ideal of corporatism consorts with industrial democracy as conceived by the most radical syndicalists. Never does Pound support their goal of the takeover by labor of the means of production and distribution. Like the majority of Fascists, he believes in the preservation of private property and in the social value of the industrial capitalist, whom he views not so much as a capitalist but as a producer or "employer" (RB, 22). As for Pound's enthusiasm for Mussolini's return to socialist and "republican" ideals at Salò,[62] it might lead one to suppose that Pound had been dissatisfied with Italian Fascism during the 1930s and early 1940s, but we have seen that in this period he had lavished the most extravagant praise upon the "corporative state." Surely there is something suspect in Pound's sudden discovery toward the end of World War II that Fascism had been unable to achieve its goals owing to its "betrayal" by internal "monopolists," "mercantile industrialists," "liberals," and the "twenty year ignorance" allegedly induced by a "putrid Italian-Jewified plutocratic press."[63] Similar to the accusations which some Italian Fascist leftists brought against the regime, these charges are probably motivated by Pound's unshakable admiration for Mussolini and his need to find scapegoats for his now manifestly catastrophic policies. Although Mussolini had been in power for over twenty years, Pound observes in the Pisan *Cantos* that he had been "hang'd dead by the heels before his thought in proposito / came into action efficiently" (78/ 482). The "ruin" of Mussolini's "20 years labor" traces to the "jactancy, vanity, [and] peculation" (77/ 470) of his associates, who are at last discovered to be "half-baked and amateur," or "mere scoundrels," selling "their country for half a million / hoping to cheat more out of the people" (80/ 495). Instead of recognizing that Mussolini himself had installed this gang of disreputables, Pound finds in them evidence of the presumed defects of the Italian national character: "and the dog-damn wop is not, save by exception, / honest in administration any more than the briton is truthful" (77/ 470). But what seems even more questionable in Pound's enthusiastic turn to the "republicanism of labor" as the true goal of Fascism is that, for all his earlier praise of "democratic" corporatism, he had in fact accepted the basic core of Mussolini's statist and anti-labor policies during the first two decades of the Fascist era.

According to David Roberts, the syndicalists had misgivings about the power of the Fascist party and its Ministry of Corporations in the supervision of labor activities: nevertheless, A. James Gregor insists that all the major syndicalist theorists accepted Mussolini's statism.[64] So did Pound, and with no apparent reservations. With some justification Pound feared that the guilds, if left to themselves, and no matter how productive, would become socially detrimental "monopolies" (SP, 176), as in the Middle Ages. This is why Pound welcomed the "liberation from the shackles of the guilds" (SP, 177) in eighteenth-century Tuscany and the American colonies. Yet Pound's antidote to guild monopoly is itself extreme and even more dangerous, for he ultimately grants the state "absolute" (SP, 306) powers. "Economic collaboration," says Pound, "is the front name and the last name of corporate organization" (RB, 324). Since Pound is certain that "the working man does NOT want to govern; he wants good government" (RB, 18), collaboration is to be implemented by the centralized state: Pound speaks of a "GUILD organization coordinated at the top, that being the only place you CAN correlate" (RB, 280). This national central determines just prices "by means of state-controlled pools of raw products" (SP, 293) and presumably is run by disinterested experts who comprehend the "continued well being of the nation" (SP, 238). When there is a "clash" (RB, 204) of interests among trades, or between capital and labor, it should be decided at the top "according to the national interest" (RB, 204). Following the Fascist Labor Charter, Mussolini says in *The Cantos*: "We ask 'em to settle between 'em / If they can't, the State intervenes" (87/ 571).

Thus, like the Guild Socialists and Fascists, Pound initially stressed localism and decentralization and ironically ended up by endowing the state with coercive, perhaps totalitarian powers.[65] For it is never made clear, either in Guild Socialist or Italian Fascist theory, whether the state is a coordinator, mediator, advisor, supervisor, theory, enforcer, or dictator in economic life.[66] Despite Pound's statement that the "CORPORATE problem . . . does NOT mean starving the workman, or breakin' him up with scab mobs" (RB, 22), he was undoubtedly aware that the supposedly disinterested Mussolini had outlawed the class struggle, given legal status only to Fascist unions, adopted a state policy of compulsory arbitration, and made strikes illegal.[67] Never once does Pound raise his voice against these policies, and one must assume that he accepted them. At the same time, Pound was either foolish or disingenuous to suppose that the Fascist party and Italian state could avoid influence from and complicity with privileged interests and groups within the social hierarchy. With the preservation of private property, and in the absence of an integral corporatism and mixed syndicates, the very concepts of organic function, social role and worth, and the national welfare could not but be biased in their determination and application. According to Adrian Lyttelton, industrialists and other employers benefited from the organization of labor under Italian Fascism.[68] Not only were the corporations dominated by the agents of the Fascist party, but in labor disputes the conciliators usually favored employers.[69] In short, Italian Fascist corporatism in practice neither eliminated nor transformed the class structure. It solidified existing relationships of social and economic domination in a supposedly organic hierarchy of roles and functions dominated and enforced by the state.

This is not to imply that Italian Fascism, as Marxists critics have argued, was no more than an instrument by which industrialists and landowners maintained their dominance over the working class. Although the capitalists had greater economic advantages and political influence than did the proletariat in Fascist Italy, Mussolini ultimately succeeded in subordinating not only labor but capital to the needs of the state. During the 1930s the Italian Fascist state successfully intervened in many sectors of the economy, and came to control a larger portion of national industry than any other government in Europe with the exception of the Soviet Union. By the late 1930s, as Mussolini more rigorously imposed his policy of autarchy, the industrialists lost their autonomy and found themselves under the state's control (Cannistraro, ed.: 277–280). Gregor argues that they had never gained independence from the autarchic state and had grown increasingly disaffected with Mussolini's regime throughout the decade (Gregor, 3: 158–160). To be sure, Mussolini's state socialism was quite different from democratic socialism, and its chief aim was totalitarian domination and imperialistic conquest. Yet one must to at least some extent distinguish Pound's idealistic conception of Italian Fascism from its reality. In fact, Pound viewed

Mussolini's intervention in industry as a major safeguard of the national welfare.

It is a mistake to believe that Pound, because he defended private property and the Italian Fascist state, was therefore in every respect a mere apologist for capitalist domination. His position on this issue is complicated by his 1941 translation of Odon Por's *Italy's Policy of Social Economics*, a work which Pound apparently endorsed yet which is more radical and anti-capitalistic than Pound's own Fascist polemics. Like Pound, Por views Fascism as a transcendence of class conflicts and a collaborative harmony of social and economic groups. But a major difference between this work and the broadcasts is that Por, instead of concentrating mainly on the financier as the embodiment of the anti-social capitalist, lashes out at a plutocratic array of speculators, industrialists, businessmen, and landowners, all pursuing excessive profits through monopolies and the exploitation of labor as a commodity. Since many capitalists lack social responsibility, Por wants the state to discipline them according the needs of the nation. In order to bring production and consumption into balance, the capitalist must follow the state's orders rather than the selfish dictates of profit and competition. To these ends Por supports the state's imposition of excess profits taxes and its determination of just prices on the basis of collective pools of goods (*ammassi*). With their installation in a state-directed economy, the capitalists are no longer "what they once were," and their "mentality" has changed; economics has ceased to be the "inexorable boss of politics."[70]

Although Pound's attacks on capitalism lack the scope and intensity of Por's, he shares Por's belief that the property owner should follow the Fascist principle that every right, including the right of property, entails a social duty. As early as *Jefferson and/or Mussolini* Pound claims that Italy "was, even in 1900, immeasurably ahead of England as far as land laws and the rights of the man who works the soil are concerned." He adds that "some of the follies and cruelties of the great English owners would not now be permitted in Italy," for such men would be shipped to the "*confino*" or exile. Pound goes on to explain that the Italian landowner is prevented from cutting down olive trees "just when he likes and can't drive the 'colonno' " or tenant farmer (the descendant, socially, of the serf) from his lands. Yet one can hardly construe Pound's position as radical or socialistic, for he goes on to observe that, while the "colonno" is not exactly a serf, despite the "persistence of feudal decorations and courtesy" (J/M, 70) in Italy, he in some sense belongs to the landlord. In effect Pound is endorsing a system of land tenure based on a modified patriarchal ideal of feudal responsibility and benevolence. Seven years later, perhaps under the influence of Por, Pound's position on land ownership allows for a greater degree of state intervention. Writing to Ronald Duncan, Pound proposes that, rather than advocating a tax on uncultivated land, Duncan should "go fascist" and "cultivate the damn land when the owner of latifundia fails to do so" (L, 342). This statement, however, by no means rejects the principle of property, but implies only that the state may control its use when the owners ignore their obligation of productivity. The fact is that Italian Fascist land policy generally favored large landowners, and it is curious, given the structure of the Fascist political and social system, that Pound supposed it might be otherwise. In any case, by the late 1930s Pound implicitly acknowledges the possibility of capitalistic rather rather than merely financial exploitation in his endorsement of the "JUST PRICE" and "ammassi" (SP, 293, 300) as administered by the Italian Fascist state. Yet his admiration for these policies does not imply a rejection of either capitalism or private profit, much less an acceptance of the theory of surplus value. Pound wants the state to purify or "chasten" (SP, 208) Mammon by defining an acceptable profit margin. This authoritarian solution, the "model" for which Pound later discovers in the state-controlled economy of Byzantium, marks the limit of his anti-capitalism.

Since Pound supports or condones severe political repression and economic exploitation, his claims to having found in Italy an organic or harmonious political system can hardly be taken seriously. In order to establish the illusion of social unanimity, Pound, like the Fascists themselves, must deflect class antagonism from the putatively organic national group. Here one sees yet another explanation for Pound's anti-Semitism. It is ideologically indispensable to Pound as he diverts attention from the true sources of social inequality and attempts to promote unity on both the national and international scale.

Pound's thought, like that of most fascist writers, "fits into the unyielding framework of national self-assertion and autonomy" (Nolte: 40). This is the reason that Pound insists that Fascist Italy and Germany should not be confused, and that he accepts fascist imperialism and harps on autarchy (RB, 151, 294). In the broadcasts, as in his articles in the *Meridiano di Roma*, Pound constantly relies on anti-Semitism and particularly on hatred of the Jewish usurer to instil in his listeners a sense of the common national interest.[71] The rootless Jewish race, like international or "wandering" Jewish loan capital, is the great enemy of the national idea, which Pound now interprets in racial terms. The Jew is "against EVERY race in Europe that takes the responsibility for being a nation" (RB, 73). "The big Jew has rotted EVERY nation he has wormed into" (RB, 59).

Despite its strong nationalistic emphasis, fascism also had international aspirations which Pound shared and within which anti-Semitism again plays a crucial role. As early as 1918 Pound asserts that the "Allied peoples had better unite" against the coming "internationalism of capital," which he identifies with "Mitteleuropa," and which he opposes to Labor in the broadest sense.[72] While this early article does not make it clear whether Mitteleuropa means Jews, by 1935, in a letter to Douglas Fox, Pound finds that "it wd/ be clever of the Nazi's [sic] to combat semitic anti-Nazi propa-

ganda by a KULTURBUND, constructive work, Italy; U.S. and GER-
MANY. . . ."[73] By the broadcasts Pound's internationalism has gained in
intensity and is linked obsessively with anti-Semitism. Not only does Pound
praise Quisling's idea of a coalition of Nordic nations under fascism,[74] but
he believes that, except for Jewish interference, there is no "fundamental
and irremediable hate" (RB, 131) between the French and the Germans.
Now Pound asks the "Producers of the world" to "unite," but "NOT under
secret control of Semitic or any other finance" (RB, 302). Fomenting "racial
enmity" (RB, 329), starving all nations, the Jews stand against "the rest of
humanity" (RB, 310).

To hold such beliefs Pound needed more than anti-Semitism. He needed
also to deny his awareness of internal social violence and estrangement
within the West. Writing to Wyndham Lewis in 1939 Pound said: "BAD
enough to have European aryans murdering each other for the sake of Willie
Wieseman [Sir William George Wiseman, British diplomat and non-Jewish
partner of Kuhn, Loeb, and Co.] and a few buggarin' kikes" (P/L, 214).[75]
The word "aryans" is a substitution. Pound had first written "aliens," thus
acknowledging the social fragmentation of Europe. Then, in an act of self-
censorship which was also a vain assertion of social unity, he had crossed it
out.[76]

Part Three

The Victim

Chapter Fifteen

The Role of the Scapegoat

Peter Nathan has argued that anti-Semitism is inseparable from the psychological process known as projection, which is the externalization of unacceptable parts of one's mental life. One cause of projection is the emergence of repressed wishes, instincts, and desires into consciousness. Because the individual interprets these as evil or forbidden, and because they induce in him fear or guilt, he is unwilling to acknowledge them. He therefore projects them onto objects and persons, who by this projection take on the alien, negative, and guilty character of the repressed wishes and desires. Projection thus enables the individual to attain freedom from mental conflict and painful introspection, to externalize his negative qualities, and to become wholly good in his own eyes, capable of identifying with his own goodness; the individual feels free to attack his projected and distorted self-image in other human beings. For Nathan, those persons and groups that are the objects of such projections tend to be made into scapegoats. They are the modern version of that creature which, in primitive and ancient times, bore responsibility for the guilt and sins of the community and whose expulsion freed it from internal evil (Nathan: 29–51).

Although post-war studies have inseparably linked anti-Semitic prejudice and projection,[1] Nathan never explains why the Jews, of all groups, are eminently suited to receive projections and suffer accusations, or why such projections should culminate in violent hostility. Indeed, Pound projects his hatred onto numerous "enemies," including the Jews, but only the Jews acquire the status of a collective plague or poison within his works.[2] Like Fenichel, Nathan argues that repressed wishes get projected onto certain groups, particularly "subject-races," such as the Jews, since subject-races "represent that part of themselves" which individuals "have had to repress" (Nathan: 34–35). However helpful, this argument stresses the subjective and is almost entirely ahistorical. It also implies that the level of anti-Semitism should stay more or less constant, whereas anti-Semitism has oscillated historically from relatively benign prejudice to murderous hostility. Unless we attribute such changes to vicissitudes in social repression, which does not seem likely, we must assume that certain historical and social situations trigger virulent anti-Semitism: plagues, depressions, wars, famine, forms of ontological catastrophe and violence, in short crisis. However much such crises may be distorted by an observer's projections, they nonetheless have a basis in historical actuality. Nor can the theory of projection account for the most important of Pound's anti-Semitic accusations, namely that the Jews cause a massive and usurious breakdown of differentiation throughout Western culture. It is not clear how this accusation is a projection of Pound's repressed wishes and desires.

Having become convinced during the 1930s of his role as a cultural prophet, Pound tried to establish intellectual and cultural distinctions amid the rising tide of usury. This enterprise coincides with the Jews' gradual emergence, with usury, as the enemy in Pound's mind of the "clean line," of all those distinctions which Pound sees as necessary for moral order, cultural hierarchy, and ritual sanctity. This suggests that Pound's scapegoating is an essential element within his project of cultural differentiation. It we can show that his anti-Semitism is a direct response to conceptual, thematic, and epistemological problems within his work, that it springs from intellectual needs for differentiation, then we can reveal once and for all what critics have denied, namely the integral relation of anti-Semitism to the whole of Pound's writing.

II.

According to René Girard, primitive religion and classical tragedy are based on the "fundamental principle" that "order, peace, and fecundity" — in short, all that men consider desirable and sacred—"depend on cultural distinctions." Girard means a system of accepted hierarchical differences, a structure of operative distinctions among men, things, and concepts: "The cultural order is . . . a regulated system of distinctions in which the differences among individuals are used to establish their 'identity' and their mutual relationships." Like Pound, Girard stresses the importance of social hierarchy and "degree" (Girard, 2: 8, 49–51).

Perhaps culture's most crucial distinction is that between the controlled, purifying, and sacred violence of ritual mimesis and the random, polluting, and no less mimetic violence which rages uncontrollably among men. Girard argues that primitive and ancient societies attribute to sacrificial ritual the continued preservation of the social order as a system of hierarchical differences. Where sacrifices are observed, there is beauty and abundance, peace and sanctity. All of these things are interpreted as signs of the sacred, gifts of the gods. The greatest threat to this order comes from the reciprocal and finally indiscriminate violence of feuds, rivalries, and vendettas. Since human violence is mimetic and contagious, once violence emerges within a community it can, like a plague or contagion, carry its infection across all social boundaries. As society is engulfed in violence, men lose faith in the powers of ritual, "pure" or sacred violence, to maintain social distinctions; impure violence even profanes ritual itself. Just as no idea, concept, belief, symbol, or doctrine is free from the taint of violent contention, so all men become unrecognized doubles of each other through acts of mutual aggression. In this way, for Girard, society reaches its apocalyptic moment or sacrificial "crisis."[3]

When all violence is reciprocal, nothing remains unpolluted, and no one is innocent or free from blame. Nonetheless, at the height of the crisis the entire community projects onto an arbitrarily chosen victim or scapegoat the blame for social disorder. Accused of mythical and monstrous Oedipal crimes such as parricide and incest—violations of the community's normal system of differences—the scapegoat represents undifferentiation and monstrosity and is thus the very embodiment of the crisis itself. Being different, he is conceived as totally monstrous, wholly other, and in this form unites the community against him (Girard, 2: 4, 8, 64, 72–85).

Since the scapegoat is "a substitute for all the members of the community," his murder puts an end to impure, arbitrary, and collective violence, reunites the community, and restores harmony and differences along with the sacred, pure, and orderly violence of ritual. In short, sacrificial and nonviolent forms of ritual are the mimetic commemoration of an initial act of generative social violence, the expulsion of the arbitrarily chosen scapegoat victim. This origin is invariably disguised by mythical explanations of social origins, and ultimately animal sacrifices are substituted for human, but the original human sacrifice underlies these customs and explanations. Religion, then, is based on misunderstandings conscious or otherwise, what Girard calls *méconnaissance*.[4]

Though the scapegoat is chosen arbitrarily, it is preferable that he be a "good conductor" of violence: an exalted figure, such as a king, at once external to and different from the community, or else a marginal or nearly exterior figure, a "foreigner," a person or group "on the fringe." Not only must the scapegoat sharply resemble the human types whom a society is willing to sacrifice, it must also resemble those persons who were original objects of violence within the community. On the other hand, the scapegoat must also produce an impression of absolute difference, for only in isolation can it absorb the great variety of the community's hostile and contradictory accusations and thus become a figure of monstrous indeterminacy. Again, apart from these requirements, the scapegoat substitutes for *all* members of the community: simply because certain groups or persons receive hostile projections does not mean that they will become full-fledged scapegoat victims. Finally, the scapegoat is most often sought among the weak and powerless, who cannot strike back in revenge, and therefore cannot plunge society back into reciprocal violence (Girard, 2: 39, 12, 13).

III.

In the late 1930s Pound asserts that nationalistic violence and social warfare threaten the organic unity of Europe. Europeans and Americans should recognize their fraternal bond against the true enemy, which proves to be usury and the Jews. During this period Pound's representation of the Jews becomes increasingly ambiguous, contradictory, and overdetermined as he projects more and more hatred upon them. As we have seen, the Jews represent both Nature and anti-Nature, excess and sterility, luxury or opulence and asceticism, paternal repression and hetaeristic freedom, history and the ahistorical, materialism and abstraction, instinctual life and the violation of the instincts. Having no fixed character or identity, they are the monstrous epitome of confusion and chaos, calling to mind Wagner's description of the Jew as the "plastic demon" of humanity.[5] Pound's projections make the Jews into figures of confusion, indeterminacy, undifferentiation, and monstrosity, in short, agents of crisis and bearers of the new and monstrous difference which characterizes the scapegoat.[6]

Yet the question still remains: why project these particular accusations onto the Jews? Though contradictory, Pound's accusations fall into an antithetical pattern and are associated with specific concepts: Nature, material wealth, sexuality, patriarchal and matriarchal authority, religion, history. These are the concepts which for various historical, social, and religious reasons have been associated with the Jews, and they do imply problems toward which Pound felt the profoundest ambivalence. Pound's scapegoating strategy is most likely to appear where his need for definition is as great as his ambivalence, where his distinctions collapse and his terms hover in uncertainty. For the sacrificial crisis is signalled by a failure of distinctions, the inability to clarify cultural values and boundaries. This failure necessitates Pound's search for a crime and a criminal, the "one enemy" responsible for "muddling and muddying . . . [his] terms" (GK, 31).

Being a marginal figure, the scapegoat is neither in nor out of the community, and because of its ambiguity is especially likely to provoke first fear and then its own victimization. To quote Mary Douglas, "all margins are dangerous"; pollution is invariably linked to that violent power which is unleashed when the lines of cosmic or social order are crossed.[7] It is also possible to extend this observation to situations apparent in the case of Jews and Orientals, both common scapegoats of the Western world. Whether as "foreigners" or as marginal members of their host societies, these groups are often associated with mysterious, dangerous, and originally foreign concepts or substances—money, gold, luxuries, books, writing, prostitution, spices, drugs, alcohol, oil, all of which are of Near Eastern provenance—whose essential value is extremely difficult to determine and toward which the West feels deep ambivalence. Like the scapegoat, each of these entities exists in a marginal area which blurs and complicates the distinction between natural and unnatural, natural and cultural, useful and useless, necessary and unnecessary, sacred and profane. On the whole, land and other "natural" forms of concrete wealth have not excited the hostility, suspicion, and passion which men have often directed toward money and gold; in the Renaissance, one hears of the *auri sacra fames*, the accursed lust for gold. Nor has man generally questioned his assumption of the transparency, presence, and naturalness of the spoken word, whereas, for all the cultural advantages of books, he has constantly feared the deformation of cultural meanings introduced by writing. Again, man has had few doubts about the inherently healthful properties of water and wheat, to use two common examples, but he has often questioned the value of such luxurious and highly prized supplements of natural alimentation as wine and pepper, which, though they may cause ulcers, also enhance the flavor of food (or disguise its rottenness). Each of these and other similarly suspicious objects, at once hated, feared, and loved, may be described as a *pharmakon* (pl. *pharmaka*) or drug. Like drugs, which are poisonous or curative depending on dosage or application, these *pharmaka* can never be given a definite moral or social status on the basis of a priori categories of right and wrong, good or bad, helpful or harmful, sacred or profane. Hence they provoke the most disturbing feelings of ambivalence and confusion in the communities that use them.[8] These objects also reflect upon those who transmit or are intimately associated with them; such groups and persons can be and have been, by association, readily identified under certain circumstances as dangerous and poisonous. There is an etymological connection between the *pharmakon*, the drug that either kills or cures, and the *pharmakos*, the scapegoat who "poisons" the community but who on his expulsion purges it of its violence and becomes in his own right a sacred and sanctifying figure (Girard, 2: 95, 36). Although etymologies are not necessarily keys to meaning, in this case the etymological link reflects the profound conceptual similarity between these words.

This is the pattern which unfolds in the next two chapters. In an attempt to overcome the inherent ambiguity of the above "drugs," Pound identifies each in its "bad" form with the Jews. But first a related problem. Girard points out that the scapegoat deflects violence from another object that the community considers sacred but that the scapegoat secretly resembles; indeed, were there no scapegoating, violence would be directed toward this object. One wonders what, in Pound's case, this object might be.

History has repeatedly revealed among men a "half-suppressed desire to place the blame for all forms of violence on women" (Girard, 2: 36). This is only one similarity between women and the Jews. Another is their recurrent association with the strange or exotic. Another is their marginal social status—the Jews' because of their foreignness, and that of women because of their subject position in a male-dominated society. So too, in Western tradition women and Jews have both been associated with most if not all of the previously mentioned *pharmaka*. Their resemblance is perhaps nowhere more evident than in the exotic image—extremely popular in the nineteenth century, as we have seen—of the luxurious Semitic vampire or courtesan. For these reasons both groups are candidates for the victimization which they have suffered in common throughout history.[9]

Critics have noted that Pound, especially in the early *Cantos*, blames women for cultural violence (Wilhelm, 2: 20–34). It is less commonly noted that Pound frequently associates women and the Near East, and that his works repeatedly suggest a secret resemblance between women, usury, and the Jews. So close is their resemblance that, for about a third of *The Cantos*, they are nearly indistinguishable from and hence interchangeable with each other. This means that each is potentially a scapegoat, whose victimization might be the basis for social order. What needs to be examined is the process by which Pound dissociates women, literally by means of violence, from the Jews.

Chapter Sixteen

Indeterminacy and Crisis, I:
The Selva Oscura

As early as *The Spirit of Romance* Pound speculated that the troubadours' sexual mysticism might derive from the "Oriental cults thronging the
Eternal City" (SR, 96) during the last days of the Roman Empire. At this
early point in his career Pound had no difficulty imagining an Oriental
influence on European sexual mysticism; it was only later, in a second
edition of *The Spirit of Romance,* that he denied such influences (SR: 18n).
Yet Pound was undoubtedly aware that Aphrodite, the dark eyelidded goddess of Canto 1, originates in the Semitic Astarte. Many of the other European mother goddesses are imports from the Semitic world, while woman-
worship in the West owes much to Oriental models. The mother goddesses
thus carry with them all the dangers, mysteries, and attractions of their place
of origin.

A good analogy is Dionysus, who appears in Canto 2. Though masculine, Dionysus is also originally an Oriental god, bringing news of wine and
orgiastic religion. Following Ovid and Euripides, Pound represents the fate
of those who fail to recognize and honor Dionysus and thus suffer his
terrifying wrath. First the sailors are turned into monstrous beasts, examples
of negative metamorphosis. Next Pentheus ignores the warning of Tiresias
and Cadmus and becomes all the more susceptible to the powers of the god:
in Ovid, as in Euripides, he visits the Bacchantes, becomes fascinated by
their rites, and is torn to pieces by Dionysus' worshippers. But while these
examples might imply complete endorsement of Dionysus and the ecstatic
powers of wine, Pound was nearly a teetotaler, and he also feared the
religions of "excess." His more likely point is that Dionysus' mysteries, like
wine itself, should be assessed properly, with reverence and also fear. Unlike
the sailors and Pentheus, men must find that proportion or balance by which
the god's violent powers are made beneficent, must find the difference between the good and bad forms of the sacred. Failure to do so will surely
provoke the "retributive forces" of Nature.

Pound considers only those cultures healthy whose rituals and customs are founded on the all-encompassing "process," Nature in its unfailing "intelligence," abundance, and "splendour" (GK, 282). If the West is to be saved, it must turn to the European mother goddesses, around whom Pound constructs a metaphorical web linking light, vegetation, fecundity, and iconic clarity: the statue of Aphrodite at Terracina; the cults of virgin Artemis and procreant Demeter; the Virgin of San Michele in Florence (adored by Guido Cavalcanti); the church in Southern France known as La Dorata (the golden); and Stefano's painting of the "Madonna in Hortulo." In Stefano's painting the radiant Madonna appears in a garden, while the epithet "La Dorata" (52/ 258) associates her with the generative light or golden rain of the divinity. Like Aphrodite or Danaë, the Virgin Mary embodies for Pound the idea of sacred parthenogenesis or virgin birth.

All of these divine images can take a negative or parodic shape. In Canto 4 Pound recalls a church "by [the] Garonne," where religion has decayed and the Virgin's procession moves "like a worm, in the crowd" (4/ 16). Since many worms reproduce parthenogenetically, this is possibly such an image. If so, the Virgin evokes the fecund but undifferentiated duplications of worms; she resembles the worm of usury in Canto 48 and the Addendum to Canto 100. This image of ritual decay also anticipates the parthenogenetic bogs of the Hell *Cantos*. The Greek inscription above London, "EIKON GES" (14/ 62), signifies "an image of the earth," specifically Gea Tellus, the Earth Mother: the feminine in its aspect of darkness, castration, and pollution. Besides the theme of woman as savior there is in Pound an antithetical theme of woman needing to be redeemed, raised into the clear light of day; as in Canto 1, where Odysseus meets his mother among the "impotent" and voiceless shades of Hades, sometimes the feminine is indistinguishable from Hell itself. In Canto 90 Alcmene and Tyro ascend into light from Hell by a protective crystal funnel:

> the crystal funnel of air
> Out of Erebus, the delivered,
>   Tyro, Alcmene, free now, ascending
> e i cavalieri,
>   ascending,
> no shades more,
>   lights among them, enkindled
>   (90/ 608–609)

The phrase "e i cavalieri" is from Canto 5 of the *Inferno*, where Helen of Troy appears ("Elena vedi," quoted in Canto 20); one may assume that Helen, formerly of the jungle, and defined in Canto 2 as "destroyer of men and cities," is at last among the redeemed souls. Tyro appears in Canto 2 (and also in Homer's Hades), while Alcmene is the mother of Hercules, with whom Pound strongly identified.

What, then, is the real difference between Stefano's luminous parthenogenetic Madonna and the dark worm in the crowd; between the fecund

Nature goddesses Demeter and Aphrodite, and EIKON GES, the parthenogenetic and polluting (and yet fecund) earth; between Pound's snake-headed
Isis of Canto 93 and the terrifying Medusa of Canto 15; between Python,
the chthonic dragon whom Apollo slays, and the Pitonessa, the Pythian
priestess to whom Pound prays in Canto 104? It is merely circular to say
that the difference between these positive and negative figures is that between reverence and irreverence for Nature or the feminine, for such an
argument offers as explanation the very thing to be explained.

Before attempting to unravel this knot, one may consider an instance in
which the feminine and Nature itself afford no clear distinctions. Canto 23
includes a brief section of Stesichorus' fragmentary poem on the journey of
Hercules to capture Geryon's cattle. Hercules, son of Zeus (as Stesichorus
calls him), is Pound's solar hero and model as a destroyer of monsters. The
following passage begins with a reference to Helios (who appears in
Stesichorus as the son of Hyperion); at the Western bounds of Ocean he
exchanges his chariot for a golden cup, on which he journeys through
darkness back to the East, there to rest in a laurel grove. The passage
concludes with another excerpt from Stesichorus, in which Hercules, having
borrowed the sun's boat on his mission to capture Geryon's cattle, likewise
enters a "shadowy laurel grove":

> With the sun in a golden cup
>   and going toward the low fords of ocean,
> Ἅλιος δ' Ὑπεριονίδας δέπας ἐσκατέβαινε χρύσεον
> Ὄφρα δὶ ὠκεανοῖο περάσας
>   ima vada noctis obscurae
> Seeking doubtless the sex in bread-moulds
> ἥλιος, ἅλιος, ἅλιος = μάταιος
> ("Derivation uncertain." The idiot
> Odysseus furrowed the sand.)
> alixantos, aliotrephès, eiskatebaine, down into,
> descend, to the end that, beyond ocean,
> pass through, traverse
>   ποτὶ βένθεα
> νυκτὸς ἐρεμνᾶς,
> ποτὶ ματέρα, κουριδίαν τ'ἄλοχον
> παῖδάς τε φίλους . . . . ἔβα δάφναισι κατάσκιον
> Precisely, the selv'oscura
>
>   (23/107–108)

The sun, or Helios, and Hercules are headed into the darkness ("ima
vada noctis obscurae" Latinizes Stesichorus). Shortly Pound introduces a
Greek series and a gloss: ἥλιος, ἅλιος, ἅλιος = μάταιος. The first word
means "sun," which in Doric dialect is ἅλιος. The second word is homony-
mous not only with an adjective meaning "of the sea," and having its root in
the Greek word for "salt," but also with the third word, which is equivalent
to μάταιος, and means "fruitless, idle, vain." In response to a commenta-
tor's puzzlement ("Derivation uncertain") over the third word, Pound sug-

gests that its meaning is contained in Odysseus' feigned insanity in ploughing sand, a futile attempt to evade the Trojan War; for the sea contains salt
and sand, both of which are fruitless, and whose sterility is evoked in
Homeric references to the "unharvestable" sea (Davenport: 395–399; Peck:
5). Yet this appeal to empirical proof to untie a textual crux hardly dispels
the uncertainty which converges in the middle term, ἅλιος, "of the sea,"
which conjoins in a single word the idea of the sun, the origin, a source of
life and plenitude, and sterility, waste, and absence. Guy Davenport observes that Stesichorus, hinting at a mystery at the heart of Nature, "felt the
tension of opposing meanings in ἅλιος, as though it were a pun, and symbolized in his poem the double nature of the word, growing and ungrowing,
light and dark, order and confusion" (Davenport: 398–399). Subsequently
Pound introduces two words with a common root and suggesting a similar
ambiguity of growth and depletion, presence and absence: alixantos,
aliotrephès, meaning "sea worn" and "sea reared" (Peck: 6). The sun's
journey, like the hero's, is into a tangled realm in which opposing ideas are
indissolubly joined. This is the "selv'oscura" —the very forest which Pound,
like Dante, had dared to enter.

The selva's connection with the feminine "jungle" is noted by Peck, who
finds a "family resemblance" between these themes.[1] In Dante "selva
oscura" means woods uninhabited and uninhabitable by man. It is thus
similar but not necessarily identical to Pound's HYLE in Canto 30, as well
as to the female "chaos" (29/ 144; PD, 204). Meaning "uncut forest," the
first epithet Pound translates as Madame Matter. Pound's idea of woman as
matter probably reflects Gourmont, who accepted Aristotle's view of the
primacy and priority of the formative masculine principle. For Aristotle the
feminine requires the differentiating mark of the phallus just as the uncut
forest requires the axe; otherwise it remains formless, uncreative, without
telos.[2]

The selva is more mysterious and troublesome than HYLE. Like modern biologists, Hercules is "doubtless seeking the sex in bread-moulds."
Pound knows that these macroscopic fungi are virtually impossible to define
or clarify. Like the microscopic and unicellular forms of fungi (the so-called
"true" bacteria), bread-moulds occupy a place in Nature which is neither
definitely animal nor definitely vegetable. They are also literally parasites, as
are the invisible bacteria: they destroy that substance, grain, which Pound
worships. Yet their existence is essential to agriculture, since they cause the
decay of plant and animal debris and assure the soil's richness. Bread-
moulds also have important medicinal properties, can kill the body's parasites. Beyond these mysteries, bread-moulds exemplify the sexual ambiguity
at the heart of primitive nature. Although some moulds or "true" fungi, like
the "true" bacteria, reproduce asexually by scission, others reproduce
through differentiated sexual parts. In short, they represent a Nature which,
without loss to its fecundity, treats sexual differentiation as a matter of

indifference. Finally, bread-moulds and other true fungi further resemble the microscopic bacteria insofar as they too grow abundantly without chlorophyll and without photosynthesis. They have no need of light and in fact abhor the solar masculine principle which Hercules represents.[3]

It is wrong to see the selva as a chaos or to think that this is why it disturbs Pound. Unlike chaos, the selva is not a state of utter darkness but is "oscura": a confused mixture of dark and light. Nor is the selva a formless emptiness or non-presence: however confused, it is a place of being, of growth and abundance. The real anxiety of the selva is that it is neither undifferentiated nor clearly differentiated, neither being nor unbeing, growing nor ungrowing, abundant nor sterile, light nor dark. All of these things at once, it collapses or blurs distinctions without eliminating them. A "penumbra, . . . mother of bogies," the selva is undecidable.

The selva thus endangers those distinctions which govern Pound's attempt to define Nature as the source of fixed cultural values. Pound associates Nature unequivocally with light, splendor, beauty, and clear distinctions; society's abundance is based on Nature's unfailing tendency toward abundance, order, and vitality. In the selva none of these distinctions holds. Just as its light is inextricable from its darkness, so it confuses natural generation and its presumed opposite, sterility or death. Simultaneously within the same process one finds fecundity and decay, growing and ungrowing, the futile weaving and re-weaving of Nature itself.[4] At the same time the selva endangers the positive status of abundance, for it is inseparable from sterility ("ungrowing") and confusion: it is an overgrowing or beclouding inimical to man.

The selva is located where the sun periodically disappears and its track or movement is unknown. For Pound the sun represents the pure, unmixed, "undivided" (SP, 307), and undifferentiated origin. It is the masculine principle or Father (Pater Helios), the source of seminal light, of growth and abundance. Pound links it to natural and orderly language and speech, the *logos:* the sun, the source of human language, is "god's mouth." The sun is also the *ground* on which all distinctions can be made, that which permits things to shine forth in their splendor and clarity; the sun must be not only over but "under it all" (85/ 544). Within this system the sun is presumably the stable, unturning center toward which all things heliotropically turn; linguistically, it is the basis for a whole cluster of themes and ideas which return ceaselessly, along a kind of metaphorical chain, back to the idea of the sun as origin. The sun should thus be understood not as a metaphor or sign within a system of signs, but as that ultimate originating term which sets the system into motion and which permits, controls, and lies under linguistic definition.[5] Yet this sun worship poses an inherent problem which emerges in the selva oscura. Whether for Pound or any other heliocentric writer, the sun, itself the origin and guarantor of truth and enemy of darkness, can never be seen directly; it is always known as a reflected light or lustre mediated by natural objects, is always represented by means of metaphors (sowing, etc.).[6] This means that the sun can never be known in itself, that the putative origin is never present, that the producer of the system of signs is itself represented in mediate form. Second, the sun, like metaphors, can turn or "trope," go out of itself, can suffer "ellipse" and "eclipse"; this is evident in the selva oscura, where the sun enters obscurity and the poet must wait for its return. The selva, then, represents any place or moment in which the origin, far from being a univocal source and presence, is feared to be absent and can be inferred only by fugitive traces: the penumbral mixture of light and shadow, the last reflected rays of the sun as it fades into darkness.[7] This passage on the selva reflects Pound's doubts over origins, his fear that, within cosmos, the differentiating solar principle has no clear temporal or ontological claim to priority—or, perhaps even worse, that priority may belong to its antithesis, the primitive feminine principle.[8]

II.

Another version of the selva oscura figures in Gourmont's *The Natural Philosophy of Love*. According to Gourmont, men are capable of individuating and "egoistic act[s]," but animals exist only to propagate their species. Gourmont is fascinated by those insects who "know life and love" in the same sexual "shiver," who know "nothing but the maternal function" in the "strictest limit" of their birthplace, who live, love, and die as a "brief apparition over flowers." Like the ephemera, which "hover in clouds above the water, among the reeds," many of these species have never "looked at the sun."[9] Nature repeatedly ignores the distinctions between Life and Death, Eros and Thanatos, generation and extinction. One recalls Bachofen's "tellurian" Nature (the swamp) and Pound's selva, as well as the Palux Laerna, where features emerge for a moment and then fade, "the face gone, generation" (16/ 69).

Gourmont was especially interested in parthenogenesis, a common form of insect and plant reproduction which occurs without the union of differentiated sexual parts—in short, feminine reproduction without the aid of the male. Though he postulates two prior metaphysical entities, the Great Male A and the Great Female B, he concludes that the earliest mode of reproduction is asexual and feminine and that the female is "primitive." *The Natural Philosophy of Love* is thus a hymn to the "singular feminism which one normally finds in Nature." The male, says Gourmont, has "slowly attained a first place not intended by Nature for him," while it is "only among mammifers and in certain groups of birds that the male is equal or superior to the female." Even where the male principle introduces difference and hence individuation into Nature, this difference usually means little; the female is "nearly always the superior individual." The male psyche is a "very small" and "clumsy" butterfly, but the female is "a huge worm." Among the termites, the female is an "enormous" and fecund "sexual tub," while the male lives "in the shadow of this formidable mountain of female power and luxury." If the female represents luxury as desirable abundance, the male represents it in its other sense of something needless, parasitic, marginal; in most cases he is a pointless "extra" or "appendix." The penis, says Gourmont, is a "useless" and "supplementary development," a "luxury and a danger."[10]

Even so, in having attained "first place," man represents "progress" and "development." By contrast with most other species, he shows pronounced sexual dimorphism, an "augmentation, an aggravation of the normal type represented by femininity," thus giving mankind its distinctive and creative character. As for women, whom Gourmont and Pound compare with insects, they conserve natural instincts (Gourmont: 58, 65–69; PD, 205). It is therefore no surprise that man—rightly, according to Gourmont and Pound—wants to extend his superiority to the rest of Nature. Aristotle argues that without the intervention of the male, the female exists in a state of formlessness and privation.

Actually, Gourmont's work suggests the opposite. Fecund beyond anything known to the male, indifferent to *telos*, reason, order, destiny, identity, to every one of man's marks, the primitive feminine carries on in its vague, spontaneous, promiscuous confusion:

> After coupling they fade as lamps when extinguished. This luminosity is, evidently, of an interest purely sexual. When the female sees the small flying star descend toward her, she gathers her wits, and prepares for hypocrite defense common to all her sex, she plays the belle and the bashful, exults in fear, trembles in joy. The fading light is symbolic of the destiny of nearly all insects, and of many animals also; coupling accomplished, their reason for being disappears and life vanishes from them. (Gourmont: 48–49)

Suspended between light and dark, growth and ungrowth, life and death, Nature's fading light resembles the selva oscura.

There is another, perhaps unexpected resemblance between the selva, which belongs to Nature, and that which is supposedly Nature's metaphysical opposite. For Nature as selva seems indistinguishable from usury: both are characterized by the absence or impermanence of the phallic mark. Pound's metaphors of usury imply castration, absence, effacement, and loss of light. Usury destroys the differences between things. The darkness of usury, portending the obliteration of the phallic trace, thus resembles the "fading light" of Nature.

It might be argued that usury differs from Nature in its unnatural barrenness, its parasitism, its hostility to the organic, its opposition to "nature's increase" (Addendum, 100/798). But in Pound's usage parasitism is an ambiguous term which, like usury, constantly shifts its ground. For instance, Pound compares usury and its effects to parthenogenesis, which one might arbitrarily describe as "sterile," and which is characteristic of many parasites, but which is nonetheless organic. The same comparison appears in the reference in the Addendum to Canto 100 to usury as "Τόκος [Tokos]." According to Carroll F. Terrell, this is Greek for usury—a correct observation, yet one that attempts to limit the word's meaning and thus to dispel its ambiguities. In Liddell and Scott usury is a secondary meaning, deriving metaphorically from "Tokos" in the sense of childbirth, parturition, the time of parturition, and offspring of men and animals: in short, natural entities and events.[11] In the Hell *Cantos* the inhabitants of usurious London breed by "scission" in the "muted light" ("luce muto," 14/ 61) of a parthenogenetic swamp; in this "bog of stupidities" the soil is "living pus, full of vermin," with "dead maggots begetting live maggots." Not only does the emergence of live maggots or worms from their dead parents suggest the coalescence of life and death in London, a repetition of the selva oscura, but it looks forward to the "great worm" which is killed in Canto 48; almost certainly symbolic of usury, this worm resembles the "worm in the crowd" in Canto 4 and Fafnir the worm in Addendum to Canto 100 (Bacigalupo: 91–92). Again usury resembles parthenogenetic or spontaneous growth, terrifying doubles from the swamp: "Fafnir the worm, / . . . Twin evil of envy, / Snake of the seven heads, Hydra, entering all things" (Addendum, 100/ 798).

Traditionally feminine, the Hydra (or octopus) belongs to the Palux Laerna, which appears in Canto 16 as an image of abortive fecundity. Amid swarms of fish, eggs, and embryos, the face is "gone" in mere "generation" and the phallic mark remains unclarified; meanwhile trout are "submerged by the eels" (16/ 69). This reference to eels prefigures Canto 51 and Geryon, who as the beast of Usury carries the "eel fisher's basket," a phrase repeated in Addendum to Canto 100 again in connection with Geryon. As for why usury resembles or recalls eels, Gourmont had noted that sexual differences are generally unnoticeable in fish, which are primitive forms of life.[12]

Finally, consider "A Visiting Card," where Pound returns to Cheng Ming, the Confucian injunction to call things by their right names. Here the profuse and "wild" vegetation of the "swamp" represents the "beclouding" (SP, 331–333) or confusion which occurs when men fail to observe Cheng Ming. But Pound's use of the swamp figure is ambiguous and finally self-contradictory. The swamp's beclouding is meant to represent the result of usury, for which Cheng Ming is the antidote. But since usury is by definition *contra naturam* and against Nature's increase, one would not expect it to be compared with the luxuriant growth of the swamp. Yet just as usury and Nature suggest fading light, here they both cause "beclouding."

It might be objected that this confusion results only from the inevitable imprecisions of figurative language; Pound's metaphors may in some instances suggest a resemblance between usury and Nature, but for him usury is in its essence quite different. This objection was anticipated by Pound, who sees metaphor as a major obstacle in the definition of usury, and even suggests that metaphor is usurious:

> "A pity that poets have used symbol and metaphor
> and no man learned anything from them
>   for their speaking in figures."
>   (Addendum, 100/ 799)

This implies that a transparent and non-metaphorical language exists; that usury is a definable referent or object; and that metaphor clouds the truth by a kind of usurious borrowing, the transference of the qualities of one thing to an altogether different thing. Thus, in order to grasp what usury is, one must speak an appropriately denotative language.

Apart from the fact that Addendum to Canto 100 is filled with proliferating metaphors for usury—syphilis, canker, wenn, worm, Hydra, slime, etc.—Pound's project of defining usury faces a major problem. For the concept of usury is already constituted, contaminated, and overdetermined by metaphor. To return to an earlier example, the Greek "Tokos," by which Pound means usury in the Addendum to Canto 100, is itself a metaphorical derivative from the ideas of growth and offspring. In fact, the metaphors for usury recapitulate the same ambiguity and confusion which characterize the selva oscura.

Jacques Derrida has observed that one meaning of *usure* is "wear and tear": erasure by rubbing, or exhaustion, the slow erosion or effacement of the images or marks on the face of the coin.[13] We have seen many instances of such associations in Pound, who fears the darkening, blurring, and "putrefaction" of images, the decline of numismatic art, the clipping or erosion of the metal substance of coins, the loss of boundaries, the thickening of lines. For Pound usury is comparable to "syphilis" and "canker," is the "slow rot eating in." In Cantos 14 and 15 he associates usury with "lost contours," "erosions." One meaning of the selva is "sea-worn," suggesting slow depletion.

Nonetheless, usury is also associated traditionally with growth, increase, expansion, the bearing of fruit (Derrida, 3: 210). One recalls Pound's other metaphors and symptoms of usury: swamp, parthenogenesis, profusion of insect and vegetable life, cancer, wenn, and excrescence. Pound thus represents usury in terms of irreconcilable opposites. Usury is a "murrain" or "marasmus" (wasting) (GK, 109) and "fat"; it comes from the arid wastes of Arabia Petraea as well as from the fecund swamp; it is sensory starvation (those who have "set money-lust / Before the pleasures of the senses," 14/ 61) and sensory overcharge; it is the economics of scarcity and also of dangerous abundance, the "profusion" (SR, 18) of "opulence" (GK, 282) and parasitic luxury. One can understand why Pound fails to define usury, since usury is an overdetermined concept in which contradictory metaphorical ideas are already embedded. Pound is not the enemy of usury per se, for he is not really sure what usury is. Rather, usury is the name which Pound gives to indistinction itself.

III.

Though a confusion, the selva is not entirely undifferentiated. As in the Hell *Cantos*, it manifests signs of previous differentiation, mediation, and origination, and hence falls (as does HYLE) under the category of the organizable. It is thus possible for the trace to be preserved or restored. Consider the Palux Laerna, where Hercules destroyed the Hydra:

> Palux Laerna,
> the lake of bodies, aqua morta,
> of limbs fluid, and mingled, like fish heaped in a bin,
> and here an arm upward, clutching a fragment of marble,
> And the embryos in flux,
>   new inflow, submerging,
> Here an arm upward, trout, submerged by the eels;
>   and from the bank, the stiff herbage
> the dry nobbled path, saw many known, and unknown,
> for an instant;
>   submerging,
> The face gone, generation.
>
> (16/ 69)

Seemingly dead, these waters contain embryos, a promiscuous profusion; though fluid, they are bordered by a solid bank or margin of stiff herbage. Though dense with mingled and fragmented bodies, their depths reveal the glimmer of cultural and personal identity. An arm raises a fragment of marble and sinks back into the water; formed faces appear, which the poet knows and identifies. Apparently changeless and self-contained, the swamp yet reveals a temporal movement. "Flux" and "generation," the new inflow of embryos, import differentiation and temporal sequence, the historical within the seemingly ahistorical swamp.

By the 1940s Pound is convinced that one region resists clarification and organization. This is the Near East, which combines the sterile and abstract desert with the sterile luxuriance of the parthenogenetic swamp:

> All that is obscure and distorted results from an almost pathological attempt to cause to conceal or to make correspond some Greek perception of the truth with some Near Eastern ambiguity.
> . . . But between the Chinese "key economic space" and the Roman key space, we find an obscurantist space. It may be said that in the Near Eastern space the tribe and the people with little sense of the State were trying for millennia to block traffic between West and East, profiting from it, raising prices, etc.[14]

As a form of the selva, the Near East resembles the feminine. Not only are many of Pound's Fatal Women Semitic (Zothar, parthenogenetic Salomé, Helen of Tyre), but the Near East and the feminine share a common promiscuity, which apart from its sexual meaning implies the absence of a fixed or definite character. Hence Pound's association of the Jews with prostitution and sexual excess. Pound also charges that the Jews use drugs and magic to reduce Gentiles to the condition of swine or cattle. To quote Von Tirpitz in the Pisan *Cantos,* the clever Jews possess a dangerous "charm" (74/ 443), a quality which they share equally with the hated English and the unredeemed Circe, who uses evil drugs and sorcery to transform Odysseus' men into swine.[15] As the Jews are associated with cultural opulence, so in Canto 39 the luxuriant and promiscuous Circe entices men with the beautiful but dangerous entanglements of her loom.

In Pound's early poetry, and for a good part of *The Cantos,* women evoke the same associations as the Jews with plague and pestilence. In "La Fraisne" Pound's speaker tells of "women / That plague and burn" (PER, 5). Later, having the voice of Schoeney's daughters and thus associated with the tangled swamp, Helen of Troy is destroyer of men and cities, "helandros" and "heleptolis" (2/6), the two Greek "hel" words linking her to the confusion of Hell (Nassar: 48–49). Blamed by Pound as by the Trojan elders for her destructive sexuality, Helen is a scapegoat figure.

Or rather, Helen is a confusing mixture. A symbol of "To Kalon" or Beauty, and thus associated with order (for Pound beauty and order are synonymous), she is also linked with the swamp, which signifies fecundity. Nor does Pound view the promiscuity of HYLE or Nature as categorically bad. In the Pisan *Cantos* Demeter appears as *porne* (prostitute), an honorific term importing the vital promiscuity of Mother Earth (Surette, 3: 214). Pound also finds it appropriate that one of the founders of the Monte dei Paschi was illegitimate (Alexander: 177). And, though Pound sometimes blames Helen for the Trojan War and for her violation of the restrictive law of marriage, he is on the side of de Maensac when, in Canto 5, he abducts the willing wife of de Tierci and defends her with arms. It is unclear, though, how such sexual freedom is compatible with patriarchal China of the later *Cantos.*

In any case, just as luxury, magic, and drugs have good properties, so there is a value in feminine promiscuity and illicit sexual love.

> It remains that man has for centuries nibbled at this idea of connection, intimate connection between his sperm and his cerebration, the ascetic has tried to withhold all his sperm, the lure, the ignis fatuus perhaps, of wanting to super think; the dope fiend has tried opium and every inferior to Bacchus, to get an extra kick out of the organ, the mystics have sought the gleam in the tavern, Helen of Tyre, priestesses in the temple of Venus, in Indian temples, stray priestesses in the streets, and probably with a basis of sanity. . . . (PD, 213–214)

Perhaps the "prototype" of "chivalric love" (SR, 91), that is illicit troubadour love, Helen of Tyre appears in Canto 92 with Theodora, a circus prostitute in early life, but who became the wife of Justinian and helped him build Hagia Sophia, dedicated to the Virgin. Mead notes that the prostitute Helen of Tyre symbolizes the human soul fallen into matter and the need for the spiritual redemption of the feminine. Surette argues that Pound lacks

Mead's prudery and finds nothing wrong with Helen's descent into matter; hence presumably Pound's approving references to temple prostitutes and Indian temples, which sometimes celebrate raw sexuality (Surette, 3: 60–65). Nonetheless, Marianne Moore correctly observed that Pound's "unprudery" is exaggerated, and such exaggeration, as here, always reveals a basic ambivalence.[16] There is a Neo-Platonic Pound who wants to escape (and dominate) matter; for Pound NOUS, the differentiating and masculine mind, "flows upward," while "HYLE, or matter, pulls down."[17]

A similar ambivalence envelops Cunizza da Romano, whose story fascinated Pound in Cantos 6, 22, and 92. After her marriage Cunizza committed adultery with the poet Sordello, was expelled from her home, and lived a life of love and wandering. In the end, though, Cunizza returned home, freed her slaves, and earned a place in Dante's *Paradiso,* among those redeemed by their love; she appears in the ninth canto in the sphere of Venus, reserved for such redeemed lovers as Folquet of Marseilles and the Canaanite (but pro-Israelite) harlot Rahab (Rehab) from Joshua 2: 1–24:

> "in questa lumera appresso"
>   Folquet, nel terzo cielo.
> "And if I see her not,
>   no sight is worth the beauty of my thought"
>   (92/ 619)

In the first line Folquet refers to Rahab, while in the second Arnaut Daniel asserts the value of troubadour love. Although Rahab, like Helen of Troy, once threw the world into confusion, now she is "radiant in this light." But Folquet's words also pertain to Cunizza. Those in the third Heaven, the Sphere of Venus, "do not repent," but rather "smile, not for ... [their] fault," but "for the Power which ordained and foresaw."[18] Here love cures its own ills.

In "A Visiting Card" (1943) Pound shows less confidence in his moral and ethical distinctions: "We must," he says "distinguish between the intellectual construction of Europe, and poison. Perhaps in re-reading the *Divina Commedia* we may find this dissociation of ideas. I cannot say. Geryon is biform. He takes you lower down. And after the eighth canto of the *Paradiso,* who understands the meaning?" (SP, 332). Since Dante enters the Sphere of Venus in the eighth canto of *Paradiso,* Pound probably refers to the ambiguous powers of love as revealed in Rahab and Cunizza. One might expect to find these two in the swamp of Hell, with Helen of Troy, and yet they appear in a heaven of light. Such inexplicable transformations suggest an ultimate inversion of values, the arbitrariness of justice, the equivalence of the way up and the way down. In his doubleness Geryon the swamp monster signifies fraud, confusion, and indistinction.

Pound further complicates the issue by treating woman as a divine or quasi-divine figure, a source of wisdom whose love can transform the poet's soul. Thanks to his beautiful "*mantram*" (SR, 96–97), the poet or troubadour attains that heightened awareness of Nature's "splendor" which he renders in song.[19] Troubadour or chivalric love thus exists on the margins of natural sexuality and is inherently ambiguous. As Pound says, its spiritual value depends on the withholding of the immediate sexual urge; repression enables the lover to grasp and to enhance poetically the spiritual value of the lady (LE, 151, SR, 90, 97). But Pound never defines the correct proportion between restraint and desire. Moreover, within this margin of restraint it is possible for the poetic imagination to create a usurious increment of value; hence the monks' charge that Cavalcanti had committed idolatry. Since troubadour love is illicit, it is also potentially destructive of patriarchal distinctions and even of the poet. In Pound's version of the story of Piere Vidal, the troubadour's adulterous passion causes him to be transformed into and hunted as a wolf—a blurring of differences between man and animal which, Girard would claim, is "always linked to violence" and social disintegration (Girard, 2: 128).

In Canto 17 troubadour love produces lyric beauty:

> Eleanor, domna jauzionda, mother of Richard,
> Turning on thirty years (wd. have been years before this)
> By river-marsh, by galleried church-porch,
> Malemorte, Correze, to whom:
> "My Lady of Ventadour
> "Is shut by Eblis in
> "And will not hawk nor hunt
>   nor get her free in the air
> "Nor watch fish rise to bait
> "Nor the glare-wing'd flies alight in the creek's edge
> "Save in my absence, Madame."
>
> (6/ 22)

Bernart de Ventadorn asks Eleanor of Aquitaine, expert in courtly love, to liberate Lady Malemorte of Correze, whose husband had imprisoned her. The passage thus repeats the theme of Helen of Troy's adultery, which appears also in connection with Eleanor (an avatar of Helen), whose mythical dalliance with Saladin in Canto 6 represents the liberation of Provençal woman from patriarchal restraints. Just as Helen is linked to Trojan Paris, so Eleanor is connected with the Near East, whence the troubadour love ethic may derive.

This passage is most ambiguous. Bernart's poem depends on his prolonged absence from the lady; were his natural desires satisfied, he would not rise to spiritual and lyric clairvoyance: the margin of restraint and repression would have vanished. This passage also forces us to ask whether Bernart is a sort of avatar of Zeus, who in Canto 4 foils patriarchal tyranny by visiting Danaë in her tower, or whether troubadour love, for all its beauty, will throw the world into confusion, as does Helen of Troy. This explains why Eleanor, like Helen of Troy or Circe, appears at the ambiguous margin of the river-marsh, with its fecundity and confusion, and the galleried church-porch, signifying the sanctity of woman (Mary). The motif of the margin is repeated in Ventadorn's lyric, which contrasts the bounded existence of the lady in her tower with her free existence at the creek's edge, amid the uncertain brightness of glare-winged flies. Dazzling man with the reflected light of the sun, these are beautiful bearers of disease, lovers of fecundity and decay, undifferentiated products of the parthenogenetic swamp.[20]

IV.

All of these problems, and the possibility of their resolution, are encapsulated in Pound's Helen of Tyre, who appears again in Canto 91 as the "pilot fish" of the poet's spirit:

> Helen of Tyre
> > by Pithagoras
> > by Ocellus
> > (pilot-fish, et libidinis expers, of Tyre . . . .
> > > > (91/ 610)

Surette says that Pound probably learned of Helen of Tyre either through G.R.S. Mead's essay on Simon Magus, or, more likely, from Mead's discussion of Simon in his *Fragments of a Faith Forgotten.*[21] In the latter work, Mead notes the early Christian allegations that Helen was a prostitute or had fallen into prostitution, after which Simon Magus rescued her from a brothel and transformed her, apparently by magic, into his mystic spouse. He seems to imply that she is a version of the Semitic temple prostitute, and in fact Pound makes this identification in his Postscript to Gourmont (Mead: 168–169).

In Mead's allegorizing interpretation, Helen signifies the moon, the human soul fallen into matter, Simon the Sun and Logos, the "mind which brings about her redemption" (Mead: 168). In Hippolytus, whom Mead mentions, Simon gives an "allegorical interpretation of the wooden horse, and Helen with the torch . . .":

> And he said that the latter was the "lost sheep," who again and again abiding in women throws the Powers in the world into confusion, on account of her unsurpassable beauty; on account of which the Trojan War came to pass through her. For this Thought took up its abode in the Helen that was born just at that time, and thus when all the Powers laid claim to her, there arose faction and war among those nations to whom she was manifested.

Later, says Hippolytus, Helen of Troy became Helen of Tyre, and lived in a Tyrian brothel. But Simon Magus "purchased her freedom," after which he pretended "that she was the 'lost sheep,' and that he himself was the Power which is over all."[22] Helen of Tyre's redemption is suggested by the phrase "et libidinis expers" ("having no part in lust") (91/ 610), which probably refers to her ascetic life after her rescue from the brothel.

The promiscuous Helen is redeemed by Simon as Circe is redeemed by

Odysseus in Cantos 39 and 47; Surette rightly suggests that Odysseus' night with Circe is related to Simon's revelation (Surette, 1: 421). But note especially Helen's doubleness. For if her beauty throws men into confusion, her liberation brings "salvation to men."[23] These contradictory roles are summed up in her epithet, the "lost sheep." This alludes to her status as scapegoat, a figure associated with social destructiveness and salvation.

The following lines from an early version of Canto 6 appeared in *The Dial* of August, 1921:[24]

> and Zion Still
> Bleating away to Eastward, the lost lamb
> Damned city.

This section of Canto 6 treats the sexual adventures of Eleanor of Aquitaine in the Near East. An avatar of both Helen of Troy and Helen of Tyre, Eleanor is also a version of the lost sheep. But why should Pound apply a minor variation of this phrase not to Eleanor but to Jerusalem and hence the Jews? Both are associated with the selva oscura, with confusion, ambiguity, destructiveness. Because of these cultural associations, they are nearly equal candidates for scapegoating.

Yet the use of "lost lamb" in Canto 6 also suggests the possibility of the transference of women's negative qualities onto the Jews. In this canto, in which Eleanor is largely a positive figure, woman is on the way to redemption and sanctity: Pound will ultimately concentrate on her socially beneficent features. Meanwhile usury, and the Jews, will be identified with those qualities which formerly they had shared with the feminine. Here is where the transformation (and projection) occurs:

> commune sepulchrum
> Aurum est commune sepulchrum. Usura, commune sepulchrum.
> helandros kai heleptolis kai helarxe.
> Hic Geryon est. Hic hyperusura.
> (46/ 234–235)

The "hel" words, formerly applied to Helen of Troy, are applied to gold and usury, both of which can readily be connected with the Jews. Without anti-Semitism, women would continue to be scapegoats too.

V.

In Canto 39, as in Homer, Odysseus is aided by Hermes in foiling Circe's "bad drugs":

> All heavy with sleep, fucked girls and fat leopards,
> Lions loggy with Circe's tisane,
> Girls leery with Circe's tisane
> κακὰ φάρμακ' ἔδωκεν [she gave them evil drugs]
> kaka pharmak edōken
> (39/ 193)

No more than the swamp is Circe completely undifferentiated or completely evil. Rather, she is ambiguous. Her ambiguity is reflected in her genealogy, since she is the daughter of Apollo, a god of light, and Perseis, a version of Persephone, linked in this case to the matriarchal world of Hell; she is also the sister of the monstrous Pasiphaë. Though dangerous, Circe's "house" of "smooth stone" (39/ 193) resembles that architecture which Pound praises in Canto 45 ("with usura / hath no man a house of good stone"), while her song of "sharp sound" (39/ 193) calls to mind the art of "bounded sounds" toward which Pound himself aspires. Circe also weaves, thus providing a soft but sophisticated comfort of civilization. When Pound calls her the goddess of the "velvet marge" (39/ 193), he evokes her fundamental undecidability: a marge or margin cannot be located, since it is a defined border—a line or edge—or the area alongside a border. Circe is like the undefined border of the Pontine Marshes.

Pound-Odysseus transforms Circe into a beneficent figure of agrarian culture: the goddess Aphrodite on her pedestal at Terracina. The feminine is finally resolvable into a positive form. In Canto 98 Helen of Troy administers Egyptian medicine to Menelaus and Telemachus; no longer a destroyer of men and cities, Helen now soothes the minds of heroes. Pound thus associates Helen with the veil of Leucothea, which enables Pound-Odysseus to find rest in the land of the Phaeacians, and the *hsin* sign, whose axe signifies cultural differentiation. The Greek below refers to *Odyssey*, IV, 220, by way of Philostratus' *Life of Apollonius of Tyana:*

> Τὰ ἐξ Αἰγύπτου φάρμακα [out of Egypt medicine]
> Leucothea gave her veil to Odysseus
>
> (98/ 684)

The redeemed Helen resembles Eleanor of Aquitaine, who in Canto 94 sucks venom "out of . . . [a] wound" (94/ 641).

Many Pound critics think that Circe's transformation results from Pound's full recognition of the sanctity of Nature and the feminine. But is it only a change of attitude which permits this decisive clarification of the "velvet marge"? In Pound such clarification can occur only through an act of essentially sacrificial violence. This violence sanctifies and excludes, separates sacred from demonic, land from the swamp.

Violence is often disguised by myth. In Canto 39 the transformation of Circe should really coincide with the moment when Odysseus threatens Circe with the cutting edge of his sword, forcing her thereby to submit to patriarchal authority. Why did Pound elide this encounter? His poem's mythology obliged him to emphasize sexual union and agrarian measure and fecundity—the harmony of man and woman. But in the next canto, as if as a result of the earlier repression, violence emerges in Pound's translation of the *Periplus of Hanno*. Hanno's conquest of the African "bayou" culminates with the murder of three promiscuous native women, whose "pelts" become sacred objects. Such sanctification is not hard to grasp once we remember that the sacrificial victim, *once dead,* is worshipped as the source of abundance, beauty, order. This explains why the dominated Circe should be worshipped as the graven Aphrodite at Terracina.[25]

Neither Canto 39 nor Canto 40 can be considered apart from Canto 41, where Mussolini, an avatar of Odysseus, drains the Pontine and other marshes, thus bringing agricultural order into the selva. Again, order can be achieved only by the decisive use of the Fascist sword or axe. These events—the encounter with Circe, Hanno's adventure, and Mussolini's swamp reclamation—occur before Pound, in Canto 46, transfers Helen's damning epithets to gold and usury.

The essential difference between the sacred and profane aspects of the feminine, between women as selva oscura and women as light, is now apparent. The first belongs to unorganized Nature; the second, to the culture of the tilled field.[26] On the one hand we have the polluting, parthenogenetic earth or swamp, EIKON GES; the terrifying snake-crowned Medusa of Canto 15; the demonic, promiscuous Circe; and Mary, as the "worm in the crowd." On the other, we have the Virgin Mary, in whom parthenogenesis becomes sacred; the goddess Demeter, who symbolizes the bounty of agriculture; the beneficent and luminous Isis, with her talismanic "ureus" (93/ 624) or crown of snakes; and Kuanon, whose stone, like Helen's drugs, "bringeth sleep," and who is associated (as is Hitler) with the "grass nowhere out of place" (74/ 435), the solar culture of the "plowed . . . field" (74/ 428–429). The same distinctions appear in the savage Python and the Pitonessa (or Pythian priestess) to whom Pound prays in Canto 104. As Zielinski observes, in its original form the untamed maternal dragon, whose cognate figure is the masculine Python, opposes the patriarchal Zeus and Apollo.[27] But once defeated by Apollo, Python becomes a sacred figure, represented by the Pitonessa or Pythoness, whose oracle stands at the site of Python's murder.[28]

Sanctification does not prevent the feminine from lapsing periodically into "confusion." Pound's anti-feminism persists in the later Cantos, in which the Taoists are associated with the "bitch . . . empress" (54/ 287) and organize promiscuous meetings in which women are conspicuous.[29] The preservation of the sanctity of the feminine requires the constant projection of its "bad" qualities onto a group that resembles it and that can be its substitute—in short the Jews.

Not only does Pound depict the Jews as essentially feminine, he tends increasingly to identify them with the bad form of substances and activities with which he earlier associated women:

> Opium Shanghai, opium Singapore
> "with the silver spilla . . .
> amber, caught up and turned . . ."
> Lotophagoi
> (Addendum to 100/ 799)

"Silver spilla" and "amber" allude to the Lotos-Eaters in Canto 20. As for the Shanghai and Singapore rackets, in the radio broadcasts Pound accuses the Jewish businessman Sassoon of controlling the opium trade in the Far East.[30] This identification of the Jews with "poison" explains why Pound warns his listeners to avoid Jewish doctors. In *Thrones* Pound complains of the flood of Near Eastern customs in Europe after the fall of Rome: "dope" is "already used, / even the snake cult, / concubines" (96/ 652). Again in Canto 103 Pound reports that dope is "already in use" (103/ 737) during the reign of the barbarian king Rothar, enemy of Byzantium. Admittedly these phrases make no mention of the Jews or the Near East, but one may infer their anti-Semitism from a passage in Canto 104, which follows Pound's attack on Disraeli's evasion of Parliamentary controls in the purchase of Suez. Pound speaks of "metal cylinders, swallowed by camels / who are then killed after passing the frontier" (104/ 739); these cylinders contain such drugs as "heroin," which brings "*PANOURGIA*" or "knavery" to barbarian and modern Europe. While the reference to concubines in Canto 96 parallels Pound's earlier notions of Jewish prostitution and syphilis, the association of the Jews with drugs is typical of his thinking in the 1950s and extends his 1934 objection to the "dyeing" of Europe with an alien Semitic mythology. Pound perhaps refers implicitly to drugs and poison, since the word *pharmakon* also means dye.[31]

The motif of poison figures again in Pound's accusation that the Jews, like Circe, practice magic and sorcery. The Greek word *pharmakon* means magician, and in Greek and Latin the words for sorcery and poison are interchangeable.[32] In the 1940s Pound finds "black magic" (SP, 320) in the Kabbala and Talmud and blames the Jews for a demonic transmutation of value and thought. He also views Freud as a kind of sorcerer or witch-doctor and, combining anti-Semitism and anti-feminism, speaks of the "un-Freudian chewess eating . . . into the creative will of her victim." Again his anti-Semitism resembles the medieval form, in which Jewish women were often accused of sorcery, and Jewish doctors were valued and feared for supposedly magical skills (Trachtenberg: 77, 91).

These attacks do not mean that Pound altogether rejects magic and drugs, for he too resorts to mental "pills" (98/ 687). Boris de Rachewiltz says that Pound's earliest poems reveal "a leaning towards magic," which "reasserts itself more strongly than ever" in old age.[33] While Confucius generally condemned occultism, Flory notes that the Chinese character 巫 , appearing in the *ling* ideogram in Canto 97, signifies "witch," "wizard," or "the rites that these perform" (Flory: 261–262). In 1954 Pound wrote to de Rachewiltz:

> Have you any more formulae (strong ones) for exorcism? —Egyptian—of demon possession. Apollonius in Philostratus merely threatens the devils but Ph / don't give formulae. . . . I will meditate re / esoteric utilities / the Isis inscription . . . is, I think, the best immediate medicine.[34]

Pound always believes that his antidotes constitute good or beneficent cultural pharmacology. If Pound, as late as the 1950s, is looking for good magic to exorcise devils, it is not hard to guess who these devils are. Along with the mysterious "usurai" and his aggressive and numerous female admirers, Pound at St. Elizabeths felt himself still under attack by the Jews, who had earlier compelled him to seek good drugs. In the broadcasts Pound speaks of "virus" (RB, 79), "bubonic plague" (RB, 74), "microbes" (RB, 125), "parasites," and "bacilli" (RB, 199), all carried by a hostile race, an "alien race" which "has wormed into the system" and "infected the world" (RB, 340). In the face of these threats, Pound thinks of "prophylaxis" (RB, 90), a cultural pharmacology or "purge" enabling the West to "maintain antisepsis" (94/ 635). "Health is CRUEL," says Pound, "or rather health is often accompanied by what seems cruelty to the bacillus" (RB, 194). He adds that "You better invent some bug poison that will eliminate him [the shyster] from your system" (RB, 196).

What drug is Pound seeking? In Canto 97 Pound again introduces the *hsin* sign, which, with its tree and axe, represents renewal and clearing, and then a cryptic question:

New fronds,

novelle piante 新

what axe for clearing?
(97/ 675)

After lamenting the loss of true mythological awareness, now degraded to mere folklore, Pound speaks of "reserpine clearing fungus" (97/ 676). He probably refers to a tranquilizing drug whose beneficent effects he discovered at St. Elizabeths, but its interest here is symbolic (Bacigalupo: 359). Besides anticipating Helen's drugs in the next canto, reserpine is related metaphorically to the mysterious axe and mythology. Axe, myth, and drug eliminate the confusion of "fungus" and establish clarity.

But what axe, and what drug, for clearing? The answer is obvious if we remember that Pound never abandoned Italian Fascism. The axe is that of Fascism, which Pound links to mythology, ritual, and powerful drugs. As in Cantos 40 and 41, it is impossible to make clear distinctions save through violence, the decisive cut of the Fascist axe.

As to the nature of "fungus," given that Pound identifies the Jews with bacilli, and that fungi appear in bacillary form,[35] it is highly probable that he refers to the Jews, the chief enemies of Poundian "antisepsis." We thus come full circle to Canto 23, where Hercules descends into darkness "seeking the sex in bread-moulds." The terror of the selva oscura is its undifferentiation. But woman is finally redeemed from "beclouding" thanks to the Fascist axe and is thus assimilated, as a sacred figure, within the patriarchal order of agriculture. The Jews, meanwhile, are not merely dissociated from the feminine; they are identified with the beclouded, unpruned, excessive, and unredeemed selva, with those permanently undifferentiated parasites which spawn at the heart of the sunless swamp. And yet, like the scapegoat, and also like bread-moulds, even in this role they are not entirely parasitic, but perform, at least for Pound, a beneficent function. For it is with their elimination—or so Pound hopes and believes—that cultural confusion and undifferentiation will be eliminated as well.

Chapter Seventeen

Indeterminacy and Crisis, II:
The Tangle of Luxury and Passion

A recurrent theme in Pound's economic writings from the 1920s onward, luxury is not only one of his most significant cultural values. It is perhaps the most revealing and troublesome of the numerous *pharmaka* which appear throughout his work. Yet there would be no reason to examine luxury here if it did not implicate usury and the Jews within its multiple ambiguities. As we shall see, Pound attacks usury and the Jews at least partly in an attempt to overcome or resolve the uncertainties of luxury itself, uncertainties which threaten to undermine his whole project of cultural definition and construction. At the same time, anti-Semitism deflects sexual and economic tensions which Pound felt increasingly over his career and with which the concept of luxury, having associations of sensuality and wealth, is almost invariably and inevitably involved.

Unlike orthodox nineteenth-century scarcity economists, Pound envisions a modern society of abundance and luxury, distribution and consumption. His model for an abundant society is the prolific, luxuriant growth of plants; man's luxury has its basis and norm in Nature's "unquenchable splendour and indestructible delicacy" (GK, 282). But the natural and vegetable metaphor opens up the possibility of the same confusion already evident in Pound's treatment of usury, Nature, women, and the Semitic world; for if luxury resembles the natural, then it resembles the luxuriant growth of the swamp, selva, or jungle, which engulfs man in the feminine substance, confuses him by its very profusion, and reveals itself paradoxically as a form of sterility and decay, even of usury itself.

In *The Natural Philosophy of Love* Gourmont defines the entire range and "diversification" of man's cultural activity, apart from the pursuit of natural necessities, as luxury or "*luxuria*." In a footnote Pound observes that *luxuria* parallels the French *luxure*, and that *luxuria* is not identical in meaning to the French word for luxury (*luxe*) but means the "exercise of pleasant lusts" (Gourmont: 281–282, 281n). Even so, lust and luxury have been associated throughout Western tradition (as in the identification of lechery and luxury with a libidinous woman) (Sekora: 44). As Pound in *The Cantos* associates *luxuria* with luxurious extravagance, so Gourmont subsumes *luxure* or lust within the category of luxury: art, spices, decoration, cosmetics, music, etc.

Although Gourmont and Pound recognize that *luxure* means lewdness, which is morally pejorative, both writers claim a definite cultural value and natural justification for luxury. This suggests that luxury, in extending life beyond bare necessities, provokes considerable moral and cultural equivocation. To borrow a term from J. Hillis Miller, luxury is "in para," on the margins or to the side of what is supposedly normal, useful, or rationally acceptable, and hence it can be judged as adventitious and parasitic (Miller: 219). But, like other parasites, luxury breaks down this distinction between natural and unnatural, inner and outer, necessary and unnecessary. As Pound and Gourmont recognize, luxury also seems to exist within the limits of permissible, desirable, and in many circumstances necessary cultural activity.

As early as 1919, in *The New Age*, Pound castigated social revolutionaries for failing to see that the luxury of the upper classes has a "beneficent" social "function" in providing a "model for living"; meanwhile, the "duty of a sane manufacturing system" is to "overproduce," so that luxuries are "within every man's reach."[1] Thus, though sometimes abused, and always judged according to a sliding historical and economic scale, luxury belongs within an economy ("function"). It is a true value, not a "parasite" or false increment (as is usury, against Nature's increase). Pound also suggests that the aristocracy's useful "function" is to distinguish good luxury from bad. Yet this appeal to an intuitive cognoscenti does not provide the principle by which to dissociate the "baroque" from the "elegant."[2] Nor does Pound explain why aristocrats, simply by belonging to a class, possess this requisite taste. Subsequently Pound refers to Doughty's *Arabia Deserta*, which contrasts the backwardness of the Semitic world with the material advantages of the Occident. While Pound often associates the Near East with material excess, he does the opposite here. This is another instance of the paradox of Semitic fecundity and aridity, a paradox analogous to that of luxury throughout Pound's thought.

Elsewhere Pound is openly hostile to luxury. In *Guide to Kulchur* usury distorts clear values by introducing a love of "luxury" and "opulence" (GK, 282) into design; luxury is thus a product of usury. In the radio broadcasts, Pound attacks luxury as the enemy of "Mediterranean sanity and beauty, order." Noting that few men can resist the lure of "getting rich," since all men "like comfort," Pound adds that "that is my weakness and I have seen men who can do without it" (RB, 194). Pound is certain that the "suggestion of luxury" coincides with a massive corruption of ethics, justice, and intellectual discriminations, a descent "toward Avernus" (RB, 193). In these instances Pound writes within what John Sekora defines as the "classical" and largely pre-eighteenth-century tradition of anti-luxury, in which luxury is attacked categorically as the enemy of civic virtue and responsibility (Sekora: 23–62). Perhaps in the end Pound belongs to the earlier tradition. In 1962 he told an interviewer that his struggle had been against modern conformity and the "propaganda of luxury."[3]

II.

In Canto 26 Pound examines Venice's development from a Gothic Eden into a plutocratic Renaissance state, the city through which Oriental luxury poured into Europe:

> And hither came Selvo, doge,
> > that first mosaic'd San Marco,
> And his wife that would touch food but with forks,
> Sed aureis furculis, that is
> > with small golden prongs,
> Bringing in, thus, the vice of luxuria. . . .
> > (26/ 122)

Next appears a luxurious pageant from the Venetian fifteenth century—an image of Venice corrupted by Renaissance opulence. Pound treats Venice as both earthly Paradise and artificial Hell, again exemplifying the ambiguities of usury and luxury. Unique in its amphibious setting, Venice is another of Pound's border places, where demarcations disappear and usury therefore inhabits.

Gold as mosaic for San Marco serves a religious and public function: Doge Selvo willingly sacrifices surplus (and hence luxurious) wealth to God, or to Pound's gods. But gold hammered into forks signifies purely private or conspicuous consumption, here called "luxuria," apparently based on a need for prestige and status. This distinction between kinds of luxury depends essentially on use. Again consider gold, ambiguous symbol of Venice throughout *The Cantos:* "In the gloom the gold / Gathers the light about it" (17/ 78), writes Pound in Canto 17. In one sense Pound sees gold as the symbol of intrinsic value: he thinks of it not as money but as a medium of art or craft, or as a divine sign, like Zeus' golden rain or Aphrodite's golden crown. In the later *Cantos*, Pound oversees the Byzantine goldsmith's craft, and as late as Canto 116 he affirms the "gold thread in the pattern" (116/ 797). But these lines from Canto 17 also evoke gold as an unnatural and Plutonian concentration of wealth, a sterile substance, a "Midas lacking a Pan" (21/ 99). Pound announces the inedibility of gold in Canto 56, and in Canto 46 he links gold with usury.

Perhaps use enables one to distinguish between good and bad luxury. One may also attempt to make this distinction by sanctifying certain luxuries and thus defining them as good in their sacred form. As Ruskin recognized, the use of gold as a religious artifact represents a highly sublimated form of religious sacrifice and ritual mimesis. No less important, it transforms a mere object of human greed and contention into an untouchable gift to God.[4] In this way the sacrifice of gold for religious purposes in Canto 26 would do what Pound claims for ritual in general: it would enable men to call things by their right names, to distinguish between good and bad luxury. Nonetheless, it is impossible to sanctify all luxury items. Nor can Pound or anyone else specify at what point such expenditure ceases to give spiritual edification and passes into luxurious idolatry. Materialism often tempts the religious-minded aesthete, as it did Guido Cavalcanti, who worshipped the "Madonna in Hortulo," and whom Pound defended against the monks' charge of idolatry (SP: 320).

Canto 26 contains a less overt kind of sanctification. Sekora notes that the attack on luxury invariably reveals a *pharmakos,* a tendency to blame luxury's bad effects on women and the foreign (Sekora: 50–51). In Canto 26 the bad forms of luxury and gold are introduced into Venice by the Doge's Greek wife, whose culture is already corrupted by the decadent Near Eastern world, and whose error (not sin) is not luxury but *luxuria* —this distinction being clear to those who retain the "Mediterranean sanity." As luxury appears in classical literature as a seductive and lecherous woman, so in *The Cantos* it is associated with vamps and courtesans. Reminiscent of Helen, Zothar, and Circe, the vain Vanoka in Canto 20 probably represents Venice as it passes into the fat, opulent, and inelegant Baroque.

By canto 46 Pound largely ceases to associate the bad form of luxury with woman, but by the 1940s he considers it an import from effeminate and Near Eastern cultures, the zone of confusion:

> Greece was disturbed by foreign doctrines; fathers and Roman senators were alarmed from time to time by the effeminacy introduced into manners: "Persicos odi, puer," etc. And Horace was anything but a puritan.[5]

Despite his assertion that Horace was not a puritan, Pound never clarifies the middle way between good and bad luxury, overabundance and scarcity. Except through strategies of projection and exclusion, he fails to stabilize luxury or resolve his ambivalence toward it.

Luxury poses an epistemological, moral, and cultural problem for Pound. Accepting the idea of the intrinsic value of objects, Pound conceives of an a priori balance between Nature and Man, each adapted to the other as healthy aliment to proper consumer. He also treats cultural consumption as analogous to the consumption of wholesome food, and implies that certain cultural objects—his "luminous details"—have permanent and unquestionable intrinsic value and "interest."[6] The function of literature, like that of money, is to "deliver" what is true and health-giving. Just as money must represent actual wealth, so words, to be valuable, must accurately represent things.

Nonetheless, in the case of cultural consumption taste must be unusually subtle, since its objects are most ambiguous and even dangerous. Especially apposite are books, which are unquestionably luxuries. Like Ruskin, Pound knows that literature, like any drug, can poison: it dispenses illusions, fosters idolatry, and conceals, falsifies, and distorts intrinsic value.[7] As bad writing is linked to usury in Addendum to Canto 100, usury is in turn compared to poisonous drugs dispensed by Jewish opium racketeers, who have turned their victims into Lotophagoi, sunk in luxurious vegetable stupor. Like Geryon, who appears in this canto, and who symbolizes usury and fraud, literature is a delusive bad drug; for "poets have used symbol and metaphor" and "no man" has "learned anything from them." To define one thing in terms of something else violates Pound's rule of calling things by their right names. Metaphor is a kind of usurious "borrowing," whereby the attributes of one thing are transferred to and confused with those of another.[8] The poet who uses metaphor is guilty of "coining," as does the usurer, a false increment of value—Ruskin's Phantasm, a mere product of the parthenogenetic imagination.[9]

Ironically, Addendum to Canto 100, like much of Pound's other writing, is saturated with figurative language, while usury itself implies conflicting metaphorical ideas. But much earlier, in Canto 20, literature already seems dangerous and undecidable. Pound associates the "sharp" and bounded song of his favorite love poets (Bernart de Ventadorn, Ovid, Cavalcanti, Propertius) with the no less sharp but seductively lethal siren's song ("ligur' aoide," 20/ 89), a promise of dangerous knowledge. In Canto 39 Circe tempts men with the "sharp sound of a song" (39/ 193), which portends danger but may also lead to sexual illumination. Similar ambiguities appear in Canto 26 in the doomed love affair between Parisina d'Este and her stepson Ugolino. Besides importing perfumes, cosmetics, and other luxuries from Venice, Parisina reads such medieval romances as inspired Paolo and Francesca to adultery. One of these books is a "Tristano," no doubt treating Tristan's adultery with Ysolt. Conscious of Dante's use of similar material, Pound suggests that Parisina's passion results from her imitation of dangerous literary models.

In *Guide to Kulchur* Pound complains that writing, thanks to its indiscriminate profusion, has become a "poison mixed in sweet cake" (GK, 309), a "drug on the market," and asks for a "divine parsimony of ideas" (GK, 294). Much later, nearly at the end of *The Cantos,* he observes: "Litterae nihil sanantes" (116/ 795), literature which cures nothing. This judgment reflects on Pound's poem, in which he finds, on final scrutiny, "many errors, / a little rightness" (116/ 797). In the same canto Pound compares his achievement with the lawgiver Justinian's. Both have left a "palimpsest," a "tangle of works unfinished" (116/ 795). This image of swamp-like confusion suggests ultimate uncertainty.

Writing, however, is a *pharmakon,* both poison and remedy. Its properties thus resemble those of the scapegoat or *pharmakos,* whose presence the community judges as poisonous or evil, but who, after the arbitrary violence of its expulsion, is held responsible for curing social ills. It also bears mentioning that the art of writing originated in the Near East, and was introduced into Greece by the Phoenicians, a Semitic people. The story of Theuth, Egyptian god of writing, in Plato's *Phaedrus,* testifies to the great anxiety and hostility which writing inspired in the Greek world.

As was noted in Chapter One, a form of literary anti-Semitism appears in Pound as early as *The Spirit of Romance.* Ovid, says Pound, is close to Nature and intrinsic value; even in treating "wonders" and "transformations" he desires "scientific accuracy" and "the definite" (SR, 15) and does nothing to invite our incredulity. But in Apuleius, a (Greek) Carthaginian of the later Empire, "the facts are nothing." What counts in Apuleius is the romantic and subjective element, the "mood," which is "everything" (SR, 16):

> One might consider Apuleius' floridity a purely oriental quality, analogous to the superficial decorations of Byzantine architecture, as distinct from its underlying structure. . . . We must look to the style for our distinction between the Latin of Apuleius and classic Latin. Restraint, which drives the master toward intensity and the tyro toward aridity, has been abandoned. The charm of neatness has lost its power; the barbaric and the Gothic mind alike delight in profusion. If Europe ends at the Pyrenees, the similarity of Apuleius' style to the later Spanish "culturismo" offers opportunity to some literary theorician for investigating the Carthagenian [sic] element in literature. (SR, 15, 17–18)

Although Apuleius' floridity is "purely oriental," Pound connects Byzantine architecture, which he came to admire, with the "Carthaginian element" in literature. He also finds "profusion" in Gothic, a European product. His cultural demarcations therefore lack precision. This passage reveals one term of the paradox of Oriental fecundity and sterility. Often associated with aridity, which Pound attributes to scarcity economics (usury) and repression, the Orient in this instance manifests floridity. The unregulated production of Semitic writing is thus comparable to the unregulated growth of vegetable nature which Pound so often praises; the usurious Orient actually resembles the natural world which it supposedly rejects. This, however, is altogether in keeping with the nature of usury, which encompasses not only absence but that material and verbal "excess" which Pound considers distinctly Semitic.

In 1932 Pound aligns the above passage with his recent distinction between the "Mediterranean sanity" and the "Hebrew disease": "Spanish point of honor, romanticism of 1830, *Crime passionel,* down to Sardou and the '90's, all date from the barbarian invasion, African and oriental inflow on Mediterranean clarity" (SR, 18n). Pound by now believes that the worst mental and literary habits of Europeans have Semitic and specifically Jewish sources. "The dirty near eastern habit of using a text instead of trying to think, cramped and distorted most of [medieval] thought. . . . Moral degradation and decay set in with . . . the revival of semitic texts as a basis of metaphor, as mythology." The Jewish hermetic texts always contained "literal, allegorical, and moral meanings together in the same expression," a clear violation (but no less so in Dante's letter to Can Grande) of Cheng Ming. Hence Pound's attack on the Talmud and Kaballa, which he believes had introduced allegory, metaphor, and symbolism into Europe, and which he associates with magic and sorcery (also present in *The Golden Ass*). In replacing self-evident truth with "interpretation," Jewish writing is the literary equivalent of usury.[10] Now one better understands why Pound attacks the "Jewish" press and insists that "not a jot or tittle of the hebraic alphabet can pass into the [European] text" (SP, 320).[11] For Pound, the Jews write with the "beclouding" ink of the Hydra (Addendum, 100/ 798), which is also an octopus.

This characterization of Pound's literary anti-Semitism is confirmed in a recent article by Andrew Parker. Drawing upon Derrida's conjunction of usury, writing, metaphor, and rhetoric, Parker shows the inseparability of this "tropological economy" and Pound's anti-Semitism. He argues that Pound's chief linguistic and cultural aim is to deny that usurious and rhetorical "excess" of meaning and deferral of original presence which deconstructionists (incautiously) take as the property of all written texts. Hence Pound's insistence on an immediate and intrinsic rather than abstract and arbitrary connection between sign and referent, that is, a precise language "grounded" on "natural" meanings and origins; his interest in the ideogram, whereby merely abstract phonetic script is replaced by a supposedly pictorial, non-phonetic, and synecdochic representation of phenomena; his hostility to metaphor, through which one thing is defined in terms of another and meaning thus wanders from its true "home"; and above all his paradoxical attitude to writing, which he views as an obstacle to presence but which he attacks by means of the written word. Another inevitable rather than "contingent" consequence of these values, according to Parker, is Pound's anti-Semitism. Although he does not supply exact textual links, Parker requires us not implausibly to suppose that Pound knew or intuited several features of post-Exilic Jewish culture, most notably the profound affinity and resemblance between Judaism and writing, at least as the deconstructionists conceive it. After the first destruction of their Temple and long displacement from their "origin" or homeland, the Jews returned to Jerusalem to "recuperate" the "lost presence" of the destroyed Temple. But this the Jews sought to accomplish through reading (and writing): under Ezra's tutelage they became the rabbinical "people of the book," for whom interpretation and textual commentary had a primary cultural and religious function. "Just as the textual sign . . . differs from and defers that which it represents," so the constantly exiled, displaced, and bookish Jews practice a "religion of difference and deferral, . . . an ethos of absence and loss conditioned by the hope for a Messiah" who is never present, always yet to come. Like the writer and his text, the Jews know only a "nomadic" existence displaced from any unequivocal origin and marked by the constant increase (and wearing out) of ever "wandering" signs. Parker notes that Pound's hatred of Jewish "excess" takes two related forms. He attacks usury as a "surplus value" which increases without reference to a world of "tangible commodities"; usury is an abhorrent mixture of presence and absence. For similar reasons Pound attacks and seeks to expel the Jewish text, which threatens to undermine his ideal of linguistic presence and adequacy. Apart from their gift for abstract allegory and metaphor, the Jews specialize in "parasitic" or "heterogenous" commentary or "interpretation" (as described above), through which the text's original and "true" meaning is supplemented, differed, and deferred (the Derridian *différance*). Parker's conclusion, which again mine parallels, is that Pound's effort to write against writing, as against the Jews and their "poison," is defeated by the return within his own text and life of that otherness and difference, Jewish and otherwise, which he seeks to repress.[12]

III.

Pound's scapegoating strategy arises from the challenge of indeterminacy and serves as his primary, indispensable means of overcoming it. This entire process is encapsulated in the concluding section of Part V of *Guide to Kulchur*. In "Chaucer was Framed?" usury is again "contra naturam," hostile to sensuality and "nature's increase," and "antithetic to discrimination by the senses" (GK, 281). But Pound's argument reveals unacknowledged difficulties when he applies the same conceptual language to Nature and usury. Against this puritanical "Miltonism [of usury]," he writes, "only the Romantic rebellion strove," and though that rebellion was "finally degraded to luxury-trade advertisements," Nature found "an advocate where none was consciously intended." The diluted Romanticism of luxury is still a victory for Nature over usury, since the "kill-joy" or usurer is "an enemy," while "exuberance," "splendour," and "delicacy" are virtually "unquenchable . . . and indestructible." So far, Nature stands against sterile usury and scarcity. But in the next paragraph there is no opposition: Usury, says Pound, is "always trying to supplant the arts and set up the luxury trades, . . . to set up richness as a criterion . . . . 'opulence' without hierarchy" (GK, 282).

Though Pound views natural growth as a sign of divine *caritas*, he also identifies it with the confusion, absence, decay, and dangerous luxuriance of the swamp. Similarly in *Guide* he at once advocates luxury and Nature's increase and attacks luxurious opulence and floridity, whose confusion resembles the swamp or selva. Perhaps in only one instance does Pound confront these problems directly. In Notes for Canto 111 he may actually be seeing Geryon for the first time:

                                    Amor
Cold [Gold]¹³ mermaid up from black water—
    Night against sea-cliffs
            the low reef of coral—
And the sand grey against undertow
        as Geryon—lured there—but in splendour,
Veritas, by anthesis, from the sea depth
        come burchiello in su la riva
The eyes holding trouble—
        no light
            ex profundis—
                    (Notes for 111/ 783)

A beautiful and splendid mermaid reveals herself first as Amor (god of sensual love), and then as Veritas, Geryon's diametrical opposites. This creature is gold—the same substance which Byzantine artists use to create the numinous ground of their paintings, but which man also hoards in Plutonian darkness. In a subsequent passage Pound mentions Rothar, who, though he "Coin'd gold," also "bumped off 8,000 Byzantines" (Notes for 111/ 783). Pound adopts the Italian phrase from Dante's description of Geryon in the *Inferno*: *"come burchiello in su la riva* (like a bark upon the shore)."¹⁴ This image places Amor or Geryon neither in nor out of the water, but indeterminately astride the margin. Further to add to her ambiguity, she is "lured" to the shore, "but in splendour." In *Guide* Pound speaks of Nature's "unquenchable splendour" (GK, 282), the luxuriant growth of vegetation. But now it is Geryon, supposedly against Nature's increase, who appears in "splendour" and is connected with natural growth: "Anthesis" refers to "the period or act of expansion of flowers."¹⁵ Geryon, the "biform" monster who "takes you lower down" (SP, 332), into the "undertow" of sexuality or of the usurious "gold bugs," emerges like a golden, expanding, and beautiful flower, the very opposite of sterile usury.

Equally ambiguous is the concluding section ("The Promised Land") of Part V of *Guide to Kulchur*. The title suggests a utopian vision of abundance, but Flory rightly notes that Pound's "self-confidence" is "at a low ebb" (Flory: 52). Observing the intellectual confusion and economic misery of his colleagues, who more resemble "misfits" than "the flower of civilization," Pound complains that knowledge has become a "job lot of odds and ends, . . . a drug on the market, . . . abundant, superhumanly abundant" (GK, 294). Ironically, though Pound labored throughout his career for the dissemination of knowledge against usurious "monopoly" and oppressive control, now he is disturbed because abundance has largely been realized. He calls for "a divine parsimony of ideas" (GK, 294), some unknown principle of order that would restore literature to its therapeutic function. Formerly luxurious in the sense of being costly, rare, or dear, books and ideas are now luxurious in the sense of being overabundant, superfluous: they are "bad" drugs which, like usury, confuse the minds of men.

To evade these problems Pound offers familiar tautologies such as "the arcanum is the arcanum" (GK, 292), thus implying that an elite group intuitively possesses its untransmissible solution. He further asserts that "certain truth exists," that "Truth is not untrue'd by reason of our failing to fix it on paper" (GK, 295). This assertion is preceded by an appeal to absent authority, the unequivocal "mille splendori" (GK, 292) of *Paradiso:* "Only in the high air and the great clarity can there be a just estimation of values" (GK, 299). Pound concludes Part V by saying that it is "as obscure as anything in my poetry" (GK, 295). He is not in his "undiscussable Paradiso," but in "hell" (GK, 292), a place associated with "tangles," "undertow" (GK, 288), passions, and the failure of moral and sexual discriminations. Here he conducts his search for an enemy and a crime.

Flory suggests that Pound's crisis cannot be dissociated from his marriage and adultery, passion and sexuality (Flory: 51, 53). In Sections 51 and 52 of *Guide* Pound discusses the "sordid matrimonial customs of England" (GK, 287), the failure of Hardy, James, and his contemporaries to work out an adequate "new code" (GK, 287) of sexual conduct, and the pressure and limitation which money introduces into sexual life. Hardy represents, oddly enough, Poundian *"joie de vivre"* (GK, 287) against repression, while James criticizes the social "undertow" (GK, 288)—a word which Pound often associates with usury, but which he now associates with "sex tangles" (GK, 288):

> ... But neither he [Hardy] nor James ignored the undertow. ... Put it also that no sane and clear code can be formulated until and unless all tangled relations between men and women have been analyzed and set in two categories: those due to money and those that are independent of it.
>
> Marriage has scarcely ever been lifted outside this zone. Neither have irregular relations. (GK, 288)

Irregular relations no doubt include promiscuity, adultery, and "polygamy" (GK, 294), while the new "code" would replace the Mosaic code, which condemns adultery, attacks natural impulse, and bolsters those Victorian values against which Hardy and James rebelled. Pound, who once praised Arnaut Daniel for his un-Hebraic indifference to codes, now desires norms of marital and promiscuous conduct (SR, 97). The need seems all the greater when one considers that Pound, from the 1920s to his death, carried on openly an adulterous liaison with Olga Rudge, a relationship that produced intense emotional conflicts in the households in which he lived.[16] Hints of this conflict appear in *The Cantos,* as in the statement, referring to women, that "somewhere in the snarl is a tenderness" (113/789). A "snarl," besides suggesting teeth, is also a "tangle." Nor is it accidental that Pound, who despised psychoanalysis, invoked as universal truth Turgenev's observation (from *A Nest of Gentle Folk*) that "the heart of another is a dark forest" (SP, 414; GK, 200). This statement explicitly links the life of the passions, and the dangers and attractions of intersubjectivity itself, with a descent into the selva oscura.

Hugh Kenner observes that we have no sense of the "fine line" which Pound and his circle were "demarking between matrimony and liberty" (Kenner, 4: 493). Pound, however, believes that such demarcations are impossible under modern conditions, in which sex is supposedly dominated altogether by "monetary" pressures. The problem is to distinguish those relations "due to money" and those that are "independent of it," to dissociate the tangle and "underbrush" (GK, 288) of usury from the tangle of human passion, dualisms which elsewhere converge inextricably in the image of the swamp. According to Pound, "80%" of his generation's (and his own) sexual problems result from the economics of usury. He adds that "until BOTH parties are free from monetary pressure, any 'solution' is impossible" (GK, 288–289).

Nonetheless, in the next section of *Guide to Kulchur* there remain persistent sexual "tangles," few of which can be satisfactorily separated from monetary pressures, and some of which have nothing to do with money at all. Pound is unable to deny man's "personal crises and cruces, that exist above or outside monetary pressure." These include "the permanent susceptibility to tragedy, the enduring tangles, situations, etc. that depend wholly on free emotion, emotion conditioned only by hungers, appetites, affinities, and durabilities" (GK, 291). Pound himself was susceptible to those "free emotions" which, independent of money, can lead to violence and tragedy; hence his fascination with Aeschylus' adulterous Agamemnon and Sophocles' adulterous Heracles in *The Women of Trachis*.[17] But though Pound reluctantly acknowledges what he elsewhere terms the "natural chaos" of man and the "unclean . . . tangle" of the swamp, he minimizes its importance and seeks the main cause of human problems in money. Since money can cure those very problems which it creates, Pound can make those distinctions which money supposedly dissolves. At the same time, by indicting money, Pound avoids acknowledging a personal crisis for which money affords no solution. Money thus arouses in Pound a deep hostility (mixed with reverence) which, if not directed outward, might lead to what Pound calls "tragedy." Instead, this tragedy—a word which, like "crises" and "cruces," implies sacrifice—is located elsewhere:

> A refusal to recognize two categories [the difference between monetary and sexual problems] leads, in novel writing, to tosh, unmitigated and blithering tosh. The only professional writing worth the name has been, for years, Crime Club, and that, I take it, is, again, instructive. The whole people having an intuition of a crime somewhere, down under the Bank of England and the greasy-mugged regents, but accepting an escape mechanism [the detective novel] of murder, burglars, and jewel-thefts.
>
> (GK, 291–292)

Pound fails to see that the escape mechanism of detective fiction resembles his own scapegoating practice. *The Cantos*, he noted, are a detective story whose villain is found to be usury in Cantos 45 and 51.[18] It is not necessary, however, for Pound over the long run to blame a dissatisfyingly bloodless abstraction such as usury or gold, for there is a connection between the *pharmakon* (in this case money) and the *pharmakos*, the "criminal" victim of a collective murder. In *Guide to Kulchur* Pound speaks of the "whole people" intuiting a crime "somewhere," and he views the pursuit of imaginary criminals as a poor substitute for an attack upon the real ones. Thus, while the instrument of the crime is money, responsibility must ultimately fall on human beings, in this case the Regents of the Bank of England. During his wartime broadcasts Pound would divert more and more blame onto the Jews, who finally figure as his "one enemy" (GK, 31). In this he is in total agreement with the "findings" of "Duce and Führer," the "two real detectives," who had solved the "crime" (RB, 156) of usury.

Chapter Eighteen

Profanation

The basis or rationale for Pound's anti-Semitic scapegoating is now deep-founded yet incomplete. Indeed, it would be extremely dubious were one to conclude that Pound came to hate the Jews so intensely mainly because of their associations with such ambiguous cultural entities as writing and luxury, or with the feminine. To be sure, such associations are important contributing factors in the scapegoating process, for they help to single out the Jews from all other groups as monstrous and hence despised figures of cultural indeterminacy. But, as Girard has shown, the necessary conditions for lethal scapegoating are massive social violence, the loss of social order and distinctions, and profanation as a result of the collapse of ritual—in short, the sacrificial crisis. It is thus necessary to show, even at the risk of some repetition, that Pound's work, and especially *The Cantos,* give special prominence to the themes of profanation, ritual, and crisis.

Writing in 1945, Pound agrees entirely with the Japanese artist Tami Kume: "*We are at the crisis point of the world*" (CON, 89). This crisis manifests itself not only in wars and economic catastrophies but in man's failure to observe the Confucian principle of Cheng Ming: "Call people and things by their [right] names; that is by the correct denominations" (GK, 16). But Cheng Ming is also a sacred principle, dependent on and originating in religious ritual. Where the rites are observed, so are true distinctions; where men fail to observe ritual procedures, social and cultural chaos will surely follow. To quote the Confucian *Analects:* "A proper man extends his study of accomplishment, he brings it into close definition for the rites . . ." (CON, 217–218). But "when the services (actions) are not brought to true focus, the ceremonies and music will not prosper; where rites and music do not flourish punishments will be misapplied, not make bullseye, and the people won't know how to move hand or foot (what to lay hand on, or stand on)" (CON, 249).

More than a destroyer of cultural distinctions, usury is the essence of profanation, leaving no aspect of religion untouched. In "A Visiting Card"

(1942) Pound speaks of history's "two forces": the first "divides, shatters, and kills, . . . falsifies . . . [and] destroys every clearly delineated symbol, . . . [destroys] not one but every religion"; the second "contemplates the unity of the mystery" and "the images of the gods," which "move the soul to contemplation and preserve the tradition of the undivided light" (SP, 306–307). Pound blames the process of desymbolization on the usurers and "Iconoclasts," a "power of putrefaction" like "the bacilli of typhus or bubonic plague" (SP, 317). Usury is a violent plague which infects everything and reduces everything to a state of undifferentiation.

In Canto 4 Pound contrasts the luminous beauty and clarity of medieval Catholic devotion with the Virgin's modern ritual near the River Garonne; the rites have decayed, and the Virgin's procession moves like a fat and ugly "worm . . . in the crowd" (4/ 16). Canto 4 anticipates the usury *Cantos,* in which usury makes the "line grow thick" and destroys "clear demarcation[s]" (45/ 229). Incapable of equalling or reviving earlier religious art (San Zeno, St. Trophime, St. Hilaire), modern man lacks a "painted paradise on his church wall," a picture "where Virgin receiveth message / and halo projects from incision" (45/ 229). To complete this catalogue of profanation, Pound writes that usurers have brought "whores for Eleusis" (45/ 230), the ancient seat of holy mysteries.

The corruption of the rites also appears in Canto 52:

> Between KUNG and ELEUSIS
> Under the Golden Roof, la Dorata
> her baldacchino
> Riccio on his horse rides still to Montepulciano
> the groggy church is gone toothless
> No longer holds against *neschek*
> the fat has covered their croziers
> The high fans and the mitre mean nothing
> Once only in Burgos, once in Cortona
> was the song firm and well given
> old buffers keeping the stiffness,
> Gregory damned, always was damned, obscurantist.
> (52/ 258)

La Dorata is a Romanesque church where the rites were once celebrated properly, with Mary enthroned. Now the Virgin's fans and the bishop's mitre mean nothing, as does the crozier, symbol of the Church's pastoral responsibility.[1] The Church has grown fat, perhaps on its usurious investments, and thus resembles the line that grows thick and the fat and profaning worm of Canto 4. Desymbolization also coincides with failure to keep the clean, firm line of religious song: Pound dislikes the Gregorian chant for its gloomy monotony. It is also significant that Pound finds the "firm song" to have been preserved in Burgos, the birthplace of the Cid. This music, which may also allude to the *Poem of the Cid,* carries the reader back to Canto 3, in which the Spanish folk hero tricks two Jewish usurers to get pay for his private army. Considered in the new perspective provided by Canto 52, the Cid emerges as an archetype of the opportunistic Mussolini. It is not clear, though, that the Cid is justified in combating usury, whose essence is fraud, by fraudulent means.[2]

In Canto 43 Pound examines the establishment, in seventeenth-century Siena, of the Monte dei Paschi, an anti-usurious bank founded on "the whole will of the people" (43/ 218).[3] Before the bank's establishment, the Sienese economy had been rotted by usury. Pound then observes the beginning of a degraded ritual:

```
          to the end:
                    four fat oxen
having their arses wiped
and in general being tidied up to serve god under my window
with stoles of Imperial purple
with tassels, and grooms before the caroccio
on which carroch six lion heads
                    to receive the wax offering
Thus arrive the gold eagles, the banners of the contrade
and boxes of candles
                    'Mn-YAWWH!!!'
said the left front ox, suddenly,
'pnAWH' as they tied on his red front band,
St. George, two hokey-pokey stands and the unicorn
                    'Nicchio! Nicch-iO-né!!'
The kallipygous Sienese females
get that way from the salite
          that is from continual plugging up hill
One box marked '200 LIRE'
                    'laudate pueri'
alias serve God with candles
with the palio and 17 banners
and when six men had hoisted up the big candle
a bit askew in the carroch and the fore ox had
been finally arse-wiped
they set off toward the Duomo, time
consumed 1 hour and 17 minutes.
```
                                        (43/ 216–217)

Pound's irreverence mocks the ineptitude of the ritual preliminaries, in which abundant excrement delays the event for over an hour. The oxen are as fat and sluggish as those sacrificial beasts clumsily slaughtered by primitive Hyksos and nomadic Jews, who never rose to a sense of discriminations. Like the ornamental and tasselled stoles of Imperial purple, the gilded eagles falsely glorify a regime which has tolerated usury and even stolen from its people (a pun on stoles?). These degraded symbols of Roman authority contrast with the anti-usurious Hitler and Mussolini, both of whom are celebrated in this part of Pound's poem. Degraded heroism figures too in the quasi-pagan horseman St. George, who is properly a chivalric killer of swamp dragons (and by implication the Hydra or serpent of usury), but who now appears alongside "hokey pokey stands" and a legendary animal.[4] Meanwhile, mechanization and calculation have corrupted the sacrificial spirit. Not only do the mechanically produced and boxed devotional candles cost 200 lire, but the procession has been delayed exactly an hour and seventeen minutes. As we have seen, throughout *The Cantos* Pound contrasts the "organic," non-linear, repeatable yet endlessly renewing mythical time of ritual with the profane, quantifiable, mechanical, and merely linear time of the modern world—a world of meaningless repetition and increasing debts, in which time is not renewed or lived but numerically accumulated and "consumed." Pound's reference to clock time removes this Sienese ritual from mythical sanctity and locates it within the profane realm of history. The phrase "serve god," echoed in *"laudate pueri,"* "praise [God], boys," is therefore ironic. Authentic religion requires the truly "solid" and renewing, perhaps the "blood rite" (25/ 118) of Ferrara or the actual burning of the fat of oxen rather than surrogate wax substances (candles made from the fat of animals). In Canto 52, in which Chinese ritual is intact, "Heaven's Son" feeds on beef and pork in the community's sacrificial meal.

Though the nature of profanation still remains vague, all of Pound's metaphors for usury imply some sort of destructive violence. Not only does the power of putrefaction "destroy the symbols," but usury "attacks continuously, the nerve centers" (SP, 317) of nations. Insofar as Pound compares usury with plague and vermin, it constitutes a multitudinous and monstrous attack on human beings, particularly by the Jews, whom Pound repeatedly associates with violent aggression and provocation. The opposition between Jewish *neschek* and the now "toothless" Church is essentially that between the all-consuming violence of usury and the ordered Communion ritual of Catholicism. Pound is thematizing the difference between sacred and profane violence, a difference which "no longer holds" in the modern world.

This recurrent association of usury with violent profanation suggests that Pound is concerned with a version of what Girard calls the sacrificial crisis. Yet Girard emphasizes that the culmination of such an event, namely the complete collapse of ritual and hierarchical distinctions, is always marked by specifically mimetic violence. The question thus arises whether the sign *par excellence* of the sacrificial crisis—what Girard terms the monstrous doubles of mimetic violence—appears in Pound's text.

II.

Canto 4 opens with compressed mythical resonance:

> Palace in smoky light,
> Troy but a heap of smouldering boundary stones,
> ANAXIFORMINGES! Aurunculeia!
> Hear me, Cadmus of Golden Prows!
>
> (4/ 13)

The first image evokes the fall of Troy, which resulted from sexual rivalry and Helen's violation of the marriage vow. It also projects forward to a bloody period of Greek history, "when the blood feud is to take its course" (Baumann: 21). One recalls the rape and murder of Philomela by Tereus, her sister's husband; the murder of Clytemnestra by her son, Orestes; and the murder of Agamemnon by his wife, Clytemnestra. Since Pound associates the Trojan War with World War I, in whose aftermath war-guilt also played a significant role, these lines probably refer to the recently concluded hostilities in Europe (Surette, 3: 27–30). In the third line, after alluding to Pindar's martial bombast ("ANAXIFORMINGES"), Pound contrasts Greek militarism and conjugal disloyalty with Catullus' Roman marriage rite (Aurunculeia is the bride in one of his poems); this rite has its Japanese analogue later in the canto in Pound's reference to the sacred pine tree at Takasago. Legend has it that the tree is inhabited by the spirits of a married couple who (like Baucis and Philemon in Greek myth) honored the gods: "The pine at Takasago / grows with the pine of Isé" (4/ 15).

The fourth line—"Hear me, Cadmus of Golden Prows!"—encompasses the preceding themes. Pound recalls that moment in Ovid when Cadmus, having killed the dragon Dirce, is commanded by Athena to sow the Dragon's teeth in a ploughed furrow, whence came the *spartoi*, builders of Thebes. This line evokes the entire Theban cycle: the killing of Dirce, the building of Thebes, the myth of Oedipus, the fraternal rivalry of Oedipus' sons, and Thebes' near destruction. It also encapsulates the entire sacrificial crisis. After Dirce's murder, Cadmus and the hierarchized *spartoi* build Thebes. But the new order is always endangered by sacrilege and profane violence, which would overturn society's operative system of distinctions. The story of Oedipus centers on parricide and incest, precisely the charges which fly during the sacrificial crisis (the Theban cycle in the Oedipus myth) and which finally attach to the scapegoat victim (Oedipus). Fraternal rivalry sets off the mimetic conflict of Eteocles and Polyneices, which ends in fratricide and nearly destroys Thebes. The first thirty *Cantos* contain numerous other examples of monstrous violence connected with undifferentiation, for instance matricide, fratricide, cannibalism, incest, and the murder of adulterous and incestuous wives and sons. Prominent among these horrors are the myth of Procne in Canto 4 and the history of the Este family in Canto 24.

The presence of the double indicates that profane violence has escalated to the point where all differences have virtually collapsed. This motif explodes into prominence in Cantos 14 and 15 (the Hell *Cantos*), in which London is a constant succession of phantasmagoric images importing filth, contamination, defilement, impurity, desymbolization, and violence.

London, or Hell, is a "great arse-hole, / broken with piles," where men plunge "jewels in mud," howling "to find them unstained." In this atmosphere of "slow rot" and "corruptio" (14/ 62–63), flies carry news (and disease), and harpies drip excrement through the air, defiling human food. When Pound tries to escape Hell he finds "nothing that might not move, /

mobile earth, a dung hatching obscenities" (15/ 65). In an earlier passage Pound surveys Hell and sees a "greasy . . . sky" (14/ 62) over Westminster. Profanation has extended to the seat of Anglican religion, which, like the Catholic Church in Canto 52, is associated with fat. Pound's disgust with the Anglican Church stems in part from John Quinn's discovery that it had invested in slum properties. In Canto 15 a clergyman appears with his "head down, screwed into the swill" (15/ 64), indicating total inversion of religious authority. Pound is equally contemptuous of the "arse-belching of preach-ers" (14/ 63), whose flatulent speech echoes the intestinal "rumbling" (15/ 64) of imperialism, and of the hypocrites who wave "the Christian symbols" (14/ 63) but do not understand them. Ian F.A. Bell rightly recognizes the appropriateness of Pound's excremental discourse in representing a world where dirt, as "matter out of place," threatens all categories and decorums, and where human speech or *logos,* properly the means of rendering reality nameable and distinct, has become interchangeable with the meaningless, shapeless, and messy emissions of the body's orifices (Bell: 61–62).

At the same time, Pound's scatalogical language signifies a world regress-ing to the level of anal sadism in its literal and deflected forms. The Anglican Church is complicit with a general social violence which has no definable source; everyone is entrapped in imitative cycles of reciprocal and unani-mous hostility. Besides prominent war profiteers, one finds the "pusillani-mous, raging" (14/ 62), "sadic mothers driving their daughters to bed with decrepitude," "sows eating their litters" (14/ 62), conservatives gaitered with "slum flesh" (15/ 64), the "agents provocateurs / The murderers of Pearse and MacDonagh" (14/ 62), "orators" (14/ 63) whipping up imperial-ism, "cowardly inciters to violence," the "courageous violent" who slash themselves "with knives" (15/ 64). Equally sensitive to latent violence, Pound mentions the "backscratchers," who appear anonymously and equally in a "great circle," and who spend their time in rituals of insincere admiration. Complaining of "insufficient attention, / the search without end, counterclaim for the missing scratch" (15/ 64–65), the backscratchers then turn backbiters: "with daggers, and bottle ends, waiting an / unguarded moment" (15/ 65). Such massive and contagious violence explains why Pound employs metaphors of contamination and plague (the "lasting pox" of Canto 15) in the Hell *Cantos* and elsewhere. The plague for Pound is what Girard calls a "transparent metaphor for . . . reciprocal violence that spreads, literally, like the plague."[5]

Pound also compares Hell to the parthenogenetic and usurious swamp. Deprived of the determinate phallic principle, Hell is filled not with human beings but parthenogenetic spawn, insects, and "liquid animals," the incestu-ous and undifferentiated generation of "EIKON GES," the maternal earth. But while parthenogenesis might serve to represent usury, usury plays a minor role in the Hell *Cantos,* in which violence predominates. On the other hand, parthenogenesis well serves to represent the spreading violence of the sacrificial crisis, which results in the loss of differentiation among human beings.

Unlike Dante's Hell, Pound's is entirely de-individualized. This loss of human identity, which Pound traces to the phallus, is reflected in imagery of effacement: the clergyman's face "screwed into the swill" (15/ 64), the unknown "faces submerged under hams" (14/ 62), and the cryptic placard in Canto 14: "THE PERSONNEL CHANGES" (14/ 62). Breeding by "scission," a monstrous self-duplication, these people are interchangeable; it makes no difference who belongs to the multitude of "newts, water-slugs, water-maggots" (14/ 61). These "doubles" suggest that Pound has represented the sacrificial crisis in advanced form. To quote Girard on the "phobia of resemblance":

> Twins invariably share a cultural identity, and they often have a striking physical resemblance to each other. Wherever differences are lacking, violence threatens. Between the biological twins and the sociological twins there arises a confusion that grows more troubled as the question of differences reaches a crisis. It is only natural that twins should awaken fear, for they are harbingers of indiscriminate violence .... As soon as the twins of violence appear they multiply prodigiously, by scissiparity, as it were, and produce a sacrificial crisis. It is essential to prevent the spread of this highly contagious disease.[6]

Pound, who likes to compare himself to primitive man, shares the primitive's phobia of resemblance (this could well define his attitude towards usury) and for the same reasons. The doubles of "scission" signify undifferentiating and profaning violence.

But does this reading of the Poundian Hell agree with the earlier one in Chapter Twelve? There it was argued that Pound, instead of recognizing his own violence against London, imagined London with hallucinatory intensity, as an enemy or other, a crowd of others. The enormous violence in the Hell *Cantos* is thus entirely a projection of Pound's own violence.

These two readings seem incompatible. Either the violence of the sacrificial crisis is real, or Pound is exaggerating London's violence, confusing what is going on outside with what is going on within. However, the earlier point was that Pound projects his violence onto London, and that such projection accounts for his exaggerated representation of the city. The truth of this would not be affected were one to acknowledge what many observers, including Pound, noticed, that England in the post-war period experienced a social and political climate of real or incipient violence. In these terms, the Hell *Cantos* would more closely resemble the sacrificial crisis, in which projection and reality, inner and outer, are no longer distinct:

> In a universe both deprived of any transcendental code of justice and exposed to violence [Girard writes], everybody has reason to fear the worst. The difference between a projection of one's own paranoia and an objective evaluation of circumstances has been worn away. (Girard, 2: 54)

The argument for projection remains valid in Pound's case. Himself part of the violent collapse of differences, Pound presents London's violence "under glass," as entirely other. When violence engulfs a society, the mutually antagonistic doubles fail to see that the mimetic reciprocity of violence has erased all differences between them. They keep fighting, each convinced of his own righteousness, in a futile effort to maintain those differences which their violence destroys.

It is evident now why Pound fears the monstrous and infectious doubles of the parthenogenetic crowd. These projected images testify to Pound's unrecognized identity—never far from his consciousness—with the violence around him. As Girard writes of the "monstrous double":

> The subject feels that the most intimate regions of his being have been invaded by a supernatural creature who besieges him without. Horrified, he finds himself the victim of a double assault to which he cannot respond. Indeed, how can one defend oneself against an enemy who blithely ignores all barriers between inside and outside? (Girard, 2: 165)

And yet, this description of the last stages of mimetic conflict corresponds only imperfectly to Pound's situation in the Hell *Cantos*. In Canto 15, Pound controls the head of the Medusa, signifying protective violence, phallic restitution, differentiation, and demarcation: castration turned against his enemies. As we shall see, the description corresponds more closely to Pound's mental condition in the broadcasts, where usury ("Twin Evil of Envy"), named as the cause of violence, and associated with the Jews, takes the form of the monstrous double.

Chapter Nineteen

"Nothing Can Save You": The Sacrifice

The examples of Hitler, Céline, and Pound confirm Horkheimer and Adorno's as well as others' observations that fascism is a modern sacrificial religion. Once recognized as projections, fascist accusations of violence against the Jews appear in their true light, as a preparation and justification of that sacrificial killing or "offering" of the "chosen foe" which lies at the "hub" of fascism. Likewise, once fascist ritualism is divested of its falsely mythical and naturalistic justification, it stands revealed as purely human aggression in its most evil form. In the "unrestricted" violence of fascism, all of civilized man's horror of "pre-history," as well as his longing for a long-vanished ritual order, is "rehabilitated as rational interest by projection onto the Jews."[1] Pound's fascism is evident as well in his attraction to the sacrificial and ritualistic order of Confucian China, which he either confused with fascism or else viewed as a model for Mussolini and Hitler.

Critics generally agree that Pound's rites create order and end that mimetic violence whose fullest presentation is in Cantos 2–7. Walter Baumann is certain that for Pound all violence is "futile," while Sister Bernetta Quinn believes that for Pound "nothing truly good comes from violence."[2] Nonetheless, in Canto 1 Odysseus sacrifices beasts that the dead may drink blood and thus speak to him; the sacrificial animals serve as a buffer between Odysseus and the clamoring dead. In Canto 26 Venice's drift into the usurious replication of cultural forms and symbols results from its lack of "the solid, the blood rite" (25/ 118) which characterizes violent Ferrara, where "confusion" is the "basis of renewals" (20/ 92). In Canto 30, Artemis' purifying rites of sacrifice involve not just the pruning of trees but the slaying of deer. In Canto 40 the murder and flaying of three native women is undoubtedly sacrificial, for this violence leads to contact with the NOUS or "gods." This is not to imply that Pound's rituals always involve animal killing, since the later Pound is also interested in an agrarian worship "without bloodshed" (Bacigalupo: 381). But Pound's suspicion of the "blood rite" follows his writings of the 1930s and 1940s, when his anti-Semitism reached its greatest intensity.

In Canto 52 Pound turns to ancient China, where social and cosmic harmony are preserved through the scrupulous observance of the *Book of Rites* (*Li Ki*):

> to this month are birds
> with bitter smell and with odour of burning
> To the hearth god, lungs of the victim. . . .
>
> To this month is SEVEN
> with bitter smell and with odour of burning
> Offer to gods of the hearth
> the lungs of the victims . . . .
>
> The lake warden to gather rushes
> to take grain for the *manes*
> To take grain for the beasts you will sacrifice . . . .
>
> Rain has now drenched all the earth
> dead weeds enrich it, as if boil'd in a boullion.
> Sweet savour, the heart of the victim . . . .
>
> Now is cicada's time,
> the sparrow hawk offers birds to the spirits.
> Emperor goes out in war car, he is drawn by white horses,
> white banner, white stones in his girdle
> eat dog and the dish is deep. . . .
>
> Tolls lowered, now sparrows, they say, turn into oysters
> The wolf now offers his sacrifice. . . .
>
> Heaven's Son [the Prince] feeds on roast pork and millet, ...
> (52/ 258–261)

Each stage of the natural cycle coincides with a sacrificial ritual. The Prince's sacrificial meal of roast pork and millet symbolically represents the communal feast which unites and harmonizes Chinese society.

Pound asserts the "immediate need" (SP, 75) of Confucius in the Western world. The great Confucian texts (*The Unwobbling Pivot, The Great Digest,* and *The Analects*), as well as the *Sacred Edict of K'ang Hsi,* are all "solid wisdom" (CON, 97). The adjective "solid," which Pound uses to describe the "blood rite" of Ferrara in Canto 26, is equally appropriate to describe Confucian thought, in which *li,* or sacrifice, plays a central role.

In the broadest sense *li* means correctness and precision in every form of human activity.[3] The "scholar-gentleman sees danger and goes thru to his fate (L. sacrifice life) . . ." (CON, 282). Confucius "put men to work as if . . . performing the Great Sacrifice" (CON, 244). *Li* implies respect for one's duties to family and superiors and hence for the distinctions among men; for the differences among musical tones (since music builds character and is essential to the rites); for the correct use of language; and for the appropriate names and procedures necessary to the correct performance of sacrificial ritual. The society that observes *li* calls things by their right names. But *li* is not merely a matter of formal adherence to procedures—it demands a spirit of sincere reverence: ". . . The real man has to look his heart in the eye even when he is alone" (CON, 47).

Confucian China recognizes man's potential for mimetic conflict and emphasizes good mimesis in politics, religion, and the family: the Prince "must have in himself not one but all of the qualities he requires from others, and must himself be empty of what he does not want from others in reflex" (CON, 61). Not only must the father imitate and obey the Prince, he must set a proper example for his sons, who are bound to obey him and who will, therefore, imitate his desires and actions. But if one's superior ignores *li* and provides a bad example, one must not imitate him; otherwise conflicts will arise and destroy hierarchy: "If you hate something in your superiors, do not practice it on those below you; if you hate a thing in those below you, do not do it when working for those over you" (CON, 67). Ideally the benevolent Prince, like the father on his lower scale, will treat "the mass of people as children," thus causing them to "stimulate each other (in good conduct) from a simple tendency toward imitation" (CON, 159).

Whether it involves the sacrifice of grain or animal victims, Confucius also values sacrificial mimesis or ritual, from which the idea of *li* derives. In *The Analects* he answers one who wanted to eliminate sheep from the sacrifice to the new moon: "He said: You, Ts'ze, love the sheep, I love the rite" (CON, 203). Elsewhere Confucius acts for the spirits or Prince (a very high honor) in "first tasting" (CON, 236) the sacrificial meat. For the Chinese, sacrifice signifies not expiation or atonement or propitiation but a free gift of gratitude to the spirits and ancestors (Ching: 172–173). Though Pound (like the later Confucians) is skeptical toward the supernatural, he countenances belief in the spirits (Smith: 57–58; CON, 191). Following Confucius, he considers the actuality of the spirits less important than that sacrifice provides the "binding cement" of society (Smith: 23).

Besides preserving "close definition," the rites create continuity between past and present. Shun "offered the sacrifices in the ancestral temple and his descendants offered them there to him" (CON, 133). The rites also promote cultural renewal. In Canto 53, Chun prays "to the spirit of Chang Ti, of heaven moving the sun and stars" (53/ 263). David Gordon comments that "On entering office Shun [Chun] made a great sacrifice to Chang Ti, the sun, moon, stars, and the four seasons" (Gordon, 3: 127). In the same canto Pound conjoins *hsin*, signifying renewal, with the personal sacrifice of Tsching. "When the silos were exhausted and after two years of sterility," Tsching "went alone to Mt. Seng-Lin," there offering himself "as a sacrifice, which produced a cloud burst and saved the crops" (Gordon, 3: 129–130).

Finally, sacrificial ritual mysteriously promotes, even establishes, the binding unity of society. In *The Great Digest* "Right action gains the people and that gives one the state" (CON, 71). Pound comments that the ideogram may have "an original sense of the people gathered at its tribal blood rite" (CON, 71n). In no sense, however, is this an indiscriminate gathering. The correct performance of the rites repeats those rules of deference and distinction which characterize society in non-sacrificial situations (Smith: 21, 91). To quote *The Great Digest*, each member of society finds his proper "rank" or "degree" during sacrificial performances, so that "even the most humble had their part in the rites" (CON, 143).[4] Thanks to sacrifice, families observe the great rule of "fraternal deference" (CON, 57), whereby each member is content with his degree:

> The harmony between elder
> and younger brother
> Is like that at the holy altar
> When the grain is offered up to the gods.
> Bring your family thus into order . . . .
> (CON, 129)

No Confucian would think of eliminating sacrifice, nor would Pound. It is indispensable not only to the establishment but to the maintenance of Pound's hierarchical conception of social harmony.

II.

Though Confucius is sure that men should sacrifice, he admits that he cannot "tell" what sacrifice exactly "mean[s]" (CON, 203). Nor is Pound altogether sure of its significance. "As to sacrifices," writes Pound in 1939,

> I think the body of notes on this subject, everything that has ever come to my attention, is just plain stupid to the point of imbecility. "Pleasing to heaven," etc. Various ideas of pleasing the spirits are all very well, but there would still be a lesson in animal sacrifice for any group that had evolved beyond primitive stages. Animals are killed now in abattoirs; the sight of a killing can remind us, in the midst of our normal semi-consciousness of all that goes on in our vile and degraded mercantilist ambience, that life exists by destruction of other life. The sight of one day's hecatomb might even cause thought in the midst of our democracy and usuriocracy. (SP, 68)

Though Pound scoffs at sacrifice as a gift to Heaven, he accepts it for practical reasons. If anything, his interpretation of sacrifice is entirely naturalistic, as in Canto 30, where Artemis speaks out against that Pity which prevents her from fulfilling her bloody and ritualistic function. Democracy and usurocracy are violations of Nature which, like Pity, permit the unfit to live and even thrive.

Unlike Pound, who admits to finding the meaning of sacrifice somewhat obscure, many critics are certain that they understand the reason for sacrifice in his works. Eugene Paul Nassar speaks of Pound's "beautiful rites" which "poeticise the earth and heavens" (Nassar: 125). But if the rites' major purpose is no more than to aestheticize or prettify Nature, then Pound would manifest that trivial, superficial, and folkloristic attitude toward ritual which he despised. Other critics take Pound more seriously and consider his rites to be sanctioned by and closely imitative of Nature.[5] By performing acts of sacrificial killing, society supposedly imitates and honors the cyclical mysteries of birth and death while promoting natural fecundity. There is warrant for this interpretation in Frazer and Confucius.[6] Again, critics such as Vasse, Dekker, and Pearlman emphasize that not only natural but cultural renewal demands the "solid, the blood rite."[7] Yet none of these critics explains a curious paradox: Why should the infusion of new blood require a dead rather than a live animal? Why should natural or cultural revivification depend necessarily on its opposite, namely death?

Pearlman wants to show that Pound's "order within," which demands sacrifice, "is based on the precise observation of the nature of things," an "awareness of nature's way."[8] Indeed, in Canto 52 Nature seems to sanction and even participate in sacrifice. In "cicada's time / the sparrow hawk offers birds to the spirits," and later "the wolf . . . offers his sacrifice" (52/ 260). Pound has penetrated to the heart of the primitive and mythical participation mystique. Man's sacrificial acts are continuous with and imitative of supposedly sacrificial occurrences in Nature.[9] One recalls *The Natural Philosophy of Love*, where natural violence is a "rite" (Gourmont: 159, 168, 171).

No doubt the Chinese conception of Yin and Yang is evident in Canto 52, as in *The Book of Rites* (Smith: 86). Sacrifice would thus dramatize the recurrent interchange of positive and negative, creation and destruction: in naturalistic terms, the lesson that life is made out of life. At the same time, Pound associates this interchange with natural justice and retribution. Pound's myths, observes Pearlman, reveal "the *moral* nature of things," above all the truth of Nemesis, that Nature "cannot be repressed or perverted for long without serious consequences" for her "violators." Artemis in Canto 30 thus "represents the mysterious power that insures the orderly procession and God-like eternal return of the seasons"; her sacrifices and rituals are "symbolic of the self-regulatory principle in Nature, the ecological balance by which nature maintains itself in a sort of timeless perfection." Pity, meanwhile, represents a human intrusion into and profanation of this ecological balance: it "violates the order of nature, whose self-regulatory pattern of birth, copulation, and death is founded upon the immanent will of the universe itself, a necessity in things that appears ruthless, perhaps, but is in fact the profoundest wisdom."[10]

To illustrate Pound's ideas of retributive justice and ecology, Pearlman notes that for Pound there is "no connection between death as a murderous violation of Nature [the Crucifixion in Canto 80] and death as a phase in the fulfillment of Nature's cyclical course (the waning of the moon [a sign of Artemis])."[11] It is difficult to see how the example of death as a consequence and fulfillment of unimpeded natural process applies to the ritual acts of sacrifice which Pound sanctions in Canto 30 under the name of Artemis. Instead of letting Nature take its course, Artemis (and her worshippers) intrude murderously within natural process, and they do so with a violence Pound admires. If Pearlman's formula is correct, Artemis' intrusions against Nature would lead to Nature's reprisal against the goddess, for in Pearlman's view Nature supposedly follows a law of compensation whereby her violators are themselves punished with violence. But since Artemis' actions go unpunished, this law of compensation has both the facts and the significance of "natural" violence turned around. According to Pearlman, not Artemis but Pity is to blame for various intrusive acts of violence against natural beings, thus preventing Nature from taking its beneficent course. In fact, the mistake of Pity lies in precisely the opposite, namely the all-too-compassionate withholding of violence, while Artemis, far from acting violently only in reprisals against Nature's enemies, is herself characteristically violent against Nature. One can only conclude that to do violence to Nature is to refrain from violence, which, as in Gourmont and Pound's broadcasts, seems to be Nature's essence.

Like Pound, Pearlman has a way of arguing that such violent actions against Nature occur with Nature's sanction. For now, though, let us question further Pearlman's assertion that Nature's ecological balance is inevitable, necessary, and self-regulating, and that Nature therefore abhors human interventions; again, Artemis would supposedly exemplify these ideas. If this theory were true, Artemis would merely look on benignly as Nature took its course, yet it is evident that she does not. By the same token, man would need only refrain from intruding into natural process in order to reap its abundant benefits. Actually, in Canto 30, man as a cultural being acts murderously upon Nature under the flimsy illusion that he himself is enacting Artemis' purifying justice and "natural" retribution. Despite Pearlman's argument that Artemis is a "necessity in things," she cannot be anything other than a name for human violence projected onto Nature. Pearlman admits that Artemis' endangered "nymphs . . . are the poetic and religious projections of a 'primitive' sensibility" for which Nature is "divine" and "often benevolent" (Pearlman, 1: 120). It seems fair to say that Artemis too is a projection, and that the source of her violence is not Nature or the gods but rather culture and man, as is shown by the poem's language: "foul," "foulnesse," "purity," and "clean" derive from a religious and cultural, not a natural lexicon.[12] Neither at Miwo nor in Nature is Artemis' "moon's axe" (106/ 755) sacrificially renewed, but in man, who only imagines the natural sanction.

Admittedly my appeal to the Nature-Culture dichotomy lacks imaginative charity towards Pound's holistic assumptions. But more is at stake here than the beautiful rites that poeticize the earth and heavens. As a didactic poet Pound wants us to take his ideas seriously. Nonetheless, his concepts of Nature and anti-Nature have been shown to be thoroughly arbitrary constructs conforming to fascist ideology. Pound's ideas also have human consequences, since an obsession with Artemisian sanctity drives him to recommend various forms of "pruning" in the broadcasts. In attacking the Jews, Pound has no doubt that the forces of Nature and the sacred are behind him and that he embodies Nature's retributive justice against a profane and unnatural force. As in Nazism, such an appeal to retributive justice or Fate, inseparable from an interest in sacrifice, is morally empty. Adorno rightly points out that the projection of morality onto "timeless" Nature disguises cultural violence, cancels personal freedom, and evades human responsibility.[13]

Still, it is only fair to consider why Pound believes that sacrificial violence conforms to Nature. Pound believes that man, if he makes a "precise observation of the nature of things," can "aid in the process," and sacrificial rituals are one way of doing so. When men imitate Artemis' actions, or perform her rituals in due season, they are aiding in the process. This is why Pearlman believes that Pound's sacrificial rites are ecological.[14]

But can one really believe that the Spartans' sacrifice of a horse on Mt. Taygetus in Canto 97, or Odysseus' sacrifice of bullocks in Hades, or the "blood rite" of Ferrara, are examples of a benign ecology? What of the assumption that sacrificial acts should be performed according to "precise observation" of Nature and in "due season"? There is nothing in Nature that clearly corresponds to sacrificial rituals, nothing in its random violence that would give rise to specific acts of sacrifice. The sacrificial acts in the *Li Ki* owe their propriety not to any definable mimetic correspondence to Nature but rather to their fitness within the symbolic (and seemingly natural) pattern by which Chinese society represents Nature to itself. Finally, if the aim of mimetic rituals is fecundity and abundance, why is this achieved through sacrificial violence, which involves death?

If Pound equivocated over sacrifice, he remained certain that Nature sanctioned it. Its origins and reasons presumably lie in the mythical past, for instance China's in Canto 52, where the great heroes make the first sacrifices and teach men how to live. Nor would Pound have been troubled by his lack of a clear explanation, for the first rule of mythical thinking is: "When you don't understand it, let it alone" (GK, 127).

There is nothing unusual in Pound's position. Girard argues that culture almost invariably appeals to Nature or myth to conceal not only the violent origins of its rituals but the truth of its own origin, which lies in acts of collective violence against the scapegoat victim; without this original act of human sacrifice, there is no social hierarchy, no ritual, no order. Let us then apply this insight of Girard's to a major question concerning the structure and development of *The Cantos*. Cantos 45 and 51 name usury as the major evil of history, while the opening of Canto 52 briefly recapitulates the state of the modern West in its fratricidal violence, greed, intellectual chaos, and desacralization. There follows a sudden transition to the hierarchical society of ancient China, which is characterized by a beautiful ritualistic harmony between man and Nature, and which looks forward to *The Cantos'* later paradisal moments. But how in fact does one move, practically speaking, out of the profane West into this beneficent sacrificial order? What would in the fullest sense permit and justify the substitution of one image of ideal beauty for another of infernal ugliness? However obscure or buried, and however unacknowledged, the real mechanism of this transition is human victimization.

III.

The opening section of Canto 52 contains this blast:

> "Goods that are needed," said Schacht (anno seidici)
> commerciabili beni, deliverable things that are wanted.
> $\qquad\qquad\qquad\qquad$ neschek is against this, the serpent
> . . . .
> ——————— sin drawing vengeance, poor yitts paying for
> ——————
> paying for a few big jews' vendetta on goyim
> . . . .
> Remarked Ben: better keep out the jews
> $\qquad$ or yr/ grand children will curse you
> jews, real jews, chazims, and *neschek*
> also super-neschek or the international racket
>
> $\qquad\qquad\qquad\qquad\qquad\qquad\qquad\qquad$ (52/ 257)

The next five lines are blacked out. They refer to the Rothschilds, as do the blacked out lines above. Hugh Kenner observes that Pound was driven to this unprintable fury by the sight of a Rothschild yacht anchored in the harbor of Rapallo (Davis: 179, 200, 207n).

In the previous canto Pound had isolated the disease of usury. Thus, in Canto 51, at a key structural turn of *The Cantos,* one finds the most virulent eruption of anti-Semitism in the poem thus far. Hjalmar Horace Greeley Schacht was a German financier and President of the Reichsbank under Hitler. Next comes the opposition between good economics and Jewish *neschek*. Pound then attributes vengeful impulses to a few "big" Jews, who cause punishment to fall on their lesser brethren. This is followed by an even broader condemnation of the Jews, falsely attributed to Benjamin Franklin.[15] "Chazims" is a distortion of the Hebrew "*chaseirim,*" meaning pig. Pound also refers in this canto to "gun-swine" (52/ 258), who certainly include Jews[16]. In the broadcasts the Jews are dirty "swine" and are characterized by "swinishness" (RB, 119, 134, 236, 240), while some of their most nefarious figures even have the faces of "pig[s]" (RB, 139). This is Pound's updated version of the medieval idea of the *Judensau.*[17]

Pound escapes into ancient China, where "Heaven's Son feeds on roast pork and millet." Since "chazims," applied to the Jews, means pigs, it is striking that the pig reappears in Canto 52 as a sacrificial victim and totemic animal. The reference to a meal of roast pork may thus allude consciously or unconsciously to the vilified Jews, from whose original victimization the new (and sublimated) ritual order emerges. One can understand why critics have invariably evaded the possible implications of this passage.[18]

Still, this reading of Canto 52 may make too much of a coincidence arising from Pound's generally faithful (though selective) translation of the *Li Ki*. Pound, however, was aware of Allen Upward's *Divine Mystery:*

> sd/ old Upward:
> "not the priest but the victim."
> (74/ 437)[19]

In *The Divine Mystery* Upward argues that primitive societies originate in the sacrifice of a scapegoat, who is interchangeably and sometimes simultaneously a God, king, genius, or pariah, and whom these societies view as the source of order, fertility, and renewal. The various historical mutations of sacrificial forms are sublimations and transformations of this originating and ordering act of sacrifice (Upward, 2: 56–59, 92–103). Hence Upward's statement, which Pound quotes in his review of *The Divine Mystery,* that "In the beginning the Goat created heaven and earth" (SP, 409).

A. D. Moody in his essay on Pound and Upward says of Pound that "the taint of the victim was not in him" (Moody: 58, 70). This statement has two meanings in context. One is that Pound, at Pisa, did not behave ignobly, as would a victim. Besides revealing contempt for victims, Moody ignores the fact that in the Pisan *Cantos* Pound twice compares himself with Christ. Moody more broadly implies that Pound and Upward have no interest or belief in the efficacy of victimization, whether of the animal or human variety, and that Pound opposes sacrifice. Yet there is a sense in which Moody's interpretation could be justified. Deeply troubled by human sacrifice, Upward insists that "the civilized conscience" must not share the "joy" of primitive man in such rites, and that man should cease to practice them. Upward is also pleased to believe that human sacrifice was largely overturned in the ancient world by the Aryans, whose great hero was the solar Hercules. Once it was discovered that the sun's vitality, rather than the dead victim, gave life to the seed, man worshipped the sun and the solar hero, his representative: he consumed the victim in sublimated and vegetarian form, as the grain—the Wheat God in whom Upward finds the Christ of the Catholic Communion. Upward argues that Hercules appeared in Greece, Asia, and Egypt, where he put an end to human sacrifices and snatched the victim from the cross. By contrast, the Jews continued for many centuries to practice human sacrifice, and carried a fetish (the Ark of the Covenant) in a box.[20]

Besides admiring and identifying with Hercules, Pound speaks with great abhorrence of human sacrifice. He objects to Mithraism because its "celebrant[s] immolated victims" (SP, 58), and later he accuses the Jews of implicitly sacrificial acts against Gentiles. As we have seen in Chapter Six, Upward may have also inspired Pound's rejection of the Crucifixion and his attempt, reminiscent of the Nazis' "positive Christianity" and life affirmation, to assimilate Christ to the figure of the rising and vital solar god. All this might confirm Moody's interpretation. But Moody would still have to explain why animal sacrifices appear so frequently in Pound's writing, and why Pound preached a lesson in animal sacrifice for modern civilization; he would also have to explain why Pound persecutes the Jews. Nor is an official condemnation of human sacrifice proof of freedom from a desire for human victims: the Nazis, who denounced Jewish brutality and praised Aryan life affirmation, did not blink at the holocaust.

Animal sacrifice is not the only kind of victimization in Pound's idealized China, nor is it necessarily the most useful for him in promoting order. The Confucians also foster social unity through hostility and violence, such as murder, against alien and heretical groups. In the Chinese *Cantos*, as in Pound's translations of *The Sacred Edict* in Cantos 98 and 99, the Buddhists and Taoists figure as the chief villains or "pest[s]" (CON, 79).[21] Indeed, their role in China resembles the Jews' in the West.[22] Repeatedly associated with the "bad" form of activities and objects which the in-group normally performs and uses, they are scapegoat victims. This resemblance again suggests how much Pound's vision of social unity and hierarchy depends on the demonization of outgroups.

The "seepage" of Buddhists and the "babbling" of "taozers" appears as early as Canto 54. Later, in Canto 98, these "groups" destroy the "five human relations," the organic bonds of political and familial deference and emulation. Concerned only with matters of the head and spirit, the Buddhists "provide no mental means for / Running an empire," and so represent "Man by negation." The Taoists are the "wholly subjective." "Babbling" of heaven and "elixir[s]" of immortality, they shift men's minds to their inner life: "The Dragon moaning, / the screaming tiger."[23] These charges resemble those which Pound brings against the Jews, whom he associates with antisocial interiority and subjectivity (Freud, Bergson), the abstract, and the invisible. The Taoists, again like the Jews, engage in magical practices, particularly exorcism; and although the Confucians and Pound do the same, the Taoists apparently practice the wrong kind. Pound also associates the Taoists with dangerous drugs or "pills" (98/ 687), with which they poison the minds of men. The Buddhists, meanwhile, are foreigners who speak a strange "argot" (99/ 701) and "barbarous lingo," "floaters" who "eat / without maintaining their homesteads" (99/ 697) (Baller: 73–80, 82). Like the Jews, these "heretical" parasites despise agriculture, which in *The Sacred Edict* is man's primary activity. In Canto 54 the Buddhist "shave-heads" and "rotters" destroy the "46 tablets" (54/ 284) that stood in Yo Lang and build them into their own temples. The Jews too allegedly destroy and appropriate Western cultural tradition.

Pound further links the Taoists and Buddhists with the political machinations of evil women, luxury, and crowd manipulation; it would be easy to find in his work equivalent or virtually identical accusations levelled against the Jews. In Canto 54 the Buddhists rose "under Hou-Chi the she empress"; in a later century they "ran the old empress / the old bitch . . ." (54/ 284, 287). In Canto 98 Pound ridicules the Taoists and then goes on to consider those who are like "mules saddled with trappings," who fall "deeper in debt every day" (98/ 687). These lines may owe something to Baller's comment, in a footnote to *The Sacred Edict*, on the expensiveness of Buddhist and Taoist masses for the dead (Baller: 62–63, 81n). Typically the scapegoat is identified with "bad" luxury. Just as Pound stresses the Jews' ability to create crowd hysteria, so the *Edict* accuses the heretical sects of inspiring "processions" and "promiscuous" meetings, which it associates with women and luxury (Baller: 77–79). Pound concisely translates Baller in Canto 99:

> But your females like to burn incense
> And buzz round in crowds and processions
> (99/ 701)

Nonetheless, Carroll F. Terrell has argued that Pound, and *The Sacred Edict* as well, are far more liberal and tolerant than these passages would suggest. Glossing the phrase "Bhud rot" (99/ 697), for example, Terrell insists that this phrase "does *not* say that all Buddhists are rotten." Rather, "if one respects the precise meaning of the words—according to the dictionary—it is clear that 'to rot' means to disintegrate from a former pristine state." Terrell adds questionably that Pound makes the "same judgment against all the great organized religions," which are reduced by "later practitioners" into a "tissue of absurd practices and superstitions." In these terms, neither Pound nor the *Edict* deplores Buddhism (or Taoism) as originally defined and exemplified by their founders but only in their decadent later forms. Neglecting Buddha's ascetic ideal, his followers build expensive monasteries and religious houses while encouraging idleness through begging. But the main idea of Buddhism was "different," as is stated in the seventh chapter of the *Edict:* "What is Buddha? Buddha is the heart . . . . If your heart is good, this *is* Buddha." Actually, Terrell's argument is based on an illusory notion of semantic precision as well as on distortion of the evidence. The phrase "Bhud rot" need not mean, and probably does not mean, that Buddhism has rotted from a pristine state. It can also have transitive force, meaning that the Buddhists (like the Jews in the West, for "Bhud rot" calls to mind Pound's notion of Jewish "putrefaction") have a rotting effect on their host cultures. This interpretation is all the more credible when one considers that Terrell is unjustified in giving the impression that Pound and the *Edict* favor Buddhism in its original form, as a religion of asceticism and the heart. Terrell quotes two passages from the *Edict* in which Buddhism is condemned precisely for these features. Buddha, it is said, abandoned "parents, wife, and children" to pursue an ascetic ideal—an act which neither the Confucians nor Pound, who attacks ascetism and believes in the primacy of the social, would praise. The seventh chapter of the *Edict,* on the heretical sects, speaks of Buddhism thus: ". . . Buddhism does not concern itself with anything in the four corners of the universe, but simply with the heart." This is a rejection, from a Confucian point of view, of a basic and original motive of Buddhism.[24]

Unquestionably a persecutory text, *The Sacred Edict* proposes the harshest measures against those "detestable fellows who . . . incite . . . cabals," teach magical arts, and "plot [and] . . . do evil" as their numbers increase. In one instance "the chief shall be strangled, and his adherents beaten a hundred heavy blows each, and transported 1,000 miles." Treating heretical sects as "flood, fire, robbers, or thieves," the *Edict* says: "If none of you people believe these heretical sects, they will not want to be driven out, they will become extinct naturally."[25] As Pound renders it: "If you don't swallow their buncombe / you won't have to drive 'em out" (98/ 688).

Ironically, the Buddhists and Taoists seem neither violent nor rebellious. Nor is it likely that any outgroup should be exclusively responsible for such massive evil. *The Sacred Edict* is thus a monument of ethnocentric intolerance, which Pound offers as a model to the modern world, and whose specific form is evident in the Chinese *Cantos:*

> MOU-TSONG drove out the taozers . . . .
> OU-TSONG destroyed hochang [Buddhist] pagodas,
>   spent his time drillin' and huntin'
> (55/ 291)

> And CHI cleared out the temples and hochang
>   cleared out 30 thousand temples
>   and that left 26 hundred
>   with 60 thousand *bonzes* [priests] and *bonzesses*
> (55/ 294)

IV.

Pound never openly acknowledges a personal desire for human victims. Nor should we expect him to endorse openly the idea that unanimous scapegoating is necessary for the restoration of the rites. Even so, in the radio broadcasts Pound's urge to human sacrifice is almost entirely overt.

The world, says Pound, is in "crisis" (RB, 107). Suffering collective panic induced by the Jews, the Western nations are transformed into an undifferentiated herd of animals fleeing a host of demons: "Are we," says Pound, "the gadarine [sic] swine, taken with collective hysteria?" (RB, 29). No less terrifying are the numerous forms of plague carried by the Jews. Insofar as plague is "universally presented as a process of undifferentiation, a destruction of specificities,"[26] it replicates the effects which Pound attributes to usury, the "power of putrefaction." Indeed, usury is itself "the virus of death" (RB, 78).

The plague is a "transparent metaphor" for the spread of "reciprocal violence." Pound therefore wants to know "what races can dwell together without constantly inciting other races to start fraternal slaughter and civil assassination" (RB, 173). This question is purely rhetorical, for Pound believes that "the non-Jew nations are shoved into wars in order to destroy themselves" (RB, 113), that the Talmud is "AIMED specifically at the destruction of all non-kike order" (RB, 118), and that "every man that dies in McArthur's army is sacrificed to [Felix] Frankfurter's friends" (RB, 79). The Jews view Gentiles as cattle, sheep, goats, and lambs, beasts used in sacrifices:

> . . . Don't die like a beast. I mean if you are dead set to be sunk in the mid-Atlantic or Pacific or scorched in the desert, at least KNOW why it is done to you.
> To die not knowing why is to die like an animal. What the kike calls you: goyim or cattle. To die like a human being you have at least to know why it is done to you. (RB, 409).

Pound denounces the "dirty, greasy old Talmud," in which "all flesh is grass for the Hebrew pasture, human material, just browsin' round, innocent as lambkins at Easter, cute an' amusin', no shame" (RB, 206). Meanwhile the usurers crucify mankind on crosses of gold: "not a mere cross this time, but a whole grill full of dozens of crosses" (RB, 341). The name of the "new (abattoir?)," Pound adds, is the world's new "uniform currency," by which the Republicans and the English are to be made into "goat[s]" (RB, 342). Now the scapegoat idea is explicit: "Thirty-two other nations are being sheparded toward shearing field and slaughter house" (RB, 342).

Unlike Pound's sacrificial rituals, Jewish sacrifice produces only carnage, profane violence. What then is the cure for this plague? It is homeopathic, controlled violence: "Health is CRUEL, or rather health is often accompanied by what seems cruelty to the bacillus" (RB, 194). The West had "better invent some bug poison that will eliminate him [the shyster] from your system" (RB, 196). Earlier, speaking of the Jews, Pound says that "nothing will save you, save a purge" (RB, 62). Yet even if "purge" implies violent elimination, its nature is not clear. Is Pound suggesting expulsion or extermination? Although tantalized by political violence, Pound is often vague, tentative, equivocal in discussing the subject, for the anti-Semitic propagandist usually knows that the open endorsement of violence will in most cases get him nowhere. Like Pound, who offers his audience images of Jewish sacrifice, he plants the seeds of vengeance in the listener's mind, without making clear what specific expression the vengeance is to take. To render insignificant his listener's violent impulses against the Jews, the anti-Semite must, like Pound, reduce them to the level of bugs and lower animals. And even while he speaks provocatively of "bug poison," "purges," and "pogroms," he must deny hatred and assert the futility of all violence.[27]

To be sure, in some broadcasts Pound opposes full-scale pogroms and even rejects pogroms altogether. In "Non-Jew" he tells his audience not to "start a pogrom. That is, an old style killing of small Jews." In a more up to date spirit, he proposes a pogrom "UP AT THE TOP," which might have "something" to be said for it, and which Pound attributes to an unspecified man of genius. But finally, Pound says, "legal measures are preferable," and the "sixty Kikes who started this war might be sent to St. Helena as a measure of world prophylaxis" (RB, 115). Nearly a year later Pound again invokes the specious and hardly practicable distinction between the harmless Jew and the "LARGE kikes" (RB, 247), the latter deserving to be expelled from the United States. Since Pound in the next broadcast observes that the "Jews have ruin'd every country they have got hold of" (RB, 256), he cannot be said to take his own distinction seriously. Nor can one accept in good faith Pound's rejection in the same broadcast of "a pogrom" (RB, 255). According to Pound, the Jewish "problem" in the United Kingdom is soluble through the presumably forced sale to the Jews of a "national home," preferably Australia, which Pound supposes that the Jews will buy at "cut-rates" (RB, 255). It is not clear how the forceful expulsion of all Jews from the United Kingdom to Australia is morally and practically distinguishable from the pogroms which Pound rejects.[28]

"Violence," a broadcast of June, 1942, is no less equivocal. Noting that American lynch law originated in "the Jewish ruin of the American South" (RB, 171)—thus blaming the Jews for the Civil War—Pound says that the "Ku Klux Klan once had a reason" (RB, 171). Admittedly, lynch law is a "manifestation of COWARDICE," and "the European sees nothing distinguished in a mob of a thousand men, chasing one man" (RB, 171); and yet:

> You would think that with all that anarchy and violence and contempt for everything, that political violence might be possible in America, yet it apparently is not.
> I am asking, I don't know the answer, does anyone in the audience, invisible audience, know the answer? You lynch the Negro, you glory in the manhunt, but you are incapable of political violence. But the degraded Finkelstein, coward and accomplice of murderers, accomplice of the men responsible for the labor conditions on the Stalin canal, put such utter swine in an official position . . . . (RB, 171)

Pound tantalizes his audience with the idea that "political violence is possible in America," as if the lynching of blacks were not a form of political violence. After introducing this false distinction, Pound presents it in another form: lynching and the manhunt are bad, while "political violence" is implicitly desirable. No one should be fooled by Pound's protestations of ignorance ("I don't know the answer"). His implication is that "Finkelstein," perhaps intended as a generic Jewish name,[29] deserves political violence.

One way Pound denies his violent impulses is by donning a mask of Enlightenment rationality, as when he appeals to Voltaire against the "cruelties of fanaticism" (RB, 92). Here he ignores what he certainly knew, that Voltaire had been a dedicated anti-Semite obsessed by fantasies of ritual murder. Pound reveals his real position in his references to Céline: "I have been readin' YET AGAIN a French author. Way out above other French authors . . . . I hear he is a doctor, been working in Paris suburbs. Seen a bit of reality" (RB, 128). Expert in diseases, cures, and eugenics, Céline knows the "stink" (RB, 129) of France and the unnatural forces which lead to the "Suicide of the Nation" (RB, 128, 129). Unfortunately, says Pound, his most recent book (probably *Some State of Affairs*) had been banned in France. Pound comments: "Don't like the SUBJECT. Some folks don't like the SUBJECT. Now WHY don't they like the subject?" Such distaste is inexplicable, since Céline is "all out to save France." Pound then repeats that "Ferdinand has GOT down to reality" (RB, 129)[30].

To determine Céline's subject, one must know his works of the late 1930s and early 1940s: *Bagatelles pour un massacre, L'École des cadavres,* and *Les Beaux draps (Some State of Affairs).* Besides *Bagatelles,* Pound in the broadcasts was probably much indebted to *L'École des cadavres,* in which Céline denounces the "negroized" and "judaized" democracies, mocks Roosevelt as "Rosenfeld," favors the Aryan "bulwark" of the Reich, and envisions intensified eugenic breeding to purify the "rotten Aryan." Pound favorably mentions Céline's eugenic ideas in the broadcasts. For Céline as for Pound, the Franco-German rivalry is a "mask" of the real conflict, namely an "implacable battle of the species . . . Negrified Jews against Whites."[31] Céline is filled with an "infinite capacity to hate . . . the Jew," saying openly what Pound only hints at in referring to him. In *Some State of Affairs,* in which Céline's maxim is "Vote for the Aryans. Urns for the Jews," he urges: "Eat the Jew."[32] Similar oral aggression appears in Pound's broadcast references to Céline: "Ferdinand," says Pound, "has GOT down to reality . . . . Next one [war] will be the last one. Gnrr, gnrrn, gnrrn, gnrr" (RB, 129). One hears the gnashing and sharpening of teeth.[33] In *Bagatelles pour un massacre* there is no mistaking Céline's "reality":[34]

Let us recall, for our pleasure and to remind ourselves, the main provisions of the *Protocols* . . . . For an Aryan, nothing is more invigorating than to read them . . . . It does more for our salvation than any number of prayers . . . .

Do you know that the executive power over the whole of world Jewry is called the "Kahal?" . . . Assembly of the Elders of Israel? . . . Our fate . . . depends entirely on the good favour of the big Jews, "the big occult ones." It's not stupid to think that our fate is certainly still being discussed in the consistories of the Kahal, as much as in the Masonic lodges, indeed much more.

In short, Frenchmen . . . you will go off to war at the moment chosen by the Baron de Rothschild . . . at the moment fixed in full agreement with his sovereign cousins in London, New York and Moscow . . . .

> I want something solid! . . . Realities! . . . Those who really are responsi-
> ble! . . . I've got a hunger! . . . an enormous hunger! . . . a world-wide hunger!
> a hunger for revolution . . . a hunger for planetary conflagration . . . for the
> mobilization of all the charnel-houses in the world! An appetite which is surely
> divine, divine! Biblical![35]

Céline presents himself as a Biblical prophet at an apocalyptic moment of
violence and victimization. He feels violent oral aggression, an enormous
hunger as he announces, "Death to the Jews" (Céline, 2: 245). This is
Céline's version of Pound's "the solid, the blood rite"—the sacrificial ritual
which, in the broadcasts, demands a human victim.

V.

But not only in the broadcasts. Written in the 1930s, Cantos 42 and 44
focus on banking and social reforms in Northern Italy: the founding of the
Monte dei Paschi of Siena (1624) and related developments in the next
century. But Pound also has a contemporary purpose. The Monte dei Paschi
Cantos reflect his increasing fascination with the social programs and rituals
of fascism, which are given numerous historical analogues in this section of
his poem.[36]

In Canto 44 the Mount continues to be managed intelligently in 1766
by the Florentine Duke Pietro Leopoldo and still later by his successor,
Ferdinand III. Hence the following celebration in Siena in 1792, in honor of
Ferdinand:

> Flags trumpets horns drums
> and a placard
>   VIVA FERDINANDO
> and were sounded all carillons
> with bombs and with bonfires and was sung TE DEUM
> in thanks to the Highest for this so
> provident law
> and were lights lit in the chapel of Alexander
>   and the image of the Madonna unveiled
> and sung litanies and then went to St. Catherine's chapel
> in S. Domenico and by the reliquary
> of the Saint's head sang prayers and
> went to the Company Fonte Giusta
> also singing the litanies
> and when was this thanksgiving ended the cortege
> and the contrade with horns drums
> trumpets and banners went to the
> houses of the various ambulant vendors, then were the sticks of the
> flags set in the stanchions on the Palace of the Seignors
> and the gilded placard between them
> (thus ended the morning)
>   meaning to start in the afternoon
>
>   (44/ 223–224)

This is a cleaner, more vigorous, and more orderly Sienese ritual than that examined earlier, in which the arses of oxen needed wiping and the procedure took over an hour to begin. Though the whole community participates, the flags of the wards (*contrade*) stand out prominently, thus emphasizing place and degree. This ritual occurs not in linear but in "mythical" time, for the rites (like the litanies) are constantly repeated and time therefore seems ever-renewing and hence timeless: "(thus ended the morning) / meaning to start in the afternoon." Indeed the afternoon is a resumption of the morning.[37]

The next passage represents increasing yet controlled ritual violence, a simulated disorder which likewise belongs to the ever-renewing and eternal present of myth; the ritual proceeds "always" to the sound of drums and trumpets:

> and the big bell and all bells of the tower in the piazza
> sounded from 8 a.m. until seven o'clock in the evening
> without intermission and next day was procession
> coaches and masks in great number
> and of every description e di tutta le qualità
>   to the sound always of drums and trumpets
> crying VIVA FERDINANDO and in all parts of the piazza
> were flames in great number and grenades burning
> to sound of bombs and of mortaretti and the shooting of
> guns and pistols and in the chapel of the Piazza
> a great number of candles for the publication of this so
> provident law and at sundown were dances
>   and the masks went into their houses
> and the captains of the ward companies,
> the contrade, took their banners to the Piazza Chapel
> where once more they sang litanies
> and cried again Ferdinando EVVIVA . . . .
>
> (44/ 224)

In order to commemorate the sacrificial crisis, rituals and festivals invariably introduce signs of the violent undifferentiation which they seek to control or dispel. The constant ringing of bells throughout the day and into the night, as well as the drums, trumpets, and gunshots, obviously violate normal patterns of life. The procession of coaches and masks encompasses every segment of the community and creates a collective impression of massive and disorderly heterogeneity, a kind of monstrous confusion. As for the bombs and grenades, though set off more or less safely here, these can claim random and arbitrary victims, as can the shooting off of pistols and the burning of torches in great numbers. Besides contrasting with Canto 43, in which the cost of candles is recorded as evidence of niggardly, sterile, and abstract calculation, such firepower symbolizes spreading and perhaps uncontrollable violence.

And yet, if in one sense the masks signify the violent doubles of undifferentiated violence, they also serve ritualistically to exorcize bad violence, as shamans are known to use masks. The appearance of the mask indicates that moment just before the quest for the victim, when violence is epidemic and can be quelled only by sacrifice.[38] Thus in Canto 44:

> and from the contrade continued the drumming
> and blowing of trumpets and hunting horns,
> torch flares, grenades and they went to the Piazza del Duomo
> with a new hullabaloo gun shots mortaretti and pistols
> there were no streets not ablaze with the torches
> or with wood fires and straw flares
> and the vendors had been warned not to show goods for
>   fear of disorder and stayed all day within doors
> or else outside Siena.
>
> (44/ 224–225)

"There were no streets not ablaze" suggests momentarily that fire had spread to the houses. Amid imagery of intensifying light, ritual nearly reaches its collectively violent climax. The hunt for the scapegoat figures implicitly in the hunting horns, reminiscent also of the huntress Artemis, who in Canto 30 oversees ritualistic pruning. Potential victims, namely the merchants and the ambulant vendors, are temporarily forced to stay indoors or (like the scapegoat) remain outside the city.

In the end, though, the Sienese ritual seems successful because it keeps violence under control. One recalls the Dantescan light imagery of "A Visiting Card": "A thousand candles together blaze with intense brightness. No one candle's light damages another's. So is the liberty of the individual in the ideal and fascist state" (SP, 306). Yet this is a questionable assertion. Canto 44 contains a reference to "wood fires," apparently burning logs. This image connects with the *hsin* sign, whose axe, tree, and woodpile signify not only cultural renewal but sacrifice, and whose meaning Pound conveys in Canto 53:

新 hsin[1]

> Day by day make it new
> Cut underbrush,
> pile the logs
> keep it growing
>
> (53/ 265)

If underbrush signifies the rubbish or excess which needs to be pruned and cleared, the logs are just the thing with which to start a wood fire, or the burning in Canto 44:

> and on June 28th came men of Arezzo
> past the Porta Romana and went into the ghetto
> there to sack and burn hebrews
> part were burned with the liberty tree in the piazza

and for the rest of that day and night
1799 anno domini
pillage stopped by superior order . . . .
(44/ 225)³⁹

One might see this action as a ritual gone wrong in its failure to control social violence and thus reject the conclusion that the Monte or Mount is also a sacrificial pyre. But consider again Canto 43, in which Pound laments the "fat" and sloth of the Sienese rites, and in which wax candles are the offering—a far cry from those pagan rituals in which the beast itself was slain. Then the left ox speaks:

'Mn-YAWWH!!!'

(43/ 216)

According to Pound, the father god of the Old Testament—Yahweh, Jehovah—"was beast."⁴⁰ In this passage a beast—the sort one would use in a sacrificial ritual—names Yahweh, which may be the beast's own name. A canto later, representatives of the Jewish god are burnt along with a liberty tree. For Pound, this would be a modern commemoration of that burning bush within which, before Moses, the Hebrew god stood at once revealed and concealed.

Sacrificial violence—once more against the Jews—is displaced and concealed in the midst of another section of *The Cantos*. Canto 48 follows the first Usury Canto as well as the decisive transference in Canto 46 of universal blame from women to gold and usury. The celebration of Italian Fascist ritual and community in Canto 48 also anticipates Canto 52 and the ritualistic order of ancient China. Now, however, Pound is no longer content to vilify such abstractions as gold and usury. Quoting an unknown source, he writes: "Bismarck / blamed american civil war on the jews; / particularly on the Rothschild / one of whom remarked to Disraeli / that nations were fools to pay rent for their credit" (48/ 241). There follows a series of passages with no overt relation to the Jews or to the previous quotation, but which are structured according to oppositions between the natural and unnatural, the vital and unvital, the fit and unfit, the new and the old: a reference to leopards known as "DIGONOS" or "twice-born," hence totemic animals of Dionysus (and Pound), the avenging Nature god; an ironic contrast between British aristocrats carefully choosing pedigreed dogs and an American President carelessly choosing a Secretary of State; a further contrast between corrupt senatorial politics in America and the wisdom of King Athelstan and the anti-usurious Romans; the navigational feats of the Polynesians, who sailed the Pacific "naturally," without the aid of maps, simply by the stars; and the displeasure of Pound's mistress Olga Rudge in the company of a luxurious and wasteful lady of means. Next comes a much longer and central passage adapted from a letter from Pound's young daughter Mary, in which she recounts, in a naive and enraptured voice, a feast day in a

Tyrolean village in the twelfth year of the Fascist Era ("dodicesimo anno E.F.," 48/ 242). Insofar as this "festa" is "bella" or beautiful, it betokens the correct performance of the rites. It is moreover the "first mass" or "nuova messa" of a young priest, and so signifies sanctification and renewal. As in Canto 44, in which torches blazed at the festival in Siena, and Canto 40, in which the sailors of Hanno-Mussolini observe the mountain fires of African savages, soon to be their victims, fire figures prominently: the "mountains are full of fires," children carry torches, the "houses were full of lights" (48/ 242). In Canto 44 the festival seemed continually to resume and renew itself in an eternal present; here too a mass and a procession take place the day after the "new mass." Cast from a child's perspective, this passage represents the culture and faith of Italian Fascism as communal ("there were a lot of people"), natural ("the *carrozze* [carriages] were full of flowers," "tree branches in the windows"), joyful, and innocent.

This illusion is dispelled by the canto's conclusion: Pound honoring fascism in its authentically violent form and as the supposed embodiment of the necessary processes of Nature. In one sense fascism is the apocalyptic wind, a natural force, which blows upon the Lido, scattering the beach costumes of a decadent, luxurious, and usurious bourgeoisie. But more important, fascism acts at the behest of Artemis and especially Dionysus, whose predatory leopards figure in this canto.[41] Pound compares the elimination of usury, now inseparable from the Jews, by Italy, Germany and Japan, with the savage destruction of a "great worm" (48/ 243) by three ants acting by intelligent instinct. In the Addendum to Canto 100, usury is a "worm" (Addendum, 100/ 798), while in the broadcasts the Jews are collectively vermin. The killing of the worm is preceded by a reference to the three warring fascist nations, symbolized as Mars, falling "to the stone bench / Where was an ox in smith's sling hoisted for shoeing." The helpless ox suggests the idea of a sacrificial victim, and in fact these lines imply the descent of Dionysian violence. Abducted by the greedy sailors in Canto 2, Dionysus causes these abusers of Nature to be transformed into beasts while their ship stands fixed, as if by magic, "slung like an ox in smith's sling" (2/ 8).[42] The same naturalistic mythology probably motivates Pound's earlier and baffling reference to the careful breeding of dogs by British aristocrats. This passage calls to mind statements in the radio broadcasts, where Pound laments that men fail to give the same attention to human breeding as British dog-fanciers give to "whiffets" and proposes Nazi-style eugenics as an implicitly "natural" solution to the Jewish corruption of the Aryan race. Eugenics, an idea which Pound had played with as early as Canto 32, is a form of sacrifice. Nonetheless, Pound has arranged this canto so that the "new mass," the sacred heart and communal feast of the fascist religion, is structurally self-contained and removed from the violence on which it depends and in which it originates. The naivete of his daughter's voice imparts to the ceremonies a speciously girlish freshness, as of virginal Artemis in one of her benign moods. As for the Jews, indispensable victims of fascist violence, they are mentioned elsewhere casually and in a seemingly irrelevant and confusing context, while the violence itself is treated symbolically and transferred from the cultural to the natural realm. Again, displacement and *méconnaissance* are at work.

VI.

Long before the fascists, other notable figures in Western culture had anticipated Pound in believing that Jews seek to perform sacrificial acts against Gentile victims. Voltaire repeatedly associates the Jews with ritual murder and asserts that they normally practiced human sacrifice in Biblical times. These accusations are probably projections. In "Genèse" Voltaire fantasizes a vengeful mass attack on two Jews supposedly responsible for bringing a plague upon Gentiles. Similarly, as Pound in the broadcasts mentions Jewish slaughterhouses and butchers, Wagner believes that the Jewish god, who preferred Abel's lamb to Cain's vegetable offering, loves sacrificial meat. This belief partly explains Wagner's turn to vegetarianism, in which he foreshadows not only Pound but Hitler, who also has no doubt that the Jews hunger for human victims.[43]

A brutal image of the Jews appears too in Upward's *The Divine Mystery,* which holds that Hebrew religion before the Babylonian exile followed Tyre and Carthage in sacrificing children to the King Moloch. Later the Jews commemorated this brutality in the "dreadful face" of the later Hebrew God, who provides the "first glimpse of Puritanism, and of the Inquisition." Contrasting Hellenism and Hebraism, Upward says that, thanks to Hercules, the Aryan Greeks replaced brutal sacrificial religions with those of solar vitality: "Even the sacrifice of animals," says Upward, "is denounced by the Hebrew prophets as soon as they feel the mild breath blowing from the North." Nonetheless, "the Israelites continued to sacrifice their children, after the Hellenes had learned to regard such rites with horror" (Upward, 2: 256, 262–263, 141, 148).

In *The Divine Mystery* Upward alludes to but does not quote this passage from First Isaiah:

> To what purpose *is* the multitude of your sacrifices unto me? saith the LORD: I am full of the burnt offerings of rams, and the fat of fed beasts; and I delight not in the blood of bullocks, or of lambs, or of he goats. When ye come to appear before me, who hath required this at your hand, to tread my courts? Bring me no more vain oblations; incense is an abomination unto me . . . . Yes, when ye make many prayers, I will not hear: your hands are full of blood.
> (1: 11–14)

Few Biblical scholars would claim that the anti-sacrificial spirit of this passage, which was probably written in the late eighth century B.C., derives from Aryan or European influences. Rather it belongs to a powerful and emergent strain within Judaic religion, one which, in its most radical form, for instance Amos 5: 22ff and Jeremiah 7: 21ff, would seem to reject the sacrificial cult unconditionally.[44] To be sure, many if not the majority of interpreters of the Isaiac passage do not believe that it goes so far as that in the rejection of sacrifice. In all likelihood its intention is closer to such texts as I Samuel 15: 22, Micah 6: 7–8, and Psalms 51: 6–19, none of which denies the legitimacy of sacrifice as such, but all of which insist on its insufficiency when unaccompanied by purity of heart and righteous deeds. Sacrifice is thus understood to be no mere substitute for piety and goodness, least of all when performed, as in the above passage, by those whose hands are guilty of "innocent" blood. The accumulation of sacrifices which Yahweh loathes cannot by itself renew the broken covenant between disobedient Israel and its god.[45] It should further be emphasized that there is perhaps from the very beginning of Biblical tradition a profound moral difference between the Hebraic conception of sacrifice and that which characterized other peoples in the ancient world. Typically in ancient religion sacrifice is conceived as a magical action which, rightly performed, controls the will of the gods. In a period of crisis, such as that which provides the historical context for First Isaiah, most ancient worshipers would either increase the volume of helpless and innocent victims—precisely the solution which Isaiah (and Yahweh) rejects—or else abandon their gods in favor of new ones. But for the ancient Hebrews sacrifice is the channel of "God's approach to man in grace and man's approach to God in responsive faith."[46]

Within the next two hundred years Hebrew religion would carry its understanding of sacrifice still further, partly as a consequence of the Babylonian Exile and the fall of the Temple of Jerusalem in 587 B.C., which subjected the Hebrews to the "great deprivation" of no longer being able to offer sacrifices. Yet it was at this point of seemingly utter degradation that the "opportunity had arisen for Israel to realize that she could now hold intimate communion with her chosen God without the instrument of a sacrificial cult."[47] Second Isaiah announces a new conception of sacrifice which powerfully reflects the sympathy of the Hebraic God not with the powerful and violent but with those who, like Israel, are chiefly victims, who have "no might" and are reduced to the abject status of a "worm."[48] This text would powerfully influence Christianity, and it may help to explain why Pound, who not infrequently compares the Jews to worms and other lower creatures, grouped Christianity with Judaism as "humiliation doctrine" (RB, 199, 214). In Second Isaiah Israel's historical destiny lies not in violent conquest or the multiplication of sacrifices but in taking on the role of the Suffering Servant, whereby the members of the Hebrew nation will voluntarily become vicarious sufferers in atonement for their own sins and those of mankind. Bernhard Anderson observes that this concept has far greater moral power than any animal sacrifice. Not only is Israel's sacrifice made voluntarily for the sake of others, but, in order to be effective, it forces the other nations to recognize that they have been self-centered in their violence and ambition and that they have allowed the Suffering Servant to suffer both at their hands and in their behalf. Ultimately, the Suffering Servant will triumph in his very abjection, for he has helped to reestablish through his own misery God's broken relation with the world—a moral covenant for which no mere animal sacrifice is adequate. Thus sacrifice becomes internalized and—in the Christian idea of the Imitation of Christ—attains a universal, collective significance.[49]

Admittedly Upward recognizes the great originality, spiritual superiority, and influences of Second Isaiah's ideas: the Suffering Servant is the "charter" of the Christian Church (Upward, 2: 288). But this recognition has little effect on Upward's spiritual elitism (which he shares with Pound), and he denies to the Jews real responsibility for this new conception of sacrifice. He argues that Second Isaiah was created under Aryan and Greek influence, "the mild breath blowing from the North." The truth of the matter is that the Jews (or Hebrews) had given up human sacrifice and had called all sacrifice into question well before human sacrifices had ceased in the Greek world.[50] The historical originality and uniqueness of the Old Testament lies partly in its rejection of sacrificial mythologies and in its sympathy toward the victim. Anti-Semitism, both in Pound and in the West, may thus be seen as a refusal to recognize the power of the Old Testament to demythologize sacrifice and to expose the arbitrariness of victimization within culture (Girard, 3: 219–220).

What is even more curious is that Pound was probably aware of both First and Second Isaiah and their critique of sacrifice. Canto 74 contains the phrase: "to redeem Zion with justice / sd/ Isaiah" (74/ 429). This is a gloss on First Isaiah, 1: 27, in which the Lord says that "Zion shall be redeemed by justice, and those in her that repent, by righteousness." Terrell points out that these words follow almost immediately the passage in which the Lord refuses the sacrificial blood of bulls and other animals.[51] In all likelihood Pound means to assert, even more thoroughly than does First Isaiah, that blood sacrifice belongs to no true system of justice, and he therefore acknowledges implicitly the value if not the originality of this Jewish ethical conception. Still, the ultimate significance of this passage from *The Cantos* must be considered in the light of Pound's notion that the Jews fail to observe their own laws, as in their practice of usury; that the "prophets ceased not to object to the conduct of . . . [their] coreligionaries" (RB, 117); and that the usurious and Talmudic Jews remain bent on the sacrifice of Gentile "cattle." Seen from this perspective, the passage hardly repudiates Pound's anti-Semitism but rather confirms it. Ignoring their own prophets, the Jews have failed to redeem Zion with justice. Instead, as this passage continues, they have sought to redeem it "on interest," to quote "David Rex, the prime s.o.b." (74/ 429). In misrepresenting the Jews' attitude toward their own laws even as he appropriates those laws for himself, as in his continued attacks on the Jews even while condemning the sacrificial impulse, Pound affords a characteristic example of what Girard calls *méconnaissance*.

Yet many of Pound's critics find nothing questionable in his fascination with the "timeless" ritual order of pre-history. For them, Pound's desire to escape history, and to reconcile man and nature in a mythical, "organic" synthesis, is altogether innocent and admirable, another compelling example of Poundian vitalism. Indeed, who would not want to cast off the degradations and deprivations of the modern world in quest of a lost natural plenitude assured by myth? Who would not prefer to exchange the abrupt and violent discontinuities of historical life for the slow and unfailing round of the seasons? In assessing these fantasies, one almost hopes that Lionel Trilling is right in saying that "the intellectual life of our culture . . . fosters a form of assent that does not involve actual credence" (Trilling: 171). Such nostalgia for prehistory is based on a sentimental misunderstanding of the violence that underlies all ritual and all mythology. To adopt Pound's form of mythical thinking, and to pursue his ideal of ritual order, is also inevitably to accept bondage to "Nature," sacrifice, and unrecognized scapegoating. To ignore the darker and concealed significance of Pound's ritualism is to embrace that *méconnaissance* which enables victimization to continue. Pound's impulse toward "organic" and "holistic" values is inseparable from his need for victims, and these, most often, are the Jews.

Part Four

Self and Other

Chapter Twenty

Pound's Gods:
Contagion, Magic, and Taboo

Pound's anti-Semitism is an overdetermined phenomenon and hence multiple in its meanings and origins. Thus far we have examined it as an ideological and intellectual construct; as a myth; as the expression of personal, social, political, and economic pressures; and as an indispensable poetic strategy within the verbal economy and formal development of *The Cantos*. What remains to be considered, even at the risk of some repetition, are the deepest and most personal roots of Pound's anti-Semitism, which lie in his religious and spiritual ideas and in his messianic conception of himself. As we shall see, Pound's quarrel with the Jews finally centers on opposing views of the nature of the divinity and of the possibility of man's access to the sacred or divine: the Jews are Pound's imagined and hated rival for the power which divinity confers. At the same time, this rivalry at once derives from and masks Pound's secret admiration and unacknowledged emulation of his Jewish enemies. Pound's conception of the divinity will begin to emerge as we interrogate an unlikely yet frequent Poundian metaphor: the bacillus.

Although Pound verges on fascism when he identifies the Jews with bacilli, his metaphor is not entirely propagandistic.[1] Once Pound adopts this cliché it takes on the distinctive color of his thought and personality. The ultimate origins and profoundest implications of his bacillus metaphor probably lie in Allen Upward's *The New Word*, which Pound deeply admired. Seeking to explain the defects of Christianity, Upward sought "the leading symptom of the disease," and then "the bacillus" (Upward, 1: 250).

In *The New Word* the source of the bacillus is Genesis. Later editing of this text cannot conceal the evil intentions toward mankind of the "jealous Elohim," whom Upward mistakenly views not as the single god of the Jews but as their supposedly original plurality of deities.[2] As for the Serpent, or Satan, he is a Promethean culture hero, bringing forbidden knowledge and "material benefit" to man and suffering immensely for his labors. Man, in consequence, suffers too; the Elohim "provide against his gaining eternal life" and entering Heaven, as in the story of the Tower of Babel (Upward, 1: 250–252). In this version of a familiar Romantic myth, Satan resembles not only Prometheus but the invariably victimized artist, Upward's and Pound's Divine Man, who brings light to a mankind sunk in superstition and terror of Nature.

Upward's conception of the Jewish deity, and the deity in general, is inconsistent. He never decides whether God is Nature, or man's projection onto Nature, or whether God is one or many; he speaks of the Man and the Men Outside. Nor does Upward decide whether God is a remote divinity or a human being (like the Divine Man); no one has "yet learned" the nature of the "Man Outside," the extent of whose interference in our lives we cannot calculate, and who may be good or bad (Upward, 1: 244, 252–256, 258, 271). Upward's fear and ambivalence toward the divine emerges in his theory of the origin of religion from a kind of paranoiac warfare between man and Nature, in which the gods reside and which they control to the detriment of man. Religion is a means of gaining power over Nature and the gods through mimetic practices such as "incantations" and "spells," "liturgies," rituals, and dances, of which the Divine Man has special knowledge (Upward, 1: 253–254).

Of all religions, Upward most associates Judaism with the idea of God as an absolute authority who, through fear and prohibitions, thwarts man's instincts and desires: "fear is the enemy that the Idealist has to fight," although "fear is the hardest word for him to understand." The remote and fearful Jewish God affronts human desire and intelligence: "If the Man Outside is a good man, then he cannot want us to fear him. He can only want us to live so that we need not fear him." Upward thus splits the idea of God into two conceptions, one an inaccessible and uncontrollable force, the other an indulgent being amenable to human control. The last of these, says Upward, is "the foe worth fighting, for when the Man Outside wrestles with us under this form he means us to prevail." No one is luckier than the Divine Man, whom the Man Outside has chosen to be his "privileged" servant, an "ambassador of the great King."[3]

Pound likes Upward's idea that "the real God is neither a cad nor an imbecile" but an amiable being. "That is," Pound adds, "a fairly good ground for religion" (SP, 405). Like Upward and Zielinski, Pound distinguishes between the good gods, indulgent and attractive to man, and the ugly and repressive Jehovah.[4] The Greek gods are known by their "beauty," while "demons" are "unbeautiful" (SP, 47), and Jehovah, as repopularized by Calvin, is a "maniac sadist" (SP, 70). Pound believes that the Italian Catholic habit of "moderation" is attributable to such prayers as the one in an Italian schoolbook which supplicates God by referring to "the hilarity of thy face" (GK, 141). In numerous other instances Pound views divinity as an attribute possessed by favored human beings. Cantos 93 and 98 contain two brief passages from Ovid's *Fasti* whose source reads: "There is a god within us; at his instigation we are fired; in this impulse inhere the seeds of the divine mind" (SP, 72). In "Quotations from Richard of St. Victor," Ovid's "god within" tallies with Richard's "certain fire within us." "When this Spirit," says Richard, "enters the rational spirit, it inflames it with its own divine ardour and transforms its qualities into its own likeness, so that it shows forth the love of its author, as is fitting" (SP, 72). Such transformations of men into the "likeness" of the divinity are desirable because the divinity is known "by . . . beauty."

Pound further echoes Upward in his belief that names are crucial if the gods are to be controlled or "handled." In "Religio," the "gods have many names. It is by names that they are handled in the tradition" (SP, 48). Upward notes in *The New Word* that primitive man gradually obtained some degree of power over the "Men Outside" through "magic spell[s]" (Upward, 1: 254). One recalls Freud's observation that among primitive men "one of the most important parts of a person is his name," and that "if one knows the name of a man or of a spirit, one has obtained a certain amount of power over the owner of the name" (Freud, 1: 78–79, 81). For Upward, who feels a profound affinity with primitive man, the most fearful aspect of the Jewish God is that he abandons Nature and conceals his name. Being incommensurable with anything else in Nature, the nameless and invisible Jewish god is beyond magical and verbal control, and this explains why Upward describes Judaism as a bacillus:

> If the Men Outside did not resent man's control they would not be human . . . . It is their sleepless dread lest man should master them by his conjurations that leads them to withhold their names from him . . . . An enchantment, it would seem, like a medieval writ, must call the defendant by his right name, or the whole process is null and void . . . . Well did those old Hebrews hide the right name of their God, calling him Lord and King and Bright One . . . . We have not yet learned the right name of the Man Outside. (Upward, 1: 256–257)

Like Upward, Pound and his circle were deeply fascinated by primitive man, and liked to think of the artist as a primitive or savage.[5] Pound thus found it easy to envisage him as equivalent to Upward's Divine Man or Wizard. Being extremely sensitive to his own "symptoms" and to external Nature, the Divine Man can magically summon spirits and dominate human crowds (Upward, 2: 2). It is thus likely that Upward inspired the Poundian manifesto in which the long-oppressed but rebellious artists turn to "the powers of the air": "We who are the heirs of the witch doctor and the voodoo . . . are about to take control." At this point, however, there is no justification for asserting that Pound's bacillus metaphor resembles Upward's. Where Upward's use of it evokes the terror of Jehovah, Pound's has no clear connection with the idea of divinity: if anything it suggests the very opposite, namely profanation and defilement by the demonic Jews. It therefore remains to be shown that Pound's God or gods are comparable to bacilli and indeed interchangeable with them in their terrifying power.

II.

Pound's only overt comparison of God or the gods to bacilli appears in "Axiomata" (1921). In contrast with Pound's "Religio," what strikes one about this text is his assertion that the divinity or divinities are inaccessible to man's knowledge. Not only are we "utterly ignorant" of the "intimate essence of the universe," we "have no proof that this God, Theos, is one, or is many, or is divisible or indivisible" (SP, 49). To be sure, the "consciousness may be aware of the effects of the unknown and of the non-knowable on the consciousness" (SP, 50), but it "is incapable of knowing why this occurs, or even in what manner it occurs, or whether it be the *theos*" (SP, 50). Pound gives an example:

> For instance: a man may be hit by a bullet and not know its composition, nor the cause of its having been fired, nor its direction, nor that it is a bullet. He may die also instantly, knowing only the sensation of shock. Thus consciousness may perfectly well register certain results, as sensation, without comprehending their nature. He may even die of a long-considered disease without comprehending its bacillus. (SP, 50)

As usual distrusting analogies, Pound notes the "confusion between a possibly discoverable bacillus and a non-knowable *theos*." He adds: "Concerning the ultimate nature of the bacillus, however, no knowledge exists; but the consciousness may learn to deal with superficial effects of the bacillus, as with the directing of bullets" (SP, 51). Though Pound attempts to dissociate two ideas, their connection remains a possibility and their resemblance seems greater than before. "No knowledge exists," says Pound, of "the ultimate nature of the bacillus." The bacillus is as inaccessible and unknowable as the divinity itself. One cannot be sure that the attack of the bacillus differs from the assault of the divinity. Nor does the difference between the bacillus and the divinity lie in man's ability to direct and control the former, presumably by inoculations, vaccines, etc., which are man's way of turning dangerous bacilli homeopathically against themselves.[6] The function of religion resembles that of inoculation: religion controls, through ritual, those violent forces which belong to the sacred. In a less skeptical mood Pound says that one "handles" the gods by their names.

Still, there appears to be a disparity between these ideas: divinity, suggesting the infinite, sublime, beneficent, holy, and universal; bacillus, the microscopic and unclean. But not all bacilli are harmful, and harmful ones can be beneficial, while in the imagination the divine and the bacillus share invisibility and incommensurability. Again, both can invade and take over a person from without, divinity in a moment of inspiration or enthusiasm, bacilli at the onset of a disease. All this explains Pound's description of "nearly all the divine attributes—i.e., infinite expansibility, infinite compressibility, infinite metamorphosability, a capacity for incarnation, now in one, now in the other of us."[7] Finally, a bacillus can engulf an entire society in the same manner as societies experience collective conversion, natural disaster, religious panic, and hysteria—that is, through contagion, mimetic in one instance, physical in the other (Girard, 2: 31). Nothing better testifies to divine violence than the capacity—one which Pound attributes to the Jews—to bring a plague upon a whole people; of this the Bible and Greek literature provide numerous examples.[8] It is now evident why, in "Axiomata," the bacillus bears the same trait as the divine—the power of violent possession, of producing the sensation of "being hit by a bullet."

The sacred is essentially ambiguous. One cannot distinguish it essentially from the manifestations of bacilli, and it has no clear a priori status good or bad. As doctors know that the effects of bacilli vary depending on dosage, witch doctors know that the gods bring good or ill depending on how they are manipulated.

III.

In speaking of the Jews as bacilli, Pound identifies them with diseases that attack the body violently and invisibly: "Microbes are exceedingly small."[9] In the broadcasts the incommensurability of microbes is terrifying: "[The] American public [is] rather like that lunatic in Pea's novel *Moscardino,* chap in gook house who just wouldn't believe that there could be enough microbes on the back of a postage stamp to knock a man cold" (RB, 91). But Pound is also speaking of what he considers moral evil; as bacilli, the Jews are the essence of profanation and pollution. For although the nineteenth century learned that "bacilli can kill," and thus "prophylaxis entered the general mind," man forgot a "theological concept" known "to the age of faith," that a "wrong idea could bring evil" (RB, 91–92). Before Ehrlich, Semmelweis, and de Kruif "[had] sought for physical heresies, for the almost invisible and, with high power microscopes, spirochete or hidden evil," the "true" medieval theologians "had sought and fought against the roots and beginnings of error" (GK, 317).

In *Crowds and Power* Canetti notes that medieval devils reappear in the nineteenth century as dangerous and mysterious bacilli. Resembling devils in "their power to harm and their concentration in enormous numbers in very small spaces," these creatures attack not the souls but the "bodies of men." And, while only a small minority has peered into microscopes and seen them, as in the case of devils everyone knows of bacilli and vaguely attempts to avoid their contact.[10] In fact, Pound's massive and obsessive fear of Jewish bacilli is not primarily a physical fear, but rather a fear of a diabolical power. Not only does Pound speak of Jewish "devilment" in the Middle Ages, but in one broadcast, after warning of bacilli, he warns of the "hosts of Belial and Jewry" (RB, 93).

Like bacilli, these satanic hosts contaminate and control others through direct contact. Pound speaks of "interlocking . . . [Jewish] directorates" (RB, 253) increasing their power through contact among themselves, of "[Jewish] psychology . . . getting power over others, by personal contact" (RB, 297), of Jewish women paralyzing their Gentile "victims" through sexual contact and "syphilis" (RB, 297). Because of Jewish contamination, the Gentiles have been transformed into hysterical cattle, sheep, and lambs, whose herds are known to succumb to infectious diseases. This demonic metamorphosis inverts that in which men gain access to the divine.

And yet, however diabolical the Jewish bacilli may seem, they also belong to the sacred. Canetti has observed that "there is nothing that man fears more than the touch of the unknown" (Canetti, 1: 1). In *Totem and Taboo* Freud similarly remarks that "touching is the first step towards obtaining any sort of control over, or of attempting to make use of a person or object." He discusses obsessional patients who, like Pound, "behave as though the 'impossible' persons and things were carriers of a dangerous infection liable to be spread by contact on to everything in their neighborhood." These patients' habits resemble the reaction of primitives to taboo objects:

> Behind all these prohibitions there seems to be something in the nature of a theory that they are necessary because certain persons and things are charged with a dangerous power, which can be transferred through contact with them, almost like an infection . . . . This power is attached to all *special* individuals, . . . and to all *uncanny* things, such as sickness and death and what is associated with them through their power of infection or contagion. (Freud, 1: 33–34, 27, 21–22)

Although Pound identifies the Jews with the "brute disorder of taboo" (SP, 150), the truth is that the Jews themselves are taboo objects in Pound's writings, and thus belong in a most ambiguous and uncanny category. As Freud notes, the word *sacer*, from which the word sacred derives, has the same double meaning as the word *taboo*, referring simultaneously to the sacred and profane. Freud adds that in more modern periods "the meaning of 'taboo' diverges in two contrary directions. To us it means, on the one hand, 'sacred,' 'consecrated,' and on the other hand 'uncanny,' 'dangerous,' 'forbidden,' 'unclean' "(Freud, 1: 18, 25, 67). Nonetheless, such distinctions have often proved troublesome. Despite our efforts to separate the good or beneficial aspect of the sacred from the terrifying demonic form (what we normally call profane or taboo), these concepts continue to resemble each other and in fact remain virtually indistinguishable in the most crucial ways. To quote Kenneth Burke: "*Sacer* [and taboo as well] might thus be more accurately translated as 'untouchable,' since the extremely good, the extremely bad, and the extremely powerful are equally 'untouchable' " (Burke: 55). From this perspective, that which is taboo is also sacred.

Upward observes of the Man (or Men) Outside that he has thus far eluded our religious comprehension, measure, and control. Incapable of giving his proper name or of calculating his interference in our lives, we may yet find him good or bad (Upward, 1: 256, 258). But man's persistent paranoia and hatred toward the God in no way lessens his reverence. "Worship," says Upward, "in the form of awe and deprecation, is paid by primitive man to everything he fears, irrespective of any theory as to its nature" (Upward, 2: 35). For the same reason the Jews must be judged as objects not only of Pound's fear but of his worship. Having identified the unknowable "*theos*" with the death-dealing bacillus, Pound comes to equate the increasingly more formidable Jews with infectious, lethal, and yet perhaps beneficent germs, with plague, violence, sorcery, and the swamp. Pound's Jews thus stand at the indeterminate point where the sacred and the taboo are indistinguishable. In *The Divine Mystery* Upward notes the same fearful ambiguity of the sacred:

> The word *divine* shows its ambiguous origin in many languages. In Russia *Bog* is the name of God; in Britain the *Bogey* Man faithfully preserves the lineaments of the Wizard as he loomed in the terrified imagination of the primeval nursery. (Upward, 2: 70)

It cannot be emphasized enough that Pound always associates the Jews with his image of their God. Like Upward's Man Outside, this image expresses an infantile fear: Jehovah is a "bogey," "daddy slap / em / with / slab." In these nursery phrases Pound connects the Jews with the bad father whom Cohn finds in medieval millenarian paranoia and the "devils" of modern anti-Semitism (Cohn, 1: 256–266). But in Pound's eyes the Jewish God stands for something far more profound though never consciously articulated. Probably more than any other deity, the invisible, transcendental, and inhuman Jewish God represents the sheer and terrible otherness of the sacred, with which Pound, for all his fears, himself craves contact. To quote Paul Ricoeur:

> . . . The religion of Israel is imbued with this conviction that man cannot see God without dying . . . . [The prophets] experience in the name of the whole [Jewish] people the incompatibility of God and man. This terror expresses the situation of sinful men before God. (Ricoeur: 63)

Here we encounter the archaic "system of defilement" and the "theme of '*possession*' that belongs to that system" (Ricoeur: 86). Undoubtedly Pound fears both possession and defilement by the Jews: "Are we," he says in the broadcasts, "the gadarine [sic] swine?" (RB, 29). But what is the connection between defilement and the sacred? To quote Ricoeur again:

> . . . In fearing defilement, man fears the negativity of the transcendent; the transcendent is that before which man cannot stand; no one can see God—at least the god of taboos and interdicts—without dying. It is from this, from this

wrath and this terror, this deadly power of retribution, that the sacred gets its character of separateness. It cannot be touched; for if it is touched—that is to say, violated— its death dealing power is unleashed. (Ricoeur: 33)

In "Axiomata" Pound had compared the divinity both to a bacillus and a deadly bullet. Later, during the period of his radio broadcasts, when he was most obsessed with fears of bacilli, Pound boasted to the studio technicians in Rome that "the bullet has yet to be made that will kill me."[11] Though raised in the Hebraic atmosphere of Protestantism, Pound repeatedly resists the moral claims and power of the wholly invisible and transcendent deity, that God who is "Wholly Other" and who thus reveals the "impotence," guilt, and "wretchedness" of sinful man (Ricoeur: 57–58). But Pound's sense of the transcendent, though banished or buried, does not disappear. It reemerges in his fear of bacillary creatures, as deadly as bullets, as invisible as the transcendent God, and who also reveal man's powerlessness before the sacred. As Pound says in the radio broadcasts: "Whom God would destroy, he first sends to the bug house" (RB, 27). This statement may trace ultimately to a fragment of Euripides', but Pound's version is most interesting for its alterations of the original. The fragment reads: "Whom God would destroy, he first drives mad."[12] In Pound's version divine destructiveness is associated not only with madness ("the bug house") but with the proliferation of bacilli ("bugs")—an association which appears elsewhere in Pound's references to psychiatrists "going bugs" and to the "swamp" or "quagmire" of the unconscious. Yet one would expect Pound, a resolute pagan, to have attributed this power to many gods. Instead, he uncharacteristically identifies it with a single deity, "God." This God is probably Jehovah, the God of monotheism.

Chapter Twenty-One

The God in the Crowd

Pound's mockery and belittlement of the Jewish God emerges early and serves a double purpose. Besides helping to promote paganism in general, it justifies Pound's personal messianic cult as the most preferable replacement for Judaism and its Christian offshoots. As Pound said in 1911, "we no longer believe that the supreme and controlling power of the universe is a bigoted old fool or a Hebrew monopoly. . . ."[1] Yet there is irony in this statement, for Pound's constant attacks on the despised Jews actually reveal his high and fearful estimation of their power and that of their patriarchal god. However much Pound claims access to the divine, Judaism and the Jews remain his most formidable enemy, rival, and obstacle. In these terms, one might view Pound's anti-Semitism as in part a revolt against the punitive parental rival and superego, a conflict between the religion of the forbidding father Jehovah and that of the messianic son.[2]

In spite of the skeptical "Axiomata," Pound persistently believes that some men can at least momentarily "become a god" (SP, 47). Consider the early "Paracelsus in Excelsis":

> "Being no longer human, why should I
> Pretend humanity or don the frail attire?
> Men have I known and men, but never one
> Was grown so free an essence, or become
> So simply element as what I am.
> The mist goes from the mirror and I see . . . ."
> (EP, 148)

Paracelsus asserts that he has penetrated the veil of phenomena (the mist) and attained unmediated or "free" experience of something superhuman and probably divine. But even when the mist has vanished from it, a mirror implies reflection, mediation. One might also argue with Girard that the mirror always implies the double and the other. Paracelsus's confirmation of his divinity requires an invidious comparison with those mere "men" who have failed to become gods. Meanwhile, Pound mediates his own divine longings through Paracelsus, who is his mirror, model, and mask. Such indirect approaches to godhead are probably necessary, for the myth of Actaeon teaches that proximity to the sacred can bring death.

In "Erat Hora," another early poem, sex transforms the speaker into the equal, even the envy of the onlooking gods:

> "Thank you, whatever comes." And then she turned
> And, as the ray of sun on hanging flowers
> Fades when the sun hath lifted them aside,
> When swiftly from me. Nay, whatever comes,
> One hour was sunlit and the most high gods
> May not make boast of any better thing
> Than to have watched that hour as it passed.
>
> (CEP, 150)

In the Provençal love lyric sexual union with the wife of an absent lord often leads to theophany: "Good Lady," says Piere Vidal, "I think I see God when I gaze on your delicate body" (SR, 96).

Pound traces chivalric love to agrarian and pagan traditions, which asserted a connection between sexuality and divinity. At Eleusis, the hierophant joined symbolically with the priestess Demeter, who acted the part of the god and goddess. Elsewhere in classical tradition mortals count it a sign of election to be sexually favored by the gods, and it is from such unions that the "man-god" comes into being. Among his numerous versions of this myth, such as Adonis and Tammuz, Pound evokes the sexual union of Anchises and Venus, whence springs the messianic culture hero, Aeneas. At the conclusion of Canto 79, Aphrodite is Cythera, the Great Mother, the divine unity underlying her numerous manifestations.

It seems reasonable to suppose a latent Oedipal content in a mythology that elevates the Great Mother and distinguishes between her good and bad forms. In *Totem and Taboo* Freud remarks that while "the notion of a man becoming a god" seems "shockingly presumptuous," this was not so in the agrarian cultures of ancient times. With the rise of agriculture the son became increasingly important, and in rebellion against the "father-gods" he "ventured upon new demonstrations of his incestuous libido," myths of "Attis, Adonis, and Tammuz," "youthful divinities enjoying the favors of mother goddesses and committing incest ... in defiance of their father" (Freud, 1: 149, 152). The Jews, however, remained mostly immune to this revolt. As Bernhard Berliner observes, the God of the Jews deifies the "super-ego" and "conscience" and "demands control of the instincts"; hence the Hebrew rejection of the matriarchal cults of the Near East.[3] Here is yet another reason why Pound, who links religion and sexuality, and who worships the mother goddesses in their purified form, should have hated and feared the patriarchal Jews.

Pound's religiosity, like his fascism, is pervaded by spiritual elitism. "The Greek gods," he says, ignored the "abstract love of mankind at large" and "loved" only "the elect, . . . the handpicked" (SP, 70). In *Guide to Kulchur* Pound freely translates Zeus' remark about Odysseus, with whom Pound identified: "A chap with a mind like THAT! the fellow is one of us. One of US" (GK, 146). When Pound praises paganism for never asserting that "everyone was fit for initiation" (SP, 56), he probably refers to the Eleusinian mysteries, whose initiate, says Plutarch, "lives with pure and holy men," and "sees on earth the crowd" of the uninitiated "crush and jostle themselves in the mud and darkness."[4] In contrast with the spiritual democracy and "humiliation doctrine" (RB, 199) of Judaism and Christianity, Confucianism is based on the idea that "order will emanate from," and that "the mandate of heaven" will fall upon, the man who "brings order into his own consciousness"; indeed, Chinese history affords "demonstrable evidence of this process" (SP, 66). Pound was no doubt thinking of himself as one of those who had received the mandate of heaven.

Light, observes Pound in his Postscript to *The Natural Philosophy of Love,* is a projection from the "brain" and "eye" of the creative genius. After comparing the genius to the Egyptian god Horus, also of the luminous eye, Pound goes on to speak of Frazer's "horned gods," and of those daring souls who, "in a primitive community," would have "risked" the dangers attending claims to godhood. "The immensely high head of the Chinese contemplative," he adds, ". . . is another stray grain of tradition" (PD, 210). Pound probably had in mind the dragon-horned culture hero Confucius, whose father, *The Cantos* report, had a cranial bump, and possibly the "electrified" (WT, 50) head of the god-victim Heracles in Sophocles' *Women of Trachis,* which Pound was to translate. The Postscript also calls to mind Pound. Since Pound associates the head of the genius with light, thought, sperm, and the phallus, his much-advertised assault on the "passive vulva" of London may be viewed as his attempt to confirm his status as a divinely-favored man. That Pound may have conceived of himself as divinely favored from childhood is suggested by the fact that as a boy he was nicknamed "Ra," which is short for Ezra and pronounced "ray," and identical with the name of the Egyptian sun-god (Stock, 3: 29). One wonders "whether Pound . . . does not sometimes wish to identify himself with the sun as the divine center of the cosmos" (Vasse: 115).

II.

Pound believed in full seriousness that modern man "may have need even of horned gods to save him, or at least of a form of thought which permits them" (PD, 206). Upward and Zielinski provided considerable support for such speculations. A "performing god," Wizard, and culture hero, Upward's Divine Man is persecuted from envy and undergoes singly the heroic "Initiation of the Saviour," which may include sacrifice. Where Judaism develops the idea of the Jewish people as the Suffering Servant, and Jesus later gives this concept universal form, Upward's Divine Man alone plays the role of Suffering Servant; his Hercules is "a man of sorrows and acquainted with grief." Meanwhile Zielinski attacks the Jews for rejecting the pagan man-god, whom a divinity fathers on a mortal woman, and who earns final apotheosis through superhuman exploits. This sounds like Hercules, who appears in Zielinski as the messianic founder of a golden age, and whom Pound took as a model.[5]

Pound's messianic quest becomes overt in the post-war period. In 1910 he wrote his mother "asking for exact information about the hour of his birth." Correlating this and "similar information" in an anonymous article in the spring issue of the *Little Review* in 1922, Pound determined exactly when the Christian era had ended and was replaced by paganism: midnight on October 29–30, 1921, or on the day (October 30) when Pound turned thirty-six and *Ulysses* was completed. The name of this new pagan age, said Pound, was "the Pound Era," a phrase which was not, as many people now may think, invented by Hugh Kenner.[6] Pound thus confirmed a prophecy made in the heyday of *Blast*, when he may have upset Wyndham Lewis by hanging a banner from the Rebel Arts Center; it read: "END OF CHRISTIAN ERA."[7]

In *The Little Review* calendar, the "END" of the "Christian era" is "followed" by the Feast of Zagreus Dionysus.[8] Thus is reversed the decadence lamented in *Mauberley*: "Christ follows Dionysus, / phallic and ambrosial." Pound's new pagan calendar is nearly contemporary with his "Cantus Planus," in which he compares himself implicitly to Zagreus and appropriates the god's totemic animals: leopards, lynxes, and cats, all of them, like the "cat-head" in the Postscript to Gourmont, signs of divinity. Here again Pound sees himself as the Dionysian Messiah of a new era: as Dionysus is born from the union of Zeus and Semele ("shot to atoms" by Zeus' light in Canto 92/ 621), in Pound's fantasy he is himself born of his mother's union with an unknown deity. Pound also associates the birth of the Italian poet Fracastorus, who had Zeus' lightning for "midwife" (5/ 20), with his own rescue from death during the blizzard of 1887. The saved child and lightning are motifs of Dionysus, the twice-born (Bacigalupo: 35–36).

Pound's calendar is an indispensable clue to his conception of himself. In Canto 9 Pound's hero Malatesta is "Poliorcetes" ("And it was his messianic year, Poliorcetes," 9/ 36). Known as Poliorcetes, "taker of cities," the Macedonian King Demetrios (336–253 B.C.) was deified as the "Saviour-God" and given honors usually reserved for Demeter and Dionysus (Feder: 295, 298). In imitation of Malatesta, with his Tempio at Rimini, Pound seeks to establish his own cult. Much later Pound's rivalry with Christianity emerges in his identification with Apollonius of Tyana, a pagan prophet of the first century A.D., and another version of the messianic child. Like Pound, who sees himself as a special advisor to Mussolini and Roosevelt, Apollonius advised emperors and kings and was charged with treason. Concluding his plea before Domitian, Apollonius told the court that he was immortal and then supposedly vanished.[9] Such fantasies of power and escape had special appeal for Pound during his confinement at St. Elizabeths.

Pound thought of himself as one of those "few intelligent spirits" whom "the Lord of the universe sends into this world in each generation" to "manage the rest" of mankind.[10] What Girard says of Nietzsche applies to Pound: one has only to substitute the word divinity for will to power:

> To write as he did, Nietzsche had to assume not only that there are undefeated champions of the will to power, but also that he must be one. His whole work is a hymn to that higher will. Had he not shared abundantly in the ultimate principle of the universe, how could he have discovered it?[11]

Numerous modern artists and geniuses have sought to be priests and even gods. Although Pound thought of Voltaire as the embodiment of anti-fanaticism, Voltaire had dreamed of founding a personal cult and a messianic era (CON, 191; Poliakov, 2, Vol. 3: 97). Nietzsche similarly sought to create his own pagan and Olympian cult, while Wagner was honored by "German youth" as a "dictator . . . in the name of the 'Chosen People,' the Germans."[12] Wagner's desire for domination was matched, as was Pound's, only by an unshakeable conviction of his moral purity.[13] In Nazism, the Germans are the Chosen People; the Jews are the Devil; and Hitler, a failed artist and Wagner-cultist, is the messiah (Viereck, 2: 287–288).

Yet Pound differs in a crucial way from most of these self-appointed messiahs. He knew that the Divine Man proves his messianic status through his "audience," his ability to control the crowd as a "performing god" (Upward, 2: 1). How else can one organize one's own cult? But for most of his career, Pound resembles the isolated and neglected Nietzsche rather than the enormously successful Wagner, Voltaire, or Hitler. Only at St. Elizabeths does Pound see a real cult develop around him, though it is neither Bayreuth, Ferney, nor Berlin. On the other hand, Pound probably surpasses these would-be Messiahs in his recognition of the risks of a messianic quest. As early as 1910 he speaks of a man who had escaped the quotidian into the clear light of the gods: ". . . Greek myth arose when someone having passed through delightful psychic experience tried to communicate it to others and found it necessary to screen himself from persecution" (SR, 92). Upward and Frazer had argued that in primitive societies the god is also victim, and that victimization is confirmation of divinity. Or as Pound said, the horned god would have been "deified, or crucified, or both."[14]

It is evident now why the Jews are not only Pound's opponent but his rival. Upward notes that the Greek "Christos" is equivalent to the Hebrew "Messiah," meaning the "anointed": the Messiah, whose head bears the holy oil, is the anointed of the Lord. In Hebrew culture he is the national warrior king, for instance Saul or David (the "prime s.o.b." Pound calls David in 74/ 429), while in Christianity this role in modified form belongs to another Jew, the pacifist Jesus Christ (Upward, 2: 97–98, 248–249). Since

Pound sought to replace Jesus, Jesus may be viewed as his rival. Since Jesus remains "alive" through his worshippers, this rivalry is real. Pound emphasizes Jesus' Jewishness, which supposedly kept him from finding "an antidote to Judaism," and which resulted in Christianity "becoming unbearable" (SP, 57). Thus Pound attacks and identifies with Jesus, who, he says, "was crucified for trying to BUST a [Jewish] racket" (RB, 188). As Zagreus, and as an anti-Semite, Pound intends to repair Jesus' failures or else suffer his fate.

There is yet another and more profound reason for Pound's anti-Semitism. Although a Jew, Jesus rebelled against the religion of his people, who denied his messianic claims and punished him with death. Obviously, if the Jews rejected the first Messiah, they will probably reject the second, namely Pound. The idea of the Messiah, notes Upward, "was a heresy against the strict monotheism which recognized no divine Person except Jehovah; it was a belief for which there was no warrant in the Law" (Upward, 2: 303).

Repeatedly Pound stresses that the Jews claim exclusive access to God and hold other religions in disdain: "The Gods made heaven and earth. Then came Jehoveh and the Jew boy. I made it, get the hell out of here" (RB, 211). The term "Jew boy" suggests that the paternal Jehovah is close only to his chosen people, his boys. To quote *The Divine Mystery*: "The Hebrew worshipper enjoys a tremendous intimacy with his God. It is this which gives to his outpourings that peculiar quality to which we rightly give the name of inspiration" (Upward, 2: 214). Upward traces this feeling to the period between Ezra and Christ, when the Jews "unfortunately" came to believe "that they were in full possession of the divine will," for "the mind of God has few secrets from the monotheist." In fact, "like his Christian representatives of today, the Jewish Pharisee firmly believed that the book of revelation was closed," and that God's "will was fully expressed in the Law of Moses." "The Chosen People had only to comply with its requirements to entitle themselves to the full benefit of the promises made to their forefathers."[15] Such privilege could could only have filled Pound with horror and envy: a rabble enjoying the full power of the divine will and tremendous intimacy with God— that which rightfully belongs to the Genius.

III.

Pound's escalating and envious rivalry with the Jews needs to be understood in the context of the poet's career. To all appearances Pound's poetic fortunes were in decline throughout the 1930s, when the supposedly megalomaniacal Jews were, at least in Pound's mind, in the ascendancy. Indeed, by the 1940s Pound was deeply frustrated and disappointed. The young Pound had been a true *enfant terrible* or "infant Gargantua" (PD, 48), like the Hercules who strangled snakes in his crib. But despite his many achievements, Pound failed to win the literary dictatorship of England. The

Vorticist adventure was interrupted by World War I, and in neither America nor England did Pound set off a Renaissance or "Risorgimento" (L, 10; Norman: 70). By 1924 Pound had retreated to the comparative isolation of Rapallo, where he moved toward fascism and saw himself as an influential political figure. Yet his abortive visit to save America proved his distance from the nation's mood, and in Italy he was ignored by Mussolini and even distrusted by Italian Fascist ministers, who found his broadcasts suspicious.[16] During the late 1930s Pound also felt unappreciated as a writer. As he told Wyndham Lewis before Lewis's visit to the U.S. in 1939: "You better do a build up of EZ / on ground that I am their most distinguished writer and they OUGHT bloodydamnwell to DO something about it" (P/L, 216–217).

It is not surprising that these disappointments of the 1930s should coincide with Pound's increasingly obsessive messianic impulse. Apart from his personally motivated propaganda for paganism, one thinks of his 1939 voyage to America, to talk sense into Roosevelt and "to keep hell from breaking loose in the world."[17] In spite of poverty, Pound managed to travel first class on the opulent Italian luxury liner *Rex,* whose name suggests the royal status accorded the Messiah or Savior. "I shall go on Rex or something large," Pound told Wyndham Lewis in a letter of March 2, 1939, for he preferred to be "2nd on colossus to capn's KaBIN on a small tub" (P/L, 206). Begun soon thereafter, Pound's broadcasts stand within a tradition of millenarian prophecy and repeatedly contain the theme of salvation, specifically from Jews; the saviors, as we have seen, are Mussolini and Hitler. Like them, Pound in his broadcasts is "curin' the world's diseases" (RB, 195), will "save what's left of America" (RB, 49). "Out of these talks," says Pound, "the young men of England and America will have to build their souls"; without them, they may "never get into life at all" (RB, 191). Like a latter-day Apollonius of Tyana, Pound thinks seriously of going to Japan as a special emissary and of conferring with Stalin (RB, 25–26; Olson: 39, 62; Heymann: 158, 175, 193). In his absolute commitment and belief in his "special . . . mission" (RB, 95), Pound resembles those millenarian leaders whom Cohn compares to paranoid schizophrenics (Cohn, 1: 265).

The following statement, which Dr. Joseph L. Gilbert delivered at Pound's trial, contains a summary of the poet's condition as Pound described it in 1945:

> When I have seen him he complained that for at least four years he felt unusually fatigued . . . and that when those symptoms of fatigue are more marked he describes his feelings at the time as being unable to get flat enough in bed . . . during long periods of interviews with him he remained reclining in bed, with the additional symptoms of restlessness, rather rapid movements about the bed, and suddenly sitting or rising to the upright sitting position, or to move quickly about from the bed to a table nearby to get some paper, book, or manuscript, and to as suddenly throw himself on the bed and again assume the reclining position. This fatigue and exhaustion, which he states was com-

pletely reducing him, as he said, to the level of an imbecile in his thinking capacity, was notwithstanding the fact that he was undergoing no amount of physical activity.

He spoke of his mental processes being in a fog, to use his own words, that he admits during these periods of severe fatigue that he was unable to undertake temporarily any mental activity, and also complained of pressure throughout various regions of the head, what he described as a feeling of hollowness, going through this gesture (indicating) with his fingers, describing the vortex of the skull, indicating that there was a feeling not only of pressure but of hollowness in that particular part of the cranium.[18]

Charles Olson observes that Pound makes a "great deal of the head," the fruitful sphere and the source of man's power (Olson: 102). But in this description the "vortex" of the skull—and here Gilbert may be quoting Pound—is powerless and empty, and Pound feels enormous external pressure concentrated at precisely this point. He was presumably in this condition during the broadcasts, when his anti-Semitism reached its height.

Pound assumes that the "great artist," as a version of the Divine Man or "performing god," "has in the end, always, his audience."[19] Thus, whether in exile or in triumph, the artist remains conscious of the crowd, the very measure of his power: "The party that follows" the artist "wins . . . . Blessed are they who pick the right artists and makers" (SP, 215). But in the late 1930s, Pound experiences widespread indifference, and this, as Girard shows, is a harder thing for the messianic artist to take than opposition.[20] Cut off and powerless, Pound is like the luckless and "lone Jew" (RB, 330) in the broadcasts. It is clear then why Pound, given the chance, broadcast from Rome. He pursues that audience which he requires in order to prove his status as Divine Man and performing god.

Yet this move occurs precisely at the moment when the "big Jews" are fulfilling the destiny which Pound predicted in 1919:

> . . . Since the lions of the Tribe of Judah gave up the sword, "beat it," metaphorically into the pawn shop, their power has steadily increased; no such suave and uninterrupted extension of power is to be attributed to any "world conquering," bellicose nation.[21]

Pound's association of the Jews with power extends to the Jewish god, whom he secretly admired. In Canto 50 Pound says of Pope Pius the Sixth that "no Jew God / wd have kept THAT in power" (50/ 247). Whereas in the previous quotation he had used the Jews as an example of non-violence, in the broadcasts they are at once violent and megalomaniac. The "Kike is out for all power" (RB, 120), and every loss of power in the West increases the power of the Jews.

Thus the Jews confirm themselves as the Chosen People. Besides controlling the passive crowds of America and England, the "Jew boy[s]" (RB, 211) have direct access to the power which their Jehovah confers. Pound remarks with disgust that the "British poisoners [of Jewish origin] have become sacred persons" (RB, 171). In another broadcast he reports that the "old bleeders will all be Christ child, and Santy Claus" (RB, 199). Since Pound himself sought to replace Christ as the divine child, one can see the envy which the last remark contains. The aged yet curiously ageless Jews possess what the aging Pound has desired all along: they have become Messiahs, like the Christ Child, and enjoy divine power. They have fulfilled the destiny promised in the *Protocols,* in which they are chosen by God himself "to reign over the world." As Pound conceives of F.D.R. as the Jews' puppet, so in the *Protocols* the Jewish elders secretly grant power to sovereigns and prepare a "universal ruler" of "Zionist blood" (*Protocols:* 24, 25, 20, 21).

In the broadcasts Pound refers to the Jews as the "oily race" (RB, 219), and to Karl Marx, inseparable in Pound's mind from his Jewishness, as "oily" (RB, 189). In an earlier essay he had condemned "hair oil boys," "hair oil organs," and "Broadway hair oil" (SP, 161–163), all implicitly references to Jewish exploiters of mass culture and merchandising. These phrases conceal an unconscious and honorific intent buried beneath the foul abuse, while their recurrence points to Pound's anxiety toward his rivals. Frazer observes that the Hebrew King or Messiah was "regarded as in a sense divine, . . . embodying Jehovah on earth," while "the application of the holy oil to his head was believed to impart to him directly a portion of the divine spirit" (Frazer: 20–21). When Pound says that the "old bleeders will be all Christ Child," he means that they will be Messiahs; and the Messiah is the anointed one, whose oiled hair symbolizes power, light, and authority. During the broadcasts Pound felt "not only . . . pressure but . . . hollowness" in his head. This remark reveals his ontological deprivation at the very moment when the Jews had supposedly received anointment.[22]

IV.

Pound's anti-Semitism involves not just Pound and his Jewish phantom but the crowd. As his anti-Semitism escalates, nothing more clearly proves his divine power than control over the passive Gentile multitudes. That the Gentile world is the disputed object in this imaginary rivalry is evident in that Pound, like his Jewish enemies, conceives of the "goyim" as a herd of domestic animals, "sheep," "pigs," and "cattle."[23] But in this rivalry the Jews have an unfair advantage. Since Pound's anti-Semitic metaphors are first applied to Gentile crowds in America and London, the Jews and Gentiles would seem in some ways predisposed to each other. Indeed, not only are the Gentile multitudes monotheistic, as are the Jews, but Jehovah "keeps a troublesome rabble in order" (SR, 95), and Protestantism is largely Judaism in disguise.

About a year before his first broadcasts Pound wrote to Ronald Duncan:

Blasted friends left a goddamn radio here yester. Gift. God damn destructive and dispersive devil of an invention. But got to be faced. Drammer has got to face it, not only face cinema. Anybody who *can* survive may strengthen inner life, but mass of apes and worms will be still further rejuiced to passivity. Hell a state of passivity? Or Limbo?

Anyhow what drammer or teeyater *wuz*, radio is. Possibly the loathing of it may stop diffuse writing. No sense in print *until* it gets to finality? Also the histrionic developments in announcing. And the million to one chance that audition will develop: at least to a faculty for picking the fake in the voices. Only stuff fit to hear was Tripoli, Sofia, and Tunis. Howling music in two of 'em and a cembalo in Bugarea.

And a double sense of the blessedness of silence when the damn thing is turned off.

Anyhow, if you're writin' for styge or teeyater up to date, you gotter measure it all, not merely against cinema, but much more against the personae now poked into every bleedin' 'ome and smearing the mind of the peepull. If anyone is a purfekk HERRRRkules, he may survive, and *may* clarify his style in resistance to the devil box. I mean if he ain't druv to *melancholia crepitans* before he recovers.

I anticipated the damn thing in the first third of Cantos and was able to do 52/71 because I was the last survivin monolith who did not have a bloody radio in the 'ome. However, like the subjects of sacred painting as Mr. Cohen said: "Vot I say iss, ve got to svallow 'em, vot I say iss, ve got to svallow 'em." Or be boa constricted. (L, 342–343)

The radio is a form of the masses, for Pound speaks of "personae" "poked into every bleedin' 'ome." To go on the radio, even to listen to it, is to enter a vast crowd.[24]

Pound was revolted by the abundant human "carrion" in Paris and London, an association partly explained by the crowd-like ubiquity of germs, which are communicated in crowds. In the above passage Pound compares the effects of the radio, in his time *the* instrument of mass communication, with those of infectious diseases; like radio waves, germs travel on the air and work their greatest effects on crowds. Infection also figures implicitly in Pound's references to survival, strength, resistance, and recovery. When Pound calls himself the "last survivin monolith," he sees himself as one who has "faced" the "devil box" and its "dispersive" multitude of voices. "Monolith" further suggests fascist rigidity, definition, and immunity, the enormous resistance and god-like power of a survivor.[25] What radio disease is Pound referring to? It is probably propaganda-induced hysteria, which sweeps through a crowd like an epidemic and turns its members into passive "apes," frightened imitators of each other. Those not favored by the gods—and Pound is the perfect Hercules to whom he refers—suffer the simultaneous transformations of the "gadarene swine, taken with collective hysteria."

And yet, ironically, Pound's response to the radio is mimetic. Although the radio reduces the masses to passivity because of histrionic developments, the "fake in the voices," to master the crowd Pound will resort to the same vocal dissimulation and histrionics. A similar mimesis (and oral aggression) is suggested when Pound refers to the devil box as the maw of a snake. The alternatives are to be devoured whole or to swallow up the enemy. Given Pound's conception of the Jews as "chews," it seems fitting that the second and preferable alternative has been proposed by one Mr. Cohen, a "Chew." As for Pound's warnings of the Jewish and "Roosevelt hysteria" (RB, 32), these hardly conceal his true purpose, which is to use the radio to induce panic in the Gentile crowd.

There is a further mimetic aspect to Pound's radio broadcasts. Pound is probably imitating Mussolini, who could "speak efficiently to the crowd / in piazza" (98/ 686), Hitler, and the proto-Fascist poet Gabriele D'Annunzio, of whom Pound said enviously that he "could move the crowd in a theater" (93/ 630). Because of their histrionic gifts, these mediumistic personalities communicated to the despised crowd "its own, deeply buried spirit" (Nolte: 372). But Pound is obviously less successful than his models; he confronts the crowd not in the theater or piazza but on the radio. Nor does Pound communicate effectively in the broadcasts. Committed to preserving his arcanum, and yet drawn to the world of *l'opinion*, Pound works at cross purposes. His broadcasts are a wierd mélange of esoteric pedantry, elliptical private reference, self-quotation, and pseudo-folksy sententiousness in the style of American populism. Finally, Pound knows that he has virtually no audience. In the supposed "maze of Jew covered American radio transmissions," it is miraculous if a single "listener" (RB, 104–105) hears him.

Thus the performing god discovers the same indifference as before. Now Pound has no need to maintain monolithic "resistance" against the crowd, or to complain of that "opposition" (L, 232) which he considered necessary to the exercise of power and personality. What Pound now perceives as resistance is really a paranoiac investment of the outer world "boundlessly with . . . [his] own content."[26] Nor can Pound remain a monolith. Because his audience is absent, Pound faces a vacuum which must be filled; and the only way to fill it is through the elaborate schizophrenic histrionics of the broadcasts, the "fake in the voices." In imitating numerous American accents—New England, Midwestern, Southern, Pennsylvanian—Pound is not just the performer but the absent, desired, and despised audience, which he incarnates through an endless succession of voices and masks (Norman: 387; Heymann: 105).

This "aping" of the crowd must increase Pound's fears of bacilli and Jews, whom he associates with the contagious transformations of crowd existence. The Jews make use of numerous Gentile "carriers" (SP, 317) or zombies, who pursue the Jewish cause; it is as if the crowd, by a kind of demonic possession, were about to be transformed into the Jewish enemy; as if the Jews, embodiment of "devilment," were about to become legion.[27] Yet simultaneously they have become "sacred persons," masters of the very crowd which Pound desired.

Chapter Twenty-Two

The Doubles

We have piled up much evidence of Pound's hatred of Jews, yet we have also begun to see that this hatred masks a curious fascination and even emulation. The Jews are not just Pound's scapegoats but his models. The example of Pound would thus confirm René Girard's argument that intense hatred and rivalry are the ultimate consequence of imitative desire, moving through stages of imitation, worship, frustration, denial, hatred, and hostility. At first the subject not only identifies with his model but worships him. But to imitate another's desires completely is to desire to replace him and appropriate his object of desire: "Imitative desire is always a desire to be Another . . . . Two desires converging on the same object are bound to clash." Thus, to his surprise, the subject suddenly discovers himself in competition with his model, and his attitude toward him changes. Because the model prevents the fulfillment of the subject's desires, he has become a dangerous rival and obstacle deserving the intensest reciprocal hatred: Girard emphasizes that men reserve genuine hatred only for someone who prevents them from satisfying a desire. Now the subject scrupulously represses or conceals all indications of his original admiring identification with his despised model. Now he seeks to belittle his mediator (and imagined oppressor), to claim that his desires are totally different from the mediator's, that the mediator is an imposter. But since the subject secretly worships the mediator and that which he possesses, he continues to imitate him, but in secret. In attacking the mediator the subject blindly attacks himself while seeking to keep his identity with the mediator from emerging into consciousness.[1]

Pound was originally committed to his father's Protestantism and received a Sunday school education in the Old Testament. As Pound admitted, not only had he "read the Bible daily in childhood" (RB, 117), but he had taken the Old Testament "for granted, and . . . with great seriousness" (GK, 330). In his teens Pound "continue[d] to study Dante and the Hebrew prophets," as he told his parents, and the prophetic stance and tone appears in his early poem "From Chebar," in which Pound is an American Ezekiel. Only later did he begin to repudiate Protestantism as a form of Judaism in disguise (Stock, 3: 28–29, 44).

Charles Olson recollected James Laughlin's conversation with Pound: "He [Laughlin] appeared to have been surprised they found him [Pound] 'insane.' I [Olson] demurred. But he [Laughlin] came back with the remark. 'But this morning he [Pound] came up with a remark like this, over the Jewish question: "It's too bad, and just when I had plans to rebuild the Temple in Jerusalem for them" ' " (Olson: 77). One recalls *The Cantos*, in which Pound, the enemy of "David Rex / the prime s.o.b.," seeks to "redeem Zion with justice" (74/ 429, 440) and again to "rebuild" (76/ 454) Zion and the Temple of Jerusalem. In fact, in Canto 74 he quotes from Jeremiah's directions (Jer. 31. 38–40) for building the city. But Pound's statement to Laughlin has a deeper significance. For can we suppose that Pound had never read the Book of Ezra?

The Book of Ezra treats the rebuilding of the Temple of Jerusalem after the Babylonian exile and the renewal of the Covenant. Priest, scribe, and great lawgiver, Ezra is known as the father of Judaism. His "greatest contribution was to establish the Pentateuch as the authoritative canon for Jewish faith and practice," and thus to define the "sacred scripture" which constitutes "the community's rule for faith and conduct." Ezra's reforms coincide with the restoration of Jerusalem and the establishment of the Jews as a tight-knit, cultic community after a long exile (Bernhard Anderson: 451–455).

The Book of Ezra is an exceedingly ethnocentric document, demanding the sharpest distinctions between Jews and non-Jews:

> And thou Ezra, after the wisdom of thy God, that *is* in thine hand, set magistrates and judges, which may judge all the people that *are* beyond the river, all such as know the laws of thy God; and teach ye then that know *them* not. And whosoever will not do the law of thy God, and the law of the king, let judgment be executed speedily upon him, whether *it be* unto death, or to banishment, or to confiscation of goods, or to imprisonment.
>
> (Ezra 7: 25–27)

Ezra's language contains imagery of filth, profanation, and defilement. He accuses those outside the cult of all sorts of abomination:

> The land, into which ye go to possess it, is an unclean land with the filthiness of the people of the lands, with their abominations, which have filled it from one end to another with uncleanness.
>
> (Ezra 9: 11)

The sin which Ezra especially deplores is mixed marriage. The Jews have contaminated their "holy seed" with that of foreigners:

> The people of Israel, and the priests, and the Levites, have not separated themselves from the people of the lands, *doing* according to their abominations . . . . For they have taken of their daughters for themselves, and for their sons; so that the holy seed have mingled themselves with the people of *those*

lands . . . . Now therefore give not your daughters unto their sons, nor take their daughters unto your sons, nor seek their peace or their wealth forever: that ye may be strong, and eat the good of the land, and leave *it* for an inheritance to your children forever.

(Ezra 9: 1, 3, 12)

The similarities between the Biblical Ezra and Ezra Pound are uncanny. Both believe themselves recipients of "the mandate of Heaven" (SP, 66). Both seek to restore an endangered tradition and to rebuild an ideal city: Ezra, the city of Jerusalem, Pound, the city of Dioce, whose "terraces are the color of stars" (74/ 425). Both seek to restore the ethnic purity and cultural inheritance of a group by forbidding contact with aliens and outsiders. Both sit in judgment on their enemies, of whom they speak in terms of abomination, filth, and contamination, and whom they condemn to banishment and even death. Both denounce false wealth and promise an age of abundance, "the good of the land." Finally, they seek to establish a body of classic and sacred texts as the lasting basis of the cultural community.[2]

Since Pound never mentions Ezra, one might explain this resemblance as coincidence. However, Pound's absorbing hatred of the Jews requires us to postulate an original identification with them, and specifically with Ezra and the other Jewish prophets. This identification traces to childhood, and is ultimately based on a linguistic principle stated by Freud in *Totem and Taboo:* children "are never ready to accept a similarity between two words as having no meaning; . . . If two things are called by similar-sounding names," there is "some deep-lying point of agreement between them" (Freud, 1: 56). In short, the young Protestant Ezra Pound once thought consciously of himself as being like the prophet whose name he bore. There is still another reason why the young Pound should have initially admired Ezra and the Jews. In *The Divine Mystery* Upward associates the Ezraic reforms and the restoration of the Temple with the Jews' new conviction of their exclusive relationship with their god; Ezra convinced them that they were the Chosen People, "in full possession of the divine will." Thanks to Ezra, the Jews claim the very privilege that Pound would claim for himself. On the other hand, the Jews' belief that "the book of revelation was closed" explains their status as obstacles. The Jews need neither a second Ezra (Pound) nor a Gentile Messiah.[3]

To obtain comparable closeness to the divinity Pound must in some sense "become a Jew." But to become a Jew is unacceptable to Pound for at least two reasons. Not only does Pound view Judaism as a religion of the herd, but every Jew must submit to circumcision, which marks his difference from other groups and which God exacts for his allegiance. While the herd violates Pound's spiritual elitism, circumcision, a form of sexual mutilation and absence, violates his estimation of the phallus. Nonetheless, these purely ideological objections and differences ultimately amount to smokescreens, self-justifications after an initial and frustrated fascination with the Jews

(Girard, 1: 73–74). The inadequacy of Pound's claims to being different from the Jews is most evident in his fears of Jewish bacilli, his castration anxiety, and his harping on Jewish circumcision and phallic absence, as if it were necessary constantly to increase the diminishing difference between himself and his enemies.[4]

II.

However much abuse Pound heaps upon the Jews, he is drawn unconsciously toward his enemies and the power which they supposedly hold. This, coupled with Pound's unacknowledged and repeated impulse to imitate Jewish behavior, is decisive proof that the Jews are his secret model. In Canto 22 Pound recalls visiting a synagogue in Gibralter in 1908 in the company of Yusuf, a Jewish guide:

> And we went down to the synagogue,
> All full of silver lamps
> And the top gallery stacked with old benches;
> And in came the levite and six little choir kids
> And began yowling the ritual
> As if it was crammed full of jokes,
> And they went through a whole book of it;
> And in came the elders and the scribes
> About five or six and the rabbi
> And he sat down, and grinned, and pulled out his snuff-box
> And snuffed up a thumb-full, and grinned,
> And called over a kid from the choir, and whispered,
> And nodded toward one old buffer,
> And the kid took him the snuff-box and he grinned,
> And bowed his head, and sniffed up a thumb-full,
> And the kid took the box back to the rabbi,
> And he grinned, e faceva bisbiglio, [whispered]
> And the kid toted off the box to
>   another old bunch of whiskers,
> And he snuffed up his thumb-full,
> And so on till they'd each had his sniff.
>
> (22/ 104–105)

In this early and comparatively innocuous instance of Pound's anti-Semitism, Jewish ritual is an amusing exercise involving whispering and sniffing; later Pound is obsessed with Jewish secrecy and smells. But so far Pound has described the ritual from outside. Next Pound sees himself as the Jews see him:

> And then the rabbi looked at the stranger, and they
> All grinned half a yard wider, and the rabbi
> Whispered for about two minutes longer,
> An' the kid brought the box over to me,
> And I grinned and snuffed up my thumb-full . . . .
>
> (22/ 105)

Pound is the stranger. The rabbi looks at him inquisitively, and then whispers something about Pound. What was said about him is not revealed, but the Jews' actions are telling. Pound is included in the service and obligingly grins and sniffs as the Jews had done earlier.[5] It seems that Pound, in being included in the ritual, had been taken for a Jew. Why else would he have been included in the ritual? How else explain his presence in the company of a Jewish guide? Indeed, why had Pound entered the synagogue? Later his guide asserts categorically what this scene renders ambiguous: "Yais, he ees a goot fello, / But after all a chew / ees a chew" (22/ 105).[6]

Horkheimer and Adorno note that every anti-Semite "basically want[s] to imitate his mental image of a Jew . . .: the argumentative movement of a hand, the musical voice painting a vivid picture of things and feelings irrespective of . . . what is said, and the nose—the physiognomic *principium individuationis* . . . ."[7] In the broadcasts Pound frequently imitates a Jewish or rather Yiddish accent: "chewisch," "yittisch" (RB, 198), "bischniscz" (RB, 229, 297). Since Pound emphasizes the undesirability of imitating the Jews, such imitation is most curious. Michael Reck recalls that Pound, when raging against Roosevelt, whom he considered a kind of Jew, "assumed a Jewish accent (for some obscure reason) and actually bit his thumb" (Reck, 1: 115). Compare Olson's memoir of St. Elizabeths:

> Pound had also performed for K [Jerome Kavka, one of Pound's psychiatrists, and a Jew] what he calls his YIDDISH CHARLESTON, composed originally for Louis Zukofsky. K says it is something! and regrets he didn't get a recording. A dance which Pound does, with gesture, movement, words. (Olson: 66)

"The Semitic," said Pound, "is excess . . . . Under stress of emotion, the Jew seems to lose his sense of reality" (SP, 86, 65).

It is understandable that Pound was not infrequently mistaken for a Jew. Although he complained that a Jewish artist, in painting his portrait, had given him a "Semitic image," the portrait was probably accurate. Noel Stock reports that an acquaintance of Pound's, seeing his portrait by Gaudier-Brzeska, thought him Jewish. In this portrait the nose, the "physiognomic *principium individuationis*," is emphasized.[8] On another occasion Pound's social behavior seemed "Jewish." As Wyndham Lewis remarked, before World War I he lunched frequently at the Vienna Cafe with "a man who had an excellent nose for Jews . . . ." Lewis's friends at the cafe thought Pound a "real Jew . . . a subtle blend, but a pukka kosher."[9] Mario Praz likewise said of Pound that he is "rumored to be a Jew."[10] All this explains Pound's eagerness to justify his worrisome Hebraic first name. "Don't worry about my biblical name," he told Douglas Fox, "English puritans emigrated to New England in 1638, mostly with names chosen from Scripture."[11]

By the 1930s Pound imitates his idea of the Jews almost instinctively, move by move. "The idea of a chosen race," says Pound, "is thoroughly semitic."[12] But what does Pound himself do? Increasingly he appeals to racial doctrines and the exclusiveness of the European community. What of Pound's accusation that the Jews are out for vengeance against the West? In response he proposes a "purge," a pogrom "up at the top." Though Pound charges that the Jews treat Gentiles as sheep or cattle, the view of men as stupid cows and sheep runs through his works. As for his accusation that the Jews create crowd "hysteria," what, if not that, is the purpose of the radio broadcasts? Consider too Pound's assertion that the Jews increase their power over Gentiles through secret and intimate contact among themselves, what Pound calls "interlocking . . . directorates" (RB, 253). His response to this supposed conspiracy is mimetic: "The world [can] . . . only be saved by a conspiracy of intelligent men" (RB, 185).[13] The power of such a conspiracy, like the Jews', depends on that intimate "contact" which Pound admires (and yet also deplores) in those elites who rule by "conversation" (RB, 149). It also depends on the "secretum," secret knowledge which assures mastery. Pound remarks of his sacred mysteries that the "cult was of the few"; he adds that the "Un-understanding and incapable of understanding what went on in temples, the gross apes destroyed them . . . ."[14] Not only does this elite and endangered cult resemble Judaism, it really stands opposed to the culture as a whole, and even in its ascendancy is isolated: "the anti-semitic church," though it "built the cathedrals" and "evolved a few clean economic ideas," existed in a "penumbra"; a "vast deal of ignorance surrounded even these few ideas."[15] Like Maurras, Pound would limit the true and vital core of a culture to an *élite généreuse* (Nolte: 145).

No less ironically, Pound associates the Jews with effacement, erosion, and fragmentation. Reducing the Western heritage to "fragments that can be sold in antique shops" (RB, 219), the Jews "cut off" all that is culturally organic in the West. Yet Pound does very nearly the same thing. Asserting that "All the Jew part of the Bible is black evil," Pound wonders "how soon one can get rid of it without killing the patient." Pound would "get rid of worst and rottenest phases first, i.e., the old testy-munk, barbarous blood sac[rifice], etc., and gradually detach Dantescan light (peeling off the Middle Ages bit by bit, that bloody swine St. Clement, etc.)" (L, 345). One is reminded of Ernst Nolte's description of Maurras, who, "like a sculptor, . . . blithely chips away from his statue of the *patrie* the bits of national history that do not correspond to the harmonious image of his goddess" (Nolte: 145). When Pound has finished peeling away the false layers of culture, of which there are many, his goddess will stand again in clear outline on her pedestal at Terracina.

III.

The symmetry of Pound's doctrines with those of the Jews is the most terrifyingly intimate sign of the "sacrificial crisis" in the broadcasts, a breakdown of differences between individuals and things, sacred and profane, through quarrels over power, divinity, sacred objects. As violence escalates, the sacred and profane are no longer distinguishable, and the antagonists become unrecognized doubles of each other.[16]

For Pound violence is always what Girard terms a "signifier of the divinity." Constantly presuming his own righteousness, Pound believes throughout the broadcasts that he is free from profane violence, that he of all men knows the violent yet sacred means to bring conflict to an end. Once he has saddled the Jews with responsibility for the plague, once they are confirmed as monsters, absolutely different, their sacrificial expulsion will restore peace. But this project of differentiation encounters problems. Since Pound's broadcasts fail to stop the war, they are just another example of random rather than divine violence. Moreover, far from becoming victims, the supposedly violent Jews have become "sacred persons," Kings of the West. Even worse, there is no longer a difference between sacred and profane violence, Gentile crowds and Jewish bacilli, rightful victors and victims. Now anyone can play the scapegoat role, and this includes Pound himself (Girard, 2: 143, 151–152, 158–159).

In the broadcasts Pound compares Gentiles to sacrificial beasts such as lambs, sheep, cattle, pigs. Projected onto the Gentile other or "goyim," such animal imagery reflects among other things Pound's increasing fear that, surrounded by Jewish persecutors, he too will become a lamb led to the slaughter: as Girard says, the "loss of distinctions between man and beast . . . is always linked to violence" (Girard, 2: 128). This fear of becoming the Jews' victim is the other side of Pound's desire to persecute them. It also follows from his imaginary competition with the Jews for divinity.

First responsible for social violence, on its murder the scapegoat becomes an object of worship. It thus resembles Upward's Divine Man, who in turn resembles Pound: "The awe inspired by the thunder extends to its representative, the visible incarnation of its power. Who shall tell what are the limits of that power, or what other dangers lurk in that trembling frame? Saint, holy, accursed, consecrated—all these words once had the same meaning: the Wizard is *tapu*" (Upward, 2: 9). Bringing dangers and immense "power," the Divine Man signifies violence and appears where the sacred and taboo merge; thus, like the Jews, he is a likely candidate for victimization. Meantime each act of violence that Pound commits against the Jews brings him nearer to his enemies. As the Jews represent sacrificial Jehovah, so Pound manifests sacrificial aggression and patriarchal rage. As Pound sees the Jews as victims, so, in tainting himself with violence, he prepares his own victimization.

In the last stages of the mimetic process, as Pound becomes more and more like his idea of the Jews, he is truly *obsessed* by his enemies: his imagined understanding of their desires becomes more profound and intimate and his hatred more intense. Even so, he insists all the more strenuously on the difference between himself and the Jews; he fails to realize that he condemns himself and his own desires in the form of the encroaching Other, toward whom he is secretly drawn. Pound's complaints of personal and ontological depletion caused by Jewish persecutors really signify "a flight toward the Other through which the substance of his being flows away." The same is true of Pound's fears of Jewish contact and bacilli, for "contagion and proximity are, after all, one and the same phenomenon" (Girard, 1: 64, 99). When Pound denounces Jewish bacilli, he reveals a secret attraction toward the Jews.

Even as he approaches, in Girard's terms, "the Other is more fascinating the less accessible he is, . . . the more he tends towards instinctive automatism." In much of literature, according to Girard, "the obscure [animal] universe is . . . that of the mediator"; victims, like Pound, of mediated desire, Stavrogin and Svidrigailov dream of spiders, snakes, and vermin (Girard, 1: 285–287). Similarly in Pound's broadcasts the Jewish bacilli belong to the "obscure universe" and live according to that automatism which parallels Pound's instinctive and automatic imitation of the Jews. These bacilli are insidious, ignoring the barriers between inside and outside, having the power to invade, gnaw, infect, and create colonies of their own within the subject; and they can kill. Finally, these bacilli are conclusive signs of the double. They proliferate endlessly, cast off endless duplicates of themselves. In the ubiquitous and encroaching terror of "Jewish" bacilli, Pound feels the proximity of the double, who now attacks him not only from without, but from within.

The bacilli are the equivalent of what Girard calls the "monstrous double," which characterizes the last stages of the sacrificial crisis, when "unrecognized reciprocity" and undifferentiation produce monsters, delirium, and "hallucinatory phenomena." Symbolizing the violent confusion of crisis, this hallucinatory being diverts attention from the fact that men have become violent doubles of each other and are thus implicated in the collapse of differences. Indeed, there is no essential difference between any of the human doubles and the monstrous double. Yet in its monstrosity the monstrous double is perceived as the alien embodiment and cause of crisis. It thus enables the antagonists to exteriorize the crisis in which they are immersed, to represent it and project it beyond themselves, to avoid their own victimization. In short, the emergence of the monstrous double means that purifying violence, the recovery of difference, is imminent: the monstrous double is another name for the scapegoat, invariably associated with monstrous undifferentiation (Girard, 2: 164, 160, 161).

The Addendum to Canto 100 was written in the early 1940s. Like the broadcasts, it is hallucinatory, filled with duplicating, proliferating monstrosities:

> The Evil is Usury, *neschek*
> the serpent . . . .
> The canker corrupting all things, Fafnir the worm,
> Syphilis of the State, of all kingdoms,
> Wart of the common-weal,
> Wenn-maker, corrupter of all things.
> Darkness the defiler,
> Twin evil of envy,
> Snake of the seven heads, Hydra, entering all things. . . .
>   (Addendum, 100/ 798)

A self-duplicating worm, usury is also syphilis, whose germs create doubles of themselves while eating away within; cancer, a monstrous duplication of cellular life; the many-headed snake, an amphibious Hydra; and "Twin evil of envy," a double.[17] These lines also imply violence, for usury attacks the state and brings death and profanation, evoked in this case as the breakdown of inner and outer: Usury "passes" the "doors of temples" and "defiles" the "grove of Paphos" (Addendum, 100 / 798). Like the scapegoat, Usury is a parasite, a wenn or cancer, a monstrous excrescence to be excised from the organic community.

Usury's accretion of monstrous qualities constitutes a new difference. It is thus possible to name, to isolate the monstrous double, just as one can name the scapegoat at the height of the crisis: "Usury, . . . *neschek,* whose name is known" (Addendum, 100/ 798). The fact remains, however, that this monstrous double is finally indistinguishable from the Jews and Pound. Pound blames the Jews for *neschek,* and Addendum to Canto 100 concludes with an attack on Jewish opium racketeers. And, since the monster is ubiquitous and pervasive, corrupting and poisoning "all things," it can penetrate, dominate, transform, and "possess" Pound:

> The subject [Girard says] feels that the most intimate regions of his being have been invaded by a supernatural creature who besieges him without. Horrified, he finds himself the victim of a double assault to which he cannot respond. Indeed, how can one defend oneself against an enemy who blithely ignores all barriers between inside and outside? This extraordinary freedom of movement permits the god—or spirit or demon—to seize souls at will. The condition called "possession" is in fact but one particular interpretation of the monstrous double. (Girard, 2: 165)

As Girard connects possession with the last stages of mimetic reciprocity, so he finds a resemblance between exorcism and ritual sacrifice (Girard, 2: 83, 123, 165, 267). Pound too has an inkling of such connections in his translation of and introduction to the Noh drama *Awoi No Uye.* When Pound refers to this play in *The Cantos,* he may be referring to his jealous relationship to the Jews. At the opening of the play, the Lady Awoi is attacked and then possessed by an evil spirit at the height of the Kami Festival. This evil spirit resembles the Princess Rokujo, who is Awoi's successful rival for the love of Prince Genji, and whom Awoi greatly hates and envies, having thoroughly absorbed her desires. It is no accident then that this spirit is indistinguishable from Awoi herself. The spirit is the image both of Rokujo and the jealous Awoi, and since this distinction is necessarily blurred, the play poses insuperable problems in representation. The breakdown of differences between Awoi and her tormenting but admired double indicates a sacrificial crisis, as does the failure of ritual at a sacred moment (the Kami Festival). For most of the play the exorcists are powerless to expel Awoi's tormentor. Only at its conclusion, when more powerful exorcists are called in, is the demon totally externalized, differentiated, and made to appear in "his true shape," that of a terrifying monster or "hannya." Once the monster is expelled order is restored: Awoi is cured of her jealousy and dies one with herself.[18]

The structure of this exorcism parallels the sacrificial crisis from aggravated reciprocity to unanimous expulsion. The character of Awoi also illustrates Girard's argument that before exorcism the possessed subject may be considered monstrous. He is, to quote Girard, "at the same time one and many beings as he reenacts the hysterical trance and the crazy mixture of differences that immediately precedes the collective expulsion."[19] Neither exactly herself nor Rokujo nor the monster, Awoi grows increasingly delirious as her torments escalate and she impersonates her monstrous invaders. She is, in short, a version of the monstrous double.

In the broadcasts Pound too is a histrionic puppet who moves only when his imaginary demons pull the strings. Such histrionics disclose his "infection" by the same Jewish bacilli which have already infected the Gentile crowds of the West. Thus infected, Pound seeks to become the crowd itself through histrionic oscillation from voice to voice, mask to mask. He seems less himself than the delirious mixture of differences which is the sacrificial crisis. Like the possessed subject, Pound "bellows like Dionysus the bull [the name of Pound, his god, and his hero Mussolini]: like a lion he is ready to devour anyone who ventures within sight" (Girard, 2: 105). At one point Pound abandons human sounds and resorts to enraged animal noises, the gnashing of teeth: "Gnrr, gnrrn, gnrrn, gnrr" (RB, 129). These sounds prepare a sacrifice in which Pound himself is the victim.[20]

IV.

Though Pound's agon with the Jews threatened to tear apart his personality, he had other models with whom he openly identified. In the later sections of *The Cantos*, written mainly at Pisa and St. Elizabeths, these kindred and sustaining spirits help Pound to preserve his ego and to create a protective history and mythology:

> To Kung, to avoid their encirclement,
> To the Odes to escape abstract yatter,
> to Mencius, Dante, and Agassiz
> for Gestalt seed,

> pity, yes, for the infected,
> > but maintain antisepsis . . . .
> > (94/ 635)

Since these lines were written at St. Elizabeths, and since Pound defined an insane person as "an animal somewhat surrounded by Jews" (Olson: 75, 55), the "their" of the first line, like the "fungus" cleared by reserpine in Canto 92, may refer to the Jews.

There is another reason that Pound resisted collapse. It was suggested earlier that his extreme anti-Semitism coincides with his increasing want of recognition and esteem. Crudely put, it is related to his lack of success. In spite of his post-war sufferings, and even because of them, Pound, as we shall see, was much more successful after the war than before it.

Nietzsche's messianic project casts light on Pound's. Nietzsche's original god and model, his openly admired and worshipped divinity, was Wagner. Inevitably, however, Wagner became Nietzsche's rival and obstacle. Each man sought the cultural dictatorship of Germany (and Europe) and the organization of his own cult; each sought to master the crowd and make it emulate his desires. But Wagner, unlike Nietzsche, was an enormous success. Where Wagner succeeded, at Bayreuth, in completely mastering the crowd and becoming the Messiah of a new religion, Nietzsche, the very prophet of the will to power, failed to win the recognition and submission which a self-proclaimed Superman supposedly deserves. The intellectual scorn which Nietzsche came to heap upon Wagner, his once worshipped and now hated model, hardly conceals his outraged vanity, his sense of humiliation and defeat. Yet the deepest blow to Nietzsche's pride came from his awareness that his failure derived not from the crowd's opposition but from its indifference. Having in the end neither opponents nor an audience against which to test his will to power, yet driven to imitate his more successful rival, Nietzsche enacted the entire conflict in solitude. As he frenziedly imitated the other, whether Wagner or the absent and desired crowd, his behavior grew increasingly histrionic and "schizophrenic." Within the closed circle of Nietzsche's mind the Dionysian superman at last became indistinguishable from Christ, the crucified.[21]

Unlike Nietzsche, Pound suffers in the end neither "complete silence" nor that general indifference which leads the would-be Messiah into madness. Eliot said of Pound in the late 1930s that he had no disciples and was "becoming forgotten."[22] But at Pisa the U.S. Army treated Pound as a special and even dangerous prisoner, and Pound's trial and its successful aftermath brought him far more attention than ever before. Besides earning the hostility of the liberal press, at St. Elizabeths Pound attracted a fairly large coterie of disciples and admirers who treated him not only as a sage but as a political victim: the crowd, or part of it, had at last come to Pound and made him the object of a cult which continues to be reflected in Pound criticism to this day.

Pound always assumes that the culture hero is followed and copied: ". . . Until a selection of the intelligentsia can organize something, until they can set up at least a model, they can not expect the 120 million or whatever million to copy it" (SP, 165). Ironically, in the radio broadcasts Pound himself imitates the crowd. By contrast, at St. Elizabeths Pound was "pleased" (Reck, 1: 101–102) to find his image multiplied in "reflex" (CON, 61) in a crowd of visitors and disciples. This is David Rattray's description of one of Pound's admirers:

> In our conversation he revealed himself as a fanatic disciple of the "Maestro"; he apes his every like and dislike, even imitates his nervous tics and manner of speaking, and way of jumping up and stalking around. (*A Casebook:* 109)

Pound had two other faithful imitators, Eustace Mullins, his sycophantic biographer, and Dallam Simpson, a "flaming redhead [like Pound] who aped Pound's thoughts, gestures, speaking manner, and beard" (Reck, 1: 102–103). Another was Noel Stock, the literary critic and Pound's biographer. Although by the 1960s Stock had come to have strong reservations about Pound, his letters to Pound at St. Elizabeths imitate Pound's conspiratorial thinking, telegraphic style, and idiosyncratic spelling: "Slow slogging to ferret out genwin masonic from the cowshit. Hard to tell yet where exactly the black magic boys wormed in."[23] Other politically active visitors and imitators during this period included T. David Horton, William Mc-Naughton, editor of the right-wing sheet *Strike,* and John Kasper, right-wing agitator and anti-integrationist (Reck, 1: 104; Mullins: 312, 314, 355).

The resemblance between Pound and his numerous doubles now posed none of the dangers of violent mimetic conflict and undifferentiation such as had resulted from Pound's close and unrecognized imitation of the Jews. During the broadcasts Pound's increasing yet denied resemblance to his enemies had been signalled by his hostility toward them as well as by his fears of their proximity, contagion, and control. The Jews were the secret and hence hated model, the unacknowledged mediators of Pound's desire. But at St. Elizabeths Pound himself was the acknowledged mediator, and imitation was not only open but controlled by Pound. A clear difference separated him from his disciples, among whom Pound was the unapproachable model and undisputed arbiter in matters of literature, economics, politics, and aesthetics (*A Casebook:* 111). Thus, while Pound's disciples were free to emulate him, he had altogether eliminated rivalry and conflict.

There is another and most important reason for Pound's success after the war. Like Upward, Pound believes that the messianic culture hero suffers social victimization, and that that victimization proves his special status; in a sense it is preferable to suffer society's torment than its indifference. At Pisa, instead of meeting indifference, Pound suffers public execration and even unjust treatment. In Canto 74 he speaks of suffering with "Barabbas and 2 thieves beside me" (74/ 436), and he introduces this idea earlier in the same canto. Besides evoking Upward's idea that the victim, not the priest, is the foundation of cultural order, these lines anticipate Pound's self-vindication in Canto 91 as a Fascist martyr, as well as his entire St. Elizabeths period, when he had the satisfaction of divinity without actually undergoing the "inconvenience of crucifixion" (SP, 412). One wonders whether Pound unconsciously sought, even conspired for, that victimization which is also the vindication of the genius.

Chapter Twenty-Three

The Return of the Swamp

The argument that Pound abandoned fascism and anti-Semitism after Pisa is clearly untenable. As we have seen, Pound's fascist ideology persists in his poetry, prose, and correspondence after 1945, as he moved into the last phase of his career. But though Pound entered and left St. Elizabeths an unregenerate fascist and anti-Semite, *Drafts and Fragments*, following *Thrones*, contain only one relatively minor example of anti-Semitism. These poems are even more remarkable for Pound's intense awareness of precisely those emotions from which much of his anti-Semitism derives. They contain repeated meditations on "pride, jealousy and possessiveness" (113/ 787); on "Fear, father of cruelty"; upon a "genealogy of the demons" (114/ 793); and on the "twisted" state of affairs in which love becomes the "cause of hate" (110/ 780). Canto 110 also gives prominence to the theme of Awoi, whose passion, as Pound said, "makes her subject to the demon possession" (NOH, 115). Finding an analogy to his own situation in Awoi's torment, Pound longs for the serenity which she finally attains. But this would require the exorcism of fear, the father of cruelty, a final dissociation of love and hate, and freedom from jealous passion and envy. It would require, in short, Pound's repudiation of anti-Semitism.

Assessing his career in a 1967 interview with Allen Ginsberg, a despondent and self-disappointed Pound said that his "worst mistake" as a writer had been the "suburban prejudice" of anti-Semitism. This is probably the first clear evidence of Pound's rejection of anti-Semitism, although he may well have repudiated it earlier in the decade, perhaps even with the publication of *Drafts and Fragments*. Pound's hatred can never be reduced to a mere error or prejudice, but despite Pound's attempt to minimize its scope and significance, the interview with Ginsberg shows that Pound understood that anti-Semitism had had a perverse and shattering effect on his achievement and life, thus giving it nearly the same importance it is given in this book. What remains to be shown is why Pound should have cast off his hatred.

Having published *Thrones* in 1959, Pound was eager to finish *The Cantos*. But he suffered increasing fatigue, inability to concentrate, failure of memory, depression, and never completed his epic (Hall: 47). Pound's depression was not entirely physical, however. Obsessed by a sense of personal and poetic failure—he would come to view *The Cantos* as a "wreck" and a "botch"[1]—Pound was plagued by feelings of remorse, a desire for forgiveness for his past errors and sins. His unexpected humility is perhaps most impressive in what now appears as the last canto, where Pound asks those whom he loves to "try to forgive / what I have made" (Notes for 117/ 802).

During a 1963 interview the Italian journalist Grazia Livi told Pound that he had come to seem a "very remote figure." She added that she "was almost afraid" of meeting him. "Afraid?" Pound asked. "I understand . . . . Everything I touch I ruin."[2] This statement calls to mind the severe judgment of the later *Cantos,* in which Pound stands among his "errors and wrecks" (116/ 796). Pound confesses himself a man who ruins everything he touches, a destroyer, whereas one motto of the late *Cantos* is "to be men not destroyers" (Notes for 117/ 803). Pound thus resembles the doomed Hercules in his translation of Sophocles' *Women of Trachis,* who returns home but carries with him the accumulated guilt of his violence and rage. It is as if he sees himself as having violated a taboo. At this stage of his life Pound also strikes a new note in judging his violence and hubris. Writing to Archibald MacLeish after his release from St. Elizabeths, Pound asks to be forgiven for "about 80% of the violent things" he had said of MacLeish's friends, and in another letter to the poet he apologizes for his "arrogance" to his "colleagues."[3] In Canto 116 Pound asserts that he is "not a demigod," that he "cannot make it cohere" (116/ 796). This is not a grandiloquent way of confessing inadequacy, but an abandonment of the project of divinity which Pound-Zagreus-Dionysus had pursued through his career.

This repudiation of divinity is probably implicit as well in some obscure lines from Notes from Canto 117. To an unknown addressee, but probably himself, Pound says: "Under the Rupe Tarpeia / weep out your jealousies—/ To make a church / or an altar to Zagreus / Son of Semele / Without jealousy / like the double arch of a window / Or some great colonnade" (p. 801). The prominence given to the sin of jealousy in this passage is difficult to explain unless one realizes that Pound, as the modern Dionysus, had sought to found his own cult, and that he was therefore not only Jesus' but Dionysus' rival. But now Pound seeks to dissociate himself from the true god, and thus he gives Dionysus' name as well as that of his mother, a sign of the god's authenticity. The Rupe Tarpeia is the rock from which the ancient Romans hurled to their death the betrayers of the Roman state. Its presence here implies Pound's guilt at having betrayed the true Roman tradition in some unspecified way, perhaps for having endorsed a regime of distinctly un-Dionysian repressiveness, or more likely for having sought to introduce a factitious Dionysus, namely himself.

The aged Pound, who had sought to replace Christianity with an arrogant, aggressive, and often pitiless pagan naturalism, now seems reconciled to Christian values.[4] One thinks of his wish for greater personal charity in Canto 116, and this passage from Alain, which Pound translated for Daniel Cory in 1968:

> [A time will come when] The spirit will be able (will know enough) to deprive itself of power, of every *kind* of power. That is the highest Kingdom. Now Calvary announces this very thing, in so eloquent, and so violent a way, that I will add no commentary whatsoever. (Cory: 36)

Cory notes that Pound was impressed and moved by this passage. Christ is no longer a rival Messiah but an unattainable model of selfless sacrifice. Now one gains sanctity not by exercising power and violence (traits eminently of Dionysus), but by repudiating and even suffering them.

If one needs proof of the sincerity of Pound's above statement, it lies in his deliberate abandonment of his greatest power: language, writing. Once the self-professed "lord of his work and master of utterance" (74/ 442), Pound from the 1960s to his death in 1972 writes almost nothing and speaks hardly at all. Perhaps this voluntary descent into a "personal inferno" is a form of atonement, perhaps a sign of Pound's fear of lapsing into his former violence.[5] Or perhaps it expresses his sense that language is inadequate to express that truth—the eloquent truth of the Crucifixion—which he alludes to but does not discuss, in his interview with Cory.

It is unclear what motivated Pound to reject and judge his *hubris;* perhaps it was the series of defeats he had suffered, perhaps his growing awareness of his own mortality, perhaps the dwindling of his mental and physical powers. One may speculate too on why Pound should have repudiated his anti-Semitism. As we have seen, the Jews had been Pound's agonistic rivals for possession of the divinity. But with Pound's recognition of his *hubris,* and his rejection of his messianic quest, this hatred has nothing to feed on, and so it vanishes.

II.

The cessation of Pound's combat with the Jews cannot be explained solely as the result of his intense remorse or spiritual illumination. When Grazia Livi interviewed Pound in 1963, she saw him as one "sinking beyond the illusory borders of the world."

> He is not any more a man, but a symbol, who keeps only formal rapport with life; not a personage, but a presence who looks at the vicissitudes of this world with a soul completely freed, already far away, already thinking in the tragic and illuminated wisdom which precedes the end.[6]

Throughout Pound's work the Jews repeatedly substitute for forms of otherness and mystery. Chief of these is the feminine, which Pound associates with the swamp, and which is characterized by ambiguity, incoherence, confusion, parthenogenesis, undifferentiation, obscurity, fecundity, decay, in short the absence, failure, or incompleteness of identity, light, and the originating phallic principle. Pound ultimately redeems the confused and "bad" form of the feminine in the middle *Cantos* by conquering the swamp and arbitrarily transferring its "bad" qualities and indeterminacy to the Jews. There is no need to rehearse again this process of repression, projection, and displacement, or to define its implicitly sacrificial character.

Yet if the Jews resemble the feminine and the swamp, they also resemble the greatest and most mysterious otherness and the greatest threat to Pound's identity in his largely silent last years: Death itself, which man, though he cannot know it directly or immediately, associates with the dissolution of differences, the cessation of language, and loss of being.[7] Note the Jews' repeated association with disease, bacilli, and violence, their identification with castration, confusion, and the undifferentiated, and the enormous fear which they inspire in Pound.[8] Just as the deadly Jews belong to the ambiguously fecund swamp, so Death is interwoven with Life, as plants emerge from the seasonal decay of the soil, or maggots or vermin live in rotting corpses. Thus, like the swamp, the Jews in the broadest sense signify not Death itself but the confusion and indetermination of opposites, the collapse of determinate meaning: birth that is not really birth, growth that is not really growth, being that is not really being, origination that is not really origination. Identified with the swamp, they stand for an endless scattering or dissemination of meaning, a movement without end or origin or center, without distinction, completeness, or identity, without the intervention of *logos*.

Nonetheless, the goal of *The Cantos* is to stand in the presence of their logocentric and phallocentric origin, a unified and all-embracing plenitude of coherent meanings: Pound would lift "the great ball of crystal" and "enter the great acorn [or *glans*] of light" (116/ 795), radiating seminal *logoi* throughout his entire poem and thus confirming its organic unity. *The Cantos* are projected as a *nostos* or return, modelled after Odysseus' journey home not only to Penelope, his possession, but to the recoverable presence, rootedness, fullness of being of an earlier self and a patriarchal origin. But because the putative origin or center (Pater Helios) is itself constantly "turning" (113/ 786), coming, going out of itself, casting off its rays and traces, it is impossible for Pound to return to the perfect semantic plenitude or full "splendour" (116/ 797) of a fixed and stable origin. He can neither "lift" the great ball of crystal nor "enter" the great acorn of light.

Failing to produce that home or enclosure which would contain or reconcile all the meanings generated within his poem, Pound's mind "jumps without building" (110/ 780), thus resembling the minds of those lesser men who lack the phallic *chih* (110/ 781) or "root." His situation reminds him of those larks at Allègre (Notes for 117/ 803), who fly toward the sun and then fall back to earth. As for *The Cantos* themselves, they are a "palimpsest—/ A little light / in great darkness" (116/ 795). Apart from the text's mingled light and dark (and predominantly dark), its original meaning has been erased or rubbed out to make place for a second layer and even for successive later ones. Such a text has lost contact with a prior meaning, which is now untraceable; it is associated with a rubbing or effacement which resembles *usure* (one thinks of Canto 14, the swamp of London, with its "lost contours" and "erosions"). Pound also speaks of *The Cantos* as a "tangle of works unfinished" (116/ 795), a telling phrase, since in Pound's vocabulary tangle also implies the labyrinthine swamp, a place without ultimate origin or *telos*. Nor can Pound appeal to the metaphorical Fascist axe in order to cut through this tangle, since Mussolini's career and that of Italian Fascism had been supposedly "wrecked for an error" (116/ 795), while the tangle itself encompasses the confusion of fascist thinking. Perhaps Death portends only the gradual process of undifferentiation and loss of hierarchy to which Pound's *Propertius* alludes and in which one can also read, at last, the dissolution of his agon with the Jews; for in the undifferentiation of impending Death, the chaos of swampy Acheron, the doubles will become one:

> When, when, and whenever death closes our eyelids,
> Moving naked over Acheron
> Upon the one raft, victor and conquered together,
> Marius and Jugurtha together,
> > one tangle of shadows.
> > > (PER, 218)

The Cantos can return to their origins only insofar as they return to that which is textually at once primordial and familiar; ironically, this is the swamp, the "home" and origin and yet the non-origin in which they begin. In the middle rather than at the beginning of the Ur-*Cantos,* as Pound casts about for a beginning and a model, he finds himself at the swamp's "border" or margin among the endlessly echoing or repeating voices of Nature:

> As well begin here. Began our Catullus:
> "Home to sweet rest, and to the waves' deep laughter,"
> The laugh they wake amid the border rushes.[9]

This, however, proved to be a false start; appropriately, the later Pound identifies the swamp with the loss or confusion of origins. The present first canto begins with the word "And" and thus offers itself not only as a beginning but a continuation. Seeking to build the poem on Homer, it transports us to what Pound recognized as the deepest and least traceable layer of the *Odyssey:* the *logos*-less world of Hades, traditionally associated with the swamp (Kenner 3: 147; L, 74). In Canto 2, Pound briefly and vainly questions whether his or Browning's treatment of the historical poet Sordello adequately represents the original figure, who in any case in the canto appears not as a presence but as a documented name, a name to be interpreted and a life to be speculated upon. Then, in an exploration of a different yet related form of indeterminacy, Pound introduces a littoral scene which belongs, or seems to belong, to prehistory, and whose fecund abundance is matched only by its instability and vagueness. In succeeding cantos the swamp appears repeatedly as a sign of unresolvable confusion. Only in Canto 41, in which Mussolini drains the Pontine Marshes, does Pound achieve the victory of the solar and differentiating principle, the originating light, phallus, *logos*.

This conquest can only be temporary, subverted not only by the historical fate of fascism but even more so by Pound's disastrous life. Grazia Livi said of the aged Pound that he was "sinking beyond the illusory borders of the world." Intentionally or not, this phrase evokes Pound's descent in the last *Cantos* into a realm indistinguishable from the swamp. This movement is anticipated as early as Canto 82 (and still earlier in Canto 47), in which Pound enters a feared realm of "softness" and engages in symbolic coition with Gea Terra the Earth Mother, the feminine as prostitute (*porne*, 80/ 494) or swamp. A form of "fluid ΧΘΟΝΟΣ ["of the earth"], strong with the undertow" (a word elsewhere associated with the confusion of usury), this goddess draws man into the earth "till one sink into thee by an arm's width" (82/ 526). Pound thus conflates the life-giving act of intercourse with the release of death and the loss of identity within Nature: "but I will come out of this knowing no one / neither they me" (82/ 526). Now truly No Man, Odysseus, Pound feels the "loneliness of death" come "upon [him] . . . for an instant" (82/ 527).

In *Rock-Drill*, following the Pisan *Cantos*, Pound temporarily integrates the swamp within his cosmic economy in the figure Ra-Set, a syncretic goddess. But later, in *Drafts and Fragments*, as Pound approaches the as yet undetermined limit between Life and Death, the defense which the Jews had earlier provided against multifarious confusion collapses and Pound once again confronts—as if by the slow return of the repressed— his earlier and once familiar symbols of alterity and uncertainty. No wonder that these cantos have an *unheimliche* quality, a disturbing mingling of the familiar and the unfamiliar. The opening line of *Drafts and Fragments* is "Thy quiet house" (110/ 777). Referring to that home which is the object of the poet's *nostos*, this is also the habitation of the Virgin Mary in the Cathedral of Santa Assunta (Assumption) on the island of Torcello. A predecessor and hence one of the numerous historical origins of Pound's beloved Venice, where the poet died in 1972, Torcello was like its successor wrested by its earliest inhabitants from the swampy chaos of the Venetian lagoon. But in the later Middle Ages, on account of malaria, the island was virtually abandoned, and it remained pestilential until modern times, when "land reclamation" once again "redeemed both soil and man" (Lorenzetti: 833). The reference to Torcello thus alerts us to some of the persistent and major problems of Pound's text: the presence of the sacrosanct feminine figure within and her emergence from the very depths of the plague-ridden swamp;

the unresolved status of luxury (and art), which is symbolized not only by the proliferant swamp but, even in the austere Cathedral of Santa Assunta, by the "gold thread in the pattern" (116/797); and the peculiar resemblance between the parthenogenetic Virgin as "Theotokos," or Mother of God, as the Virgin of Torcello is known, and "Tokos," or usury, which Pound identifies with the abundant parthenogenesis of swamp creatures, and from which, as he well knew, derived many of the most seductive splendors of Venetian civilization.[10]

Bacigalupo observes that the "quiet house" is also the home of Pound's anima ("Alma") figure, the white goddess Leucothea.[11] But this appropriation of matriarchal sanctity as well as of an original, untainted, and undifferentiated purity (white) of the central self is immediately brought within the play of language. Leucothea is known only as a readable trace or track, through her veil (*kredemnon*, 96/651), which conceals and reveals, and the transitory foam or spume that she leaves on the surface of the waves. In the fourth line of this canto Pound announces that he is "all for Verkehr without tyranny" (110/777). A plea for the free "interaction" or intercourse among the "materials" of his poem (Bacigalupo: 463)—and hence an invitation, intended or not, to the persistently troublesome destabilization of meaning—this line is also Pound's self-serving personal plea for sexual freedom (a vaguely defined requirement of his "paradiso terrestre," Notes for 117/802), specifically his freedom to move from one woman (his wife Dorothy, his Penelope figure), to another (Olga Rudge, the Circe of *The Cantos*, and Marcella Spann), and back again. Pound's actual relation with the feminine remains of an ambivalent as well as promiscuous and hence undefined character; it implies a constant movement from one house to another (Compare Pater Helios's "turning" movement among the "Houses of Heaven" in Canto 113). Nor are these houses quiet. Later in *Draft and Fragments* Pound alludes to woman and domestic life in terms of abstract generality: "Somewhere in the snarl is a tenderness" (113/789). Snarl, implying the vicious baring of teeth, also implies the "tangle" of the swamp, the persistent labyrinth of sexual passion beyond extrication.[12]

This confrontation with the feminine confusion appears elsewhere. To return to the previous example: "Sea, over roofs, but still the sea and the headland. / And in every woman, somewhere in the snarl is a tenderness" (113/789). Typically feminine, as elsewhere in Pound,[13] the sea is in this instance outside the limits of the feminine enclosure, is over the roofs of the houses, as if to overwhelm them. The promontory or headland, as at Terracina where the goddess's statue stands, inscribes the phallus permanently and prominently within natural geography; snarl, meanwhile, refers not only to the dangerous teeth of marine Scylla in Canto 47, but to the swamp as the direct opposite of the promontory's protrusive definition. Pound speaks later of "Their dichotomies (feminine) present in heaven and hell / Tenthrils training / caught in rocks under wave" (114/791–792).

Besides evoking woman as a polyvalent profusion of unpruned meanings ("trailing"), this image calls to mind the feminine Hydra or octopus in Canto 29, or else woman as sunless and aimless movement, a "drift of weed in the bay" (29/ 144). She remains a danger to passing ships exactly like the eel-infested Sargasso Sea. Finally, in Canto 111 the feminine Amor is now a "cold" and ambiguous "mermaid" who threatens (as do usury and the earlier Gea Terra) to submerge man in a fluid "undertow." To add to her ambiguity, Pound associates her with the usurious and unnatural beast Geryon (who is "biform," and "takes you lower down," SP, 332), and with the "splendor" and growth ("anthesis") of flowers. This sinister creature appears at the undefined border between the sea and the land, is "like a bark upon the shore [*come burchiello in su la riva*]" (Notes for 111/ 783).

When Pound wrote these lines he had passed his seventieth birthday and stood on the brink of poetic exhaustion and physical debility. What then is his fate amid this increasing uncertainty, as he moves "al poco giorno / ed al gran cerchio d'ombra" (to a short day / and a great circle of shade) (116/ 787)? It seems, at least at first, that he is bound finally by the limits of the tellurian confusion, the selva oscura he had sought to defeat: Death awaits him, as it awaits everything else in Nature.[14] There is perhaps an irony in the concluding lines of the fragmentary Canto 112:

> Artemisia
> Arundinaria
> Winnowed in fate's tray

 neath

 luna

(112/ 785)

These two substances figure in the sacrificial and purificatory ceremony of the Celestial Female among the Na-Khi of China: artemisia implies for the syncretizing Pound Artemis, inaccessible goddess of Nature's purity, while arundinaria is a "reedy substance . . . used to build the cane-brake tray that is supposed to winnow . . . life" (Wilhelm, 2: 172). Again Pound refers to the swamp and to the governance of that other cyclical goddess Fortuna, who is "hidden as eel in sedge [a form of marsh grass]," and who like Artemis governs "all neath the moon" (97/ 676), that is material or tellurian Nature. Repeatedly Pound associates Artemis with purity, sacrifice, the clarification of distinctions, and natural retribution. As Artemis is elsewhere associated with the sacrificial axe (and thus with Italian Fascism), here she is linked with the more traditionally familiar scythe according to the well-known idea that all flesh is grass and that in the end all life is exchanged for Death (Bachofen: 28, 57, 125–126). Artemis makes the distinctions between Life and Death which Pound had earlier presumed to make himself. But since Artemis detests all dying things, laments that "nothing is now clean slayne / but rotteth away," the aging and decaying Pound is one of her likely victims; he will be winnowed in the futile circle of Fate's tray, felled by Nature's scythe which is also a waning moon. This is the inevitable consequence of Pound's submission to the idea of natural retribution. Although Pound does not offer himself openly as victim according to the Artemisian law, the sacrifice he had once pursued is, as he approaches death, turned implicitly against himself.[15]

At the very end of Canto 110 Pound refers to "the oval moon" (110/ 781). Besides signifying yet again the changeful Artemis, this evokes the feminine egg of generation and implies yet another confrontation with the "female principle of the world."[16] But while it is no surprise that the egg is associated with Fortuna, it also symbolizes the god Neptune, who appears at the opening of Canto 116 (Bachofen: 31–32):

> Came Neptunus
> > his mind leaping
> > > like dolphins,
> These concepts the human mind has attained.
> To make Cosmos—
> to achieve the possible—
>
> > > > (116/ 795)

The opening of Canto 110, referring to "the harl, feather-white, as a dolphin on sea-brink" (110/ 777), and anticipating a voyage, probably implies Neptune. But the god's appearance in the last *Cantos* requires explanation, for he has not been prominent in the poem thus far, except perhaps as a negative figure: spiteful enemy of Odysseus, violator of Tyro. To be sure, Pound alludes to (but does not necessarily endorse) Gemistos Plethon's idea that all things stem "from Neptune" (83/ 528). But this idea would contradict Pound's more usual assumption, that the sea is feminine.

Neptune's new and positive prominence is another of the unexpected reversals of the last *Cantos*. Just as there is an immutable solar phallus, associated with pure light, so there is a phallus of the tellurian and aquatic depths: the sea also contains Neptune, a male god. In contrast with the sun, Neptune represents "the generative, lifegiving, and fructifying principle . . . in its tellurian aspects"; it is he who "stands beside the primordial female egg . . . and works in the moist depths of matter," and who, "in conjunction with Apollo, . . . laid the foundations of Troy's walls deep in the earth." Hence the significance of salt, to which Pound refers in the fragment of Canto 115 ("the salt hay whispers to tide's change," 115/ 794); it is the sea-god's sperm, which fecundates the land. Hence too Pound's reference to the mind of Neptunus leaping like dolphins and the making of cosmos; "came" in this context has perhaps a sexual significance, implying the cast of the god's mental and physical seed (for in Pound these are interchangeable). It is no less appropriate for men to make cosmos, for Neptune is a builder of walls (phallic objects, as noted elsewhere). Like the egg, the dolphins are signs of Neptune, and their leaping in this passage as in classical tradition expresses the idea of "the eternally rising and forever receding waves of existence": the same meaning as Pound finds in the "wave pattern" (29/145) at Excideuil, or in "the crozier's curve [that] runs in the wall" (110/777), or in the disappearing wake of a boat, the last two images appearing with dolphins in Canto 110; for as Pound says, "what has been shall be, / flowing, ever unstill" (113/787). This too is in keeping with the nature of tellurian Neptune, who belongs to the realm of eternal change, not the realm of light.[17]

If Pound is thus ruled by the law of matter, in which life flows into death, and death into life, in an endless, indivisible, and inexorable process, the most he can hope for is not the persistence of identity, which is impossible, and even less an ascent to the light, but rather to contribute in dying to the preservation and renewal of Nature's vitality, the great scheme of daedal changes that always remain the same. Indeed, this is one possible interpretation of sacrifice in Pound's works. Nor is such submission to death altogether unattractive to Pound, whose thought is often anti-transcendental. In Canto 6 Guillaume of Poitiers, the originator and disseminator of troubadour art, imagines his dead body fertilizing the soil: "The stone is alive in my hand, the crops / will be thick in my death-year" (6/21). Later, in the ritual coition in Canto 47, Pound writes: "Hast'ou a deeper planting, doth thy death year / Bring swifter shoot? / Hast thou entered more deeply the mountain?" (47/238). This passage, as noted earlier, anticipates the descent to "fluid" earth in Canto 82, in which Pound's sexual union with Gea Terra is equated with Death: "Where I lie let the thyme rise / and basilicum / let the herbs rise in April abundant" (82/526). Pound is a self-sacrifice, a version of what Frazer and other anthropologists term the foundation victim, from whose body arises a new era ("thyme" puns on time) and a new civilization ("herbs" puns on urbs).

Given his nostalgia for the earth, and given his suspicion of the transcendental impulse, Pound might prefer to ignore "spirits" so long as he has some link to "sun and serenitas" (113/786); but "the hells move in cycles / No man can see his own end" (113/787). Even in his confession that he is no demigod, the hope of transcendence still lives on in Pound—a longing for the realms of light, or at least a purgatorial transformation of his long-suffering spirit. Such is the implication of the dolphins in Canto 110, who appear at the "seabrink" (110/777); this alludes to a voyage done or, more likely, about to begin, for in classical tradition the dolphin conveys souls across the seas to the Elysian Fields. More mysterious is the vision which succeeds Pound's disturbing image of the "gold mermaid" Amor: "Soul melts into air, / Anima into aura, / Serenitas" (Notes for 111, 783). This passage is reminiscent of the ending of Canto 110: "Awoi or Komachi, / the oval moon" (110/781). While the oval moon implies the cycles of generation, in the Noh plays that bear these characters' respective names these women conquer their overwhelming pride (exactly as does Pound) and attain a final spiritual serenity in Death. To quote *Awoi No Uye:* "Pity has melted her heart, and she has gone into Buddha. Thanksgiving" (NOH, 121).

The Noh drama *Kakitsubata,* which Pound translated in 1917, and to which he returns at several points in the later *Cantos,* shares with the last two works a theme of transcendence, the restoration of love and identity in the spirit world. In Canto 110 Pound perhaps alludes to Aphrodite, whose colors are saffron and gold: "Yellow iris in that river bed" (110/ 778) (Eisenhauer: 253). But this line also alludes to the Lady Kakitsubata, who had loved the poet Narahira, and who, because the poet had written an acrostic on the iris and had remembered her while passing an iris marsh, had chosen to manifest herself in the shape of that "swamp" (NOH, 123) flower and in that particular place. She is, then, the flower of "remembrance" (NOH, 125), specifically of her love of the poet, and thus symbolizes the power of love to reveal and preserve traces of immortal spirituality, the world of "splendour." For in fact Kakitsubata is an immortal spirit; though she manifests herself each year "anew" (NOH, 129) as those "flowers Kakitsubata / that flare and flaunt in their marsh" (NOH, 128), she really transcends the limited existence of these plants without memory and "without mind" (NOH, 126). To quote Pound, "she demonstrates the 'immortality of the soul' or the 'permanence or endurance of the individual personality' by her apparition—first, as a simple girl of the locality, secondly, in the ancient splendours" (NOH, 130). At the end of the play, as she prepares to join her lover Narahira (also an immortal spirit), she asks for "a light that will not lead to darkness" (NOH, 128). When her spirit at last vanishes, "[melting like Awoi] into Buddha," it leaves its mere bodily "apparition," which is "the cracked husk of the locust" (NOH, 130). Kakitsubata, traced in the swamp flower, finds her way back to the light.

Kakitsubata contributes to *The Cantos'* necessarily provisional but final speculations on the nature of reality and spirit, the status of the origin, the possibility of transcendence. It also contributes to a key reversal in the pattern of reversals in these last poems. Perhaps for having remembered a token of Aphrodite in the heart of the swamp, Pound can now look upon its fecund confusion with acceptance and even love:

> A blown husk that is finished
> > but the light sings eternal
> A pale flare over marshes
> > where the salt hay whispers to tide's change
> Time, space,
> > neither life nor death is the answer
> > > (from 115/ 794)

This "blown husk" is reminiscent of the ending of *Kakitsubata,* in which the lady, departing for the spirit world, leaves only "the cracked husk of the locust." The poet's identification with Kakitsubata is further suggested by the otherwise cryptic lines: "Time, space, / neither life nor death is the answer." Now Pound looks for answers which, if they exist at all, exist beyond the world of change. But Pound does not scorn, fear, or seek to dominate the littoral setting before him; he exults in its beauty, whether of the swamp or of the light. The "pale flare over marshes" evokes the flowers of love and remembrance of Kakitsubata, which "flare and flaunt in their marsh." They are also signs of Aphrodite ("Yellow iris in that river bed"), goddess of immortal beauty and love. The spermatic Neptunian salt mingling with and fecundating the hay (rushes or marsh grass) evokes the perpetual intermingling of tellurian Nature. As for "the light" that "sings eternal," although it may seem at first to refer to the fecundating sun, its origin is ambiguous, for "light" is perhaps equivalent to "flare," in which case the light derives from the presumably heliotropic swamp flowers. In keeping with the speculative mode of this poem, one must at least entertain the possibility that the light emanates from within the marsh itself. If so, it is the traditional *ignis fatuus*, which is produced from the spontaneous combustion of swamp gases (formed by the decomposition of matter and perhaps implied in "flare"), and which leads men to destruction. Hence the neatly placed preposition "over," suggesting one further border place, and leaving in doubt the actual source of light.

It is fair to say that Pound, at the conclusion of *The Cantos*, and in perhaps the most extraordinary of the reversals we have been examining, turns the once feared swamp and its products into a symbol and instrument of the powers of divine love and grace. This metamorphosis is no doubt inspired by *Kakitsubata*, but probably more so by the first canto of *Purgatorio*. As Dante stands with Virgil and Cato on the eastern shore of the Mount of Purgatory, Virgil washes Dante's face with dew from the grass and girds him with a reed or rush which he plucks from the margin of the sea. To quote Sinclair's translation:

> There he girded me as the other had bidden. O marvel! for as was the lowly plant he chose such did it spring up again immediately in the first place where he had plucked it.[18]

The unbidden and spontaneous generation of plants, as if by parthenogenesis, becomes a symbol of an unexpected grace, renewal, purity, a sign of divine abundance and love. The reed is an indispensable token of Dante's fitness to ascend the Mount of Purgatory, from which he will further ascend to the light of Paradise. In Pound as well the products of the swamp provide a no less indispensable means by which he will regain charity and, after long suffering, return to the light:

> Charity I have had sometimes,
>   I cannot make it flow thru.
> A little light, like a rushlight
>   to lead back to splendour.
>   (116/ 797)[19]

Still there remains the actual terror and uncertainty of Death, the unnameable and unspeakable; the poem can chart only the poet's approach to, not his entrance into, this last mystery or "arcanum" (Notes for 117 et seq./ 803). If this means that *The Cantos* cannot really conclude, one can nonetheless choose from among its last scattered fragments its most appropriate if tentative ending—that which most adequately traces its trajectory into the mysterious poetic silence of Pound's last years. The best ending is to be found in the very last of the dated fragments, which Flory reproduces in her study of Pound (Flory: 195, 198). In this brief statement, Pound recalls Canto 23's borrowing from Stesichorus, where Hercules, son of Zeus, solar hero, and once Pound's alter ego, follows "in periplum" the fading Western track of the sun to the "low fords of ocean," and then descends into the mysterious "selva oscura" or swamp, where all opposites are inextricably mingled: "ima vada noctis obscurae":

> 28 Sept
>   1960
> for a long pull
>   & a
>   long
>   wane
> ima vada
>   noctis
>   obscurae

Now not knowing if he shall rise, like the ever "turning" sun, into that other "arcanum" of dawn, no longer assured of his status as solar hero, with admirable stoicism and heroic will-power the poet chooses to journey not by sail but by oar into the "lowest depths of dark night."

Chapter Twenty-Four

*"All Will Be Judged"**

This book has attempted to show the inadequacy of the familiar description of Pound's fascism and, more particularly, his anti-Semitic hatred as the mere passing consequence of his exasperation with a few Jewish financiers. Like most anti-Semitism, that of Pound is not primarily motivated by economic beliefs, nor is it confined to Pound's so-called "big Jews." Nor is it merely a "suburban prejudice," as Pound described it, but is a massive ideological hatred conforming to the criteria of modern anti-Semitism. It asserts the existence of a transhistorical, pernicious Semitic essence, manifesting itself not only in religious doctrines but in the cultural and biological form of race. The emergence of this obsession in Pound's writings of the 1930s (and even earlier) assures that he will finally attack not just "big Jews" but "Jewry" itself.

In spite of the extraordinary richness and sometimes unsurpassed beauty of his verse, Pound's anti-Semitism and fascism throw his achievement into deep shadows. By his 1940s broadcasts over Rome Radio, Pound did not hesitate to express violent hostility against the Jews, at some points covertly but unmistakably recommending their extermination, at other points endorsing their mass expulsion or "purgation" from the West. But in addition to enlisting his abilities in the service of a brutal, retrograde, and largely incoherent ideology, Pound interwove that ideology within the texture of his major poem. As we have seen, Pound's fascist broadcasts and his poetry cannot be separated. Far from consisting of historically incidental and detachable opinions, themes, ideas—in short, of "mere" ideology— anti-Semitism and fascism are embedded inextricably in Pound's poetic language, in his web of metaphors and images.

Thus we have seen that anti-Semitism and fascism figure in *The Cantos*, as elsewhere in Pound, not only at the local verbal level but structurally, as

---

*"At the Grave of Henry James," in *The Collected Poetry of W. H. Auden* (New York: Random House, 1945), p. 130, ll. 133–138.

indispensable strategies and solutions within his effort to overcome the threat of the "swamp" by imagining a fascist utopia, an organic, ritualistic, hierarchical society based on "Nature," mythological values, and Cheng Ming, or "correct denominations." The conquest and redemption of woman in the Odysseus-Hanno-Mussolini episodes in Cantos 39, 40, and 41, and the transference of woman's asocial qualities of "confusion" and "evil" to usury and the Jews, constitute a fascist myth of order. Whether as usurers, rootless cosmopolitans, sterile rationalists and demythifiers, or symbols of anti-Nature, or else as the very embodiment of monstrous indetermination and confusion, the Jews come to represent all that Pound would eliminate from his ideal society. No wonder then that Canto 52, in which Pound escapes to the ritualistic, "organic," and unchanging hierarchy of ancient China, opens with an extraordinarily violent attack on the Jewish people, who allegedly prevent the attainment of this ideal in the West. In this example, as in the broadcasts and elsewhere in Pound's poetry and prose, the Jews are the "foundation" victim and scapegoat, through whose elimination a desacralized and denaturalized modern world would supposedly return to myth, hierarchy, and beauty. The means of Jewish elimination is necessarily the Italian Fascist axe, which brings clarity and distinction, restores the processes of Nature, and promotes a vital mythological awareness. Pound thus stands as the major example in modern literature of fascist nostalgia for prehistoric society, for myth, ritual, sacrifice. Pound's ideal social order, no less than that of the Nazis, requires continued violence against outgroup scapegoats, and these include not only Jews but Buddhists and Taoists, who in Pound's China take the place of the Jews and represent a comparable "confusion."

The "genealogy" of Pound's hatred has been shown to be tangled, various, intricate; his anti-Semitic ideology has no single cause or explanation, but rather reflects the full complexity and development of his emotional, intellectual, and psychological life. Nonetheless, I would give special importance to Pound's logocentric and phallocentric outlook, his identification of the sun with language and paternity, and his related commitment to such patriarchal and agrarian values as the authenticity of names and demarcations and the rightfulness of ownership and property (both of which are linked conceptually to the idea of propriety). In seeking to banish the non-agrarian and castrating Jews from the agricultural West, Pound would not merely dispel a power of darkness and obscurity; he would restore Europe to its authentic paternal inheritance and connect it once more with its patriarchal (and solar) origins. This project of restoration has a number of historical and traditional sources, the chief of which are Christianity and, even more important, Hellenism. Although Pound is by no means a Christian, and although his anti-Semitism is not exclusively religious but social and cultural, he feels a deep nostalgia for the Catholic Middle Ages, when the Jew figured as an alien and enemy within a closed, corporate, and religiously homogeneous society. This nostalgia goes far to explain his attraction to fascism, which held a similar corporate ideal, and which in a sense updated the medieval accusations against the Jews. As for Hellenism, Pound reveres Greek and Roman civilization and sharply contrasts paganism with Hebraic tradition; he also accepts no less enthusiastically the Voltairean idea that the authentic cultural roots of Europe lie in Greece and Rome. In this way Pound prepares himself for Zielinski and Frobenius and for the ultimate embrace of fascist anti-Semitism.

Nor can one forget as an essential psychological element in this "genealogy" Pound's repeated tendency to project his own violence and megalomania onto the Jews and to use anti-Semitism as a means of deflecting his own fears of social marginality and alienation; in attacking the Jews Pound reproaches himself in a different guise. Again, as perhaps the deepest and fundamental root of Pound's hatred, one finds it hard to overemphasize Pound's messianic ambition and his secret imitation of the sacred and untouchable Jews: during the broadcasts Pound is locked in a mimetic and paranoiac combat with his earliest models and rivals in pursuit of the divinity.

In perhaps the broadest sense, Pound's anti-Semitism stems from a massive and persistent fear, which Pound called the "father of cruelty," and which, as he implies, fathers "the genealogy of the demons." One thinks of how Pound's castration anxiety is linked to his terror of the paternal Jewish deity. Yet this fear is best understood not in its specific examples but more generally, as a characteristic feature of Pound's fascism.

Ernst Nolte has shown that fear underlies the ideologies of Maurras and Hitler.[1] Maurras feared the destruction of beauty in the world, Hitler the ultimate defeat of Germany at the hands of anti-Nature. Generally speaking, fascism manifests a profound fear and intolerance of the vague, inchoate, and incommensurable, of all that seems to it mysterious and ambiguous, indefinite and confused. This overdetermined fear extends to the unconscious, to the frightening isolation of the individual soul or conscience, to repressed and yet ever familiar periods of national and personal history, to the ever-present world of microbes, to the body's vegetable-like tropisms, to the invisible realm of the spirit, the sacred; it would extend as well to pure thought or the imagination, to all those abstract and transcendental tendencies which lead men away from the concrete and given, the familiar here and now. The fascist fears all that seems violently threatening to the individual ego, to assertive and definite masculine values, to the stable or immanent society or home in which the ego seeks to find and preserve its being. One is tempted to say that this massive and confused fear is that of foreignness, of the Other, in a multitude of aspects and in the abstract. But in another sense this fear is not that of foreignness per se, or of foreignness as something definitely external, but rather of that which only seems to be entirely foreign but which is really intimate, familiar, all too close to home: an uncanny and uncertain presence within the self or society. Whatever form it takes, this fear turns inevitably to hate (phobia means both fear and aversion), a hatred of everything with which the fear itself is associated. This explains why fascism so frequently embodies its fear and hatred in the Jew, the foreigner par excellence who yet lives society's midst. Because of a variety of alien and often contradictory cultural traits and associations, and through the process of projection, the mysterious Jew condenses and crystallizes this multitude of fears and, in representing them, seems to afford the possibility of their elimination. To eliminate the Jew would be to eliminate confusion itself.

Pound, like Hitler, is a phobic personality. Almost from the very start his work contains images of indistinct and contaminating creatures, alternately or interchangeably insects and human beings, but in either case representatives of a confused otherness, leaving their slimy trails on the face of the earth. Nor can one doubt Pound's massive fear and hatred of the vague, the confused, the ambiguous, the undifferentiated, the unknown. His hero and model is Hercules, for whom the purpose of culture (as in Pound's translation of Sophocles' *The Women of Trachis*) is to assert, violently if necessary, clear demarcations—to banish chaos, to destroy monsters, to exorcise the vague and incommensurable. Having chosen this Herculean task at an early point in his career, Pound confronts the same forms of confusing alterity which trouble the mind of fascism: the unconscious, the isolated self and conscience, the mystery of feminine nature, philosophical abstraction and speculation, metaphysics, the transcendental spirit, the world of microbes — a vast forest of uncertain meanings and ideas in which Pound himself is lost and from which he must escape. Pound turns to fascism because he shares not only its deep fear of indeterminacy but also its central desire, which is to banish the indeterminate from social life and the mind of man. As in fascism, in Pound's works the ultimate sign of such fearful indeterminacy is the Jew. A symbol of virtually every form of dangerous otherness—the threat of disease, labyrinthine inwardness, instinctual passion, the vagina dentata, a plague of vermin, satanic magic, divine violence—the Jew is by projection Pound's very embodiment of confusion itself. It is he against whom Pound unleashes his Herculean rage, as if to destroy in the Jew his own confusion. In Pound as in fascism the projection of evil and socially undesirable qualities onto this familiar/foreigner has the same function and effect: no longer himself but a "plastic demon," an unquestioned symbol of monstrous otherness and frightful indeterminacy, the defenseless Jew is the most likely and obvious candidate for scapegoating in periods of social upheaval and undifferentiating violence.

Despite the centrality of the Jew in fascist ideology, anti-Semitism by no means exhausts the fascist implications of Pound's work. For if throughout this book we have tried as much as possible to avoid relying on simple ideological schemata and categories, seeking rather to convey the uniqueness of Pound's mind and language as of his political development, we have shown that much of his thinking on politics, society, religion, and culture repeatedly falls within the typology of Italian and German fascism. This is true of many Poundian beliefs and values which critics do not generally consider fascistic, and which they prefer to treat separately or else apolitically—Pound's anti-monotheism, his reverence for the concrete and natural manifold, his emphasis on hierarchy, his suspicion of abstraction and transcendence, his glorification of myth and ritual, his agrarianism, his patriarchy, his anti-feminism, his solar religion, his abhorrence of usury, to give only a few examples. All of these taken together form a typical, mutually reinforcing fascist constellation. To treat them in isolation, without regard for their political implications and their interconnection with the whole of Pound's thought, is to place them within a partial perspective and to distort their full ideological significance. Bacigalupo is entirely correct when he describes *The Cantos* as "the sacred poem of the Nazi-Fascist millennium."[2]

If Pound belongs within the fascist ideology, he likewise shares its massive confusion and contradictions, which are embodied in his metaphors and images, the form and content of his works. Repeatedly Pound's ideology is problematized and undercut by his text; our task has been in large part to reveal these hiatuses in meaning. Not the least of Pound's contradictions is the disparity between his hope of installing an homogeneous, "organic," and "totalitarian" culture around a single luminous image (a religious and ritual object such as the goddess of Terracina) and the poem's final status as an aggregate of some bright and other terrifying images, a work that approaches totality only through numerical inclusiveness rather than through the all-embracing mythical symbol. Besides mirroring the ideology and policy of fascism, *The Cantos* mirror what fascism tried violently and desperately to overcome, the fragmentation of modern culture.

I would point still more emphatically to a telling and typically fascist contradiction in Pound's work. Pound persists in his apparently conservative appeal to an all-encompassing and normative Nature. This "process" is for Pound the objective, permanent, and immanent basis for a totalitarian, hierarchical, and all-inclusive society. At the same time, according to the principle that individuals and groups should preserve and augment their own being, Nature demands the preservation of "naturally occurring" social and biological groups, in short races. As it turns out, instead of constituting a demonstrable totality or universally observed norm, Pound's Nature and this natural society are constantly beset by numerous social and political enemies and various forms of intellectual and social disease: democracy, socialism, communism, libertarianism, metaphysics, abstraction, all of which Pound comes to associate with the Jews. So strong are these enemies of the natural that they implicitly and paradoxically constitute a force of anti-Nature. Moreover, because the natural and totalitarian society is itself a utopian ideal, Pound must abandon his conservatism and pursue his utopia through extreme political measures, which involve dubious human interven-

tions into natural process such as racial breeding or eugenics and the maintenance of racial barriers. To repeat our earlier questions: If Nature is the
basis of the totalitarian society, why does that society not exist naturally,
without the need of man's intervention? Why are the forces of Nature,
supposedly immanent and objective, so obviously beleaguered by Manichean combat with a negative principle? These questions, implicit but unan-
swered in Pound's works, utterly destroy his claim that "the way," or "process," is "one." Far from being inclusive, Pound's Nature like his hierarchical society is a contemporary historical construct based on a narrow conception of human life and human possibility.

It is equally difficult to accept Pound's persistent claims to have envisioned an equitable, benevolent, and harmonious society. A sharp disparity
exists between Pound's ideal of social unity and the latent or overt
violence—and not only against outgroups such as the Jews—on which it
depends. Given the increasing rigidity, hierarchism, and authoritarianism of
his politics, Pound's platitudinous appeal to the Confucian *ling*, or benevolence, loses all credibility. Nor is Pound any more convincing in his claim
that this society exists in harmony with Nature and in accordance with
natural laws. According to Pound, the link between man and Nature is
supplied by ritual sacrifice, which has a natural sanction, and which imitates
natural occurrences. A reading of Pound shows that this natural sanction is
mythical and that there is nothing in Nature to correspond to human sacrificial acts. In Pound, as in the actual world, if Girard's speculations are
correct, sacrifice is an essentially arbitrary form of cultural violence which
while masquerading as Nature only reflects the violence within culture itself.
Originating in a forgotten act of human sacrifice, it always carries with it the
submerged threat of violence against those members of the social hierarchy
who violate "natural" order or degree. If such ritualistic violence resembles
Nature in any sense, it is only insofar as it permits religion and social
authority to lay claim for its own purposes to the fear and terror with which
external Nature is often associated in the mind of primitive man; and in this
context one should note not only the presence of the thunder or fear sign as
a symbol of "natural" retribution and sacred institutions in *The Cantos* but
the general function of ritual as a means of intimidation in the many versions of fascism.[3] Although Pound pretends to have found in Nature a
retributive and sacrificial force of fate and justice, an agency on the order of
Dante's *contrapasso*, this fearful power has no objective validity but is
another name, justification, and mythical smokescreen for the enormous
power of social domination and vengeance which Pound arbitrarily arro-
gates to fascism and himself. Pound, whose whole social system is founded
on the necessity of calling things by their right names, did not always follow
his own advice.

The Poundian utopia contradicts itself in other ways. It is doubtful that
Pound's paganism any more than the Nazi solar mythology entirely be-

speaks life affirmation: the Jews' indispensable role as victims casts a shadow over Pound's religion of solar vitality and natural renewal. Nor is it true that this paganism really achieves a true restoration, as Pound claims, of man's long-severed contact with Nature and instinct. The harmony or identity ("two halves of the tally") which Pound envisions between Man and Nature, culture and instinct, is repeatedly belied not only by his advocacy of repressive and authoritarian regimes but by his fascist attack against what he calls "the natural chaos of man"—a phrase which, in context, encompasses the passions and instincts, the human unconscious. It is equally doubtful that Pound, through ritual and other means, has succeeded in eliminating from his work the tension between myth (or Nature) and history. Throughout his writings there appears a persistent conflict between his desire to negate (actually to conceal) history and return to Nature by means of myth and ritual, and his support of movements committed to technological advancement and renovation and the control and domination of Nature. Similarly, Pound's use of myths and rituals to evoke the "true" content of historical events (such as the fascist revolution), rather than transmitting archetypal or primitive truth, transparently involves the historically sophisticated (that is to say modernist) manipulation of mythical materials for historical purposes. This literary and high-tech modernist appropriation of mythology, as in Pound's efficient streamlining of the *Li Ki* in Canto 52, bears a resemblance to the Nazis' equally efficient but far more deadly absorption of myths and rituals within the constantly renovating framework of modern mechanization, technology, and production. In Pound, as in fascism, the "revolt of nature" is appropriated and exploited in the interests of domination.[4]

Ultimately it is the Jews who most fully embody and reveal the contradictions of Pound's thought. The fascist and Poundian conception of the Jews is inconsistent and self-contradictory, being based on a multitude of projections and reflecting the ambivalence and confusion of the fascist subject. Yet once the process of projection and scapegoating is recognized and understood, it is possible to read in fascist anti-Semitism the confusion of fascist thought itself. In Pound it is not enough that the regressive and reptilian Jews should allegedly destroy history; at the same time they must be representatives of anti-Nature, above all in their hostility to myth and their aggressive modernity in thought and commerce. If these contradictory accusations are never reconciled in Pound's thought, the reason is that Pound (like fascism) never clarifies or resolves his allegiance to the two opposing worlds of history and myth. Instead, he turns to violence against the ambiguous Jews as a means of masking his ideological equivocation. In the eyes of fascism as in Pound the Jews do not merely represent the forces of ascetic repressiveness and paternal authority which the instinctual revolt of the fascist sons denies; they also represent the instinctual life itself, the unconscious chaos of the swamp, which fascism fears, and which it unleashes only in the form of violence against the "naturally depraved" Jews. Thus the attack on the Jews again belies the fascist and Poundian claim of a return to Nature, which it cannot embody except in a mythological and sacrificial rather than actual form.

It must be emphasized that the essential contradictoriness of Pound's fascism is not to be found in any specific anti-Semitic accusation. It is revealed most strikingly in the Jews' central function within his ideology, which is to represent the massiveness and omnipresence of Poundian and fascist fears. In whatever form, the demonic Jew provides the most compelling argument not for Pound's naturalistic and totalitarian claims, but for his true and primary and essentially fascist impulse, which is fearfully to eliminate and exclude.

In assessing the value of Pound's social, political, cultural, and economic thought, one cannot avoid an overwhelming conclusion. Apart from Pound's technical expertise in many literary and aesthetic matters, much of it, when not merely superficial, is manifestly a tissue of absurdities, dangerous half-truths, contradictions, self-delusions, home-spun platitudes, untested and conceited assertions and dogmas. It is simply astonishing that Pound's apologists and sincere admirers continue to treat it with such reverence.

Yet such reverence has its reasons. Perhaps only a few Pound critics, whether consciously or not, find Pound's ideology and attitudes to be truly attractive. For the most part Pound critics are aesthetes who lack such historical, political, and psychological knowledge and interest as would enable them to recognize the total complex of fascist attitudes even when, as in Pound's work, it stares them in the face. This is a disturbing sign, it seems to me, in contemporary academic life.

Still, none of the above explanations accounts altogether for critics' high estimation of Pound's cultural values in combination with their obvious failure to inquire into his overt impulse to scapegoat Jews (as well as Buddhists and Taoists) even to the point of expulsion and extermination. This failure results not from historical ignorance but from *méconnaissance,* that blindness to violence which characterizes culture as a whole, and to which, according to Girard, culture owes its existence. Put simply, critics have chosen "the essential 'idolatry' of all human culture."[5] If this view of Pound seems forced, it should be remembered that Pound, like Hitler, believed that Western culture could be saved by the sacrificial elimination of the Jews; as Pound said, the Nazis "wiped out bad manners in Germany." Nor should one suppose that Pound's high cultural values are necessarily incompatible with barbarism. The rough and violent side of Pound, as well as his idolatry of culture, was recognized decades ago by Yvor Winters when he described Pound as "a barbarian on the loose in a museum."[6]

II.

It may seem that this book is unfair to Pound insofar as it stresses his "bad side." If this is so, my only answer is that my subject has been Pound's anti-Semitism and fascism. It may also seem that my treatment of Pound emphasizes only his confusion and that it locates his value only in the revelation of the social contradictions of fascism; for the rest, Pound would appear as an aesthetic failure and a dangerous intellectual renegade. A broader, more careful, and more tolerant assessment of Pound is yet necessary because of critics' tendency either to praise him excessively and uncritically, in complete disregard of the poetic significance of his politics, or else to condemn his work virtually in its entirety, as if his ideology had thoroughly vitiated it.

Tom Scott carries to an extreme an idolatrous attitude common to many Pound apologists. Pound, he argues, is the misunderstood victim of "repressed hatred" and "lust for revenge," of the masses' inability to see that his politics, rather than being fascistic or anti-Semitic, are visionary and poetical, a "dream of the kingdom of poetry on earth."[7] Unable to recognize its own guilt, and needing scapegoats for fascism, the anti-poetic public chooses the guiltless Pound as its victim, Pound thus emerging as a kind of Socrates or Jesus, a modern crucified saint.[8] Despite the absurdity of such arguments, and for all his errors concerning Pound's politics, Scott rightly notes a profound hostility to Pound, a hostility which appears not just in the public but in responsible critics. To be sure, Irving Howe is to be commended for having in 1949 insisted on the importance of Pound's fascism to our judgment of his work. But Howe would refuse to Pound more than the Bollingen Prize. He believed that Pound's ideology as such demands what would amount to a total quarantine and devaluation of his work. Pound, he said, "by virtue of his public record and utterances, is beyond the bounds of our intellectual life."[9] In this refusal of an intellectual identity to Pound, this banishment beyond the pale, this decontamination of American cultural life from Pound's dangerous influence, one recognizes a version of that scapegoating strategy to which Scott refers.

Ironically, the cultural banishment and neglect of Pound by many liberal critics has had a positive effect on the development of Pound's reputation, at least in some circles. For although Howe's and Scott's views of Pound seem radically opposed, they are really dependent on each other in subtle ways and constitute the two aspects of the indivisible process of victimization and apotheosis which we have examined in this book. The Pound cult would probably not have attained its present proportions if the liberal critics, instead of merely condemning and ignoring Pound's poetry for its overt ideological evil, had fully elucidated the intimate relation between his poetry and politics. This strategy, had it been carried out in the years following the Bollingen controversy, would have prevented any facile and sophistic apologetic dissociation of Pound's poetry and ideology, and it would have made it all the more difficult to exonerate and then apotheosize Pound. But the liberal critics, by at once condemning, ignoring and failing to explain Pound, have unwittingly fostered other critics' attempts to turn him into a kind of cultural god. In truth Pound is neither a god nor an outcast. While his idolators ignore his complicity with violence, his enemies ignore their own critical violence and ironically repeat against Pound the very scapegoating strategy for which he is condemned. This is not to exempt my book, and perhaps all criticism, from some degree of violence or aggression towards its subject. Yet my intention in criticizing Pound has never been to achieve what would in any case turn out to be an impossible goal, namely his cultural banishment. Undoubtedly Pound will remain a questionable figure, but he can be questioned only within the bounds of our intellectual life.

By no means do I believe that *The Cantos* should be condemned categorically. It is possible to find generous, affirmative, and humanistic ways of reading them. Of course, there always remains their poetic beauty and the fascination of their verbal texture—the mere explicability which in much of contemporary criticism has become virtually a standard of value in itself. It is also entirely possible to read *The Cantos* as an autobiographical poem in which the autobiographical impulse finally displaces history and ideology and wins for both the poet and the poem a truly tragic illumination: "I am not a demigod, / I cannot make it cohere." In these lines Pound rejects the spiritual elitism which had drawn him to fascism and those messianic aspirations which had led him into a protracted and psychologically destructive agon with the Jews. *The Cantos* would emerge in this reading as a tragedy of Pound's character, a tragedy whose catharsis lies in Pound's final recognition of his own confusion and *hubris*. But this reading would require us to restore the true significance of the word *hubris*.[10]

Nor should we suppose that either *The Cantos* or Pound's prose is altogether vitiated by an allegiance to a repressive and contradictory ideology. To the contrary, it is possible to argue that the "official" opinions of a text or author are mere "surface phenomena." Such an argument would not follow the New Critical disparagement of ideas as such. It would follow the Marxist idea that in spite of the conscious intent of an author, and beyond his ideological aims, which may themselves be reactionary or repressive, a text can offer "renewed access to some essential source of life."[11] In short, a writer can be secretly at war with his ideology. As much as he claims to resolve all social contradictions in a "specious harmony" and premature unity, as does Pound, his works may actually "express the idea of harmony negatively, by embodying the contradictions, pure and uncompromised," in their "innermost structure." This is a good description of *The Cantos*. So too, as much as a writer officially supports domination, repression, or the status quo, his works can belie that allegiance through their resistance to social pressure, their personal claims to the ideal of happiness, and their measure of utopian protest.[12]

It is well known that Pound repeatedly denounced ideologies and systems. In one sense this attitude comes to intersect with Italian Fascism's claim to leave all avenues open, but in another it reflects Pound's genuine (and finally paranoid) distrust of received opinions and pre-packaged and pre-coordinated knowledge, especially that disseminated by the modern media and universities. No matter what one thinks of it as a reliable instrument of knowledge, Pound's ideogrammic method, characterized by the heaping together of concrete particulars to form new and unexpected inter-relations, represents a deliberate avoidance of an imposed system. This is one reason that *The Cantos,* as an idiosyncratic and largely autodidactic "paideuma," sometimes reveal truth and beauty and wisdom which the trained specialist overlooks or ignores. Though Pound in the later *Cantos* endorses an apparently regimented system of education (ancient China), his poem, like his other works, continues to demand the student's active participation in the process of understanding. Thus the subjective, which Pound generally distrusts in his ideology, asserts itself in his work and is perhaps its main inspiration.

It is also necessary to qualify our earlier description of Pound as a cultural idolator. Pound rarely succumbs to one of the least attractive forms of cultural idolatry, that which values culture for its own sake and thus treats it as the equivalent of the museum.[13] As Pound suggests, the word *diletto,* meaning delight, and the related word dilettante, have pejorative meaning only when, as in the modern world, mechanization and systematization have transformed culture into a joyless activity and a specialized form of experience.[14] In Pound's view the classic example of such idolatry is the Prussian or Germanic ideal, whereby (to follow Pound's parody) culture becomes academic regimentation at the behest of the state and scholarship degenerates into a deadly concentration on trivia. Though they celebrate a repressive politics, *The Cantos* never lose sight of joy, pleasure, and leisure as the true goal of culture. Thus in Canto 20:

> "Noigandres, eh, *noi*gandres,
> "Now what the DEFFIL can that mean!"
> Wind over the olive trees, ranunculae ordered,
> By the clear edge of the rocks
> The water runs, and the wind scented with pine
> And with hay-fields under sun-swath.
> Agostino, Jacopo and Boccata.
> You would be happy for the smell of that place
> And never tired of being there, either alone
> Or accompanied.
> Sound: as of the nightingale too far off to be heard.
> Sandro, and Boccata, and Jacopo Sellaio;
> The ranunculae, and almond,
> Boughs set in espalier,
> Duccio, Agostino; *e l'olors—*
> The smell of that place—*d'enoi ganres.*

> Air moving under the boughs,
> The cedar there in the sun,
> Hay new cut on hill slope,
> And the water there in the cut
> Between the two lower meadows; sound,
> The sound, as I have said, a nightingale
> Too far off to be heard.
> And the light falls, *remir*,
> from her breast to thighs.
>
> (20/ 90)

Like much of *The Cantos*, this passage connects culture with an image of utopian happiness and with resistance to various forms of control and renunciation. It thus maintains an uneasy relationship with that totalitarianism which Pound, mistakenly, summons as a preserver of cultural vitality. Nor is it possible to accept as entirely accurate our earlier argument that Pound's works, like some versions of fascism, reflect an opposition to transcendence and a longing for immanence. Admittedly Pound constantly attacks transcendental modes of thought. He believes that man, rather than reaching toward an "absolute whole,"[15] or seeking to transcend the natural world and the familiar givens of human nature, should properly confine his attention to the natural manifold, the bounded and concrete, to the individual divinities in Nature, to what already and "really" exists. Furthermore, Pound considers it "natural" for man not to transcend his specific human nature but to preserve his own being—an ideal not so much of individual freedom as of allegiance to the locally originating, immediate, and preexisting values of the social (and racial) group. From such beliefs follows Pound's fearful hatred of Jewish monotheism as of all transcendental and universal absolutes and values, among which belongs money in its abstract forms. The danger of such spiritual, philosophical, and commercial abstractions is that they tend to universalize the concept of human nature and in transforming it disrupt the enclosed unity of the traditional society. Here is why Pound was increasingly hostile to modernization and the emancipation process and why he was increasingly attracted to tribal, ethnocentric, anticosmopolitan, stratified, and even xenophobic societies.

Yet Nolte observes that Charles Maurras, though staunchly hostile to transcendence and to absolute and universal morality, did not completely belong to "the world for which he was fighting."[16] This is even more true of Pound, in whom the rejected impulse of transcendence asserts itself variously and inexorably. As obvious as it may seem, Pound's commitment to social criticism, which always implies resistance to the merely given, is a mode of transcendence. The same can be said of Pound's hatred of dogma and tyranny, which, while contradictory, contains a genuine if largely individualistic element of protest. One also recalls the reformist, Enlightenment, and even utopian element in Pound's thought; his pleas for the dissemination of knowledge to overcome both provincial and urban backwardness;

and the enormous *hubris* of his desire to found a personal cult, a desire which, while it is in one sense a manifestation of fascist spiritual elitism, also reveals that the anti-Romantic Pound had absorbed the example of Romantic individualism. When Pound appeals to the individual rather than the social conscience in defense of his broadcasts, he provides evidence not so much of his Confucianism as of his despised Protestant upbringing.

The best and most satisfying testimony of Pound's transcendence are *The Cantos* themselves. I am not thinking primarily of Pound's visions of utopian happiness or his attempts to evoke an "absolute whole" and a permanent realm of values—the NOUS, the "high air" in which universal values are measured, the "great ball of crystal," the "undiscussible Paradiso," the "Thrones" of judgment—although all these are highly significant.[17] *The Cantos,* insofar as they are the product of an uprooted, cosmopolitan, self-conscious, capacious, and highly exacerbated sensibility, a mind freely conversant with and dependent on a multitude of cultural traditions, testify to Pound's early and in many ways successful attempt to transcend the narrow limits of his American cultural origins. In their attempt to unify vast portions of the world's cultural heritage, they suggest just the sort of sensibility which would have been out of place in the ethnocentric and regimented China of the later *Cantos.*[18] One can only conclude that Pound's ideological resistance to transcendence reveals an extraordinary (but by no means atypical) lack of self-knowledge, particularly of the circumstances to which he owed his personal and poetic identity; to some extent it amounts to a negation, a deliberate limitation of self. In another sense, it reflects again Pound's enormous fear, which in this instance extends to the potentially democratic or socialist future, a world supposedly filled with "rabble" led by Jews, those who "dazzle men with talk of tomorrow." Finally, it reflects Pound's nomadic, marginal, and essentially undefined social position, in short, his alienation, which gives rise to longings for familiarity and rootedness, and which, the future being closed off, Pound can appease only with images of an archaic, ethnocentric, and vanished past. Fortunately, in spirit and in perspective *The Cantos* often rise above and at the same time undercut the narrow ideology which Pound imposes upon them.

Notes

Chapter One: Introduction

1 Pound, quoted from *Patria Mia* in Chace, p. 7.

2 Pound to Lincoln Kirstein, ed. of *Hound and Horn*, April, 1930, Beinecke Rare Book and Manuscript Library, Yale University.

3 Pound, "Hunger Fighters," *New English Weekly*, 22 Feb. 1934, p. 452; "American Notes," *New English Weekly*, 21 Nov. 1935, p. 105; "What Price the Muses Now," *New English Weekly*, 24 May, 1934, pp. 130–132; "American Notes," *New English Weekly*, 5 March, 1936, p. 405; "American Notes," *New English Weekly*, 26 March, 1936, p. 465; "The Return of the Native, II," *New English Weekly*, 9 April, 1936, p. 510. As late as 1938 Pound said that "international usury contains more Calvinism, Protestant sectarianism than Judaism." See Stock, 3, p. 479.

4 See Pound's letter to the editor, *New English Weekly*, 24 May, 1934, p. 144, and Pound, "Organicly Speaking," *New English Weekly*, 26 Dec. 1935, p. 211. By 1934 the anti-Semitic tendency of the British Union of Fascists had turned into an official and sometimes brutal campaign against the Jews. See Cross, pp. 78, 102, 116, 118, 119–128, 149–161, 166.

5 Pound to John Drummond, 6 March, 1934, Beinecke Rare Book and Manuscript Library, Yale University.

6 Pound, "Demarcations," *British Union Quarterly*, 1 (Jan.-April, 1937), p. 37.

7 Pound, "Ecclesia," *Townsman*, 2 (Nov. 1939), p. 4; "Problemi da risolvere," *Meridiano di Roma*, VIII (14 Feb. 1943), p. 1.

8 Pound, "Statues of Gods," *Townsman*, 2 (Aug. 1939), p. 14; Pound, quoted in Norman, p. 228.

9 Pound, "Race," *New English Weekly*, 15 Oct. 1936, pp. 12–13.

10 See Pound, "Money and Irving Fisher," *New English Weekly*, 5 Jan. 1939, p. 195; Pound's Aug.-Sept., 1939 letter to Wilson is in the Beinecke Rare Book and Manuscript Library, Yale University.

11 For "disease incarnate" ("malattia incarnata"), see Norman, p. 373.

12 See Gordon, 1, p. 357; Wilhelm, 2, p. 183.

13 For "martyr," see Weyl, in *A Casebook*, p. 15.

14 E. Fuller Torrey, M.D., confirms the persistence of Pound's anti-Semitism and fascism at St. Elizabeths. See Torrey, p. 226.

15 See the discussion of the Ezra Pound Conference at the University of Keele in Kayman, p. 465.

16 See Chace, pp. 7, 20; Loftus, pp. 347–354; Vasse, p. 324; Ferkiss, 2, pp. 358–367.

17 See Emery, pp. 66–67, quoting Duarte de Montalegre; Kenner, 3, pp. 464–

465; Wykes-Joyce, "Some Considerations arising from Ezra Pound's Conception of the Bank," in Russell, ed., pp. 225–226; Surette, 3, p. 5; Vasse, p. 324; Brooke-Rose, p. 250; Flory, p. 81; Kimpel and Eaves, 2, pp. 61, 67.

18 Emery, pp. 6–9, 11, 17, 21–22; Chace, p. 81; Charlesworth (Gelpi), pp. 9–17.

19 See Handlin, pp. 323–344; Hofstadter, 2, pp. 61, 68, 69, 300–302.

20 Three scholars have stressed and perhaps finally exaggerated religious factors: Trachtenberg, p. xii; Poliakov, 2, Vol. III, p. viii; Cohn, 2, p. 79; Hook, pp. 462–482, esp. 464.

21 Heymann, p. 75; Bergonzi, pp. 1195–1196. Perhaps the most serious example of such evasiveness and even deception is Carroll F. Terrell's two volume *A Companion to the Cantos of Ezra Pound*, which, with its extensive references and exegetical apparatus, will probably become the chief engine of Pound scholarship in the coming decades. In the preface to the first volume Terrell asks for a "temperate evaluation" of Pound on the basis of his work rather than the negative yet presumably inaccurate "public image of the poet" as a fascist and anti-Semite. This disavowal of partisanship and "apologetics" is dubious, since Terrell ignores or deemphasizes to the point of triviality the whole issue of Pound's anti-Semitism. Indeed, he even seeks to give the impression that Pound is not anti-Semitic. Nor does Terrell pay sufficient attention to the many ways in which fascism informs the ideology of *The Cantos*. For him, the radio broadcasts belong on the farthest margins of Pound's corpus. See Terrell, Vol. I, p. ix, and *passim*. See also my forthcoming review of Terrell in *Resources for American Literary Study*.

22 Dr. E. Fuller Torrey has argued convincingly that Pound, with help, faked insanity to escape prosecution. See Torrey, *passim*. Political controversy shadowed Pound as late as 1972, the year of his death, when he was nominated for but finally denied the Emerson-Thoreau Medal awarded annually by the American Academy of Arts and Sciences. The decisive factor in the decision was the judges' opinion that Pound's anti-Semitic and fascist pronouncements disqualified him from receiving a humanistic award. See Heymann, pp. 309–311.

23 Library of Congress Press Release No. 542, Feb. 20, 1949, quoted in *A Casebook*, pp. 44–46.

24 Davis, in *A Casebook*, p. 56; Viereck, in *A Casebook*, p. 96.

25 Graff, pp. 94, 108, 109, 15, 34, 140.

26 Tate, quoted in Davis, in *A Casebook*, p. 80.

27 Howe, Shapiro, and Davis, all in the *Partisan Review* Symposium, "The Question of the Pound Award," included in *A Casebook*, pp. 59–60, 61, 58.

28 Davis's and Viereck's position resembles Gerald Graff's in *Poetic Statement and Critical Dogma*, p. 27. Sammons, pp. 146–147, similarly cautions against the reification of the extrinsic and intrinsic; he quotes Viktor Žmegač who argues that "externals can become immanent and formal aspects internal impulses."

29 For "scaffolding," see Graff's discussion of I. A. Richards' and Cleanth Brooks's use of this New Critical notion, pp. 89–90.

30 MacLeish unjustifiably refers to Pound's opinions as "they," as something apart from "he," thus freeing Pound from responsibility for his opinions. He also praises Pound's poem for its compelling "image" of the true incoherence of the modern world. Thus, thanks to the fallacy of imitative form, MacLeish transforms incoherence into a mimetic virtue, while covertly introducing extrinsic criteria in order to justify Pound. See Archibald MacLeish, *Poetry and Opinion: The Pisan Cantos of Ezra Pound*, (Urbana: Univ. of Illinois Press, 1950), quoted in *A Casebook*, pp. 87–91. For a penetrating criticism of MacLeish's argument, see Graff, pp. 172–179. Michael André Bernstein also stresses the impossibility of "refining out of existence" *The Cantos'* "polemic and pedagogic dimension," its "ideas," its claims to "verifiable propositions." See Bernstein, p. 129n.

31 See Pearlman, 1, *passim*; see also Jerome Mazzaro's review of three books on Pound in *Criticism*, 24 (1976), pp. 388–391. Mazzaro quotes from Eugene Paul Nassar's *The Cantos of Ezra Pound: The Lyric Mode*.

32 Shapiro, in *A Casebook*, pp. 61–63; Pound, quoted in Stock, 2, p. 91.

33 T.S. Eliot, quoted in Alexander, p. 125.
34 G.S. Fraser, in Russell, ed., p. 185; Kimpel and Eaves, 2, p. 67.
35 Henry Swabey, in Russell, ed., pp. 201, 202.
36 Flory, pp. 4, 5, 49, 56, 59–83. See also Woodward, p. 48. Woodward speaks of the "true Pound" as a kind of benevolent and unaggressive Taoist.
37 See Reck, 2, p. 116; Duarte de Montalegre, in Emery, pp. 66–67; Kimpel and Eaves, 2, p. 56. Houston Stewart Chamberlain affords a typical example of this sort of anti-Semitic apologetics. See Geoffrey Field, p. 186.
38 See Fraser, in Russell, ed., p. 185; Reck, 1, p. 116; Wilhelm, 2, p. xvi; Brooke-Rose, p. 250; Kimpel and Eaves, 2, p. 57. By contrast, John Lauber argues effectively for the "centrality" of anti- Semitism and fascism in *The Cantos*. In his view, "the anti-Semitism of *The Cantos* cannot be dismissed as an aberration." See Lauber, p. 14. Confining himself mainly to Pound's critical prose and explicitly ideological writing, Andrew Parker argues with equal effectiveness for anti-Semitism as an essential rather than "contingent phenomenon" within Pound's system of thought and cultural enterprise. See Andrew Parker, pp. 103–128.
39 See Lander, p. 85; Dekker, p. xv.
40 This positivistic approach reaches its culmination in Kimpel and Eaves's "Ezra Pound's Anti-Semitism." In an attempt to prove the insignificance of anti-Semitism in *The Cantos,* they gather what they consider to be a comprehensive collection of Jewish and anti-Semitic "references" from the poem. Jewish references, they conclude, appear on only thirty-one pages, while only forty-five lines, less than ".002" of the poem, can be called anti-Semitic. Kimpel and Eaves's most serious error does not lie in the fact that they fail to recognize gross anti-Semitic attitudes in some passages (see for instance their views of Canto 35) or that they overlook a large number of passages with anti-Semitic import. Nor is it in failing to recognize those passages whose context and implication is anti-Semitic, or in which Pound's reviled Buddhists and Taoists, for the sake of political convenience, take the place of the Jews. The real difficulty is that their technique of statistical and content analysis cannot do justice to a subject which requires painstaking attention to verbal and metaphorical nuance, unconscious intentions and displacements, cultural antecedents and analogues, ideological purposes, and literary and historical contexts. Above all, their quantitative approach cannot explain the essential place of anti-Semitism within the linguistic and psychological economy of *The Cantos*. Anti-Semitism is not a detachable fraction of Pound's text, nor is it reducible to a mere fact or series of facts; it is a problem of Pound's work and personality as a whole. The limitations of Kimpel and Eaves's method are manifest if one takes its assumptions to their logical conclusion. One might estimate a scale of relative anti-Semitism among leading literary and political figures by determining a percentage of their anti-Semitic references in relation to the total quantity of their literary output. For instance: Pound, .002 per cent (a count of Pound's prose would no doubt increase this figure, which in any case is inaccurate); Wagner, perhaps half of one per cent; Voltaire, perhaps one per cent; Céline, perhaps one and a half per cent; Mosley, perhaps two; Hitler, almost three . . . . It might thus be possible to conclude that Hitler was "no more than" three per cent anti-Semitic. The use of such reifying statistical devices borrowed from the social sciences gives the illusion of precision while encouraging the abdication of thought. See Kimpel and Eaves, 2, pp. 59, 66–67.
41 A harsh critic of Pound during the Bollingen controversy, Irving Howe resumed his attack during the debate over Pound's candidacy for the Emerson-Thoreau Medal in 1972: "Pound wished none of us [Jews] personal harm; his rantings against the Jews were utterly *abstract,* a phantasm of ideology that is a major dimension of their terribleness." Quoted in Heymann, p. 310. But the idea that Pound's anti-Semitism is a phantasm is also misleading, since it suggests that his image of the Jews is entirely divorced from the reality of individual Jews or Jewish culture. While Pound's anti- Semitism contains mythical elements, his representation of the Jews is not a complete distortion, nor did he completely misread the significance of the Jews in the West. On this point, see Pulzer, pp. 14–15; Reichsmann, p. 37.

42 Recently Lewis Hyde has made a fruitless attempt to read Pound's anti-Semitism mythically. Ignoring its complex historical, ideological, and personal origins, and absorbing it within the vague realm of mythical archetypes and Jungian "shadows," Hyde argues that Pound's concept of the Jews has "little to do" with actual Jews but is an "elaboration" of the "classical Hermes." See Hyde, pp. 246, 247, 250, and my essay, "Ezra Pound and Hermes," *San José Studies*, 12 (Fall, 1986), pp. 83–104.

43 Reck, 1, p. 116; the comparison of Pound with Milton and Dante appears in Heymann, pp. 179, 194.

44 See Pound to T. David Horton, 6 Jan., 1958, in the Beinecke Rare Book and Manuscript Library, Yale University; see also Cornell, p. 192: at his trial Pound shouted that he was "opposed to Fascism."

45 Recent historians recognize the difficulty of giving a "clear definition of fascism" as a movement or ideology, for there is apparently no "absolutely common identity" uniting the various fascisms. To quote George L. Mosse, "the old model of fascism" as a "monolith" has "broken down . . . . There were profound differences between German national socialism and Italian Fascism," above all on the issues of race, modernization, and corporatism. Other historians, and the fascists themselves, view Nazism as the most strikingly "alien" and "divisive" element. See Mosse, with Michael A. Ledeen, 7, p. 17; 8, p. 159; Eugen Weber, 2, pp. 44, 46, 141–143; Allardyce, pp. 367–388; Gregor, 2, pp. 1338–1347; Ledeen, p. 165; Wiskemann, pp. 99–100; De Felice, pp. 15, 91–92, 95, 105. On the other hand, Stanley Payne warns against a "radically nominalist approach that insists on the inherent difference of all the radical nationalist movements of interwar Europe." Like other historians, such as Renzo de Felice, he considers it possible to speak of "generic fascism" and a "fascist minimum," although in many cases the differences between the movements are more important than their similarities. See Payne, pp. 195–196. For a good summary of fascism that in my view maintains an untrivial "minimum of conceptual unity," see Bernt Hagtvet and Reinhard Kühnl, "Contemporary Approaches to Fascism: A Survey of Paradigms," in Larsen et al., eds., p. 27.

46 Nolte, p. 40; Zeev Sternhell, "Fascist Ideology," in Laqueur, ed., pp. 356–357; Eugen Weber, 2, p. 69. Italian Fascism is problematic. Although Italy was not culturally anti-Semitic, and although Mussolini showed disdain for Nazi racism in the 1920s and 1930s, by 1938 the Fascist government had for a variety of reasons instituted unpopular racial laws against the Jews. But on the whole racism is far less prominent in Italian Fascism than in Nazism, and takes not a rigidly biological but rather "spiritual" or "nationalistic" form. See Ledeen, pp. 110, 134, 149. See also below, Chapters Ten and Eleven.

47 Often implicit in Pound's attacks on the Jews, the charge of parasitism is overt in his letter of 21 Dec., 1934, to Fred R. Miller: "NO jew any good on his own, got to have a partner, or got to have an Aryan to parasite ON." Quoted in Kimpel and Eaves, 2, p. 57.

48 Miller notes that "parasite" is a "word 'in para' ": ". . . 'Para' is a double antithetical prefix signifying at once proximity and distance, similarity and difference, interiority and exteriority, something inside a domestic economy and at the same time outside it, something simultaneously this side of a boundary line, threshold, or margin, and also beyond it, equivalent in status and also secondary and subsidiary, submissive, as of guest to host, slave to master. A thing in 'para,' moreover, is not only simultaneously on both sides of the boundary line between inside and out. It is also the boundary line itself, the screen which is a permeable membrane connecting inside and outside. It confuses them with one another, allowing the outside in, making the inside out, dividing and joining them. It also forms an ambiguous transition between one and the other. Though a given word in 'para' may seem to choose univocally one of these possibilities, the other meanings are always there as a shimmering in the word which makes it refuse to stay still in a sentence. The word is like a slightly alien guest within the syntactical enclosure where all words are family friends together." See J. Hillis Miller, "The Critic as Host," in *Deconstruction and Criticism*, p. 219. Although the accusation of parasitism generally figures within

a strategy of differentiation and exclusion, whether from a community, home, or text, and although the parasite is thus implicitly conceived as marginal and adventitious, this strategy is called in question not just by the parasite's prior existence within the community but, above all, by the fact that it is itself necessary, indispensable within the process of differentiation. As Miller says, the parasite is not only within and beyond the margin: it can also be the margin itself. Thus, in Pound, the parasitic Jews might well be taken to create the "permeable" distinction or margin between the organic community and that which threatens to disrupt or confuse its fixed values. Similarly, in Pound criticism, the imputation of parasitism to anti-Semitism enables the critic to make a distinction between those meanings which are authentic and acceptable and those which are alien to and disruptive of the verbal economy of Pound's writing.

49 Ernst Simmel, "Anti-Semitism and Mass Psychopathology," in Simmel, ed., p. 55.

50 W.B. Yeats, quoted in Norman, p. 353.

51 However, David I. Goldstein has established the place of anti-Semitism in Dostoyevsky's Russian or Pan-Slavic ideology, and he shows that this calls in question the authenticity of Dostoyevsky's Christianity, which is a major theme and value in his novels. Eliot largely keeps his relatively mild anti-Semitism out of his work, and when he refers to the Jews, they appear as general symbols or else as unpleasant examples of rootless modernism and cosmopolitanism. Although distasteful, this practice does not raise anti-Semitism to a major position in ideological or formal terms. See Goldstein, *passim*. On Eliot's anti-Semitism, see Morris, pp. 173–182.

52 See Viereck, in *A Casebook*, p. 98.

53 Friedrich Nietzsche, 3, p. 77.

54 Kimpel and Eaves mistakenly seek to divorce the broadcasts from Pound's more "literary" production. Ignoring the frequent intersection of the broadcasts' themes with those of the poetry, they also refuse to recognize that the broadcasts provide a context within which to determine Pound's more obscure intentions in *The Cantos*. Yet certainly they will not deny that the same man wrote both works. Furthermore the fact that the broadcasts are more blatantly anti-Semitic than the poetry does not necessarily make the poetry less anti-Semitic in its aims and implication. Rather, one goes to the broadcasts to discover those impulses which the decorum of English verse— which is to say not Pound's moral sense but merely his good taste—often prevented him from expressing with complete openness in *The Cantos*.

55 There is a good reason especially for treating Pound from a Freudian and Marxist perspective. For all his emphasis on the concrete particular, Pound repeatedly insists on the need for coordinated, organic, and inclusive knowledge: each branch of knowledge should be connected with all other branches. But Pound is extraordinarily arbitrary in his view of what constitutes good, useful, relevant, or organic knowledge; if anything, the true tendency of his thought is not to include but to exclude. Just as Pound (in the fascist manner) condemns entire historical periods as worthless or factitious, he resists violently but with little argumentative justification intellectual positions he does not like. Of these, Freudianism and Marxism, the chief manifestations of *"the kikery"* (91/ 614), have the most conspicuous place. Pound's uncritical and irrational dismissal of Freudianism and Marxism may originate in his fear of their demonstrable power to demystify his ideology and poetic text. Such power of demystification motivates and justifies my use of Freudian and Marxist approaches. For Pound on organic knowledge, see LE, pp. 15, 19, 62, 77; SP, pp. 190–191.

56 Alan Durant rightly deplores critics' "unacknowledged complicity with Pound's founding aesthetic principles," particularly his notions of "precision in language" and his simplistic empiricism. See Durant, pp. 7, 9, 11, 8–19, 42–43, 45–46, 50, 58–60.

57 Of all intellectual traditions, Pound probably most preferred that of the ruling mandarin bureaucracy of Confucian China, who stand at a far remove from the tradition of Western philosophy as it descends from the Greeks. Max Weber observes that the very concepts of *logos* and *dialectic* are "absolutely alien" to

Chinese philosophy. Shunning speculation and system, Chinese thinking manifests a "categorical manner" (most congenial to Pound) and an overriding interest in practical problems. In Weber's view it remained "stuck" in the pictorial and descriptive (again qualities congenial to Pound), in "matter-of-fact illustrations and parables," rather than developing the rational and discursive power of logical argumentation. Weber would seem to consider as deficiencies of the logical and critical spirit the very qualities which Pound most admires in Confucian thought. Given Pound's later emphasis on the cultivation and preservation of mainly local traditions, it seems ironic that he went "so far to burn incense" (99/ 698). See Max Weber, "The Chinese Literati," in Gerth and Mills, eds., pp. 431–433.

58 Although the title of this book implicitly places Pound's ideology under the category of myth, myth and ideology are not identical. Ben Halperin notes that myths normally refer to deceptive or distorting social beliefs whose origin is irrational or unconscious and whose function is the preservation of the status quo. Ideologies claim rational justification or truth and attempt to mould future action. Still, Halperin finds these concepts to be similar and even comparable. Not only do all ideologies manifest some degree of irrationality, distortion, and deception, but, as in fascism and Pound especially, they often make an irrational appeal to mythology by means of symbols and images. See Ben Halperin, pp. 134–135, 136–137, 143–144; Mannheim, p. 144.

59 As Eliot suggests in his discussion of Joyce in "Ulysses—Order and Myth," the modern artist can use a mythical pattern to support his work— a position which acknowledges not so much the truth or archetypal value of myth as its practical (and finally arbitrary) purpose. But other artists and critics, such as Pound, make greater truth claims for myth. One of the most effective attacks on the attraction to myth in modern culture is Philip Rahv's "The Myth and the Powerhouse," which argues that Pound, "wholly in the throes of 'mythicism,' " manipulates myth for historical and ideological ends. See Rahv, pp. 3–21.

Chapter Two: The Jews as Negative Principle
1 Not only does Pound identify the *logos* or word with intelligence, essence, and the Good, but he ascribes to what Jacques Derrida defines as "a Platonic schema that assigns the origin and power of speech, precisely the *logos*, to the paternal position." Pound also associates (rather than strictly equates) the Good with light and more specifically the sun, which figures as "the origin of all *onta*, responsible for their appearing and their coming into *logos*, which both assembles and distinguishes them." For Pound, as for Plato, the sun "is more than the essential; it produces essence, being, and appearing; the essence of that which is." Because the sun is a minister and symbol of *logos*, and because it is identified with the father, it is also the governing "ground" (the sun is "under it all," 85/ 544), the luminous "center" from which proper and distinct meanings and truths derive. Thus Pound's logocentrism and solar worship manifest what Derrida would call a "longing for a center," an "authorizing pressure" which, operating at once within and outside the system it controls, "spawns" categorical and "hierarchical oppositions" in language and thought. These meanings and oppositions depend on a relation to or contact with the sun, the origin, presence; and they threaten to collapse whenever that origin or presence is called in question, whenever its traces are absent, obscured, or confused. See Derrida, "Plato's Pharmacy," in Derrida, 3, pp. 77, 82, 86; "White Mythology: Metaphor in the Text of Philosophy," in Derrida, 4, pp. 218–219, 242–244, 250–251, 267. See also Gayatri Spivak's "Translator's Preface" to Derrida, 1, pp. lxviii–lxix, and Derrida's "Structure, Sign, and Play in the Discourse of the Human Sciences," in Richard Macksey and Eugenio Donato, eds., pp. 247–272.

2 See Pound, SP, p. 333, where he introduces the Cheng Ming ideogram (which also appears at the end of Canto 51), enjoining men to call things by their right names. My discussion above is also indebted to Durant, p. 54.

3 According to Derrida, the idea of the Logos is related metaphorically to a complex of ideas including the sun, capital (money and head), agriculture, the action

of sowing or planting, generation and growth— again, paternity and origination. See "Plato's Pharmacy," pp. 81–83.

4 See Remy de Gourmont, p. 114. See also Pound's postscript to that work, which is included in PD, esp. p. 204. In Canto 30 Pound refers to the feminine as HYLE, meaning "wood, uncut forest, matter," thus implying that the feminine is to be ordered and marked by the masculine. The subtleties of Aristotle's arguments will be treated later.

5 Note the concluding sentence of Lacan's essay, "The Signification of the Phallus": "The function of the phallic signifier touches here on its most profound relation: that in which the Ancients embodied the [Nous] and the [Logos]." See Lacan, p. 291. Alan Durant grasps (through Lacan) the major importance of Pound's phallocentrism and its relation to his ideas of signification as well as to his politics. See Durant, pp. 91, 103–107.

6 See Olson, p. 102. "Pound makes a lot of the head. You can see that he thinks of it as a pod." Pound's notion of the head revives the root meaning of the word cerebral, which has the same root as Ceres and cereal, and which suggests the brain's germinal power and fecundity.

7 See PD, p. 203. Pound is responding to a speculation of Gourmont's in *The Natural Philosophy of Love*, p. 99: "There might be, perhaps, a certain correlation between complete and profound copulation and the development of the brain."

8 See J/M, pp. 66–67; see also the opening of the Pisan *Cantos* (Canto 74), where Pound, speaking of the martyred Mussolini, writes: "that maggots shd/ eat the dead bullock." In death Il Duce is no longer a bull but a bullock, that is a castrated young bull.

9 Pound, quoted in Norman, p. 373.

10 See the radio broadcasts, pp. 31, 176, on the homestead. Mussolini too believed that "in Italy it is important to build homesteads." Quoted in Delzell, p. 20.

11 Like Pound, Mussolini defends the patriarchal family as the basis of private property and hereditary succession, without which supposedly there can be no human welfare or civilization. See Mussolini, p. 111.

12 See Pound, CON, pp. 53–55, 63–65, and 141, on familial order and duty.

13 Pound to Marianne Moore, circa December, 1934, Beinecke Rare Book and Manuscript Library, Yale University.

14 Voltaire, "Genèse," translated as "Genesis" by Pound in PD; see p. 169.

15 Sieburth comments on this passage and the Jews' presumed hatred of light in "Ideas into Action: Pound and Voltaire," pp. 378–379.

16 William Cookson, Introduction to Pound, SP, p. 9.

17 Pound repeatedly blames the Jews for undermining literal meanings through needlessly elaborate and abstract methods of interpretation, the most pernicious of which is in his view allegory. He may have had in mind the Jew Philo Judaeus, who was famous for his allegorical method. However, in this Philo was influenced not by the rabbis but by Pound's beloved Greeks, among whom the allegorical method originated. As Frederick C. Grant observes, the rabbis pursued literal and tropological meanings, as did other learned men of the ancient world, but "as a rule they did not practice or encourage" allegory. See Grant, p. 127, and Sandmel, pp. 4, 15, 17–28.

18 Pound's argument and use of Old Testament sources is virtually identical to that of early Christians against the Jews. See Parkes, 2, pp. 115–116.

19 Compare Nietzsche on the bad infuence of priests in *The AntiChrist*, in Nietzsche, 2, pp. 611–612, 630–631.

20 See Pound, letter to R. McNair Wilson, April, 1934, Beinecke Rare Book and Manuscript Library; "Pastiche: The Regional. XVI," *New Age*, 6 Nov. 1919, p. 16.

21 In "Ezra Pound to the Falsifiers," published in *Secolo d'Italia* in Jan. 1959, Pound refers to the "heretical scoundrel Calvin" as the "alias of Cauein, or Cohen, philo-usurer. . . ." Quoted in Heymann, p. 265.

22 Nietzsche's attack on the Jewish "falsification of Nature" resembles Pound's. The Judeo-Christian god is the "deity of decadence, gelded in his most virile virtues and instincts, [who] becomes of necessity the god of the physiologically

retrograde, of the weak." See *The AntiChrist,* in Nietzsche, 2, pp. 592–593, 588–589, 583–585.

23 See for instance GK, p. 340, and CON, p. 216, from the *Analects.* On the Jewish attitude toward original sin, see Maccoby, p. 61; Grant, p. 63.

24 According to Ernst Simmel, the Jews transformed God into a "spiritual collective superego" demanding "greater mental sacrifice than the human race can afford." Houston Stewart Chamberlain and Nietzsche attack Judaism as the source of our religious conceptions of evil, sin, guilt, atonement, vengeance, and punishment. For Nietzsche, Judaism (and its heir, Christianity) thwarts the passions, kills joy, promotes priestly tyranny, and altogether destroys the possibility of culture. See Simmel, "Anti-Semitism and Mass Psychopathology," pp. 50, 60–61, and Bernhard Berliner, "On Some Religious Motives of Anti-Semitism," pp. 79, 82, in Simmel, ed.; Nietzsche, "The Dawn," pp. 77, 79, 87, and *The AntiChrist,* in Nietzsche, 2, pp. 594–599.

25 Pound, "A Problem of (Specifically) Style," *New English Weekly,* 22 Nov. 1934, p. 127.

26 See Pound, LE, pp. 154–155; Canto 92, p. 620. "For up till now," says Pound, mathematics "had been the research into reality. But with the peculiar filth of the present age even mathematics shot out into unreality" (GK, 130). We have "too much . . . talk about vibrations and infinites" (SP, 78). See also "Method," *New English Weekly,* 18 March 1937, p. 447: "A lot of what had hitherto been 'last elements' were and are still being split up by microscopes and by chemistry."

27 Céline, whom Pound praises and quotes in his radio broadcasts (RB, 128, 129), likewise identifies the Jews with cold reason and lifeless, unspontaneous abstraction. Hence he shares Pound's obsessive fear of the Jewish presence within the Western university and educational system. See Céline, 1, pp. 57, 69; 2, pp. 32, 232–233; Kristeva, p. 184. For Céline, the Sorbonne is a "ghetto."

28 Pound, "Ecclesia," *Townsman,* 2 (Nov. 1939), p. 5.

29 Pound, quoted in Heymann, p. 236; Berezin, p. 269, and Maccoby, p. 69. On the link in Pound's thought between religious monopoly (monotheism, in Pound's interpretation) and financial monopoly, see Sieburth, 1, p. 379. Following George Simmel's *The Philosophy of Money,* Peter Nicholls notes the structural and psychological resemblance between the monotheistic idea and the money form, the second of which attains its "abstract purity" in the rate of interest. For Simmel, this resemblance helps to explain the religious and clerical animosity towards money and especially usury. Simmel furthermore finds a clear relation between the "specific ability and interest" of the Jews in the sphere of money and their "monotheistic schooling." According to Nicholls, Pound's awareness of this resemblance provides the logic not only for his equation in his wartime writings between Hebrew monotheism and monopoly but for his identification of the Jews with abstract thought. See Simmel, p. 237; Nicholls, pp. 153, 247n.

30 Discussing Pound's use of "Jewsury" in relation to his linguistic assumptions and practices, Andrew Parker shows the "ultimate inseparability of the word's separate parts." See "Ezra Pound and the 'Economy of Anti-Semitism,' " p. 111. Medieval and Renaissance Jews took to money-lending because of their exclusion from crafts and agriculture; their existence as usurers also served a true and lasting need within the Gentile community. However, to the extent that Pound in the 1930s and 1940s often treats usury and capitalism as interchangeable entities, he can be said to blame the Jews for capitalism. There is thus a resemblance between Pound's thinking and Werner Sombart's in *The Jews and Modern Capitalism,* in which Sombart argues that the Jews are primarily responsible for creating the spirit and techniques of modern economic life. But unlike Pound, Sombart does not limit his definition of capitalism to usury or finance. Sombart's thesis receives its classic refutation in Max Weber, 2, pp. 358–361.

31 Nelson, pp. xix-xx. Implicit in the Deuteronomic law is the permissibility of taking *marbith* or *tarbith,* the fair increase which Pound mentions favorably above, from brothers. There is, however, another text, Leviticus 25: 35–37, which "proscribes increase or interest of any sort (*marbith* or *tarbith,* as well as *neshek*), from

brothers." This text goes farther in proscribing interest than does Pound, who always seeks to define the difference between the just and unjust increment. See Nelson, p. xx, and note. In the Pisan *Cantos* (Canto 74, pp. 434, 440) Pound alludes not to this passage from Leviticus but to 19: 35, which requires the Jews to "do no unrighteousness in judgment, in meteyard, in weight, or in measure." Pound thus acknowledges the Jews' interest in economic justice in spite of his belief that they disregard their own laws.

32 For accusations of Jewish tribalism because of the Deuteronomic law, and the role of ascendent usury in the formation of a modern society of "universal otherhood," see Nelson, pp. xv-xvii, xx-xxiin, 99–100, 110–113.

33 Pound, "Anti-Semitism," *New English Weekly*, 14 May, 1936, pp. 99–100.

34 Actually, it was the Christians who, independently of the Jews, first introduced legislation against divergence of belief. "Rabbinic Judaism," writes James Parkes, "was prepared to be exceedingly intolerant in matters of practice, but in many cases, including usually any question of belief, 'punishment' was left to the Almighty." See *Judaism and Christianity*, p. 120.

35 For the attack on the Talmud, see the first chapter of Katz, 2, pp. 13–33, and Mosse, 6, pp. 138–141. The nineteenth-century French anti-Semite Gougenot des Mousseaux believed that the "immoral" Talmud had replaced Mosaic Law among the Jews. See Byrnes, p. 114. Céline gives maliciously distorted versions of the Talmud in his anti-Semitic diatribes. See Céline, 1, pp. 72, 204, 212, 255, 291; 2, p. 166; Knapp, p. 244n.

36 See Pound, GK, p. 60: "When a given hormone defects, it will defect throughout the whole system."

37 See Nietzsche, "The Dawn," pp. 76–79, and *The AntiChrist*, pp. 592–593, in Nietzsche, 2. My guess is that Pound derived these ideas not from Nietzsche, whom he did not admire, but from Ernest Renan, whose *Averroès and Averroism* fed his anti-Semitism, and whose *St. Paul*, pp. 300–325, sharply distinguishes Paul's harsh teaching from Jesus' message of love.

38 Gay uses this phrase to describe the Enlightenment and its offshoots. See Gay, *The Enlightenment, An Interpretation: The Rise of Modern Paganism.*

39 Poliakov, 2, Vol. III, p. 459, and Lebzelter, pp. 1–3.

40 See for instance Reck, 1, pp. 86–87, recounting an incident at St. Elizabeths.

41 Pound, "Pity," *Action*, No. 139, Oct. 15, 1938, p. 16. See also the radio broadcasts, pp. 397, 388.

42 See Gordon, 1, p. 355; Kimpel and Eaves, 2, p. 61.

43 Hermann Goering, quoted in Charles Y. Glock and Rodney Stark, eds., p. 101: "I determine who is a Jew." For Leuger, see Mosse, 6, pp. 141–142. Pound's notion of the "non-Jewish kike" (RB, 115) resembles the French anti-Semite Edouard Drumont's concept of the "judaïsant," the "fellow traveler" or "virtual Jew." See Wilson, p. 422. In the early 1940s Pound was an avid reader not only of Drumont but of Céline, who speaks of "synthetic" Jews and "Jewified" ("enjuivés") Aryans. See Céline, 1, pp. 125, 135; 2, pp. 66, 97, 138.

44 For a concise treatment of the influence of psychological and neurotic factors in the formation of personal and social ideologies on the "objective" level, see the discussion of Freud and Wilhelm Reich in Lorrain, pp. 83–88.

Chapter Three: The Jews, Castration, and Usury

1 Stock, 3, p. 444. For Leese, see Cross, pp. 63–65; for Lewis, see Eris, p. 53.

2 Pound to Douglas Fox, April 7, 1936, in the Beinecke Rare Book and Manuscript Library, Yale University.

3 Frazer, pp. 3–30, 263–298; Zielinski, 1, pp. 76–83, 84–85, 92.

4 For the Greeks' and Romans' dislike of the Attis cult and its rites of mutilation, and their far greater acceptance of the cult of the Great Mother (Cybele), see Vermaseren, pp. 32, 41, 43, 94, 96–98, 101, 112, 177–180.

5 See for instance the lines "Their Punic faces dyed in the Gorgon's lake," from *Homage to Sextus Propertius*, and his gloss in L, p. 149.

6 Pound to R. McNair Wilson, March, 1934, Beinecke Rare Book and Manuscript Library, Yale University.

7 See Berliner, "Some Religious Motives of Anti-Semitism," in Simmel, ed., p. 79.

8 Davie, 1, p. 76; Durant, pp. 130–131, 139–140, 151.

9 At least once Pound suggests that Jewish culture is characterized by castrating mothers. See Sieburth, 2, p. 89. In his letters Pound combines these conflicting associations of demonic patriarchy and matriarchy in a phrase: "that bitch Moses" (L, 182).

10 The image of the demonic Jewess, and the association of the Jews with sexual lust and prostitution, is typical of late nineteenth-century French anti-Semitism. See Wilson, pp. 584–585, 590–594.

11 Pound's obsession with syphilis and its identification with the Semitic world appears early in his career. See Weyl, in A Casebook, p. 7. Both fascinated by and fearful of syphilis, Hitler associates the Jews with venereal disease, sexual immorality, prostitution, and the destruction of Germany's offspring. See Waite, pp. 27, 23, 24; Hitler, pp. 59, 246–247, 251, 255–256; Nolte, pp. 509–511; Hitler, quoted in Reich, pp. 81–82. Edouard Drumont and Céline, two noted French anti-Semites, also link the Jews with venereal disease and prostitution. See Wilson, p. 586; Céline, 1, pp. 120–122, 126; 2, p. 34; 3, pp. 60, 142.

12 Freud, 7, p. 116; see also Loewenstein, p. 34.

13 In some cases, however, Pound prints the word "Jews" not in lower case but entirely in capitals. This gesture of "warning" to the Gentile world paradoxically indicates Pound's deep awe and admiration of the Jews' presumed power. See for instance Kimpel and Eaves, 2, p. 67.

14 E. Fuller Torrey recognizes the connection between Pound's anti-Semitism and his horror of circumcision; however, he fails to link such horror explicitly to castration fear. See Torrey, pp. 144–145.

15 For Lacan on the phallus, see Écrits: A Selection, passim. See especially "The Significance of the Phallus," pp. 281–291. My discussion of Lacan is much indebted to Lemaire, pp. xviii-xix, 7, 53–54, 58–62, 82–89, 95, 164–166. Alan Durant gives a systematic reading of Pound through Lacan in Ezra Pound, Identity in Crisis, passim. Durant argues that Pound seeks to repudiate castration and lack by fetishizing the phallus, and so to return to the narcissistic and pre-symbolic state of undifferentiation (identification or "integration," PD, 204, with the phallus) which precedes the castration complex; indeed, the reason Pound repeatedly (and vainly) inscribes the phallus in The Cantos is to abolish the fact of difference and to foreclose the possibility of lack. Durant also traces to phallocentrism such Poundian ideas as the fixity of the ego, a transcendental logos, the identity of subject and object in the act of looking, the coalescence of signifier and signified, and the existence of a centrally organized and hierarchical world of self-evident meanings. Perhaps the greatest value of Durant's study lies in his demonstration that Pound's quest for mimetic and denotative language, a language to "deny the unconscious," is constantly undercut by the differential and unconscious operations of metaphor and metonymy, which reintroduce difference, absence, and "lack" within Pound's signifying chains. But unlike this study, Durant's is primarily psychological and barely touches on Pound's anti-Semitism and politics. At the same time, Durant is mainly concerned with what Lacan might call the "psychotic" or potentially psychotic Pound, who seeks to annihilate difference in "foreclusion" and to escape from the symbolic order into the Imaginary. My focus is on a probably more typical and certainly not insane Pound, who stresses the differentiating role of language, craft, and sex, and who has a horror of undifferentiation and resemblance. This Pound knows the phallus only as a constantly endangered differentiating trace, the sign of the Nous or paternal light. For him the greatest terror lies not in differentiation but in the loss of difference, for the loss of the phallic trace also portends the disappearance of the origin itself. I discuss Durant's book at length in my "The Poet as Fascist: Pound's Politics and his Critics," Review, 6 (1984), pp. 275–302.

16 Many German and French anti-Semitic ideologists, including the Nazis,

attributed to the Jews' desert origins their non-agrarian habits and supposed sterility of various kinds. See Poliakov, 1, pp. 274, 286; Mosse, 1, pp. 4–5; Wilson, pp. 267–279; Céline, 1, pp. 59, 69, 170, 192. Writing in the *Meridiano di Roma* of 3 March, 1941, Pound asserted that the Jew Henry Morgenthau, Secretary of the Treasury under Franklin D. Roosevelt, was "unable to run a fruit-growing concern." Quoted in Heymann, p. 98.

17 Mussolini's demographic policies encouraged large families in order to avoid the "biologic death" of the Italian people. See Gregor, 3, pp. 265–280, esp. 285, 289; William S. Halperin, p. 64. For the Nazis' emphasis on breeding large populations, see Nolte, p. 291.

18 Late nineteenth-century French anti-Semites similarly feared the destruction of private property by Jewish "nomads." See Wilson, p. 352.

19 See Hitler, pp. 51, 65, 155, 156, 168, 215, 382. See also Nolte, p. 419; Cecil, pp. 20, 24–25, 69. According to Céline, Rothschild, Marx, and Trotsky belong to the same international Jewish conspiracy, while Communism is a fraud played by the Jews upon the Aryan proletariat. See Céline, 1, pp. 47, 50, 51, 78, 81, 152–153, 259, 279, 281, 288; 2, pp. 130, 141, 183–185; 3, p. 70.

20 See GK, p. 357, and SP, pp. 214–215, 290, 295–297; Kenner, 3, p. 558.

21 Pound, quoted in Norman, p. 352; Pound, "Demarcations," *British Union Quarterly*, 1 (Jan.-April, 1937), p. 39. Many conservatives, proto-fascists, and fascists believe that the modern press is under the corrupting control of the Jews. The list would include Jacob Burckhardt, Edouard Drumont, Wagner, Houston Stewart Chamberlain, Hitler, Céline, and many American right-wing agitators. See Mosse, 4, p. 58; Katz, 2, p. 294; Viereck, 2, p. 118; Geoffrey Field, pp. 99, 134; Hitler, p. 244; Céline, 1, pp. 49, 66, 268, 278; 2, pp. 25, 35; 3, p. 46; Lowenthal and Guterman, p. 56.

22 Derrida, "White Mythology," in *Margins of Philosophy*, p. 210. See also Pound, GK, p. 94.

23 Girard, 2, p. 60; Malinowski, pp. 88–91.

24 But as Durant notes in a discussion of Canto 28, p. 137, Pound is no less concerned with the coin's weight, which is "its guarantee of value." See Durant, p. 115.

25 Mussolini frequently emphasizes "virility" as a political value, while one of the major aims of Italian Fascism was to redeem Italy's so-called "mutilated victory" in World War I. See Mussolini, pp. 97, 122, 126, 144, 163; Delzell, p. 2.

Chapter Four: Medievalism, Corporatism, and Totalitarian Culture

1 For Pound on guilds, see J/M, p. 5; SP, p. 298; radio broadcasts, pp. 47, 18, 19, 204, 52.

2 Among numerous examples, see LE, p. 211, and "A Visiting Card," in SP, p. 323.

3 Although Pound in the broadcasts implies the medieval or at least medieval-izing character of Italian Fascism, he is elsewhere careful to emphasize that the movement was more than an impractically romantic attempt to reconstitute a pre-modern past. Writing in the *New English Weekly* in May, 1935, Pound views the Italian Fascist economy as a "great resurrection of guildism, not furnished with William Morris' medieval tapestries and upholsteries, but brought very much up to date." In any case, Pound like other Italian Fascists has difficulty in reconciling the medieval idea of self-regulating guilds with modern centralization and political abso-lutism, and he at least as frequently appeals to the tradition of the Roman state in his Fascist polemics. According to Gioacchino Volpe, the official historian of Italian Fascism, the movement in its early days manifested a strong impulse to return to the corporate life of the Middle Ages, a society of independent citizen-producers in which the arts and crafts were given a prominent place. These values are reminiscent of Pound's claim that Italian Fascism had made good on the medievalizing and aesthetic dreams of Ruskin and Morris. But Volpe points out with no apparent regret that Italian Fascism ultimately rejected this kind of neo-medievalism in favor of

greater state control. Fearing that the guilds would become monopolistic and self-interested, as in the Middle Ages, the Italian Fascist state would not allow itself to be undermined by the independence of producers' associations. Volpe's fears of guild monopoly against the national interest were shared by Pound as well as by Mussolini and his chief ideologue Alfredo Rocco, who viewed the Middle Ages as a period of anarchy and decentralization and who preferred to legitimate a strong Fascist state by invoking Roman tradition. The appeal to medievalism and a decentralized guild structure is more prominent in the corporate theory of the French right-wing theorist de La Tour du Pin, whom Pound somewhat admired, and whom George L. Mosse treats as a kind of national socialist. It is possible, though, to find Italian Fascists who connect their movement with the Catholic traditions of justice and economics as well as with the Middle Ages. As for whether Italian Fascist corporatism or syndicalism is mainly medieval in inspiration, a recent authority treats it as a peculiar offshoot of Marxism, and hence as a distinctly modern phenomenon. See Volpe, pp. 147–148; Pound, SP, p. 176; "The Italian Score," *New English Weekly,* 23 May, 1935, p. 107. For Mussolini on the Roman tradition of Italian Fascism, see Finer, p. 191; for Rocco, see "The Political Doctrine of Fascism," trans. Dino Bigongiari, in *Man and Contemporary Society,* pp. 1029–1032. For French corporate theory and its medievalism, see Nolte, pp. 74–75, and Elbow, pp. 11–80. Pound somewhat praises de La Tour du Pin's anti-usury in "American Notes," *New English Weekly,* 16 April, 1935, pp. 5–6; de La Tour du Pin is characterized as a national socialist in Mosse, 6, p. 138. For Catholicizing and medievalizing tendencies among Italian Fascists, see Lyttelton, p. 321; Roberts, p. 303. For the Marxist rather than medieval emphasis of syndicalism, see Roberts and Gregor, 3, pp. 3–31.

4 Matthew Little has attempted to show that Pound's "peculiar" use of the word "totalitarian" does not imply his support of despotic, absolutist, or totalitarian rule, that is, a government empowered to control every aspect of social and cultural life. Not "specifically" political in content and largely free of political implications, Pound's term implies a holistic and organic approach to learning and culture. Pound desires a "total culture" in the sense of a comprehensive, organic, hierarchical order, as in Jefferson and especially the medieval theologians (Little's example). But Little fails to consider how Pound expects to achieve his stated goals within the fragmented and pluralistic culture of the twentieth century. As the Italian Fascists and Nazis understood, the aim of a totalitarian and "national culture" (this phrase is Pound's in SP, p. 161) can be achieved only through revolutionary and totalitarian political means. Similarly, if the use of words is linked necessarily to intentions, actions, and contexts, as Pound and many modern linguists hold, then Pound's use of "totalitarian" is by no means free of political implications. His support of an absolute and hierarchical state, as of its dictator, party, and party army, are inseparable from and indispensable to his project of restoring the totalitarian unity of culture. So too are his attacks on the Jews. See Little, pp. 147–156. On the other hand, Cohen's description of the later medieval political and social ideal as totalitarian does not altogether consort with modern notions of total political domination; medieval (and Confucian) civilization is probably best understood not as a form of totalitarianism but as a traditionalist authoritarian hierarchy. It is also true that Italian Fascism, which probably gave the world the word "totalitarianism" and aspired toward this ideal, was much less totalitarian in practice than were the Nazis and the Stalinists. See Arendt, Vol. III, pp. 6–7.

5 The social philosophy of Pound and Italian Fascism is discussed at greater length in Chapter Fourteen.

6 Trachtenberg, pp. xii, 5; Cohn, 1, pp. 15–16.

7 Although religious factors play a major role in Pound's anti-Semitism, the ideological and emotional roots of his hatred are not exclusively or even mainly located in medieval Catholicism or in any other religion. Hannah Arendt rightly criticizes Norman Cohn in his *Warrant for Genocide* for treating modern anti-Semitism primarily as a kind of updated medievalism. Yet she too is reductive in emphasizing a few exclusively modern political, economic, and social causes, such as the Jews' loss of prestige, the rise of the masses, and the breakdown of the nation

state. See Arendt, Vol. I, pp. 36–37. For an excellent refutation of Arendt's thesis, see Gager, p. 267.

8 For this distinction, see Lebzelter, pp. 1–3. See also Guido Kisch, "The Jews in Medieval Law," and Waldemar Gurian, "Anti-Semitism in Modern Germany," in Pinson, ed., pp. 107–108, 218.

9 An aspect of this tradition is explored in Cohn, 1, *passim*. See also Webb, pp. 125–143, 213–343.

10 Pound, "Germany Now," *New English Weekly*, 26 Sept. 1935, p. 399; "Ecclesia," *The Townsman*, 2 (Nov. 1939), p. 4. Compare Lewis, 1, p. 122.

11 Pound's statement raises the question whether the medieval Church was ideologically anti-Judaic or anti-Semitic and whether modern Western anti- Semitism originates in Christian antiquity. The second question became especially pressing after World War II, when many feared that Christianity was the chief source of modern anti-Semitism. Jeremy Cohen, cited above, shows that the early medieval Church adopted on ethical grounds a policy of toleration of Jews. Nor can Western anti-Semitism be said to originate in Christian (and pagan) antiquity except in what John G. Gager calls a "highly restricted sense." But though Gager shows that early Christianity was not universally anti-Judaic, he also quotes a number of Biblical scholars who believe that an element of anti-Judaism is rooted in the New Testament and that it contributed heavily to later anti-Semitism. In the words of M. Reuther, anti-Judaism fulfilled "an intrinsic need of Christian self-affirmation" and became a "part of Christian exegesis." See Gager, pp. 9, 13, 20, 32–34, 103–104, 135, 147, 151, 153, 160, 172–173, 202, 267.

12 Trachtenberg, pp. 17, 23, 40, 47, 82, 90, 97–101, 102–104, 109ff, 137, 140–155, 180, 185, 211, 254n.

13 Kimpel and Eaves, 2, pp. 57, 58. Oswald Mosley also distinguishes between dangerous "big" Jews and harmless "little" Jews—a distinction which Céline explicitly rejects and which is usually ignored in anti-Semitic practice. See Cross, p. 127; Céline, 2, p. 34. Chace, pp. 226–232n, provides brief biographical descriptions of some of the prominent Jews attacked in Pound's broadcasts. Although Pound probably reserves his deepest hatred for Jewish financiers such as the Rothschilds, the Schiffs, the Warburgs, Sir Alfred Beit, and Kuhn, Loeb, and Co., he also vilifies Jewish merchants, philanthropists, men of letters, industrialists, publishers, politicians, stock-analysts, and presidential advisers. This list includes the Sassoons, the Isaacs, the Warburgs, Baron Israel Moses Sieff, Sir Harry Lawson, Webster Levy-Lawson, Lord Leslie Hore-Belisha, Bernard Baruch, and Henry Morgenthau, Jr. Incidentally, many of Pound's Jewish "enemies" are also objects of attack in Céline's anti-Semitic writings. See Céline, 1, pp. 210, 211, 281, 288; 2, pp. 30, 43, 62, 75, 77, 160, 161, 167, 184; 3, p. 70.

14 For another of Pound's assertions of the Jews' collective responsibility, see Torrey, p. 143.

15 Hitler, p. 58; Pound, quoted in Kimpel and Eaves, 2, p. 59. For the relation between the Black Death and the appearance of exterminatory anti-Semitism, see Cohn, 2, pp. 138–139. Pound's accusations resemble those of Céline, whose anti-Semitic pronouncements he much admired, and for whom the Jews are synonymous with vermin, plague, decay, and "cancer mondial." See Céline, 1, pp. 42, 68, 96, 98, 101, 132, 177, 226, 228, 247; 2, pp. 41, 139, 153; 3, pp. 59, 69.

16 RB, 120. In Canto 35 one learns that when Jews "have high cheek- bones / they are supposed to be Mongol" (35/ 174). This passage probably alludes to the generally rejected theory that East European Jews descend from the Tartar or Turkish tribe of Khazars, a notion which Arthur Koestler resurrects in *The Thirteenth Tribe: The Khazar Empire and its Heritage* (New York: Random House, 1976). In Canto 96, p. 657, as he surveys the events of the reign (610–641 A.D.) of Emperor Heraclius, Pound mentions among the barbarian hordes who assaulted the sacred city of Byzantium the "Turks called Khazars": "Turcos quos Cazaros vocant." This phrase, which derives from the *Mixed History* of Landulphus Sagax, is probably code language for the Jews. Lewis, 1, p. 38, similarly links the Jews and "Tartary," while Céline views the Jews as Mongol or Asiatic. See Céline, 1, pp. 68, 69, 118; 2, p. 80.

17 For Pound's attacks on the Jewish drug rackets, see the radio broadcasts, pp. 3, 17, 21, 43; see also Pound, "Problemi da risolvere," *Meridiano di Roma*, VIII (14 Feb. 1943), p. 1, and Canto 74, p. 437: "but poison, *veleno* / in all the veins of the commonweal." Céline similarly believes that the Jews push drugs and alcohol as a means of corrupting the French people. He is also highly critical and fearful of Jewish doctors. See Céline, 1, pp. 68, 93, 101, 143–150, 309–310; 2, pp. 138, 208.

18 For Hitler's fear of blood poisoning, see Waite, pp. 150–156, 471. Drumont also identifies the Jews with blood poisoning and pollution. See Wilson, pp. 488, 491.

19 For Pound's colonial ancestors and his pride in his family's distinguished history, see Wilhelm, 4, pp. 1–65.

20 Pound alludes to such a violation in the Adams *Cantos*. Visiting a church in Holland, John Adams notices "a tapestry: number of jews stabbing the wafer / blood gushing from it" (65/ 376). While the original passage may not have anti-Semitic intent, Pound's reflects his prejudices, as in his contemptuous spelling of "Jews" in lower case.

21 Richard Thurnwald, *Economics in Primitive Communities*, quoted in Desmonde, p. 76.

22 Pound, "The Inedible," *Townsman*, 3 (Feb. 1940), p. 2.

23 Allen Upward, 2, pp. 56–59, 92–109. Upward, however, was gratified by the sublimation of the rites of human sacrifice into a rite in which grain or bread was consumed in place of the body of the god.

24 Pound also connects food with patriarchal authority and money, which is properly in the hands of the king and ruler, and which is "the power to amass and distribute" (GK, 42) society's abundance. To maintain the purity of the coinage is to maintain, through food, the organic life of society. See also Desmonde, pp. 37, 124, 20–21.

25 See Ernst Simmel, "Anti-Semitism and Mass Psychopathology," in Simmel, ed., pp. 51, 55–58, and Loewenstein, p. 76. See also Trachtenberg's observation in *The Devil and the Jews*, p. 100, that in the Middle Ages both secular and ecclesiastical codes often forbade Christians to purchase meat and other foodstuffs from Jews on the grounds "that they might have been poisoned."

26 Voltaire, "Ezekiel," *Philosophical Dictionary*, p. 197.

27 See also Norman, p. 379, quoting Pound.

28 Céline similarly charges that the Jews attack the entrails of the Aryan peoples and nations. See Céline, 1, pp. 68, 87, 130.

29 Simmel, "Anti-Semitism and Mass Psychology," pp. 58–63.

30 Pound, quoted in Norman, p. 374.

31 Loewenstein, pp. 76, 99–106, 190–191; Simmel, "Anti-Semitism and Mass Psychopathology," pp. 55–57.

32 Hitler, quoted in Simmel, "Anti-Semitism and Mass Psychopathology," p. 63; *Mein Kampf*, p. 452.

33 Simmel, "Anti-Semitism and Mass Psychopathology," p. 65. Pound's projection of oral aggression onto the Jews is ironic in view of the Jewish religion, which expresses "disapproval of the devouring instinct" and the totemic feast "by placing the taboo of 'Kosher' (unclean) on Christian food." According to one theory, the Jews prohibited the eating of pork because swine attended the pagan Mother goddesses of the Near East, whom the Jews (and Pound to some extent) abhorred. It is therefore ignorant and vicious for Pound to refer to the Jews as "swine" (RB, 119, 240). See Simmel, p. 61, and Berliner, "On Some Religious Motives of Anti-Semitism," in Simmel, ed., pp. 80–81.

34 Pound, "La guerra degli usurai," *Meridiano di Roma*, VII (3 May, 1942), p. 1. Referred to alternately in the broadcasts as "Franklin D. Frankfurter Jewsfeld" (RB, 223), "Rosenfeld" (RB, 60), "Frank Rosenstein" (RB, 102), Roosevelt is the architect of the "new Jew Roosevelt oosalem" (RB, 228), a wierd and sinister amalgam of Communism and usury. Pound wants America to get rid of "the kikes AND Mr. Roosevelt" (RB, 246), "Roosevelt and his Jews" (RB, 105). In Canto 86, p. 568, Pound mocks Roosevelt with an undistinguished type face meant to capture the

supposed essence of the man; see the phrase "HE / talks." This lettering contrasts with the bold Roman type which introduces Mussolini's major symbolic exploit, the draining of the Pontine Marshes, at the opening of Canto 41. Céline also treats Roosevelt as a Jew or as an accomplice of Jewish advisers and financiers. See Céline, 1, pp. 50, 152; 2, pp. 47, 60–61; 3, p. 31.

35 Reck, 1, p. 115. Compare Hitler's behavior, reported in Simmel, "Anti-Semitism and Mass Psychopathology," p. 43, and that of the anti-Semitic Mussolini, reported in Michaelis, p. 181.

Chapter Five: The Enlightenment and Orientalism

1 Hugh Kenner, "Ezra Pound and the Light of France," in *Gnomon: Essays on Contemporary Literature*, pp. 263–279. For a brief discussion of Voltaire's anti-Semitism as an influence on Pound, see Sieburth, 1, pp. 371–379. Sieburth overemphasizes hatred of monotheism as a cause of Pound's anti-Semitism.

2 Hertzberg, p. 299; Horkheimer and Adorno, p. 169.

3 See Vox, pp. 101–109; Schwarzfuchs, *passim*. However, in the radio broadcasts, p. 207, Pound notes that "Napoleon wanted to be real nice to the Hebrews, and they ditched him."

4 For an account of these uprisings, see Procacci, p. 261.

5 Although Pound, in GK, p. 254, and J/M, p. 43, gives qualified praise to the Declaration of the Rights of Man and its concept of negative liberty, by the radio broadcasts, p. 316, he believes that liberty entails positive duties, as in Italian Fascism. For Pound's view of the French Revolution, see also the radio broadcasts, pp. 207, 241, 254.

6 See Jacob Katz, 2, pp. 24–25; Poliakov, 2, Vol. III, pp. 86–99, esp. 98; Hertzberg, pp. 284–290.

7 Hertzberg, pp. 299–307; Poliakov, 2, Vol. III, p. 87. Louis-Ferdinand Céline praises Voltaire's anti-Semitism in his pro-Nazi *L'École des cadavres*, p. 205.

8 Voltaire, "Genesis," in *The Philosophical Dictionary*, p. 220.

9 Voltaire, quoted in Poliakov, 2, Vol. III, p. 89; Hertzberg, p. 303.

10 See PD, p. 174; the radio broadcasts, p. 253, where Pound speaks of a Jewish allegory "against procreation"; and Poliakov, 2, Vol. III, p. 89, on Voltaire's notion of the Jews' "sterile intellect."

11 Pound, PD, pp. 172–174; Voltaire, "Ezekiel," in *The Philosophical Dictionary*, p. 199. Pound recommends "Ezekiel" in PD, p. 185n.

12 The charge that Judaism is a sacrificial religion figures frequently in anti-Semitic writing. But though the early Hebrews certainly performed blood sacrifices, over the course of Jewish history sacrifice is rejected or else internalized through morality and the conscience. In modern Judaism prayer is the primary form of man's relationship with God. See Albright, pp. 266–267, 329–333; Grant, pp. 39, 66.

13 See Poliakov, 2, Vol. III, pp. 88–89; Voltaire, "Torture," in *The Philosophical Dictionary*, pp. 394–395.

14 Said, *passim*. See also Schwab, *passim*.

15 Said, pp. 145, 32–33, 38–39, 47, 48, 105–106, 6, 56, 188, 21, 97, 137–138.

16 See the first chapter of Renan's *Averroès et l'Averroisme: essai historique*, 4 ed.

17 Pound, "Pastiche: The Regional. IX," *New Age*, 11 Sept. 1919, p. 336. Compare Lewis, 1, p. 136.

18 Pound to Wyndham Lewis, 15 Dec., 1936, in P/L, p. 192. Pound was responding to Lewis's letter of 13 Dec., 1936, in which Lewis had asked: "What was the name—and address—of that bloke I met in Barbary?" Pound's reply: "Paolo Zappa wuz the guy wot you met in the jungle."

19 See Davenport, p. 359, and Espey, pp. 39–40, 100.

20 Flaubert, 2, p. 9 (Krailsheimer's introduction); see also pp. 91, 79.

21 Said, pp. 6, 167, 180, 187, 190.

22 Bacigalupo, p. 283. The Fatal Woman is almost invariably exotic and for-

eign, for instance Slavic, Italian, Greek, or Roman. Generally, however, she is, as Mario Praz says, of "fabulous Oriental background," and is often Jewish or Canaanitic. See Praz's compendious chapter, "La Belle Dame Sans Merci," in his classic, The Romantic Agony, 199–300, esp. pp. 200, 205, 213–216, 222–223, 240, 250–253, 256–257, 272, 282n, 283.

23 For Swinburne and Wilde, see Praz, pp. 250, 252, 256–257.

24 Praz, pp. 200, 213–214, 222, 240, 256–257.

25 Pound said that "Laforgue's 'Salomé' is the real criticism of Salammbo" (LE, 406). Undoubtedly he admired it as a parodistic means of eliminating the ornamental and marmoreal element from European prose.

26 Laforgue, "Salomé," in Moralités légendaires, pp. 119–120.

27 Laforgue, pp. 130–140, 144–146.

Chapter Six: Modern Anti-Semitism and Millenarianism: Zielinski, Frobenius, Rosenberg, and the Protocols

1 Pound, "Total War on 'Contemplatio,' " Edge, 1 (Oct. 1956), p. 20.

2 Zielinski, 1, passim; 2, passim. The translations from Zielinski are mine.

3 Zielinski, 1, pp. 7–12, 21–22, 24, 30–31, 43, 49; 2, p. 222.

4 Zielinski, 2, p. 36; 1, pp. 17, 25–31.

5 Zielinski, 1, pp. 14–15, 50–58; 2, p. 17.

6 The argument for the authentically non-Hebraic character of Christianity appears in the Nazi ideologist Alfred Rosenberg, who advanced it in the interests of a "vital" Nazi paganism and "positive" Christianity, and whose arguments were refuted by the Catholic Church in a famous debate; it also figures in Ernest Renan as in a number of proto-Nazi and Nazi (or fascist) theorists, among them Lagarde, Wagner, Houston Stewart Chamberlain, Haeckel, and Drieu la Rochelle. See Nolte, p. 68; Mosse, 6, pp. 100, 103, 88, 128–149; Soucy, 2, pp. 181–182; Viereck, 2, pp. 168, 286–287. For Céline, by contrast, Christianity is inherently Jewish, and must be replaced by a "white religion." A racial anti-Semite, he has no patience with the earlier anti-Semitic charge that the Jews had killed Christ. See Céline, 2, p. 223; 3, pp. 80–82.

7 Zielinski, 1, pp. 17, 76–78; 2, pp. 99, 108.

8 Zielinski, 1, pp. 76–83, 85–86, 92. Similar facts and conclusions concerning the opposition between European moderation and Oriental "excess" can be found in Frazer, pp. 299, 263, 266, 298, 301, 270, and Vermaseren, pp. 32, 96–97, 101, 112, 177. See also Peter Whigham's Poundian translation of Catullus, Carm., lxiii, in The Poems of Catullus, pp. 136–139, in which the speaker is a castrated follower of the Attis cult.

9 Zielinski, 1, pp. 92, 94, 19–22, 26; 2, p. 108.

10 Jesus says this in the Sermon on the Mount; see Matthew 5: 17. There is no foundation for Zielinski's argument that true Christianity is non-Jewish in origin and spirit. Frederick C. Grant shows Christianity's "indebtedness" to Judaism in its monotheism, its emphasis on divine revelation, and its eschatology, which contrasts with Greek cyclicism. Jesus' ethics, about which Zielinski and Pound say little, are "authentically Jewish," going back to the Old Testament, while early Christianity has a "basically Jewish nature, character, antecedents, and outlook." Zielinski's and Pound's strong emphasis on the man-god is excessively "Christological," to use Grant's term, whereas the "total Christian faith" that descends from Judaism gives primacy to the monotheistic idea. Admittedly one can find considerable evidence of anti-Judaism in the Gospels, as John G. Gager shows. However, this does not refute the argument that much of Christianity, especially its ethical teaching, is rooted in Judaism. Acknowledging what Jules Isaac calls the "fundamentally Jewish character of early Christianity," Gager points out that both Christianity and Judaism based their case against each other on the Hebrew Bible. Among other Christian texts, even the anti-Judaic Gospel of St. John presupposes a "significant level of familiarity with the beliefs and practices of first-century Judaism." When Marcion attempted, as Pound would later, to dissociate the Old from the New Testament, this proposal by

the most extreme of the radical anti-Judaizers was "roundly rejected." Christianity would not "sever once and for all . . . its ideological connection with Israel." Nor was Marcion any more successful in eliminating from the Synoptic Gospels and Pauline letters supposedly corrupt quotations and allusions to the Old Testament. One plausible explanation of Christian anti-Judaism (and later anti-Semitism) is that it expresses the Christian need to establish self-identity by sharp differentiation from a parent religion which it fears it too much resembles and upon which it feels itself a parasite. Anti-Semitism, to quote Rudolf Loewenstein, is the Christian's "reaction" to his "moral debt to the Jews." See Grant, pp. ix-xi, xiii, xiv-xvi, 4, 12, 19, 26, 28, 29, 119, 130; Gager, pp. 15, 20, 134, 135, 153, 160, 162.

11 Dekker, p. 78; Pound, quoted in Stock, 3, p. 478.

12 Stock, 3, p. 520. For Pound's idea of the Paideuma and his debt to Frobenius for this concept, see "For a New Paideuma," in SP, p. 284. Pound probably implies the compatibility of Frobenius with fascism in Canto 74, p. 436: "And the only people who did anything of any interest were H. [Hitler], M. [Mussolini] and / Frobenius der Geheimrat / der im Baluba das Gewitter gemacht hat."

13 See Joseph Campbell's introduction to Bachofen, p. lv.

14 For the Culture-Civilization distinction in *Volkisch* thinking, see Mosse, 1, p. 6, and Fritz Stern, pp. 90, 246. For the Jew as symbol of mere "civilization" rather than "culture," see Mosse, 4, pp. 36, 57.

15 For Frobenius's influence on the second volume of *The Decline of the West*, see Hughes, 1, p. 134. For Spengler's statement of the Culture-Civilization distinction, see *The Decline of the West*, pp. 24–27, 73–75, 182–183, 413–414. Spengler considered cross-cultural influences destructive of the organic unity and vitality of individual cultures. Despite some probably accidental affinities with Spengler, Pound rejected his apparent cultural fatalism while viewing some cross-cultural influences as positive. See Surette, 2, pp. 109–110, 112–113. Actually, Spengler's pessimism was not absolute but guarded, and in this respect it reveals a striking resemblance to Pound's thought. Although Spengler feared the decline of *Kultur* into *Civilization*, and despite his complaints of numerous modern evils such as rationalism, mechanism, impersonality, and abstraction, he differs from the nineteenth-century *Volkisch* theorists in refusing to dissociate technology in its essence from the vitalism, intuition, and wilful productivity which for him characterizes *Kultur* as the spontaneous and magical expression of the German soul. If technology stands for creativity and man's mastery over Nature, then for Spengler, as for Pound, the real disease of modern civilization is unproductive money, whose symbol as the calculating Jew. Thus technology, far from belonging inherently to *Civilization* in all its soulless intellectuality, has a truly personal and mystic character, and once freed from monetary control and placed in proper hands will again express German "blood and tradition." In short, Spengler imagines as do numerous other German reactionaries of his age a dubious reconciliation between technology and *Kultur* and through it the reversal of a morbid historical process. A similar mentality may be seen in Pound, who decries money as the destroyer of organic social relations, and who, instead of recognizing that advanced technology is part of the same process of rationalization, views it as compatible with his cultural aim of establishing a new *Gemeinschaft* under fascist auspices. For this revision of conventional views of Spengler, see Herf, pp. 49–69.

16 See Welke, pp. 415–417. For further discussion of Frobenius, see Read, pp. 299–301; Harmon, pp. 30–36. Is is evident that Frobenius's hopes for the restoration of *Kultur* do not encompass, as in Spengler, the possibility of a reconciliation with modern technology.

17 Fritz Stern, p. 246n. In fairness to Pound, the distinction between Culture and Civilization has been taken seriously by at least two noted contemporary writers. Theodor Adorno, who was somewhat influenced by Spengler, retained these concepts in his attack against modernity and mass culture; see Jay, 2, pp. 106, 111, 114–115. Although he acknowledges its vagueness, Fernand Braudel does not altogether dismiss the distinction in *On History*, trans. Sarah Matthews (Chicago: Univ. of Chicago Press, 1980), pp. 177–184, and indeed he makes use of it in his *Civiliza-*

tion Materielle et Capitalisme, XVe-XVIIIe siècle, I (Paris: Armand Colin, 1967), pp. 9–77.

18 Pound to Lewis, 1939, Beinecke Rare Book and Manuscript Library, Yale University; radio broadcasts, pp. 79, 402–405; see also Pound to Douglas Fox, Dec. 1936, Beinecke Rare Book and Manuscript Library.

19 Rosenberg, pp. 83–84.

20 Rosenberg, pp. 115, 47–49, 56–57; see also Hitler, p. 64.

21 Rosenberg, p. 199. Pound too despised the Weimar "democracy" and praised Hitler for having recognized that it was filled with "Jew puke" (RB, 140). England, said Pound, "set up a Jew government in Germany and the Germans HAD to get rid of it, or die" (RB, 147).

22 For proto-Nazi and Nazi solar occultism, connected with the ideas of myth, sacrifice, and seasonal rebirth, see Mosse, 1, pp. 71–72, 82, 197, and Cohn, 1, pp. 176, 169.

23 Pound, "Statues of Gods," *The Townsman,* 2 (Aug. 1939), p. 14.

24 Materer, 1, p. 47. Torrey, pp. 139, 307–308n, notes that Pound signed another letter with a swastika, and that on other occasions he closed with "Heil Hitler, yrs. Ez." Solar mythology figures in conjunction with pro-Nazism in Henri de Montherlant's *Solstice de juin,* in which the German swastika, symbolizing the solar wheel, triumphs over France at the moment of the summer solstice. See Mehlman, pp. 3, 16.

25 Nietzsche, *The AntiChrist,* in Nietzsche, 2, pp. 612, 614, 617. For Goethe's interpretation of Christianity and the Cross, see Löwith, pp. 14–26.

26 Rosenberg, pp. 68, 100, 72; Viereck, p. 286. Rosenberg specifically rejects the crucifix as "representing Christ's suffering." See Cecil, p. 85. The charge that Paul had Judaized Christianity is most ironic. In this century Paul is often viewed as the most influential of the early anti-Judaisers. He is the "apostolic witness" for those types of Christianity which in the second and third century attempted to "sever all ties between Christianity and Judaism." See Gager, pp. 172–173, 183–184, 191, 256–257.

27 Zielinski closely links Christ to the later pagan Sol Invictus, which he derives in turn from the universal worship of the god Apollo in the Hellenistic world. See *La Sibylle,* p. 95. However, Zielinski is in error. Though the monotheistic idea was "found in increasing measure and emphasis in Greek philosophy and religion" in the later ancient world, the movement toward monotheism "did not sharply impinge upon early Christianity but went its own way, reaching its climax in the worship of *Sol Invictus,* the unconquerable sun." See Grant, p. 29.

28 Cohn, 1, pp. 15, 16, 17, 21–25; 2, pp. 30–33, 84, 85, 72.

29 Cohn, 2, pp. 108–109; see also the discussion of Moeller van den Bruck in Fritz Stern, pp. 320–325.

30 Hitler, pp. 326, 65, 214; see also Nolte, p. 525.

31 The standard work on the *Protocols* is Norman Cohn's *Warrant for Genocide.* Like the *Protocols,* the myth of the mysterious Jewish organization known as the Kahal originated in Russia, being the invention of the police spy and Jew turned Christian, Jacob Brafman. According to Brafman in *The Book of the Kahal* (1869), the Kahal was a Jewish organization or fraternity which "aimed at enabling Jewish traders to oust their Christian competitors and in the end to acquire possession of all the property of Christians." In actuality, the Kahal, which was abolished in Russia in 1844, was no more than a community organization through which Jews attained a certain degree of self-government. For the *Protocols,* see Cohn, 1, pp. 25–168; for the Kahal, see pp. 53–54. See also Carlebach, *Karl Marx and the Radical Critique of Judaism,* p. 202, quoting A. L. Patkin, *The Origins of the Russian-Jewish Labor Movement* (Melbourne and London, 1947), p. 49.

32 Cohn discusses Ford in *Warrant for Genocide,* pp. 103, 158. For Ford on the *Protocols,* see Lee, pp. 27–29, 37, 56, 63, 64; Lee notes Ford's extreme fear of the *Protocols* and his influence on Adolf Hitler. Pound's admiration for Ford's anti-Semitism is evident in the broadcasts, pp. 98, 273.

33 See the third section of Zielinski, 1, entitled "La Sibylle et la Fin de Rome,"
pp. 97–110, 124–125, 113–115.

34 For "martyr," see Weyl, in *A Casebook,* p. 15; for "Joan of Arc" and
"saint," see Norman, p. 396. The description of Hitler as a "Joan of Arc" perhaps
echoes Lewis, 2, pp. 76, 122.

35 See Terrell, Vol. II, p. 198.

36 See Pound's letter to Fernando Mezzasoma, Minister of Popular Culture for
the Italian Fascist Republican Government at Salò, Feb. 27, 1944: "The Germans are
strong because they believe they can create a new order . . . they believe that they can
establish a just peace for a thousand years to come . . . ." Quoted in Heymann, p. 333.

37 For Pound's references to the *Protocols* in the radio broadcasts, see pp. 159,
200, 212, 241–242, 283–284. Although the *Protocols* are a forgery, an awareness
of this fact does not deter rabid anti-Semites from believing in them; rather, the fact
that they are a forgery only confirms their truth. In this Pound's logic is identical to
Hitler's. See the radio broadcasts, p. 283; Hitler, p. 307; and Pearlman, 3, pp. 467–
468; 4, p. 109.

38 See *The Protocols and World Revolution: Including a Translation and
Analysis of the Meetings of the Zionist Men of Wisdom* (Boston: Small and Maynard, 1920). Pound probably owned or had seen a copy of this edition. See the radio
broadcasts, p. 241.

39 Pound refers to the Kahal in the radio broadcasts, pp. 60, 86, 111, 113, 115,
118, 189, 219, 311. The Kahal also figures prominently in Céline's anti-Semitic
paranoia, which helped to feed Pound's. See Céline, 1, pp. 285, 288; 2, pp. 43, 142,
163.

40 Stock, 3, p. 496. For Fry, see Cohn, 1, pp. 70–71, 167. For Brafman, to
whom Pound refers in the broadcasts, p. 330, see Cohn, 1, pp. 53–54, and Fry, pp.
20n, 25n, 27n, 203–205. Brafman's "revelations" about the Jews are contained in
his *Book of the Kahal* and *Jewish Brotherhoods.* For Fry on the conspiratorial Kahal
(and Talmud), see *Waters Flowing Eastward,* pp. 18, 20–25, 28–30, 31, 32, 34, 44,
60, 81, 204, 205. According to Fry, who reproduces the text of the *Protocols* in Part
II of *Waters Flowing Eastward,* the Jews are the motivating force behind the French
and the Russian Revolutions, through which they aim at the total destruction of
private property, the bourgeoisie, and Western culture. The Kahal, however, victim-
izes Gentiles and Jews alike, for it is in reality the instrument of a greedy and
megalomaniac gang of Jewish high-priests, financiers, and politicians. As in Pound,
these include the Rothschilds, Sassoons, Warburgs, Monds, Bernard Baruch, and
Kuhn, Loeb, and Co., whose two main centers of operation are London and New
York. Fry believes that Jews controlled United States policy during the Wilson
administration, that the Russian Revolution, like the Zionist movement, masks the
interests of Jewish finance, and that Roosevelt's Brain Trust consists of Jewish
radicals secretly advancing the Communist cause. As for the *Protocols,* Fry argues
that "the claim of the Jews that the Protocols are forgeries is in itself an admission of
their genuineness." See Fry, pp. 31, 32, 35, 44, 45, 51, 54, 55, 56–57, 57n, 61–62,
74, 74n, 80, 81, 92–96, 107, 111, 126. Part III of Fry's book attempts to show that
the British Empire and the United States during the 1920s and 1930s are threatened
with "Sovietization" at the hands of the socialist Fabian Society and the British
Labour Party, both of which are supposedly directed by predominantly Jewish
"Illuminati" who also infest the American universities. Their victory would result in
the elimination of private property, the imposition of heavy taxes, the reduction of
the Gentile population to slavery under the "Dole," and the elevation of the Jews to
international dominance. See Fry, pp. 219–220, 222–230. Fry's dubious and often
paradoxical accusations would have had a powerful appeal for Pound. In the broadcasts he also relies on at least two other of Fry's allegations, that in New York City
all meat is slaughtered by Jewish butchers as part of a Jewish monopoly, and that the
firm of Small and Maynard, which published an edition of the *Protocols* in 1920, fell
into financial difficulties immediately thereafter. See Fry, pp. 29, 105; Pound, RB,
pp. 241, 331.

41 Carroll F. Terrell is correct in pointing out that the exact meaning of the reference to nickel is unclear. See Terrell, Vol. II, p. 725. However, Pound may be referring to the supposed machinations of the Jewish Mond Family, whose fortunes were based heavily on chemical industries, and whose perhaps most illustrious figure, Ludwig Mond, helped to improve world steel production through his discovery in 1890 of a process of extracting nickel and adding it to steel. Pound's implication would then seem to be that Finland, which the "Judaic" Soviet Union invaded in World War II, is valuable to the Monds as a source of nickel, and that they have helped to orchestrate the war in order to achieve their own selfish ends. For Ludwig Mond, see Barraclough, p. 46. The Addendum also contains this elliptical line, to which Pound resorted (as in Canto 52) to escape libel: "S. . . . . . doing evil in place of the R. . . . ." The first initial probably refers to the Jewish businessman Victor Sassoon, who in the broadcasts dominates the opium trade, and who here replaces the Rothschilds as a primary villain and leader of the Kahal.

42 Noel Stock to Pound, November 15, 1956, Beinecke Rare Book and Manuscript Library, Yale University. Although Stock's letters to Pound in the 1950s indicate his interest in and even agreement with some of Pound's racist and political ideas, it must be emphasized that they reflect only his earliest and unformed views as a literary critic and scholar, during the period in which he was Pound's impressionable Australian disciple. Since the publication of *Poet in Exile* in 1964, Stock has been a severe critic of Pound's racism and fascism, and he has been quick to point out instances in which Pound's work is marred by erroneous or questionable historical, cultural, and political theories. Few critics have done more than Stock to explain Pound's links with fascism. The reader should keep this in mind in considering the excerpts from Stock's correspondence quoted elsewhere in this book. Stock discusses his years as Pound's disciple in "Ezra Pound in Melbourne 1953–57," *Helix* 13/14, *Ezra Pound in Melbourne*, pp. 159–178.

Chapter Seven: Bachofen and the Conquest of the Swamp
1 Pound, "Ecclesia," *The Townsman*, 2 (Nov. 1939), p. 4.
2 Pound, "Non sacrificate ad uno spirito che non vi appartiene," *Meridiano di Roma*, (28 Jan. 1940), p. 1; "Statues of Gods," *The Townsman*, 2 (Aug. 1939), p. 14.
3 See Waite, p. 111; Hitler, pp. 62–63, 95, 255; Rosenberg, pp. 70, 51, 199.
4 Maurice Bardèche, quoted in Soucy, 1, p. 55.
5 Maurras, 3, pp. 209–215, 217, 219, 225–230; Nolte, pp. 140–143, 169. Although Louis-Ferdinand Céline was neither a fascist sympathizer nor a vicious anti-Semite when he wrote *Journey to the End of the Night* (1932) (English ed. New Directions, 1983, trans. Ralph Manheim), the novel anticipates his later politics, nowhere more impressively than in its extended representation of the swamp or jungle. Arriving at Fort Gono[rrhea], capital of the French African colony of Bambola-Bragamance, the anti-hero Bardamu encounters everywhere the jungle's putrefying, deliquescent, debilitating power. Rats and maggots gnaw away constantly and invisibly at the works of man; going nowhere, government roads "soon vanished under a dense growth of vegetation," while numerous Frenchmen are lost each year in the "swamp." Disgusted with the colony's miscegenous and syphilitic director, tortured by malarial fever, delirium, heat, humidity, and mosquitoes, Bardamu is himself nearly submerged in the "swollen, wildly aggressive vegetation in the garden," "floral and verbal excess," "moist green gloom." These passages reflect Céline's contempt not only for French colonialism but for the myriad corruptions and weaknesses of post-war France. See pp. 107, 108, 113, 114, 115, 122, 123, 140. By 1937, Céline had come to blame this multifarious decay on the Jews, one of whose primary characteristics is "viscosity," and who supposedly seek to submerge Western and Aryan origins, the authentic "patrimoine autochthone," in an "Asiatic" flood. See Céline, 1, pp. 68, 96, 180, 183, 296; 2, pp. 80, 94; 3, p. 81. Céline refers to the Jewish Hydra in *Les Beaux draps*, p. 78.

6 See Bachofen, pp. 227–228, 70, 89–90, 162–163. For Aeschylus, see Said, pp. 21, 56–57.

7 See Weigert-Vowinkel, pp. 349–353, and Joseph Campbell's introduction to Bachofen, pp. xxx-xxxii, xlix, liv.

8 Bachofen, pp. iv, xiv, xix, xxv, 27–28, 93, 61–62, 57, 59, 28, 78.

9 Bachofen, pp. 35–37, 59, 60, 102, 80, 94, 95.

10 Bachofen, pp. 39, 63, 91–92, 110–111, 97–98.

11 Bachofen, pp. 1, 89–91, 117–118, 99, 100, 102.

12 Bachofen, pp. 224, 228, 231–232, 234–235, 237–239, 116.

13 Fromm, "The Significance of the Theory of Mother Right for Today," in *The Crisis of Psychoanalysis: Essays on Freud, Marx, and Social Psychology*, p. 106.

14 Bachofen, pp. 91, 94–95, 97, 181n, 191. Bachofen alludes to Atalanta, the "*Schoeneia virgo*, the daughter of Schoenus the rush man, [who finally] renounces her proud freedom and resigns herself to her new fate" under the conditions of marriage and agriculture. Recapitulating the major themes announced in the first part of his poem, Pound links Helen and Atalanta in Canto 102, p. 730: " 'for my [Helen's] bitch eyes' in Ilion / copper and wine like a bear cub's / in sunlight, thus Atalanta." But though she rejected patriarchal controls, Atalanta had before her marriage dedicated herself to Artemisian purity, as Helen had not.

15 See Walter Houghton and G. Robert Stange, eds., *Victorian Poetry and Poetics* (Boston: Houghton Mifflin, 1968), p. 409n. The editors comment on the third line of Matthew Arnold's "To a Friend" —"saw the Wide Prospect [Europe] and the Asian Fen." Here, in Arnold's reference to Homer, the tangled and ahistorical world of Asia is contrasted implicitly with the prospect of the Greek and European future.

16 Girard, 2, p. 60, quoting from Malinowski, pp. 88–91.

17 For Hermes, and the *hermae* as phallic symbols, see William Smith, ed., p. 602; Athanassakis, p. 89n. The golden bough mentioned in Canto 16 looks back to Hermes' "golden bough of Argicida" (1/ 15) in Canto 1. Pound identifies Hermes in his bad form with the greedy urban huckster-shyster, such as Baldy Bacon, the parodistic "miraculous Hermes" (12/ 54) of Canto 12. For the good and bad Hermes, see Brown, *passim*. Lewis Hyde, pp. 244–257, misleadingly claims that Pound's image of the Jews is virtually identical with that of the "classical Hermes."

18 Bachofen, pp. 95, 41.

19 Horkheimer and Adorno, pp. 69, 70.

20 There is an analogue to the opposition between Circe as swamp sorceress and Circe as exalted religious ikon in Maurras's "L'étang de Marthe et les hauteurs d'Aristarche." Like Circe, the evil Semitic prophetess Martha belongs to the murky depths of the swamp. Her opposite for Maurras is the Ephesian woman Aristarche, who brought Hellenic culture to the region of Marseilles in ancient times and established upon the sunlit heights shrines dedicated to Ephesian Diana (Artemis), goddess of purity. As in Pound, Jewish darkness and confusion are contrasted with the Greek religion of light. See Maurras, 3, pp. 217–219, 231–232.

21 See the dangerous and feminine Geryon, who is also Amor, in Notes for Canto 111, p. 783.

22 Fromm, "The Theory of Mother Right and its Relevance for Social Psychology," in *The Crisis of Psychoanalysis*, pp. 116–121, 112. Compare Reich, pp. 86–87.

23 Fromm, "The Theory of Mother Right and its Relevance for Social Psychology," pp. 130–131.

24 Pound, "Non sacrificate ad uno spirito che non vi appartiene," p. 1: "Tutto quello ch è oscuro e contorto, risulta da un tentativo quasi patologico di far coprire o far corrispondere qualche percezione greca della verità, con qualche ambiguità vicino-orientale.

Nelle leggi di Antonino Pio, di Costantino Imperatore, di Giustiniano abbiamo i più elevati concetti di giustizia . . . . Ma fra 'lo spazio economico chiave' cinese e lo spazio chiave romano, troviamo uno spazio oscurantista. Si dice che nello spazio vicino orientale le tribù e i popoli di scarso senso statale cercavano da milleni di ostacolare il traffico fra occidente ed oriente approfitandone, alzando i prezzi, etc.

La Grecia era turbata da dottrine estranee, i padre ed i senatore romani ogni tanto si allarmavano per le mollezze introdotte nei costumi: 'Persicos odi, puer,' etc."

25 Pound, Canto 46, p. 234; Canto 78, pp. 479–480; Canto 87, p. 570; Canto 94, p. 635. The opposition between Rome and the Near East appears as late as Canto 103. By means of a parallel construction, Pound associates the struggle of the agrarian homestead against Communism, which he considers essentially Asiatic, with Rome's struggle against the Near East: "Homestead versus kolschoz / Rome versus Babylon" (103/732).

26 See Cannistraro, ed., pp. 305–306; Claudio Segré, The Fourth Shore: The Italian Colonization of Libya (Chicago: Univ. of Chicago Press, 1974). Italy's three other shores were the Tyrrhenian, Adriatic, and Sicilian. In Italy's Policy of Social Economics, 1939–1940, which Pound translated in 1941, Odon Por refers to Italian land "reclamation" in Libya, "where swamps disappear giving place to flourishing colonies that recall the fairest and most prosperous stretches of the mother country." See Por, 3, p. 106. On the ideal of "Romanità" in Italian Fascism and its effect on political and cultural life, see Cannistraro, ed., pp. 461–463.

27 Rosenberg, pp. 55–57. According to Zielinski, 1, p. 98, the destruction of Jerusalem was "un des petits faits de la grande histoire romaine."

28Mussolini also exaggerated not only the economic and political importance but the originality of his land reclamation projects. However, they had an immense symbolic, propagandistic, and politically legitimating function within Italian Fascism. See Nolte, p. 286.

29 Bachofen visited and described the Pontine Marshes. See Die Landschaften Mittelitaliens (Basel: Verlag Benno Schwabe, 1945), p. 357, quoted in d'Erme et al., p. 19.

30 In 1936 Gaetano Salvemini argued statistically that the draining of the Pontine Marshes was an ill-advised and economically wasteful propaganda stunt. See Salvemini, pp. 296, 296n. In view of Pound's much advertised interest in conservation and ecology, whereby man "aids" natural process, it is also ironic that recent observers have come to view the draining of the Pontine Marshes as an ecological disaster resulting from machine fetishism and man's impulse to dominate Nature. See d'Erme et al., pp. 9–21, 34. The authors of this work recognize the longstanding link between Circe, Monte Circeo, and the mysteries of the Pontine Marshes. They add, however, that after Mussolini's "bonifica" or land reclamation Circe no longer "inhabited" the region. Her presence, like her myth, had "perished" along with the swamps of which she had been the immemorial symbol. See p. 56.

31 Bachofen, pp. 11, 41, 42. One of usury's distinguishing characteristics, according to Dante, is to destroy "walls and arms" ("rompe i muri e l'armi," as Pound quotes Inferno, 17. 2, in SP, p. 329).

32 Despite Mussolini's much-advertised concern for the peasant, his "ruralism" was opportunistic while his land reclamation projects and agricultural programs favored large landowners. See Lyttelton, pp. 352, 353; Cannistraro, ed., pp. 63, 162–163. Writing in 1940, in a work translated by Pound, the Italian Fascist economist-journalist Odon Por claimed that the Italian Fascists had "assaulted" the regressive feudal latifundia system, which favored large landowners, and had distributed farms to Italian peasants. Such a scheme might satisfy Pound's general demand for the homestead, but in the same work Por acknowledged that many peasants were not yet in possession of the promised lands and that landowners had not been expropriated but rather required to establish responsible and "collaborative" relations with the new colonists. These conditions sound like a disguised repetition of those feudal relations which Pound praises in unguarded moments. See Por, 3, pp. 32, 100, 108–115, 108n, 190–191. For another favorable view of Italian Fascism as an agrarian revolution, see Gioacchino Volpe, pp. 51–52, 123, 151, 153, 157. An official historian of the Italian Fascist movement, Volpe praises Mussolini's "bonifica integrale" for eliminating malaria and providing the basis for "rural democ-

racy." Pound apparently admired Volpe's work; see Heymann, p. 146. The "Volpi" to whom Pound refers is probably Volpe.

33 By the late 1920s, Italian Fascism's anti-feminist ideology had been solidified: the natural task of woman is to bear children and stay at home. According to Mussolini, woman is "passive" and does not "count" in the state. Political, social, and cultural anti-feminism is typical of Nazism, which would send woman "back to work at the spinning wheel and the weaving loom." See Gregor, 3, pp. 281–291; Cannistraro, ed., pp. 202–203; Mosse, 2, p. 20.

34 The *fasces*, which in ancient times were born by the lictors before the magistrates of the Roman Republic, symbolize judicial power and authority. The Italian Fascists were aware of the symbolic relation between the *fasces* and the draining of the Pontine Marshes. One of the towns built upon the reclaimed swampland was Littoria (now Latina), meaning "city of the lictors." See Nolte, p. 266, and Melograni, p. 229.

Chapter Eight: Waddell and Aryan Tradition

1 Reno Odlin, letter to the Editor, *Paideuma*, 8 (Spring, 1979), p. 175. See also French, p. 142.

2 Strauss, *passim;* Freud, 3, pp. 142–143.

3 Richard Sawyer, one of the few scholars to examine Pound's relation to Waddell, argues that Waddell's pan-Sumerian theme is "so far-fetched that it can hardly be taken seriously." However, Sawyer is "convinced that Pound actually was taken in by Waddell's 'histories,' and that he did expect his reader to regard these particular works as constituting a fairly reliable record of an ancient civilization's extensive influence and cultural advancement." The rescue of Waddell's theories from obscurity is thus essential to Pound's struggle against "darkness" and the "historical blackout" promoted by usurers. As for Pound's "deeper purpose" in using Waddell, Sawyer finds oblique connections, which this chapter seeks to extend and clarify, between Waddell's Sumerian Paradise and the utopia of Italian Fascism. Still, it is a stunning fact that Sawyer omits all reference to Waddell's manifest anti-Semitism and never once suggests the appeal which Waddell's Aryan prejudices undoubtedly had for the racist Pound. Besides ignoring the anti-Semitic implications of Waddell's and Pound's solar mythology, and its links with Nazi thinking, Sawyer proposes that Pound intends a favorable comparison between Menes's enlightened economics and statecraft in Canto 94 and the plan in the Book of Jeremiah to "redeem Zion with justice" (74/ 429), as Pound describes it in the Pisan *Cantos*. In Sawyer's misleading account, which is corrected in this chapter, the Aryan Sumerians and Jews are equally admirable to Pound in their devotion to the principles of "solar justice," commercial honesty, and hatred of sacrificial bloodshed. See Richard Sawyer, pp. 90–91.

4 Waddell, 2, pp. vii-x, 19–24, 29, 86, 100, 130, 135, 154, 169–170, 172–173, 176–177.

5 The myth of Aryan migration from an Aryan or Indian homeland traces to the Enlightenment, its purpose being to replace the traditional Christian and Western conception of Semitic origins: no longer would Europeans trace their ancestry to Jewish Adam. Voltaire helped to fabricate these ideas. As in Pound, the Aryan migration in one theory follows the sun's course (Pound's "periplum"). See Poliakov, 1, pp. 188, 191, 197, 209, 256, 259; Barzun, pp. 135–146. See also Mosse, 6, pp. 39–46. Wyndham Lewis speculates inconclusively on the "Aryan" theory of the origins of world civilization in *Hitler*, pp. 134–135.

6 Waddell's ideas concerning Sumeria bear some resemblance to those of Houston Stewart Chamberlain, whom Nazi ideologists found indispensable. See Chamberlain, Vol. I, pp. 369–370.

7 Waddell, 2, pp. 34–35, 40.

8 Waddell, 2, pp. x, 13, 29, 30, 34, 44, 88, 108, 133, 135, 176–177.

9 On the somewhat confusing derivation of this lion head in Waddell, see Richard Sawyer, pp. 86–87n.

10 Pound reverses Jesus' intention in Matthew 5: 18: "For verily I say unto you, Till heaven and earth pass, one jot or tittle shall in no wise pass from the law, till all be fulfilled."

11 Waddell, 2, pp. 50, 86, 21, 146, 165, 171. Though Waddell was neither a Nazi nor specifically a Nordic supremacist, his ideas of the widespread diffusion of Aryan culture, agriculture, and solar religion have many analogues in the writings of the Nazi ideologist Alfred Rosenberg. Like Waddell, Rosenberg traces the cultural greatness of Egypt, Phoenicia, Sumeria, and Central Asia to Aryan sources. See Rosenberg, pp. 33–72. For a detailed discussion of the similarities between Waddell and Rosenberg, see my "Ezra Pound, L. A. Waddell, and the Aryan Tradition of *The Cantos*," *Modern Language Studies*, 25 (Spring, 1985), pp. 74–75.

12 Waddell, 2, pp. 86, 50–51, 163–166.

13 Noted in Stock, 1, p. 255; see also Waddell, 1, p. 42. For the Indian origins of the Gothic arch, see p. 103n.

14 Pound, quoted in Norman, p. 373.

15 See Bacigalupo, p. 360, on this passage. However, according to Terrell, Vol. II, p. 622, San Vio is a church in Venice, while the eyes are those of "Old Ziovan," who is mentioned along with the church in Canto 83, p. 532.

16 Here Pound resembles Alfred Rosenberg, who attacks Jewish "legalism" and claims that "any people which needs a complex law code and commentary lacks a natural morality of its own." These charges "can be traced back to certain statements of the early Christian philosopher Justin Martyr (A.D.c.100- c. 165). . . ." See Rosenberg, pp. 14, 184.

17 For Apollonius' revulsion from sacrifice, see Philostratus, Vol. I, Conybeare's Introduction, p. xiii, and pp. 23–24, 89, 519; Vol. II, pp. 325–327.

18 Bacigalupo, p. 248. For Apollonius' advocacy and practice of vegetarianism, see Philostratus, Vol. I, pp. 19–21, 61; Vol. II, pp. 39, 305. There would seem to be vegetarian implications in the Latin translation, included in Canto 100, p. 715, of a Greek account of Alexander the Great's conversation with Indian Brahmins; the translation, entitled *De Moribus Brahmanorum*, was probably made by St. Ambrose. See Terrell, Vol. II, p. 648. Hitler's vegetarianism is discussed in Waite, pp. 20, 28, 49, 126. For Wagner's "Aryan" and "Christian" vegetarianism, and his hatred of "carnivorous Jews," see Poliakov, 1, p. 312. The fascist Arnold Leese combined vegetarianism with a horror of Jewish butchers (comparable to Pound's in the radio broadcasts, pp. 331, 342); see Cross, p. 63.

19 Richard Sawyer discusses the source of these lines; see p. 90.

20 Pound undoubtedly knew that Alexander the Great was thirty-three, not thirty-eight, when he died. This is probably a misprint for thirty-three, so that Alexander, dead at the same age as Jesus Christ, figures here as the alternative Messiah (Hitler, the Führer, was also messianic) of Europe. See Hesse, p. 182.

21 Terrell, Vol. II, p. 584.

22 Thus far Pound critics have largely ignored King Edward I's anti-Semitism, just as they have sought to explain away the anti-Semitism of Pound's hero Sir Edward Coke (1552–1634), who incorporated elements of Edward's anti-Semitic legislation (Statutum de Judeismo) in the *Second Institutes of the Laws of England*. Canto 107, p. 759, quotes from Coke's *Second Institutes* a law, in Latin, forbidding the donation and sale of land to Jews; however, Pound elides the incriminating word "Judaeis" ("to the Jews"). Curiously, David Gordon finds no anti-Semitism in this passage. Nor does Carroll F. Terrell find anti-Semitism in two other documents excerpted from the *Second Institutes* in Canto 108, p. 765. One excerpt derives from Coke's discussion of the Statutum de Judeismo: "Divers had banished / but the usuries, no King before him." This alludes to the banishment of Jews by various earlier kings, and the unprecedented prohibition of Jews from the practice of usury by King Edward I. The other excerpt is taken from an act passed in 1290, the eighteenth year of King Edward's reign, and concerns property lost to legal heirs because of usury. Terrell comments that the act goes on to define limits to usury and leads to acts to protect the Jews, for whereas King John had treated them harshly, Edward I attempted to remedy such injustice. This conclusion is highly misleading.

To be sure, King Edward, after his prohibition of the Jews from taking usury, sought to emancipate them economically by diverting them into agriculture, trade, and other productive channels. However, Edward did not emancipate the Jews socially, and so put them at a distinct disadvantage in business. Jews could enter neither the burgesses nor the trades, and many, especially the poorer ones, faced starvation. Given their straitened circumstances, it is understandable that some Jews did in fact resort to highway robbery and to coin-clipping, as Pound remarks disapprovingly in the broadcasts. Terrell also fails to mention that Edward continued to impose extraordinary levies on the impoverished Jews; that in 1278 he had all English Jews arrested, 293 of whom were hanged the following year; and finally, that in 1290 he expelled the Jews from England. It is to this event that Pound, quoting Coke in the Statutum de Judeismo, refers in Canto 107, p. 765, in the phrase "was 1500 three score." This cryptic figure is the number of Jews who were expelled. As if to deny the fact of expulsion, Terrell says that these Jews "left the country under the anti-usury law," thus suggesting that they might have stayed had they been allowed to practice usury. As we have seen, Pound gives a similar interpretation in the radio broadcasts, which Terrell never mentions in discussing these passages. See Sir Edward Coke, *The Second Part of the Institutes of the Laws of England* (1642; rpt. Garland, 1979), pp. 506–509; Gordon, 2, pp. 280–282; Terrell, Vol. II, pp. 698, 705, 706; Roth, pp. 68–90. Bacigalupo, p. 451, does not evade the anti-Semitism in these and other passages in the Coke *Cantos*.

Chapter Nine: Nature, Race, and History, I

1 Pound expresses this idea in a memorable phrase: "Nemus aram vult" (SP, 332), the grove calls for the column (or altar).

2 Pearlman, 1, pp. 21, 24, 26, 27, 28–30; Vasse, pp. 256–265.

3 Quoted in Heymann, p. 97.

4 Pound's view of Mussolini as "*artifex*" agrees with Mussolini's conception of himself: ". . . Mussolini said that politics must be like art." See Mosse, 5, p. 205, and Volpe, p. 105. Gioacchino Volpe, author of an official history of the Italian Fascist movement published in 1932, acknowledged the double impulse of Italian Fascism toward "organicist" conservatism and revolution, yet he insisted that this amounted not to confusion or contradiction but to a "fusion of historical sense and revolutionary spirit." See Volpe, pp. 9, 116–117, 136, 164.

5 Burckhardt, pp. 1–6, 26–28, 49, 52. Pound refers to this work in SP, pp. 22, 201.

6 See Mussolini, quoted in Finer, p. 109; Nolte, pp. 206, 247. Pound's powerful attraction to Mussolini may be seen in the fact that, apart from his visit to the Palazzo Venezia in 1933, he wrote to Il Duce over fifty times. The nine letters which Heymann has selected from this correspondence are chiefly concerned with finance and monetary policy. See Heymann, pp. 317–327.

7 Walter Benjamin, "The Work of Art in the Age of Mechanical Reproduction," in *Illuminations*, pp. 243–244. Apart from its aesthetic emphasis, Pound would have admired Italian Fascism for at least two other "stylistic" reasons: its proclaimed unification of thought and action, which consorts with Pound's well-known slogan praising "ideas into action"; and its supposed abandonment of political rhetoric in favor of hard, direct, and concise speech. Mussolini, says Volpe, "repudiated the eloquence [,] 'verbose, prolix, inconclusive [,]' of the democrats and had created an eloquence 'essentially Fascist; that is choice, biting, sincere, and hard.' " However, this description is difficult to square with Mussolini's frequently florid and inflated pronouncements. See Volpe, pp. 161, 80.

8 Germino, p. 123; Gregor, 3, pp. 54, 112; Mussolini, p. 144.

9 Mannheim, pp. 136, 137n; Finer, p. 109. For many years historians have regarded Italian Fascism (and other versions) as virtually lacking an ideology. They point to its negative and reactive character, its irrationalistic cult of action, its glorification of political and historical open-endedness and opportunism, the contradiction between its actions and its professed intentions, and the apparent incoher-

ence of its political ideas. Historians have also tended to view Italian Fascist ideas as little more than *ex post facto* justifications or rationalizations of Fascist actions. More recently Zeev Sternhell has rightly observed that few if any political movements attain consistency in word and deed, and he joins other historians in acknowledging if not the full intellectual coherence of Italian Fascism then at least the existence of intellectual patterns within it. According to A. James Gregor, Italian Fascism has a coherent and plausible "rationale," an impressively arguable ideological foundation comparable to that of Marxism. In contrast, Adrian Lyttelton affirms Mannheim's early view of Italian Fascism as the most irrational and least coherent of modern political ideologies. See Zeev Sternhell, "Fascist Ideology," in Laqueur, ed., pp. 319–320; Mannheim, pp. 135, 136, 136n, 137, 137n; Cassels, pp. 55, 71; Lyttelton, pp. 364–367, 499–500n; Gregor, 1, pp. 90–92, 199–200; 4, p. 237.

10 On Italian Fascist technocracy, see Lyttelton, p. 76. See also Pound, SP, p. 53.

11 Pound, "Atrophy of the Leninists, I," *New English Weekly*, 2 July, 1936, p. 227; J/M, pp. 94, 98; for Palmerston, see also "Demarcations," *British Union Quarterly*, 1 (Jan.-April, 1937), p. 38. Despite their shared anti-Communism, Pound and Mussolini reveal a profound respect for Lenin as a charismatic leader of the masses and dynamic political artist (though ultimately a failed one.) This admiration reflects what Nolte describes as the partial resemblance between Russian Communism and Italian Fascism as revolutionary mass movements, and the "mysterious proximity and distance" between Lenin and Mussolini. Although Mussolini was against all forms of Bolshevism, if he had to "choose" one version he "would prefer that of Lenin, because it was of gigantic, barbaric, universal proportions." It is therefore understandable that Pound, at least in the 1930s, sometimes links Italian Fascism not only with Lenin but with Marxism as a whole. See Nolte, pp. 204–209, 247, 265, 279, 308–309; Pound, J/M, p. 72.

12 Hyam Maccoby also makes this point in his excellent "The Jews as Anti-Artist: The Anti-Semitism of Ezra Pound," p. 64. Pound refers to the Jews' "inter-uterine mode of life" in a letter to Louis Zukofsky. See Kimpel and Eaves, 2, p. 57.

13 I agree entirely with the analysis of Charles Berezin in "Poetry and Politics in Ezra Pound," p. 267. The identification of the Jews with the "formless wobble" of feminine indecisiveness and confusion appears in the once famous *Sex and Character* (*Geschlecht und Charackter*, 1903), by the Jewish anti-Semite Otto Weininger. See *Sex and Character*, pp. 301–330 (Chapter Thirteen, "Judaism"). This work influenced Joyce's distinctly positive characterization of the somewhat ambisexual Jew Leopold Bloom. See Richard Ellmann, *James Joyce* (New York: Oxford Univ. Press, 1959), p. 471. For the link in Nietzsche between the Jews and the feminine, see Derrida, 2, p. 69. See also Lewis, 1, p. 41.

14 Bush, p. 58. See also Canto 99, p. 698, and Canto 100, p. 719, both concerned with Confucian China: "Peace comes of good manners"; " 'Peace grips the earth in good manners.' " For the Jews' antagonistic and critical relation to middle class culture, see John Murray Cuddihy's dyspeptic but brilliant *The Ordeal of Civility: Freud, Marx, Levi-Strauss and the Jewish Struggle with Modernity, passim.*

15 Phyllis Bottome, quoted in Norman, p. 173.

16 Terrell, Vol. I, pp. 136, 138.

17 Pound, "Private Worlds," *New English Weekly*, 2 May, 1935, pp. 48–49. In "Ezra Pound to the Falsifiers," published in *Secolo d' Italia* in Jan. 1959, Pound asserts his "utter contempt" for Freud, whose work is a "poison." Quoted in Heymann, p. 265.

18 Houston Stewart Chamberlain devoted a whole section of *The Foundations of the Nineteenth Century* to what he called the "Chaos of Peoples." For Chamberlain, Vienna is the most vivid representation of this debilitating racial mixture. See Geoffrey Field, pp. 114–115.

19 Pound refers to the "sewers" of Vienna in a 1953 letter to Denis Goacher in the Beinecke Rare Book and Manuscript Library at Yale; no month or day is given.

20 Quoted in Kimpel and Eaves, 2, p. 58.

21 Pound associates the Jews, the stomach, and animal lust in a remark to John Quinn. New York, said Pound, had been usurped by "a million Jews who are walking appetites." Quoted in Torrey, p. 69.

22 Durant, p. 108; Pound, L, p. 266; Céline, 1, pp. 305–306; Hughes, 2, pp. 9–10. See also the Italian Fascist propagandist Vittorio Guerriero, "Il Dottor Freud," in del Buono, ed., p. 253. Disgusted by aimless introspection, homosexuality, and other "satanic liberties" allegedly promoted by Freud, Guerriero is gratified by the "purifactory" book-burnings of Hitler, whose revolution had "fortunately swept away all of this [Freudian] trash and obscenity." As for Fascist Italy, Guerriero predicts the "virtual termination" of the ideas of the paradoxically satanic yet "absurd" Doctor Freud.

23 Durant notes Pound's criticism that Joyce's "mittel europa humour runs to the other [anal] orifice." See P/J, p. 158, and Durant, p. 149. Pound later refers to Mitteleuropa as "the privy that stank Franz Joseph" (48/ 247), identifies the Jews with gold, stench, and guilt, and denounces the "*dung flow*" of "*the kikery*" (91/ 614) of Marx and Freud. His connection in the later *Cantos* of the "anal" Jews with homosexuality follows logically his familiar identification of sodomy and the "sterile" generation of usury. See Kimpel and Eaves, 2, p. 66.

24 Pound combines anti-Semitism, anti-feminism, and anti-psychiatry in his phrase "pussyKiKeatrists," which he "used for psychiatrists." See Torrey, pp. 250–251.

25 See Fenichel, "Elements of a Psychoanalytic Theory of Anti- Semitism," in Simmel, ed., p. 22. Pound identifies the Jews with burdensome memory and its evasion in his caricature of the Jew "Brennbaum" in *Hugh Selwyn Mauberley*. At rare moments one can read in the face of this rootless dandy "the heavy memories of Horeb, Sinai, and the forty years." It was at Horeb, the mountain of God, that Jehovah addressed the terrified Moses from a burning bush; Sinai is the mountain where Moses received the Ten Commandments. In an effort to become sartorially rather than morally "impeccable," this dandy has attempted in the most trivial way and with only partial success to cast off the weight of the Mosaic concept of guilt and sin. It is not irrelevant that the lapsed Protestant Pound was himself dandyish for much of his career.

26 Pound, quoted in Chace, p. 12.

27 See Nathan, p. 83; Mosse, 1, p. 316.

28 Gourmont, pp. 8, 261–273: "One must not be gulled by the scholastic distinction between instinct and intelligence; man is as full of instincts as the insect most visibly instinctive; he obeys them by methods more diverse, that is all there is to it."

29 Carlyle, 2, pp. 183–197.

30 Heymann, pp. 257, 273–274. Carlyle celebrates "rhythmic" and automatized "dancing" under the direction of the "Drill-Sergeant" in "Shooting Niagara: And After?" See *Carlyle's Works*, XVI, *Critical and Miscellaneous Essays*, IV, pp. 458–460.

31 See Pound's anonymous contribution to *Strike* (circa 1956 or 1957), reproduced in "Ezra Pound, Anonymous Contributions to *Strike*," *Paideuma*, 3 (1974), p. 393: "G. Vattuone's *L'Uomo e la Malattia Mentale* . . . contains at least two suggestions: First that the patient be led to forget himself; second that he stop attributing his troubles to present external causes . . . ."

Chapter Ten: Nature, Race and History, II

1 See Pound to Albert Mockel, June 14, 1935, in the Beinecke Rare Book and Manuscript Library, Yale University. Pound finds Maurras "ignorant," meaning that he knows nothing about money and ignores finance capital. Actually, Maurras calls for the banishment of usury as part of his national programme in his 1899 royalist declaration, "Dictator and King"; see McClelland, ed., p. 233. He also sought to prove, as Pound did in his later career, the "complicity between international finance and international revolution"; see Nolte, p. 165. The resemblance

between Pound's and Maurras's ideas was recognized by Peter Whigham, who wrote to Pound at St. Elizabeths. See his letter of June 29, 1954, and July 10, 1954, also in the Beinecke Library. Besides praising Maurras, Whigham mentions Joseph de Maistre, the fountainhead of French conservative and reactionary thought after the French Revolution.

2 There is much to suggest that Maurras, with his monarchistic and Catholic emphasis and his lack of a large movement or mass appeal, is a radical conservative and reactionary traditionalist. Alan Cassels observes that *Action Française*, of which Maurras was the leader, "can at best be called proto-fascist." However, Nolte and Peter Viereck believe that Maurras and *Action Française* passed into fascism through their acceptance of mass violence and toleration of the Nazi takeover of France. Nolte also makes clear Maurras's profound ideological affinity with Hitler and Mussolini (especially Hitler), and he observes that, for all his vaunted conservatism, Maurras repeatedly and arbitrarily attacked as "un-French" the whole political and social legacy of the French Revolution, in short, the actual roots of his own reactionary philosophy. This raises serious doubts about the real extent of Maurras's conservatism. Maurras, says Nolte, "was the first man in Europe who as a thinker and a politician drove conservatism beyond the limits separating it from incipient fascism." Robert Soucy similarly argues in a discussion of Maurras that "the lines between Fascism and conservatism in France were . . . blurred." As for Pound, although Hugh Kenner views him as a radical conservative, he too casts aside his most immediate historical roots and condemns what he considers the virtually total ideological factitiousness of American politics and civilization since the Civil War. According to Pound, American civilization "collapsed" (SP, 162) in the 1860s, when the whole nation was "sold" (RB, 56) to the Rothschilds and other Jewish usurers, with "sub-kikes assistin' " (RB, 165). The American people had "killed each other off to make room for the vermin" (RB, 75). At this point began the "period of despair" (SP, 147) and "infection" (RB, 75), the "progressive falsification of America" (RB, 40), with the "nation in the hands of the enemy" (SP, 321), the "legislatures" (RB, 103) rendered impotent, and the nation no longer "worth inhabiting" (P/L, 288). "Perhaps after Lincoln's death," speculates Pound, "there was no United States Republic" (RB, 75). In any case, after the "debacle of American culture individuals had to emigrate in order to conserve such fragments of American culture as had survived" the "usurocracy" (SP, 161). Though clothed in the language of conservatism, this last statement goes far to explain the motivation for Pound's revolutionary fascism. Besides showing his alienation from contemporary America and his rejection of the continuity of American history, it typifies his arrogant appropriation for himself and his revolutionary elite of a supposedly misplaced, devalued, but authentic American tradition: Pound's intellectual gang, the "conspiracy of intelligent men" (RB, 185), has its analogue in Maurras's culturally privileged though beleaguered and misunderstood minority, the *élite généreuse*. Likewise, Pound's idea of replacing the individual franchise in America with guilds and voting rights according to profession is consistent with fascism's attempt to obliterate the longstanding and consensual tradition of the French Revolution and its conception of citizenship. Later we will examine the importance of this discontinuity in Pound's thought. See Maurras, in McClelland, ed., pp. 215–238; Eugen Weber, 1, pp. 526–527; Sauer, "National Socialism: Totalitarianism or Fascism?", and Cassels, "Janus: The Two Faces of Fascism," in Turner, ed., pp. 103–104, 82; Payne, pp. 14–16, 27–28; Nolte, pp. 24, 123; Viereck, p. 62; Soucy, pp. 33–34; Pound, GK, p. 264; RB, pp. 51, 56, 61, 103, 111.

3 See Maurras, 2, pp. 19–21, 45, 48; McClelland, ed., pp. 231, 251, 254, 282; Nolte, p. 187.

4 Maurras, 2, p. 20; McClelland, ed., pp. 216, 217, 264–266, 269, 285, 287, 290; Nolte, pp. 142, 159, 182, 183; Curtis, p. 89; Eugen Weber, 1, p. 9.

5 Maurras, 2, pp. 18, 4, 5, 20, 21; McClelland, ed., pp. 219–220, 250, 242, 252, 255; Curtis, pp. 80, 84–85, 87, 88; Nolte, p. 142; Tannenbaum, 1, p. 68.

6 Pound, quoted in Norman, p. 396.

7 Two other ideological positions which Pound favors, autarchy and eugenics, are in Karl Popper's view characteristic products of naive monism. See Popper,

Vol. I, pp. 57, 59, 60, 61, 62, 63, 68–71, 87, 171–173, 182, 188; Pound, SP, pp. 85–87.

8 Canto 86, p. 453: "B[itch] yr/progress"; see also Pound, SP, pp. 76, 154, 155, 196, 198, 202, 268. For Pound's attack on ideology, see SP, p. 158: "And the lesson is . . . against raw ideology, which Napoleon, Adams, Jefferson, were up against." See also Canto 33, p. 160.

9 See Mosse, 8, pp. 5, 12, 163–164. Pound's endorsement of a hierarchy of function is implicit in J/M, p. 106: "I do not think the best men are excluded in Italy." See also pp. 115, 123.

10 See Pound, "Demarcations," *British Union Quarterly,* 1 (Jan.-April, 1937), p. 37; SP, pp. 336–337.

11 See Fritz Stern, p. 89. It must be emphasized that fascism was not a mere reaction to liberalism or a counter-revolution against Marxism but an alternative revolutionary movement, an independent effort to transform the basis of modern society. It is not true that the only authentic revolutions are leftist. See Rhodes, p. 219; Eugen Weber, 2, *passim;* esp. pp. 26–27, 48, 139–141; "Revolution? Counter-revolution? What Revolution?" in Laqueur, ed., pp. 443–445.

12 Nolte, pp. 418, 524, 528–529; Hitler, pp. 257, 58. Compare Eugen Weber, Introduction to *The European Right: A Historical Profile,* ed. Weber and Hans Roggers, p. 8: "Certainly, even when its language is optimistic, the underlying mood of the Right, particularly the extreme Right, is pessimistic and especially appropriate to a threatened or declining society, to men and social groups that feel disillusioned or resentful."

13 In 1933 Mussolini expressed an identical view in conversation with Emil Ludwig, to whom Il Duce looked "extraordinarily Napoleonic": "Naturally every imperium has its zenith. Since it is always the creation of exceptional men, it carries within it the seeds of its own decay. Like everything exceptional, it contains ephemeral elements. It may last one or two centuries, or no more than ten years. The will to power." See Emil Ludwig, *Talks with Mussolini,* excerpted in Salomone, ed., p. 211.

14 Nolte, p. 60. Nolte speaks specifically of Christian conservatism, but I am extending the problem to radical conservatism in general. See also pp. 528–529.

15 According to Pound, Leibniz "was the last philosopher who 'got hold of something,' his unsquashable monad may by now have been pulverized into subelectrons, it may have been magnified in the microscope's eye to the elaborate structure of a solar system, but it holds as a concept. . . . If you let go of it, you are wafted out among mere nomenclatures" (GK, 74). Pound's identification of Leibniz as an intellectual watershed is accurate. However, as Paul Hazard points out in *The European Mind, 1680–1715,* pp. 409–411, Leibniz's metaphysics (like his calculus) is "based on the infinitely little, the imperceptible, the inapprehensible, the obscure." As suspicious of Descartes's Cogito as of his geometry, Leibniz as psychologist emphasizes the mind as a self-enclosed world or monad containing within itself the infinite and unconscious. By contrast, Pound affirms the Cogito, fears the unconscious, and prefers geometry to algebra.

16 Pound, "Ecclesia," *Townsman,* 2 (Nov. 1939), p. 5.

17 As Pound associates the Jews with slime, swamps, and viscous dissolution, in *Mein Kampf* Hitler identifies them with the "jelly-like slime" of the dialectical method, an anti-categorical form of thinking in which an idea or concept, inseparable from its antithesis, is transformed into something other than itself. See Hitler, pp. 62–63. In GK, p. 201, Pound seems to disparage the dialectical method, which is entirely foreign to his categorical manner of thinking.

18 Nolte, pp. 185, 186, 187, quoting Maurras; Curtis, pp. 86–88; Maurras, 1, pp. lxxii, lxxxix; 2, pp. 8, 4, 7; McClelland, ed., pp. 247, 242, 246; Sutton, pp. 18, 19, 22.

19 Pound's acceptance of cultural and racial pluralism within world culture does not make him any less a fascist. For all his anti-Semitism and his belief in Nordic supremacy, Alfred Rosenberg espoused a similar ideal, and was therefore disturbed by Hitler's extermination of various races in Eastern Europe. See Arendt, Vol. III, p. 79n.

20 Pound to R. McNair Wilson, March, 1934, Beinecke Rare Book and Manuscript Library, Yale University.

21 There is an affinity throughout this section between Pound and Nietzsche, who condemns Christianity for metaphysical abstraction, spiritual inwardness, social irresponsibility, otherworldliness, and general disparagement of natural existence. None of this implies that Nietzsche was a fascist, although Nolte reminds us that he prepared the way for certain forms of fascist thinking. Already in Nietzsche one finds the opposition between Judaism and Rome which appears in Mussolini, Hitler, Rosenberg, and Pound. See Nietzsche, *The AntiChrist*, in Nietzsche, 2, pp. 601, 585, 592–595, 618, and Nolte, p. 296.

22 Alfred Rosenberg especially objected to the universalism of the New Testament, which cuts across ethnic, national, and class lines. See Cecil, p. 85.

23 See Nolte, p. 513; Reichsmann, p. 196. In his admiration and imitation of Catholic order, Hitler contrasts sharply with Chamberlain and Rosenberg. See Cecil, p. 90.

24 Horkheimer and Adorno, p. 12. An infantile fear and hatred of the incommensurable appear in Pound's "Studies in Contemporary Mentality, V," *New Age*, 13 Sept. 1913, p. 426: "The first clever Semite who went out for monotheism made a corner in giantness. He got a giant 'really' bigger than all other possible giants." Quoted in Sieburth, 2, p. 89.

25 Maurras, quoted in Nolte, pp. 186, 145, 168–169.

26 Maurras (and Pound too) is in accord with Nietzsche, for whom the monotheistic god oversees the democratic and socialistic movements of the ancient and modern world. The identification of Christianity with socialism appears in Flaubert's correspondence, in a passage underlined by Pound in his personal copy. Renan and even Engels also found these movements worthy of comparison. See Nietzsche, *The AntiChrist*, in Nietzsche, 2, pp. 585, 619, 647; Sieburth, 2, pp. 163–164; Engels, "On the History of Early Christianity," in Feuer, ed., pp. 168–170. For Céline, socialism springs from an essentially Jewish Christianity. See Céline, 2, pp. 134–135.

27 See also Stock, 3, pp. 497, 520. According to Stock, Pound inscribed this question on a banner which he made for the Italian Fascist regime.

28 Drumont, Maurras, and Céline also blame the Jews for the French Revolution. See Wilson, pp. 349–350; Nolte, p. 169; Céline, 2, pp. 38, 153, 219.

29 Céline similarity identifies the Jews with the revolutionary doctrines of humanitarianism and progress, or "*l'Avenir*," all of which amounts in his view to an ideological fraud. See Céline, 1, pp. 76, 78, 93, 102, 122, 128, 279; 2, pp. 128, 220, 222.

30 The phrase "plastic demon" is Richard Wagner's; see Pois, Introduction to Rosenberg, p. 15. The idea of the single enemy is in Hitler, p. 118.

31 See Pound, "Sulla Propaganda," *Meridiano di Roma*, VII (6 June, 1943), p. 1. Although Pound is referring specifically to the usurer, in an earlier article he had referred to "la catene della finanza internazionale giudaica Rothschildiana." See "Ob pecuniae scarcitatem," *Meridiano de Roma*, VII (7 June, 1942), p. 1.

32 "Sulla Propaganda," p. 1. Céline similarly charges that democracy in the United States (as well as democracy in general) only camouflages Jewish interests; indeed, he believes as Pound does that both the United States and England have become essentially Jewish. See Céline, 1, pp. 51, 176, 245, 246; 2, pp. 45–47, 49, 66, 94, 152, 160–161.

33 The statement that "liberty is not a right but a duty" ("La libertà non è un diretto: è un dovere") is from Mussolini; see Terrell, Vol. II, p. 417. The extreme emphasis on duties over rights is typical of Italian Fascism and appears in the works of its chief ideologue Giovanni Gentile. Arguing that individualism is incompatible with the nation, and attempting to link the values of Italian Fascism with the Risorgimento, Gentile traces this doctrine to the liberal Mazzini (for instance his *Doveri de Uomo* or *Duties of Man*). According to Nolte, Mazzini's critique of the theory of rights which descends from the French Revolution marks the Risorgimento as the first and only victory of critical liberalism in Europe. It should be added that the belief that social rights entail social duties appears in the conservative Ruskin as in

certain theories of socialism, for instance the works of R. H. Tawney. See Lyttelton, p. 376; Nolte, p. 195; Tawney, *The Acquisitive Society* (New York: Harcourt, Brace, and World, 1948), *passim*. However, Herman Finer rightly observes that Mazzini, unlike the Fascists, conceived of duties in a liberal sense, as exercised by free men and citizens, while Lyttelton finds Gentile's ideas incompatible with Mazzini's humanitarianism. The difference between Mazzini's ideals and those of Italian Fascism is evident in his theory of labor organization. Not only did Mazzini favor voluntary associations of free citizens within trades or professions rather than medieval style corporations, he opposed labor organizations similar to those established by the Fascist state, which provided the members of each trade and profession with their sole recognized means of economic and political representation. Although participation in such organizations was not compulsory under Italian Fascism, it was nearly so for all practical purposes, since the Italian worker had no preferable alternative; in any case he had to pay dues to his designated syndicate even if he was not officially a member. Besides annihilating the liberal concept of citizenship, as Mazzini recognized, such associations would either tend to "tyrannical monopoly" or, as in Italian Fascism, fall "subject to the despotism of the State," to a "hierarchy arbitrarily constituted" and "ignorant of the needs and aptitudes" of labor. By giving a "legal form to the oppression of minorities," they would "deprive a dissatisfied workman of every possibility of getting work." Hence Mazzini insists, as the Fascists would not, on the "liberty to withdraw oneself, without doing harm to the association." For Mazzini's conception of duties and individual freedoms, see Finer, pp. 183–184; Salvemini, pp. 19, 25–27, 28, 30, 33, 35, 45, 46, 49, 92–94, 97–98, 135; Mazzini, pp. 8, 10, 11, 12, 41, 51, 57, 58, 68, 77–80, 93–94, 109–111.

Pound's relation to Mazzini and the Risorgimento is equivocal and complicated by his desire to claim the Risorgimento for Italian Fascism. Writing in 1944, at the height of his support for Mussolini, Pound proclaims that the "Italian Risorgimento was a light in the world. That light will shine again." Pound also praises Mazzini's "doctrine of duties" as the "bedrock of his sainthood," quotes his *Duties of Man* on banks and storehouses, and views Italian Fascism as the continuation of the Risorgimento. See Pound, quoted in Heymann, p. 141; Pound, SP, 312, 314, 351; radio broadcasts, pp. 313, 316. Nonetheless, in SP, 312, written in 1942, Pound observes that, having been a "Cavourian," he had "long neglected" Mazzini. As the originator of the "Historic Right" and the bureaucratic state of modern Italy, Cavour has often been contrasted with the more liberal Mazzini, and indeed in recent years the extent of Cavour's liberalism has itself been called in question, most notoriously by Denis Mack Smith. But in any case one may be sure that Pound, as a self-confessed "Cavourian," had sympathy with the offical Fascist view that "Cavour was no true liberal, that Victor Emmanuel [first King of Italy after its unification] was an ideological forerunner of Mussolini, and that their Kingdom of Piedmont-Sardinia had to be extolled as 'the most authoritarian, the most *reactionary*, the most military and indeed the most *militaristic* state in the Italian peninsula.'" Pound's preference for Cavour over Mazzini is explicit in *Guide to Kulchur*, in which Pound discusses the numerous virtues of (state-approved) educational text-books in Fascist Italy: "It is impossible to tell everything in one school book, if Mazzini is not attacked for fanaticism, his constructive acts are recorded, and Cavour is praised with masterly succinctness: through deep study and long travels he came to understand the needs of the Italian people. . . . As head of govt. he improved with wise provisions the condition of agriculture, industry, and commerce . . ." (GK, 142). Although Pound like other Fascists is willing to acknowledge some of Mazzini's achievements, he finds him to be a political extremist or "fanatic"; this is in all likelihood a somewhat oblique reference to Mazzini's liberalism. Cavour's greatness, by contrast, lies implicitly in his statism and hence his anticipation of Mussolini and Italian Fascism. Like Il Duce in *Jefferson and/or Mussolini*, and despite the fact that he had strong doubts about the desirability of unifying Northern and Southern Italy, Cavour has a paternalistic regard for and presumed understanding of the diverse needs of the Italian people. At the same time, Cavour is responsible for establishing a strong state dedicated to the promotion of Italy's economic welfare. As for Cavour's parliamentary liberalism, Pound the anti-parliamentarian finds it less an expression of his political ideology than a momentary necessity of nineteenth-century politics: "Cavour [like Mussolini] worked in circumstance," observes Pound later in *Guide*, "various need to use a parliamentary system" (GK, 227). Indeed, Cavour's greater achievement in Pound's view was more conservative than liberal, namely to have laid the groundwork for a rapprochement between the Italian state and the Roman Catholic Church, precisely what Mussolini achieved in the Lateran Pact of 1929 (GK, 76, 164). Pound's deeper suspicions toward Mazzini may be inferred from his paranomastic remark of 1943, in a letter in praise of Mussolini's newly-founded Salò Republic, that "It seems that 'Mazzinian' in many cases means 'Mason.' " This absurd statement discredits Mazzini in linking his thought (quite properly) to the liberalizing French Revolution, whose doctrine of rights Fascism sought radically to transform, and which Pound, as we shall see later in this chapter, identifies with a conspiracy of Jews and Masons. See Procacci, pp. 325, 328; Denis Mack Smith, p. x; Pound, quoted in Heymann, p. 326. Finally, in his view of the rights of labor Pound stands equivocally and probably disingenuously at a far remove from Mazzini. Defending the Italian Fascist labor organizations as economically and politically preferable to what he considers irresponsible American unions, Pound observes that "EVERY man of whatever trade or profession has the OPTION of joining up with his *sindicato* [syndicate]; he don't have to, but if he wants to be represented directly, that is the method" (RB, 102). With that facile "directly" Pound evades what he probably knew, that other forms of "indirect" representation, economic or political, would have not the slightest significance or effect in Fascist Italy, that the freedom he grants the worker is the freedom *not* to be represented. Pound goes on to assert dubiously that even non-members will be "looked after" by the *sindicato*, presumably on the equally dubious assumption that all participants in a trade necessarily share more or less the same interests.

The Italian Fascists showed no consistency in defining their relation to the Risorgimento and Mazzini. As the Risorgimento belonged to the detested nineteenth century, the heyday of liberalism, some Fascists were "happy" and "proud" to criticize the earlier movement, and to claim that Fascism had "accomplished something greater." Mussolini, however, shared Gentile's position that Fascism had brought the Risorgimento to its culmination. Yet this claim was possible only through a distortion of the evidence, specifically by taking Mazzini's passing critique of the French Revolution out of context, in order to prove that the Risorgimento was neither liberal nor democratic. Although he shared the pride of other Italian Fascists in being labeled "anti-Risorgimento," Gioacchino Volpe found in Fascism many of the Risorgimento's motives, such as the "cult of some of its men . . ., also national passion and the subordination of liberty to the independence, unity, and greatness of the country." In short, Volpe values the Risorgimento only insofar as it anticipates Italian Fascist leader-worship, nationalism, and authoritarianism. See Volpe, p. 162; Nolte, pp. 320–321, 322; Mussolini, p. 82.

The relation of the Risorgimento to Italian Fascism has been contested, some historians, such as Luigi Salvatorelli, viewing Fascism as the shameful betrayal of the Risorgimento's liberal ideals and goals, others, such as Denis Mack Smith, tracing the emergence of Fascism to the Risorgimento's weakness as a liberalizing and democratizing force. It is perhaps best to follow A. William Salomone, who treats Fascism not as the fulfillment or logical outcome of the Risorgimento but as the closure of its finest "possibilities." See Salvatorelli, *passim;* Salomone, ed., pp. 9–11, 15, 29–30, 53, 55, 89–99, 103–123, 124–148.

34 See Nolte, p. 51, and Finer, p. 192. Like many reactionaries, Pound suspects that modern liberalism and "chaos" are fomented by a conspiracy of Jews, Freemasons, and Illuminati. See Pound, radio broadcasts, pp. 114, 115, 289, and Noel Stock, letters to Pound, Dec. 23, 1956, and Nov. 15, 1955, in the Beinecke Rare Book and Manuscript Library, Yale University. In his anti-Semitic polemics Céline frequently attacks the Masons, whom he believes to be under Jewish control, and whom he blames for the French Revolution. See Céline, 1, pp. 78, 96, 97, 99, 134, 138, 287, 294, 295; 2, pp. 14, 30, 31, 38, 39, 41, 70, 93, 98, 219–220, 272; 3, p. 78.

Lesley Fry, on whom Pound relies in the broadcasts, speaks of socialist and Marxist Jews as "Illuminati." See Fry, pp. 222, 223. The standard work on the Jews and Freemasons is Katz, 1. See also Katz, 2, p. 295; Cohn, 1, pp. 26, 28, 44–51; Hitler, p. 315; and *The Protocols of the Elders of Zion*, p. 15, in which the Jews use the slogan "Liberty, Equality, and Fraternity" to stir the mob, destroy hierarchy, and gain power for themselves.

35 By the 1930s Mussolini viewed Fascism as a "universal phenomenon" and "article for export." See Diggins, p. 88; Ledeen, pp. xviii, xix, 19, 23, 24, 62, 104, 89–90. Ledeen notes that such interest in universality did not lessen Mussolini's nationalistic emphasis. In the early 1930s Gioacchino Volpe made the familiar claim that Italian Fascism was not for export, yet he went on to assert that it might have a wide influence elsewhere and even envisioned an international or universal fascism. See Volpe, pp. 165–166.

36 In 1937 Pound professed neutrality on the issue of the Spanish Civil War, finding it to be of "no more importance than the draining of some mosquito swamp in deepest Africa." However, this statement probably contains a concealed bias in favor of Mussolini's intervention on the side of Franco's fascist (or right-wing) armies. As he did on at least two other occasions in the 1930s, Pound identifies Spain with Africa, in whose pestilent "bayou[s]" Mussolini had recently undertaken the civilizing mission celebrated in Canto 40. Pound also links Spain with swamps and malaria, two of the leading symbolic enemies of Italian Fascism as a political and cultural movement. Despite the opacity and equivocation of his position in the 1930s, Pound's real and ultimate attitude toward the Spanish Civil War is evident in Canto 105, p. 746: "And Muss. saved, rem salvavit, / in Spain / il salvabile." See Stock 1, p. 173; Weyl, in *A Casebook*, p. 15; Heymann, pp. 77, 222; Pound, SR, p. 18n. In a letter of 28 Nov., 1935 or 1936, to T. C. Wilson, Pound refers to Spain as "AFRICAN." This letter is in the Beinecke Rare Book and Manuscript Library, Yale University.

37 Nolte, pp. 187–189, 537–543, 553. Again note the resemblance between Pound and Nietzsche, who, though by no means a fascist, laid the groundwork for the fascist attack on transcendence.

38 Cassels, "Janus: The Two Faces of Fascism," and Turner, "Fascism and Modernization," in Turner, ed., pp. 76, 125–126. Wyndham Lewis astutely makes the same point in *The Hitler Cult*, pp. 50–51.

39 Cassels, "Janus: The Two Faces of Fascism," p. 72; Mosse, 5, p. 192. However, this characterization of Nazism requires qualification. As Jeffrey Herf has recently shown, there existed within Nazism a sizable and very influential group of ideologists, engineers, and politicians who envisioned technology, once rescued from Jewish financial control and directed by the state, as altogether compatible with the spiritual needs of the German people. See Herf, pp. 152–235.

40 Mosse, quoted in Ledeen, p. 165.

41 Kitchen, 2, pp. 141–142, 145–146; Cassels, "Janus: The Two Faces of Fascism," pp. 72, 76; Gregor, 3, pp. xii, 59, 61, 100, 110, 133, 134–135; Sarti, pp. 1029–1045, esp. 1029, 1031; Delzell, p. 9; De Felice, pp. 68, 83; Roberts, pp. 309, 311, 314. Other historians continue to view fascism as a largely reactionary and anti-modernizing movement. See for instance Maier, p. 513; Wohl, p. 585. Weiss, *The Fascist Tradition*, argues that fascism was a conservative revolution and hence anti-modern.

42 There was, however, an element of nostalgia in Italian Fascism for medieval guilds and Catholic corporatism. See Chapter Four, footnote four.

43 Cassels, "Janus: The Two Faces of Fascism," p. 74; see also Roberts, p. 57.

44 In 1922 Mussolini exultantly predicted a century of right-wing "Restoration." The Right would "completely destroy" the "movement that Napoleon had aroused among the nations of Europe," in short the legacy of "1789." But in his "Doctrine of Fascism," published in 1932, Mussolini condemned as reactionary the "De Maistrian" goal of turning the clock back to 1789. See Lyttelton, ed., pp. 52, 64.

45 Mosse, 7, p. 95; Eugen Weber, 2, p. 139; Roberts, pp. 272, 273, 304; De Felice, p. 102.

46 Mosse, 5, pp. 5–7, 11, 13; 8, pp. 162–164. Mosse is indebted to J. L. Talmon, *The Rise of Totalitarian Democracy.* See also De Felice, pp. 105–106.

47 Mosse, 7, pp. 105–106; 8, pp. 240–241; Ledeen, pp. 149–153; De Felice, pp. 55–56; Volpe, p. 161.

48 De Felice, pp. 95–96; Ledeen, p. 150.

49 Gregor, 1, pp. 209. Gregor observes that biological racism, if accepted, would have destroyed the "coherence" of Italian Fascist ideology. See also Ledeen, pp. 152–153.

50 In his "Doctrine of Fascism," Mussolini disparages utopias as unrealistic. Adrian Lyttelton argues that Italian Fascism, with its doctrine of "permanent conflict," could not be utopian, but that the racial community of the Nazis was a utopia. See Lyttelton, ed., pp. 13, 48–49.

51 Quoted in Wees, pp. 114–115.

52 Pound also praises the Futurist Marinetti in this chapter of J/M, p. 107. However, Henry A. Turner Jr. follows James Joll's suggestion that the Italian Futurists tended to attribute an "autonomous existence" to the products of industrial society. Insofar as they wanted the products of industry without an industrial society, they resembled the Nazis. To a great degree this description fits Pound as well. See Turner, "Fascism and Modernization," pp. 126, 138n.

53 Pound's admiration for technology in combination with his insistence on pre-modern and agrarian examples of cultural rootedness results in a paradox (or contradiction) similar to that which appears in such noted early twentieth-century German reactionaries as Spengler and Ernst Jünger. Jeffrey Herf observes that these writers succeeded in dispelling the longstanding German social and intellectual prejudice against technology by representing the machine and industry as compatible with such cherished conservative values as vitalism, the soil, personal creativity, inwardness, and the organic community. Herein lies the core of what Herf, without limiting the term to the German example, describes as "reactionary modernism." As noted above, the same paradox appears in Nazism, which drew upon the thought of its conservative precursors in the Weimar Republic. See Herf, *passim;* he mentions Pound on p. 47.

54 Although he does not connect Pound with Talmon's "totalitarian democracy," Forrest Read finds links between his fascism and his support of the American and French Revolutions; see Read, pp. 47, 194, 221, 228, 242, 243, 354.

55 See Kappel, p. 60; Kimpel and Eaves, pp. 81, 86, 91, 92.

56 See Talmon, pp. 86, 282; Payne, p. 180. On the historical and ideological resemblance between Bonapartism and fascism, see Kitchen, pp. 70, 72. However, Kitchen points out important differences between Bonapartism and fascism, and his chief example is not Napoleon Bonaparte but Louis Napoleon, whose high taxes Pound thought oppressive and whose deceptive political strategies he did not admire. See Canto 85, p. 549, and Canto 100, p. 720. On the other hand, in Canto 78, p. 477, and SP, 313, Pound praises Napoleon and Mussolini for waging "economic war" against such Jewish usurers as the Rothschilds and the Monds. Pound also praises the Code Napoleon in Canto 44, p. 227, Canto 100, p. 713, and in the radio broadcasts, p. 197.

57 See Read, pp. 225, 295, 224; Hofstadter, "The Pseudo-Conservative Revolt," in Daniel Bell, ed., pp. 79, 80; Pound, J/M, pp. 41–46.

58 See Michaelis, *passim;* Gregor, 1, pp. 258–259; Berardini, pp. 449–451; Cannistraro, ed., pp. 28–30; Volpe, pp. 121, 141, 153. In a letter to Jackson McLow, Pound claims that the "dirtiest smear of all was to try to call Mussolini an anti-sem." Quoted in Heymann, p. 223. However, Pound stands on record as having told an Italian Jew that Mussolini's racial laws were "the right thing." See David Anderson, p. 440.

59 Gourmont, p. 71; the passage from Gourmont is slightly altered in paraphrase.

60 See Hampshire, pp. 46, 54; Spinoza was an apostate from Judaism. See also Berliner, in Simmel, ed., pp. 81–82. According to Terrell, Vol. I, p. 185, glossing the phrase *"naturans"* (47/ 237), "Creative nature" was called *natura naturans* by Jo-

hannes Scotus Erigena, one of Pound's favorite philosophers. See also Canto 94, p. 637, in which Apollonius of Tyana remarks, in Greek, on the universe as a "living" and all-engendering "creature."

61 See the Italian Fascist philosopher Giovanni Gentile, quoted in Delzell, p. 93; Sternhell, "Fascist Ideology," in Laqueur, ed., p. 344.

62 Mussolini, "The Doctrine of Fascism," in Lyttelton, ed., pp. 53–54.

63 Tannenbaum, 2, pp. 49, 54, 133. See also the well-known though highly questionable interpretation of Barrington Moore in *Social Origins of Dictatorship and Democracy: Lord and Peasant in the Making of the Modern World.* Moore argues that fascism in both Germany and Italy was a form of conservative modernization, inspired by a feudal hierarchy rather than by the bourgeoisie.

64 Michael André Bernstein notes that Pound's ancient China is an ideally "closed" or self-contained society. He quotes Canto 85, p. 593: "All there by the time of I Yin / All roots by the time of I Yin." See Bernstein, pp. 54–55.

65 Pound admires Ovid partly because he sings of the "mystery of the presence of a permanent and unchanging principle throughout all the seeming flux of the universe, in which things come into existence, grow, reproduce, age, and die." See Charlesworth, p. 89. Louis Agassiz, another of Pound's intellectual heroes, asserted against the evolutionists "Ovidian metamorphosis within a cosmic synchrony." See Sieburth, 2, p. 152; Bell, pp. 102, 115–116, 185–188.

66 Maurras, 1, p. li, quoted in Nolte, p. 183. A fascination with the circle as symbol of the ahistorical unites Pound, Maurras, Eliot, and Lewis. See Materer, 1, p. 28.

Chapter Eleven: Nature, Race, and History, III

1 Gourmont, p. 71. See also Norman, pp. 289–290, quoting Pound in *The Exile*, No. 2, which contains this quotation from Gourmont.

2 See Stock, 3, pp. 325–326. In his broadcasts Pound observes that after Gourmont's death the French were "biologically fixed." He attributes the same perception of dangerous biological stasis and uniformity to Céline, whose eugenics proposals he endorses. See radio broadcasts, pp. 101, 114, 127, 131–132. The biological stasis of France supposedly coincides with its "wreckage . . . under yidd control" (RB, 290) in the 1930s. Pound probably refers to the government of the French Premier Leon Blum, a Jew and a Socialist, to whom he devotes these mocking lines in the Pisan *Cantos:* "Pétain defended Verdun while Blum / was defending a bidet" (80/ 494). According to Terrell, Vol. II, p. 430, the "bidet" is probably the Banque de la France, which Blum reorganized. In the Pisan *Cantos* Pound refers cryptically to Pétain, the leader of Vichy France, and Pierre Laval, another Vichy collaborator with the Nazis, as "gli onesti" (76/ 460). In the broadcasts Pound is also pro-Vichy, although he registers the qualification that "the Vichy radio is twisty, it is trying to hold on to France, and double cross the Axis . . ." (RB, 5).

3 Gourmont, pp. 233–234; Davie, 1, p. 76.

4 For fascism's cult of toughness and its disdain of "decadence" and the comfortable life, see Nathan, p. 52. See also Soucy, 2, pp. 290, 95.

5 Quoted in Heymann, p. 141.

6 Emery and Rosenthal, quoted in Pearlman, 1, p. 117; George Dekker, "Myth and Metamorphosis: Two Aspects of Myth in *The Cantos,*" in Eva Hesse, ed., pp. 284–285; Pearlman, 1, p. 120.

7 Nietzsche, 1, pp. 165–176; Scheler, pp. 119–123.

8 The axe and moon are followed in Canto 106 by the verb "HREZEIN," Greek for "to perform ritual" or "to sacrifice," which suggests that Nature's retributive course is somehow bound up with a human sacrificial order. The connection between the moon's axe and fascism in Canto 106 is further strengthened by an immediately preceding reference to the construction of a temple to "APHRODITE EUPLOIA" on the promontory of Zephyrium near Alexandria by the "high admiral" Callicrates; this voyager intersects not only with Odysseus, who transforms Circe into the goddess Aphrodite on her promontory at Terracina, but with Musso-

lini, who drains the marshes at Circeo (thanks to the Italian Fascist axe). The passage on Hitler in Canto 90, p. 606, opening with a reference to the pure stream of Castalia ("like the moonlight"), perhaps carries with it the idea of Artemisian purity as well as the idea of a retributive justice working in cyclical process.

9 Nolte, pp. 551–558; Nietzsche, *The AntiChrist*, in Nietzsche, 2, pp. 570, 583–584, 572–573. Charles Maurras too despised pity as an example of Jewish influence on Christianity. See Sutton, pp. 36–37.

10 Pound, quoted in Heymann, p. 74.

11 For the theme of natural retribution, and the uses to which Pound puts Fortuna, goddess of cyclical Nature, see Flory, pp. 238–239, especially on the Chinese "thunder" or "fear" sign.

12 Hitler, pp. 287, 132, 289, 247; see also Nolte, p. 529.

13 Hitler, quoted in Kolnai, p. 437; Hitler, p. 131; Nolte, p. 363.

14 Hitler, pp. 135, 296, 214, 285, 151, 284, 285, 392; Gerald K. Smith, *The Cross and the Flag*, quoted in Lowenthal and Guterman, p. 94. Noel Stock mentions Smith's *The Cross and the Flag* to Pound in a letter of Nov. 15, 1956, Beinecke Rare Book and Manuscript Library, Yale University. Heymann, p. 78, notes that Pound was in touch with Smith in the 1930s. Although Mussolini did not emphasize race in his ideology, he believed that there was "No life without shedding blood." Quoted in Nolte, p. 210. The emphasis on natural struggle and racial survival also figures in Drieu la Rochelle and Céline. See Soucy, 2, pp. 243, 289; Céline, 1, p. 60. According to Abraham Maslow, p. 403, such "tough-minded Darwinian realism" characterizes the authoritarian personality.

15 See Kolnai, pp. 482–489; Lowenthal and Guterman, p. 93; Pound, SP, pp. 165, 248.

16 Pound, "Race," *New English Weekly*, 15 Oct. 1936, p. 12.

17 For the sources of Pound's eugenic thinking in John Adams, nineteenth-century "progressives," and Theognis of Megara, see Stock, 3, p. 509; Terrell, Vol. I, p. 130; and Canto 33, p. 160, where John Adams, alluding to Theognis of Megara's "stallions," writes of breeding both thoroughbred sheep and an American aristocracy. Among twentieth-century American racial theorists and eugenicists, Pound is indebted to Theodore Lothrop Stoddard, whom he praises in RB, pp. 168, 363. A rabid white and especially Nordic supremacist, Stoddard envisions world history as a "Darwinian" struggle between races for self-preservation and dominance. Although the white race had retained its world mastery at the turn of the century, its position is endangered by nationalistic wars (chiefly World War I), indicating the loss of racial "solidarity" among the white nations; the greater rate of increase in population among the colored and especially the Asiatic races; and socialism, which preserves the unfit and thus undermines civilization. Stoddard deplores the "melting pot" of racial "hybridization" in America, since it corrupts the older Anglo-Saxon colonial stock and favors inferior stocks of immigrant whites and other races; the result is a "bog." The solution to these dangers is to establish "dikes" against Asiatic and non-Nordic immigration and a "humane" eugenics program aimed at creating a "super-race" and "neo-aristocracy." For Stoddard, an admirer of the eugenic ideas of Theognis of Megara, the modern conflict is between socially applied biology and an atavistic, levelling Bolshevism. He finds the methods of German fascism excessive, yet he shares many of its beliefs. See Stoddard, *The Rising Tide of Colour against White World Supremacy; The Revolt Against Civilization: The Menace of the Under-Man; Clashing Tides of Colour*.

18 The phrase in Canto 94, p. 641 on the "melting pot" is inspired by Apollonius of Tyana's admiring remarks on Sparta, which had "prevented strangers from settling within its borders." According to Apollonius, Lycurgus, who had made the law, acted not out of "boorish exclusiveness," but out of a desire to "keep the institutions of Sparta in their original purity by preventing outsiders from mingling in her life." See Philostratus, Vol. II, p. 85; Terrell, Vol. II, p. 585. Though it would serve to justify exclusion of Jews, the law as thus described is not racist but ethnocentric; however, Pound's construction of it has racist implications. It is also worth remembering that Plato, the first philosopher of the "closed society," pre-

ferred Sparta over all other states in the belief that its institutions had changed least from their original form. See Popper, Vol. I, pp. 35–36.

19 Pound to Kasper, 1956, no month or date given, Beinecke Rare Book and Manuscript Library, Yale University.

20 *Edge*, 4 (March, 1957). Pound's racial doctrines are adumbrated in "Anima Sola," from *A Lume Spento* (1908). Pound "sit[s] in the vale of fate," where "the three Eumenides / Take justice at . . . [his] hands." He is, moreover, the "life blood's ward," while "the blood of light is the god's delight" (CEP, 20).

21 Homer, *The Odyssey*, trans. Robert Fitzgerald (New York: Doubleday Anchor, 1961), pp. 186–187, Book 10, ll. 285–347.

22 Flaubert told Sainte-Beuve that he believed the *Periplus* to be a Greek document (the extant work is in Greek), and in defense of this opinion he said that no Oriental was capable of the clarity and accuracy which the *Periplus* reveals. Pound thus had no qualms about including a Semitic source prominently in his poem. See Sieburth, 2, p. 166.

23 Pearlman, 1, p. 164; Surette, 3, p. 140.

24 Pearlman, 1, p. 166. The possibility of an Ethiopian invasion had been recognized in Italy for several years before the event. See Enzo Santarelli, "The Economic and Political Background of Fascist Imperialism," in Sarti, ed., pp. 166, 168, 172. For Pound's favorable view of the invasion, see Stock, 3, p. 435. Reck, 1, p. 123, reports that Pound told Mrs. Pound after the invasion that Mussolini had lost the feeling for the people (see Canto 86, p. 560: "Lost the feel of the people"). This statement consorts oddly, however, with the enthusiasm of Canto 40 and with Pound's later "Gold and Work" (1943), in which Pound's Italian Fascist utopia partly owes its economic health to imports from its "African possessions" (SP, 337). In "An Introduction to the Economic Nature of the United States," written in Italian in 1944, Pound compares Italy's acquisition of colonies in Africa with the American conquest of the frontier: "The romance of the covered wagon, clipper of the prairies, finds its analogy in the Italian colonization in Africa" (SP, 177). In the radio broadcasts, pp. 57, 234, 309, Pound further praises Italy's "colonial empire" and its "perfectly arranged productive system" (RB, 234), which constitutes "real colonization" (RB, 57) as opposed to rapacious English imperialism. Since Pound supported Mussolini's concept of national self-sufficiency or autarchy as a worthy alternative to the imperialism and greed of other states, his support of Italian Fascist imperialism is contradictory. The contradiction appears within a single sentence of this essay: "Peanuts could bring self-sufficiency in food to Italy or, rather to its empire, for these 'monkey nuts' would grow better in Cyrenaica" (SP, 319). It is well established that Mussolini was finally driven to his often contemplated policy of autarchy as a result of the sanctions Italy suffered as a consequence of the invasion of Ethiopia; it is also well known that the ultimate purpose of autarchy was to prepare Italy for Mussolini's projected imperialistic wars. With typical blindness toward fascist violence, Pound chose to misinterpret the sanctions as an act of aggression by the Allies, motivated by resentment of Italy's "ambition to achieve economic liberty— the liberty of not getting into debt" (SP, 341). According to Pound, not the Italian Fascists but England and America pursue policies of economic and militaristic imperialism, whose real ends are concealed by the lies of the Jewish media. See the broadcasts, pp. 44–47, 60, 83, 85, 94, 138, 159, 304–307. See also Pound's translation of Por, 3, pp. 32, 40, 45, in which Por denies that Mussolini's policy of autarchy is a preparation for war.

25 Despite his and other Italian Fascists' mockery of the "soft" bourgeoisie, Mussolini saw a place for the bourgeois within Italian Fascism and denied that capitalism had concluded its historical cycle: Italy had a bourgeois, capitalist "task." Edward R. Tannenbaum considers the Italian Fascist attack on the bourgeoisie an "ideological front." See Tannenbaum, 2, pp. 70–71, 168. See also Gregor, 3, pp. 88, 91, 128–129, 163; 4, pp. 188, 201, 212, 217, 239.

26 The "misshapen men swifter than horses" are probably blacks, whom Pound views as "fine animal[s]" and associates with horses in PD. He also identifies them with a kind of pre-intellectual "feel" (PD, 31), ironically the same sort of

power which he ascribed to the "savage" modern artist in the "forest" of the modern world.

27 Compare Hitler, whose phobia of smells and hatred of perfumes is directly related to his anti-Semitism; Hitler objects to the use of perfumes on the grounds that they conceal the distinguishing smells of different races. See Waite, p. 156. According to Martin Jay, 1, pp. 239–240, in 1938 the Nazi psychologist E. R. Jaensch defined the so-called J-Type of personality, a personality which reflected fascist values. This type "was defined by its unwavering rigidity." Its opposite was the S-Type, "for synaesthesia, the capacity to confuse senses, which he [Jaensch] equated with the effete, vacillating uncertainty of the democratic mentality."

28 The Italian imperialism celebrated in Canto 40 was a partial consequence of Mussolini's demographic policies. Canto 40 is thus linked ideologically to Canto 45, in which Pound, like Mussolini, inveighs against birth control. See Gregor, 3, pp. 289–290; Cassels, p. 59.

29 This confusion probably reflects Pound's racist ideas, whereby blacks assimilate to the ape. The same confusion appears in Voltaire, one of Pound's most important mentors in racial thinking. See Poliakov, 1, p. 176.

30 Pearlman, 5, p. 426; Pound, GK, pp. 38, 41.

31 Mircea Eliade, quoted in Molnar, p. 153.

32 The tension between myth and history reappears in the last line of Canto 40: "hung this [presumably the book containing Hanno's narrative] with his map in their temple." This line must be understood in relation to a distinction which Pound makes in Canto 59 and which is often implicit in his work: "periplum [Pound's odd form of *periplus*], not as land looks on a map / but as sea bord seen by men sailing" (59/324). For Pound the word *periplus* properly applies to Hanno's voyage as a lived experience in all its concrete diversity, irregularity, and unpredictability. In this sense the *periplus* apparently belongs to the world of Nature and myth. The map, meanwhile, is as McLuhan tells us an historical invention which represents man's transformation of continuous and differentiated reality into an isomorphic abstraction; historically it is inseparable from man's effort to gain dominance over Nature. One might thus view it as the spatial counterpart not of cyclical Nature or myth but of History, linear or chronological time in its uniform and irreversible succession of moments. McLuhan further points out that advances in the art of map-making contributed significantly to the acceleration of the historical process in Europe and the disruption by Europeans of the pre-historical cultural rhythms of tribal groups: in short, exploration, colonization, and empire. Mussolini's forces used maps in 1935, and these led not to the ahistorical NOUS but to the invasion of Ethiopia. Pound's choice of the word "map" marks a key moment of equivocation between History and Nature (or myth). On the other hand, such equivocation is perhaps already implicit in *periplum*, for Pound notwithstanding, "*periplum*" and "map" are not mutually exclusive. See McLuhan, pp. 16–21, 28; Harmon, p. 149n.

33 In neither Pound's thought nor in Italian Fascism can the invasion of Ethiopia be dissociated from anti-Semitism. In *The Origins of Totalitarianism* Hannah Arendt argues a general thesis linking racial anti-Semitism and colonialism. This link appears in Italian Fascism, whose imperialistic policies dictated racial laws in Ethiopia in 1935 and the extension of similar laws to Italian Jews in 1938. Pound identifies the Jews and Africa as early as July, 1921, in "Kongo Roux," which he published in a Dadaist journal. Pound speaks of the Jews as "totem de tribu SHEENY, Yid, taboo." The link between blacks and Jews appears later in the broadcasts, pp. 207, 285. In the 1930s Pound justified Italy's "civilizing" mission in Ethiopia on the grounds that the Ethiopians were merely "black Jews"; he alluded almost certainly to the Falasha tribe of Ethiopians, who are in fact Jewish, and he may also have been thinking of the claim of Haile Selassie, as the "Lion of Judah," to be descended from Solomon. Mussolini too identified the Jews with Africa. After the invasion of Ethiopia he envisioned the possibility not of Jewish "persecution" but "separation," a policy of "controlled" Jewish immigration to "certain districts" in Ethiopia and Somaliland. Implicitly these regions of desert and jungle are appropriate environments for the Jews. On Arendt, see Wilson, pp. 446n, 469. See also Torrey, pp. 141,

148; Michaelis, pp. 85, 156, 174, 181, 191, 195. On Italian Fascist racism in Ethiopia, see Luigi Preti, "Fascist Imperialism and Racism," in Sarti, ed., pp. 188–193. The link between Jews and blacks also appears in Lewis, 1, p. 39, and in Céline, 1, pp. 68, 182, 186, 188, 192; 2, p. 25.

Chapter Twelve: America and London
    1 Chace, p. 8: in *Patria Mia*, notes Chace, publishers are among the chief "culprits." See also Pound, letter to the editor, *New English Weekly*, 7 July, 1932, p. 92; and "Mr. Eliot's Quandaries," *New English Weekly*, 29 March, 1934, p. 558.
    2 Pound, quoted in Espey, p. 38.
    3 Pound, quoted in Chace, p. 6. Chace, p. 7n, notes that the published version of *Patria Mia* (1950) omits Pound's statement that "the Jew alone can retain his detestable qualities, despite climatic conditions." Canetti, p. 179, describes the Jews as a "crowd symbol."
    4 Something of Pound's optimism persists in "L'Homme Moyen Sensuel" in *Personae*, where he praises the immigrants' "animal invigorating carriage" (PER, 245), and in "Imaginary Letters" (PD, 56), where Villerant speaks of the "splendour of their [the immigrants'] vigorous . . . animality." An ominous note, however, appears in "Indiscretions," where Pound mentions a character of Kipling's who had "summarized the effects of the 'War' ('60–65) as extermination of the Anglo-Saxon race in America in order that the Czeko-Slovaks might inherit Boston Common" (PD, 30); Pound refers to the same passage in the radio broadcasts, pp. 61, 173. Nonetheless, Pound's early view of America contrasts with the first visit of the young provincial Maurras to Paris and that of Hitler to Vienna, the polyglot and multi-racial capital of the Austro-Hungarian empire. See Nolte, p. 91, and Hitler, pp. 123, 56.
    5 Pound, "What America has to Live Down, III–IV," *New Age*, 5 Sept., 1918, p. 297.
    6 Reminiscent of Pound's conception of a passive, feminized America, the girl in "Ortus" also calls to mind his later pejorative references to the Near East as a maternal place of vague, undisciplined growth. The link is suggested in Pound's discussion of the poem in L, p. 21: " 'Ortus' means 'birth' or 'springing out' same root in 'orient'." But "orient" thus also has a positive significance, not only because it implies generation, which Pound celebrates, but because the Orient encompasses both the Near East and China, the land of the rising sun, which had recently captured Pound's attention. The vague figure in "Ortus" simultaneously evokes disorder and solar energy, the double and contrary aspects of Pound's East.
    7 Quoted in Torrey, p. 75.
    8 Norman, pp. 212, 265.
    9 See P/J, p. 147.
    10 According to Kimpel and Eaves, 2, p. 65, there is "only one Jew" among the damned of the Hell *Cantos*.
    11 Gourmont, pp. 21–22, 24–27, 35, 58, 79, 38, 64, 68.
    12 Freud, "Medusa's Head," p. 105, in *Collected Papers*, ed. James Strachey, Vol. V.
    13 Freud, "Medusa's Head," p. 105.
    14 Hutchins, pp. 80, 90, 96, 142. Pound participated in the alteration of the magazine title *The New Freewoman* to *The Egoist* at the beginning of 1914. As Durant comments, "in such an alteration the challenge of political liberation for women is replaced by the assurance of the ego's self-possession." See Durant, pp. 106–107.
    15 Despite their apparent sympathy with the suffragettes between 1910 and 1914, the Vorticists admired not so much their political stance as their impulse towards destructive violence and disruption. See Wees, pp. 17–18, 19, 190. Pound combines anti-feminism and Vorticism in a letter of 1915 to Wyndham Lewis: "My invaluable helpmeet [Dorothy Pound] suggests that the Thursday dinners [to discuss *Blast*] would maintain an higher intellectual altitude if there were a complete and

uncontaminated absence of women. She offers to contribute her own absence to that total and desirable effect." Pound defines a male-dominated hierarchy within which totality and completeness are paradoxically achieved through the characteristic absence of the "contaminating" feminine.

16 See Nathan, pp. 52–82, and Soucy, 2, p. 342.

17 See Pound, letter of 1937 to Alice Amdur, Beinecke Rare Book and Manuscript Library, Yale University; see also J/M, pp. 48–49.

18 Robert, pp. 45–46; Pound, "Private Worlds," *New English Weekly*, 2 May, 1935, pp. 48–49. The identification of the crowd with the instincts is typical of conservative thought, the most striking instance of which is probably Gustave Le Bon's *The Crowd* (1895), which Freud knew and which had some influence on his work. See Freud, 5, pp. 4–15.

19 Kenner, 1, p. 127, quoted in Dekker, p. 12n. Dekker's view of the Hell *Cantos* resembles mine, but he does not give details; for him, they are "a projection of Pound's disgust." See Dekker, p. 13.

20 See Kenneth Burke, *Attitudes Towards History* (Los Altos, California, 1959), pp. 50, 37, quoted in Vasse, p. 179.

21 Schneidau, pp. 8, 21, 44, 65. See also Dasenbrock, pp. 91–94.

22 Materer, 2, p. 202, quoting Pound, "Affirmations, II. Vorticism," *New Age*, 14 Jan. 1915, p. 298.

23 See North, p. 110, and Cork, Vol. I, p. 255.

24 See Worringer, *passim;* North, pp. 111, 112, esp. 113–114. On the Vorticists and Worringer, see also Dasenbrock, pp. 53–56. However, in spite of the Vorticists' emphasis on aesthetic "deadness" and geometrical abstraction, Dasenbrock argues against the standard critical opinion that Vorticism rejects representation and turns its back on life and the world.

25 For Pound, Vorticism originates in Imagism and is its intensification. See Wees, p. 187. A motivation for Vorticism's attraction to geometrical forms is suggested in *Abstraction and Empathy*, pp. 14–15. According to Worringer, in geometric forms empathy, the tendency "toward the organic, cannot have determined artistic volition." The urge toward abstraction is based on "fear."

26 Horkheimer and Adorno, "Elements of Anti-Semitism," in *Dialectic of Enlightenment*, pp. 187–190.

Chapter Thirteen: Persecution and Power

1 Paul Rosenfeld, "The Case of Ezra Pound," *American Mercury*, January, 1944, LVIII, pp. 98–102, reprinted in Homburger, ed., p. 353.

2 Norman, p. 460; Terrell, 1, p. 370; Olson, pp. 75, 55.

3 Pound, quoted in Moody, p. 64. This essay, though misleading, is the most thorough discussion of Pound's relation to Upward. Also useful is Knox, pp. 72–88.

4 Upward, 1, pp. 245, 19, 16; 2, pp. 1–5; Pound, SP, pp. 403–406; Upward, quoted in Moody, pp. 63, 62, and the same essay, p. 62.

5 See Pound, "Salutation the Third," in *Blast 1: Review of the Great English Vortex*, p. 45.

6 There is the suggestion of a doubling or splitting of personality in *Some Personalities*, p. 186: Upward observes that he had been unable "to carry on the work begun in *The New Word* . . . . The respite [the writing of *The Horoscope of Man*] proved illusory. I am again leading a double life." Five years later Upward committed suicide. In his introduction to *The Divine Mystery* (1915: rpt. Santa Barbara, California: Ross-Erikson, 1976), p. xxiii, Robert Duncan finds in Upward something comparable to a "schizophrenic disorder." This self-division is reflected in Upward's emotional oscillations throughout *Some Personalities*, in which the phrase "double life" appears three times. Upward is at once certain of his extraterrestrial origin and divine mission and painfully aware of public indifference; snobbishly contemptuous of his audience and in obvious and pathetic need of social recognition and esteem; overpoweringly ambitious and yet both frustrated and self-satisfied in

his personal failure and insurmountable obscurity. This is not to deny that Upward constantly couches his megalomania in irony and humorous self-deprecation, but the self-irony wears thin after his repeated comparisons of himself to Confucius, H. G. Wells, Newton, Shakespeare, Darwin, Dickens, Carlyle, Gladstone, Nietzsche, Poe, Mary Baker Eddy, Shelley, Themistocles, Socrates, Buddha, St. Paul, and Spinoza. As in *The New Word*, Upward puns on his own name, referring to the "upward march of man." Moody, p. 63, is surely wrong in claiming that Upward (and Pound as well) desired to form a civilization not upon his own genius but the "genius of things." See *Some Personalities*, pp. 3–31, 45, 49–61, 71, 88, 89, 128, 151–153, 162, 167, 175–184, 186, 208, 240, 243, 256, 259–260, 266, 299, 300–302.

7 René Girard, "Strategies of Madness—Nietzsche, Wagner, and Dostoyevsky," in *'To Double Business Bound': Essays on Literature, Mimesis, and Anthropology*, pp. 61–83. Pound's histrionics as well as his simultaneous antagonism and attraction to the "bourgeois" public has a close analogue in those nineteenth-century French Bohemians and romantics who, as Cesar Graña observes, had a powerful influence on the style of modern artistic rebels. See Graña, pp. 19–20, 41, 53, 54–55, 68, 69, 72–80, 87–88, 110–113, 136, 141–154, 179, 181, 186, 188. His entire book is extremely useful for an understanding of Pound and Upward.

8 Pound to Michael Roberts, July, 1937, Beinecke Rare Book and Manuscript Library, Yale University.

9 Fenichel, "Elements of a Psychoanalytic Theory of Anti-Semitism," in Simmel, ed., pp. 15–26; Freud, "The Uncanny," in *Collected Papers*, Vol. IV, pp. 368–407; Reichsmann, pp. 40–41, 55. See also Horkheimer, *Eclipse of Reason*, pp. 114–117; Horkheimer and Adorno, pp. 179–186; and Martin Jay's summary of Theodor Adorno's unpublished paper (1940): ". . . Adorno had proposed one of his more speculative hypotheses, half historical, half meta-historical. The pre-Diaspora Jews, he argued, had been a nomadic, wandering people, 'the secret gypsies of history.' The abandonment of this mode of life in favor of a sedentary existence, which had come with the development of agriculture, had been achieved at a terrible price. The Western concepts of work and repression were intertwined with the post-nomadic attachment of man to the soil. A subterranean memory of the wandering Jew, however, persisted in Western culture. This image of the Jew, Adorno held, 'represents a condition of mankind which did not know labor, and all later attacks on the parasitic, consumptive character of the Jews are simply rationalizations.' In other words, the Jew embodied the dream of gratification without toil, a dream whose frustration resulted in the displacement of fury onto those who seemed to have realized its promise." See Jay, 1, p. 232. As for the European gypsies, it is rarely noted that they were nearly totally wiped out by the Nazis during World War II.

10 Fenichel, "Elements of a Psychoanalytic Theory of Anti-Semitism," pp. 23, 24. The themes of sacrifice and victimization are written into the rituals and celebrations surrounding the Feast of St. John. See Bush, pp. 111, 121–122.

11 Quoted in Davie, 2, pp. 46–49.

12 Pound, "The Revolt of Intelligence. V," *New Age*, 8 Jan., 1920, p. 153.

13 Pearlman, 3, p. 415, recognizes the similarity between Pound's and the Jews' nomadism. Similar social anxieties, along with psychological confusion and projection, appear in the anti-Semitic Houston Stewart Chamberlain. See Geoffrey Field, pp. 47–48. See also Stonequist, *passim*.

14 As early as 1910 Pound had written: "One must hack through a shell of indifferentism if one is to startle anyone into attention." Quoted in Mary de Rachewiltz, 2, p. 163. The need to provoke opposition was also strong in A. R. Orage and Wyndham Lewis, and Pound himself recognized Lewis's urge to destructive violence. See Hutchins, p. 105; Chace, p. 11; Materer, 1, pp. 30–31, 56, 53.

15 Noted by Norman, p. 47, and Makin, pp. 29–35.

16 Bottome, quoted in Norman, p. 173.

17 Stock, 1, p. ix. See also Richard Aldington, quoted in Norman, p. 213.

18 Aldington, quoted in Norman, p. 213.

19 Pound, quoted in Chace, pp. 11–12, from *Poetry*, 5 Oct. 1914, pp. 29–30.

20 Pound to Lewis, July (?), 1920: "*Our* opinion of Instig.[ations] can only be that it is crowd-police work intended to keep the mob in order; and that opinion *shd.* be kept to ourselves"; Pound to Lewis, 5 Dec., 1936: "Let's cop the PoLICEman's elmet." See P/L, pp. 126–127, 190.

21 For a discussion of the idea of the free and classless intelligentsia, see Mannheim, pp. 10–13, 259, and *passim.* Unlike Pound, who would merge the intelligentsia through constant "selection" (LE, 319) with the social aristocracy or "beau monde," Mannheim hopes (with excessive optimism) that the mixed intelligentsia will attain a position beyond class and ideology. There is an analogue for Pound's cultural elite in Charles Maurras, whose elitist ideal also resembles that of Confucian China. See Tannenbaum, 1, p. 78.

22 Pound, quoted in Stock, 3, p. 299, and in Norman, p. 360. Pound's "conspiracy of intelligent men" resembles the Italian Fascist conception of a revolutionary, meritocratic, and technocratic middle class elite. On Italian Fascist elites, see Gregor, 3, pp. 219–223; Lyttelton, p. 76; Volpe, pp. 18, 23, 29, 51, 74, 136, 156, 159. Although Volpe believes as do Pound and Mussolini in the energetic minority that "made history," he insists no less strongly that Italian Fascism is a mass movement, a spiritual force within the nation, rather than the simple product of a directing elite. According to Arendt, Vol. III, p. 74: "The totalitarian movements have been called 'secret societies established in broad daylight.' "

23 See Terrell, Vol. II, p. 655.

24 See the radio broadcasts, pp. 39, 62, 65, 74, 75, 89, 97, 105, 113; GK, 241–242; Canto 74, p. 426.

25 Canetti, p. 290, and also 207. An obsession with controlling distance, both physical and psychic, characterizes paranoiacs and rulers. See Canetti, pp. 206–207, and Norman, p. 314, on Pound's only visit (in 1933) to Mussolini. For all of Pound's interest in the dissemination of knowledge, he did not abandon his idea of the secretum or the elite. To borrow an idea from Nolte's description of Charles Maurras, Pound developed in a democratic age of the powerful press and the supremacy of "*l'opinion.*" Thus, as a social and political type, Pound remains a product of mass society and mass politics. Unlike his heroes, Jefferson and Adams, who ruled "by conversation," Pound could not avoid some kind of more direct contact with the masses which he despised but sought to control. In some ways his situation is reminiscent of that of many fascist intellectuals who turned to fascism because they saw it as primarily favorable to elites, only to discover that it was really a mass movement. See Nolte, p. 188, and Mosse, "Fascism and the Intellectuals," in Woolf, ed., p. 222.

26 See Delmore Schwartz, "Ezra Pound and History," *New Republic,* 8, Feb. 1960, CXLII, pp. 17–19, reprinted in Homburger, ed., p. 450. The phrase "domination of benevolence" is from the dust-jacket of *Thrones de los Cantares* and refers to *Section: Rock-Drill.*

27 Pound, quoted in Norman, p. 227.

28 Pound to T. S. Eliot, Sept. 25, 1935, Beinecke Rare Book and Manuscript Library, Yale University.

29 Pound to Basil Bunting, May, 1935, Beinecke Rare Book and Manuscript Library, Yale University.

30 See also Pound, RB, 245. Like other fascists, such as Céline, Mussolini is fond of imagery of individual survival amid massive human decay. See Mussolini, quoted in Finer, p. 110. Wyndham Lewis often depicts himself as the "only live man amid a pile of corpses." See Dasenbrock, pp. 176, 178, 180.

31 Canetti, p. 227, and p. 247, on the "plague hero," and p. 275. See also Hamilton, p. 27.

32 Pound's mistaken translation of goyim as cattle may derive from Drumont's *La Dernière Bataille:* in which the Jews supposedly view *goyim* as the "seed of cattle." See Wilson, pp. 409–410. In *Waters Flowing Eastward* Fry claims that *goyim,* though normally translated as "heathen," means "animals" in its derogatory sense and that it is "usually a term of offense and contempt." See Fry, pp. 23, 130.

33 De Rachewiltz, 1, p. 158; Canetti, p. 85.

34 Canetti, p. 210. Pound agrees entirely with Plato, the first great advocate of the "closed society," that the art of ruling is a kind of herdsmanship involving training and breeding. See Popper, Vol. I, pp. 50–51.

35 Nolte, p. 518, notes "those numerous statements in *Mein Kampf* which display a frank and lordly contempt for the masses and depict their inertia and feminine nature with a cynical eye." See also Hitler, pp. 183, 42. According to Mosse, p. 212, Mussolini "likened the crowd to a herd of sheep until it is organized." Finer, p. 109, quotes this statement by Mussolini: "*With this human material everything is possible*, even a masterpiece, when, in the men who have been placed on high by the Nation, there is a spasm of art, and not merely the routine practice of an ordinary job." Il Duce's language conflates sex, politics, and artistic creation, as in Pound. Here is the basis for Mussolini's observation that "The crowd loves strong men. The crowd is like a woman." See Emil Ludwig, *Talks with Mussolini*, excerpted in Salomone, ed., p. 214; see also p. 225.

36 Pound, "Pastiche: The Regional. VIII," *New Age*, 28 Aug., 1919, p. 300.

37 For Pound's loneliness and humiliations in boyhood and adolescence, see Torrey, pp. 24–31.

Chapter Fourteen: Society, Economics, and Politics

1 On vermin as symbols of despised brothers or the social "horde," see Theodor Adorno, "Freudian Theory and the Pattern of Fascist Propaganda," in Arato and Gebhardt, eds., p. 131.

2 Pound, "Pastiche: The Regional. XIV," *New Age*, 23 Oct. 1919, p. 432; "Mr. Eliot's Solid Merit," *New English Weekly*, 12 July 1934, pp. 298–299; Pound to Lewis or Eliot, Beinecke Rare Book and Manuscript Library, Yale University.

3 Pound to Eliot, Beinecke Rare Book and Manuscript Library, Yale University.

4 Pound, "Mr. Eliot's Solid Merit," p. 298.

5 Pound to Lewis, August 3, 1939, Beinecke Rare Book and Manuscript Library, Yale University. Pound apparently refers to the publishing company of Allen and Unwin.

6 Pound, quoted in Norman, p. 309.

7 C. H. Douglas, 1, pp. 14, 86–87; Finlay, pp. 106–111; Kenner, 3, pp. 301–317.

8 For Marx's theory of crises, see Joan Robinson's comments on *Capital*, Vol. II, p. 365 (London, 1907) in *An Essay on Marxian Economics*, p. 47, and E. E. Nemmers, *Hobson and Underconsumption* (Amsterdam: North-Holland, 1956), p. 15. See also C. H. Douglas, 2, pp. 3, 6, 22, 25, 31–32, 34–35, 41, 46, 50–51.

9 C. H. Douglas, 1, pp. 111, 115, 65–67, 58, 63, 36, 32; 2, pp. 6, 9, 22, 25, 31–32, 34–35, 41, 46, 50–51; Kenner, 3, pp. 306–307.

10 Finlay, pp. 97–108; Pound, SP, pp. 211–212, and "Jean Barral is With Us," *New English Weekly*, 5 Dec. 1935, pp. 146–147.

11 Douglas, 2, pp. 6, 19, 46–47, 86, 90, 91–92, 101, 104, 106, 107, 109, 121, 124–125, 128–134, 138–139, 142–143; 1, pp. 5–6, 110–141; see also Pound's review of *Economic Democracy*, which first appeared in *The Little Review*, April, 1920, and which is reprinted in SP, pp. 210–212, and his "Social Credit and the Fine Arts: A Practical Application," which first appeared in *The New Age*, March 20, 1922, pp. 284–285, in EPVA, pp. 146–147. Arguing against common misinterpretations of Pound's economics, Dennis R. Klinck shows that Douglas's theory of Social Credit proposes not national but local or decentralized control of credit. By contrast Pound favored nationalization, as in Mussolini's takeover of the Italian banking system—a measure which in Douglas's view must result in the state's wasteful monopoly of finance for its own ends. See Klinck, "Pound, Social Credit, and the Critics," *Paideuma*, 5 (Fall, 1976), pp. 227–230, 234–235. For Douglas's hatred of centralized organization, see Finlay, *Social Credit*, pp. 102, 103, 104, 129, 131, 237–238, 246, 252.

12 See Pound, "The Revolt of Intelligence, X," *New Age*, 18 March, 1920, p. 318.

380/THE GENEALOGY OF DEMONS

13 Pound, "Jean Barral is with Us," p. 147.

14 On Douglas's anti-Semitism, and the anti-Semitic coloring of the *New Age,* see Finlay, pp. 103–105, and Holmes, pp. 209–210. But though Douglas was anti-Semitic, the Social Credit movement disavowed anti-Semitism.

15 Pound, "Profili Americani," *Meridiano di Roma,* V (29 Dec. 1941), pp. 1–2. For Douglas, see also Webb, pp. 131, 134.

16 See Ernst Simmel, ed., introduction to *Anti-Semitism: A Social Disease,* p. xxi; Ackerman and Jahoda, pp. 63–64, 75; Horkheimer and Adorno, "Elements of Anti-Semitism," in *Dialectic of Enlightenment,* pp. 170, 173–175; Joseph Greenblum and Leonard Pearlman, "Vertical Mobility and Prejudice," in Bendix and Lipset, eds., pp. 480–491; Bettelheim and Janowitz, pp. 137–145; Bell, ed., pp. 27n, 91, 309, 310, 226, 360; Fritz Stern, pp. 84–85, 93–94; Hofstadter, 2, pp. 60–61; Wilson, p. 637.

17 Critics have often assumed a close connection between Pound and American Populism, whose heyday coincided with his early years, and the majority of whose adherents derived from a beleaguered middle and especially lower-middle class. At the same time, Pound's affinity with Populism is often believed to provide a powerful motivation for his later economics and politics. As a political movement, Populism combined liberal or progressive and conservative elements: on the one hand, a desire for major monetary and social reforms, many of which it helped to realize, and, on the other, a strongly agrarian, nativist, and paranoid strain reflected in Manichean fantasies and a fear of financial conspiracy. According to some historians, the conservative or right-wing component of Populism took a radical and extremist turn in the twentieth century and issued in an "American Fascism" or at least proto-fascism typified by such demagogic advocates of "plebiscitary" and statist politics as Governor (later Senator) Huey Long of Louisiana and Father Charles Edward Coughlin. If Oscar Handlin is correct, the nativist strain of Populism was also responsible in the 1890s for the first significant wave of political and economic anti-Semitism in the United States. In two recent essays David Murray and Peter Brooker have shown independently that Pound shares with Populism an overwhelming interest in increased economic distribution along with the belief that this goal requires an increase in the money supply: otherwise, the small farmer, businessman, and industrial laborer must remain in the grip of money power and special interests. Although the Populists sought a bimetallic monetary standard, whereas Pound rejects the use of metal as a basis of currency, his reliance on the derogatory term "gold-bug" (87/ 572) in *The Cantos* reflects typical Populist usage, referring to a financial conspiracy supposedly centered in Wall Street and London and masterminded by such bankers as the Rothschilds. For the Populists, as for Pound (and the fascists), society is divided according to a simplistic and dangerous opposition between the forces of good, consisting of producers or "businessmen" of all classes, and the forces of evil, consisting chiefly of a parasitic class of financial monopolists. It is therefore understandable that Pound in the broadcasts refers favorably to Bryan's Cross of Gold speech; that the Usury *Cantos,* as Brooker notes, "throb with the nervous tension" of Bryan's speeches; and that one of Pound's favorite historical works, *The Law of Civilization and Decay,* which postulates the increasing dominance of money-power in modern history, was used as Populist propaganda in the election of 1896. Other ideological elements typical of Populism and Pound (as well as fascism) include a modified primitivism, an ideal of a golden age free of plutocratic villainy, a cult of the soil (as opposed to urban finance and cosmopolitanism), and a nostalgia for mythical, cyclical time. According to Brooker, not only do Huey Long and Father Coughlin typify "American Fascism" as a form of "compromised" Populism, but Pound's favorable view of these demagogues in the 1930s, simultaneously with his growing admiration of Mussolini and Hitler, is best understood as a sinister development from his Populist attitudes. Huey Long resembles Mussolini in his appeal to the "general will," his anti-plutocratic rhetoric, and his successful implementation of some much-advertised welfare programs. But though Long's leftist policies were, to quote Lipset and Raab, "in the populist tradition," and though he received much of his early support from former Populist strongholds, his politics reveal other features which are not typical of Populism and which mark them

as right-wing extremist, perhaps as even embryonically fascist. The virtual and self-professed dictator of Louisiana, Long resembles Mussolini in his control of the judiciary and press and, notwithstanding his claims to look after the common man, his covert alliance with capital against labor. Besides Long's authoritarian statism and his reliance on the principle of unquestioned leadership, other aspects of his politics—for instance, the appeal (however hypocritical) to lower class interests, the absence of nativism, and the eschewal of conspiracy theory— differentiate him from the Populists. Still, Long does not share the anti-Semitic and anti-Communist obsession typical of fascism and Pound. In the view of Lipset and Raab, Long is best understood not as a fascist but as a pure demagogue of neither the left nor the right—although they believe that, had he not been assassinated in 1935, he would have moved inevitably toward fascism. As for Father Coughlin, he seems more readily identifiable as a revolutionary fascist than does Long and closer in spirit to Pound. Like Long, Coughlin derived his considerable political following through a direct appeal to the masses of the lower class, chiefly by means of radio speeches which bristle with themes familiar to readers of Pound's broadcasts: anti-Semitism, anti-Communism, hatred of Roosevelt and the New Deal, fear of international financial conspiracy and other forms of monopoly, the necessity of government control and ownership of banks, the virtues of state capitalism, the rejection of labor's right to strike, and the glories of the anti-usurious and Catholic Middle Ages. See Pearlman, 3, pp. 466–479; Ferkiss, 1, pp. 173–197; 2, p. 359–367; Hofstadter, 1, pp. 5, 17–21, 60–93, 95–96, 168; 2, pp. 61, 68, 69, 300–302; Hicks, pp. 315–320; Handlin, pp. 323–344; Murray and Brooker, in Bell, ed., pp. 71–74, 14–20; Lipset and Raab, pp. 154, 167–189, 189–202; Rogin, pp. 212–213; Pound, RB, p. 80; "Senator Long and Father Coughlin: Mr. Ezra Pound's Estimate," *Morning Post,* 17 April, 1935, p. 14; "As for Huey, . . . ," *New English Weekly,* 12 Sept., 1935; "Again the Rev. Coughlin," *New English Weekly,* 24 Oct. 1935, p. 26. For arguments against the identification of Populism and anti-Semitism, see Pollack, 1, pp. 76–80; 2, pp. 391–403. For a less strong qualification of this identification, see Tucker, p. 107. Lipset and Raab observe that the Populist Party was "clearly not anti-Semitic," but that it existed within a climate of increasing anti-Semitism; see pp. 92–104.

On the evidence of Pound's writings, it is impossible to deny his affinities with Populism and "American Fascism." Even so, not only is it difficult to determine a precise biographical or sociological basis for this connection, but its extent and importance should not be exaggerated, especially as an explanation of Pound's anti-Semitism and fascism. According to Brooker, Pound's family supported the Populists against the Republicans in the election of 1892; one might also make something of the fact that Populism was fairly strong in the Middle West, whence one prominent branch of Pound's family derived. However, James J. Wilhelm, perhaps the best authority on Pound's early years, argues that Pound's family was not in favor of Populism in the 1890s, and he rightly doubts that Pound's attacks on Wall Street and Jewish financiers can be attributed significantly to Populist influences, much less to Pound's "suburban" origins; indeed, no simple historical explanation suffices for Pound's anti-Semitism. Nor is there reason to think that the Wisconsin background of Thaddeus Pound would have necessarily predisposed him or his son's family to Populism. Hofstadter notes that the older middle West, of which Wisconsin is a part, gave little support to Populism in 1892, and that in 1896, when Bryan ran on the Democratic ticket, he was nonetheless unable to carry the state. In fact, Wisconsin was too developed economically to lend full support to an agrarian-centered Populism. What is more, for Pound the most admirable aspect of Thaddeus Pound's career in the Middle West was his substantial contribution as an entrepreneur to the development of the railroads, which were one of the leading targets of Populist hatred. Finally, Pound is by no means in sympathy with every aspect of Populism. As Murray notes, the immediate effect of Populism on Pound was lessened by its appeal to the silver interests and its overwhelming concern for the common man. Despite his pose as a Middle-American rube in the broadcasts, an opportunistic and overplayed pitch to nativist prejudice, Pound could not have truly admired the anti-intellectualism, anti-elitism, and anti-Europeanism which typifies both Populism and Father

Coughlin's brand of "American Fascism." In actuality his fascism reveals its deepest affinity with the hierarchical and culturally elitist traditions of European conservatism. In short, the ideological panoply of American Populism is much too limited to account for the complexity of Pound's political, social, and economic thought. See Brooker and Murray in Bell, ed., pp. 14–15, and 71; Wilhelm, 3, pp. 20, 42, 73, 75; and Hofstadter, in Ionescu and Gellner, eds., p. 23.

18 Pound, quoted from the cover of *Blast* in Norman, p. 147.

19 For Mussolini's incorporation of scientists, professionals, artists, and writers within state-controlled syndicates, see Gregor, 3, p. 234; Salvemini, p. 99. David Roberts observes that Italian Fascism held out the hope of social, economic, and psychological security for an endangered " 'humanistic' petty bourgeoisie." See "Petty Bourgeois Fascism in Italy: Form and Content," in Larsen et al., eds., p. 337. Gioacchino Volpe, whose history of Italian Fascism Pound admired, offers an openly pro-bourgeois interpretation of the movement. He criticizes the "levelling" socialists for seeking to "dissolve" the middle class as a governing class, and he denies that the bourgeoisie consists only of social "parasites." Rather, the "reawakened" bourgeoisie is the ruling class by "right and duty." It furthermore constitutes the real and ideal unity of the nation, for not only is it open to all, but it holds spiritual values supposedly identical to those held by all other classes. See Volpe, pp. 37, 39, 40, 49, 50.

20 Barkun, pp. 7, 20, 31, 32, 35–36, 37, 45, 52, 54–55, 74, 75, 79, 145–154. For the distinction between clinical and social or political paranoia, see Gilbert, pp. 270–271.

21 Barkun, pp. 53, 159, 163: "[Disaster] . . . reduces much of the disparity between the social isolates and the rest of the community. . . . In this suddenly opened and democratized atmosphere, individuals who led formerly separate lives identify with each other."

22 Pound, "Private Worlds," *New English Weekly,* 2 May 1935, pp. 48–49; "Leaving out Economics," *New English Weekly,* 31 Jan., 1935, p. 331; GK, p. 157.

23 Pound, "American Notes," *New English Weekly,* 5 Sept., 1935, p. 325. See also Pound, "Private Worlds," pp. 48–49.

24 Pound, "Last Words on Economic Democracy," *New English Weekly,* 7 May 1936, pp. 69–70. Following J. L. Talmon, Dante L. Germino defines Italian Fascism as a form of "political messianism." See "Italian Fascism and its Place in Political Thought," pp. 118, 120n. Pound may also have been drawn to Italian Fascism out of a deep-felt sympathy for the underdog, since Italy, a self-styled "proletarian" nation, considered itself to have been cheated and betrayed by the plutocratic great powers during the negotiations of the Versailles Treaty. Italy's resentments helped to create a climate within which fascism could emerge. Apart from his lifelong hatred and contempt of Woodrow Wilson, Pound repeatedly denounces the Versailles Treaty for its unfairness to the Axis nations; by the radio broadcasts he views it as nothing more than an instrument of Jewish financiers and gun-runners. His admiration for Gabriele D'Annunzio stems partly from the fact that D'Annunzio, in anticipation of Italian Fascist violence and style, and in defiance of the Treaty, conquered and held Fiume for fifteen months. See Carsten, pp. 45–52; Pound, J/M, pp. 33, 51; RB, pp. 21, 42, 102, 136, 236, 244, 259, 305; LE, p. 192.

25 See Arendt, Vol. III, p. 35; see also Pearlman, 4, pp. 114–115. Fascism gained power in Italy and Germany through the support of only a minority of the population, and it had no footing in any particular class. However, historians agree that it was nonetheless a mass movement, and they also recognize that the middle and lower-middle classes dominated its ranks and leadership. See G. Germani, "Fascism and Class," in Woolf, ed., pp. 71–75, 89; De Felice, "Italian Fascism and the Middle Class," pp. 312–317; and Roberts, "Petty Bourgeois Fascism in Italy: Form and Content," pp. 337–347, in Larsen et al., eds. Roberts summarizes other historians' analysis of the class origins of fascism. See also Mosse, 1, p. 7. Fredric Jameson traces Wyndham Lewis's "Proto-Fascism" to his fundamentally petit bourgeois outlook aggravated by increasing social emargination and fear of submergence in the masses. See Jameson, 2, pp. 15–17, 113–114, 115–116, 129, 131.

26 Horkheimer and Adorno, "Elements of Anti-Semitism," in *Dialectic of Enlightenment*, p. 173; see also Eugen Weber, 2, pp. 66–68.

27 See for instance Pound, "Pastiche: The Regional, IX," *New Age*, 11 Sept., 1919, p. 336; "Mr. T. S. Eliot's Quandaries," *New English Weekly*, 26 April, 1934, p. 48; "Mr. Eliot's Solid Merit," *New English Weekly*, 12 July 1934, p. 298. In L, p. 257, Pound speaks of the "god damn capitalist psychology" as a "disease that has eaten in thru every interstice of the mind" and condemns "capitalist literature."

28 Pound, quoted in Berezin, "Poetry and Politics in Ezra Pound," p. 264.

29 The distinction between producers of whatever class and exploiters, between "good" productive capital and parasitic finance, plays a major ideological role in Italian Fascism, especially among those syndicalists of the Italian fascist "left" among whom Mussolini began his political career and with whom Pound manifests certain affinities. See De Grand, pp. x, 29; Roberts, pp. 196, 311.

30 Berezin, p. 276; Douglas, 2, p. 137.

31 See also Pound, SP, p. 233: "It would be possible to attack the 'rights' or 'privileges' of capital without attacking the rights or privileges of property." In the same volume, p. 342, Pound writes: "All trade hinges on money. All industry hinges on money. Money is the pivot. It is the middle term. It stands midway between industry and workers." See also I, pp. 143, 153, 263. For rare instances in which Pound denounces the profit motive as a general principle, see SP, p. 91, on Mencius, and RB, pp. 109, 182. Compare Douglas, 1, pp. 65, 67. Nonetheless, Pound does not reject the idea of profit. Rather he would limit profits according to the just price while reminding the capitalist of his social obligations.

32 Mosse, 6, pp. 151–152. Inspired by medieval examples, a similar distinction between capital and usury appears in the nineteenth-century corporatist de La Tour du Pin; see Nolte, p. 75. Pound, GK, p. 96, endorses de La Tour du Pin's characterization of the nineteenth century as the "age of usury"; however, in SP, pp. 155, 272, 280, he says that he failed to comprehend money. Pound also discusses de La Tour du Pin in "American Notes. Time Lag," *New English Weekly*, 18 April, 1935, pp. 5–6. This article, however, precedes the virulent period of Pound's anti-Semitism, and he criticizes the undocumented assertion that the Jews are responsible for usury, Calvin, and Voltaire. Pound adds that de La Tour du Pin was incapable of thinking of "money," by which Pound means monetary reforms and mechanisms. For a summary of de La Tour du Pin's "organicist" corporative doctrines, his anti-usury, and his anti-Semitism, see Elbow, pp. 53–80. Other French anti-Semites of the late nineteenth and early twentieth century distinguished between good and bad capital (finance) and attacked those who consumed without producing. See Wilson, p. 265.

33 Hitler, pp. 209, 234–235. Pound mentions Feder admiringly in the broadcasts, pp. 213, 280–281, noting that Hitler had approved of Feder's idea that " 'A great deal of purchasing power is allocated for reasons other than the performance of useful labor.' " Feder is thus enlisted to contradict the Marxist theory of economic value and to provide confirmation of Douglas's idea of the "increment of association." According to Heymann, Pound was in touch with Feder in the 1930s. See Heymann, p. 78. In a letter of Nov. 10, 1953 (in the Beinecke Rare Book and Manuscript Library, Yale University), Denis Goacher alerts Pound to Feder's works and points out the similarities between Feder's economic thought and Pound's. For a sampling of Feder's ideas, see Barbara Miller Lane and Leila J. Rupp, eds., pp. 27–30, 33–40. Denouncing the "Bondage of Interest," Feder attacked finance, international loan capital, and non-productive capital. As a corporatist philosopher of "The Social State," and hence a member of the "left wing" of Nazism in the 1920s, Feder proposed not only to abrogate the national debt but to nationalize credit and certain industries. But Hitler had little stomach for this kind of socialism, and Feder descended into obscurity in the 1930s. See Cassels, "Janus: The Two Faces of Fascism," p. 75; Weiss, p. 17.

34 Pound, "The Nazi Movement in Germany," *Townsman*, 2 (April 1939), p. 12. See also Lewis, 1, p. 147.

35 Mosse, p. 151; Edouard Drumont, quoted in Tannenbaum, 1, p. 16; and Nolte, p. 75. Pound refers approvingly to Drumont in RB, pp. 179, 199.

36 Evidence of Pound's Marxist flirtation appears in Canto 33. The most extensive study of Pound's interest in Marxism is Chapter Two of Nicholls, pp. 47–59; see also pp. 24–25, 79, 80, 81, 234–235n. During the 1920s Pound discovered the *New Masses* even as he was drawn to fascism. Having read Marx's *Capital* by the early 1930s, he contributed to a variety of left-wing magazines until 1937. Pound frequently drew parallels between the Russian and Fascist Revolutions while attempting to persuade the left that Mussolini's policies—for instance, banking reforms, the shortening of the working week, the war on tuberculosis, national dividends in rice and macaroni, rent reductions, government price-fixing—were sufficiently socialistic. Even so, Nicholls recognizes the ultimate incompatibility of Pound's views with Marxism. An article by Pound in *The New Masses* offended its editor, Mike Gold, for its ignorance of and aesthetic approach to industrial conditions. The theories of Major Douglas lessened the urgency of Marx's concept of economic crisis as an inherent structural defect of capitalism by blaming it on finance and simple "perversions" of capitalist ownership. They also differ from Marx's thought in their excessive emphasis on distribution and consumption, as if the essential problems of production had been solved. Like Berezin, noted above, Nicholls points out the divergence between Marxist theory and Pound's assumption that capital and property are essentially different. As for Marx's labor theory of value, Pound rejects it with two arguments: that economic value derives not only from labor but from Nature; and that the contribution of labor to the formation of value is heavily supplemented in modern times by the community's cultural and technological inheritance.

37 See Pound, "Pastiche: The Regional. XIV," *New Age*, 23 Oct., 1919, p. 422: "The Revolt of Intelligence, VII," *New Age*, 22 Jan. 1920, p. 187; "Last Words on Economic Democracy," *New English Weekly*, 7 May, 1936, pp. 69–70; letter to John Drummond, March 6, 1934, Beinecke Rare Book and Manuscript Library, Yale University. See also SP, pp. 172–173, in which Pound "refutes" the idea that class war exists in America by pointing anecdotally to the harmonious reunion of a "typical American family" after eight generations: "we find all sorts of conditions—rich and poor." The family was the Wadsworths, relatives of Pound on his mother's side, and largely made up of members of the middle and upper-middle class.

38 Hitler similarly attributes to the Jews that "inner estrangement . . . between employer and employee . . . which later leads to political class division." "The better acquainted I became with the Jew," he says, "the more forgiving I inevitably became toward the worker." See Hitler, pp. 314, 63, 382. The same idea appears in Lewis, 1, pp. 74–75, and Céline, 3, pp. 72–73. According to Douglas, 2, p. 137, the financier is largely responsible for class division and unrest.

39 Pound, "Sulla Propaganda," *Meridiano di Roma*, VIII (6 June, 1943), p. 1.

40 Max Wykes-Joyce, "Some Considerations Arising from Ezra Pound's Conception of the Bank," in Peter Russell, ed., pp. 225–226; Davis, p. 154. For Pound's admiration for Mussolini's financial reforms, see "American Notes," *New English Weekly*, 2 April, 1936, p. 489; "Intellectual Money," *British Union Quarterly*, 1 (April-June 1937), pp. 24–34; "The Italian Score," *New English Weekly*, 23 May, 1935, p. 107; J/M, p. 117. In Canto 41, p. 202, Mussolini tells financial malefactors that he will send them to the "*confine*" (*confino*, imprisonment or exile). Unlike Douglas, Pound advocated the nationalization of credit, and was therefore encouraged by Mussolini's takeover and centralization of banking in Italy. Actually, these reforms did not so much redistribute wealth as enable the government to finance its projects more easily, as Douglas had predicted. For Douglas's objections to such schemes, see *Credit-Power and Democracy*, pp. 57, 63, 53–54, and Pound, SP, pp. 279, 294. For Mussolini's reforms, see De Grand, p. 155; Gregor, 1, pp. 300–301; 3, pp. 142, 144. For a highly favorable view of Fascist financial policies by a writer whom Pound knew and admired, see Odon Por, *Finanza Nuova: Problemi e soluzioni* (Firenze: Felice de Monnier, 1940). Influenced by Douglas's argument that private banks create artificial scarcity by sabotaging purchasing power through the manipulation of the currency, Por distinguishes between "plutocratic" and state-controlled banking. The first reaps exorbitant profits through interest charges while promoting wars and debts; the second finances production and distribution within a

state-directed corporate economy and according to the real needs of the nation. Like Douglas and Pound, Por attacks the gold standard and seeks to establish money and credit on the nation's actual wealth; meanwhile, the state must fix prices according to the store of available, collectivized goods. Por's interest in Douglas and the just price, the Wörgl experiment in local money, Marco Polo's discovery of Chinese paper money, and the reforms of the Reichsbank, probably reflect the influence of Pound, whom Por mentions. Por also wrote *Politica economico-sociale in Italia* (Firenze: Sansoni, A., 1940), which Pound translated as *Italy's Policy of Social Economics* in 1941.

41 Walter Hampden, quoted in Norman, p. 326. See also Douglas, 2, pp. 53–54, 57, 80–81, 84; Pound's reviews of 1920, "Economic Democracy" and "Probari Ratio," in SP; and Heymann, pp. 77–78, on Gorham Munson's and Douglas's views of Pound's position. For Pound's and Douglas's hatred of Prussianism, see especially pp. 207: "Fabianism and Prussianism alike give grounds for what Major Douglas has ably synthesized as 'a claim for the complete subjection of the individual to an objective which is externally imposed on him'. . . ." However, in his later career Pound would grant large authority to the state. Writing to R. McNair Wilson on Dec. 22, 1935, Pound said: "I am not going to be 'handled' as a tame sheep in the Soc/Cr [Social Credit] herd" (this letter is in the Beinecke Rare Book and Manuscript Library, Yale University). In RB, p. 123, Pound says: ". . . No, I am not a social creditor. . . . I am a national money man."

42 Pound critics have failed to note that Silvio Gesell, one of Pound's monetary gurus, was also one of "the prophets of Volkish thought," a leader of the free land movement in Germany before the First World War, an advocate (as was Pound) of the free flow of money, and the architect of a Germanic utopia. An opponent of usury, Gesell helped pave the way for Nazism. For Gesell, see Mosse, 1, pp. 110, 120; Gesell's most important work is *The Natural Economic Order*, trans. Philip Pye (London: Peter Owen, 1958).

43 For Pound on the just price, the decline of the feudal system and medieval crafts, and the importance of the responsibilities and duties of the feudal overlord, see GK, pp. 30, 48, 261, and the radio broadcasts, pp. 55, 67, 197. For Pound, the Italian Fascist idea that liberty is a duty rather than a right, as well as the Fascist ideal of function, have a medieval basis. He also blames Jewish usury for the destruction of chivalry and the "feudal system." Douglas reveals a qualified admiration for the Middle Ages in *Economic Democracy*, pp. 90–91.

44 Mosse, 6, p. 138; Tannenbaum, 1, p. 21.

45 See de La Tour du Pin, quoted in Tannenbaum, 1, p. 83n. For the just price, see Mosse, 6, p. 138; for distributive justice, see Canto 93, p. 627; GK, p. 335; and Earle Davis, p. 150.

46 The English Guild Socialists generally espoused an organic and functional theory of society, but the two chief groups within the movement differed in the extent of their socialist and democratic sympathies. The dominant group, represented by G.D.H. Cole, is usually viewed as socialistic and democratic, one of its chief aims being the "encroaching control" and final takeover of capitalist industry by the workers. The less influential group within Guild Socialism is represented by A.R. Orage, who, as editor of the *New Age*, sponsored Major Douglas's credit schemes while helping to provide Pound with an education in economics. Although the *New Age* is often described as the official publication of Guild Socialism, the journal was strongly colored by Orage's scornfully elitist (and Nietzschean) view of democracy, the trades union movement, traditional socialism, class warfare, and Cole's concept of the workers' encroaching control of industry. Alan Robinson observes that Orage's program for social reform was based, like that of A. J. Penty, perhaps the founder of Guild Socialism, on "a form of neo-feudalist, hierarchial guild organization." It is therefore understandable that Orage accepted for publication in the *New Age* J. M. Kennedy's articles on "Tory Democracy" as well as Ramiro de Maeztu's on the theory of a hierarchical, functional, and organic society. Orage's views probably influenced Pound as strongly as they did Douglas, who found the labor movement opposed to the best interests of society, and whose dislike

of socialist democracy and basic acceptance of capitalism led Cole to accuse him of being "no Guildsman." Orage, on the other hand, charged that the National Guilds League, whose leading figure was Cole, had been "captured for Communism" after World War I. None of this is meant to imply that Orage was a fascist or proto-fascist, for while Italian Fascism similarly emphasized hierarchy, preserved private capitalism, and denied control of industry to the workers, both Orage and Douglas denounced the kind of statism which Pound came to embrace in Mussolini. Still, it is worth remarking that Ramiro de Maeztu suffered political assassination for his support of fascism (or proto-fascism) in Spain, and that A. J. Penty, under the delusion that he had found "industrial democracy," nearly ended up in the Italian Fascist camp in the 1930s. See Martin, pp. 200, 201, 227, 228; Wright pp. 28, 84; Glass, pp. 27–28, 42, 43; Carpenter, pp. 65, 127, 128, 135, 268; Finlay, pp. 49, 68–70; Robinson, p. 105; Douglas, 2, p. 3.

47 Gregor, 3, p. 26; Pound, J/M, p. 94; Volpe, pp. 14, 23, 57, 85, 136, 142.

48 Pound, GK, pp. 52, 191–192; J/M, p. 44; SP, pp. 207–209, 210–212; "Jean Barral is with Us," p. 211; Volpe, pp. 20, 37–39, 56–57, 64.

49 For Pound's organic and fascistic conception of society and politics, and his hatred of Communist collectivism, see "Organicly Speaking," New English Weekly, 26 Dec., 1935, p. 211. For Italian Fascist organicism see also Por, 3, pp. 54, 147, 202, and Volpe, pp. 6, 57, 126, 136.

50 For Italian Fascism's claims to transcend class, see Lyttelton, p. 50; William S. Halperin, p. 58; Volpe, pp. 20, 24, 51, 75, 80, 136. See also Pound, SP, p. 294, and Por, 1, p. 13; 3, pp. 52, 53, 60, 61. Earle Davis, p. 51, notes that Pound admired Por's guild concepts, and that his Guilds and Cooperatives in Italy (1923) received the blessing of Orage's group and also contained an appendix by G. D. H. Cole, perhaps the leading Guild Socialist. For the Italian Fascist ideal of gerarchia or hierarchy, see Finer, pp. 12, 38; Lyttelton, p. 75. In J/M, Italian Fascism implicitly corresponds to the "gerarchia . . . in nature" (J/M, 116, 85).

51 Pound, I, pp. 145–146. Fascism sought openly to overturn and replace the liberal concept of citizenship. See Gregor, 3, p. 106; Salvemini, p. 109. The difference between the liberal concept of citizenship and that of Italian Fascism may be seen in the following statement by Gioacchino Volpe: "Work is the supreme qualification that entitles a man to full citizenship." The statement can be taken to mean that only those persons are entitled to full citizenship who perform economic functions within producers' associations designated and sanctioned by the state. See Volpe, p. 75.

52 For Guild Socialist thought and its difficulties with the problem of centralized state authority, see Ulam, pp. 80–95. For the movement within Italian Fascism from syndicalist and guild ideas of corporate self-determination to the theory of the state, see Finer, pp. 206, 494, 519. Critics often ignore the fact that Pound's interest in the Byzantine Book of the Prefect in the later Cantos reflects not his transhistorical values but his continuing commitment to Italian Fascist corporatism and statism. Seeking a deep-rooted Fascist "tradition," other Italian Fascists were similarly drawn to the state-directed and corporate economy of the late Roman period, whence Pound's Byzantium derives. See Walbank, pp. 46–47n.

53 For the Italian Fascist idea of class collaboration, see Finer, p. 52; Lyttelton, p. 50; Gregor, 4, pp. 7, 208, 217, 223.

54 Roberts, p. 265; Lyttelton, p. 331. Finer, pp. 503–509, analyzes the Charter of Labor.

55 G. Lowell Field, pp. 90–91, 95, 96, 137, 138, 141, 182–185, 194–200. See also Gregor, 3, pp. 183–196, 196–197, 200–202. Against all the evidence, Por, 3, pp. 163, 186–187, argues that workers were an influential force within the corporations, and that the corporations had major political influence.

56 See Roberts, pp. 18–19, 55, 196, 252, 253, 256, 265, 311; Lyttelton, pp. 310, 326–327; Gregor, 3, pp. 3–63. In the radio broadcasts, p. 353, Pound defends the fascist form of socialism and, much like Céline in L'École des cadavres (Céline, 2: 108), claims that its achievements for the national welfare far surpass those of the Communists in Russia. Pound salutes "his Excellency" Edmondo Rossoni, Italian

Fascist minister of agriculture and forests, in GK, pp. 40, 166–167, 246, 272, 274, 277; Canto 101, p. 726. However, Pound appears to admire Rossoni mainly for his "Confucian" interest in agricultural reforms and production in the 1930s, rather than for his early activities as a Fascist labor organizer.

57 The Nazi Party included a corporate "left wing" in its early days. Led by Gregor and Otto Strasser, it emphasized medieval guilds, the necessity of credit, the nationalization of industry, and the evils of unproductive capital, especially finance capitalism. Although Hitler shared some of these values, he rejected corporatism as alien to a Führerstaat. See Mosse, 4, pp. 119, 121, 128, 130, 135, 136; Cecil, p. 57; Hamilton, p. 131; Weiss, p. 17.

58 For Pound's sympathies with the Italian Fascist "left" during World War II, see Chilanti, pp. 235, 238–239, 242. In Canto 79, p. 470, Pound quotes Chilanti's twelve-year-old daughter, who wanted to do away with the shifty Count Ciano, Mussolini's son-in-law and Italian Fascist minister of foreign affairs, "with a pinch of insecticide." The "left" fascists believed that Italian Fascism had been betrayed by "capitalism," by which they meant mainly "money" or finance, and which they blamed for the catastrophe of the war. Yet it must be stressed that Pound's politics, however peculiar in its so-called "leftism," remained Fascistic.

59 Roberts, pp. 184–185, 190–191, 206; Lyttelton, pp. 45–46, 75, 310–313, 323, 347–349; Salvemini, p. 427.

60 On the Italian Fascist return to socialist "origins" at Salò, and Mussolini's "humanism of labor," see Gregor, 1, pp. 283–309. Gregor believes that in his later career Mussolini was moving toward a thoroughgoing socialism and had thus alienated many capitalists.

61 See also the line " 'alla' non 'della' in Il Programma di Verona" (78/ 478). Pound is thinking of Article 15 of the Program Manifesto of the Fascist Republican Party, which refers to not "merely a right of property, but a right to property." See Gregor, 1, pp. 387–391, on the Manifesto.

62 See Pound, quoted in Heymann, pp. 143, 148, 326, 333.

63 See Pound, quoted in Heymann, pp. 326, 332, 336.

64 Roberts, pp. 288, 289, 291; Gregor, 3, pp. 206–207.

65 One of the ironies of Pound's politics is that he often praises political decentralization. Moreover, despite his obvious sympathy with Italian Fascism's professed statist and totalitarian aims, he views it as being in some ways a decentralizing movement. In the 1920s Pound inveighs against Prussian and Communist collectivism and denounces modern bureaucracy as the "flail of Jehovah," while in *Guide to Kulchur* he stresses the necessity of observing the "borderline between public and private things" (SP, 207–212, 217; GK, 192). Pound's praise of guilds and syndicates at least partly reflects his conception of them as largely autonomous organizations which protect the individual against the encroachments of the state; a similar view of professional and other associations as local and self-determining establishments may be seen in Charles Maurras. In Canto 48 Pound implicitly (and most dubiously) identifies Italian Fascism with the Albigensians, who refused to "be under Paris" (48/ 243) but ultimately succumbed to centralizing power. Although Pound deviates from Douglas in supporting Mussolini's nationalization of banking, he favors the Wörgl monetary experiment in Austria, a rebellion against the tyranny of centralized banks. According to Guy Davenport, Pound is essentially a conservative who dreams of a "decentralized America, a simple, taxless federation of states, ruled by laws, locally passed and locally enforced." For Pound, these conditions are especially beneficial to artistic production, for in his view art is properly "local" (87/ 570), an expression of the peculiar social and geographical conditions of a region or place, as in the decentralized city-states of the Italian Renaissance. Nor does Pound necessarily view Mussolini as single-mindedly statist, claiming that his aim as dictator is first to establish a government strong enough to achieve "justice," and then to move at a "reasonable pace" toward the Jeffersonian ideal of a government "which governs least" (J/M, 45). Yet these values are difficult to square with Pound's acceptance elsewhere of Mussolini's "absolute" (SP, 306) and "totalitarian" (SP, 158) state and in particular of his intervention in the Italian economy, which was

inconceivable without an extensive bureaucracy. *Guide to Kulchur* contains the statement that "in Italy the trouble is not too much state authority but too little" (GK, 254). Apart from Mussolini, many of the leading figures of *The Cantos*, for instance Napoleon, Antoninus Pius, and Justinian, represent centralizing authority, while the Byzantium celebrated toward the end of the poem is characterized by a guild system controlled by a strong state. Even Pound's much admired Chinese mandarins must be viewed as bureaucrats, although Pound probably supposes that their aesthetic and literary qualifications lift them far above the plane of the bland and technocratic modern functionary. Never does Pound reconcile the tension (or contradiction) in his thought between statism and decentralization, but it is possible that his wide-angle view of Italian Fascism as simultaneously statist and decentralizing is influenced by Gioacchino Volpe's claim that Mussolini had achieved or would ultimately achieve an ideal balance between government authority and the local and corporate self-determination of social and professional groups. Noting the strong decentralizing impulse of Fascism during the early days of the syndicates, Volpe asserts quite dubiously that Mussolini visualized the state as having the "minimum of material" but the "maximum of moral functions"—an assertion which consorts neither with Mussolini's practice nor with Volpe's own statism. Volpe's equivocation, if not confusion, is evident in his typically Italian Fascist belief that "the nation is a unit realized in the state," and in his desire for the state to become "the hub and centre of every national activity": "all within the state, nothing without or against the state." See Davenport, "Ezra Pound: 1885–1972," *Arion* [new series], Vol. 1, 1 (1973), pp. 188–196, quoted in Heymann, p. 83; Volpe, pp. 14, 35, 76, 77, 65, 139; McClelland, ed., pp. 217–220. For *The Cantos'* increasing emphasis on state control, see Nicholls, pp. 110–111, 149.

66 See the Italian Fascist Charter of Labor, Declaration IX, quoted in Delzell, p. 122: "[State] intervention may take the form of supervision, of promotion, or of direct management." Volpe, p. 146, describes the state as the director of labor and employers.

67 Earle Davis, pp. 153, 157; Finer, pp. 492–498; Lyttelton, pp. 317, 319–320, 324, 329; Salvemini, pp. 32, 37, 76. According to Salvemini, Edmondo Rossoni, one of Pound's heroes on the Fascist "left," had no difficulty in acknowledging that "Fascist unions are nothing but instruments of the [Fascist] Party." Indeed, Rossoni was one of the "inventors" of this system of labor organization.

68 Lyttelton, pp. 319–320. See also Salvemini, pp. 417, 27, 64–66.

69 William S. Halperin, pp. 56–57; Cassels, pp. 57–58; Weiss, p. 101; Lyttelton, p. 331.

70 See Por, 3, pp. 15–17, 49, 51, 55, 56, 68, 70, 77, 83–88, 154, 170–172.

71 Apart from anti-Semitism, Pound uses essentially the same argument as he had used in 1920, when he proposed "dividing the country just below the great financial rings, the arrangers of credit." See "The Revolt of Intelligence, X," *New Age*, 18 March, 1920, p. 318. Pound repeats this idea in "Atrophy of the Leninists, II," *New English Weekly*, 9 July, 1936, p. 250; according to Pound, all but usurers are the "exploited."

72 Pound, "What America Has to Live Down, III-IV," *New Age*, 5 Sept., 1918, p. 298.

73 Pound to Douglas Fox, 3 April, 1936, Beinecke Rare Book and Manuscript Library, Yale University.

74 See Pound, radio broadcasts, pp. 403–405. For Quisling's dream of a "Greater Nordic Peace Union," see Hayes, p. 153.

75 Pound believed William Wiseman to have been the head of British Intelligence before he joined the New York banking firm of Kuhn, Loeb, and Co. In Canto 100 Wiseman figures as a powerful behind-the-scenes adviser in the coordination of American participation at Versailles and in the formation of the League of Nations, which Pound detested. See Terrell, Vol. II, p. 645. For Wiseman's influential career as a diplomat, see Fowler, *passim*. Incidentally, Wiseman was not Jewish.

76 This alteration is not given in Materer's transcript of this letter of Aug. 3, 1939 in *Pound/Lewis*, p. 214. My source is a xerox of the letter contained in the

Beinecke Rare Book and Manuscript Library, Yale University. Given the ultimately lethal implications of this statement, it is interesting that Pound, as Materer reports, typed it in red.

Chapter Fifteen: The Role of the Scapegoat

1 To name just a few studies of anti-Semitic projection: Ackerman and Jahoda, pp. 55–60; Parkes, pp. 82–86; Simmel, "Anti-Semitism and Mass Psychopathology," pp. 50–57; Douglas Orr, "Anti-Semitism and the Psychopathology of Everyday Life," pp. 85–95; and Else Frenkel-Brunswik and R. Nevitt Sanford, "The Anti-Semitic Personality: A Research Report," pp. 96–124, all in Simmel, ed.; Horkheimer and Adorno, pp. 185–190. Projection is also a category in the famous "F Scale" used by post-war researchers to measure authoritarian tendencies; see Adorno et al., *The Authoritarian Personality*, Part I, Ch. VII, pp. 222–228.

2 Despite numerous instances of anti-Semitic scapegoating and projection in his work, Pound himself referred to scapegoating as "common to all cowards." See "Ecclesiastical History," *New English Weekly*, 5 July, 1934, pp. 272. Pearlman, 4, pp. 113–114, argues that Pound's refusal of introspection leads him to project his own unacknowledged impulses onto the Jews. For the problem of why the Jews in particular are repeatedly chosen as scapegoats, see Fenichel, "Elements of a Psychoanalytic Theory of Anti-Semitism," in Simmel, ed., pp. 14–24; and Morse and Allport, pp. 228–229.

3 Girard, 2, pp. 11, 24, 61, 36–38, 49, 8–10, 31, 34, 39–47, 127.

4 Girard, 2, pp. 8, 31, 63–65, 68–69, 94–103, 250–273. Robert Parker similarly views ritual purification as a science of "division," separating sacred from profane. See his *Miasma: Pollution and Purification in Early Greek Religion*, pp. 18–31, 325–326.

5 Richard Wagner, quoted by Robert Pois in his Introduction to Rosenberg, p. 15. The same "plastic," excessively mobile, and monstrous image of the "hydra-headed" Jew appears in Wagner's disciple Houston Stewart Chamberlain and in the French anti-Semite Drumont. See Geoffrey Field, p. 193; Wilson, pp. 493, 634. See also Céline, 1, pp. 102–103, 127; 2, pp. 34, 108–109, 142, 216, 222; 3, p. 142.

6 Conspicuous among the accusations of nineteenth-century French anti-Semites was that the infinitely plastic and mobile Jews had destroyed hierarchy. See Wilson, pp. 493, 633, 634.

7 See Mary Douglas, pp. 48, 115, 116, 117, 118, 136, 145.

8 For the *pharmakon*, see Jacques Derrida, "Plato's Pharmacy," in Derrida, 3, pp. 63–171, esp. p. 70.

9 Leschnitzer, pp. lx, 98. See also Venetia Newall, "The Jew as Witch Figure," in Newall, ed., p. 107. Mary Douglas compares witches to beetles, spiders, and Jews. Living in the "non-structure," that is the "cracks" of a house or social order, these beings have an ambiguously marginal or "interstitial" status. See Douglas, pp. 124–126. After the Jews, "inferior" or "defective" German women were among the most prominent scapegoats of Nazi racism. See Gisela Bock, "Racism and Sexism in Nazi Germany: Motherhood, Compulsory Sterilization and the State," in Renata Bridenthal et al., eds., pp. 271–296.

Chapter Sixteen: Indeterminacy and Crisis, I: The Selva Oscura

1 Peck, pp. 13, 5–8. Odysseus' journey, as in Canto 1, is into the realm of the mothers. See the lines quoted from Stesichorus in Canto 23: ποτὶ ματέρα, to his mother, κουριδίαν τ᾽ ἄλοχον and bed mate in marriage, παῖδάς τε φίλοις and dear children.

2 Brooke-Rose, p. 218. For Aristotle, see *The Generation of Animals (De Generatione Animalium)*, Book I, 715b16, 716a14, in Vol. V of *The Works of Aristotle*, ed. J. A. Smith and W. D. Ross (Oxford: Clarendon Press, 1958). See also *Physics (Physica)*, Book II, 193b20, and *Metaphysics (Metaphysica)*, Book V, 1002b22; 1023a; Book VI, 1032a12; Book IX, 1046a32; Book X, 1055a34; Book

XII, 1070b11, in Vols. II and VIII of *The Works of Aristotle,* ed. W. D. Ross (Oxford: Clarendon Press, 1948, 1966).

3 Sarles et al., pp. 3–5, 39–45; Uvarov and Chapman, eds., pp. 159, 38; Schery, p. 301; Kelly and Hite, p. 12.

4 The selva oscura resembles what Bachofen calls "tellurian creation." See Bachofen, pp. 24–30, 31–39, 55–61.

5 This entire paragraph is indebted to Derrida's "White Mythology: Metaphor in the Text of Philosophy," in Derrida, 4, esp. pp. 218–219, 240, 242–244, 250–251, 267, 268–269.

6 The same darkness at the absolute of sunlight, "blindness at the heart of vision," undermines the pro-Nazi solar mythology of Henri de Montherlant in *Solstice de juin.* See Mehlman, pp. 13–16.

7 Compare SP, p. 79: "In every cranny of the West there is a mildew of books that start from nowhere." In the "mildew" (fungus without need of the sun) of terms, language has lost track of its ultimate origins in the light, "starts from nowhere," fails to originate at all.

8 Many critics argue that the Taoist Pound fully accepts natural process as the interpenetration of complementary opposites: man should revere Nature, either aiding it or permitting it to take its course. Actually, for much of his career Pound struggles if not against Nature then against that aspect of it which he conceives as anti-Natural: the bog or swamp. There is, however, a long-delayed moment of integration and dissociation in Canto 91: "The Princess Ra-Set has climbed / to the great knees of stone" (91/ 611). Pound combines the Egyptian principles of good and evil: Ra, the god of light (whose name is identical to Pound's childhood nickname), and the evil Set (or Typhon), a swamp god. But though these deities are combined, they remain distinguished: where formerly in the selva oscura light and dark were intermingled, now splendor and darkness are clearly dissociated. The hyphen is the decisive cut which Pound is looking for; in a single stroke of mythopoesis Pound conquers the confusion of the selva. Boris de Rachewiltz notes that Pound's source for Ra-Set is an Egyptian text in which Set is liberated by Isis, now reconciled with her former enemy. Ra thus represents the sun, Set the swamp, and Isis, whom Pound associates with the moon (Isis-Luna), that aspect of the feminine which is positive insofar as it is marked by the sun's reflective light—a distinction which also appears in Bachofen. See de Rachewiltz, "Pagan and Magic Elements in Ezra Pound's Work," in Hesse, ed., pp. 180–181; Fontenrose, pp. 177–193, esp. pp. 185–187; and Bachofen, pp. 115, 27–28. For the fusion of sun and moon, masculine and feminine, within *The Cantos,* see Woodward, pp. 35–36; Woodward is much indebted to Pearlman's longer argument in *The Barb of Time.*

9 Gourmont, pp. 7–10, 14, 15, 16, 17.

10 Gourmont, pp. 21–31, 35–39, 40, 44, 45, 79.

11 Terrell, Vol. II, p. 724; Henry George Liddell and Robert Scott, *Greek-English Lexicon* (Oxford: Clarendon Press, 1961), p. 1803.

12 Gourmont, p. 53. Compare Pound's "Portrait d'Une Femme," in which sterile and usurious femininity is evoked as a "Sargasso Sea." Ernest Jones notes that Freud, the discoverer (or inventor) of the castration complex, was interested in his early career in solving the riddle of the sex of eels. See Jones, Vol. I, p. 38.

13 See Derrida, "White Mythology," pp. 209–217. Derrida's discussion of *usure* situates itself within the context of late nineteenth-century French literary aesthetics, a context which includes Remy de Gourmont and even Pound. Derrida opens with a critique of Anatole France's *Le Jardin d'Epicure,* in which France terms metaphysics "white mythology," and in which he argues that all abstract and metaphysical words and ideas are metaphorical and usurious substitutes for originally concrete images and words. They are, he says, essentially dead metaphors, words from which all actual and concrete meaning has been removed. Such words are like worn coins whose images ("heads") have been effaced and whose value, through a kind of erosion (*usure*), has been reduced nearly to nothing. The same assumptions about concrete language, the same distrust of metaphorical abstraction, and the

same metaphorical equation between language and coining, appear in Gourmont and Pound. See Sieburth, 2, pp. 67, 76, and Pound, SP, p. 361.

14 Pound, "Non sacrificate ad uno spirito che non vi appartiene," *Meridiano di Roma*, V (28 Jan. 1940), p. 1. In a letter of March 11, 1940 to T. S. Eliot, Pound speaks of the Near and Middle East as an objectionable "middle" cultural zone between two distinct cultural entities: "It is the neither east nor west that is lousy." See Kimpel and Eaves, 2, p. 58.

15 According to Kimpel and Eaves, Von Tirpitz refers to the English and probably the Jews. They also quote a letter in which Pound warns of the "individual charm and great plausibility" of certain Jews. See "Ezra Pound's Anti-Semitism," p. 65.

16 Marianne Moore, quoted in Dekker, p. 93.

17 See Flory, p. 11, and Wilhelm, 2, p. 85. A further and unrecognized ambivalence appears in the Cavalcanti essay, in which Pound, contrasting the physical health and moderation of Provence with the Hebrew and "Hindoo" (LE, 150) diseases of "anti-flesh" (LE, 154), associates the former with "the bare wall" (LE, 151) and the latter with "bulbous" (LE, 151), ornamental, and "niggled sculpture" (LE, 150). Asceticism and material excess hardly fit. Nor does Pound's association of Bengalese temples comport with Indian asceticism and a Gandhian hatred of the body; an earlier reference to erotic Indian temples in PD suggests that Pound was aware that the "niggled" Bengalese sculpture to which he refers celebrates the jungle-like tangle of promiscuous sexuality. To complete the paradox, Pound attributes the healthy, clean, but nonetheless restrained physicality of Provence to geographical aridity: "Perhaps out of a sand-swept country, the need of interior harmony" (LE, 151). But Pound never makes the same claims for the desert-dwelling Jews.

18 John D. Sinclair, trans., *The Divine Comedy of Dante Alighieri*, Vol. III, *Paradiso* (London: Oxford Univ. Press, 1948), Canto 9, ll. 104–107, pp. 136–137.

19 Alexander, p. 59; Makin, pp. 170, 246.

20 In his essay on Arnaut Daniel, Pound refers to the troubadour's "XVIth Canto," which contains "the classic reference to the Palux Laerna" (LE, 142). See LE, pp. 142, 143, 144.

21 Surette, 3, pp. 60–62; 1, p. 419.

22 See Surette, 1, pp. 420, 421; Mead, p. 169.

23 The phrase derives from the "Simonian" system of Irenaeus. See Mead, p. 169.

24 Quoted in Surette, 3, p. 30.

25 The covertly sacrificial significance of the Circe episode may be inferred from Pound's mention in Canto 47 of the herb "Molü" (47/ 237) or *moly* which in Homer is given to Odysseus by Hermes as a magical protection against Circe's charms. In Canto 53 Pound compares *moly* to the Chinese "Tsing-mo" (53/ 267), which David Gordon describes tautologically as a herb that is "only used in sacrifices because of its sacred nature." See Gordon, 3, p. 127.

26 Many of the conclusions reached in this chapter find support in a recent article by Angela Elliott. She points out that Pound's beloved goddesses Kuanon and Isis, whom he combines in the luminous syncretic figure Isis Kuanon, are both cognate with the Virgin Mary. These beneficent figures are also associated with light and even the *logos;* each is, to quote Madame Blavatsky, one of the "female Logoi," or else the "energy" of the *logos* as it activates material Nature. Hence their association with the moon. Another version of the feminine in its exalted form is the Princess Ra-Set, who appears in Canto 91, and who signifies the fusion of the masculine (solar) and feminine (lunar) principles. In further confirmation of the links we have established between women, Jews, and the Semitic world, Elliott shows that Pound may have partly derived his conception of divine femininity from Islamic and especially Jewish mystical sources. In certain texts of Arab mysticism God is incarnate in women, a notion which Pound believed had influenced the troubadours. Yet Pound was probably more indebted to the Jewish Zohar, a Kabbalistic text, for the idea of the feminine principle as the "Shekhinah." Associated with light and the

moon, and appearing in unredeemed and redeemed form, the Shekhinah achieves redemption only through reunion and reconciliation with the masculine principle. Zothar, identified with the confusion of the jungle in Canto 20, may represent the Shekhinah in its "exile," as Isis represents it in its redemption. Elliott also suggests that some might find it odd that Pound, "notorious" for his anti-Semitism, should rely on a Jewish text in *The Cantos*, and especially for the purpose of promoting matriarchal religion; but this seems less strange in view of the constant resemblance in his works between women and the Jews. The strength of Elliott's essay is in showing that the late Pound sought to eliminate "sexism" and to correct patriarchal values in his theology. However, in relying on such mystical catchphrases as the "unredeemed feminine" and the "fusion" of sun and moon, she ignores the prior and largely concealed violence which underlies such "redemptive" syntheses and which finally undermines their theological liberalism. See Elliott, pp. 327–356.

27 Zielinski, 1, pp. 19–22. In Rosenberg's Nazi mythology the luminous, patriarchal, and authentically "Greek" Zeus and Apollo defeat the dark, matriarchal, and chthonic deities of the Near East. See Reich, pp. 85–88, 91–95. It is also interesting that in Canto 85 Pound alludes to Orestes' trial for the crime of matricide in the *Eumenides*. The trial was decided in his favor by the vote of the patriarchal Athena, mentioned in Canto 87, p. 571.

28 The Homeric *Hymn to Apollo*, which Pound undoubtedly knew, contains the earliest known record of Apollo's combat with a dragon at Delphi. Having gone to Delphi to lay the foundations of his temple, Apollo fought a she dragon (*drakaina*) beside a spring and killed her with an arrow from his bow. Though still the victim of Apollo, in later versions of the myth the dragon is generally male and is called Python. This myth encompasses the idea of demonic parthenogenesis, the precise opposite of Poundian, Apollonian, and patriarchal values: the Delphian *drakaina* has in her keeping Python's cognate figure, the terrible Typhon, to whom Hera, with the assistance of Ge, the Earth-Mother, gave birth by parthenogenesis in envy of Zeus' androgenesis of Athena, and whose slayer is Apollo, god of light. In view of Pound's fear and distrust of the pre-agricultural chthonian powers, and his obsessive horror of putrefaction, it is worth noting that in some myths Python is the son of Ge, and that the name Python derives from the Greek *pythein*, meaning to rot, and referring to the rotting corpse of the sacrificed serpent. According to Joseph Fontenrose, just as the divine hero Apollo is related to Hercules in his various manifestations, so Python is linked not only to Typhon but more remotely to the monstrous Geryon and the Hydra. These are variants within a comprehensive "combat myth" which celebrates the victory of cosmos over the forces of death and chaos, the "dragon enemy." It would be a mistake, however, to interpret Pound's use of these myths transhistorically and thus mythically, rather than giving prominence to their immediate historical context and significance. See Fontenrose, pp. 13–15, 18, 21–22, 47–49, 59, 71–72, 78, 82, 91–93, 95, 217, 228–230, 334, 337, 356–358.

29 See Pound, Canto 99, p. 701, concerning the evil influence of Buddhists and Taoists on the Chinese masses: "But your females like to burn incense / and buzz round in crowds and processions. . . ."

30 Pound, RB, pp. 3, 17, 21, 43, 88, 208, 246; L, p. 346.

31 Brooke-Rose, p. 149; Trachtenberg, p. 98. In his correspondence of the 1950s, Pound repeatedly charges the Jews with pushing drugs to the young. His letters and the Pisan *Cantos* also refer to the Jew as an extraneous, dangerous, and yet often necessary creative "stimulant" for the otherwise stupefied *goyim*. See Kimpel and Eaves, 2, p. 65.

32 Brooke-Rose, p. 149; Trachtenberg, p. 98.

33 De Rachewiltz, "Pagan and Magic Elements in Ezra Pound's Works," in Hesse, ed., p. 177.

34 Pound, quoted in de Rachewiltz, "Pagan and Magic Elements in Ezra Pound's Works," p. 180.

35 William Bowen Sarles describes bacteria as "microscopic, unicellular fungi of the class Schizomycetes; they contain no clorophyll, and reproduce asexually by fission." He goes on to list the bacillus among the shapes of "true bacteria," which

would imply that bacilli are also a form of fungi. Martin Frobisher too speaks of "fission fungi or bacteria," which would include bacilli. On the other hand, Florene Kelly and K. Eileen Hite refer to bacteria as being on the borderline between true fungi, which include bread moulds and protozoa. But these problems of definition can only serve to reinforce the monstrousness of bacilli and other related microorganisms in Pound's eyes. See Sarles et. al., p. 3; Frobisher, p. 32; Kelly and Hite, p. 12.

Chapter Seventeen: Indeterminacy and Crisis, II: The Tangle of Passion and Luxury

1 Pound, pp. 216–217, quoting from "Pastiche: The Regional. XV," *New Age*, 8 Jan. 1920.

2 Jo Brantley Berryman believes that Pound succeeds in performing this dissociation by means of the phrase "simplex munditiis" ("plain in her neatness," simple elegance, Horace, *Odes* I, 5), which he applies to the "trim-coifed" (1/ 3) Circe in Canto 80, p. 494. According to Berryman, just as Pound defines two Circes good and bad, so he distinguishes elegance in the sense of simplicity and purity from bad elegance, namely luxurious or unnecessary embellishment, whether in economics or writing. Thus the following lines from Canto 80 represent a "whole set" of economic and linguistic "values": "To communicate and then stop, that is the law of discourse / To go far and come to an end / simplex munditiis, as the hair of Circe / perhaps without the munditiis / as the difference between the title page in old Legge / and some of the elegant fancy work." Actually, far from clarifying the categorical values or "laws" to which Berryman and Pound refer, this passage undermines them through its equivocation. Undoubtedly aware that "simplex munditiis" might be construed as a redundancy, and thus marked by the very verbal excess which it condemns, Pound cannot decide at what point his own communication should come to a stop before generating its own needless supplementation of meaning: the word "munditiis" is perhaps superfluous. Nor does Pound offer a definition of elegance or simplicity, much less a law. Instead, he complicates the matter through a perhaps necessary analogy, in which the presumed principle of simplicity is illustrated in terms of a difference which is not itself defined by any prior principle. Attempting to be simple, Pound has added to, supplemented his discourse with difference—a process of analogy and metaphor which might be indefinitely extended. This example opens up a question which these and other chapters explore, namely the relation between usury and luxury on the one hand and the endless proliferation of Pound's language on the other. See Berryman, pp. 18–19.

3 Pound, quoted in Flory, p. 260, from Hall, pp. 22–51.

4 Ruskin, *The Works of John Ruskin,* ed. E. T. Cook and Alexander Wedderburn (London: George Allen, 1903–1912), Vol. 8, pp. 27–53.

5 Pound, "Non sacrificate ad uno spirito che non vi appartiene," *Meridiano di Roma,* V (28 Jan., 1940), p. 1.

6 Pound, ABC, pp. 33, 35; GK, pp. 21, 57, 98. See also Pound on the category of "donative works" in SP, pp. 25, 30.

7 Ruskin, *Works,* Vol. 17, pp. 164–165.

8 For the notion of metaphor as a kind of borrowing, see César Chesnau Du Marsais, *Traité des tropes,* Ch. 2, X, quoted in Derrida, "White Mythology," p. 253.

9 Ruskin, *Works,* Vol. 17, pp. 208–210.

10 Pound, "Ecclesia," *Townsman,* 2 (Nov., 1939), p. 4; "Problemi da risolvere," *Meridiano di Roma,* VIII (14 Feb. 1943), p. 1. See especially Pound's 1957 letter to R. McNair Wilson, in the Beinecke Rare Book and Manuscript Library, Yale University: "Any mass of savage records, hoisted to word of God, wd / be poisonous. Interpretation, using text as authority for something other than plain meaning of the words." Modern Jews are equally blameworthy in taking Gentile names, another violation of Cheng Ming to which Pound objects in the broadcasts. For the Jew to "change" (RB, 297) his name violates the patriarchal and linguistic law of the "proper," as when "Mrs. Rabinovitch" becomes "Mrs. Perkins" (RB, 257), and Henry Levy Lawson becomes Lord Burnham. The English, says Pound, should con-

sider the "patronymics of some of . . . [their] peers; I mean the names that they
started life with, or that their parents started life with" (RB, 257). The Jews' linguistic desecrations extend beyond writing to the spoken word. Disturbed by the disappearance of "pure" Indian dialects on the North American continent, which perhaps
forebodes the fate of American English, Pound remarks that Henry James "already
noticed a change in New York phonetics" (RB, 189). Pound probably alludes to
those passages in *The American Scene* in which James, feeling a profound sense of
"dispossession" in confronting the "Hebrew conquest of New York," discusses the
effect upon American speech of the great wave of European immigrants, specifically
the Jews. See James, pp. 86, 132, 138–139. Céline affords another and in some ways
similar example of literary anti-Semitism, charging that the Jews not only control but
corrupt French literature through their conspiratorial cliquishness, inveterate abstraction, empty stylistic formalism, indifference to the vitality of spoken language, and
lack of authentic and spontaneous feeling. See Céline, 1, pp. 68–69, 166–170, 172,
175, 177, 178–179, 183–184, 190, 196, 218.

11 Glossing this and other passages by Pound, Andrew Parker quotes Maurice
Blanchot's statement that the elimination of the Jews would require not merely their
extermination but the obliteration of their written traces. See Parker, p. 103.

12 Parker, pp. 113, 114, 115, 118–119, 120.

13 This mermaid is "gold" in earlier editions, "cold" in that of 1972; see
Wilhelm, 2, pp. 179–180; Bacigalupo, p. 482, accepts "gold."

14 Dante, *The Divine Comedy of Dante Alighieri*, trans. John D. Sinclair, Vol.
I, *Inferno* (New York: Oxford, 1948), Canto 17, ll. 19–20: "Come tal volta stanno a
riva i burchi / che parte sono in acqua e parte in terra. . . ."

15 James Wilhelm and Bacigalupo note that "anthesis" is a crux, since the
printed version differs from the typescript, which gives "antithesis." Though he
senses the poet's perceptual disturbance in this passage, Wilhelm assumes that "Antithesis" is correct, apparently believing that Geryon or Fraud must be the opposite
of Veritas. Bacigalupo finds "antithesis" more persuasive than "anthesis" on the
same grounds, but notes that the connection between "splendour" and vegetation is
frequent in Pound, and that "anthesis" therefore "makes some sense." He also notes
that Pound did not care to correct this apparent error in the galleys of *Drafts and
Fragments*. In my opinion, "anthesis" makes as much or more sense than "antithesis," since it fits into the pattern which Bacigalupo notes, that of "inversion." See
Bacigalupo, p. 483, and Wilhelm, 2, pp. 179–180.

16 De Rachewiltz, 1, pp. 259–260, 243–244, 301, 305–306.

17 Pound's view of his own marriage was perhaps complicated by Gourmont's
ambiguous or at least extremely flexible interpretation of sexual promiscuity and the
human couple in *The Natural Philosophy of Love* (Pound's guide to "natural"
conduct). See Gourmont, pp. 199–218.

18 See Bacigalupo, p. 59, quoting D. G. Bridson, "Interview with Ezra Pound,"
in *New Directions in Prose and Poetry*, 17 (1961), p. 172. See also Pound, quoted in
Sieburth, 2, pp. 120–121, Canto 46, p. 231, where Helen's attributes are transferred
to usury, and pp. 187, 262.

Chapter Eighteen: Profanation

1 Pound refers to the Virgin Mary's fans "in the Easter Mass at Siena" in a
discussion of the anti-Semitic Zielinski in RB, p. 411.

2 Since each is engaged in fraud, the Jewish usurer and the Cid are mimetic
doubles in Canto 3: it is impossible to justify one or the other's actions without
arbitrary favoritism. In the end, though, Pound dissociates the Cid and the usurer as
examples respectively of good and bad fraud, heroic and ignoble action. The basis of
this distinction lies not in logic but in the Cid's very act of predation against the Jews.
Through this act, which the community accepts and by which it benefits, the Jews are
transformed into scapegoats and identified with fraud in its unacceptable form;
without this act of violence, there would be no distinction between good and bad
fraud. According to Girard, the scapegoat substitutes for an object which might

originally have suffered the violence of the community. It is interesting that the Cid's victimization of the Jews takes place while he himself is an outlaw and outcast charged (mistakenly) with crimes against his king. In another sense the Cid is a folk hero who can do no wrong, whose ignoble means are justified by noble ends, namely the good of the community. To borrow a distinction of Norman O. Brown's, the Cid is the "good" Hermes, a distributor of wealth, while the Jew is the "bad" Hermes of the marketplace, a greedy shyster. See Brown, *passim.*

3 The anti-usurious Monte dei Paschi, the "New Mountain" erected in Canto 42, anticipates not only Mussolini but the King's Mountain (Königsberg) from which Hitler, in Canto 51, announces banking reforms and a new mode of existence for the "folk" mentioned in Cantos 42–44.

4 St. George figures as the enemy of the Jewish dragon in the anti-Semitic propaganda of the British Imperial Fascist League. See Lebzelter, p. 81. St. George also tallies with Simone Martini's painting of the triumphant Sienese warrior Guidoriccio da Folignano in Canto 52, p. 258: "Riccio on his horse rides still to Montepulciano." Guidoriccio in turn links up with the resurgent ("rides still") modern condottiere and dragon-killer Mussolini.

5 Girard, "The Plague in Literature and Myth," in Girard, 3, p. 139.

6 Girard, 2, p. 57. In "Imaginary Letters," Pound's thinly disguised alter ego Walter Villerant (a name suggestive of ranting and vilification) surveys the same London milieu as appears in the Hell *Cantos*: "Stupidity is a pest, a bacillus, an infection, a raging lion that does not stay in one place but perambulates. When two fools meet, a third springs up instanter between them, a composite worse than either begetter" (PD, 64). Here we have imagery of massive infection, violence ("a raging lion"), doubles ("two fools"), generation ("begetter"), and a monstrous mixture ("composite").

Chapter Nineteen: "Nothing Can Save You": The Sacrifice

1 Adorno, "Anti-Semitism and Fascist Propaganda," in Simmel, ed., p. 136; Horkheimer and Adorno, p. 186. Although not openly interested in ritual murder, Maurras makes it clear that the beauty, hierarchy, and order of his goddess France depend on sacrifice: "The whole world would be less good if it contained fewer mysterious victims whose sacrifice contributed to its perfection." Such victimization remains mysterious only if the victims—the lower classes and the Jews—fail to grasp its arbitrariness. One sees why Maurras described democracy as false; it was, he said, "not prepared to sacrifice anyone." Similarly, in *Mein Kampf* the new Nazi Germany is based on the necessity of sacrifice; the immorality of democracy and the Jews is that both deny this great sacrificial law. One recalls Pound's idea that sacrifice might have educative value in a degraded democratic society, and his appeal to Artemis, a figure reminiscent of Maurras's goddess France and Hitler's "cruel queen" of wisdom. Nor does Pound, any more than his fellow fascists, confine sacrifice to the Jews. For him, Italian Fascism is a "faith" ("fede," 78/ 478) whose most devout practitioners will gladly sacrifice themselves. To quote the "commandante della piazza" in Canto 41: "Noi ci facciam sgannar [scannar] per Mussolini [we would let ourselves be butchered for Mussolini]" (41/ 202). See Maurras, 3, p. 214; Volpe, pp. 96, 118; Nolte, p. 218, 219, 529; Hitler, pp. 151, 301, 313–314, 132; and Hitler, quoted in Nolte, p. 525.

2 Baumann, pp. 29, 33; Sister Bernetta Quinn, *Motive and Method in The Cantos of Ezra Pound*, pp. 83–85, quoted in Baumann, p. 19.

3 According to H. G. Creel, *li* originally meant "to sacrifice"; one sacrificed in order to obtain the gods' blessings. Confucius later conceived of *li* as "the whole complex of conventional and social usage, which he endowed with a *moral* connotation. Thus combined, the sanctions of morality and courtesy reinforced each other." See Creel, pp. 32–34, and Baller, ed., p. 100.

4 A good illustration of how ritual promotes respect for close definition is in Canto 52, pp. 259–260, in the instructions given to the inspector of dye-works. In the *Yüeh Ling* (Section II, Part III, 9) it is necessary to maintain close definition of the

colors because the dyers "furnish the materials for the robes used at the sacrifices in the suburbs and ancestral temple; for flags and their ornaments; and for marking the different degrees of rank as high or low." See *Li Ki: Book of Rites,* Vol. I, trans. James Legge (Hyde Park, N.Y.: University Press Books, 1967), p. 278. Pound's source was the translation of S. Couvreur, S. J., Vol. I, p. 368.

5 Vasse, p. 256; Dekker, p. 35.

6 Flory, p. 163; Smith, p. 58.

7 Dekker, p. 35; Vasse, pp. 106–107; Pearlman, p. 37.

8 Pearlman, 1, p. 136. See also Nassar, pp. 66–67.

9 These sacrificial acts performed by animals also appear in the fourth book of the *Li Ki (Yüeh Ling).* Legge's gloss on the otter's sacrifice applies to all the other instances: "What is said about the otter is simply a superstitious misinterpretation of its habit of eating only a small part of its prey, and leaving the rest on the bank." See Legge, ed., pp. 251, 283–284, 292; Couvreur, Vol. I, pp. 332, 373, 385.

10 Pearlman, 1, pp. 50–51, 123, 118. Pearlman also sees a connection between Pound's idea of Nature and Emerson's idea of compensation. According to James J. Wilhelm, Pound's insistence on preserving the "beauty of nature" not only qualifies him as a forerunner of contemporary environmentalism and the ecology movement but serves as evidence of his liberalism. This statement is based on the mistaken notion that liberalism and ecology go hand in hand. This century's greatest and most effective political proponent of ecology was probably Adolf Hitler, whose mystified conception of retributive Nature resembles Pound's. See Wilhelm, 1, p. 158. On Nazi environmentalism and the return to the soil, see Alan Cassels, "Janus: The Two Faces of Fascism," p. 87n; Wolfgang Sauer, "National Socialism: Totalitarianism or Fascism?", p. 106; Henry A. Turner, Jr., "Fascism and Modernization," pp. 122–123, 136–138n, in Turner, ed.

11 Pearlman, 1, p. 277. Pound's "ethical" conception of Nature sometimes leads to poetic absurdity. Imprisoned at Pisa, Pound remains certain of never having violated the natural order or of having failed to act in "due season": "neither Eos nor Hesperus [the morning and evening stars] has suffered wrong at my hands" (79/488). After the violence and anti-Semitism of *The Cantos* and radio broadcasts, such self-justifications are empty and irrelevant. Pound often verges on ethical vacuity, but in this case he is in the very center of it.

12 Pearlman makes it clear that Canto 30 has ultimately to do with human violence. See *The Barb of Time,* p. 119.

13 One can say of Pound what Adorno says of Spengler's mythical glorification of Fate and Cosmos in *The Decline of the West:* "The return of what is always the same, in which such a doctrine of fate terminates, is . . . nothing but the perpetual reproduction of man's guilt toward man. The concept of fate, which subjects man to blind domination [by Nature or cosmos] reflects the domination of man toward man. Whenever Spengler speaks of fate he means the subjection of one group by another." See *Prisms,* p. 70. See also Bernstein, pp. 100, 113. It is also worth noting that *The Cantos* endorse the fatalism of the later, disappointed Mussolini. Canto 86 contains the phrase "All that has been, is as it should have been" (86/564), while in Canto 87 Pound quotes an unidentified source: " 'What has been should have' " (87/572). According to Nicholls, pp. 183, 250n, these lines render the opening passage of Mussolini's *Notebook of Thoughts in Ponza and La Maddalena,* written toward the end of Il Duce's life, and translated by Pound in *Edge,* 7 (March, 1957), pp. 10–26, under the title "In Captivity: Notebook of Thoughts in Ponza and La Maddalena." The passage reads: "All that has happened, should have. Had it been contrary to what should have been, it would not have happened." However, while such fatalism is characteristic of many versions of fascist thinking, it is difficult to square with Mussolini's (and Pound's) tendency in more optimistic moments to emphasize the power of the will to form circumstance and its freedom from deterministic schemes.

14 Pearlman, 1, pp. 118–120, 136. The *Li Ki* contains some seemingly ecological prescriptions. See Legge, ed., Vol. 1, pp. 255, 256, 260, 270, 271, 273; Couvreur, I, pp. 336, 337, 344, 356, 357, 360.

15 Davis, p. 180, points out that this lie appears in the *Handbuch der*

Judenfrage by Theodore Fritsch (who incidentally may have coined the term anti-Semitism). Pound's source, however, was *Liberation*, published in Asheville, North Carolina, as noted by Lander, p. 84. Céline relies on the same false evidence in *L'École des cadavres*, p. 206.

16 Pound attacks numerous munitions-makers and gun-sellers, including the Harvey United States Steel Co., Vickers-Armstrong (England), Schneider-Creusot (France), Krupp (Germany), and Mitsui (Japan). However, he reserves his deepest hatred for the Greek-born international gun-seller Sir Basil Zaharoff, whom Pound without evidence assumes to be Jewish. Zaharoff figures in *The Cantos* as the endlessly opportunistic Zenos ("foreigner") Metevsky, whose true homeland is wherever he can do business. Metevsky is the very type of the demonic, deracinated, "cosmopolitan" Jew. For Zaharoff and Metevsky, see Davis, pp. 19, 22, 25, 55, 128. See also Pound, SP, pp. 222, 267; Canto 18, pp. 80–82; Canto 38, pp. 187, 188, 191; Canto 93, p. 627.

17 Terrell, Vol. I, p. 201; see also Chace, p. 80. On the *Judensau,* see Trachtenberg, pp. 26, 47, 218.

18 See for instance the casual approach of Alexander, p. 184. It may be relevant to this passage that the pig had great importance in the Eleusinian mysteries, which are central to Pound's conception of the true European religion, and to which he refers in Canto 52 only a few lines before his translation of the *Book of Rites.* The commonest of sacrificial animals, the pig figured on the autonomous coinage of Eleusis as the sign and symbol of her mysteries, in short, as a kind of totemic animal at once adored and reviled. During the rite of purification at Eleusis each participant had with him his own *pharmakos* or pig, driving it before him, and finally bathing with it in the sea. To quote Jane Harrison, the "pig of purification was itself purified." Morever, in the lesser Eleusinia the "principal rites" of the first stages of initation "consisted in the sacrifice of a sow," which the "mystae" had previously purified by washing in the Cantharus River. See Harrison, pp. 152–153; William Smith, ed., p. 453.

19 The lines from Canto 74 are the focus of critical disagreement between A. D. Moody and Bryant Knox, whose interpretation I basically accept. See Knox, p. 76; Moody, pp. 58, 70.

20 Upward, 2, pp. 98, 99, 131, 109, 116, 140, 103, 119, 59, 139–142, 228–229.

21 The Chinese *Cantos* are based largely on the chronicle of the eighteenth-century French Jesuit Joseph de Mailla, who ignores as Pound does the extent to which Confucianism incorporates Taoism and Buddhism. See Gordon, 4, p. 397; Kenner, 3, p. 456.

22 John Lauber also finds the "equivalent" of the Jews in the Buddhists and Taoists of the Chinese *Cantos.* See Lauber, p. 11.

23 For the quotations from *The Cantos* in this paragraph, see 54/280, 288; 98/687; 99/702, 696; 54/288.

24 Terrell, Vol. II, pp. 630, 631, 638, 640.

25 Baller, pp. 83, 84, 86–87, 125. The "hochang" or Buddhists also resemble the Jews not only in their pursuit of nullity and emptiness but also, again paradoxically, in their overproduction. Just as the Jews are characterized as "spawn" and "hordes" of various sorts, so the "hochang" breed "like rabbits / half a million in one province only" (56/302). See Durant, p. 137.

26 Girard, "The Plague in Literature and Myth," in Girard, 3, p. 136.

27 The same strategy of false denial appears in Hitler and in the American reactionary and right-wing agitator. See Hitler, p. 58, and Lowenthal and Guterman, pp. 99, 4–8.

28 Stock, 3, p. 479, notes that with the approach of war Pound took an increasing interest in Jewish matters and read more and more anti-Semitic tracts, one of which advocated Mosley's proposal that the Jews be sent to Madagascar. Actually, the plan originates with Hitler. For the Madagascar scheme, see Lebzelter, pp. 61–62, 79–80, 97; Poliakov, 1, p. 309.

29 The index to the broadcasts gives no reference for Finkelstein.

30 Céline's works of the late 1930s and early 1940s refer constantly to the moral, political, cultural, and biological degeneracy which the Jews have supposedly inflicted on France. See Céline, 1, pp. 88, 90; 2, pp. 80, 82; 3, p. 68; these are only a few examples. Céline refers to the "suicide" of the French nation in *L'École des cadavres* (1938), pp. 88, 91. He claims that France will commit suicide if it enters the next war, for its victory will benefit only the Jews, while the Germans, with their powerful war-machine and sense of mission, also stand a good chance of winning. Hence France should remain neutral or, as Pound quotes from *L'École* in RB, p. 128, the next war will be the "last ONE." See Céline, 2, pp. 91, 94.

31 See McCarthy, 1, pp. 139–169, esp. pp. 153–155, 161. Not only are Céline's anti-Semitic accusations identical to Pound's, his relation to the Jews reveals mimetic features similar to those discussed in Part Four.

32 Knapp, pp. 93, 108, and pp. 124, 127, quoting Céline, 3, pp. 124, 127.

33 Pound's gnashing of teeth is probably inspired by Céline, 2, p. 91.

34 André Gide viewed *Bagatelles* as a "stylistic exercise, a parody of anti-Semitism." Patrick McCarthy, though he acknowledges the "overwhelming" anti-Semitism of Céline's pamphlets, wonders whether *Bagatelles*, with all its exaggeration, is to be taken seriously. Jeffrey Mehlman argues correctly that Céline's anti-Semitism is no "mask," and in any case Pound had no doubts about his meaning. See Mehlman, pp. 64, 127n; McCarthy, pp. 139, 143, 168.

35 Céline, quoted in Cohn, 1, p. 250. The original passages may be found in Céline, 1, pp. 279, 285, 288–289.

36 In Canto 42 the Sienese, with the aid of their Prince (Ferdinand II), intend to "erect a New Mountain" (42/ 211) or bank to combat pervasive usury and taxation. Symbolizing abundance and masculine authority, this bank will lend to "folk of / ANY CONDITION" (42/ 211) and is founded on "the whole will of the people" (43/ 218), while Ferdinand himself is associated with the Holy Roman Empire ("Ferd. I [II] / Roman Emperor as elected," 43/ 216). As a result of these reforms, the pasture lands are saved, order is restored, and the "grass [is] nowhere out of place" (43/ 219). In Canto 51, likewise, Hitler is a bank reformer (like Mussolini) and a modern day version of the Holy Roman Emperor. Speaking (through his minister Rudolf Hess) from Königsberg, the King's Mount, perhaps the very source from which "seed" are "blown" (92/ 618) in Canto 92, he defines a "modus vivendi" for the folk or "volkern" and sees to it that the "grass" —meaning both Nature and the people—is "nowhere out of place" (51/ 251). Later, in Canto 52, Pound praises the anti-usurious legislation of Hjalmar Schacht, Hitler's finance minister, and in Canto 90 Hitler appears as a bringer of "rain" (90/ 606) to the parched multitudes of Europe. Another link with fascism appears in Pound's identification of the Sienese reforms with the cause of youth; the Monte dei Paschi is opposed to the idea that "to be young is to suffer. / Be old and be past that" (42/ 213). Fascism too presented itself (as Pound's broadcasts reveal) as a young man's movement, opposing energetic youth to the moribund older generation. In Canto 44 we find these lines: "so that the echo turned back on my mind: Pavia: / Saw cities move in one figure, Vicenza, as depicted / San Zeno by Adige . . ." (42/ 213). This is no doubt an historically tele-scoped vision of the whole of Italy (and even the whole of Europe) swept by eco-nomic and social reforms, one of which is the placing of "the guilds under common tribunal" (44/ 227), in short the disinterested and mediating state: Pound, with the benefit of hindsight (which here masquerades as prophetic foresight) views the re-forms of Pietro Leopoldo of Tuscany in the eighteenth century as a prefiguration first of Napoleon's radical and centralizing innovations in Northern Italy and then of Italian Fascism and corporatism. In Canto 42 is the rhetorical question: "Have you a place on the Hill, sir?" (42/ 214). The emphasis on "place" picks up the idea of Italian Fascist *gerarchia* or hierarchy. Again, in Canto 44 we learn that Ferdinand III of Tuscany "declared against exportation / thought grain was to eat" (44/ 223). This probably alludes obliquely to Mussolini's frequently announced policy of *autarchia* or autarchy, which Pound emphasized in his economic writings of the 1930s, and which Mussolini officially instituted after the sanctions resulting from his invasion of Ethiopia. However, Ferdinand's measures against importation do not conform with

his predecessor Pietro Leopoldo's policy of free trade, and Tuscany in the 1800s remained true to free trade principles, as shown by Procacci, p. 273. In Canto 43, Pound makes something of the fact that two prostitutes, presumably as a result of the economic reforms instituted in Siena, had been removed from the book of public women; these examples may thus import a familiar fascist theme which repeatedly appears in Pound's prose and broadcasts, namely the inseparable relationship between usury and the moral and biological evils of prostitution and the need to purify society of syphilis. Finally, there is an obvious similarity—to be examined in greater detail below—between the continuous mass celebrations in honor of Ferdinand III in Canto 44 and the hysterical mimetic rituals carried out by Mussolini from his balcony overlooking the Piazza Venezia. The Monte dei Paschi *Cantos* point toward the successful organization, mobilization, and nationalization of the masses along the lines of fascist cult and ritual. Fascist ritual is treated by Horkheimer, pp. 92–127 ("The Revolt of Nature"); Cassirer, pp. 277–296 ("The Technique of Modern Political Myths"); Mosse, 5, pp. 1, 4, 9, 195, 199, 203–206, 207–208, 211–212, esp. Chapter Four, "Public Festivals," pp. 73–99. Generally speaking, though, in Italian Fascism mass ritual and the "nationalization of the masses" did not have the "decisive role" which they played in Nazism. See De Felice, pp. 40, 75–76.

37 The political transcendence of merely linear or chronological time is well described by Walter Benjamin in an essay of 1940: "The awareness that they are about to make the continuum of history explode is characteristic of the revolutionary classes at the moment of their action. The great revolution [the French Revolution] introduced a new calendar. The initial day of a calendar serves as a historical time-lapse camera. And, basically, it is the same day that keeps recurring in the guise of holidays, which are days of remembrance. Thus the calendars do not measure time as clocks do; they are monuments of a historical consciousness of which not the slightest trace has been apparent in Europe for the past hundred years. In the July revolution an incident occurred which showed this consciousness still alive. On the first evening of fighting it turned out that the clocks in towers were being fired on simultaneously and independently from several places in Paris." However, Benjamin seems mistaken in suggesting that this experience had been absent in Europe for decades. The same attempt to explode the continuum of history can be found in the ritual celebrations led by the revolutionary messiahs Hitler and Mussolini, the second of whom initiated a new calendar which Pound followed. See "Theses on the Philosophy of History," in *Illuminations*, pp. 263–264.

38 See Girard, 2, pp. 166–167. Compare Pound, Canto 74, p. 448: "Where the masks come from, in the Tirol, / in the winter season / searching every house to drive out the demons."

39 The burning of Jews with the liberty tree is perhaps foreshadowed as early as Pound's caricature of "Brennbaum" in *Hugh Selwyn Mauberley*. Conjoining the German "brennen," meaning "to burn," and the German "baum," meaning "tree," Brennbaum's name evokes the arid, sunburnt desert, an environment hostile to Nature and the presumed source of his cultural sterility. Brennbaum is also burdened with the "heavy memories of Horeb and of Sinai." Horeb is the Biblical "mountain of God," where a terrified Moses heard Jehovah speak from a burning bush. One might then speculate that, for Pound, the immolation of Jews with the liberty tree unconsciously commemorates and even appeases their vengeful and fearful God Jehovah.

40 Pound to R. McNair Wilson, March, 1934, Beinecke Rare Book and Manuscript Library, Yale University.

41 When Pound refers to Hitler as a "Joan of Arc," he implicitly transforms him into an Artemis figure. The connection between Joan of Arc and Artemis lies in their common youthfulness and virginity, their love of pastoral solitude (Joan of Arc was a shepherdess and lover of forests before her military career), their associations with visionary experience, and their gift for violence and bloodshed, though for sacred ends. It is therefore appropriate that the canto in which Pound celebrates the "Lorraine girl" (91/ 617) as a visionary also contains anti-Semitic and pro-fascist themes. See Norman, p. 396.

42 Although the relationship between Dionysus and fascism figures somewhat obliquely in Canto 48, it is made explicit at the opening of Canto 74, where Mussolini is "DIGENES," a misspelling (perhaps deliberate) of "DIGONOS," the traditional epithet which Pound applies to Dionysus in Canto 48. The convergence of Mussolini and the god is all the more plausible in view of the fact that Pound often likens Mussolini to a bull, and that the bull is one of the forms taken by Dionysus. But whereas in Cantos 2 and 48 Dionysus' victims are identified with oxen, in Canto 74 the assassinated Mussolini has himself been transformed into a "bullock" (74/ 425). Strictly speaking, a bullock is a castrated young bull, but in view of the fact that Mussolini was in his sixties at the time of his assassination, he might better have been described as an ox, which refers to a castrated older bull. In any case, Mussolini's new role as victim connects him with Dionysus not in the god's aspect of conqueror or predator but as the (scape-) goat which suffered dismemberment or *sparagmos*. Pound would seem inadvertently to have suggested a truth which he never fully understood, that the participants in violence are doubles and hence potentially interchangeable as conquerors or victims: like Dionysus, Mussolini is both bull and ox (or goat). But, as A. D. Moody observes, for Pound the once-potent Mussolini is properly understood as the untouchable "solar missionary," the human repository of the sun's vitality, the virtual equivalent of the solar god of agrarian religion. As such, he has become the mistaken victim of sacrificial violence which Pound claims to reject but which, as Moody fails to recognize, he would prefer to inflict upon other, less exalted objects, chiefly the Jews. See Moody, p. 69. In Canto 48 Pound reinforces the sacrificial theme with references to solar religion and the boundary stone of agricultural civilization, the ritualistic and hierarchical order which the Jews oppose and which fascism would restore through violence. An immediately preceding passage commemorates Pound's visit to the Provençal citadel of Montségur, which in his view had been the center of a medieval solar cult, and whose destruction he blames on usurious Paris. Passing through the Provençal landscape, Pound finds relics of a decayed agrarian order: "the stair there still broken," a wheatfield, a milestone, and an "altar to Terminus" (48/ 243). Terminus is the Roman god of the boundary stone and in the broadest sense of limits, distinctions; each year the Romans sacrificed to Terminus and thus affirmed the boundaries over which the god presided. His appearance here testifies to agricultural civilization as an ideal order, the antithesis of Jewish civilization in its boundless confusion and greed. Still within the same landscape, Pound observes that the "sun cuts light against evening," and that the "light shaves grass into emerald" (48/ 243). The votive object of the Provençal cult, and the ultimate source of beauty, bounty, purity, and distinctions, the sun dissociates light from darkness, conquers the selva oscura, in a metaphorical act of violence: it "cuts." Once again Pound provides sacrifice with an illusory natural sanction. In the succeeding passage, discussed in the text, Pound embodies the sun's ordering and purifying violence in fascism. For Terminus, see William Smith, ed., p. 602; *Oxford Classical Dictionary*, ed. N.G.L. Hammond and H.H. Scullard (Oxford: Clarendon Press, 1970), p. 1045.

43 Voltaire, quoted in Poliakov, 2, Vol. III, pp. 88–89; Katz, 2, pp. 39–40; Voltaire, "Genesis," in Pound, PD, p. 183. For Wagner, see Poliakov, 2, Vol. III, p. 448, and Viereck, 2, p. 119; for Hitler's vegetarianism, see Waite, pp. 20, 28, 126.

44 Kaiser, 1, p. 15; Delitzsch, pp. 91–92.

45 Kaiser, 1, pp. 14–17; 2, pp. 31–34; John F.A. Sawyer, pp. 14–16; Clements, pp. 32–33; Delitzsch, p. 95. Kaiser, 1, p. 24n, leads one to believe that the majority of commentators find the passage not to reject sacrifice "in principle" but to be concerned with "cultic regulations connected with a particular situation."

46 Bernhard Anderson, p. 424.

47 Knight, pp. 104–105; Sawyer, p. 14.

48 The text of the Book of Isaiah is accepted as consisting of two parts, the first of which, known as First Isaiah, and comprising chapters 1–39, is mainly the work of an eighth-century prophet. Chapters 40–66 are attributed for the most part to another and even greater prophet whose real name is unrecorded and who has come to be known as Second or Deutero-Isaiah. He lived more than 150 years after his

namesake. See Bernhard Anderson, pp. 261–263. The quoted passages are from Isaiah, 40: 29–29; 41: 14.

49 See Isaiah, 48: 1–7; 52: 13–15; 53: 1–12; Bernhard Anderson, pp. 408, 411, 413, 414–427; Albright, pp. 326–333; Herbert, pp. 10–14, 240.

50 Girard, 2, pp. 293–294n. Zielinski emphasizes the violently vengeful and fanatical qualities of the Jews while insisting that "a human sacrifice cannot be reconciled with the religio-moral feeling of historic Greece." See Zielinski, 2, pp. 36, 134, 215, 216.

51 Terrell, Vol. II, p. 368.

Chapter Twenty: Pound's Gods: Contagion, Magic, and Taboo

1 For the appearance of this metaphor in proto-fascism, see Fritz Stern, pp. 3, 93. See also Nolte, pp. 170, 600n; Hitler, quoted in Poliakov, 1, p. 1.

2 No doubt because the Hebrew word *elohim* means "gods," Upward treats the Hebrew deity as singular and plural. But the Hebrew word is entirely consistent with monotheism: "The Israelites took over the Canaanite plural, *elohim* 'gods,' in the sense of 'God'." See Albright, p. 214.

3 Upward, 1, pp. 244, 240–242. The splitting of the father figure, and the identification of the bad or forbidding father with Jehovah, is characteristic of anti-Semitism. See Loewenstein, p. 31, and Loeblowitz-Lennard, p. 36.

4 See Zielinski, 2, pp. 130, 17, 217; 1, pp. 50–58.

5 See Lewis and Pound, quoted in Materer, p. 201. See also Pound in *Blast*, II, "Et Faim Saillir le Loup des Boys": "Cowardly editors threaten, / Friends fall off at the pinch, the loveliest die. / This is the path of life, this is my forest." Quoted in Flory, p. 69.

6 Pound's reference to the "directing of bullets" also has medical significance. It picks up the idea of the "magic bullet," the cure for syphilis discovered by Paul Ehrlich, whom Pound praises in the broadcasts, in which the Jews are repeatedly associated with syphilitic infections. Incidentally, Ehrlich was Jewish.

7 Quoted in Sieburth, 2, pp. 88–89, from "Pastiche. The Regional, XVII," *New Age*, 13 Nov., 1919, p. 32.

8 Sontag, pp. 39–40; Robert Parker, Chapter Eight, "Divine Vengeance and Disease," pp. 235–236.

9 Pound, "American Notes," *New English Weekly*, 11 July, 1935, pp. 245–246.

10 Canetti, p. 47. Canetti confirms our earlier view that Pound's anti-Semitism is in some ways a variation on the medieval form, in which the Jews are persecuted as devils and demons. Hitler, who speaks of the "personification of the devil" in the "living shape of the Jew," assimilates Jewish devils to hordes of bacilli, and compares his struggle against the Jewish virus and the "invisible Jewish state" to the work of Pasteur and Koch. See Cohn, 2, pp. 76, 35; 1, pp. 15, 252; Hitler, pp. 324, 58; Nolte, pp. 524, 513.

11 Quoted in Torrey, p. 166.

12 In ancient Greek culture the gods often bring madness. See Robert Parker, pp. 235, 243, 244–248. For the possible sources of Pound's statement, see Boswell's *Life of Johnson*, Vol. IV, ed. G. B. Hill and J. F. Powell (Oxford: Clarendon Press, 1934), pp. 181–182n.

Chapter Twenty-One: The God in the Crowd

1 Pound, letter to *New Age*, quoted in Hutchins, p. 84.

2 Pound's anti-paternal revolt should not be exaggerated. Like his fascism, his anti-Semitism is a "condensation of the most contradictory tendencies," namely "instinctual rebellion directed against the authorities, and the cruel suppression and punishment of this instinctual rebellion, directed against oneself." Thus the Jews represent not just Jehovah but the unconscious growth of the feminine swamp, both of which need to be overcome. Similarly, Pound identifies with the paternal authority of fascism. These tensions appear in the radio broadcasts, where Pound praises

fascist youth against "old bleeders" (Jews and moribund politicians) (RB, 16, 17, 18, 199), who, like Freud's primal father, "want all the young gals for themselves" (RB, 16), and in which he is the wise patriarch: "Come back and tell Papa" (RB, 200, 162). See Fenichel, "Elements of a Psycho-Analytic Theory of Anti-Semitism," in Simmel, ed., p. 20; for the fascist cult of youth, see Mosse, 3, pp. 18–19.

3 Berliner, "On Some Religious Motives of Anti-Semitism," in Simmel, ed., p. 79.

4 Plutarch, quoted in Surette, 3, pp. 238–239.

5 Upward, 2, pp. 4, 141–142, 307–308; Zielinski, 1, pp. 6–11. The man-god idea appears in Pound as early as the poem "Anima Sola" from *A Lume Spento* (1908); Pound calls himself "a weird untamed" and invokes "Loneliness" as "Thou cup of the God-man's own" (CEP, 20).

6 Stock, 3, p. 323; Bacigalupo, pp. 33–34. For a detailed discussion of the *Little Review* calendar, see Read, pp. 35–45.

7 Pound, quoted in Materer, 1, p. 22.

8 Pound, quoted in Bacigalupo, p. 33n.

9 By identifying himself with Apollonius, Pound satisfies his vanity while indirectly disclaiming responsibility for crimes for which he had been charged by the U.S. government. Endowed with absolute purity of conscience and superhuman powers of divination, Apollonius had no doubts about his divine status and his messianic mission in the Roman world. His birth was miraculous, and at his death he reportedly ascended into heaven. As Pound is obsessed with ridding the world of plagues, Apollonius saved Ephesus from plague by locating its source in a demon disguised first as a beggar and then as a dog. Although Apollonius repeatedly disavowed animal and human sacrifice, the stoning of the dog appears to be a covert version of the socially purifying murder of the *pharmakos*. During his trial at Rome, Apollonius stood accused of conspiracy against Domitian and, most interesting in view of Pound's covert sacrificial impulse in the broadcasts, of the sacrifice of an Arcadian boy. But Apollonius proved himself innocent of conspiracy and bloodshed and turned the charges against his accusers: not Apollonius but Domitian was "convicted." Pound holds the same attitude towards Roosevelt, and in the later *Cantos* he ostentatiously disavows blood sacrifice while affirming the purity of his conscience. Pound even finds an analogy between Apollonius' tormentors and his own Jewish "enemies." Apollonius' rival was the philosopher Euphrates, who preferred money to wisdom, and who conspired to bring Apollonius to trial in Rome. In Canto 94 Pound transforms him into an honorary Jew, the "schnorrer Euphrates" (94/ 640). After his trial Apollonius returned to Greece in triumph and was joined by his faithful "Band." One thinks of Pound's much less triumphant return to Italy and his establishment, beginning at St. Elizabeths, of his own cult. See Philostratus, Vol. I, pp. 13, 269, 363, 367, 457, 503; Vol. II, pp. 63, 157, 187, 257, 281, 283, 315, 317, 323, 333–339, 371, 385, 401.

10 Pound, quoted in Chace, pp. 10–11, from *Poetry*, 5 (Oct. 1914), pp. 29–30.

11 Girard, "Strategies of Madness—Nietzsche, Wagner, Dostoyevsky," in Girard, 3, p. 70.

12 For Nietzsche's messianism, see Girard, "Strategies of Madness," *passim*; Nietzsche, quoted in Viereck, 2, p. 9.

13 See Wagner, quoted in Poliakov, 2, Vol. III, pp. 449–450.

14 In *The Divine Mystery*, pp. 9, 35, the Divine Man is both sacred and accursed, in short "*tapu*" or taboo, like the scapegoat victim.

15 Upward, 2, p. 287. Upward's conception of the Jews' intimacy with their deity tallies with Freud's views in *Moses and Monotheism*, p. 134.

16 See Stock, 3, pp. 468–469, on Pound's disappointment and depression on his trip to America; see pp. 510–511, on the response of the Italian Fascist ministers to Pound. See also Heymann, pp. 99, 102.

17 Pound, quoted in Norman, p. 360.

18 Dr. Gilbert's testimony is quoted in Norman, pp. 411–412.

19 Pound, quoted in Chace, pp. 10–11, from *Poetry*, 5 (Oct. 1914), pp. 29–30.

20 Girard, "Strategies of Madness," pp. 72–73.

21 Pound, "Pastiche: The Regional, XVI," *New Age*, Nov. 6, 1919, p. 16.

22 I concur here with Pearlman, 3, pp. 469, 473, 477, 478. Noting the resemblance between Pound's conspiratorial fantasies and his conception of a Jewish plot to control the world, Pearlman argues that Pound's hatred of the Jews marks a profound envy of their presumed power. He also argues that Pound's anti-Semitism, linked to his desire for power, inevitably increases as his literary reputation falls to its lowest ebb. Again one finds a parallel between Pound's and Céline's anti-Semitism. Not only does Céline refer to the Jews' superior manliness, fearlessness, and resourcefulness, he believes that they have attained apotheosis, god-like power over the whole world. According to Julia Kristeva, Céline conceives of the Jew "not so much as a father" but as a "preferred son, chosen, availing himself of paternal power." Lacking for nothing, the enviable and mysterious Jew is capable of being everything and everywhere. See Céline, 1, pp. 102, 127, 180, 182, 255, 270, 327; 3, pp. 141, 142; Kristeva, pp. 181–182.

23 Power over man and Nature figures in Pound's "The Ballad of the Goodly Fere," whose subject is Jesus Christ, the very Savior whom Pound sought to replace. In his intimate relation to and power over the elements, Pound's Jesus resembles Upward's Divine Man; the speaker at once compares Jesus to the sea at Genseret and views him as the sea's master ("Like the sea that he cowed at Genseret"). Jesus is equally a master of crowds. Besides exulting in Jesus' righteous anger against the money changers (an anticipation of Pound's usury theme)—"I ha' seen him drive a hundred men / Wi' a bundle of rods swung free" —the speaker twice mentions that he "ha' seen him cow a thousand men." The spirit of the poem seems not Christian but pagan, and indeed Pound's use of the word "cow" is foreign to the spirit of the Sermon on the Mount. The poem anticipates the radio broadcasts, in which Pound, as the Performing God, attempts to control the human "sheep" and "cows" and implicitly attacks Christian "humiliation doctrine" (RB, 199) in the interests of fascist paganism. See PER, pp. 33–34.

24 See Ellul, p. 7: ". . . The listener to a radio broadcast, though actually alone, is nevertheless part of a large group, and he is aware of it. Radio listeners have been found to exhibit a mass mentality. All are tied together and constitute a sort of society in which all individuals are accomplices and influence each other without knowing it."

25 See Carsten on Mussolini, p. 74: by his policy of ostracism and exclusion, says Carsten, "Mussolini attempted to transform the nation into a 'block of granite,' into a 'monolith.' "

26 Horkheimer and Adorno, "Elements of Anti-Semitism," *Dialectic of Enlightenment*, p. 190.

27 Céline similarly conceives of the Aryan multitudes as puppets or robots manipulated by the Jews. See Céline, 1, pp. 130, 184, 194; 2, pp. 26–27.

Chapter Twenty-Two: The Doubles

1 Girard, 2, pp. 146–148; "The Mimetic Desire of Paolo and Francesca," in 3, pp. 3–4; 1, pp. 83, 10–11, 41.

2 Pound's resemblance to and identification with Ezra is noted by Robert Lowell in his *Notebook, 1967–1968*, where Lowell remembers a conversation with T. S. Eliot at St. Elizabeths; see Bacigalupo, p. 134n. See also Durant, p. 117, who does not, however, define this relationship as one of rivalry, and Andrew Parker, p. 119. According to Parker, Pound's "hostility toward Judaism" signifies his "irreducible" Jewishness, which is confirmed in his name.

3 Writing to Joyce in 1915 about a Jewish artist's objectionably "semitic" portrait of himself, Pound said that the likeness may resemble his face "as it may have been years ago" (P/J, 35).

4 Thus far the best study of the similarity between Pound and the Jews is Daniel Pearlman, "Ezra Pound: America's Wandering Jew." More recently Lewis Hyde has examined Pound and the Jews as doubles. However, Hyde follows neither a Girardian nor Freudian method but speaks in murky Jungian terms of the Jews as

Pound's "shadow," a part of himself which he should have acknowledged. Thus reducing the Jews to the status of a psychological archetype or mythical symbol (the transhistorical Hermes), Hyde ignores the historical roots and specific psychological content of Pound's anti-Semitism. It becomes a mere symptom of Pound's failure to communicate with vague spiritual essences. See *The Gift*, pp. 251–256. Timothy Materer examines Pound as double in "Doppelgänger: Ezra Pound in his Letters," pp. 241–256. Employing the familiar but limited model of the split personality rather than Girard's theory of doubling through mimetic conflict, Materer makes no mention of Pound's anti-Semitism or the broadcasts. He does, though, note Pound's lack of fixed identify throughout his career. According to Charles Olson, whom Materer quotes, Pound is the "tragic Double of our day." See pp. 242–243, 246.

5 Yet Kimpel and Eaves exaggerate in saying that Pound's rendition of his visit to the synagogue "certainly is not hostile." In fact it conveys fascination mingled with belittlement. Pound's contempt is not lessened by his later statement, noted by Kimpel and Eaves, that the service in the synagogue was one of the only two examples of the worship of God that he could remember. Pound's contempt for the Jews is entirely compatible with his fascination and respect for them. See Kimpel and Eaves, 2, p. 62.

6 According to Stock, 3, p. 74, Yusuf Benamore was extremely helpful to the young and impoverished poet in Gibraltar in 1908, and may have invested Pound's limited funds so that Pound could live on the interest. James J. Wilhelm, 3, pp. 191–192, says that in these transactions Pound came "perilously close to the commerce of Usura."

7 Horkheimer and Adorno, "Elements of Anti-Semitism," in *Dialectic of Enlightenment*, p. 184. Lowenthal and Guterman, pp. 79–80, similarly observe that mimicking is "perhaps one of the most crucial anti-Semitic stimuli," and that "the condemnation of Jewish expressiveness" by American right-wing agitators is often "accompanied by its caricaturing imitation." Indeed, hostile mimesis is the only way in which the agitators can carry out their secret desire to be like the Jews, pp. 79–80. As for the nose as the Jews' individuating feature, it figures thus in Pound's caricature of "Brennbaum" in *Hugh Selwyn Mauberley*. Although Brennbaum has sought to conceal his Jewishness by dandifying himself, his identity is manifest when the "daylight fell/ level across [his] . . . face" (PER, 193). Pound probably means that the sun has revealed the outline of Brennbaum's nose, the unmistakable mark of his race. Just as the Jews will later emerge in Pound's works as the enemies of the light and sun, in this poem the light symbolizes truth and makes it possible to define "natural" distinctions and origins. Incidentally, the model for Brennbaum was Max Beerbohm, whom Pound mistook as Jewish.

8 Stock, *The Life of Ezra Pound*, p. 444. The acquaintance was Arnold Leese, the rabid British fascist and anti-Semite.

9 This anecdote is given in Eris, p. 53, after Louis Simpson's recounting of it in *Three on the Tower*.

10 Praz, quoted in Bacigalupo, pp. 83–84.

11 Pound to Douglas Fox, April 7, 1936, Beinecke Rare Book and Manuscript Library, Yale University.

12 Pound, "Germany Now," *New English Weekly*, 26 Sept. 1935, p. 399.

13 Mimesis of the enemy is typical of Pound, as in the broadcasts, p. 13, and in his September 1954 letter to Denis Goacher (in the Beinecke Rare Book and Manuscript Library, Yale University). Nathan, pp. 116–117, describes Nazism as "in many ways . . . a form of Judaism." On this point see Arendt, Vol. III, pp. 5, 31, 56 ff., 75, 76; Hitler, p. 312; Nolte p. 523; Lewis, 2, pp. 19, 32, 123. Céline openly admires the Jews' racial pride and endurance, qualities he finds lacking in the Aryan; see Céline, 1, p. 129; 3, p. 142. For anti-Semitic mimesis of the Jews, see also Geoffrey Field, pp. 187–188, on Chamberlain, and Poliakov, 2, Vol. III, p. 97, on Voltaire. Ironically, although Pound himself unconsciously imitated the Jews, he recognized that Hitler, having been "bitten" by the "dirty jew mania," had taken the Jews as his model in his quest for "world dominion." This is not to imply that

Judaism is megalomaniacal, but that Pound and Hitler conceived it as such. See Kimpel and Eaves, 2, p. 59.

14 Pound, "Statues of Gods," *Townsman*, 2 (Aug. 1939), p. 14.

15 Pound, "Ecclesia," *Townsman*, 2 (Nov. 1939), p. 4.

16 Girard, 2, p. 47. An alternative explanation of Pound's anti-Semitic paranoia is suggested in *Totem and Taboo*, in which Freud traces the paranoiac's persecutor to the esteemed and feared father; paranoia would thus involve repressed but reemergent instincts of incest and parricide. Girard argues against Freud that the instinctual desire for the mother (the Oedipus complex) is a fiction, and that incestuous desires, when they do arise, do so not from instinct but from imitation of the father. Where paternal "law" is enforced, there is no conflictual imitation between father and son. Paranoiac behavior thus develops within a mimetic and not necessarily familial relation. However, anti-Semitism may be considered a special case, since in Pound as in European tradition the Jew is rarely divorced from the image of the bad or persecuting father. Such an argument is in no way undermined by the fact that Pound's father (Homer Pound) seems to have been indulgent and diffident, for these qualities, far from lessening Pound's feeling of repression by the harsh paternal superego, would only have increased them, as Freud shows. One might therefore assert that Pound, who vilifies the "sadistic" Jehovah and denies any such "immediate parenthood" (SP, 70), identifies the Jew not with his own father but with the stern and terrifying father imago—an interpretation which finds support in the obvious infantilism of his association of Jehovah with "giants" and "bogeys." See Freud, 1, p. 50; 6, p. 77n; Girard, 2, pp. 169–222; Cohn, 1, pp. 256–260; Norman, pp. 327.

17 Compare SP, p. 265, in which Pound inveighs against Calvinism, which had revived the "brutal mythology of the Hebrews" and "distilled a moral syphilis through the whole body of society." In the same paragraph Pound writes: "Dr. Hackett found two kinds of mosquito. No difference under the strongest microscope; but they lay different kinds of eggs, one virulent with malaria, the other innocuous. . . ." Incidentally, malaria imports the swamp.

18 Pound and Ernest Fenollosa, *The Classic Noh Theater of Japan*, esp. pp. 113–115. The above summary follows Pound's misunderstanding of the play. In the original the action is much simpler than Pound believes: not Awoi but the Princess Rokujo is jealous, and there are no mimetic doubles. Pound has made the work more subtle psychologically. See Keith, p. 201. It is also worth noting that Pound viewed the Noh drama as a form of religious ritual or ceremony. See Bush, pp. 105–106.

19 Girard, "Delirium as System," in Girard, 3, p. 96; 2, p. 165.

20 Heymann refers to Pound's "torrid rage" in the broadcasts, his "ranting at a low-pitched roar," and, most important in view of Girard's characterization of the sacrificial crisis as a dehumanizing loss of distinctions, his "bizarre vocal inflections, making it impossible for transcribers to distinguish between words." See Heymann, pp. 105–106. Pound's violently animalistic mimetic behavior in the broadcasts helps to disclose the themes of sacrifice and doubling secreted in the Addendum to Canto 100, which was written during the same period and which is filled with the same anxieties as the broadcasts. As we have seen, the Addendum expresses Pound's horror of economic and linguistic indeterminacy, the monstrous essence of which is usury. Alluding again to the amphibious Geryon, the beast of usury and Fraud, in whose "folds" lie a "thousand dead" like the tangled bodies of eels, Pound then beseeches the "Crystal" or "clarity" to descend into the confusion of his "labyrinth" (Addendum, 100/ 799). Insofar as a labyrinth constantly doubles and folds back upon itself, thus preventing progress or escape, it resembles the constricting serpentine coils of Geryon, which in turn symbolize the labyrinthine vortex of Dante's Inferno. This is all the more interesting in view of two facts. Here, as elsewhere, Pound would rely implicitly on the sacrificial axe of Italian Fascism to destroy Geryon and thus to extricate himself and the world from the labyrinth. Moreover, the word *labrys*, whence "labyrinth" derives, originally meant axe. The *labrys*, though, is a *double* axe, the sign of patriarchal Zeus' worship at Labraunda in Caria,

while the labyrinth itself is known as the House of the Double Axe. This object, like the place it signifies, evokes the essential doubleness of violence, which can be both sacred and profane. The reference to "the labyrinth" in the Addendum also evokes *the* most famous labyrinth of antiquity, that of Crete, at whose center was to be found the Minotaur, half man and half bull—and in this sense a secret double of the belligerent man-god Pound and his heroic Messiah Mussolini, the bull. The Cretan labyrinth, and the myth of Ariadne's thread, reappears in Canto 93, in which Pound speaks of entering "the presence at sunrise / up out of hell, from the labyrinth / the path wide as a hair" (93/632). According to William H. Desmonde, in ancient Crete the slaying of the Minotaur was originally connected with the worship of the holy bull, which represented Zeus and Dionysus, and which was also sacrificed in rituals as a substitute for the father: a profane impulse purified through religion. The means of this killing was the double axe, a holy object often found in close connection with the head of the bull. All of these associations, of which Pound was probably aware on some level, again suggest that in the Addendum Pound is looking for the victim, the monstrous double, the center ("Here is the core of evil") of the labyrinth, but that he remains unaware that in his bull-like aggression he is preparing this role for none other than himself. See W. H. Matthews, *Mazes and Labyrinths: Their History and Development* (New York, 1970), pp. 34, 176, quoted in Fellows, pp. xiii-xiv; Desmonde, pp. 103, 106, 118, 165.

21 Girard, "Strategies of Madness—Nietzsche, Wagner, Dostoyevsky," *passim*.

22 T. S. Eliot, quoted in Bacigalupo, p. 32.

23 Noel Stock to Pound, December 13, 1956, Beinecke Rare Book and Manuscript Library, Yale University.

Chapter Twenty-Three: The Return of the Swamp

1 "Wreck" is from Canto 116, p. 796; for "botch," see Flory, p. 285, quoting Daniel Cory's interview with Pound.

2 Grazia Livi, in the March, 1963 issue of *Epoca,* quoted in Meacham, p. 203.

3 Pound, quoted in Meacham, p. 183.

4 This is not to suggest that Pound had abandoned paganism, for the later *Cantos* allude reverently to such pagan gods as Dionysus, Artemis, and Neptune. Pound reaffirms to the end one of the major goals of his career, namely a unification of Christianity and paganism: the Madonna and the pagan mother goddesses remain compatible in these last poems. One sees Pound's persistent syncretism in the previously quoted lines from Canto 117 et. seq., in which Pound would "make a church / or an altar to Zagreus / . . . like the double arch of a window / Or some great colonnade." Like the colonnade, this double arch is spacious enough to accommodate Jesus and Dionysus.

5 For "personal inferno," see Donald Hall, *Remembering Poets,* p. 183, quoted in Flory, p. 286.

6 Livi, quoted in Meacham, p. 203.

7 In *La Dernière Bataille* Edouard Drumont views the Jew as the agent, even the personification, of Death: "Men . . . throw themselves on the Jews to die there. . . . Each person once had his Death close by him. Each person had close to him his Jew. . . . He breaks down their vital parts, he decomposes them to corpses, he puts them into the contortions of final agony." Quoted in Wilson, p. 429.

8 Pound links death and castration in an early statement to William Carlos Williams: "The phallus in many cases ceases to rise even before death comes on." Quoted in Torrey, p. 276. During his old age Pound suffered sexual debility.

9 Quoted in Bush, p. 55.

10 On Torcello, see Lorenzetti, pp. 833–841; Pignatti, pp. 20–25. What seems no less uncanny in Pound's last Venetian years is that, living in the quiet San Gregorio section of the city, he often took long and undisturbed walks along the promenade known as the Zattere, which looks out for its entire extent upon the wide Canale della Giudecca and, in the farther distance, the self-contained section of

Venice known as the Giudecca. Since the Middle Ages the Giudecca has been the city's Jewish Quarter. Admittedly the appeal of San Gregorio (and the adjoining San Trovaso) section of Venice for Pound had much to do with the fact that he began his poetic career there in 1908, and that his "return to origins" lent a quality of circularity and seeming completeness to his literary and personal life; to quote Canto 76: "things have ends and beginnings" (76/ 462). But in view of the major role which anti-Semitism had played in Pound's life and in the determination of his fortunes, one suspects that, for probably unrecognized psychological reasons, Pound was drawn to an urban geography which, apart from its evident associations with the swamp's multifarious ambiguities, embodied his persistent fascination with and distance from the Jews. On Pound's last years in Venice, see Heymann, pp. 275, 296–298, 300–301, 305–309, 311–314.

11 Bacigalupo, p. 461, points out that in the typewritten draft of Canto 110 the opening line is addressed to Alma Pulnoua, a distortion of "Pronoia" or "Patrona."

12 In *Discretions,* p. 305, Pound's daughter Mary de Rachewiltz speaks of the difficulties of his domestic life after his return to Italy from the United States.

13 For the feminine character of the sea in Pound, see Durant, p. 104.

14 For the inherent mixture and futility of tellurian creation, whose symbols are the wheel, the circle, and the swamp, see Bachofen, pp. 33–34, 27.

15 A hint of sacrifice, however, is in Canto 110, where Pound speaks of water where "the winter olive is taken" (110/ 779), and five lines later writes cryptically, "Neath this altar now Endymion lies." He alludes to the mortal who fell in love with the moon goddess. Although Artemis is a figure of light, she only reflects the light of the sun, and the moon is after all a tellurian body. The moon, moreover, is a central symbol not of that stage of culture in which the phallic or paternal principle triumphs absolutely, but rather of the Demetrian stage of agriculture, characterized by tellurian creation and the dominance of the matriarchal principle. In this stage the phallic sun is acknowledged not as the "immutable source of light," for instance Apollo or Helios, but as "forever fluctuating between rising and setting, coming into being and passing away." The masculine god of this stage is the phallic Dionysus, who like Pound (his alter ego) belongs to Nature and must therefore always confront "a night of death." In the Demetrian stage human identity likewise succumbs to the "law of matter," the "one fatum" ("Fate's tray," as Pound has it) that "coming into being and passing away run side by side." Men are like the leaves of the trees, which are interchangeably alike, doomed to perish, and which therefore do not need to be named. See Bachofen, pp. 25–30, 33–34, 114–115, 122–134. In Pound's last major translation, of Sophocles' *Women of Trachis,* the solar hero Hercules is inadvertently poisoned by his wife Deianera by means of a garment soaked in the blood of the swamp Hydra. Hercules chooses to immolate himself upon a sacrificial pyre.

16 Bacigalupo, quoting William Carlos Williams, p. 480.

17 For Neptune or Poseidon, see Bachofen, pp. lv, 41, 63, 114, 122–129, 132, 144n, 177n, 180, 203. The ancient Mediterranean myth of the phallus of the depths is apparently preserved in the civic mythology of Venice, where Pound lived both before and after his confinement at St. Elizabeths, and to which he refers frequently in *Drafts and Fragments* as in the earlier *Cantos* as an archetype of the whole enterprise of civilization. To this day the Venetians celebrate the wedding of Venice and the Sea. Contrary to the common assumption that Venice plays the role of husband, in this ceremony the city is the Sea's bride, as in Giambattista Tiepolo's great painting of *Venice and Neptune* in the Palazzo Ducale. See Lorenzetti, pp. 13, 20; Pound, Canto 26, p. 124.

18 John D. Sinclair, trans., *The Divine Comedy of Dante Alighieri,* Vol. II, *Purgatorio* (London: Oxford Univ. Press, 1958), Canto 1, ll. 134–138, pp. 24–25: "Quivi mi cinse sì, com'altrui piacque: / oh maraviglia! chè qual elli scelse / l'umile pianta, cotal si rinaque / subitamente là onde l'avelse."

19 A rushlight is a candle whose wick is made of twisted marsh grass. Although he does not place it within a pattern of reversals, Wilhelm notes the possible connection between Dante's reed in *Purgatorio* and Pound's rushlight. See Wilhelm, 2, pp. 195, 198.

Chapter Twenty-Four: "All Will Be Judged"

1 Nolte, pp. 88–89, 140–143, 507–513. See especially p. 141: "Fear has been an underlying element of the intellectual history of Europe for the last hundred years." Compare Hans Roggers's judgment of proto-fascist movements in *The European Right,* pp. 587–588: "In the final reckoning, however, and in spite of some shrewd appreciations of the needs of the contemporary world, the Right represents not the wave of the future but a nihilistic hostility to modernity, a fear of the unfamiliar, and an infantile yearning for protection (through nation, race, boundless power, and aimless activism) against dark and only dimly comprehended forces that lurk and threaten on all sides."

2 Bacigalupo, p. x.

3 See Canto 86, p. 566, and Canto 96, p. 656.

4 For the Fascist "revolt of nature," see Horkheimer, pp. 118–123, and Horkheimer and Adorno, p. 185.

5 Girard, "An Interview with René Girard," p. 185.

6 Yvor Winters, *In Defense of Reason* (New York: The Swallow Press and William Morrow Company, 1947), p. 480.

7 Scott, pp. 50, 55.

8 Scott, pp. 50–54.

9 Irving Howe, quoted in *A Casebook,* p. 60. The scapegoating strategy is even more overt in Karl Shapiro's "The Scapegoat of Modern Poetry," in *In Defense of Ignorance* (New York: Random House, 1965), p. 85. After an attack on Pound, Shapiro says that he is "a scapegoat certainly."

10 See Girard, 2, pp. 134–135, 155–156.

11 Jameson, 1, p. 119. This idea is developed more recently in Jameson's *Fables of Aggression: Wyndham Lewis, The Modernist as Fascist,* for instance p. 14: Jameson reads Lewis's " 'fascism' " as a "protest against the reified experience of an alienated social life, in which, against its own will, it remains formally and ideologically locked."

12 Jay, pp. 180, 194.

13 Adorno, p. 23: "But the greatest fetish of cultural criticism is the notion of culture as such."

14 Pound, LE, p. 55.

15 Nolte, p. 542.

16 Nolte, pp. 188–189.

17 See McNaughton, p. 151.

18 According to William Harmon, in *Guide to Kulchur* the "idea of *paideuma*" comprehends a "world civilization that transcends time and space." See Harmon, p. 43. Sieburth notes that Pound pursued a Goethean ideal of "Weltliteratur" while following Voltaire's idea of "universal history" —"history as a plenum, as a record of the total endeavour of the human spirit." See Sieburth, 1, pp. 375, 383.

Works Consulted

BOOKS BY POUND:
ABC of Reading. New York: New Directions, 1960.
A Lume Spento. New York: New Directions, 1965.
The Cantos. New York: New Directions, 1972.
The Classic Noh Theater of Japan. New York: New Directions, 1959.
The Collected Early Poems of Ezra Pound. Edited by Michael John King. New York: New Directions, 1976.
Confucius. New York: New Directions, 1958.
Ezra Pound and the Visual Arts. Edited by Harriet Zinnes. New York: New Directions, 1980.
"Ezra Pound Speaking": Radio Speeches of World War II. Edited by Leonard W. Doob. Westport, Conn.: Greenwood Press, 1978.
Gaudier-Brzeska. New York: New Directions, 1970.
Guide to Kulchur. New York: New Directions, 1970.
Impact: Essays on Ignorance and the Decline of American Civilization. Edited by Noel Stock. Chicago: Henry Regnery, 1960.
Jefferson and/or Mussolini. New York: Liveright, 1935.
The Letters of Ezra Pound, 1907–1941. Edited by D. D. Paige. New York: Harcourt, Brace, 1950.
Literary Essays of Ezra Pound. Edited by T. S. Eliot. London: Faber and Faber, 1954.
Pavannes and Divagations. New York: New Directions, 1958.
Personae: The Collected Poems of Ezra Pound. New York: New Directions, 1959.
Pound/Joyce: The Letters of Ezra Loomis Pound to James Joyce, with Pound's Essays on Joyce. Edited by Forrest Read. New York: New Directions, 1967.
Pound/Lewis: The Letters of Ezra Pound and Wyndham Lewis. Edited by Timothy Materer. New York: New Directions, 1985.
Selected Prose of Ezra Pound: 1909–1965. Edited by William Cookson. New York: New Directions, 1973.
The Spirit of Romance. New York: New Directions, 1968.
The Women of Trachis. London: Neville Spearman, 1956.

ARTICLES BY POUND:
"Affirmations. II. Vorticism." *New Age*, XVI (14 January, 1915), 277–278.
"Studies in Contemporary Mentality. V." *New Age*, XXI (13 September, 1917), 425–427.

"What America Has to Live Down, III-IV." *New Age*, XXIII (5 September, 1918), 297–298.
"Pastiche: The Regional. VIII." *New Age*, XXV (28 August, 1919), 300.
"Pastiche: The Regional. IX." *New Age*, XXV (11 September, 1919), 336.
"Pastiche: The Regional. XVI." *New Age*, XXVI (6 November, 1919), 16.
"The Revolt of Intelligence. V." *New Age*, XXVI (8 January, 1920), 153–154.
"The Revolt of Intelligence. VII." *New Age*, XXVI (22 January, 1920), 186–187.
"The Revolt of Intelligence. VIII." *New Age*, XXVI (4 March, 1920), 287–288.
"The Revolt of Intelligence. X." *New Age*, XXVI (18 March, 1920), 318–319.
"Hunger Fighters." *New English Weekly*, IV (22 February, 1934), 451–452.
"Mr. Eliot's Quandaries." *New English Weekly*, IV (29 March, 1934), 558–559.
"Mr. T. S. Eliot's Quandaries." *New English Weekly*, V (26 April, 1934), 48.
"What Price the Muses Now." *New English Weekly*, V (24 May, 1934), 130–132.
"Ecclesiastical History (Or the Work Always Falls on Papa)." *New English Weekly*, V (5 July, 1934), 272–273.
"Mr. Eliot's Solid Merit." *New English Weekly*, V (12 July, 1934), 297–299.
"A Problem of (Specifically) Style." *New English Weekly*, VI (22 November, 1934), 127–128.
"Leaving Out Economics (Gesell as Reading Matter)." *New English Weekly*, VI (31 January, 1935), 331–333.
"Senator Long and Father Coughlin: Mr. Ezra Pound's Estimate." *Morning Post*, 17 April, 1935, p. 14.
"American Notes. Time Lag." *New English Weekly*, VII (18 April, 1935), 5–6.
"Private Worlds." *New English Weekly*, VII (2 May, 1935), 48–49.
"The Italian Score." *New English Weekly*, VII (23 May, 1935), 107.
"American Notes." *New English Weekly*, VII (11 July, 1935), 245–246.
"American Notes." *New English Weekly*, VII (5 September, 1935), 325.
"As for Huey . . . ." *New English Weekly*, VII (12 September, 1935), p. 345.
"Germany Now." *New English Weekly*, VII (26 September, 1935), 399.
"American Notes." *New English Weekly*, VIII (21 November, 1935), 105.
"Again the Rev. Coughlin." *New English Weekly*, VIII (24 October, 1935), p. 26.
"Jean Barral is with Us." *New English Weekly*, VIII (5 December, 1935), 146–147.
"Organicly [sic] Speaking." *New English Weekly*, VIII (26 December, 1935), 211–212.
"American Notes." *New English Weekly*, VIII (5 March, 1936), 405.
"American Notes." *New English Weekly*, VIII (26 March, 1936), 465.
"American Notes." *New English Weekly*, VIII (2 April, 1936), 489–490.
"The Return of the Native, II." *New English Weekly*, VIII (9 April, 1936), 510.
"Last Words on Economic Democracy." *New English Weekly*, IX (7 May, 1936), 69–70.
"Anti-Semitism." *New English Weekly*, IX (14 May, 1936), 99–100.
"Atrophy of the Leninists, I." *New English Weekly*, IX (2 July, 1936), 227–228.
"Atrophy of the Leninists, II." *New English Weekly*, IX (9 July, 1936), 249–250.
"Race." *New English Weekly*, X (15 October, 1936), 12–13.
"Method." *New English Weekly*, X (18 March, 1937), 446–447.
"Demarcations." *British Union Quarterly*, 1 (January-April, 1937), 35–40.
"Intellectual Money." *British Union Quarterly*, 1 (April-June, 1937), 24–34.
"Pity." *Action*, No. 139, October 15, 1938, 16.
"Money and Irving Fisher." *New English Weekly*, XIV (5 January, 1939), 195.
"The Nazi Movement in Germany." *Townsman*, 2 (April, 1939), 12–13.
"Statues of Gods." *Townsman*, 2 (August, 1939), 14.
"Religio." *Townsman*, 2 (November, 1939), 4–5.

"The Inedible." *Townsman*, 3 (February, 1940), 2.
"Non sacrificate ad uno spirito che non vi appartiene." *Meridiano di Roma*, V (28 January, 1940).
"Profili Americani." *Meridiano di Roma*, V (29 December, 1940).
"La guerra degli usurai." *Meridiano di Roma*, VII, (3 May, 1942).
"Ob pecuniae scarcitatem." *Meridiano di Roma*, VII (7 June, 1942).
"Problemi da risolvere." *Meridiano di Roma*, VIII, (14 February, 1943).
"Sulla Propaganda." *Meridiano di Roma*, VIII (6 June, 1943).
"Total War on 'Contemplatio.' " *Edge*, 1 (October, 1956), 19–20.
"Ezra Pound, Anonymous Contributions to *Strike*." *Paideuma*, 3 (Winter, 1974), 389–400.

OTHER WORKS:
Ackerman, Nathan, and Jahoda, Marie. *Anti-Semitism and Emotional Disorder*. New York: Harper and Row, 1956.
Adorno, Theodor et. al. *The Authoritarian Personality*. New York: Harper and Row, 1950.
Adorno, Theodor. *Prisms*. Translated by Samuel and Shierry Weber. Cambridge: MIT Press, 1981.
Albright, William Foxwell. *From the Stone Age to Christianity: Monotheism and the Historical Process*. New York: Doubleday, 1957.
Alexander, Michael. *The Poetic Achievement of Ezra Pound*. Berkeley, California: University of California Press, 1979.
Allardyce, Gilbert. "What Fascism was Not: Thoughts on the Deflation of a Concept." *American Historical Review*, 84 (April, 1979), 367–388.
Allport, Floyd H. and Morse, Nancy C. "The Causation of Anti-Semitism: An Investigation of Seven Hypotheses." *Journal of Psychology*, 34 (July, 1952), 197–234.
Anderson, Bernhard. *Understanding the Old Testament*. Englewood Cliffs, New Jersey: Prentice Hall, 1966.
Arato, Andrew, and Gebhardt, Eike, eds. *A Frankfurt School Reader*. New York: Urizen, 1978.
Arendt, Hannah. *The Origins of Totalitarianism*. 3 vols. New York: Harcourt, Brace, 1968.
Athanassakis, Apostolos N. *The Homeric Hymns*. Baltimore: Johns Hopkins University Press, 1976.
Bachofen, Johann. *Myth, Religion, and Mother Right: Selected Writings of J. J. Bachofen*. Translated by Ralph Manheim. Princeton: Princeton University Press, 1967.
Bacigalupo, Massimo. *The Forméd Trace: The Later Poetry of Ezra Pound*. New York: Columbia University Press, 1980.
Baller, F. W. *The Sacred Edict: With a Translation of the Colloquial Rendering*. Shanghai: China Inland Mission, 1924.
Barkun, Michael. *Disaster and the Millennium*. New Haven: Yale University Press, 1974.
Barraclough, Geoffrey. *An Introduction to Contemporary History*. Penguin: Harmondsworth, 1967.
Barzun, Jacques. *Race: A Study in Modern Superstition*. New York: Harcourt Brace, 1937.
Baumann, Walter. *The Rose in the Steel Dust: An Examination of the Cantos of Ezra Pound*. Coral Gables, Florida: University of Miami Press, 1970.
Bell, Daniel, ed. *The Radical Right*. New York: Doubleday, 1964.

Bell, Ian F.A. *Critic as Scientist: The Modernist Poetics of Ezra Pound.* London: Methuen, 1981.

Bell, Ian F.A., ed. *Ezra Pound: Tactics for Reading.* London: Barnes and Noble, 1982.

Benda, Julien. *The Treason of the Intellectuals.* Translated by Richard Aldington. New York: W. W. Norton, 1969.

Bendix, Reinhard, and Lipset, Seymour M., eds. *Class, Status, and Power.* Glencoe: The Free Press, 1953.

Benjamin, Walter. *Illuminations.* Edited by Hannah Arendt; translated by Harry Zohn. New York: Harcourt, Brace, Jovanovich, 1968.

Berardini, Gene. "The Origins and Development of Racial Anti-Semitism in Italy." *Journal of Modern History,* 49 (September, 1977), 431–453.

Berezin, Charles. "Poetry and Politics in Ezra Pound." *Partisan Review,* 48, 2 (1981), 262–279.

Bergonzi, Bernard. "From Imagism to Fascism." *Times Literary Supplement,* 24 September, 1976, 1195–1196.

Bernstein, Michael André. *The Tale of the Tribe: Ezra Pound and the Modern Verse Epic.* Princeton: Princeton University Press, 1980.

Berryman, Jo Brantley. *Circe's Craft: Ezra Pound's Hugh Selwyn Mauberley.* Ann Arbor: UMI Research Press, 1983.

Biddiss, Michael Denis. *Father of Racist Ideology: The Social and Political Thought of Count Gobineau.* New York: Weybright and Talley, 1970.

Blast 1: Review of the Great English Vortex. 1914; rpt. Black Sparrow Press, 1981.

Blish, James. "Rituals on Ezra Pound." *Sewanee Review,* 58 (April- June, 1950), 185–226.

Bridenthal, Renata et al., eds. *When Biology Became Destiny: Women in Weimar and Nazi Germany.* New York: Monthly Review Press, 1984.

Brooke-Rose, Christine. *A ZBC of Ezra Pound.* Berkeley: University of California Press, 1971.

Brown, Norman O. *Hermes the Thief: The Evolution of a Myth.* New York: Random House, 1969.

Burckhardt, Jacob. *The Civilization of the Renaissance in Italy.* Translated by S. C. G. Middleton. Vienna: Phaidon, 1937.

Burke, Kenneth. *The Philosophy of Literary Form.* Baton Rouge: Louisiana State University Press, 1941.

Bush, Ronald. *The Genesis of Ezra Pound's Cantos.* Princeton: Princeton University Press, 1976.

Byrnes, Robert F. *Anti-Semitism in Modern France: The Prologue to the Dreyfus Affair.* New Brunswick, New Jersey: Rutgers University Press, 1950.

Canetti, Elias. *Crowds and Power.* Translated by Carol Stewart. New York: Viking, 1962.

Cannistraro, Philip V., ed. *Historical Dictionary of Fascist Italy.* Westport, Conn.: Greenwood Press, 1982.

Carlebach, Julius. *Karl Marx and the Radical Critique of Judaism.* London: Routledge and Kegan Paul, 1978.

Carlyle, Thomas. *Critical and Miscellaneous Essays,* IV. In *Carlyle's Works,* XVI, Boston: Estes and Lauriat, 1888.

_____. *Sartor Resartus.* Edited by C.F. Herrold. New York: Odyssey, 1937.

Carpenter, Niles. *Guild Socialism: An Historical and Critical Analysis.* New York: D. Appleton, 1922.

Carsten, F. L. *The Rise of Fascism.* Berkeley: University of California Press, 1969.

Cassels, Alan. *Italian Fascism.* New York: Thomas Crowell, 1968.

Cassirer, Ernst. *The Myth of the State*. New Haven: Yale University Press, 1946.

Cecil, Robert. *The Myth of the Master Race: Alfred Rosenberg and Nazi Ideology*. London: B. T. Batsford, 1972.

Céline, Louis-Ferdinand. *Bagatelles pour un massacre*. Paris: Editions Denoël, 1937.
   L'École des cadavres. Paris: Editions Denoël, 1938.
   Les Beaux draps. Paris: Nouvelles Editions Françaises, 1941.
   Journey to the End of the Night. Translated by Ralph Manheim. New York: New Directions, 1983.

Chace, William. *The Political Identities of Ezra Pound and T.S. Eliot*. Stanford: Stanford University Press, 1973.

Chamberlain, Houston Stewart. *The Foundations of the Nineteenth Century*, 2 vols. London: John Lane, 1911.

Charlesworth, (Gelpi) Barbara. "The Tensile Light: A Study of Ezra Pound's Religion." M.A. Thesis: University of Miami, Coral Gables, Florida, 1957.

Chilanti, Felice. "Ezra Pound among the Seditious in the 1940's." *Paideuma*, 6 (Fall, 1977), 235–250.

Ching, Julia. *Confucianism and Christianity: A Comparative Study*. Tokyo: Kodansha International, 1977.

Christie, Richard, and Jahoda, Marie, eds. *Studies in the Scope and Method of 'The Authoritarian Personality'*. Glencoe: The Free Press, 1954.

Clements, R. E. *Isaiah, 1–39*. Grand Rapids, Michigan: William B. Eerdmans, 1980.

Cohen, Jeremy. *The Friars and the Jews: The Evolution of Medieval Anti-Semitism*. Ithaca: Cornell University Press, 1982.

Cohn, Norman. *Warrant for Genocide: The Myth of the Jewish World Conspiracy and the Protocols of the Elders of Zion*. New York: Harper and Row, 1967.
   The Pursuit of the Millennium: Revolutionary Millenarians and Mystical Anarchists of the Middle Ages. New York: Oxford University Press, 1971.

Cork, Richard. *Vorticism and Abstract Art in the First Machine Age*. 2 vols. Berkeley: University of California Press, 1976.

Cornell, Julian. *The Trial of Ezra Pound*. New York: John Day, 1966.

Cory, Daniel. "Ezra Pound: A Memoir." *Encounter*, 30 (May, 1968), 30–39.

Craig, Cairns. *Yeats, Eliot, Pound, and the Politics of Poetry*. Pittsburgh: University of Pittsburgh Press, 1982.

Creel, H. G. *Chinese Thought: From Confucius to Mao-Tse Tung*. New York: New American Library, 1953.

Cross, Colin. *The Fascists in Britain*. New York: St. Martin's Press, 1963.

Cuddihy, John Murray. *The Ordeal of Civility: Freud, Marx, Lévi-Strauss, and the Jewish Struggle for Modernity*. New York: Basic Books, 1974.

Curtis, Michael. *Three Against the Third Republic: Sorel, Barrès, and Maurras*. Princeton: Princeton University Press, 1954.

Dasenbrock, Reed Way. *The Literary Vorticism of Ezra Pound and Wyndham Lewis: Towards the Condition of Painting*. Baltimore: Johns Hopkins University Press, 1985.

Davenport, Guy. "A Reading of I-XXX of *The Cantos* of Ezra Pound." Dissertation: Harvard University, 1968.

Davie, Donald. *Ezra Pound: Poet as Sculptor*. New York: Oxford University Press, 1964.
   Ezra Pound. Harmondsworth: Penguin, 1976.

Davis, Earle. *Vision Fugitive: Ezra Pound and Economics*. Lawrence, Kansas: University of Kansas Press, 1968.

De Felice, Renzo. *Fascism: An Informal Introduction to its Theory and Practice*. New Brunswick, New Jersey: Transaction, 1976.

De Grand, Alexander. *Italian Fascism: Its Origins and Development.* Lincoln, Nebraska: University of Nebraska Press, 1982.

Dekker, George. *The Cantos of Ezra Pound: A Critical Study.* New York: Barnes and Noble, 1963.

Del Buono, Oreste, ed. *Eia, Eia, Eia, Alalà: La Stampa Italiana sotto il Fascismo, 1919–1943.* Milan: Feltrinelli, 1971.

Delitzsch, F. *Isaiah.* Volume VII of C. F. Kiel and F. Delitzsch, *Commentary on the Old Testament,* 10 volumes. 1890; rpt. William B. Eerdmans, 1980.

Delzell, Charles F., ed. *Mediterranean Fascism, 1919–1945.* New York: MacMillan, 1970.

De Rachewiltz, Mary. *Discretions.* Boston: Little Brown, 1971.

———. "Fragments of an Atmosphere." *Agenda,* 17 (Autumn, 1979), 157–170.

Derrida, Jacques. *Of Grammatology.* Translated by Gayatri Spivak. Baltimore: Johns Hopkins University Press, 1976.

———. *Spurs: Nietzsche's Styles.* Translated by Barbara Harlow. Chicago: University of Chicago Press, 1979.

———. *Dissemination.* Translated by Barbara Johnson. Chicago: University of Chicago Press, 1980.

———. *Margins of Philosophy.* Translated by Alan Bass. Chicago: University of Chicago Press, 1982.

Desmonde, William H. *Magic, Myth, and Money: The Origins of Money in Religious Ritual.* Glencoe, Illinois: The Free Press, 1962.

Diggins, John P. *Mussolini and Fascism: The View from America.* Princeton: Princeton University Press, 1972.

Douglas, C. H. *Economic Democracy.* New York: Harcourt, Brace, and Howe, 1920.

———. *Credit-Power and Democracy.* London: Cecil Palmer, 1921.

Douglas, Mary. *Purity and Danger: An Analysis of Concepts of Pollution and Taboo.* Harmondsworth: Penguin, 1966.

Durant, Alan. *Ezra Pound, Identity in Crisis: A Fundamental Reassessment of the Poet and his Work.* Brighton: Harvester, 1981.

Ehrenpreis, Irwin. "Love, Hate, and Ezra Pound." *New York Review of Books,* 23 (May 27, 1976).

Eisenhauer, Robert G. "Jeweller's Company: Topaz, Half-Light, and Bounding Lines in *The Cantos.*" *Paideuma,* 9 (Fall, 1980), 249–270.

Elbow, Matthew H. *French Corporative Theory, 1789–1948: A Chapter in the History of Ideas.* 1953; rpt. Octagon, 1966.

Eliade, Mircea. *Myths, Rites, Symbols: A Mircea Eliade Reader.* Vol. I. Edited by Wendell C. Beane and William G. Doty. New York: Harper and Row, 1975.

Elias, Norbert. *The Civilizing Process.* Translated by Edmund Jephcott. New York: Urizen, 1978.

Eliot, T. S. *After Strange Gods: A Primer of Modern Heresy.* New York: Harcourt, Brace, 1934.

Elliott, Angela. "Pound's 'Isis Kuanon': An Ascension Motif in *The Cantos.*" *Paideuma,* 14 (Spring, 1985), 327–356.

Ellul, Jacques. *Propaganda: The Formation of Men's Attitudes.* Translated by Konrad Kellen and Jean Lerner. New York: Alfred Knopf, 1965.

Emery, Clark. *Ideas into Action: A Study of Pound's Cantos.* Coral Gables, Florida: University of Miami Press, 1958.

Eris, Albert. "Portrait of the Artist as a Mass Murderer." *Midstream,* 22 (February, 1976), 50–60.

Espey, John J. *Ezra Pound's Mauberley: A Study in Composition.* Berkeley: University of California Press, 1974.

Feder, Lillian. *Ancient Myth and Modern Poetry.* Princeton: Princeton University Press, 1971.

Fellows, Jay. *Ruskin's Maze: Mastery and Madness in his Art.* Princeton: Princeton University Press, 1981.

Ferkiss, Victor. "Ezra Pound and American Fascism." *Journal of Politics,* 17 (May, 1955), 173–197.

———. "Populist Influences on American Fascism." *Western Political Quarterly,* 10 (June, 1957), 350–373.

Feuer, Lewis B., ed. *Marx and Engels: Basic Writings on Politics and Philosophy.* New York: Doubleday, 1959.

Field, Geoffrey. *Evangelist of Race: The Germanic Vision of Houston Stewart Chamberlain.* New York: Columbia University Press, 1981.

Field, G. Lowell. *The Syndical and Corporative Institutions of Italian Fascism.* New York: Columbia University Press, 1938.

Finer, Herman. *Mussolini's Italy.* 1935; rpt. Grosset and Dunlap, 1965.

Finlay, John. *Social Credit: The English Origins.* Montreal: McGill-Queens University Press, 1972.

Flaubert, Gustave. *Three Tales.* Translated by Robert Baldick. Harmondsworth: Penguin, 1961.

———. *Salammbô.* Translated by A. J. Krailsheimer. Harmondsworth: Penguin, 1977.

Flory, Wendy. *Ezra Pound and The Cantos: A Record of Struggle.* New Haven: Yale University Press, 1980.

Fontenrose, Joseph. *Python: A Study of Delphic Myth and its Origins.* Berkeley: University of California Press, 1980.

Fowler, W. B. *British-American Relations, 1917–1918: The Role of Sir William Wiseman.* Princeton: Princeton University Press, 1969.

Frazer, Sir James. *Adonis, Attis, Osiris.* Part IV, Vol. 1, of *The Golden Bough.* London: MacMillan, 1919.

French, William. "Peacocks in Pound Land." *Paideuma,* 13 (Spring, 1984), 139–148.

Freud, Sigmund. *Totem and Taboo.* Translated by James Strachey. New York: W.W. Norton, 1950.

———. *Collected Papers.* Vol. V. Edited by James Strachey. New York: Basic Books, 1954.

———. *The Interpretation of Dreams.* Translated by James Strachey. New York: Basic Books, 1958.

———. *Collected Papers.* Vol. IV. Translated by Joan Riviere. New York: Basic Books, 1959.

———. *Group Psychology and the Analysis of the Ego.* Translated by James Strachey. New York: W. W. Norton, 1959.

———. *Civilization and its Discontents.* Edited and Translated by James Strachey. New York: W. W. Norton, 1961.

———. *Moses and Monotheism.* Translated by Katherine Jones. New York: Vintage, 1967.

Frobisher, Martin. *Fundamentals of Bacteriology.* Philadelphia: W.B. Saunders, 1944.

Fromm, Erich. *The Crisis of Psychoanalysis: Essays on Freud, Marx, and Social Psychology.* Greenwich, Connecticut: Fawcett, 1970.

Fry, Lesley. *Waters Flowing Eastward.* Chatou, France; British American Press, 1934.

Gage, John J. *In the Arresting Eye: The Rhetoric of Imagism.* Baton Rouge: Louisiana State University Press, 1981.

Gager, John G. *The Origins of Anti-Semitism: Attitudes Towards Judaism in Pagan and Christian Antiquity.* Princeton: Princeton University Press, 1983.

Gay, Peter. *The Enlightenment. An Interpretation: The Rise of Modern Paganism.* New York: Alfred Knopf, 1966.

Germino, Dante. "Italian Fascism and its Place in Political Thought." *Midwest Journal of Political Science,* 8 (May, 1964), 109–126.

Gilbert, G. M. *The Psychology of Dictatorship.* New York: The Ronald Press, 1950.

Girard, René. *Deceit, Desire, and the Novel.* Translated by Yvonne Freccero. Baltimore: Johns Hopkins University Press, 1965.

  Violence and the Sacred. Translated by Patrick Gregory. Baltimore: Johns Hopkins University Press, 1977.

  "To Double Business Bound": Essays on Literature, Mimesis, and Anthropology. Baltimore: Johns Hopkins University Press, 1978.

  "An Interview with René Girard." *Diacritics,* 8 (Spring, 1978), 31–54.

Glass, S. T. *The Responsible Society: The Ideas of the English Guild Socialists.* London: Longman's, 1966.

Glock, Charles Y, and Stark, Rodney, eds. *Christian Beliefs and Anti-Semitism.* New York: Harper and Row, 1966.

Goldstein, David I. *Dostoyevsky and the Jews.* Austin, Texas: University of Texas Press, 1981.

Gordon, David. "An Interview: Meeting E. P. and then . . . .' " *Paideuma,* 3 (Spring, 1974), 139–148.

  "Edward Coke: The Azalea is Grown." *Paideuma,* 4 (Fall and Winter, 1975), 223–229.

  "The Sources of Canto LIII." *Paideuma,* 5 (Spring, 1976), 123–152.

  " 'Confucius, Philosophe': An Introduction to the Chinese *Cantos* 52–61." *Paideuma,* 5 (Winter, 1976), 387–403.

Gourmont, Remy de. *The Natural Philosophy of Love.* Translated by Ezra Pound. New York: Boni and Liveright, 1922.

Graff, Gerald. *Poetic Statement and Critical Dogma.* Evanston, Illinois: Northwestern University Press, 1972.

Graña, César. *Bohemian versus Bourgeois: French Society and the French Man of Letters in the Nineteenth Century.* New York: Basic Books, 1964.

Grant, Frederic C. *Ancient Judaism and the New Testament.* New York: MacMillan, 1959.

Gregor, A. James. *The Ideology of Fascism: The Rationale of Totalitarianism.* New York: The Free Press, 1969.

  "Understanding Fascism: A Review of Some Contemporary Literature." *American Political Science Review,* 67 (December, 1973), 1332–1347.

  Italian Fascism and Developmental Dictatorship. Berkeley: University of California Press, 1979.

  Young Mussolini and the Intellectual Origins of Fascism. Berkeley: University of California Press, 1979.

Hall, Donald. "Ezra Pound: An Interview." *Paris Review,* 28 (Summer and Fall, 1962), 22–51.

Halperin, Ben. " 'Myth' and 'Ideology' in Modern Usage." *History and Theory,* 1, 2 (1961), 129–149.

Halperin, William S. *Mussolini and Italian Fascism.* Princeton: Van Nostrand, 1964.

Hamilton, Alistair. *The Appeal of Fascism.* London: Anthony Blond, 1971.

Hampshire, Stuart. *Spinoza.* Harmondsworth: Penguin, 1951.

Handelman, Susan. "Jacques Derrida and the Heretic Hermeneutic." In *Displacement: Derrida and After,* ed. Mark Krupnick. Bloomington: Indiana University Press, 1983.

Handlin, Oscar. "American Views of the Jew at the Opening of the Twentieth

Century." *Publications of the American Jewish Historical Society,* 40 (June, 1951), 323–344.

Harmon, William. *Time in Ezra Pound's Works.* Chapel Hill, North Carolina: University of North Carolina Press, 1977.

Hayes, Paul M. "Quisling's Political Ideas." *Journal of Contemporary History,* 1, 1 (1966), 145–157.

Hazard, Paul. *The European Mind, 1680–1715.* Translated by J. Lewis May. Cleveland and New York: New World Publishing Company, 1969.

Herbert, A. S. *The Book of the Prophet Isaiah: Chapters 40–66.* Cambridge: Cambridge University Press, 1980.

Herf, Jeffrey. *Reactionary Modernism: Technology, Culture, and Politics in Weimar and the Third Reich.* Cambridge: Cambridge University Press, 1984.

Hertzberg, Arthur. *The French Enlightenment and the Jews.* New York: Columbia University Press, 1968.

Hesse, Eva. "Notes and Queries." *Paideuma,* 4 (Spring, 1975), 182.

Hesse, Eva, ed. *New Approaches to Ezra Pound.* Berkeley: University of California Press, 1969.

Heymann, C. David. *Ezra Pound: The Last Rower.* New York: Viking, 1976.

Hicks, John. *The Populist Revolt: A History of the Farmer's Alliance and the People's Party.* Minneapolis: University of Minnesota Press, 1931.

Hitler, Adolf. *Mein Kampf.* Translated by Ralph Manheim. Boston: Houghton Mifflin, 1971.

Hofstadter, Richard. *The Age of Reform: From Bryan to F.D.R.* New York: Alfred A. Knopf, 1955.

——— *The Paranoid Style in American Politics.* New York: Random House, 1967.

Holmes, Colin. *Anti-Semitism in British Society, 1876–1939.* London: Holmes and Meier, 1979.

Homburger, Eric, ed. *Ezra Pound: The Critical Heritage.* London: Routledge and Kegan Paul, 1972.

Hook, Sidney. "Reflections on the Jewish Question." *Partisan Review,* 16 (May, 1949), 463–482.

Horkheimer, Max. *Eclipse of Reason.* New York: Oxford University Press, 1947.

Horkheimer, Max, and Adorno, Theodor. *Dialectic of Enlightenment.* Translated by John Cumming. New York: Herder and Herder, 1972.

Hughes, H. Stuart. *Oswald Spengler: A Critical Estimate.* New York: Charles Scribner's, 1952.

——— *The Sea-Change: The Migration in Social Thought, 1930–1965.* New York: Harper and Row, 1975.

Hutchins, Patricia. *Ezra Pound's Kensington: An Exploration, 1885–1913.* Chicago: Henry Regnery, 1968.

Hyde, Lewis. *The Gift: Imagination and the Erotic Life of Property.* New York: Random House, 1983.

Ionescu, Ghita, and Gellner, Ernest, eds. *Populism: Its Meaning and National Characteristics.* London: MacMillan, 1969.

James, Henry. *The American Scene.* New York: Horizon, 1967.

Jameson, Fredric. *Marxism and Form.* Princeton: Princeton University Press, 1971.

——— *Fables of Aggression: Wyndham Lewis, The Modernist as Fascist.* Berkeley: University of California Press, 1979.

Janowitz, Morris, and Bettelheim, Bruno. "Ethnic Tolerance: A Function of Social and Personal Control." *American Journal of Sociology,* 4 (July, 1949), 137–145.

Jay, Martin. *The Dialectical Imagination: A History of the Frankfurt School and the Institute for Social Research.* Boston: Little Brown, 1973.

    Adorno. Cambridge: Harvard University Press, 1984.

Jones, Ernest. *The Life and Work of Sigmund Freud.* 2 vols. New York: Basic Books, 1953.

Kaiser, Otto. *Isaiah, 1–12: A Commentary.* Translated by R. A. Wilson. Philadelphia: Westminster, 1976.

    Isaiah, 1–12: A Commentary. Revised Version. Translated by John Bowden. Philadelphia: Westminster, 1983.

Kappel, Andrew J. "Napoleon and Talleyrand in *The Cantos.*" *Paideuma,* 11 (Spring, 1982), 55–78.

Katz, Jacob. *Jews and Freemasons in Europe, 1723–1939.* Translated by Leonard Oschry. Cambridge: Harvard University Press, 1970.

    From Prejudice to Destruction: Anti-Semitism, 1700–1933. Cambridge: Harvard University Press, 1980.

Kayman, Martin. "The Keele Conference." *Paideuma,* 5 (Winter, 1976), 461–468.

Keith, Nobuko Tsukui. "*Aoi no Ue* and *Kinuta:* An Examination of Ezra Pound's Translations." *Paideuma,* 8 (Fall, 1979), 199–214.

Kelly, Florene and Hite, K. Eileen. *Microbiology.* New York: Appleton Century Crofts, 1949.

Kenner, Hugh. *The Poetry of Ezra Pound.* Norfolk, Connecticut: New Directions, 1951.

    Gnomon: Essays on Contemporary Literature. New York: McDowell, Obolensky, 1958.

    The Pound Era. Berkeley: University of California Press, 1971.

    "D. P. Remembered." *Paideuma,* 2 (Winter, 1973), 485–493.

Kimpel, Ben, and Eaves, T. C. "The Source of Canto L." *Paideuma,* 8 (Spring, 1979), 81–93.

    "Ezra Pound's Anti-Semitism." *South Atlantic Quarterly,* (Winter, 1982), 56–59.

Kitchen, M. "August Thalheimer's Theory of Fascism." *Journal of the History of Ideas,* 34 (January-March, 1973), 67–78.

    "Ernst Nolte and the Phenomenology of Fascism." *Science and Society,* 38 (Summer, 1974), 130–149.

Klinck, Dennis R. "Pound, Social Credit, and the Critics." *Paideuma,* 5 (Fall, 1976), 227–240.

Knapp, Bettina L. *Céline: Man of Hate.* University, Alabama: University of Alabama Press, 1974.

Knight, George A. F. *Deutero-Isaiah: A Theological Commentary on Isaiah, 40–55.* New York: Abingdon Press, 1965.

Knox, Bryant. "Allen Upward and Ezra Pound." *Paideuma,* 3 (Spring, 1974), 72–88.

Koestler, Arthur. *The Thirteenth Tribe: The Khazar Kingdom and its Heritage.* New York: Random House, 1976.

Kolnai, Aurel. *The War Against the West.* New York: Viking, 1938.

Kristeva, Julia. *Powers of Horror: An Essay on Abjection.* Translated by Leon Roudiez. New York: Columbia University Press, 1982.

Lacan, Jacques. *Écrits: A Selection.* Translated by Alan Sheridan. New York: W. W. Norton, 1977.

Laforgue, Jules. *Moralités légendaires.* Paris: Librairie de la Revue Independante, 1887.

Lander, Jeannette. *Ezra Pound.* New York: Frederick Ungar, 1971.

Lane, Barbara Miller, and Rupp, Leila J., eds. *Nazi Ideology before 1933: A Documentation.* Austin, Texas: University of Texas Press, 1978.

Laqueur, Walter, ed. *Fascism: A Reader's Guide.* Berkeley: University of California Press, 1976.

Larsen, Stein Ugelvik et al., eds. *Who Were the Fascists: Social Roots of European Fascism.* Bergen: Universitetsforlaget, 1980.

Lauber, John. "Pound's *Cantos:* A Fascist Epic." *Journal of American Studies,* 12 (April, 1978), 3–21.

Lebzelter, Gisela. *Political Anti-Semitism in England, 1918–1939.* New York: Holmes and Meier, 1978.

Ledeen, Michael Arthur. *Universal Fascism: The Theory and Practice of the Fascist International, 1928–1936.* New York: Howard Fertig, 1972.

Lee, Albert. *Henry Ford and the Jews.* New York: Stein and Day, 1980.

Lemaire, Anika. *Jacques Lacan.* Translated by David Macey. London: Routledge and Kegan Paul, 1977.

Leschnitzer, Rudolf. *The Magic Background of Modern Anti-Semitism: An Analysis of the German-Jewish Relationship.* New York: International Universities Press, 1956.

Lewis, C.S. *The Discarded Image.* London: Cambridge University Press, 1967.

Lewis, Wyndham. *Hitler.* London: Chatto and Windus, 1931.

　　　The Hitler Cult. London: J. R. Dent, 1939.

Li Chi, ou Mémoires sur les bienséances et les cérémonies, 2 vols. Translated by S. Couvreur, S.J. Ho Kien Fou: Imprimerie de la Mission Catholique, 1913.

Li Ki, Book of Rites, Vol. I. Translated by James Legge. Hyde Park, New York: University Press Books, 1967.

Lipset, Seymour Martin, and Raab, Earl. *The Politics of Unreason: Right-Wing Extremism in America, 1790–1970.* New York: Harper and Row, 1970.

Little, Matthew. "Pound's Use of the Word *Totalitarian.*" *Paideuma,* 11 (Spring, 1982), 147–156.

Loeblowitz-Lennard, Henry. "The Jews as Father Symbol." *Psychoanalytic Quarterly,* 16 (1947), 33–38.

Loewenstein, Rudolf. *Christians and Jews: A Psychoanalytic Study.* New York: International Universities Press, 1952.

Loftus, Beverly J. G. "Ezra Pound and the Bollingen Prize: The Controversy in Periodicals." *Journalism Quarterly,* 39 (Summer, 1962), 347–354.

Lorenzetti, Giulio. *Venice and its Lagoon.* Translated by John Guthrie. Trieste: Edizioni Lint, 1985.

Lorrain, Jorge. *The Concept of Ideology.* Athens, Georgia: University of Georgia Press, 1979.

Lowenthal, Leo, and Guterman, Norbert. *Prophets of Deceit: A Study of the Techniques of the American Agitator.* New York: Harper and Row, 1949.

Löwith, Karl. *From Hegel to Nietzsche: The Revolution in Nineteenth-Century Thought.* New York: Holt, Rinehart, Winston, 1964.

Lyttelton, Adrian. *The Seizure of Power: Fascism in Italy, 1919–1929.* New York: Charles Scribner's, 1973.

Lyttelton, Adrian, ed. *Italian Fascisms from Pareto to Gentile.* New York: Harper and Row, 1973.

Maccoby, Hyam. "The Jews as Anti-Artist: The Anti-Semitism of Ezra Pound." *Midstream,* 22 (March, 1976), 59–71.

Macksey, Richard, and Donato, Eugenio, eds. *The Structuralist Controversy: The Languages of Criticism and the Sciences of Man.* Baltimore: Johns Hopkins University Press, 1970.

MacLeish, Archibald. *Poetry and Opinion: The Pisan Cantos of Ezra Pound.* Urbana, Illinois: University of Illinois Press, 1950.

Maier, Charles S. "Some Recent Studies of Fascism." *Journal of Modern History,* 48 (September, 1976), 506–521.

Makin, Peter. *Provence and Pound.* Berkeley: University of California Press, 1978.

Malinowski, Bronislau. *The Father in Primitive Psychology.* New York: W. W. Norton, 1927.

Mannheim, Karl. *Ideology and Utopia: An Introduction to the Sociology of Knowledge.* Translated by Louis Wirth and Edward Shils. New York: Harcourt Brace, 1936.

Martin, Wallace. *The New Age under Orage: Chapters in English Cultural History.* New York: Barnes and Noble, 1967.

Maslow, A. H. "The Authoritarian Character Structure." *Journal of Social Psychology,* 18 (1943), pp. 401–411.

Materer, Timothy. *Vortex: Pound, Eliot, and Lewis.* Ithaca: Cornell University Press, 1979.

⎯⎯⎯ "Doppelgänger: Ezra Pound in his Letters." *Paideuma,* 11 (Fall, 1982), 241–256.

Maurras, Charles. *Le chemin de Paradis: Contes Philosophiques.* Paris: E. de Boccard, 1921.

⎯⎯⎯ *Romantisme et revolution.* Paris: Nouvelle Librairie Nationale, 1922.

⎯⎯⎯ *Athinea: D'Athènes a Rome.* Paris: Flammarion, 1926.

Mazzini, Joseph (Giuseppe). *The Duties of Man and other Essays.* Translated by Ella Noyes and Thomas Okey. London: J.M. Dent, 1929.

McCarthy, Patrick. *Céline.* Harmondsworth: Penguin, 1977.

McClelland, J. S., ed. *The French Right: From Maistre to Maurras.* New York: Harper and Row, 1962.

McLuhan, Marshall. *The Gutenberg Galaxy: The Making of Typographic Man.* New York: New American Library, 1962.

McNaughton, William. "A Note on Main Form in the Cantos." *Paideuma,* 6 (Fall, 1977), 147–152.

Meacham, Harry. *The Caged Panther: Ezra Pound at St. Elizabeths.* New York: Twayne, 1967.

Mead, G.R.S. *Fragments of a Faith Forgotten.* New Hyde Park, New York: University Press Books, 1960.

Mehlman, Jeffrey. *Legacies of Anti-Semitism in France.* Minneapolis: University of Minnesota Press, 1983.

Melograni, Piero. "The Cult of the Duce in Mussolini's Italy." *Journal of Contemporary History,* 11 (October, 1976), 221–237.

Michaelis, Meir. *Mussolini and the Jews: German-Italian Relations and the Jewish Question in Italy.* Oxford: Clarendon Press, 1978.

Miller, J. Hillis. "The Critic as Host." In *Deconstruction and Criticism.* New York: The Seabury Press, 1979.

Molnar, Thomas. *The Counter-Revolution.* New York: Funk and Wagnalls, 1969.

Moody, A. D. "Pound's Allen Upward." *Paideuma,* 4 (Spring, 1975), 55–70.

Moore, Barrington. *The Social Origins of Dictatorship and Democracy: Lord and Peasant in the Making of the Modern World.* Boston: Beacon, 1966.

Morris, J. A. "T. S. Eliot's Anti-Semitism." *Journal of European Studies,* 2 (June, 1972), 173–182.

Mosse, George L. *The Crisis of German Ideology: Intellectual Origins of the Third Reich.* New York: Grosset and Dunlap, 1964.

Nazi Culture: Intellectual, Cultural, and Social Life in the Third Reich. New York: Grosset and Dunlap, 1966.

"The Genesis of Fascism." *Journal of Contemporary History*, 1, 1, (1966), 14–26.

Germans and Jews: The Left, the Right, and the Search for a 'Third Force' in Pre-Nazi Germany. New York: Howard Fertig, 1970.

The Nationalization of the Masses: Political Symbolism in Germany from the Napoleonic Wars through the Third Reich. New York: Howard Fertig, 1975.

Toward the Final Solution: A History of European Racism. New York: Howard Fertig, 1978.

Nazism: A Historical and Comparative Analysis of National Socialism. New Brunswick, New Jersey: Transaction, 1978.

Masses and Man: Nationalist and Fascist Perceptions of Reality. New York: Howard Fertig, 1980.

Mullins, Eustace. *This Difficult Individual, Ezra Pound.* New York: Fleet, 1961.

Mussolini, Benito. *My Autobiography.* New York: Charles Scribner's, 1926.

Nassar, Eugene Paul. *The Cantos of Ezra Pound: The Lyric Mode.* Baltimore: Johns Hopkins University Press, 1975.

Nathan, Peter. *The Psychology of Fascism.* London: Faber and Faber, 1943.

Nelson, Benjamin. *The Idea of Usury: From Tribal Brotherhood to Universal Otherhood.* Chicago: University of Chicago Press, 1969.

Newall, Venetia, ed. *The Witch Figure.* London and Boston: Routledge and Kegan Paul, 1973.

Nicholls, Peter. *Ezra Pound: Politics, Economics, and Writing: A Study of The Cantos.* Atlantic Highlands, New Jersey: Humanities Press, 1984.

Nietzsche, Friedrich. *The Birth of Tragedy and the Genealogy of Morals.* Translated by Francis Golffing. New York: Doubleday, 1956.

The Portable Nietzsche. Edited by Walter Kaufmann. New York: Viking, 1967.

On the Genealogy of Morals and Ecce Homo. Translated by Walter Kaufmann. New York: Vintage, 1976.

Nilus, Serge et al. *The Protocols and World Revolution: Including a Translation and Analysis of the Protocols of the Meetings of the Zionist Men of Wisdom.* Boston: Small and Maynard, 1920.

Nolde, John T. "The Sources for Canto LIV: Part Two." *Paideuma*, 6 (Spring, 1977), 45–98.

Nolte, Ernst. *Three Faces of Fascism.* Translated by Leila Vennewitz. New York: New American Library, 1965.

Norman, Charles. *Ezra Pound.* New York: MacMillan, 1960.

North, Michael. *The Final Sculpture: Public Monuments and Modern Poets.* Ithaca: Cornell University Press, 1985.

O'Connor, William Van, and Stone, Edward, eds. *A Casebook on Ezra Pound.* New York: Thomas Crowell, 1959.

Olson, Charles. *Charles Olson and Ezra Pound. An Encounter at St. Elizabeths.* Edited by Catherine Seelye. New York: Viking, 1975.

Parker, Andrew. "Ezra Pound and the 'Economy' of Anti-Semitism." *Boundary/ 2*, 11 (Fall-Winter, 1983), 103–128.

Parker, Robert. *Miasma: Pollution and Purification in Early Greek Religion.* Oxford: Clarendon Press, 1983.

Parkes, James. *The Enemy of the People: Anti-Semitism.* New York: Penguin, 1946.

Judaism and Christianity. Chicago: University of Chicago Press, 1948.

   The Conflict of the Church and the Synagogue: A Study of the Origins of Anti-Semitism. Cleveland and New York: World Publishing Company, 1961.

Payne, Stanley. *Fascism: Comparison and Definition.* Madison, Wisconsin: Univ. of Wisconsin Press, 1980.

Pearlman, Daniel. *The Barb of Time: On the Unity of Ezra Pound's Cantos.* New York: Oxford University Press, 1969.

   "Alexander del Mar in *The Cantos:* A Printout of the Sources." *Paideuma,* 1 (Winter, 1972), 161–180.

   "Ezra Pound: America's Wandering Jew." *Paideuma,* 9 (Winter, 1980), 461–480.

   "The Anti-Semitism of Ezra Pound." *Contemporary Literature,* 22 (Winter, 1981), 104–115.

   "Fighting the World: The Letters of Ezra Pound to Senator William E. Borah of Idaho." *Paideuma,* 2 (Fall and Winter, 1983), 419–426.

Peck, John. "Pound's Lexical Mythography: King's Journey and Queen's Eye." *Paideuma,* 1 (Spring and Summer, 1972), 3–36.

Philostratus. *The Life of Apollonius of Tyana,* 2 vols. Translated by F.C. Conybeare. Cambridge: Harvard University Press, 1948.

Pignatti, Terisio. *Venice.* Translated by Judith Landry. New York: Holt, Rinehart, Winston, 1971.

Pinson, Koppel S., ed. *Essays on Anti-Semitism.* New York: Conference on Jewish Relations, 1946.

Poliakov, Leon. *The Aryan Myth: A History of Racist and Nationalistic Ideas in Europe.* Translated by Edmund Howard. Edinburgh: Chatto, Heinemann, 1974.

   The History of Anti-Semitism. 3 vols. Translated by Miriam Kochan. New York: Vanguard, 1975.

Pollack, Norman. "The Myth of Populist Anti-Semitism." *American Historical Review,* 68 (1962), 76–80.

   "Handlin on Anti-Semitism: A Critique of 'American Views of the Jew.' " *Journal of American History,* 51 (December, 1964), 391–403.

Popper, Karl. *The Open Society and its Enemies.* 2 vols. Princeton: Princeton University Press, 1963.

Por, Odon. *Fascism.* Translated by Emily Townshend. New York: Alfred Knopf, 1923.

   Finanza Nuova: Problemi e soluzioni. Firenze: Felice le Monnier, 1940.

   Italy's Policy of Social Economics, 1939–1940. Translated by Ezra Pound. Bergamo: Istituto Italiano d'Arti Grafiche, 1941.

Praz, Mario. *The Romantic Agony.* Translated by Angus Davidson. New York: Oxford University Press, 1970.

Procacci, Giuliano. *History of the Italian People.* Translated by Anthony Paul. Harmondsworth: Penguin, 1970.

Pulzer, Peter. *The Rise of Political Anti-Semitism in Germany and Austria.* New York: John Wiley, 1964.

Rahv, Philip. *The Myth and the Powerhouse.* New York: Farrar, Straus, Giroux, 1966.

Ramsey, Warren. *Jules Laforgue and the Ironic Inheritance.* New York: Oxford University Press, 1953.

Read, Forrest. *'76: One World and The Cantos of Ezra Pound,* Chapel Hill, North Carolina: University of North Carolina Press, 1981.

Reck, Michael. *Ezra Pound: A Close-Up.* New York: McGraw Hill, 1967.

   "A Conversation between Ezra Pound and Allen Ginsberg." *Evergreen Review,* 55 (June, 1968).

Reich, Wilhelm. *The Mass Psychology of Fascism.* Translated by Vincent Carfagno. New York: Farrar, Straus, Giroux, 1970.

Reichsmann, Eva G. *Hostages of Civilization: The Social Sources of National Socialist Anti-Semitism.* Boston: Beacon, 1951.

Renan, Ernest. *St. Paul.* Translated by Ingersoll Lockwood. New York: G. W. Carleton, 1869.

    Averroès et l'Averroisme: essai historique, 4 ed. Paris: Calmann Levy, 1882.

Rhodes, James. *The Hitler Movement: A Modern Millenarian Revolution.* Stanford: Hoover Institutions Press, 1980.

Ricoeur, Paul. *The Symbolism of Evil.* Translated by Emerson Buchanan. Boston: Beacon, 1969.

Robert, Marthe. *From Oedipus to Moses: Freud's Jewish Identity.* Translated by Ralph Manheim. New York: Doubleday, 1976.

Roberts, David. *The Syndicalist Tradition and Italian Fascism.* Chapel Hill, North Carolina: University of North Carolina Press, 1979.

Robinson, Alan. *Symbol to Vortex: Poetry, Painting, and Ideas, 1885–1914.* New York: St. Martin's Press, 1985.

Robinson, Joan. *An Essay on Marxian Economics.* London: MacMillan, 1966.

Rocco, Alfredo. "The Political Doctrine of Fascism." Translated by Dino Bigongiari. In *Man and Contemporary Society.* New York: Columbia University Press, 1962.

Rogin, Michael Paul. *The Intellectuals and McCarthy: The Radical Specter.* Cambridge, Mass.: MIT Press, 1967.

Rosenberg, Alfred. *Race and Race History and Other Essays.* Edited by Robert Pois. New York: Harper and Row, 1970.

Roth, Cecil. *A History of the Jews in England.* Oxford: The Clarendon Press, 1949.

Ruskin, John. *The Works of John Ruskin.* 39 vols. Edited by E.T. Cook and Alexander Wedderburn. London: George Allen, 1903–1912.

Russell, Peter, ed. *An Examination of Ezra Pound.* Norfolk, Connecticut: New Directions, 1950.

Said, Edward. *Orientalism.* New York: Vintage, 1978.

Salomone, A. William, ed. *Italy from the Risorgimento to Fascism: An Inquiry into the Origins of the Totalitarian State.* New York: Doubleday, 1970.

Salvatorelli, Luigi. *The Risorgimento.* Translated by Mario Domandi. New York: Harper and Row, 1970.

Salvemini, Gaetano. *Under the Axe of Fascism.* London: Victor Gollancz, 1936.

    Mazzini. Translated by I. M. Rawson. Stanford: Stanford University Press, 1957.

Sammons, Geoffrey. *Practical Criticism and Literary Sociology.* Bloomington, Indiana: Indiana University Press, 1978.

Sandmel, Samuel. *Philo of Alexandria: An Introduction.* New York: Oxford University Press, 1979.

Sarles, William Bowen et al. *Microbiology: General and Applied.* New York: Harper and Row, 1951.

Sarti, Roland. "Fascist Modernization: Traditional or Revolutionary?" *American Historical Review,* 75 (April, 1970), 1029–1045.

Sarti, Roland, ed. *The Axe Within: Italian Fascism in Action.* New York: Franklin Watts, 1974.

Sartre, Jean-Paul. *Anti-Semite and Jew.* Translated by George J. Becker. New York: Schocken, 1948.

Sawyer, John F. A. *Isaiah.* Volume I. Philadelphia: Westminster, 1984.

Sawyer, Richard. "To Know the Histories: L.A. Waddell's Sumer and Akkad." *Paideuma,* 14 (Spring, 1975), 79–94.

Scheler, Max. *Ressentiment.* Translated by W. Holdheim. New York: The Free Press, 1961.

Schery, Robert. *Plants for Man.* Englewood Cliffs, New Jersey: Prentice Hall, 1972.

Schmidt, Carl. *The Corporate State in Action: Italy Under Fascism.* New York: Oxford University Press, 1939.

Schneidau, Herbert. *Ezra Pound: The Image and the Real.* Baton Rouge: Louisiana State University Press, 1968.

Schwab, Raymond. *The Oriental Renaissance: Europe's Rediscovery of India and the East, 1680–1880.* Translated by Gene Patterson-Black and Victor Reinking. New York: Columbia University Press, 1984.

Schwarzfuchs, Simon. *Napoleon, the Jews, and the Sanhedrin.* London: Routledge and Kegan Paul, 1979.

Scott, Tom. "The Poet as Scapegoat." *Agenda,* 7 (Spring, 1969), 49–58.

Sekora, John. *Luxury: The Concept in Western Thought, Eden to Smollet.* Baltimore: Johns Hopkins University Press, 1977.

Shapiro, Karl. *In Defense of Ignorance.* New York: Random House, 1965.

Sieburth, Richard. "Ideas into Action: Pound and Voltaire." *Paideuma,* 6 (Winter, 1977), 365–390.

   Instigations: Ezra Pound and Remy de Gourmont. Cambridge: Harvard University Press, 1978.

Simmel, Ernst, ed. *Anti-Semitism: A Social Disease.* New York: International Universities Press, 1946.

Simmel, George. *The Philosophy of Money.* Translated by Tom Bottomore and David Frisby. London: Routledge and Kegan Paul, 1978.

Smith, D. Howard. *Chinese Religions.* London: Weidenfield and Nicolson, 1968.

Smith, Denis Mack. *Victor Emmanuel, Cavour, and the Risorgimento.* London: Oxford University Press, 1971.

Smith, William, ed. *A Dictionary of Greek and Roman Antiquities.* London: John Murray, 1982.

Sombart, Werner. *The Jews and Modern Capitalism.* Translated by M. Epstein. Glencoe: The Free Press, 1957.

Sontag, Susan. *Illness as Metaphor.* New York: Farrar, Straus, Giroux, 1978.

Soucy, Robert. "The Nature of Fascism in France." *Journal of Contemporary History,* 1, 1 (1966), 27–55.

   Fascist Intellectual: Drieu la Rochelle. Berkeley: University of California Press, 1979.

Spengler, Oswald. *The Decline of the West* (abr.). Translated by Charles Francis Atkinson. New York: Alfred Knopf, 1962.

Stern, Fritz. *The Politics of Cultural Despair: A Study in the Rise of the Germanic Ideology.* New York: Doubleday, 1965.

Stern, Richard. "A Memory or Two of Mr. Pound." *Paideuma,* 1 (Winter, 1972), 215–219.

Stock, Noel. *Poet in Exile: Ezra Pound.* Manchester: Manchester University Press, 1964.

   Reading the Cantos: A Study of Meaning in Ezra Pound. New York: Pantheon, 1966.

   The Life of Ezra Pound. New York: Avon, 1970.

   "Ezra Pound in Melbourne, 1953–57." *Helix* 13/14, *Ezra Pound in Melbourne,* 159–178.

Stoddard, Theodore Lothrop. *The Rising Tide of Colour Against White World-Supremacy.* New York: Charles Scribner's, 1920.

   The Revolt Against Civilization: The Menace of the Under-Man. New York: Charles Scribner's, 1923.

Clashing Tides of Colour. New York: Charles Scribner's, 1935.

Stonequist, Everett V. *The Marginal Man: A Study in Personality and Culture Conflict*. New York: Scribner's, 1937.

Strauss, Leo. *Persecution and the Art of Writing*. 1942; rpt. Greenwood, 1973.

Surette, Leon. "Helen of Tyre." *Paideuma*, 2 (Winter, 1973), 419–421.

    "A Case for Occam's Razor: Pound and Spengler." *Paideuma*, 6 (Spring, 1977), 109–113.

    A Light from Eleusis: A Study of Ezra Pound's Cantos. New York: Oxford University Press, 1979.

Sutton, Michael. *Nationalism, Positivism, and Catholicism: The Politics of Charles Maurras and French Catholics, 1890–1914*. Cambridge: Cambridge University Press, 1982.

Talmon, J. L. *The Rise of Totalitarian Democracy*. Boston: Beacon, 1952.

Tannenbaum, Edward R. *The Action Française: Die-Hard Reactionaries in Twentieth-Century France*. New York: John Wiley, 1962.

    The Fascist Experience: Italian Society and Culture, 1922–1945. New York: Basic Books, 1972.

Terrell, Carroll F. "St. Elizabeths." *Paideuma*, 3 (Winter, 1974), 363–379.

    A Companion to the Cantos of Ezra Pound. 2 vols. Berkeley: University of California Press, 1980, 1984.

Torrey, E. Fuller. *The Roots of Treason: Ezra Pound and the Secret of St. Elizabeths*. New York: McGraw Hill, 1984.

Trachtenberg, Joshua. *The Devil and the Jews: The Medieval Conception of the Jew and its Relation to Modern Anti-Semitism*. New Haven: Yale University Press, 1943.

Trilling, Lionel. *Sincerity and Authenticity*. Cambridge: Harvard University Press, 1972.

Tucker, William. "Ezra Pound, Fascism, and Populism." *Journal of Politics*, 18 (February, 1956), 105–107.

Turner, Jr., Henry A., ed. *Reappraisals of Fascism*. New York: Franklin Watts, 1975.

Ulam, Adam B. *Philosophical Foundations of English Socialism*. Cambridge: Harvard University Press, 1952.

Upward, Allen. *The New Word: An Open Letter Addressed to the Swedish Academy in Stockholm on the Meaning of the Word Idealist*. New York: Mitchell Kennerly, 1910.

    The Divine Mystery: A Reading of the History of Christianity Down to Time of Christ. Boston: Houghton Mifflin, 1915.

    Some Personalities. Boston: Cornhill, 1922.

Uvarov, E. B., and Chapman, D. R., eds. *Dictionary of Science*. Middlesex: Penguin, 1977.

Vasse, William. "Traveler in a Landscape: The Structure of History in Ezra Pound's *Cantos*." Dissertation: University of California, Berkeley, 1969.

Vermaseren, Maarten. *Cybele and Attis: The Myth and the Cult*. London: Thames and Hudson, 1977.

Viereck, Peter. *Conservatism*, Princeton: Van Nostrand, 1956.

    Metapolitics; The Roots of the Nazi Mind. New York: Capricorn, 1965.

Volpe, Gioacchino. *History of the Fascist Movement*. Rome: Soc. An. Poligrafica Italiana, 1936.

Voltaire, *The Philosophical Dictionary*. Translated by Theodore Besterman. London: Penguin, 1971.

Vox, Maximilian. *Napoleon*. New York: Grove Press, 1960.

Waddell, L. A. *Indo-Sumerian Seals Deciphered: Discovering Sumerians of the Indus*

Valley as Phoenicians, Barats, Goths, and Famous Vedic Aryans, 3100–2300 B.C.. London: Luzac, 1925.

    Egyptian Civilization: Its Sumerian Origin and Real Chronology and Sumerian Origin of the Egyptian Hieroglyphs. London: Luzac, 1930.

Waite, Robert G. L. *The Psychopathic God: Adolf Hitler*. New York: New American Library, 1977.

Walbank, Frank W. *The Decline of the Roman Empire in the West*. New York: Henry Schumann, 1953.

Webb, James. *The Occult Establishment*. La Salle, Illinois: Open Court Publishing Co., 1976.

Weber, Eugen. *Action Française: Royalism and Reaction in Twentieth-Century France*. Stanford: Stanford University Press, 1964.

    Varieties of Fascism: Doctrines of Revolution in the Twentieth Century. Princeton: Van Nostrand, 1964.

Weber, Eugen, and Roggers, Hans. eds. *The European Right: A Historical Profile*. Berkeley: University of California Press, 1964.

Weber, Max. *From Max Weber: Essays in Sociology*. Edited by Hans Gerth and C. Wright Mills. New York: Oxford University Press, 1946.

    General Economic History. Translated by Frank Knight. Glencoe: The Free Press, 1950.

Wees, William C. *Vorticism and the English Avant Garde*. Toronto: University of Toronto Press, 1972.

Weigert-Vowinkel, Edith. "The Cult and Psychology of the Magna Mater from the Standpoint of Psychoanalysis." *Psychiatry*, 1 (August, 1938), 347–378.

Weininger, Otto. *Sex and Character*. London: William Heinemann, 1906.

Weiss, John. *The Fascist Tradition: Radical Right-Wing Extremism in Modern Europe*. New York: Harper and Row, 1967.

Welke, Robert J. "Frobenius: Pound—Some Quick Notes." *Paideuma*, 2 (Winter, 1973), 415–417.

Wilhelm, James J. *Dante and Pound: The Epic of Judgment*. Orono, Maine: University of Maine Press, 1974.

    The Later Cantos of Ezra Pound. New York: Walker, 1977.

    The American Roots of Ezra Pound. New York: Garland, 1985.

Wilson, Stephen. *Ideology and Experience: Anti-Semitism in France at the Time of the Dreyfus Affair*. Rutherford, New Jersey: Fairleigh Dickinson University Press, 1982.

Wiskemann, Elizabeth. *Fascism in Italy: Its Development and Influence*. London: MacMillan, 1969.

Witemeyer, Hugh. *The Poetry of Ezra Pound: Forms and Renewal 1908–1920*. Berkeley: University of California Press, 1969.

Wohl, Robert. Review of De Felice, *Fascism: An Informal Introduction to its Theory and Practice*. *Journal of Modern History*, 51 (September, 1979), 584–586.

Woodward, Anthony. *Ezra Pound and the Pisan Cantos*. London: Routledge and Kegan Paul, 1980.

Woolf, S. J., ed. *The Nature of Fascism*. New York: Vintage, 1969.

Worringer, Wilhelm. *Abstraction and Empathy*. Translated by Michael Bullock. New York: International Universities Press, 1953.

Wright, A. W. *G.D.H. Cole and Socialist Democracy*. Oxford: Clarendon, 1979.

Zielinski, Thaddeus. *La Sibylle: trois essais sur la religion antique et le christianisme*. Paris: F. Rieder, 1924.

    The Religion of Ancient Greece. Translated by George Rapall Noyes. London: Oxford University Press, 1926.

Index